CHILTON BOOK COMPANY

REPAIR MANUAL

CHEVY CAVALIER
BUICK SKYHAWK
CADILLAC CIMARRON
PONTIAC 2000
OLDS FIRENZA
1982-87

All U.S. and Canadian front wheel drive models

President GARY R. INGERSOLL
Senior Vice President, Book Publishing and Research RONALD A. HOXTER
Vice President and General Manager JOHN P. KUSHNERICK
Editor-in-Chief KERRY A. FREEMAN, S.A.E.
Managing Editor DEAN F. MORGANTINI, S.A.E.
Senior Editor RICHARD J. RIVELE, S.A.E.
Senior Editor W. CALVIN SETTLE, JR., S.A.E.
Editor MARTIN J. GUNTHER

CHILTON BOOK COMPANY
Radnor, Pennsylvania
19089

CONTENTS

GENERAL INFORMATION and MAINTENANCE

ENGINE PERFORMANCE and TUNE-UP

ENGINE and ENGINE OVERHAUL

EMISSION CONTROLS

FUEL SYSTEM

CHASSIS ELECTRICAL

SAFETY NOTICE

Proper service and repair procedures are vital to the safe, reliable operation of all motor vehicles, as well as the personal safety of those performing repairs. This book outlines procedures for servicing and repairing vehicles using safe, effective methods. The procedures contain many NOTES, CAUTIONS and WARNINGS which should be followed along with standard safety procedures to eliminate the possibility of personal injury or improper service which could damage the vehicle or compromise its safety.

It is important to note that repair procedures and techniques, tools and parts for servicing motor vehicles, as well as the skill and experience of the individual performing the work vary widely. It is not possible to anticipate all of the conceivable ways or conditions under which vehicles may be serviced, or to provide cautions as to all of the possible hazards that may result. Standard and accepted safety precautions and equipment should be used during cutting, grinding, chiseling, prying, or any other process that can cause material removal or projectiles.

Some procedures require the use of tools specially designed for a specific purpose. Before substituting another tool or procedure, you must be completely satisfied that neither your personal safety, nor the performance of the vehicle will be endangered.

Although the information in this guide is based on industry sources and is as complete as possible at the time of publication, the possibility exists that the manufacturer made later changes which could not be included here. While striving for total accuracy, Chilton Book Company cannot assume responsibility for any errors, changes, or omissions that may occur in the compilation of this data.

PART NUMBERS

Part numbers listed in this reference are not recommendations by Chilton for any product by brand name. They are references that can be used with interchange manuals and aftermarket supplier catalogs to locate each brand supplier's discrete part number.

SPECIAL TOOLS

Special tools are recommended by the vehicle manufacturer to perform their specific job. Use has been kept to a minimum, but where absolutely necessary, they are referred to in the text by the part number of the tool manufacturer. These tools can be purchased, under the appropriate part number, from the Service Tool Division, Kent-Moore Corporation, 1501 South Jackson Street, Jackson, MI 49203, or an equivalent tool can be purchased locally from a tool supplier or parts outlet. Before substituting any tool for the one recommended, read the SAFETY NOTICE at the top of this page.

ACKNOWLEDGMENTS

The Chilton Book Company expresses its appreciation to the General Motors Corporation for their generous assistance.

Information has been selected from General Motors shop manuals, owners manuals, service bulletins and technical training manuals.

Manufactured in the United States of America
  34567890   765432109

Chilton's Repair Manual: Cavalier/Skyhawk/Cimarron/2000/Firenza 1982–87
ISBN 0-8019-7839-4 pbk.
Library of Congress Catalog Card No. 87-47937

General Information and Maintenance

1

HOW TO USE THIS BOOK

Chilton's Repair Manual for GM J-Car is intended to help you learn more about the inner workings of your vehicle and save you money on its upkeep and operation.

The first two chapters will be the most used, since they contain maintenance and tune-up information and procedures. Studies have shown that a properly tuned and maintained car can get at least 10% better gas mileage than an out-of-tune car. The other chapters deal with the more complex systems of your car. Operating systems from engine through brakes are covered to the extent that the average do-it-yourselfer becomes mechanically involved. This book will not explain such things as rebuilding the differential for the simple reason that the expertise required and the investment in special tools make this task uneconomical. It will give you detailed instructions to help you change your own brake pads and shoes, replace spark plugs, and do many more jobs that will save you money, give you personal satisfaction, and help you avoid expensive problems.

A secondary purpose of this book is a reference for owners who want to understand their car and/or their mechanics better. In this case, no tools at all are required.

Before removing any bolts, read through the entire procedure. This will give you the overall view of what tools and supplies will be required. There is nothing more frustrating than having to walk to the bus stop on Monday morning because you were short one bolt on Sunday afternoon. So read ahead and plan ahead. Each operation should be approached logically and all procedures thoroughly understood before attempting any work.

All chapters contain adjustments, maintenance, removal and installation procedures, and repair or overhaul procedures. When repair is not considered practical, we tell you how to remove the part and then how to install the new or rebuilt replacement. In this way, you at least save the labor costs. Backyard repair of such components as the alternator is just not practical.

Two basic mechanic's rules should be mentioned here. One, whenever the left side of the car or engine is referred to, it is meant to specify the driver's side of the car. Conversely, the right side of the car means the passenger's side. Secondly, most screws and bolts are removed by turning counterclockwise, and tightened by turning clockwise.

Safety is always the most important rule. Constantly be aware of the dangers involved in working on an automobile and take the proper precautions. See the section in this chapter Servicing Your Vehicle Safely and the SAFETY NOTICE on the acknowledgment page.

Pay attention to the instructions provided. There are 3 common mistakes in mechanical work:

1. Incorrect order of assembly, disassembly or adjustment. When taking something apart or putting it together, doing things in the wrong order usually justs cost you extra time; however, it CAN break something. Read the entire procedure before beginning disassembly. Do everything in the order in which the instructions say you should do it, even if you can't immediately see a reason for it. When you're taking apart something that is very intricate (for example, a carburetor), you might want to draw a picture of how it looks when assembled at one point in order to make sure you get everything back in its proper position. (We will supply exploded view whenever possible). When making adjustments, especially tune-up adjustments, do them in order; often, one adjustment affects another, and you cannot expect even satisfactory results unless each adjustment is made

only when it cannot be changed by any order.

2. Overtorquing (or undertorquing). While it is more common for over-torquing to cause damage, undertorquing can cause a fastener to vibrate loose causing serious damage. Especially when dealing with aluminum parts, pay attention to torque specifications and utilize a torque wrench in assembly. If a torque figure is not available, remember that if you are using the right tool to do the job, you will probably not have to strain yourself to get a fastener tight enough. The pitch of most threads is so slight that the tension you put on the wrench will be multiplied many, many times in actual force on what you are tightening. A good example of how critical torque is can be seen in the case of spark plug installation, especially where you are putting the plug into an aluminum cylinder head. Too little torque can fail to crush the gasket, causing leakage of combustion gases and consequent overheating of the plug and engine parts. Too much torque can damage the threads, or distort the plug which changes the spark gap.

There are many commercial products available for ensuring that fasteners won't come loose, even if they are not torqued just right (a very common brand is Loctite®). If you're worried about getting something together tight enough to hold, but loose enough to avoid mechanical damage during assembly, one of these products might offer substantial insurance. Read the label on the package and make sure the products is compatible with the materials, fluids, etc. involved before choosing one.

3. Crossthreading. This occurs when a part such as a bolt is screwed into a nut or casting at the wrong angle and forced. Cross threading is more likely to occur if access is difficult. It helps to clean and lubricate fasteners, and to start threading with the part to be installed going straight in. Then, start the bolt, spark plug, etc. with your fingers. If you encounter resistance, unscrew the part and start over again at a different angle until it can be inserted and turned several turns without much effort. Keep in mind that many parts, especially spark plugs, used tapered threads so that gentle turning will automatically bring the part you're treading to the proper angle if you don't force it or resist a change in angle. Don't put a wrench on the part until its's been turned a couple of turns by hand. If you suddenly encounter resistance, and the part has not seated fully, don't force it. Pull it back out and make sure it's clean and threading properly.

Always take your time and be patient; once you have some experience, working on your car will become an enjoyable hobby.

TOOLS AND EQUIPMENT

Naturally, without the proper tools and equipment it is impossible to properly service you vehicle. It would be impossible to catalog each tool that you would need to perform each or any operation in this book. It would also be unwise for the amateur to rush out and buy an expensive set of tool on the theory that he may need on or more of them at sometime.

The best approach is to proceed slowly gathering together a good quality set of those tools that are used most frequently. Don't be misled by the low cost of bargain tools. It is far better to spend a little more for better quality. Forged wrenches, 10 or 12 point sockets and fine tooth ratchets are by far preferable to their less expensive counterparts. As any good mechanic can tell you, there are few worse experiences than trying to work on a truck with bad tools. Your monetary savings will be far outweighed by frustration and mangled knuckles.

Begin accumulating those tools that are used most frequently; those associated with routine maintenance and tune-up.

In addition to the normal assortment of screwdrivers and pliers you should have the following tools for routine maintenance jobs:

1. SAE (or Metric) or SAE/Metric wrenches-sockets and combination open end-box end wrenches in sizes from $\frac{1}{8}$" (3 mm) to $\frac{3}{4}$" (19 mm) and a spark plug socket ($\frac{13}{16}$" or $\frac{5}{8}$" depending on plug type).

If possible, buy various length socket drive extensions. One break in this department is that the metric sockets available in the U.S. will all fit the ratchet handles and extensions you may already have ($\frac{1}{4}$", $\frac{3}{8}$", and $\frac{1}{2}$" drive).

2. Jackstands for support.

3. Oil filter wrench.

4. Oil filler spout for pouring oil.

5. Grease gun for chassis lubrication.

6. Hydrometer for checking the battery.

7. A container for draining oil.

8. Many rags for wiping up the inevitable mess.

In addition to the above items there are several others that are not absolutely necessary, but handy to have around. these include oil dry, a transmission funnel and the usual supply of lubricants, antifreeze and fluids, although these can be purchased as needed. This is a basic list for routine maintenance, but only your personal needs and desire can accurately determine you list of tools.

The second list of tools is for tune-ups. While the tools involved here are slightly more sophisticated, they need not be outrageously expensive. There are several inexpensive tach/dwell

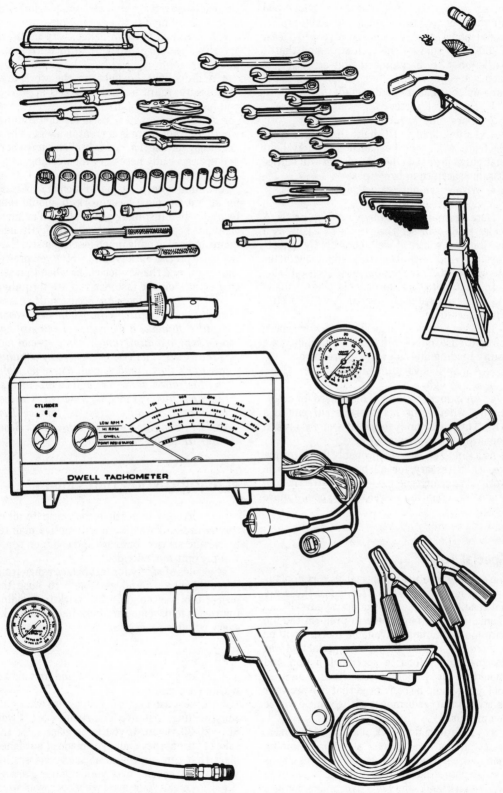

You need only a basic assortment of hand tools for most maintenance and repair jobs

meters on the market that are every bit as good for the average mechanic as a $100.00 professional model. Just be sure that it goes to a least 1,200-1,500 rpm on the tach scale and that it works on 4, 6, 8 cylinder engines. (A special tach is needed for diesel engines). A basic list of tune-up equipment could include:

1. Tach/dwell meter.
2. Spark plug wrench.
3. Timing light (a DC light that works from the truck's battery is best, although an AC light that plugs into 110V house current will suffice at some sacrifice in brightness).
4. Wire spark plug gauge/adjusting tools.
5. Set of feeler blades.

Here again, be guided by your own needs. A feeler blade will set the points as easily as a dwell meter will read well, but slightly less accurately. And since you will need a tachometer anyway. . . well, make your own decision.

In addition to these basic tools, there are several other tools and gauges you may find useful. These include:

1. A compression gauge. The screw-in type is slower to use, but eliminates the possibility of a faulty reading due to escaping pressure.
2. A manifold vacuum gauge.
3. A test light.
4. An induction meter. This is used for determining whether or not there is current in a wire. These are handy for use if a wire is broken somewhere in a wiring harness.

As a final not, you will probably find a torque wrench necessary for all but the most basic work. The beam type models are perfectly adequate, although the newer click type are more precise.

Special Tools

Normally, the use of special factory tools is avoided for repair procedures, since these are not readily available for the do-it-yourself mechanic. When it is possible to preform the job with more commonly available tools, it will be pointed out, but occasionally, a special tool was designed to perform a specific function and should be used. Before substituting another tool, you should be convinced that neither your safety nor the performance of the vehicle will be compromised.

• A hydraulic floor jack of at least 1½ ton capacity. If you are serious about maintaining your own car, then a floor jack is as necessary as a spark plug socket. The greatly increased utility, strength, and safety of a hydraulic floor jack makes it pay for itself many times over through the years.

• A compression gauge. The screw-in type is slower to use but it eliminates the possibility of a faulty reading due to escaping pressure.

• A manifold vacuum gauge, very useful in troubleshooting ignition and emissions problems.

• A drop light, to light up the work area (make sure yours is Underwriter's approved, and has a shielded bulb).

• A volt/ohm meter, used for determining whether or not there is current in a wire. These are handy for use if a wire is broken somewhere and are especially necessary for working on today's electronics-laden vehicles.

As a final note, a torque wrench is necessary for all but the most basic work. It should even be used when installing spark plugs. The more common beam-type models are perfectly adequate and are usually much less expensive than the more precise click type on which you pre-set the torque and the wrench clicks when that setting arrives on the fastener you are torquing).

NOTE: *Special tools are occasionally necessary to perform a specific job or are recommended to make a job easier. Their use has been kept to a minimum. When a special tool is indicated, it will be referred to by a manufacturer's part number. and, where possible, an illustration of the tool will be provided so that an equivalent tool may be used. The tool manufacturer and address is: Service Tool Division Kent-Moore 29784 Little Mack Roseville, MI 48066-2298*

SERVICING YOUR CAR SAFELY

It is virtually impossible to anticipate all of the hazards involved with automotive maintenance and service, but care and common sense will prevent most accidents.

The rules of safety for mechanics range from "don't smoke around gasoline," to "use the proper tool for the job." The trick to avoiding injuries is to develop safe work habits and take every possible precaution.

Dos

• Do keep a fire extinguisher and first aid kit within easy reach.

• Do wear safety glasses or goggles when cutting, drilling, grinding or prying, even if you have 20-20 vision. If you wear glasses for the sake of vision, they should be made of hardened glass that can serve also as safety glasses, or wear safety goggles over your regular glasses.

• Do shield your eyes whenever you work around the battery. Batteries contain sulphuric acid. In case of contact with the eyes or skin, flush the area with water or a mixture of water

Always support the car on jackstands when working underneath it

and baking soda and get medical attention immediately.

• Do use safety stands for any undercar service. Jacks are for raising vehicles; safety stands are for making sure the vehicle stays raised until you want it to come down. Whenever the car is raised, block the wheels remaining on the ground and set the parking brake.

• Do use adequate ventilation when working with any chemicals or hazardous materials. Like carbon monoxide, the asbestos dust resulting from brake lining wear can be poisonous in sufficient quantities.

• Do disconnect the negative battery cable when working on the electrical system. The secondary ignition system can contain up to 40,000 volts.

• Do follow manufacturer's directions whenever working with potentially hazardous materials. Both brake fluid and antifreeze are poisonous if taken internally.

• Do properly maintain your tools. Loose hammerheads, mushroomed punches and chisels, frayed or poorly grounded electrical cords, excessively worn screwdrivers, spread wrenches (open end), cracked sockets, slipping ratchets, or faulty droplight sockets can cause accidents.

• Likewise, keep your tools clean; a greasy wrench can slip off a bolt head, ruining the bolt and often ruining your knuckles in the process.

• Do use the proper size and type of tool for the job being done.

• Do when possible, pull on a wrench handle rather than push on it, and adjust you stance to prevent a fall.

• Do be sure that adjustable wrenches are tightly closed on the nut or bolt and pulled so that the face is on the side of the fixed jaw.

• Do select a wrench or socket that fits the nut or bolt. The wrench or socket should sit straight, not cocked.

• Do strike squarely with a hammer; avoid glancing blows.

• Do set the parking brake and block the drive wheels if the work requires the engine running.

Don'ts

• Don't run the engine in a garage or anywhere else without proper ventilation-EVER! Carbon monoxide is poisonous; it takes a long time to leave the human body and you can build up a deadly supply of it in your system by simply breathing in a little every day. You may not realize you are slowly poisoning yourself. Always use power vents, windows, fans or open the garage doors.

• Don't work around moving parts while wearing a necktie or other loose clothing. Short sleeves are much safer than long, loose sleeves; hard-toed shoes with neoprene soles protect your toes and give a better grip on slippery surfaces. Jewelry such as watches, fancy belt buckles, beads or body adornment of any kind is not safe working around a car. Long hair should be tied back under a hat or cap.

• Don't use pockets for toolboxes. A fall or bump can drive a screwdriver deep into your body. Even a wiping cloth hanging from the back pocket can wrap around a spinning shaft or fan.

• Don't smoke when working around gasoline, cleaning solvent or other flammable material.

• Don't smoke when working around the battery. When the battery is being charged, it gives off explosive hydrogen gas.

• Don't use gasoline to wash your hands; there are excellent soaps available. Gasoline may contain lead, and lead can enter the body through a cut, accumulating in the body until you are very ill. Gasoline also remove all the natural oils from the skin so that bone dry hands will such up oil and grease.

• Don't service the air conditioning system unless you are equipped with the necessary tools and training. The refrigerant, R-12, is extremely cold when compressed, and when released into the air will instantly freeze any surface it contacts, including your eyes. Although the refrigerant is normally non-toxic, R-12 becomes a deadly poisonous gas in the presence of an open flame. One good whiff of the vapors from burning refrigerant can be fatal.

• Don't use screwdrivers for anything other than driving screws! A screwdriver used as an prying tool can snap when you least expect it, causing injuries. At the very least, you'll ruin a good screwdriver.

• Don't use a bumper jack (that little ratchet, scissors, or pantograph jack supplied with the car) for anything other tan chaining a flat!

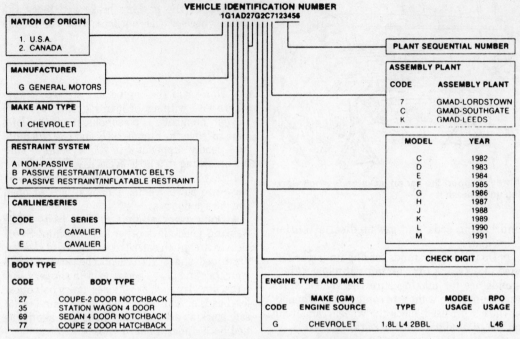

VEHICLE IDENTIFICATION NUMBER
1G1AD27G2C7123456

NATION OF ORIGIN

1. U.S.A.
2. CANADA

MANUFACTURER

G GENERAL MOTORS

MAKE AND TYPE

1 CHEVROLET

RESTRAINT SYSTEM

A NON-PASSIVE
B PASSIVE RESTRAINT/AUTOMATIC BELTS
C PASSIVE RESTRAINT/INFLATABLE RESTRAINT

CARLINE/SERIES

CODE	SERIES
D	CAVALIER
E	CAVALIER

BODY TYPE

CODE	BODY TYPE
27	COUPE-2 DOOR NOTCHBACK
35	STATION WAGON 4 DOOR
69	SEDAN 4 DOOR NOTCHBACK
77	COUPE 2 DOOR HATCHBACK

PLANT SEQUENTIAL NUMBER

ASSEMBLY PLANT

CODE	ASSEMBLY PLANT
7	GMAD-LORDSTOWN
C	GMAD-SOUTHGATE
K	GMAD-LEEDS

MODEL	YEAR
C	1982
D	1983
E	1984
F	1985
G	1986
H	1987
J	1988
K	1989
L	1990
M	1991

CHECK DIGIT

ENGINE TYPE AND MAKE

CODE	MAKE (GM) ENGINE SOURCE	TYPE	MODEL USAGE	RPO USAGE
G	CHEVROLET	1.8L L4 2BBL	J	L46

Explanation of a typical Vehicle Identification Number

These jacks are only intended for emergency use out on the road; they are NOT designed as a maintenance tool. If you are serious about maintaining your car yourself, invest in a hydraulic floor jack of a least 1½ ton capacity, and at least two sturdy jackstands.

SERIAL NUMBER IDENTIFICATION

Vehicle

The vehicle identification number is a seventeen place sequence stamped on a plate attached to the left front of the instrument panel, visible through the windshield.

Body

The body style identification plate is located on the front bar, just behind the right headlamp.

Engine

The engine VIN code is stamped on a pad at various locations on the cylinder block.

Transaxle

The manual transaxle identification number is stamped on a pad on the forward side of the transaxle case, between the upper and middle transaxle-to-engine mounting bolts. The auto-

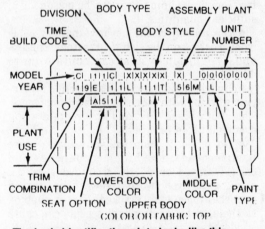

The body identification plate looks like this

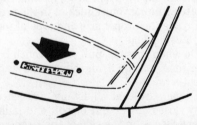

The VIN plate is visible through the windshield

matic transaxle identification number is stamped on the oil flange pad to the right of the oil dipstick, at the rear of the transaxle. The au-

Engine Code

Code	Cu. In.	Liters	Cyl.	Fuel Sys.	Eng. Mfg.
G	110 (OHV)	1.8	4	2 bbl	Chevrolet
O	110 (OHC)	1.8	4	TBI	Pontiac
J	110 (OHC)	1.8	4	MFI Turbo	Pontiac
B	122 (OHV)	2.0	4	①	Chevrolet
P	122 (OHV)	2.0	4	TBI	Chevrolet
M	122 (OHC)	2.0	4	MFI Turbo	Chevrolet
1	122 (OHV)	2.0	4	TBI HO	Chevrolet
K	122 (OHC)	2.0	4	TBI	Chevrolet
W	173	2.8	V6	MFI	Chevrolet

The seventeen digit Vehicle Identification Number can be used to determine engine identification and model year. The tenth digit indicates model year, and the fourth digit indicates engine code.
NOTE: Some 1983–85 Canadian models with the 2.0 Liter engine use a 2 bbl carburetor
HO—High Output
OHV—Overhead Valve engine
OHC—Overhead Cam engine
TBI—Throttle Body Injection
MFI—Multi-Port Fuel Injection
① 1982: 2 bbl
   1983 and later: TBI

Model Year

Code	Year
B	1981
C	1982
D	1983
E	1984
F	1985
G	1986
H	1987

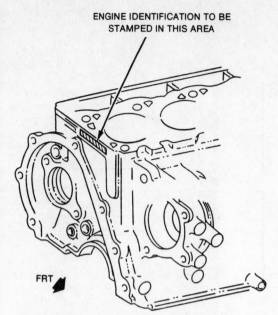

ENGINE IDENTIFICATION TO BE
STAMPED IN THIS AREA

FRT

Engine serial number location—1.8L OHV

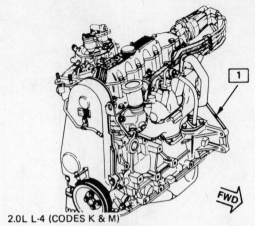

2.0L L-4 (CODES K & M)

Engine serial number locations—1.8L, 2.0L OHC

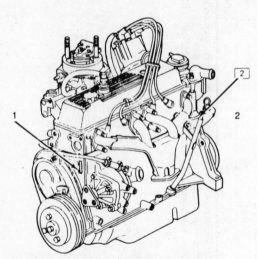

Engine serial number locations—2.0L OHV

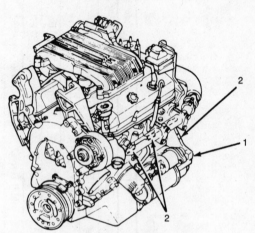

Engine serial number locations—2.8L V6

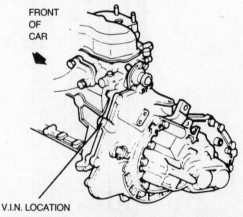

FRONT
OF
CAR

V.I.N. LOCATION

76 mm 4 speed manual transaxle serial number location

tomatic transaxle model code tag is on top of the case, next to the shift lever.

ROUTINE MAINTENANCE

Routine maintenance is the self-explanatory term used to describe the sort of periodic work necessary to keep a car in safe and reliable working order. A regular program aimed at monitoring essential systems ensures that the car's components are functioning correctly (and will continue to do so until the next inspec-

tion, one hopes), and can prevent small problems from developing into major headaches. Routine maintenance also pays off big dividends in keeping major repair costs at a mini-

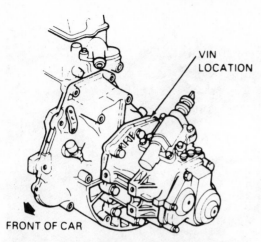

76 mm 5 speed manual transaxle serial number location

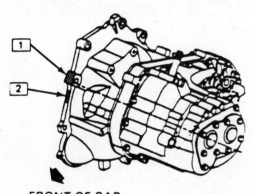

Getrag 5 speed manual transaxle serial number location

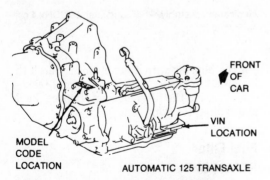

Automatic transaxle serial number location

mum, extending the life of the car, and enhancing resale value, should you ever desire to part with your new J-car.

The J-cars require less in the way of routine maintenance than any cars in recent memory.

However, a very definite maintenance schedule is provided by General Motors, and must be followed not only to keep the new car warranty in effect, but also to keep the car working properly. The Maintenance Intervals chart in this chapter outlines the routine maintenance which must be performed according to intervals based on either accumulated mileage or time. Your J-car also came with a maintenance schedule provided by G.M. Adherence to these schedules will result in a longer life for your car, and will, over the long run, save you money and time.

The checks and adjustments in the following sections generally require only a few minutes of attention every few weeks; the services to be performed can be easily accomplished in a morning. The most important part of any maintenance program is regularity. The few minutes or occasional morning spent on these seemingly trivial tasks will forestall or eliminate major problems later.

Air Cleaner

All the dust present in the air is kept out of the engine by means of the air cleaner filter element. Proper maintenance is vital, as a clogged element not only restricts the air-flow, and thus the power, but may also cause premature engine wear.

The filter element should be cleaned at least every 15,000 miles and replaced every 50,000 miles; more often if the car is driven in dry, dusty areas. The condition of the element should be checked periodically; if it appears to be overly dirty or clogged, shake it, if this does not help, the element should be replaced.

NOTE: *The paper element should never be cleaned or soaked with gasoline, cleaning solvent or oil.*

Unscrew the wingnut and remove the air cleaner housing lid

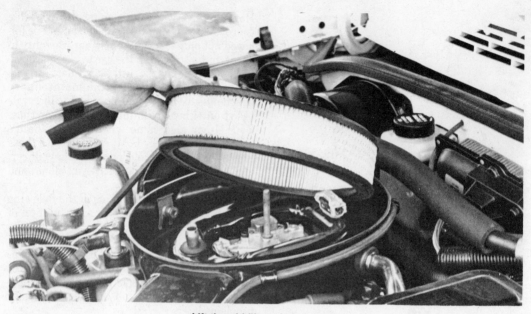

Lift the old filter element out

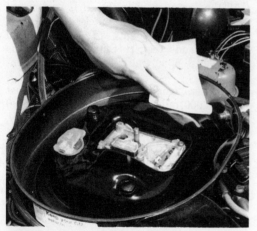

Always wipe out the inside of the housing before installing a new element

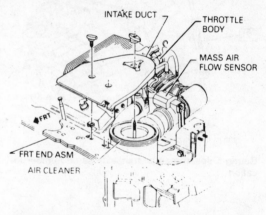

Air cleaner assembly—1987 and later 2.0L OHV 4 cylinder engine

CLEANING OR REPLACING THE FILTER ELEMENT

On most engines the air cleaner is located in the center of the engine compartment, directly over the carburetor or throttle body. On some 1987 and later 4-cyl. engines the air cleaner is more conveniently located toward the front of the engine compartment with an air duct connected to the throttle body.

1. Unscrew the wing nut on top of the air cleaner and then lift off the housing lid.

2. Lift out the filter element and shake the dirt out of it. If it remains clogged, replace it with a new one.

3. Before reinstalling the filter element, wipe out the housing with a damp cloth. Check the lid gasket to ensure that it has a tight seal.

4. Position the filter element, replace the lid and tighten the wing nut.

Fuel Filter

REPLACEMENT

Carbureted Engines

CAUTION: *Never smoke when working around gasoline! Avoid all sources of sparks or ignition. Gasoline vapors are EXTREMELY volatile!*

All models have a fuel filter located within the carburetor body. The fuel filter has a check valve to prevent fuel spillage in the event of an

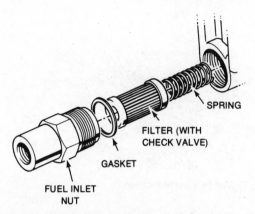

The fuel filter is located behind the large inlet nut on the carburetor

accident. When the filter is replaced, make sure the new one is of the same type. All filters are of the paper element type. Replace the filter every 15,000 miles.

1. Place a few absorbent rags underneath the fuel line where it joins the carburetor.

2. Disconnect the fuel line connection at the fuel inlet nut.

3. Unscrew the fuel inlet nut from the carburetor. As the nut is removed, the filter will be pushed part way out by spring pressure.

4. Remove the filter and spring.

5. Install the new spring and filter. The hole in the filter faces the nut.

6. Install a new gasket on the inlet nut and install the nut into the carburetor. Tighten securely.

7. Install the fuel line. Tighten the connector to 18 ft.lb. (24 Nm.) while holding the inlet nut with a wrench.

8. Start the engine and check for leaks.

Fuel Injected Engines

CAUTION: *Never smoke when working around gasoline! Avoid all sources of sparks or ignition. Gasoline vapors are EXTREMELY volatile!*

An in-line filter can be found in the fuel feed line attached to the rear crossmember of the vehicle.

1. Release the fuel system pressure.

2. Place absorbent rags under the connections and disconnect the fuel lines.

NOTE: *Always use a back-up wrench anytime the fuel filter is removed or installed.*

3. Remove the fuel filter from the retainer or mounting bolt.

4. When installing, always use a good O-ring at the coupling locations and torque the fittings at 22 ft.lb.. Start the engine and check for leaks.

NOTE: *The filter has an arrow (fuel flow direction) on the side of the case, be sure to install it correctly in the system, the with arrow facing away from the fuel tank.*

Fuel Pressure Release

CAUTION: *To reduce the risk of fire or personal injury, it is necessary to relieve the fuel system pressure before servicing the fuel system.*

MAKE SURE FILTER IS SNAPPED SECURELY INTO BRACKET.

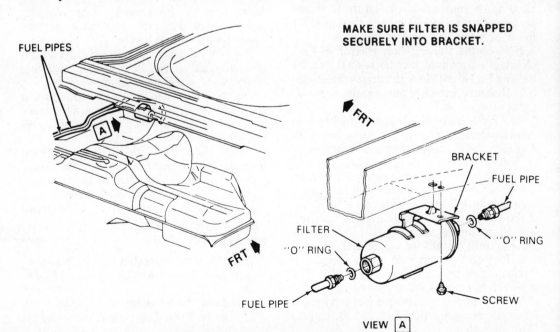

Fuel filter assembly—fuel injected engines

Carbureted Engines

To release the fuel pressure on the carbureted system, remove and replace the fuel tank cap.

Throttle Body Injection (TBI)

1983-86 1.8L and 2.0L (OHC)
1983-84 2.0L (OHV)

1. Remove the fuel pump fuse from the fuse block.
2. Crank the engine. The engine will run until it runs out of fuel. Crank the engine again for 3 seconds making sure it is out of fuel.
3. Turn the ignition off and replace the fuse.

1985-86 2.0L (OHV)

The TBI injection systems used on the 1985-86 engines contain a constant bleed feature in the pressure regulator that relieves pressure any time the engine is turned off. Therefore, no special relieve procedure is required, however, a small amount of fuel may be released when the fuel line is disconnected.

CAUTION: *To reduce the chance of personal injury, cover the fuel line with cloth to collect the fuel and then place the cloth in an approved container.*

Never smoke when working around gasoline! Avoid all sources of sparks or ignition. Gasoline vapors are EXTREMELY volatile!

1987-88 2.0L (OHV)
1987-88 2.0L (OHC)

The TBI Model 700 used on these engines contains no constant bleed feature to relieve pressure as the 1985-86 models therefore, the following procedure must be followed:

1. Place the transmission selector in Park (Neutral on manual transmissions), set the parking brake and block the drive wheels.
2. Disconnect the fuel pump at the rear body conncector.

CAUTION: *A small amount of fuel may be released after the fuel line is disconnected. To reduce the chance of personal injury, cover the fuel line with cloth to collect the fuel and then place the cloth in an approved container.*

Never smoke when working around gasoline! Avoid all sources of sparks or ignition. Gasoline vapors are EXTREMELY volatile!

3. Start the engine and allow it to run a few seconds until it stops for lack of fuel.
4. Engage the starter for three seconds to dissipate fuel pressure in the lines. The fuel connections are now safe for servicing.
5. When pressure is relieved and servicing is complete, reconnect the fuel pump at the rear body connector.

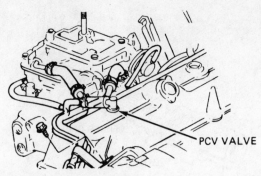

Typical PCV valve location

Port Fuel Injection (PFI)

1. Connect a J-34730-1 fuel gage or equivalent to the fuel pressure valve. Wrap a shop towel around the fitting while connecting the gage to avoid spillage.
2. Install a bleed hose into an approved container and open the valve to bleed the system pressure.

CAUTION: *Never smoke when working around gasoline! Avoid all sources of sparks or ignition. Gasoline vapors are EXTREMELY volatile!*

PCV Valve

The Positive Crankcase Ventilation (PCV) valve regulates crankcase ventilation during various engine running conditions. At high vacuum (idle speed and partial load range) it will open slightly and at low vacuum (full throttle) it will open fully. This causes vapors to be drawn from the crankcase by engine vacuum and then sucked into the combustion chamber where they are dissipated.

The PCV valve must be replaced every 30,000 miles. Details on the PCV system, including system tests, are given in Chapter Four.

The valve is located in a rubber grommet in the valve cover, connected to the air cleaner housing by a large diameter rubber hose. To replace the valve:

1. Pull the valve (with the hose attached) from the rubber grommet in the valve cover.
2. Remove the valve from the hose.
3. Install a new valve into the hose.
4. Press the valve back into the rubber grommet in the valve cover.

PCV Filter

The PCV filter is located in the air cleaner housing and must be replaced every 50,000 miles.

1. Remove the air cleaner housing lid.
2. Slide back the filter retaining clip and remove the old filter.

3. Install the new filter, replace the retaining clip and replace the housing lid.

Evaporative Emissions System

Check the evaporative emission control system every 15,000 miles. Check the fuel vapor lines and the vacuum hoses for proper connections and correct routing, as well as condition. Replace clogged, damaged or deteriorated parts as necessary.

For more details on the evaporative emissions system, please refer to Chapter Four.

Battery

The J-cars have a maintenance free battery as standard equipment, eliminating the need for fluid level checks and the possibility of specific gravity tests. Nevertheless, the battery does require some attention.

Once a year, the battery terminals and the cable clamps should be cleaned. Remove the side terminal bolts and the cables and the battery terminals with a wire brush until all corrosion, grease, etc. is removed and the metal is shiny. It is especially important to clean the inside of the clamp thoroughly, since a small deposit of foreign material or oxidation there will prevent a sound electrical connection and inhibit either starting or charging. Special tools are available

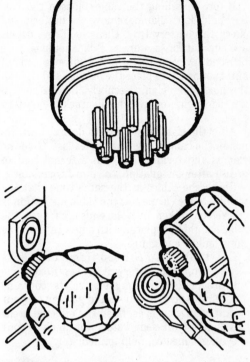

A special tool is available for cleaning the side terminals and clamps

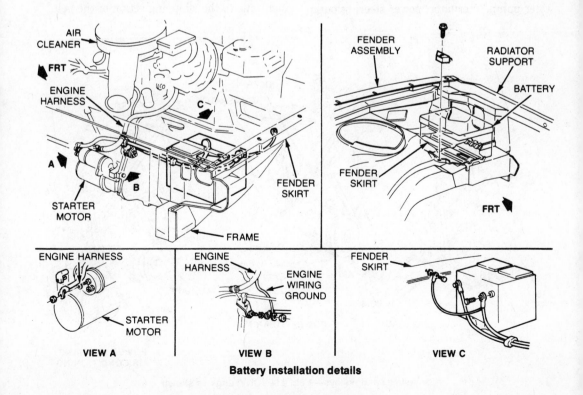

Battery installation details

for cleaning the side terminal clamps and terminals.

Before installing the cables, loosen the battery hold-down clamp, remove the battery, and check the battery tray. Clear it of any debris and check it for soundness. Rust should be wire brushed away, and the metal given a coat of anti-rust paint. Replace the battery and tighten the hold-down clamp securely, but be careful not to overtighten, which will crack the battery case.

After the clamps and terminals are clean, re-install the cables, negative cables last. Give the clamps and terminals a thin external coat of grease after installation, to retard corrosion.

Check the cables at the same time that the terminals are cleaned. If the cable insulation is cracked or broken, or if the ends are frayed, the cable should be replaced with a new cable of the same length and gauge.

CAUTION: *NOTE:* Keep flame or sparks away from the battery; it gives off explosive hydrogen gas. Battery electrolyte contains sulphuric acid. If you should get any on your skin or in your eyes, flush the affected areas with plenty of clear water; if it lands in your eyes, get medical help immediately.

Standard Drive Belts
BELT TENSION

Every 12 months or 15,000 miles, check the water pump, alternator, power steering pump (if so equipped), and air conditioning compressor (if so equipped) drive belts for proper tension. Also look for signs of wear, fraying, separation, glazing and so on, and replace the belts as required.

Belt tension should be checked with a gauge made for the purpose. If a gauge is not available, tension can be checked with moderate thumb pressure applied to the belt at its longest span midway between pulleys. If the belt has a free span less than twelve inches, it should deflect approximately $1/8$-$1/4''$. If the span is longer than twelve inches, deflection can range between $1/8$-$3/8''$.

1. Loosen the driven accessory's pivot and adjustment bolts. The pivot bolts are the bolts that enable the accessory to move in the either direction for adjustment. The adjustment bolts are the bolts in the slotted brackets.

2. Move the accessory toward or away from the engine until the tension is correct. You can use a wooden hammer handle or a broomstick as a lever, but do not use anything metallic.

3. Tighten the bolts and recheck the tension. If new belts have been installed, run the engine for a few minutes, then recheck and readjust as necessary.

It is better to have belts too loose than too tight, because overtight belts will lead to bearing failure, particularly in the water pump and alternator. However, loose belts place an extremely high impact load on the driven component due to the whipping action of the belt.

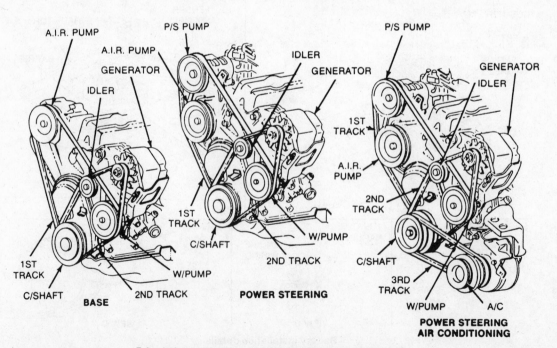

Drive belts and pulleys—1.8L, 2.0L (OHV) engines shown

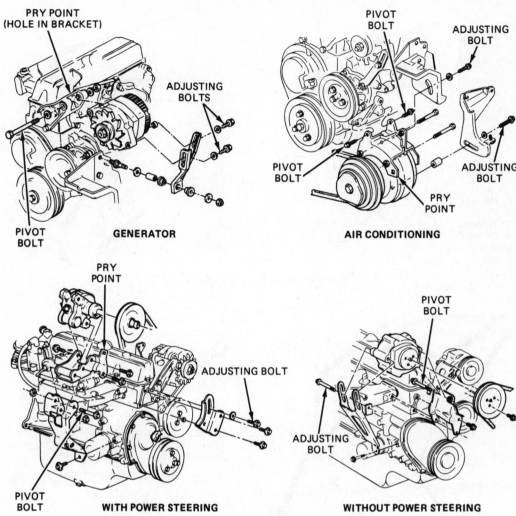

Drive belt adjustment points—1.8L, 2.0L (OHV) engines shown

Serpentine Belts

Models equipped with the V6 engine and most 1987 and later engines use a single (serpentine belt) to drive all engine accessories. The serpentine belt driven accessories are rigidly mounted with belt tension maintained by a spring loaded tensioner assembly. The belt tensioner has the ability to control belt tension over a fairly broad range of belt lengths. However, there are limits to the tensioner's ability to compensate for varying lengths of belts. Poor tension control and/or damage to the tensioner could result with the tensioner operating outside of its range.

INSPECTION

1. If fraying of the belt is noticed, check to make sure both the belt and the tensioner assembly are properly aligned and that the belt edges are not in contact with the flanges of the tensioner pulley.

2. If, while adjusting belt tension, tensioner runs out of travel, the belt is stretched beyond adjustment and should be replaced.

3. If a whining is heard around the tensioner or idler assemblies, check for possible bearing failure.

NOTE: *Routine inspection of the belt may reveal cracks in the belt ribs. These cracks will not impair belt performance and therefore should not be considered a problem requiring belt replacement. However, the belt should be replaced if belt slip occurs or if sections of the belt ribs are missing.*

REPLACEMENT

To replace the belt push (rotate) the the belt tensioner and remove the belt. Use a 15mm

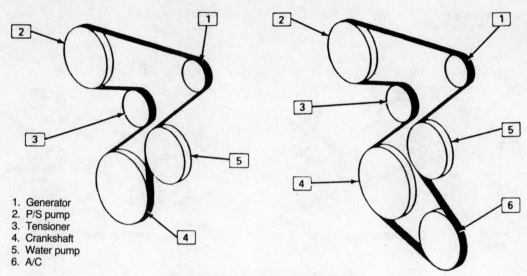

1. Generator
2. P/S pump
3. Tensioner
4. Crankshaft
5. Water pump
6. A/C

Serpentine belt routing 2.0L (OHV) engine

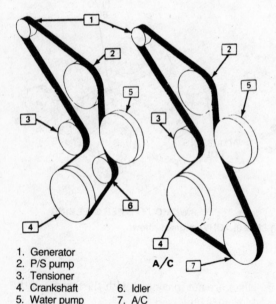

1. Generator
2. P/S pump
3. Tensioner
4. Crankshaft
5. Water pump
6. Idler
7. A/C

Serpentine belt routing 2.8L V6 engine

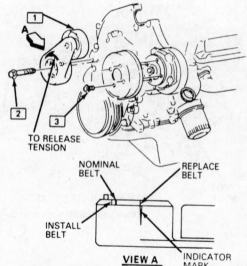

1. Tensioner
2. 48–60 N·m (35–44 ft. lbs.)
3. 20–30 N·m (14–22 ft. lbs.)

Serpentine belt tensioner 2.0L (OHV) engine

socket on the 4-cyl. engines and a ¾″ open end wrench on the V6 engines.

Hoses

Upper and lower radiator hoses and all heater hoses should be checked for deterioration, leaks and loose hose clamps every 15,000 miles. To remove the hoses:

1. Drain the radiator as detailed later in this chapter.

2. Loosen the hose clamps at each end of the hose to be removed.

3. Working the hose back and forth, slide it off its connection and then install a new hose if necessary.

4. Position the hose clamps at least ¼″ from the end of the hose and tighten them.

NOTE: *Always make sure that the hose clamps are beyond the bead and placed in the center of the clamping surface before tightening them.*

How to Spot Worn V-belts

V-Belts are vital to efficient engine operation—they drive the fan, water pump and other accessories. They require little maintenance (occasional tightening) but they will not last forever. Slipping or failure of the V-belt will lead to overheating. If your V-belt looks like any of these, it should be replaced.

Cracking or weathering

This belt has deep cracks, which cause it to flex. Too much flexing leads to heat build-up and premature failure. These cracks can be caused by using the belt on a pulley that is too small. Notched belts are available for small diameter pulleys.

Softening (grease and oil)

Oil and grease on a belt can cause the belt's rubber compounds to soften and separate from the reinforcing cords that hold the belt together. The belt will first slip, then finally fail altogether.

Glazing

Glazing is caused by a belt that is slipping. A slipping belt can cause a run-down battery, erratic power steering, overheating or poor accessory performance. The more the belt slips, the more glazing will be built up on the surface of the belt. The more the belt is glazed, the more it will slip. If the glazing is light, tighten the belt.

Worn cover

The cover of this belt is worn off and is peeling away. The reinforcing cords will begin to wear and the belt will shortly break. When the belt cover wears in spots or has a rough jagged appearance, check the pulley grooves for roughness.

Separation

This belt is on the verge of breaking and leaving you stranded. The layers of the belt are separating and the reinforcing cords are exposed. It's just a matter of time before it breaks completely.

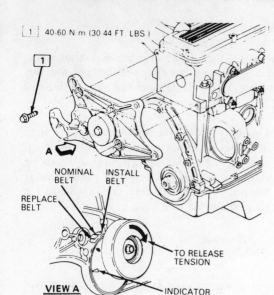

Serpentine belt tensioner 2.8L V6 engine

Air Conditioning
GENERAL SERVICING PROCEDURES

The most important aspect of air conditioning service is the maintenance of a pure and adequate charge of refrigerant in the system. A refrigeration system cannot function properly if a significant percentage of the charge is lost. Leaks are common because the severe vibration encountered in an automobile can easily cause a sufficient cracking or loosening of the air conditioning fittings; as a result, the extreme operating pressures of the system force refrigerant out.

The problem can be understood by considering what happens to the system as it is operated with a continuous leak. Because the expansion valve regulates the flow of refrigerant to the evaporator, the level of refrigerant there is fairly constant. The receiver/drier stores any excess of refrigerant, and so a loss will first appear there as a reduction in the level of liquid. As this level nears the bottom of the vessel, some refrigerant vapor bubbles will begin to appear in the stream of liquid supplied to the expansion valve. This vapor decreases the capacity of the expansion valve very little as the valve opens to compensate for its presence. As the quantity of liquid in the condenser decreases, the operating pressure will drop there and throughout the high side of the system. As the R-12 continues to be expelled, the pressure available to force the liquid through the expansion valve will continue to decrease, and, eventually, the valve's orifice will prove to be too

much of a restriction for adequate flow even with the needle fully withdrawn.

At this point, low side pressure will start to drop, and severe reduction in cooling capacity, marked by freeze-up of the evaporator coil, will result. Eventually, the operating pressure of the evaporator will be lower than the pressure of the atmosphere surrounding it, and air will be drawn into the system wherever there are leaks in the low side.

Because all atmospheric air contains at least some moisture, water will enter the system and mix with the R-12 and the oil. Trace amounts of moisture will cause sludging of the oil, and corrosion of the system. Saturation and clogging of the filter/drier, and freezing of the expansion valve orifice will eventually result. As air fills the system to a greater and greater extent, it will interfere more and more with the normal flows of refrigerant and heat.

From this description, it should be obvious that much of the repairman's time will be spent detecting leaks, repairing them, and then restoring the purity and quantity of the refrigerant charge. A list of general precautions that should be observed while doing this follows:

1. Keep all tools as clean and dry as possible.
2. Thoroughly purge the service gauges and hoses of air and moisture before connecting them to the system. Keep them capped when not in use.
3. Thoroughly clean any refrigerant fitting before disconnecting it, in order to minimize the entrance of dirt into the system.
4. Plan any operation that requires opening the system beforehand, in order to minimize the length of time it will be exposed to open air. Cap or seal the open ends to minimize the entrance of foreign material.
5. When adding oil, pour it through an extremely clean and dry tube or funnel. Keep the oil capped whenever possible. Do not use oil that has not been kept tightly sealed.
6. Use only refrigerant 12. Purchase refrigerant intended for use in only automatic air conditioning systems. Avoid the use of refrigerant 12 that may be packaged for another use, such as cleaning, or powering a horn, as it is impure.
7. Completely evacuate any system that has been opened to replace a component, or that has leaked sufficiently to draw in moisture and air. This requires evacuating air and moisture with a good vacuum pump for at least one hour. If a system has been open for a considerable length of time it may be advisable to evacuate the system for up to 12 hours (overnight).
8. Use a wrench on both halves of a fitting that is to be disconnected, so as to avoid placing torque on any of the refrigerant lines.

How to Spot Bad Hoses

Both the upper and lower radiator hoses are called upon to perform difficult jobs in an inhospitable environment. They are subject to nearly 18 psi at under hood temperatures often over 280°F., and must circulate nearly 7500 gallons of coolant an hour—3 good reasons to have good hoses.

Swollen hose

A good test for any hose is to feel it for soft or spongy spots. Frequently these will appear as swollen areas of the hose. The most likely cause is oil soaking. This hose could burst at any time, when hot or under pressure.

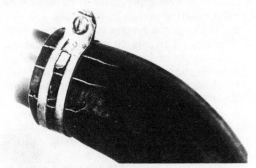

Cracked hose

Cracked hoses can usually be seen but feel the hoses to be sure they have not hardened; a prime cause of cracking. This hose has cracked down to the reinforcing cords and could split at any of the cracks.

Frayed hose end (due to weak clamp)

Weakened clamps frequently are the cause of hose and cooling system failure. The connection between the pipe and hose has deteriorated enough to allow coolant to escape when the engine is hot.

Debris in cooling system

Debris, rust and scale in the cooling system can cause the inside of a hose to weaken. This can usually be felt on the outside of the hose as soft or thinner areas.

9. When overhauling a compressor, pour some of the oil into a clean glass and inspect it. If there is evidence of dirt or metal particles, or both, flush all refrigerant components with clean refrigerant before evacuating and re-charging the system. In addition, if metal particles are present, the compressor should be replaced.

10. Schrader valves may leak only when under full operating pressure. Therefore, if leakage is suspected but cannot be located, operate the system with a full charge of refrigerant and look for leaks from all Schrader valves. Replace any faulty valves.

Additional Preventive Maintenance Checks
ANTIFREEZE

In order to prevent heater core freeze-up during A/C operation, it is necessary to maintain permanent type antifreeze protection of + 15°F, or lower. A reading of –15°F is ideal since this protection also supplies sufficient corrosion inhibitors for the protection of the engine cooling system.

NOTE: *The same antifreeze should not be used longer than the manufacturer specifies.*

RADIATOR CAP

For efficient operation of an air conditioned car's cooling system, the radiator cap should have a holding pressure which meets manufacturer's specifications. A cap which fails to hold these pressures should be replaced.

CONDENSER

Any obstruction of or damage to the condenser configuration will restrict the air flow which is essential to its efficient operation. It is therefore a good rule to keep this unit clean and in proper physical shape.

NOTE: *Bug screens are regarded as obstructions.*

CONDENSATION DRAIN TUBE

This single molded drain tube expels the condensation, which accumulates on the bottom of the evaporator housing, into the engine compartment. If this tube is obstructed, the air conditioning performance can be restricted and condensation buildup can spill over onto the vehicle's floor.

SAFETY PRECAUTIONS

Because of the importance of the necessary safety precautions that must be exercised when working with air conditioning systems and R-12 refrigerant, a recap of the safety precautions are outlined.

1. Avoid contact with a charged refrigeration system, even when working on another part of the air conditioning system or vehicle. If a heavy tool comes into contact with a section of copper tubing or a heat exchanger, it can easily cause the relatively soft material to rupture.

2. When it is necessary to apply force to a fitting which contains refrigerant, as when checking that all system couplings are securely tightened, use a wrench on both parts of the fitting involved, if possible. This will avoid putting torque on refrigerant tubing. (It is advisable, when possible, to use tube or line wrenches when tightening these flare nut fittings.)

3. Do not attempt to discharge the system by merely loosening a fitting, or removing the service valve caps and cracking these valves. Precise control is possible only when using the service gauges. Place a rag under the open end of the center charging hose while discharging the system to catch any drops of liquid that might escape. Wear protective gloves when connecting or disconnecting service gauge hoses.

4. Discharge the system only in a well ventilated area, as high concentrations of the gas can exclude oxygen and act as an anaesthetic. When leak testing or soldering, this is particularly important, as toxic gas is formed when R-12 contacts any flame.

5. Never start a system without first verifying that both service valves are back-seated, if equipped, and that all fittings throughout the system are snugly connected.

6. Avoid applying heat to any refrigerant line or storage vessel. Charging may be aided by using water heated to less than 125° to warm the refrigerant container. Never allow a refrigerant storage container to sit out in the sun, or near any other source of heat, such as a radiator.

7. Always wear goggles when working on a system to protect the eyes. If refrigerant contacts the eyes, it is advisable in all cases to see a physician as soon as possible.

8. Frostbite from liquid refrigerant should be treated by first gradually warming the area with cool water, and then gently applying petroleum jelly. A physician should be consulted.

9. Always keep refrigerant drum fittings capped when not in use. Avoid sudden shock to the drum, which might occur from dropping it, or from banging a heavy tool against it. Never carry a drum in the passenger compartment of a car.

10. Always completely discharge the system before painting the vehicle (if the paint is to be baked on), or before welding anywhere near refrigerant lines.

Air Conditioning Tools and Gauges
Test Gauges

Most of the service work performed in air conditioning requires the use of a set of two gauges, one for the high (head) pressure side of the system, the other for the low (suction) side.

The low side gauge records both pressure and vacuum. Vacuum readings are calibrated from 0 to 30 inches and the pressure graduations read from 0 to no less than 60 psi.

The high side gauge measures pressure from 0 to at least 600 psi.

Both gauges are threaded into a manifold that contains two hand shut-off valves. Proper manipulation of these valves and the use of the attached test hoses allow the user to perform the following services:

1. Test high and low side pressures.
2. Remove air, moisture, and contaminated refrigerant.
3. Purge the system (of refrigerant).
4. Charge the system (with refrigerant).

The manifold valves are designed so they have no direct effect on gauge readings, but serve only to provide for, or cut off, flow of refrigerant through the manifold. During all testing and hook-up operations, the valves are kept in a closed position to avoid disturbing the refrigeration system. The valves are opened only to purge the system of refrigerant or to charge it.

When purging the system, the center hose is uncapped at the lower end, and both valves are cracked open slightly. This allows refrigerant pressure to force the entire contents of the system out through the center hose. During charging, the valve on the high side of the manifold is closed, and the valve on the low side is cracked open. Under these conditions, the low pressure in the evaporator will draw refrigerant from the relatively warm refrigerant storage container into the system.

Service Valves

For the user to diagnose an air conditioning system he or she must gain "entrance" to the system in order to observe the pressures. There are two types of terminals for this purpose, the hand shut off type and the familiar Schrader valve.

The Schrader valve is similar to a tire valve stem and the process of connecting the test hoses is the same as threading a hand pump outlet hose to a bicycle tire. As the test hose is threaded to the service port the valve core is depressed, allowing the refrigerant to enter the test hose outlet. Removal of the test hose automatically closes the system.

Extreme caution must be observed when removing test hoses from the Schrader valves as some refrigerant will normally escape, usually under high pressure. (Observe safety precautions.)

Some systems have hand shut-off valves (the

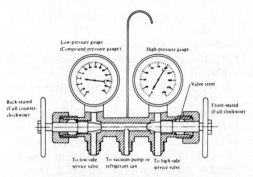

Typical manifold gauge set

stem can be rotated with a special ratcheting box wrench) that can be positioned in the following three ways:

1. FRONT SEATED — Rotated to full clockwise position.

   a. Refrigerant will not flow to compressor, but will reach test gauge port. COMPRESSOR WILL BE DAMAGED IF SYSTEM IS TURNED ON IN THIS POSITION.

   b. The compressor is now isolated and ready for service. However, care must be exercised when removing service valves from the compressor as a residue of refrigerant may still be present within the compressor. Therefore, remove service valves slowly observing all safety precautions.

2. BACK SEATED — Rotated to full counter clockwise position. Normal position for system while in operation. Refrigerant flows to compressor but not to test gauge.

3. MID-POSITION (CRACKED) — Refrigerant flows to entire system. Gauge port (with hose connected) open for testing.

USING THE MANIFOLD GAUGES

The following are step-by-step procedures to guide the user to correct gauge usage.

1. WEAR GOGGLES OR FACE SHIELD DURING ALL TESTING OPERATIONS. BACKSEAT HAND SHUT-OFF TYPE SERVICE VALVES.

2. Remove caps from high and low side service ports. Make sure both gauge valves are closed.

3. Connect low side test hose to service valve that leads to the evaporator (located between the evaporator outlet and the compressor).

4. Attach high side test hose to service valve that leads to the condenser.

5. Mid-position hand shutoff type service valves.

6. Start engine and allow for warm-up. All testing and charging of the system should be done after engine and system have reached normal operation temperatures (except when using certain charging stations).

7. Adjust air conditioner controls to maximum cold.

8. Observe gauge readings.

When the gauges are not being used it is a good idea to:

a. Keep both hand valves in the closed position.

b. Attach both ends of the high and low service hoses to the manifold, if extra outlets are present on the manifold, or plug them if not. Also, keep the center charging hose attached to an empty refrigerant can. This extra precaution will reduce the possibility of moisture entering the gauges. If air and moisture have gotten into the gauges, purge the hoses by supplying refrigerant under pressure to the center hose with both gauge valves open and all openings unplugged.

SYSTEM CHECKS

CAUTION: *Do not attempt to charge or discharge the refrigerant system unless you are thoroughly familiar with its operation and the hazards involved. The compressed refrigerant used in the air conditioning system expands and evaporates (boils) into the atmosphere at a temperature of –21.7°F (–29.8°C) or less. This will freeze any surface that it comes in contact with, including your eyes. In addition, the refrigerant decomposes into a poisonous gas in the presence of flame.*

Some models utilize a C.C.O.T. system which does not include a sight glass. The (C.C.O.T.) Cycling Clutch Orfice Tube refrigeration system is designed to cycle the compressor on and off to maintain desired cooling and to prevent evaporator freeze.

Some 1986 and all 1987 models use a 5-cylinder compressor which does not cycle.

NOTE: *If your car is equipped with an aftermarket air conditioner, the following system checks may not apply.*

The air conditioning system on these cars has no sight glass.

1. Run the engine until it reaches normal operating temperature.

2. Open the hood and all doors.

3. Turn the air conditioning on, move the temperature selector to the first detent to the right of COLD (outside air) and then turn the blower on HI.

4. Idle the engine at 1,000 rpm.

5. Feel the temperature of the evaporator inlet and the accumulator outlet with the compressor clutch engaged.

6. Both lines should be cold. If the inlet pipe is colder than the outlet pipe, the system is low on charge. Do not attempt to charge the system yourself.

DISCHARGING THE SYSTEM

CAUTION: *Perform operation in a well-ventilated area.*

When it is necessary to remove (purge) the refrigerant pressurized in the system, follow this procedure:

1. Operate air conditioner for at least 10 minutes.

2. Attach gauges, shut off engine and air conditioner.

3. Place a container or rag at the outlet of the center charging hose on the gauge. The refrigerant will be discharged there and this precaution will avoid its uncontrolled exposure.

4. Open low side hand valve on gauge slightly.

5. Open high side hand valve slightly.

NOTE: *Too rapid a purging process will be identified by the appearance of an oily foam. If this occurs, close the hand valves a little more until this condition stops.*

6. Close both hand valves on the gauge set when the pressures read 0 and all the refrigerant has left the system.

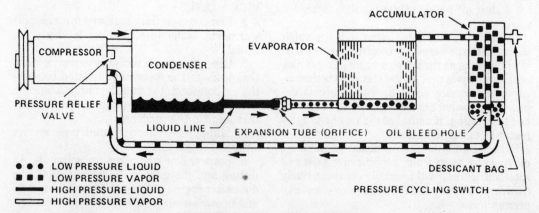

LOW PRESSURE LIQUID
LOW PRESSURE VAPOR
HIGH PRESSURE LIQUID
HIGH PRESSURE VAPOR

Typical C.C.O.T. A/C system (1982–86)

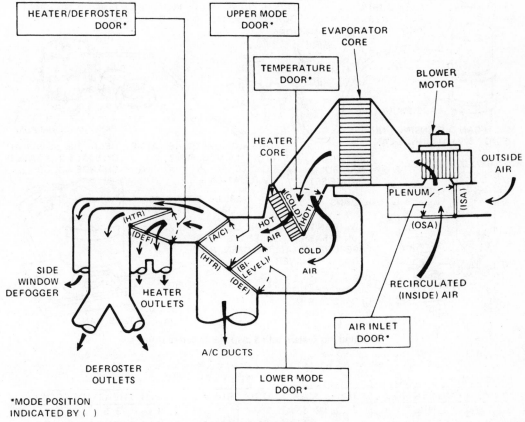

Typical A/C air flow

EVACUATING THE SYSTEM

Before charging any system it is necessary to purge the refrigerant and draw out the trapped moisture with a suitable vacuum pump. Failure to do so will result in ineffective charging and possible damage to the system.

Use this hook-up for the proper evacuation procedure:

1. Connect both service gauge hoses to the high and low service outlets.

2. Open high and low side hand valves on gauge manifold.

3. Open both service valves a slight amount (from back seated position), allow refrigerant to discharge from system.

4. Install center charging hose of gauge set to vacuum pump.

5. Operate vacuum pump for at least one hour. (If the system has been subjected to open conditions for a prolonged period of time it may be necessary to "pump the system down" overnight. Refer to "System Sweep" procedure.)

NOTE: *If low pressure gauge does not show at least 28 in.Hg within 5 minutes, check the system for a leak or loose gauge connectors.*

6. Close hand valves on gauge manifold.

7. Shut off pump.

8. Observe low pressure gauge to determine if vacuum is holding. A vacuum drop may indicate a leak.

SYSTEM SWEEP

An efficient vacuum pump can remove all the air contained in a contaminated air conditioning system very quickly, because of its vapor state. Moisture, however, is far more difficult to remove because the vacuum must force the liquid to evaporate before it will be able to remove it from the system. If a system has become severely contaminated, as, for example, it might become after all the charge was lost in conjunction with vehicle accident damage, moisture removal is extremely time consuming. A vacuum pump could remove all of the moisture only if it were operated for 12 hours or more.

Under these conditions, sweeping the system with refrigerant will speed the process of moisture removal considerably. To sweep, follow the following procedure:

1. Connect vacuum pump to gauges, operate it until vacuum ceases to increase, then continue operation for ten more minutes.

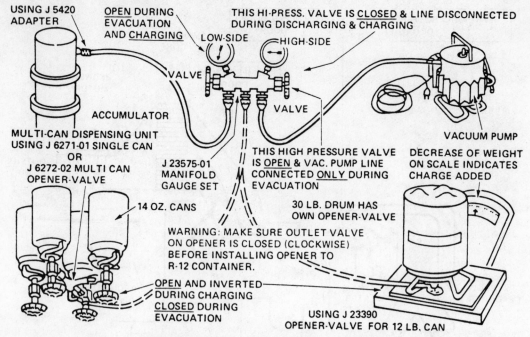

Charging the system with a disposable can or drum

VACUUM VALVE LOGIC		MODE LEVER POSITION						
PORT	CONNECTION	OFF	MAX	NORM	BI-LEVEL	VENT	HEAT	DEFROST
1	INPUT	3,5	2,3,4	3,4	3	3,4	3,5	5
2	OSA RECIRC	VENT	VAC	VENT	VENT	VENT	VENT	VENT
3	DEFROST	VAC	VAC	VAC	VAC	VAC	VAC	VENT
4	A/C MODE	VENT	VAC	VAC	VENT	VAC	VENT	VENT
5	HEAT MODE	VAC	VENT	VENT	VENT	VENT	VAC	VAC

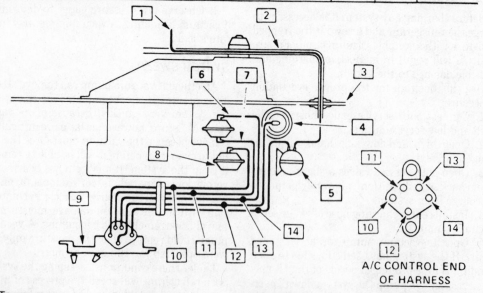

1. To eng. source
2. A/C elec. harn.
3. Dash panel
4. OSA/recirc
5. Vacuum tank
6. Heater
7. A/C
8. Defrost
9. A/C control
10. Def. (blue)
11. A/C mode (yellow)
12. OSA/recir. (orange)
13. Heater (red)
14. Input (violet)

A/C vacuum diagram, 1982–85 Cimarron, 1982–86 Cavalier, Sunbird, Firenza, Skyhawk

2. Charge system with 50% of its rated refrigerant capacity.

3. Operate system at fast idle for ten minutes.

4. Discharge the system.

5. Repeat twice the process of charging to 50% capacity, running the system for ten minutes, and discharging it, for a total of three sweeps.

6. Replace drier.

7. Pump system down as in Step 1.

8. Charge system.

CHARGING THE SYSTEM

CAUTION: *Never attempt to charge the system by opening the high pressure gauge control while the compressor is operating. The compressor accumulating pressure can burst the refrigerant container, causing sever personal injuries.*

When charging the CCOT system, attach only the low pressure line to the low pressure gauge port, located on the accumulator. Do not attach the high pressure line to any service port or allow it to remain attached to the vacuum pump after evacuation. Be sure both the high and the low pressure control valves are closed on the gauge set. To complete the charging of the system, follow the outline supplied.

1. Start the engine and allow to run at idle, with the cooling system at normal operating temperature.

2. Attach the center gauge hose to a single or multi-can dispenser.

3. With the multi-can dispenser inverted, allow one pound or the contents of one or two 14 oz. cans to enter the system through the low pressure side by opening the gauge low pressure control valve.

4. Close the low pressure gauge control valve and turn the A/C system on to engage the compressor. Place the blower motor in its high mode.

5. Open the low pressure gauge control valve and draw the remaining charge into the system. Refer to the capacity chart at the end of this section for the individual vehicle or system capacity.

PORT	CONNECTION	OFF	MAX	NORM	BI-LEVEL	VENT	HEAT	DEFROST
VACUUM VALVE LOGIC				MODE LEVER POSITION				
1	INPUT	3,5	2,3,4	3,4	3	3,4	3,5	5
2	OSA RECIRC	VENT	VAC	VENT	VENT	VENT	VENT	VENT
3	DEFROST	VAC	VAC	VAC	VAC	VAC	VAC	VENT
4	A/C MODE	VENT	VAC	VAC	VENT	VAC	VENT	VENT
5	HEAT MODE	VAC	VENT	VENT	VENT	VENT	VAC	VAC

1. To eng. source
2. A/C elec. harn.
3. Dash panel
4. OSA/recirc
5. Vacuum tank
6. Heater
7. A/C
8. Defrost
9. A/C control
10. Def. (blue)
11. A/C mode (yellow)
12. OSA/recirc. (orange)
13. Heater (red)
14. Input (violet)

A/C vacuum diagram, 1987 Cavalier

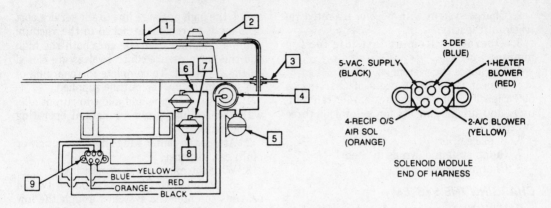

VACUUM VALVE LOGIC		MODE LEVER POSITION						
PORT	CONNECTION	OFF	MAX	NORM	BI-LEVEL	VENT	HEAT	DEFROST
1	INPUT	3,5	2,3,4	3,4	3	3,4	3,5	5
2	OSA RECIRC	VENT	VAC	VENT	VENT	VENT	VENT	VENT
3	DEFROST	VAC	VAC	VAC	VAC	VAC	VAC	VENT
4	A/C MODE	VENT	VAC	VAC	VENT	VAC	VENT	VENT
5	HEAT MODE	VAC	VENT	VENT	VENT	VENT	VAC	VAC

1. To eng. source
2. A/C elec. harn.
3. Dash panel
4. OSA/recirc valve
5. Vacuum tank
6. Heater valve
7. A/C valve
8. Defrost valve
9. Vacuum connector

A/C vacuum diagram, 1986–87 Cimarron

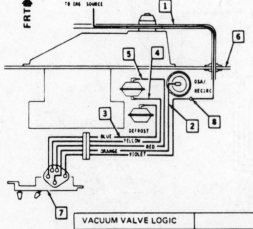

1. VIOLET — 1. INPUT SOURCE
2. ORANGE — 2. AIR INLET VALVE
3. BLUE — 3. DEFROST
4. YELLOW — 4. A/C MODE
5. RED — 5. HEATER MODE
6. COWL
7. A/C CONTROL ASSEMBLY
8. VACUUM CHECK VALVE

VACUUM VALVE LOGIC		MODE LEVER POSITION						
PORT	CONNECTION	OFF	MAX	NORM	BI-LEVEL	VENT	HEAT	DEFROST
1	INPUT	3,5	2,3,4	3,4	3	3,4	3,5	5
2	AIR INLET	VENT	VAC	VENT	VENT	VENT	VENT	VENT
3	DEFROST	VAC	VAC	VAC	VAC	VAC	VAC	VENT
4	A/C MODE	VENT	VAC	VAC	VENT	VAC	VENT	VENT
5	HEATER MODE	VAC	VENT	VENT	VENT	VENT	VAC	VAC

A/C vacuum diagram, 1987 Sunbird, Firenza, Skyhawk

Troubleshooting Basic Air Conditioning Problems

Problem	Cause	Solution
There's little or no air coming from the vents (and you're sure it's on)	• The A/C fuse is blown • Broken or loose wires or connections • The on/off switch is defective	• Check and/or replace fuse • Check and/or repair connections • Replace switch
The air coming from the vents is not cool enough	• Windows and air vent wings open • The compressor belt is slipping • Heater is on • Condenser is clogged with debris • Refrigerant has escaped through a leak in the system • Receiver/drier is plugged	• Close windows and vent wings • Tighten or replace compressor belt • Shut heater off • Clean the condenser • Check system • Service system
The air has an odor	• Vacuum system is disrupted • Odor producing substances on the evaporator case • Condensation has collected in the bottom of the evaporator housing	• Have the system checked/repaired • Clean the evaporator case • Clean the evaporator housing drains
System is noisy or vibrating	• Compressor belt or mountings loose • Air in the system	• Tighten or replace belt; tighten mounting bolts • Have the system serviced

Sight glass condition
  Constant bubbles, foam or oil streaks
  Clear sight glass, but no cold air
  Clear sight glass, but air is cold
  Clouded with milky fluid
	
	• Undercharged system
	
	• No refrigerant at all
	• System is OK
	• Receiver drier is leaking dessicant
		
		• Charge the system
		
		• Check and charge the system
		
		• Have system checked

Large difference in temperature of lines	• System undercharged	• Charge and leak test the system
Compressor noise	• Broken valves • Overcharged • Incorrect oil level • Piston slap • Broken rings • Drive belt pulley bolts are loose	• Replace the valve plate • Discharge, evacuate and install the correct charge • Isolate the compressor and check the oil level. Correct as necessary. • Replace the compressor • Replace the compressor • Tighten with the correct torque specification
Excessive vibration	• Incorrect belt tension • Clutch loose • Overcharged • Pulley is misaligned	• Adjust the belt tension • Tighten the clutch • Discharge, evacuate and install the correct charge • Align the pulley
Condensation dripping in the passenger compartment	• Drain hose plugged or improperly positioned • Insulation removed or improperly installed	• Clean the drain hose and check for proper installation • Replace the insulation on the expansion valve and hoses
Frozen evaporator coil	• Faulty thermostat • Thermostat capillary tube improperly installed • Thermostat not adjusted properly	• Replace the thermostat • Install the capillary tube correctly • Adjust the thermostat
Low side low—high side low	• System refrigerant is low • Expansion valve is restricted	• Evacuate, leak test and charge the system • Replace the expansion valve
Low side high—high side low	• Internal leak in the compressor—worn	• Remove the compressor cylinder head and inspect the compressor. Replace the valve plate assembly if necessary. If the compressor pistons, rings or

Troubleshooting Basic Air Conditioning Problems (cont.)

Problem	Cause	Solution
Low side high—high side low (cont.)		cylinders are excessively worn or scored replace the compressor
	• Cylinder head gasket is leaking	• Install a replacement cylinder head gasket
	• Expansion valve is defective	• Replace the expansion valve
	• Drive belt slipping	• Adjust the belt tension
Low side high—high side high	• Condenser fins obstructed	• Clean the condenser fins
	• Air in the system	• Evacuate, leak test and charge the system
	• Expansion valve is defective	• Replace the expansion valve
	• Loose or worn fan belts	• Adjust or replace the belts as necessary
Low side low—high side high	• Expansion valve is defective	• Replace the expansion valve
	• Restriction in the refrigerant hose	• Check the hose for kinks—replace if necessary
	• Restriction in the receiver/drier	• Replace the receiver/drier
	• Restriction in the condenser	• Replace the condenser
Low side and high side normal (inadequate cooling)	• Air in the system	• Evacuate, leak test and charge the system
	• Moisture in the system	• Evacuate, leak test and charge the system

6. Close the low pressure gauge control valve and the refrigerant source valve, on the multi-can dispenser. Remove the low pressure hose from the accumulator quickly to avoid loss of refrigerant through the Schrader valve.

7. Install the protective cap on the gauge port and check the system for leakage.

8. Test the system for proper operation.

FREON CAPACITIES:
- 4-cyl. engines: 2.25 lbs.
- V6 engines: 2.50 lbs.

Leak Testing the System

There are several methods of detecting leaks in an air conditioning system; among them, the two most popular are (1) halide leak-detection or the "open flame method," and (2) electronic leak-detection.

The halide leak detection is a torch like device which produces a yellow-green color when refrigerant is introduced into the flame at the burner. A purple or violet color indicates the presence of large amounts of refrigerant at the burner.

An electronic leak detector is a small portable electronic device with an extended probe. With the unit activated the probe is passed along those components of the system which contain refrigerant. If a leak is detected, the unit will sound an alarm signal or activate a display signal depending on the manufacturer's design. It is advisable to follow the manufacturer's instructions as the design and function of the detection may vary significantly.

CAUTION: *Care should be taken to operate either type of detector in well ventilated areas, so as to reduce the chance of personal injury, which may result from coming in contact with poisonous gases produced when R-12 is exposed to flame or electric spark.*

Windshield Wipers

For maximum effectiveness and longest element lift, the windshield and wiper blades should be kept clean. Dirt, tree sap, road tar and so on will cause streaking, smearing and blade deterioration if left on the glass. It is advisable to wash the windshield carefully with a commercial glass cleaner at least once a month. Wipe off the rubber blades with the wet rag afterwards. Do not attempt to move the wipers back and forth by hand; damage to the motor and drive mechanism will result.

If the blades are found to be cracked, broken or torn, they should be replaced immediately. Replacement intervals will vary with usage, although ozone deterioration usually limits blade life to about one year. If the wiper pattern is smeared or streaked, or if the blade chatters across the glass, the blades should be replaced. It is easiest and most sensible to replace them in pairs.

There are basically three different types of wiper blade refills, which differ in their method of replacement. Your J-Car could come originally equipped with either one of the first two types, Anco® or Trico®. The first type (Anco®) has two release buttons, approximately ⅓ of

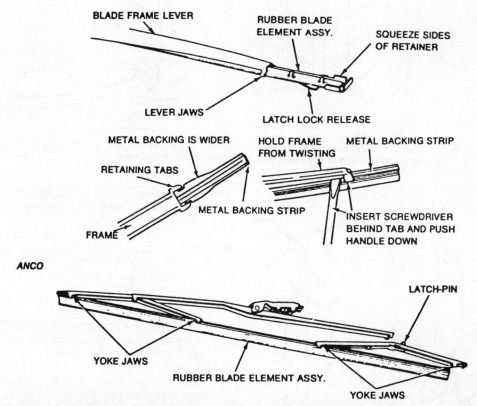

TRICO

BLADE FRAME LEVER

RUBBER BLADE
ELEMENT ASSY.

SQUEEZE SIDES
OF RETAINER

LEVER JAWS

LATCH LOCK RELEASE

METAL BACKING IS WIDER

HOLD FRAME
FROM TWISTING

METAL BACKING STRIP

RETAINING TABS

METAL BACKING STRIP

FRAME

INSERT SCREWDRIVER
BEHIND TAB AND PUSH
HANDLE DOWN

ANCO

LATCH-PIN

YOKE JAWS

RUBBER BLADE ELEMENT ASSY.

YOKE JAWS

The rubber element can be changed without replacing the entire blade assembly; your J-car may have either one of these types of blades

the way up from the ends of the blade frame. Pushing the buttons down releases a lock and allows the rubber blade to be removed from the frame. The new blade slides back into the frame and locks in place.

The second type (Trico®), has two metal tabs which are unlocked by squeezing them together. The rubber blade can then be withdrawn from the frame jaws. A new one is installed by inserting it into the front frame jaws and sliding it rearward to engage the remaining frame jaws. There are usually four jaws; be certain when installing that the refill is engaged in all of them. At the end of its travel, the tabs will lock into place on the front jaws of the wiper blade frame.

The third type is a refill made from polycarbonate. The refill has a simple locking device at one end which flexes downward out of the groove into which the jaws of the holder fit, allowing easy release. By sliding the new refill through all the jaws and pushing through the slight resistance when it reaches the end of its travel, the refill will lock into position.

Regardless of the type of refill used, make sure that all the frame jaws are engaged as the refill is pushed into place and locked. The metal blade holder and frame will scratch the glass if allowed to touch it.

Tires and Wheels
INFLATION

Tires should be checked weekly for proper air pressure. A chart, located either in the glove compartment or on the driver's or passenger's door, gives the recommended inflation pressures. Maximum fuel economy and tire life will result if the pressure is maintained at the highest figure given on the chart. Pressures should be checked before driving since pressure can increase as much as six pounds per square inch (psi) due to heat buildup. It is a good idea to have you own accurate pressure gauge, because not all gauges on service station air pumps can be trusted. When checking pressures, do not neglect the spare tire. Note that some spare tires require pressures considerably higher than those used in the other tires.

While you are about the task of checking air pressure, inspect the tire treads for cuts,

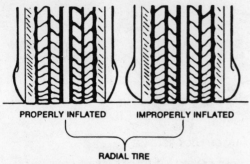

PROPERLY INFLATED   IMPROPERLY INFLATED

RADIAL TIRE

Don't judge a radial tire's pressure by its appearance. An improperly inflated radial tire looks similar to a properly inflated one

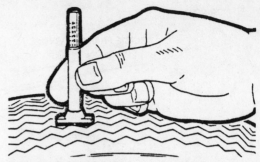

Inexpensive gauges are also available for measurement of tread wear

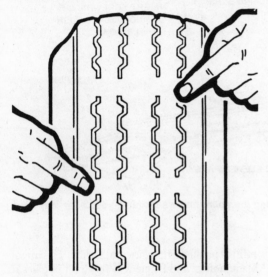

Tread wear indicators will appear as bands across the tread when the tire is due for replacement

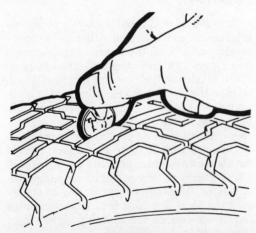

You can use a penny for tread wear checks; if the top of Lincoln's head is visible in two adjacent grooves, the tire should be replaced

bruises and other damage. Check the air valves to be sure that they are tight. Replace any missing valve caps.

Check the tires for uneven wear that might indicate the need for front end alignment or tire rotation. Tires should be replaced when a tread wear indicator appears as a solid band across the tread.

TIRE DESIGN

When buying new tires, give some thought to the following points, especially if you are considering a switch to larger tires or a different profile series:

1. All four tires must be of the same construction type. This rule cannot be violated, Radial, bias, and bias-belted tires must not be mixed.

2. The wheels should be the correct width for the tire. Tire dealers have charts of tire and rim compatibility. A mis-match will cause sloppy handling and rapid tire wear. The tread width should match the rim width (inside bead to inside bead) within an inch. For radial tires, the rim should be 80% or less of the tire (not tread) width.

3. The height (mounted diameter) of the new tires can change speedometer accuracy, engine speed at a given road speed, fuel mileage, acceleration, and ground clearance. Tire manufacturers furnish full measurement specifications.

4. The spare tire should be usable, at least for short distance and low speed operation, with the new tires.

5. There shouldn't be any body interference when loaded, on bumps, or in turns.

TIRE ROTATION

Tire rotation is recommended every 6,000 miles or so, to obtain maximum tire wear. The pattern you use depends on whether or not you car has a usable spare. Radial tires should not be cross-switched (from one side of the car to the other); they last longer if their direction of rotation is not changed. Snow tires sometimes have directional arrows molded into the side of

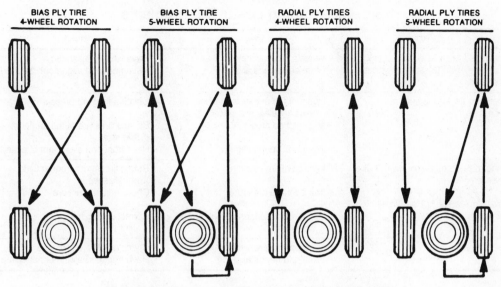

| BIAS PLY TIRE 4-WHEEL ROTATION | BIAS PLY TIRE 5-WHEEL ROTATION | RADIAL PLY TIRES 4-WHEEL ROTATION | RADIAL PLY TIRES 5-WHEEL ROTATION |

Tire rotation diagrams; radials must never be cross switched

the carcass; the arrow shows the direction of rotation. They will wear very rapidly if the rotation is reversed. Studded tires will lose their studs if their rotational direction is reversed.

NOTE: *Mark the wheel position or direction or rotation on radial tires or studded snow tires before removing them.*

CAUTION: *Avoid overtightening the lug nuts to prevent damage to the brake disc or drum. Alloy wheels can also be cracked by* *overtightening. Use of a torque wrench is highly recommended.*

STORAGE

Store the tires at the proper inflation pressure if they are mounted on wheels. Keep them in a cool dry place, laid on their sides. If the tires are stored in the garage or basement, do not let them stand on a concrete floor; set them on strips of wood.

Troubleshooting Basic Wheel Problems

Problem	Cause	Solution
The car's front end vibrates at high speed	• The wheels are out of balance • Wheels are out of alignment	• Have wheels balanced • Have wheel alignment checked/adjusted
Car pulls to either side	• Wheels are out of alignment • Unequal tire pressure • Different size tires or wheels	• Have wheel alignment checked/adjusted • Check/adjust tire pressure • Change tires or wheels to same size
The car's wheel(s) wobbles	• Loose wheel lug nuts • Wheels out of balance • Damaged wheel • Wheels are out of alignment • Worn or damaged ball joint • Excessive play in the steering linkage (usually due to worn parts) • Defective shock absorber	• Tighten wheel lug nuts • Have tires balanced • Raise car and spin the wheel. If the wheel is bent, it should be replaced • Have wheel alignment checked/adjusted • Check ball joints • Check steering linkage • Check shock absorbers
Tires wear unevenly or prematurely	• Incorrect wheel size • Wheels are out of balance • Wheels are out of alignment	• Check if wheel and tire size are compatible • Have wheels balanced • Have wheel alignment checked/adjusted

Troubleshooting Basic Tire Problems

Problem	Cause	Solution
The car's front end vibrates at high speeds and the steering wheel shakes	• Wheels out of balance • Front end needs aligning	• Have wheels balanced • Have front end alignment checked
The car pulls to one side while cruising	• Unequal tire pressure (car will usually pull to the low side) • Mismatched tires • Front end needs aligning	• Check/adjust tire pressure • Be sure tires are of the same type and size • Have front end alignment checked
Abnormal, excessive or uneven tire wear See "How to Read Tire Wear"	• Infrequent tire rotation • Improper tire pressure • Sudden stops/starts or high speed on curves	• Rotate tires more frequently to equalize wear • Check/adjust pressure • Correct driving habits
Tire squeals	• Improper tire pressure • Front end needs aligning	• Check/adjust tire pressure • Have front end alignment checked

Recommended Lubricants

Lubricant	Classification
Engine Oil	SF, SF/CC or SF/CD
Engine Coolant	Mixture of water and a good quality Ethylene Glycol base anti freeze
Brake System and Master Cylinder	DOT 3
Parking Brake Cables	Chassis grease meeting requirements of GM 6031-M
Power Steering System & Pump Reservoir	GM Power Steering Fluid, Part No. 1050017 or equivalent
Manual Steering Gear	Chassis grease meeting requirements of GM 6031-M
Automatic Transaxle	DEXRON® II Automatic Transmission Fluid
Automatic Transaxle Shift Linkage	Engine oil
Manual Transaxle	DEXRON® II Automatic Transmission Fluid (4 spd.) 5W30 engine oil (5 spd.)
Clutch Linkage Pivot Points	Engine oil
Floor Shift Linkage	Engine oil
Chassis Lubrication	Chassis grease meeting requirements of GM 6031-M
Windshield Washer Solvent	GM Optikleen Washer Solvent, Part No. 1051515 or equivalent
Hood Latch Assembly a. pivot and spring anchor b. release pawl	a. Engine oil b. Chassis grease meeting requirements of GM 6031-M
Hood and Door Hinges	Engine oil
Body door hinge pins, station wagon tailgate hinge and linkage, station wagon folding seat, fuel door hinge, rear compartment hinges	Engine oil
Key Lock Cylinders	WD-40 Spray lubricant or equivalent

Tire Size Comparison Chart

"Letter" sizes			Inch Sizes	Metric-inch Sizes		
"60 Series"	"70 Series"	"78 Series"	1965–77	"60 Series"	"70 Series"	"80 Series"
			5.50-12, 5.60-12	165/60-12	165/70-12	155-12
		Y78-12	6.00-12			
		W78-13	5.20-13	165/60-13	145/70-13	135-13
		Y78-13	5.60-13	175/60-13	155/70-13	145-13
			6.15-13	185/60-13	165/70-13	155-13, P155/80-13
A60-13	A70-13	A78-13	6.40-13	195/60-13	175/70-13	165-13
B60-13	B70-13	B78-13	6.70-13	205/60-13	185/70-13	175-13
			6.90-13			
C60-13	C70-13	C78-13	7.00-13	215/60-13	195/70-13	185-13
D60-13	D70-13	D78-13	7.25-13			
E60-13	E70-13	E78-13	7.75-13			195-13
			5.20-14	165/60-14	145/70-14	135-14
			5.60-14	175/60-14	155/70-14	145-14
			5.90-14			
A60-14	A70-14	A78-14	6.15-14	185/60-14	165/70-14	155-14
	B70-14	B78-14	6.45-14	195/60-14	175/70-14	165-14
	C70-14	C78-14	6.95-14	205/60-14	185/70-14	175-14
D60-14	D70-14	D78-14				
E60-14	E70-14	E78-14	7.35-14	215/60-14	195/70-14	185-14
F60-14	F70-14	F78-14, F83-14	7.75-14	225/60-14	200/70-14	195-14
G60-14	G70-14	G77-14, G78-14	8.25-14	235/60-14	205/70-14	205-14
H60-14	H70-14	H78-14	8.55-14	245/60-14	215/70-14	215-14
J60-14	J70-14	J78-14	8.85-14	255/60-14	225/70-14	225-14
L60-14	L70-14		9.15-14	265/60-14	235/70-14	
	A70-15	A78-15	5.60-15	185/60-15	165/70-15	155-15
B60-15	B70-15	B78-15	6.35-15	195/60-15	175/70-15	165-15
C60-15	C70-15	C78-15	6.85-15	205/60-15	185/70-15	175-15
	D70-15	D78-15				
E60-15	E70-15	E78-15	7.35-15	215/60-15	195/70-15	185-15
F60-15	F70-15	F78-15	7.75-15	225/60-15	205/70-15	195-15
G60-15	G70-15	G78-15	8.15-15/8.25-15	235/60-15	215/70-15	205-15
H60-15	H70-15	H78-15	8.45-15/8.55-15	245/60-15	225/70-15	215-15
J60-15	J70-15	J78-15	8.85-15/8.90-15	255/60-15	235/70-15	225-15
	K70-15		9.00-15	265/60-15	245/70-15	230-15
L60-15	L70-15	L78-15, L84-15	9.15-15			235-15
	M70-15	M78-15				255-15
		N78-15				

Note: Every size tire is not listed and many size comparisons are approximate, based on load ratings. Wider tires than those supplied new with the vehicle, should always be checked for clearance.

FLUIDS AND LUBRICANTS

Fuel and Engine Oil Recommendations

Oil

The SAE (Society of Automotive Engineers) grade number indicates the viscosity of the engine oil, and thus its ability to lubricate at a given temperature. The lower the SAE grade number, the lighter the oil; the lower the viscosity, the easier it is to crank the engine in cold weather.

The API (American Petroleum Institute) designation indicates the classification of engine oil for use under given operating conditions. Only oils designated for use Service SF should be used. Oils of the SF type perform a variety of functions inside the engine in addition to the basic function as a lubricant. Through a balanced system of metallic detergents and polymeric dispersants, the oil prevents the formation of high and low temperature deposits, and also keeps sludge and dirt particles in suspension. Acids, particularly sulfuric acid, as well as other by products of combustion, are neutralized. Both the SAE grade number and the API designation can be found on the top of the oil can.

NOTE: *Non-detergent or straight mineral oils must never be used. Oil viscosities should be chosen from those oils recommended for the lowest anticipated temperatures during the oil change interval.*

Multi-viscosity oils offer the important advantage of being adaptable to temperature ex-

USE THESE SAE VISCOSITY GRADES

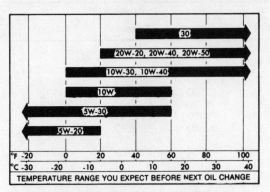

NOTICE: DO NOT USE SAE 5W-20 OILS FOR CONTINUOUS
HIGH-SPEED DRIVING. 5W-30 OILS MAY BE USED
UP TO 100°F (38°C)

Oil viscosity chart; multi-viscosity oils offer greater temperature latitude

tremes. They allow easy starting at low temperatures, yet give good protection at high speeds and engine temperatures. This is a decided advantage in changeable climates or in long distance touring.

Fuel

All G.M. J-cars must use unleaded fuel. The use of leaded fuel will plug the catalyst rendering it inoperative, and will increase the exhaust back pressure to the point where engine output will be severely reduced. The minimum octane for all engines is 91 RON. All unleaded fuels sold in the U.S. are required to meet this minimum octane rating.

Use of a fuel too low in octane (a measurement of anti-knock quality) will result in spark knock. Since many factors affect operating efficiency, such as altitude, terrain, and air temperature and humidity, knocking may result even though the recommended fuel is being used. If persistent knocking occurs, it may be necessary to switch to a slightly higher grade of unleaded gasoline. Continuous or heavy knocking may result in serious engine damage, for which the manufacturer is not responsible.

NOTE: *Your car's engine fuel requirement can change with time, due to carbon buildup, which changes the compression ratio. If your car's engine knocks, pings, or runs on, switch to a higher grade of fuel, if possible, and check the ignition timing. Sometimes changing brands of gasoline will cure the problem. If it is necessary to retard timing from specifications, don't change it more than a few degrees. Retarded timing will reduce power output and fuel mileage, and will increase engine temperature.*

Engine
OIL LEVEL CHECK

The engine oil level should be checked at every fuel stop, or once a week, whichever occurs more regularly. The best time to check is when the engine is warm, although checking immediately after the engine has been shut off will result in an inaccurate reading, since it takes a few minutes for all of the oil to drain back down into the crankcase. If the engine is cold, the engine should not be run before the level is checked. The oil level is checked by means of a dipstick, located at the front of the engine compartment:

1. If the engine is warm, it should be allowed to sit for a few minutes after being shut off to allow the oil to drain down into the oil pan. The car should be parked on a level surface.

2. Pull the dipstick out from its holder, wipe it clean with a rag, and reinsert it firmly. Be sure it is pushed all the way home, or the reading you're about to take will be incorrect.

3. Pull the dipstick again and hold it horizontally to prevent the oil from running. The dipstick is marked with Add and Full lines. The oil level should be above the Add line.

4. Reinstall the dipstick.

If oil is needed, it is added through the capped opening in the cylinder head cover. One quart of oil will raise the level from Add to Full. Only oils labeled SF should be used; select a viscosity that will be compatible with the temperatures expected until the next drain interval. See the Oil and Fuel Recommendations section later in this chapter if you are not sure what type of oil to use. Check the oil level again after any additions. Be careful not to overfill, which will lead to leakage and seal damage.

Typical engine oil dipstick

The oil level on the dipstick must always be above the 'ADD' line. 1 quart will raise the level from the 'ADD' line to the 'FULL' line

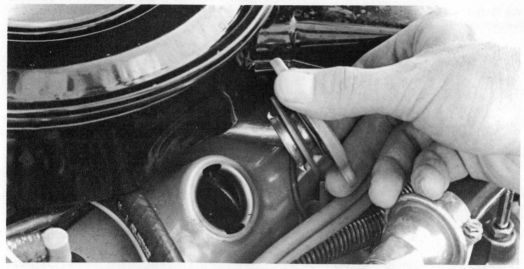

Add oil through the capped filler hole in the cylinder head cover

OIL AND FILTER CHANGE

CAUTION: *The EPA warns that prolonged contact with used engine oil may cause a number of skin disorders, including cancer! You should make every effort to minimize your exposure to used engine oil. Protective gloves should be worn when changing the oil. Wash your hands and any other exposed skin areas as soon as possible after exposure to used engine oil. Soap and water, or waterless hand cleaner should be used.*

If you purchased your J-car new, the engine oil and filter should be changed at the first 7,500 miles or 12 months (whichever comes first), and every 7,500 miles or 12 months thereafter. You should make it a practice to change the oil filter at every oil change; otherwise, a quart of dirty oil remains in the engine every other time the oil is changed. The change interval should be halved when the car is driven under severe conditions, such as in extremely dusty weather, or when the car is used for trailer towing, prolonged high speed driving, or repeated short trips in freezing weather.

1. Drive the car until the engine is at normal operating temperature. A run to the parts store for oil and a filter should accomplish this. If the engine is not hot when the oil is changed, most of the acids and contaminants will remain inside the engine.

2. Shut off the engine, and slide a pan of at least six quarts capacity under the oil pan. Throw-away aluminum roasting pans can be used for this.

3. Remove the drain plug from the engine oil pan, after wiping the plug area clean. The drain plug is the bolt inserted at an angle into the lowest point of the oil pan.

4. The oil from the engine will be HOT. It will probably not be possible to hold onto the drain plug. You may have to let it fall into the pan and fish it out later. Allow all the oil to drain completely. This will take a few minutes.

5. Wipe off the drain plug, removing any traces of metal particles. Pay particular attention to the threads. Replace it, and tighten it snugly.

6. The oil filter is at the back of the engine. It is impossible to reach from above, and almost as inaccessible from below. It may be easiest to remove the right front wheel and reach through the fender opening to get at the four cylinder oil filter. Use an oil filter strap wrench to loosen the oil filter; these are available at auto parts stores. It is recommended that you purchase

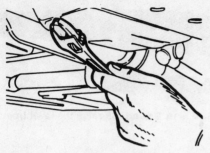

The oil drain plug is located at the lowest point of the oil pan

Apply a thin film of clean oil to the new gasket to prevent it from tearing upon installation

one with as thin a strap as possible, to get into tight areas. Place the drain pan on the ground, under the filter. Unscrew and discard the old filter. It will be VERY HOT, so be careful.

7. If the oil filter is on so tightly that it collapses under pressure from the wrench, drive a long punch or a nail through it, across the diameter and as close to the base as possible, and use this as a lever to unscrew it. Make sure you are turning it counterclockwise.

8. Clean off the oil filter mounting surface with a rag. Apply a thin film of clean engine oil to the filter gasket.

9. Screw the filter on by hand until the gasket makes contact. Then tighten it by hand an additional ½-¾ turn. Do not overtighten.

10. Remove the filler cap on the rocker (valve) cover, after wiping the area clean.

11. Add the correct number of quarts of oil specified in the Capacities chart. If you don't have an oil can spout, you will need a funnel. Be certain you do not overfill the engine, which can cause serious damage. Replace the cap.

12. Check the oil level on the dipstick. It is normal for the level to be a bit above the full mark. Start the engine and allow it to idle for a few minutes.

CAUTION: *Do not run the engine above idle speed until it has built up oil pressure, indicated when the oil light goes out.*

Check around the filter and drain plug for any leaks.

13. Shut off the engine, allow the oil to drain for a minute, and check the oil level.

After completing this job, you will have several quarts of filthy oil to dispose of. The best thing to do with it is to funnel it into old plastic milk containers or bleach bottles. Then, you can either pour it into the recycling barrel at the gas station (if you're on good terms with the attendant), or put the containers into the trash.

Manual Transaxle

FLUID RECOMMENDATION AND LEVEL CHECK

The fluid level in the manual transaxle should be checked every 12 months or 7,500 miles, whichever comes first.

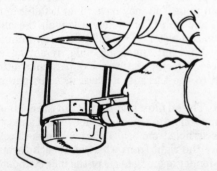

Use an oil filter strap wrench to remove the oil filter; install the new filter by hand

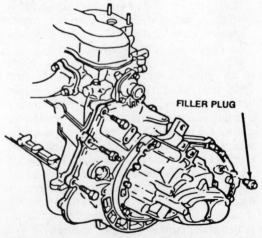

FILLER PLUG

Some models use a filler plug to check the level of the manual transaxle lubricant

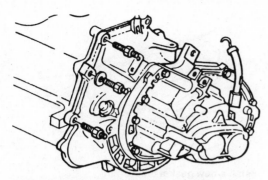

All models use a dipstick to check the level of the manual transaxle lubricant

NOTE: *Certain models may be equipped with a dipstick for checking the fluid level. If so, remove the dipstick when the transaxle is cold and check the level.*

1. Park the car on a level surface. The transaxle should be cool to the touch. If it is hot, check the level later, when it has cooled.

2. Remove the dipstick from the left side of the transaxle.

3. If lubricant is needed, add DEXRON®II transmission fluid in the 4-speeds and 5W-30 engine oil in the 5-speeds, through the filler tube until the level is correct.

4. When the level is correct, reinstall the dipstick firmly.

DRAIN AND REFILL

The fluid in the manual transaxle normally does not require changing, however you may want to chnge it if the car is used under severe conditions.

1. The fluid should be hot before it is drained. If the car is driven until the engine is at normal operating temperature, the fluid should be hot enough.

2. Remove the filler plug (or dipstick) from the left side of the transaxle to provide a vent.

3. The drain plug is located on the bottom of the transaxle case. Place a pan under the drain plug and remove it.

CAUTION: *The fluid will be HOT. Push up against the threads as you unscrew the plug to prevent leakage.*

4. Allow the fluid to drain completely. Check the condition of the plug gasket and replace it if necessary. Clean off the plug and replace, tightening it until snug.

5. Fill the transaxle with fluid through the fill or dipstick tube. The 4-speed uses DEXRON®II automatic transmission fluid. All 5-speeds use 5W-30 engine oil. You will need the aid of a long neck funnel or a funnel and a hose to pour through.

6. Use the dipstick to gauge the level of the fluid.

7. Replace the filler plug or dipstick and dispose of the old fluid in the same manner as you would old engine oil.

Take a drive in the car, stop on a level surface, and check the oil level.

Automatic Transaxle

FLUID RECOMMENDATION AND LEVEL CHECK

The fluid level in the automatic transaxle should be checked every 12 months or 7,500 miles, whichever comes first. The transaxle has a dipstick for fluid level checks.

1. Drive the car until it is at normal operating temperature. The level should not be checked immediately after the car has been driven for a long time at high speed, or in city traffic in hot weather; in those cases, the transaxle should be given a half hour to cool down.

2. Stop the car, apply the parking brake, then shift slowly through all gear positions, ending in Park. Let the engine idle for about five minutes with the selector in Park. The car should be on a level surface.

3. With the engine still running, remove the

Automatic transaxle fluid dipstick and filler tube location

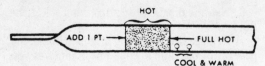

Automatic transaxle dipstick markings

dipstick, wipe it clean, then reinsert it, pushing it fully home.

4. Pull the dipstick again and, holding it horizontally, read the fluid level.

5. Cautiously feel the end of the dipstick to determine the temperature. Note that on the J-cars the cool and warm level dimples are above the hot level area. If the fluid level is not in the correct area, more will have to be added.

6. Fluid is added through the dipstick tube. You will probably need the aid of a spout or a long-necked funnel. Be sure that whatever you pour through is perfectly clean and dry. Use an automatic transmission fluid marked DEXRON®II. Add fluid slowly, and in small amounts, checking the level frequently between additions. Do not overfill, which will cause foaming, fluid loss, slippage, and possible transaxle damage. It takes only one pint to raise the

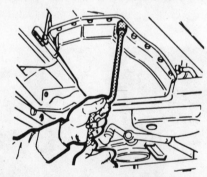

Loosen the pan bolts and allow one corner of the pan to tilt slightly to drain the fluid

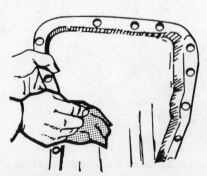

Clean the pan thoroughly with gasoline and allow it to air dry completely

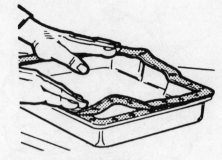

Install a new gasket on the pan

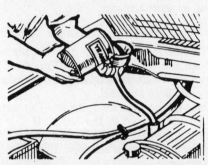

Fill the transaxle with the required amount of fluid. Do not overfill. Check the fluid level and add fluid if necessary

level from Add to Full when the transaxle is hot.

DRAIN AND REFILL

The fluid should be changed according to the schedule in the Maintenance Intervals chart. If the car is normally used in severe service, such as stop and start driving, trailer towing, or the like, the interval should be halved. If the car is driven under especially nasty conditions, such as in heavy city traffic where the temperature normally reaches 90 °F, or in very hilly or mountainous areas, or in police, taxi, or delivery service, the fluid should be changed every 15,000 miles (24,000 km.).

The fluid must be hot before it is drained; a 20 minute drive should accomplish this.

1. There is no drain plug; the fluid pan must be removed. Place a drain pan underneath the transaxle pan and remove the pan attaching bolts at the front and sides of the pan.

2. Loosen the rear pan attaching bolts approximately four turns each.

3. Very carefully pry the pan loose. You can use a small prybar for this if you work CAREFULLY. Do not distort the pan flange, or score the mating surface of the transaxle case. You'll be very sorry later if you do. As the pan is pried loose, all of the fluid is going to come pouring out.

4. Remove the remaining bolts and remove the pan and gasket. Throw away the gasket.

5. Clean the pan with solvent and allow it to air dry. If you use a rag to wipe out the pan, you risk leaving bits of lint behind, which will clog the dinky hydraulic passages in the transaxle.

6. Remove and discard the filter and the O-ring seal.

7. Install a new filter and O-ring, locating the filter against the dipstick stop.

8. Install a new gasket on the pan and install the pan. Tighten the bolts evenly and in rotation to 12 ft.lb. (16 Nm.). Do not overtighten.

9. Add approximately 4 qts. (3.8 L) of DEXRON®II automatic transmission fluid to the transaxle through the dipstick tube. You will need a long necked funnel, or a funnel and tube to do this.

10. With the transaxle in Park, put on the parking brake, block the front wheels, start the engine and let it idle. DO NOT RACE THE EN-GINE. DO NOT MOVE THE LEVER THROUGH ITS RANGES.

11. With the lever in Park, check the fluid level. If it's OK, take the car out for a short drive, park on a level surface, and check the level again, as outlined earlier in this chapter. Add more fluid if necessary. Be careful not to over-fill, which will cause foaming and fluid loss.

NOTE: *If the drained fluid is discolored (brown or black), thick, or smells burnt, serious transmission troubles, probably due to overheating, should be suspected. Your car's transaxle should be inspected by a reliable transmission specialist to determine the problem.*

Cooling System
FLUID RECOMMENDATION AND LEVEL CHECK

CAUTION: *Never remove the radiator cap under any conditions while the engine is running! Failure to follow these instructions could result in damage to the cooling system or engine and/or personal injury. To avoid having scalding hot coolant or steam blow out of the radiator, use extreme care when removing the radiator cap from a hot radiator. Wait until the engine has cooled, then wrap a thick cloth around the radiator cap and turn it slowly to the first stop. Step back while the pressure is released from the cooling system. When you are sure the pressure has been released, press down on the radiator cap (still have the cloth in position) turn and remove the radiator cap.*

Dealing with the cooling system can be dangerous matter unless the proper precautions are observed. It is best to check the coolant level

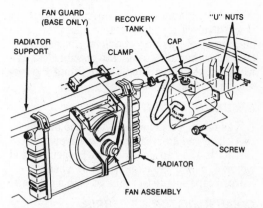

The coolant recovery tank is at the right front of the engine compartment

in the radiator when the engine is cold. The cooling system has, as one of its components, a coolant recovery tank. If the coolant level is at or near the FULL COLD line (engine cold) or the FULL HOT line (engine hot), the level is satisfactory. Always be certain that the filler caps on both the radiator and the recovery tank are closed tightly.

In the event that the coolant level must be checked when the engine is hot on engines without a coolant recovery tank, place a thick rag over the radiator cap and slowly turn the cap counterclockwise until it reaches the first detent. Allow all hot steam to escape. This will allow the pressure in the system to drop gradually, preventing an explosion of hot coolant. When the hissing noise stops, remove the cap the rest of the way.

If the coolant level is found to be low, add a 50/50 mixture of ethylene glycol-based anti-freeze and clean water. On older models, coolant must be added through the radiator filler neck. On newer models with the recovery tank, coolant may be added either through the filler neck on the radiator or directly into the recovery tank.

CAUTION: *Never add coolant to a hot engine unless it is running. If it is not running you run the risk of cracking the engine block.*

If the coolant level is chronically low or rusty, refer to Cooling System Troubleshooting Chart at the end of this chapter.

At least once every 2 years, the engine cooling system should be inspected, flushed, and re-filled with fresh coolant. If the coolant is left in the system too long, it loses its ability to prevent rust and corrosion. If the coolant has too much water, it won't protect against freezing.

The pressure cap should be looked at for signs of age or deterioration. Fan belt and other drive belts should be inspected and adjusted to the proper tension. (See checking belt tension).

Hose clamps should be tightened, and soft or cracked hoses replaced. Damp spots, or accumulations of rust or dye near hoses, water pump or other areas, indicate possible leakage, which must be corrected before filling the system with fresh coolant.

CHECK THE RADIATOR CAP

While you are checking the coolant level, check the radiator cap for a worn or cracked gasket. It the cap doesn't seal properly, fluid will be lost and the engine will overheat.

Worn caps should be replaced with a new one.

CLEAN RADIATOR OF DEBRIS

Periodically clean any debris — leaves, paper, insects, etc. — from the radiator fins. Pick the large pieces off by hand. The smaller pieces can be washed away with water pressure from a hose.

Carefully straighten any bent radiator fins with a pair of needle nose pliers. Be careful —

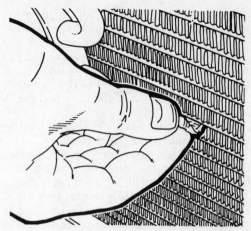

Clean the front of the radiator of any bugs, leaves, or other debris at every yearly coolant change

the fins are very soft. Don't wiggle the fins back and forth too much. Straighten them once and try not to move them again.

DRAIN AND REFILL

Completely draining and refilling the cooling system every two years at least will remove accumulated rust, scale and other deposits. Coolant in late model trucks is a 50/50 mixture of ethylene glycol and water for year round use. Use a good quality antifreeze with water pump lubricants, rust inhibitors and other corrosion inhibitors along with acid neutralizers.

1. Drain the existing antifreeze and coolant. Open the radiator and engine drain petcocks, or disconnect the bottom radiator hose, at the radiator outlet.

CAUTION: *When draining the coolant, keep in mind that cats and dogs are attracted by the ethylene glycol antifreeze, and are quite likely to drink any that is left in an uncovered container or in puddles on the ground. This will prove fatal in sufficient quantity. Always drain the coolant into a sealable container. Coolant should be reused unless it is contaminated or several years old.*

2. Close the petcock or reconnect the lower hose and fill the system with water.

3. Add a can of quality radiator flush.

4. Idle the engine until the upper radiator hose gets hot.

5. Drain the system again.

6. Repeat this process until the drained water is clear and free of scale.

7. Close all petcocks and connect all the hoses.

8. If equipped with a coolant recovery system, flush the reservoir with water and leave empty.

9. Determine the capacity of your coolant

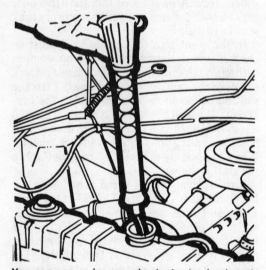

You can use an inexpensive tester to check antifreeze protection

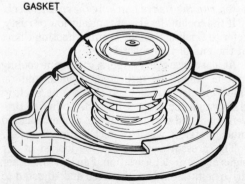

GASKET

Check the condition of the radiator cap gasket

system (see capacities specifications). Add a 50/50 mix of quality antifreeze (ethylene glycol) and water to provide the desired protection.

10. Run the engine to operating temperature.

11. Stop the engine and check the coolant level.

12. Check the level of protection with an antifreeze tester, replace the cap and check for leaks.

Master Cylinder

FLUID RECOMMENDATION AND LEVEL CHECK

Once a month, the fluid level in the brake master cylinder should be checked.

1. Park the car on a level surface.

2. Clean off the master cylinder cover before removal.

3. The cover simply snaps onto the master cylinder body. Use your thumbs to press up on the two tabs on the side of the cover to unsnap it. Remove the cover, being careful not to drop or tear the rubber diaphragm underneath. Be careful also not to drip any brake fluid on painted surfaces; the stuff eats paint.

NOTE: *Brake fluid absorbs moisture from the air, which reduces effectiveness, and will corrode brake parts once in the system. Never leave the master cylinder or the brake fluid container uncovered for any longer than necessary.*

4. The fluid level should be about ¼" below the lip of the master cylinder well.

5. If fluid addition is necessary, use only extra heavy duty disc brake fluid meeting DOT 3 specifications. The fluid should be reasonably fresh because brake fluid deteriorates with age.

6. Replace the cover, making sure that the diaphragm is correctly seated.

If the brake fluid level is constantly low, the system should be checked for leaks. However, it is normal for the fluid level to fall gradually as

The proper brake fluid level is approximately ¼ in. below the lip of master cylinder

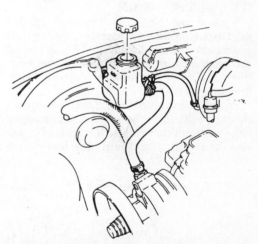

The power steering pump reservoir is located at the back of the engine compartment

the disc brake pads wear; expect the fluid level to drop not more than ⅛" for every 10,000 miles of wear.

Steering Gear

The rack and pinion steering gear used on the J-cars is a sealed unit; no fluid level checks or additions are ever necessary.

Power Steering Pump

The power steering hydraulic fluid reservoir is attached to the firewall at the back of the engine compartment. It is a translucent plastic container with fluid level markings on the outside. Check the fluid level every 12 months or 7,500 miles, whichever comes first. If the level

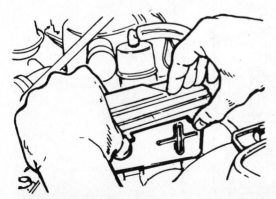

Use thumb pressure to remove the brake master cylinder cover

is low, add power steering fluid until it is correct. Be careful not to overfill as this will cause fluid loss and seal damage.

Windshield Washer Fluid

Check the fluid level in the windshield washer tank at every oil level check. The fluid can be mixed in a 50% solution with water, if desired, as long as temperatures remain above freezing. Below freezing, the fluid should be used full strength. Never add engine coolant antifreeze to the washer fluid, because it will damage the car's paint.

Chassis Greasing

There are only two areas which require regular chassis greasing: the front suspension components and the steering linkage. These parts should be greased every 12 months or 7,500 miles (12,000 Km.) with an EP grease meeting G.M. specification 6031M.

If you choose to do this job yourself, you will need to purchase a hand operated grease gun, if you do not own one already, and a long flexible extension hose to reach the various grease fittings. You will also need a cartridge of the appropriate grease.

Press the fitting on the grease gun hose onto the grease fitting on the suspension or steering linkage component. Pump a few shots of grease into the fitting, until the rubber boot on the joint begins to expand, indicating that the joint is full. Remove the gun from the fitting. Be careful not to overfill the joints, which will rupture the rubber boots, allowing the entry of dirt. You can keep the grease fittings clean by covering them with a small square of tin foil.

Chassis Lubrication

Every 12 months or 7,500 miles (12,000 km.), the various linkages and hinges on the chassis and body should be lubricated, as follows:

TRANSAXLE SHIFT LINKAGE

Lubricate the manual transaxle shift linkage contact points with the EP grease used for chassis greasing, which should meet G.M. specification 6031M. The automatic transaxle linkage should be lubricated with clean engine oil.

HOOD LATCH AND HINGES

Clean the latch surfaces and apply clean engine oil to the latch pilot bolts and the spring anchor. Use the engine oil to lubricate the hood hinges as well. Use a chassis grease to lubricate all the pivot points in the latch release mechanism.

DOOR HINGES

The gas tank filler door, car door, and rear hatch or trunk lid hinges should be wiped clean

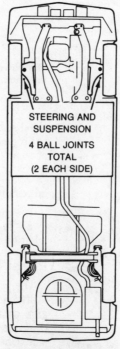

STEERING AND SUSPENSION

4 BALL JOINTS TOTAL (2 EACH SIDE)

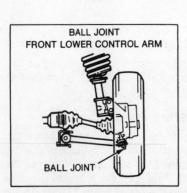

BALL JOINT FRONT LOWER CONTROL ARM

BALL JOINT

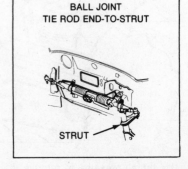

BALL JOINT TIE ROD END-TO-STRUT

STRUT

Lubrication points

and lubricated with clean engine oil. Silicone spray also works well on these parts, but must be applied more often. Use engine oil to lubricate the trunk or hatch lock mechanism and the lock bolt and striker. The door lock cylinders can be lubricated easily with a shot of silicone spray or one of the may dry penetrating lubricants commercially available.

PARKING BRAKE LINKAGE

Use chassis grease on the parking brake cable where it contacts the guides, links, levers, and pulleys. The grease should be a water resistant one for durability under the car.

ACCELERATOR LINKAGE

Lubricate the carburetor stud, carburetor lever, and the accelerator pedal lever at the support inside the car with clean engine oil.

TRAILER TOWING

General Recommendations

Your car was primarily designed to carry passengers and cargo. It is important to remember that towing a trailer will place additional loads on your vehicle's engine, drive train, steering, braking and other systems. However, if you find it necessary to tow a trailer, using the proper equipment is a must.

Local laws may require specific equipment such as trailer brakes or fender mounted mirrors. Check your local laws.

Trailer Weight

The weight of the trailer is the most important factor. A good weight-to-horsepower ratio is about 35:1, 35 lbs. of GCW (Gross Combined Weight) for every horsepower your engine develops. Multiply the engine's rated horsepower by 35 and subtract the weight of the car passengers and luggage. The result is the approximate ideal maximum weight you should tow, although a a numerically higher axle ratio can help compensate for heavier weight.

Hitch Weight

Figure the hitch weight to select a proper hitch. Hitch weight is usually 9-11% of the trailer gross weight and should be measured with the trailer loaded. Hitches fall into three types: those that mount on the frame and rear bumper or the bolt-on or weld-on distribution type used for larger trailers. Axle mounted or clamp-on bumper hitches should never be used.

Check the gross weight rating of your trailer. Tongue weight is usually figured as 10% of gross trailer weight. Therefore, a trailer with a maximum gross weight of 2,000 lb. will have a maximum tongue weight of 200 lb. Class I trailers fall into this category. Class II trailers are those with a gross weight rating of 2,000-3,500 lb., while Class III trailers fall into the 3,500-6,000 lb. category. Class IV trailers are those over 6,000 lb. and are for use with fifth wheel trucks, only.

When you've determined the hitch that you'll need, follow the manufacturer's installation instructions, exactly, especially when it comes to fastener torques. The hitch will subjected to a lot of stress and good hitches come with hardened bolts. Never substitute an inferior bolt for a hardened bolt.

Cooling
ENGINE

One of the most common, if not THE most common, problems associated with trailer towing is engine overheating.

If you have a standard cooling system, without an expansion tank, you'll definitely need to get an aftermarket expansion tank kit, preferably one with at least a 2 quart capacity. These kits are easily installed on the radiator's overflow hose, and come with a pressure cap designed for expansion tanks.

Another helpful accessory is a Flex Fan. These fan are large diameter units are designed to provide more airflow at low speeds, with blades that have deeply cupped surfaces. The blades then flex, or flatten out, at high speed, when less cooling air is needed. These fans are far lighter in weight than stock fans, requiring less horsepower to drive them. Also, they are far quieter than stock fans.

If you do decide to replace your stock fan with a flex fan, note that if your car has a fan clutch, a spacer between the flex fan and water pump hub will be needed.

Aftermarket engine oil coolers are helpful for prolonging engine oil life and reducing overall engine temperatures. Both of these factors increase engine life.

While not absolutely necessary in towing Class I and some Class II trailers, they are recommended for heavier Class II and all Class III towing.

Engine oil cooler systems consist of an adapter, screwed on in place of the oil filter, a remote filter mounting and a multi-tube, finned heat exchanger, which is mounted in front of the radiator or air conditioning condenser.

TRANSMISSION

An automatic transmission is usually recommended for trailer towing. Modern automatics have proven reliable and, of course, easy to operate, in trailer towing.

The increased load of a trailer, however, causes an increase in the temperature of the automatic transmission fluid. Heat is the worst enemy of an automatic transmission. As the temperature of the fluid increases, the life of the fluid decreases.

It is essential, therefore, that you install an automatic transmission cooler.

The cooler, which consists of a multi-tube, finned heat exchanger, is usually installed in front of the radiator or air conditioning compressor, and hooked inline with the transmission cooler tank inlet line. Follow the cooler manufacturer's installation instructions.

Select a cooler of at least adequate capacity, based upon the combined gross weights of the car and trailer.

Cooler manufacturers recommend that you use an aftermarket cooler in addition to, and not instead of, the present cooling tank in your radiator. If you do want to use it in place of the radiator cooling tank, get a cooler at least two sizes larger than normally necessary.

NOTE: *A transmission cooler can, sometimes, cause slow or harsh shifting in the transmission during cold weather, until the fluid has a chance to come up to normal operating temperature. Some coolers can be purchased with or retrofitted with a temperature bypass valve which will allow fluid flow through the cooler only when the fluid has reached operating temperature, or above.*

Handling A Trailer

Towing a trailer with ease and safety requires a certain amount of experience. It's a good idea to learn the feel of a trailer by practicing turning, stopping and backing in an open area such as an empty parking lot.

PUSHING AND TOWING

The J-cars may not be pushed or towed to start, because doing so may cause the catalytic converter to explode. If the battery is weak, the engine may be jump started, using the procedure outlined in the following section.

Your J-car may be towed on all four wheels at speeds less than 35 mph (60 km/h) for distances up to 50 miles (80 km). The driveline and steering must be normally operable. If either one is damaged, the car may not be flat-towed. If the car is flat-towed (on all four wheels), the steering must be unlocked, the transaxle shifted to Neutral, and the parking brake released. Towing attachment must be made to the main

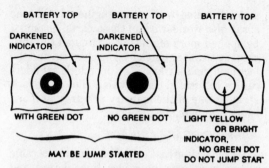

Check the appearance of the charge indicator on top of the battery before attempting a jump start; if it's not green or dark, do not jump start the car

structural members of the chassis, not to the bumpers or sheetmetal.

The car may be towed on its rear wheels by a wrecker; make sure that safety chains are used. J-cars with manual transaxles may be towed on their front wheels, for short distances and at low speeds. Be sure the transaxle is in Neutral. Cars with automatic transaxles should not be towed on their front wheels; transaxle damage may result. If it is impossible to tow the car on its rear wheels, place the front wheels on a dolly.

JACKING AND HOISTING

The J-cars are supplied with a scissors jack for changing tires. This jack engages in notches behind the front wheel and forward of the rear wheel under the rocker flange. This jack is satisfactory for its intended purpose; it is not meant to support the car while you go crawling around underneath it. Never crawl under the car when it is supported by only the scissiorsjack.

The car may also be jacked at the rear axle between the spring seats, or at the front end at the engine cradle crossbar or lower control arm. The car must never be lifted by the rear lower control arms.

The car can be raised on a four point hoist which contacts the chassis at points just behind the front wheels and just ahead of the rear wheels, as shown in the accompanying diagram. Be certain that the lift pads do not contact the catalytic converter.

It is imperative that strict safety precautions be observed both while raising the car and in the subsequent support after the car is raised. If a jack is used to raise the car, the transaxle should be shifted to Park (automatic) or First (manual), the parking brake should be set, and the opposite wheel should be blocked. Jacking should only be attempted on a hard level surface.

JUMP STARTING A DEAD BATTERY

The chemical reaction in a battery produces explosive hydrogen gas. This is the safe way to jump start a dead battery, reducing the chances of an accidental spark that could cause an explosion.

Jump Starting Precautions

1. Be sure both batteries are of the same voltage.
2. Be sure both batteries are of the same polarity (have the same grounded terminal).
3. Be sure the vehicles are not touching.
4. Be sure the vent cap holes are not obstructed.
5. Do not smoke or allow sparks around the battery.
6. In cold weather, check for frozen electrolyte in the battery. Do not jump start a frozen battery.
7. Do not allow electrolyte on your skin or clothing.
8. Be sure the electrolyte is not frozen.
CAUTION: *Make certain that the ignition key, in the vehicle with the dead battery, is in the OFF position. Connecting cables to vehicles with on-board computers will result in computer destruction if the key is not in the OFF position.*

Jump Starting Procedure

1. Determine voltages of the two batteries; they must be the same.
2. Bring the starting vehicle close (they must not touch) so that the batteries can be reached easily.
3. Turn off all accessories and both engines. Put both cars in Neutral or Park and set the handbrake.
4. Cover the cell caps with a rag—do not cover terminals.
5. If the terminals on the run-down battery are heavily corroded, clean them.
6. Identify the positive and negative posts on both batteries and connect the cables in the order shown.
7. Start the engine of the starting vehicle and run it at fast idle. Try to start the car with the dead battery. Crank it for no more than 10 seconds at a time and let it cool off for 20 seconds in between tries.
8. If it doesn't start in 3 tries, there is something else wrong.
9. Disconnect the cables in the reverse order.
10. Replace the cell covers and dispose of the rags.

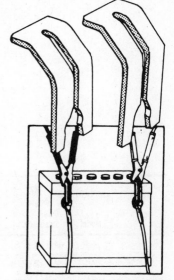

Side terminal batteries occasionally pose a problem when connecting jumper cables. There frequently isn't enough room to clamp the cables without touching sheet metal. Side terminal adaptors are available to alleviate this problem and should be removed after use.

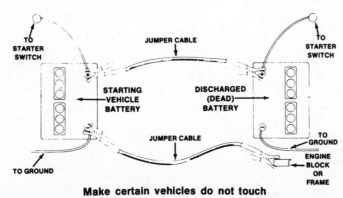

TO STARTER SWITCH   JUMPER CABLE   TO STARTER SWITCH

STARTING VEHICLE BATTERY   DISCHARGED (DEAD) BATTERY

TO GROUND   JUMPER CABLE   TO GROUND   ENGINE BLOCK OR FRAME

Make certain vehicles do not touch

This hook-up for negative ground cars only

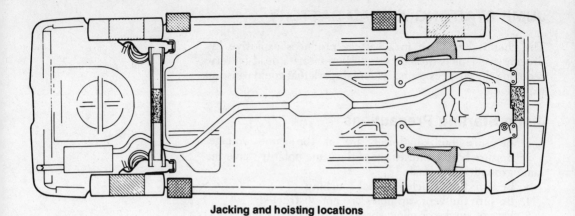

Jacking and hoisting locations

Capacities

Year	Model	No. Cylinder Displacement cu. in. (liter)	Engine Crankcase With Filter	Engine Crankcase Without Filter	Transmission (pts.) 4-Spd	Transmission (pts.) 5-Spd	Transmission (pts.) Auto. ⑥	Drive Axle (pts.)	Fuel Tank (gal.)	Cooling System (qts.)
1982	All	4-110 (1.8)	4.0	4.0	5.9	—	10.5	—	14	8.0
	All	4-122 (2.0)	4.0	4.0	5.9	—	10.5	—	14	8.3
1983	All	4-110 (1.8)	①	①	—	5.0	10.5	—	14	7.9
	All	4-122 (2.0)	4.0	4.0	5.9	—	10.5	—	14	8.3
	All	6-173 (2.8)	4.0	4.0	6.0	—	10.0 ②	—	14 ③	12.0
1984	All	4-110 (1.8)	①	①	—	5.0	10.5	—	14	7.9
	All	4-122 (2.0)	4.0	4.0	5.9	—	10.5	—	14	8.3
	All	6-173 (2.8)	4.0	4.0	6.0	—	8.0	—	14 ③	12.4
1985	All	4-110 (1.8)	①	①	—	5.0	10.5	—	14	7.9
	All	4-122 (2.0)	4.0	4.0	5.9	—	10.5	—	14	8.3
	All	6-173 (2.8)	4.0	4.0	6.0	—	8.0	—	14 ③	12.4
1986	All	4-110 (1.8)	①	①	5.9	5.3	8.0	—	14	7.9
	All	4-122 (2.0)	4.0	4.0	5.9	—	8.0	—	14	8.3
	All	6-173 (2.8)	4.0	4.0	6.0	—	8.0	—	14	12.4
1987	All	4-122 (2.0)	4.0	4.0	6.0	④	8.0	—	13.6	8.8
	All	6-173 (2.8)	4.0	4.0	5.36	—	8.0	—	14 ③	11.4

① Add 3 quarts, check oil level at dipstick and add as necessary
② Cimarron 8.0 pints
③ Cimarron 16.0 gallons
④ Isuzu: 5.3
  Muncie: 4.1

Maintenance Intervals Chart

Intervals are for number of months or thousands of miles, whichever comes first.

NOTE: *Heavy-duty operation (trailer towing, prolonged idling, severe stop and start driving) should be accompanied by a 50% increase in maintenance. Cut the interval in half for these conditions.*

Maintenance	Service Interval
Air cleaner (Replace)	30,000 mi. (48,000 km.)
PCV filter element (Replace)	50,000 mi. (48,000 km.)
PCV valve (Replace)	30,000 mi. (48,000 km.)
Power steering (Check)	12 mo/7,500 mi. (12,000 km.)
Belt tension (Adjust)	12 mo/15,000 mi. (24,000 km.)
Engine oil and filter (Change)	12 mo/7,500 mi. (12,000 km.)
Fuel filter (Change)	15,000 mi. (24,000 km.)
Manual transaxle 　Check 　Change	 12 mo/7,500 mi. (12,000 km.) 100,000 mi (160,000 km.)
Automatic transaxle 　Check 　Change (including filter)	 12 mo/7,500 mi. (12,000 km.) 100,000 mi. (160,000 km.)
Engine coolant 　Check 　Change	 Weekly 24 mo/30,000 mi. (24,000 km.)
Chassis lubrication	12 mo/7,500 mi. (12,000 km.)
Rotate tires	7,500 (12,000 km.)
Brake fluid (Check)	12 mo/7,500 mi. (12,000 km.)
Spark plugs and wires, 　ignition timing, idle speed	30,000 mi. (48,000 km.) See Chapter Two

Engine Performance and Tune-Up

2

TUNE-UP PROCEDURES

In order to extract the full measure of performance and economy from your car's engine it is essential that it be properly tuned at regular intervals. Although the tune-up intervals have been stretched to limits which would have been thought impossible a few years ago, periodic maintenance is still required. A regularly scheduled tune-up will keep your car's engine running smoothly and will prevent the annoying minor breakdowns and poor performance associated with an untuned engine.

A complete tune-up should be performed at the interval specified in the Maintenance Intervals chart in Chapter 1. This interval should be halved if the car is operated under severe conditions, such as trailer towing, prolonged idling, continual stop-and-start driving, or if starting and running problems are noticed. It is assumed that the routine maintenance described in the first chapter has been kept up, as this will have a decided effect on the results of a tune-up. All of the applicable steps should be followed in order, as the result is a cumulative one.

If the specifications on the tune-up label in the engine compartment of your J-car disagree with the Tune-Up Specifications chart in this chapter, the figures on the sticker must be used. The label often reflects changes made during the production run.

Spark Plugs

Spark plugs ignite the air and fuel mixture in the cylinder as the piston reaches the top of the compression stroke. The controlled explosion that results forces the piston down, turning the crankshaft and the rest of the drive train.

The average life of a spark plug in a J-car is 30,000 miles. Part of the reason for this extraordinarily long life is the exclusive use of unleaded fuel, which reduces the amount of deposits within the combustion chamber and on the spark plug electrodes themselves, compared with the deposits left by the leaded gasoline used in the past. An additional contribution to long life is made by the HEI (High Energy Ignition) System, which fires the spark plugs with over 35,000 volts of electricity. The high voltage serves to keep the electrodes clear, and because it is a cleaner blast of electricity than that produced by conventional breaker-points ignitions, the electrodes suffer less pitting and wear.

Nevertheless, the life of a spark plug is dependent on a number of factors, including the mechanical condition of the engine, driving conditions, and the driver's habits.

When you remove the plugs, check the condition of the electrodes; they are a good indicator of the internal state of the engine. Since the spark plug wires must be checked every 15,000 miles, the spark plugs can be removed and examined at the same time. This will allow you to keep an eye on the mechanical status of the engine.

A small deposit of light tan or rust-red material on a spark plug that has been used for any period of time is to be considered normal. Any other color, or abnormal amounts of wear or deposits, indicates that there is something amiss in the engine.

The gap between the center electrode and the side or ground electrode can be expected to increase not more than 0.001" every 1,000 miles under normal conditions.

When a spark plug is functioning normally or, more accurately, when the plug is installed in an engine that is functioning properly, the plugs can be taken out, cleaned, regapped, and reinstalled in the engine without doing the engine any harm.

When, and if, a plug fouls and begins to misfire, you will have to investigate, correct the cause of the fouling, and either clean or replace the plug.

There are several reasons why a spark plug

will foul and you can learn which is at fault by just looking at the plug. A few of the most common reasons for plug fouling, and a description of the fouled plug's appearance, are shown in the Color Insert section.

Spark plugs suitable for use in your car's engine are offered in a number of different heat ranges. The amount of heat which the plug absorbs is determined by the length of the lower insulator. The longer the insulator, the hotter the plug will operate; the shorter the insulator, the cooler it will operate. A spark plug that ab-sorbs (or retains) little heat and remains too cool will accumulate deposits of oil and carbon, because it is not hot enough to burn them off. This leads to fouling and consequent misfiring. A spark plug that absorbs too much heat will have no deposits, but the electrodes will burn away quickly and, in some cases, pre-ignition may result. Pre-ignition occurs when the spark plug tips get so hot that they ignite the fuel/mixture before the actual spark fires. This premature ignition will usually cause a pinging sound under conditions of low speed and heavy

Tune-Up Specifications

Year	VIN	No. Cylinder Displacement cu. in. (liter)	Spark Plugs Type	Gap (in.)	Ignition Timing (deg.) MT	AT	Compression Pressure (psi)	Fuel Pump (psi)	Idle Speed (rpm) MT	AT	Valve Clearance In.	Ex.
1982	F	4-110 (1.8)	R-42TS	0.045 ①	12B	12B	NA	4.5–6.0	②	②	Hyd.	Hyd.
	B	4-122 (2.0)	②	②	②	②	NA	4.5–6.0	②	②	Hyd.	Hyd.
1983	O	4-110 (1.8)	R-42XLS6	0.060	8B	8B	NA	9–13	②	②	Hyd.	Hyd.
	J	4-110 (1.8)	R-42CXLS	0.035	②	②	NA	12	②	②	Hyd.	Hyd.
	P	4-122 (2.0)	R-42CTS	0.035	②	②	NA	12	②	②	Hyd.	Hyd.
	B	4-122 (2.0)	R-42CTS	0.035	—	12B	NA	12	②	②	Hyd.	Hyd.
	W	6-173 (2.8)	R-42CTS	0.045	②	②	NA	9–13	②	②	Hyd.	Hyd.
1984	O	4-110 (1.8)	R-44XLS	0.060	8B	8B	NA	9–13	②	②	Hyd.	Hyd.
	J	4-110 (1.8)	R-42CXLS	0.035	②	②	NA	12	②	②	Hyd.	Hyd.
	P	4-122 (2.0)	R-42CTS	0.035	②	②	NA	12	②	②	Hyd.	Hyd.
	W	6-173 (2.8)	R-42CTS	0.045	②	②	NA	9–13	②	②	Hyd.	Hyd.
1985	O	4-110 (1.8)	R-44XLS	0.060	8B	8B	NA	9-13	②	②	Hyd.	Hyd.
	J	4-110 (1.8)	R-42CXLS	0.035	②	②	NA	12	②	②	Hyd.	Hyd.
	P	4-122 (2.0)	R-42CTS	0.035	②	②	NA	12	②	②	Hyd.	Hyd.
	W	6-173 (2.8)	R-42CTS	0.045	②	②	NA	9–13	②	②	Hyd.	Hyd.
1986	O	4-110 (1.8)	R-44XLS6	0.060	8B	8B	NA	9–13	②	②	Hyd.	Hyd.
	J	4-110 (1.8)	R-42CXLS	0.035	②	②	NA	12	②	②	Hyd.	Hyd.
	P	4-122 (2.0)	R-42CTS	0.035	②	②	NA	12	②	②	Hyd.	Hyd.
	W	6-173 (2.8)	R-42CTS	0.045	②	②	NA	9–13	②	②	Hyd.	Hyd.
1987	M	4-122 (2.0)	R42XLS6	0.060	②	②	NA	NA	②	②	Hyd.	Hyd.
	1	4-122 (2.0)	FR3LM	0.035	②	②	NA	10–12	②	②	Hyd.	Hyd.
	K	4-122 (2.0)	R44XLS6	0.060	②	②	NA	10	②	②	Hyd.	Hyd.
	W	6-173 (2.8)	R43LTSE	0.045	②	②	NA	9–13	②	②	Hyd.	Hyd.

NOTE: The underhood specifications sticker often reflects tune-up specifications changes made in production. Sticker figures must be used if they disagree with those in this chart.
Part numbers in this chart are not recommendations by Chilton for any product by brand name
B—Before top dead center
NA—Not available at time of publication
① Certain models may use 0.035 in. gap. See underhood specifications sticker to be sure
② See underhood specifications sticker

Troubleshooting Engine Performance

Problem	Cause	Solution
Hard starting (engine cranks normally)	• Binding linkage, choke valve or choke piston	• Repair as necessary
	• Restricted choke vacuum diaphragm	• Clean passages
	• Improper fuel level	• Adjust float level
	• Dirty, worn or faulty needle valve and seat	• Repair as necessary
	• Float sticking	• Repair as necessary
	• Faulty fuel pump	• Replace fuel pump
	• Incorrect choke cover adjustment	• Adjust choke cover
	• Inadequate choke unloader adjustment	• Adjust choke unloader
	• Faulty ignition coil	• Test and replace as necessary
	• Improper spark plug gap	• Adjust gap
	• Incorrect ignition timing	• Adjust timing
	• Incorrect valve timing	• Check valve timing; repair as necessary
Rough idle or stalling	• Incorrect curb or fast idle speed	• Adjust curb or fast idle speed
	• Incorrect ignition timing	• Adjust timing to specification
	• Improper feedback system operation	• Refer to Chapter 4
	• Improper fast idle cam adjustment	• Adjust fast idle cam
	• Faulty EGR valve operation	• Test EGR system and replace as necessary
	• Faulty PCV valve air flow	• Test PCV valve and replace as necessary
	• Choke binding	• Locate and eliminate binding condition
	• Faulty TAC vacuum motor or valve	• Repair as necessary
	• Air leak into manifold vacuum	• Inspect manifold vacuum connections and repair as necessary
	• Improper fuel level	• Adjust fuel level
	• Faulty distributor rotor or cap	• Replace rotor or cap
	• Improperly seated valves	• Test cylinder compression, repair as necessary
	• Incorrect ignition wiring	• Inspect wiring and correct as necessary
	• Faulty ignition coil	• Test coil and replace as necessary
	• Restricted air vent or idle passages	• Clean passages
	• Restricted air cleaner	• Clean or replace air cleaner filler element
	• Faulty choke vacuum diaphragm	• Repair as necessary
Faulty low-speed operation	• Restricted idle transfer slots	• Clean transfer slots
	• Restricted idle air vents and passages	• Clean air vents and passages
	• Restricted air cleaner	• Clean or replace air cleaner filter element
	• Improper fuel level	• Adjust fuel level
	• Faulty spark plugs	• Clean or replace spark plugs
	• Dirty, corroded, or loose ignition secondary circuit wire connections	• Clean or tighten secondary circuit wire connections
	• Improper feedback system operation	• Refer to Chapter 4
	• Faulty ignition coil high voltage wire	• Replace ignition coil high voltage wire
	• Faulty distributor cap	• Replace cap
Faulty acceleration	• Improper accelerator pump stroke	• Adjust accelerator pump stroke
	• Incorrect ignition timing	• Adjust timing
	• Inoperative pump discharge check ball or needle	• Clean or replace as necessary
	• Worn or damaged pump diaphragm or piston	• Replace diaphragm or piston

Troubleshooting Engine Performance (cont.)

Problem	Cause	Solution
Faulty acceleration (cont.)	• Leaking carburetor main body cover gasket	• Replace gasket
	• Engine cold and choke set too lean	• Adjust choke cover
	• Improper metering rod adjustment (BBD Model carburetor)	• Adjust metering rod
	• Faulty spark plug(s)	• Clean or replace spark plug(s)
	• Improperly seated valves	• Test cylinder compression, repair as necessary
	• Faulty ignition coil	• Test coil and replace as necessary
	• Improper feedback system operation	• Refer to Chapter 4
Faulty high speed operation	• Incorrect ignition timing	• Adjust timing
	• Faulty distributor centrifugal advance mechanism	• Check centrifugal advance mechanism and repair as necessary
	• Faulty distributor vacuum advance mechanism	• Check vacuum advance mechanism and repair as necessary
	• Low fuel pump volume	• Replace fuel pump
	• Wrong spark plug air gap or wrong plug	• Adjust air gap or install correct plug
	• Faulty choke operation	• Adjust choke cover
	• Partially restricted exhaust manifold, exhaust pipe, catalytic converter, muffler, or tailpipe	• Eliminate restriction
	• Restricted vacuum passages	• Clean passages
	• Improper size or restricted main jet	• Clean or replace as necessary
	• Restricted air cleaner	• Clean or replace filter element as necessary
	• Faulty distributor rotor or cap	• Replace rotor or cap
	• Faulty ignition coil	• Test coil and replace as necessary
	• Improperly seated valve(s)	• Test cylinder compression, repair as necessary
	• Faulty valve spring(s)	• Inspect and test valve spring tension, replace as necessary
	• Incorrect valve timing	• Check valve timing and repair as necessary
	• Intake manifold restricted	• Remove restriction or replace manifold
	• Worn distributor shaft	• Replace shaft
	• Improper feedback system operation	• Refer to Chapter 4
Misfire at all speeds	• Faulty spark plug(s)	• Clean or replace spark plug(s)
	• Faulty spark plug wire(s)	• Replace as necessary
	• Faulty distributor cap or rotor	• Replace cap or rotor
	• Faulty ignition coil	• Test coil and replace as necessary
	• Primary ignition circuit shorted or open intermittently	• Troubleshoot primary circuit and repair as necessary
	• Improperly seated valve(s)	• Test cylinder compression, repair as necessary
	• Faulty hydraulic tappet(s)	• Clean or replace tappet(s)
	• Improper feedback system operation	• Refer to Chapter 4
	• Faulty valve spring(s)	• Inspect and test valve spring tension, repair as necessary
	• Worn camshaft lobes	• Replace camshaft
	• Air leak into manifold	• Check manifold vacuum and repair as necessary
	• Improper carburetor adjustment	• Adjust carburetor
	• Fuel pump volume or pressure low	• Replace fuel pump
	• Blown cylinder head gasket	• Replace gasket
	• Intake or exhaust manifold passage(s) restricted	• Pass chain through passage(s) and repair as necessary
	• Incorrect trigger wheel installed in distributor	• Install correct trigger wheel

Troubleshooting Engine Performance (cont.)

Problem	Cause	Solution
Power not up to normal	• Incorrect ignition timing	• Adjust timing
	• Faulty distributor rotor	• Replace rotor
	• Trigger wheel loose on shaft	• Reposition or replace trigger wheel
	• Incorrect spark plug gap	• Adjust gap
	• Faulty fuel pump	• Replace fuel pump
	• Incorrect valve timing	• Check valve timing and repair as necessary
	• Faulty ignition coil	• Test coil and replace as necessary
	• Faulty ignition wires	• Test wires and replace as necessary
	• Improperly seated valves	• Test cylinder compression and repair as necessary
	• Blown cylinder head gasket	• Replace gasket
	• Leaking piston rings	• Test compression and repair as necessary
	• Worn distributor shaft	• Replace shaft
	• Improper feedback system operation	• Refer to Chapter 4
Intake backfire	• Improper ignition timing	• Adjust timing
	• Faulty accelerator pump discharge	• Repair as necessary
	• Defective EGR CTO valve	• Replace EGR CTO valve
	• Defective TAC vacuum motor or valve	• Repair as necessary
	• Lean air/fuel mixture	• Check float level or manifold vacuum for air leak. Remove sediment from bowl
Exhaust backfire	• Air leak into manifold vacuum	• Check manifold vacuum and repair as necessary
	• Faulty air injection diverter valve	• Test diverter valve and replace as necessary
	• Exhaust leak	• Locate and eliminate leak
Ping or spark knock	• Incorrect ignition timing	• Adjust timing
	• Distributor centrifugal or vacuum advance malfunction	• Inspect advance mechanism and repair as necessary
	• Excessive combustion chamber deposits	• Remove with combustion chamber cleaner
	• Air leak into manifold vacuum	• Check manifold vacuum and repair as necessary
	• Excessively high compression	• Test compression and repair as necessary
	• Fuel octane rating excessively low	• Try alternate fuel source
	• Sharp edges in combustion chamber	• Grind smooth
	• EGR valve not functioning properly	• Test EGR system and replace as necessary
Surging (at cruising to top speeds)	• Low carburetor fuel level	• Adjust fuel level
	• Low fuel pump pressure or volume	• Replace fuel pump
	• Metering rod(s) not adjusted properly (BBD Model Carburetor)	• Adjust metering rod
	• Improper PCV valve air flow	• Test PCV valve and replace as necessary
	• Air leak into manifold vacuum	• Check manifold vacuum and repair as necessary
	• Incorrect spark advance	• Test and replace as necessary
	• Restricted main jet(s)	• Clean main jet(s)
	• Undersize main jet(s)	• Replace main jet(s)
	• Restricted air vents	• Clean air vents
	• Restricted fuel filter	• Replace fuel filter
	• Restricted air cleaner	• Clean or replace air cleaner filter element
	• EGR valve not functioning properly	• Test EGR system and replace as necessary
	• Improper feedback system operation	• Refer to Chapter 4

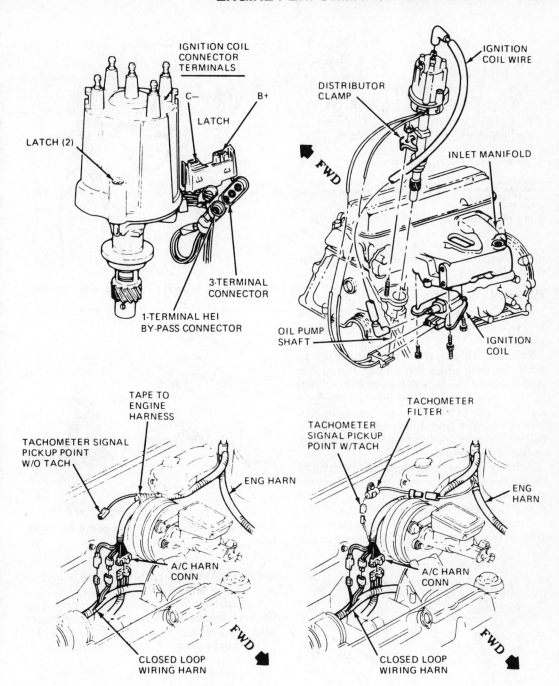

IGNITION COIL
CONNECTOR
TERMINALS

C—   B+

LATCH

LATCH (2)

3-TERMINAL
CONNECTOR

1-TERMINAL HEI
BY-PASS CONNECTOR

IGNITION
COIL WIRE

DISTRIBUTOR
CLAMP

INLET MANIFOLD

FWD

OIL PUMP
SHAFT

IGNITION
COIL

TAPE TO
ENGINE
HARNESS

TACHOMETER SIGNAL
PICKUP POINT
W/O TACH

ENG HARN

A/C HARN
CONN

CLOSED LOOP
WIRING HARN

FWD

TACHOMETER
FILTER

TACHOMETER
SIGNAL PICKUP
POINT W/TACH

ENG
HARN

A/C HARN
CONN

CLOSED LOOP
WIRING HARN

FWD

load. In severe cases, the heat may become high enough to start the fuel/air mixture burning throughout the combustion chamber rather than just to the front of the plug. In this case, the resultant explosion (detonation) will be strong enough to damage pistons, rings, and valves.

In most cases the factory recommended heat range is correct; it is chosen to perform well under a wide range of operating conditions. However, if most of your driving is long distance, high speed travel, you may want to install a spark plug one step colder than standard. If most of your driving is of the short trip variety, when the engine may not always reach operating temperature, a hotter plug may help burn

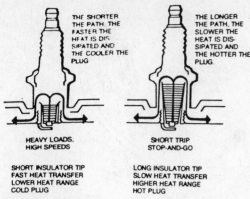

THE SHORTER THE PATH, THE FASTER THE HEAT IS DISSIPATED AND THE COOLER THE PLUG.

THE LONGER THE PATH, THE SLOWER THE HEAT IS DISSIPATED AND THE HOTTER THE PLUG.

HEAVY LOADS, HIGH SPEEDS

SHORT TRIP STOP-AND-GO

SHORT INSULATOR TIP
FAST HEAT TRANSFER
LOWER HEAT RANGE
COLD PLUG

LONG INSULATOR TIP
SLOW HEAT TRANSFER
HIGHER HEAT RANGE
HOT PLUG

Spark plug heat range

off the deposits normally accumulated under those conditions.

REMOVAL

1. Number the wires with pieces of adhesive tape so that you won't cross them when you replace them.

2. The spark plug boots have large grips to aid in removal. Grasp the wire by the rubber boot and twist the boot ½ turn in either direction to break the tight seal between the boot and the plug. Then twist and pull on the boot to remove the wire from the spark plug. Do not pull on the wire itself or you will damage the carbon cord conductor.

3. Use a ⅝" spark plug socket to loosen all of the plugs about two turns. A universal joint installed at the socket end of the extension will ease the process.

If removal of the plugs is difficult, apply a few drops of penetrating oil or silicone spray to the

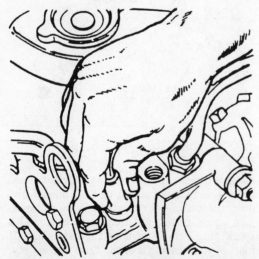

Twist and pull on the rubber boot to remove the spark plug wires; never pull on the wire itself

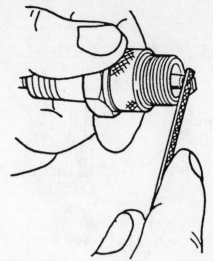

Plugs that are in good condition can be filed and reused

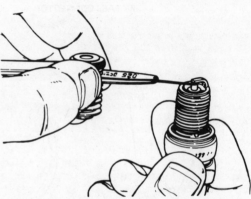

Always use a wire gauge to check the electrode gap

area around the base of the plug, and allow it a few minutes to work.

4. If compressed air is available, apply it to the area around the spark plug holes. Otherwise, use a rag or a brush to clean the area. Be careful not to allow any foreign material to drop into the spark plug holes.

5. Remove the plugs by unscrewing them the rest of the way.

INSPECTION

Check the plugs for deposits and wear. If they are not going to be replaced, clean the plugs thoroughly. Remember that any kind of deposit will decrease the efficiency of the plug. Plugs can be cleaned on a spark plug cleaning machine, which can sometimes be found in service stations, or you can do an acceptable job of cleaning with a stiff brush. If the plugs are cleaned, the electrodes must be filed flat. use an ignition points file, not an emery board or the

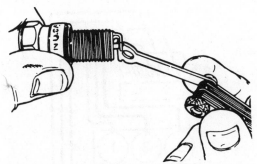

Adjust the electrode gap by bending the side electrode

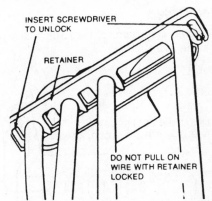

INSERT SCREWDRIVER TO UNLOCK

RETAINER

DO NOT PULL ON WIRE WITH RETAINER LOCKED

Unlock the plastic retainers to replace the spark plug wires

like, which will leave deposits. The electrodes must be filed perfectly flat with sharp edges; rounded edges reduce the spark plug voltage by as much as 50%.

Check spark plug gap before installation. The ground electrode (the L-shaped one connected to the body of the plug) must be parallel to the center electrode and the specified size wire gauge (see Tune-Up Specifications) should pass through the gap with a slight drag. Always check the gap on new plugs, too; they are not always set correctly at the factory. Do not use a flat feeler gauge when measuring the gap, because the reading will be inaccurate. Wire gapping tools usually have a bending tool attached. Use that to adjust the side electrode until the proper distance is obtained. Absolutely never bend the center electrode. Also, be careful not to bend the side electrode too far or too often; it may weaken and break off within the engine, requiring removal of the cylinder head to retrieve it.

INSTALLATION

1. Lubricate the threads of the spark plugs with a drop of oil or a shot of silicone spray. Install the plugs and tighten them hand tight. Take care not to cross-thread them.

2. Tighten the spark plugs with the socket. Do not apply the same amount of force you would use for a bolt; just snug them in. These spark plugs do nut use gaskets, and over-tightening will make future removal difficult. If a torque wrench is available, tighten to 7-15 fft.lb.

NOTE: *While over-tightening the spark plug is to be avoided, under-tightening is just as bad. If combustion gases leak past the threads, the spark plug will overheat and rapid electrode wear will result.*

3. Install the wires on their respective plugs. Make sure the wires are firmly connected. You will be able to feel them click into place. Spark plug wiring diagrams are in Chapter Three if you get into trouble.

CHECKING AND REPLACING SPARK PLUG WIRES

Every 15,000 miles, inspect the spark plug wires for burns, cuts, or breaks in the insulation. Check the boots and the nipples on the distributor cap. Replace any damaged wiring.

Every 45,000 miles or so, the resistance of the wires should be checked with an ohmmeter. Wires with excessive resistance will cause misfiring, and may make the engine difficult to start in damp weather. Generally, the useful life of the cables is 45,000-60,000 miles.

To check resistance, remove the distributor cap, leaving the wires in place. Connect one lead of an ohmmeter to an electrode within the cap; connect the other lead to the corresponding spark plug terminal (remove it from the spark plug for this test). Replace any wire which shows a resistance over 30,000Ω. The following chart gives resistance values as a function of length. Generally speaking, however, resistance should not be considered the outer limit of acceptability.

- 0-15": 3,000-10,000
- 15-25": 4,000-15,000
- 25-35": 6,000-20,000
- Over 35": 25,000

It should be remembered that resistance is also a function of length; the longer the wire, the greater the resistance. Thus, if the wires on your car are longer than the factory originals, resistance will be higher, quite possible outside these limits.

When installing new wires, replace them one at a time to avoid mixups. Start by replacing the longest one first. Install the boot firmly over the spark plug. Route the wire over the same path as the original. Insert the nipple firmly onto the tower on the distributor cap, then install the cap cover and latches to secure the wires.

Firing Orders

To avoid confusion, replace the spark plug wires one at a time.

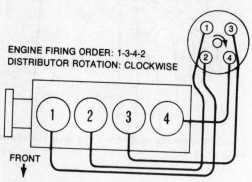

ENGINE FIRING ORDER: 1-3-4-2
DISTRIBUTOR ROTATION: CLOCKWISE

FRONT

Chevrolet 110 cu. in. (1.8L), 122 cu. in. (2.0L) 4 cyl (OHV), 1982—86
Firing order: 1—3—4—2
Distributor rotation: clockwise

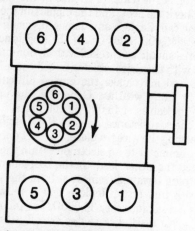

Chevrolet 173 cu. in. (2.8L) V6, 1984—86
Firing order: 1—2—3—4—5—6
Distributor rotation: clockwise

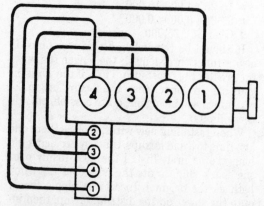

Chevrolet 122 cu. in. (2.0L) 4 cyl (OHV), 1987
Firing order: 1—3—4—2 (Distributorless)

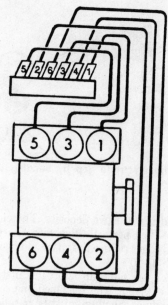

Chevrolet 173 cu. in. (2.8L) V6, 1987
Firing order: 1—2—3—4—5—6 (Distributorless)

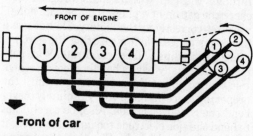

FRONT OF ENGINE

Front of car

Pontiac 110 cu. in. (1.8L), 122 cu. in. (2.0L) 4 cyl. (OHC)
Firing order: 1—3—4—2

GM DELCO-REMY HIGH ENERGY IGNITION (HEI)

General Information

The High Energy Ignition distributor is used on all engines. The ignition coil is either mounted to the top of the distributor cap or is externally mounted on the engine, having a secondary circuit high tension wire connecting the coil to the distributor cap and interconnecting primary wiring as part of the engine harness.

The High Energy Ignition distributor is equipped to aid in spark timing changes, necessary for Emissions, Economy and performance. This system is called the Electronic Spark Timing Control (EST). The HEI distributors use a magnetic pick-up assembly, located inside the distributor containing a permanent magnet, a pole piece with internal teeth and a pick-up coil. When the teeth of the rotating timer core and pole piece align, an induced voltage in the pick-up coil signals the electronic module to open the

Electronic Ignition/Fuel Injection System Application Chart

Manufacturer	Year	Model	Engine cu. in. (liter)	VIN	Electronic Ignition System	Fuel Injection System
Buick	1982–86	Skyhawk	110 (1.8)	O	HEI/EST	TBI
			110 (1.8)	J	HEI/EST	MPI-Turbo
			122 (2.0)	P	HEI/EST	TBI
	1987–88	Skyhawk	122 (2.0)	K	HEI/EST	TBI
			122 (2.0)	M	HEI/EST	MPI
			122 (2.0) HO	1	HEI/EST	TBI
Cadillac	1982–85	Cimarron	122 (2.0)	P	HEI/EST	TBI
	1986	Cimarron	122 (2.0)	P	HEI/EST	TBI
			173 (2.8)	W	HEI/EST	MPI
	1987–88	Cimarron	173 (2.8)	W	HEI/EST	MPI
Chevrolet	1982–86	Cavalier	122 (2.0)	P	HEI/EST	TBI
	1985–86	Cavalier	173 (2.8)	W	HEI/EST	MPI
	1987–88	Cavalier	122 (2.0)	1	DIS	TBI
			173 (2.8)	W	DIS	MPI
Oldsmobile	1982–86	Firenza	110 (1.8)	O	HEI/EST	TBI
			122 (2.0)	P	HEI/EST	TBI
	1986–87	Firenza	173 (2.8)	W	HEI/EST	MPI
	1987–88	Firenza	122 (2.0)	K	HEI/EST	TBI
			122 (2.0) HO	1	HEI/EST	TBI
Pontiac	1982–84	2000, Sunbird	110 (1.8)	O	HEI/EST	TBI
			110 (1.8)	J	HEI/EST	MPI-Turbo
			122 (2.0)	P	HEI/EST	TBI
	1985–86	Sunbird	110 (1.8)	O	HEI/EST	TBI
			110 (1.8)	J	HEI/EST	MPI-Turbo
	1987–88	Sunbird	122 (2.0)	K	HEI/EST	TBI
			122 (2.0)	M	HEI/EST	MPI-Turbo

coil primary circuit. As the primary current decreases, a high voltage is induced in the secondary windings of the ignition coil, directing a spark through the rotor and high voltage leads to fire the spark plugs. The dwell period is automatically controlled by the electronic module and is increased with increasing engine rpm. The HEI System features a longer spark duration which is instrumental in firing lean and EGR (Exhaust Gas Recirculation) diluted fuel/air mixtures. The condenser (capacitor) located within the HEI distributor is provided for noise (static) suppression purposes only and is not a regularly replaced ignition system component.

All spark timing changes in the HEI (EST) distributors are done electronically by the Electronic Control Module (ECM), which monitors information from the various engine sensors, computes the desired spark timing and signals the distributor to change the timing accordingly. With this distributor, no vacuum or centrifugal advances are used.

HEI SYSTEM PRECAUTIONS

Before going on to troubleshooting, it might be a good idea to take note of the following precautions:

Timing Light Use

Inductive pick-up timing lights are the best kind of use with HEI. Timing light which connect between the spark plug and the spark plug wire occasionally (not always) give false readings.

Spark Plug Wires

The plug wires used with HEI systems are of a different construction than conventional wires. When replacing them, make sure you get the correct wires, since conventional wires won't carry the voltage. Also, handle them carefully to avoid cracking or splitting them and never pierce them.

Tachometer Use

Not all tachometers will operate or indicate correctly when used on a HEI system. While some tachometers may give a reading, this does not necessarily mean the reading is correct. In addition, some tachometers hook up differently from others. If you can't figure out whether or not your tachometer will work on your car, check with the tachometer manufacturer. Dwell readings, or course, have no significance at all.

HEI System Testers

Instruments designed specifically for testing HEI systems are available from several tool manufacturers. Some of these will even test the module itself.

Troubleshooting

NOTE: *An accurate diagnosis is the first step to problem solution and repair. For several of the following steps, a HEI spark tester, tool ST 125, which has a spring clip to attach it to ground. Use of this tool is recommended, as there is more control of the high energy spark and less chance of being shocked. If a tachometer is connected to the TACH terminal on the distributor, disconnect it before proceeding with this test.*

SECONDARY CIRCUIT

Testing

SECONDARY SPARK

1. Check for spark at the spark plugs by attaching the HEI spark tester, tool ST 125, to one of the plug wires, grounding the HEI spark tester on the engine and cranking the starter.

2. If no spark occurs on one wire, check a second. If spark is present, the HEI system is good.

3. Check fuel system, plug wires, and spark plugs.

4. If no spark occurs from EST distributor, disconnect the 4 terminal EST connector and recheck for spark. If spark is present, EST system service check should be performed.

NOTE: *Before making any circuit checks with test meters, be sure that all primary circuit connectors are properly installed and that spark plug cables are secure at the distributor and at the plugs.*

Distributor Component Testing

DISTRIBUTOR WITH SEPARATE COIL TYPE ONE

NOTE: *This type distributor has no vacuum or centrifugal advance mechanism and has the pick-up coil mounted above the module. This distributor is used with the EST system.*

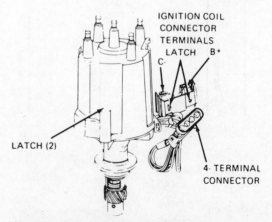

IGNITION COIL
CONNECTOR
TERMINALS
LATCH B+
C.

LATCH (2)

4- TERMINAL
CONNECTOR

HEI/EST distributor, type one distributor

Testing

IGNITION COIL

1. Disconnect the primary wiring connectors and secondary coil wire from the ignition coil.

2. Using an ohmmeter on the high scale, connect one lead to a grounding screw and the second lead to one of the primary coil terminals.

3. The reading should be infinite. If not, replace the ignition coil.

4. Using the low scale, place the ohmmeter leads on both the primary coil terminals.

5. The reading should be very low or zero. If not, replace the ignition coil.

6. Using the high scale, place one ohmmeter lead on the high tension output terminal and the other lead on a primary coil terminal.

7. The reading should NOT be infinite. If it is, replace the ignition coil.

Testing

PICK-UP COIL

1. Remove the rotor and pick-up coil leads from the module.

2. Using an ohmmeter, attach one lead to the distributor base and the second lead to one of the pick-up coil terminals of the connector.

3. The reading should be infinite at all times.

4. Position both leads of the ohmmeter to the pick-up terminal ends of the connector.

5. The reading should be a steady value between 500-1500Ω.

6. If not within the specification value, the pick-up coil is defective.

NOTE: *While testing, flex the leads to determine if wire breaks are present under the wiring insulation.*

IGNITION MODULE

Because of the complexity of the internal circuitry of the HEI/EST module, it is recommended the module be tested with an accurate module tester.

It is imperative that silicone lubricant be used under the module when it is installed, to prevent module failure due to overheating.

NOTE: *The module and the Hall Effect switch (if used) can be removed from the distributor without disassembly. To remove the pick-up coil, the distributor shaft must be removed to expose a waved retaining ring (C-washer) holding the pick-up coil in place.*

HALL EFFECT SWITCH

The Hall Effect Switch, when used, is installed in the HEI distributor. The purpose of the switch is to sense engine speed and send the information to the Electronic Control Module

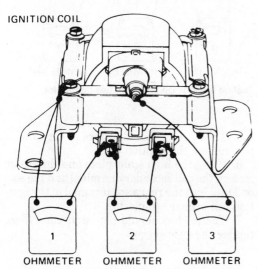

IGNITION COIL

1 2 3

OHMMETER   OHMMETER   OHMMETER

Testing the ignition coil, type one distributor

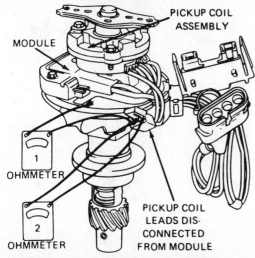

TESTING PICKUP COIL

PICKUP COIL ASSEMBLY

MODULE

1

OHMMETER

2

OHMMETER

PICKUP COIL LEADS DISCONNECTED FROM MODULE

Testing the pick-up coil, type one distributor

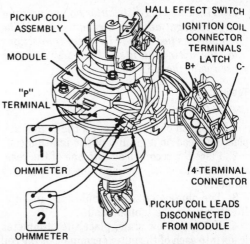

PICKUP COIL ASSEMBLY

MODULE

"P" TERMINAL

HALL EFFECT SWITCH

IGNITION COIL CONNECTOR TERMINALS
LATCH
B+   C-

1

OHMMETER

2

OHMMETER

4-TERMINAL CONNECTOR

PICKUP COIL LEADS DISCONNECTED FROM MODULE

Testing the Hall Effect Switch, type one distributor

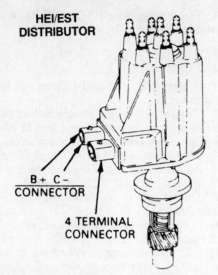

HEI/EST DISTRIBUTOR

B + C –
CONNECTOR

4 TERMINAL
CONNECTOR

HEI/EST distributor, type two distributor

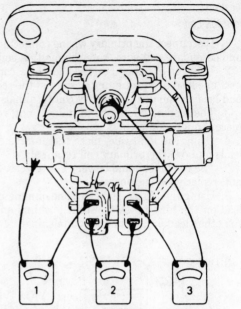

OHMMETER   OHMMETER   OHMMETER

1   2   3

Testing the ignition coil, type two distributor

(ECM). To remove the Hall Effect Switch, the distributor shaft must be removed from the distributor.

Testing

1. Remove the switch connectors from the switch.

2. Connect a 12 volt battery and voltmeter to the switch. Note and follow the polarity markings.

3. With a knife blade inserted straight down and against the magnet, the voltmeter should read within 0.5 volts of battery voltage. If not, the switch is defective.

4. Without the knife blade inserted against the magnet, the voltmeter should read less than 0.5 volts. If not, the switch is defective.

DISTRIBUTOR WITH SEPARATE COIL TYPE TWO

NOTE: *This type distributor has no vacuum or centrifugal advance mechanisms and the module has two outside terminal connections for the wiring harness. This distributor is used with the EST system.*

Testing

IGNITION COIL

1. Using an ohmmeter set on the high scale, place one lead on a ground of the ignition coil.

2. Place the second lead into one of the rearward terminals of the ignition coil primary connector.

3. The ohmmeter scale should read infinite. If not, replace the ignition coil.

4. Using the low scale, place the ohmmeter leads into each of the outer terminals of the coil connector.

5. The reading should be zero or very low. If not, replace the ignition coil.

6. Using the high scale, place one ohmmeter lead on the coil secondary terminal and the second lead into the rearward terminal of the ignition coil primary connector.

7. The reading should not be infinite. If so, replace the ignition coil.

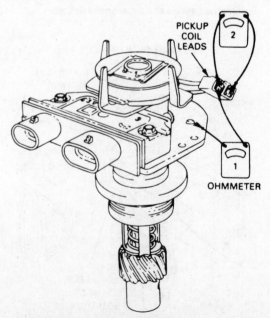

PICKUP
COIL
LEADS

2

1

OHMMETER

Testing the pick-up coil, type two distributor

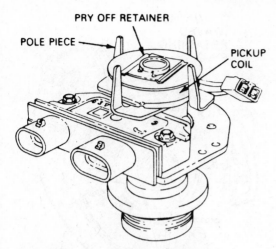

Pick-up coil removal, type two distributor

Testing

PICK-UP COIL

1. Remove the rotor and pick-up leads from the module.

2. Using an ohmmeter, connect one of the leads to the distributor base.

3. Connect the second lead to one of the pick-up coil lead terminals

4. The reading should be infinite. If not, the pick-up coil is defective.

NOTE: *During the ohmmeter tests, flex the leads by hand to check for intermediate opens in the wiring.*

5. Connect both ohmmeter lead to the pick-up coil terminals at the connector.

6. The reading should be of one steady value, 500-1500Ω.

7. If the reading is not within specifications, the pick-up coil must is defective.

Testing

IGNITION MODULE

Because of the complexity of the internal circuitry of the HEI/EST module, it is recom-

mended the module be tested with an accurate module tester.

It is imperative that silicone lubricant be used under the module when it is installed, to prevent module failure due to overheating.

NOTE: *The module can be removed without distributor disassembly. To remove the pick-up coil, the distributor shaft must be removed. A retainer can then be removed from the top of the pole piece and the pick-up coil removed.*

DISTRIBUTOR WITH SEPARATE COIL TYPE THREE W/TANG DRIVE

NOTE: *This distributor is used with the EST system. The unit is mounted horizontally to the valve cover housing and is driven by the camshaft, through a tang on the distributor shaft.*

Testing

IGNITION COIL

1. Using an ohmmeter set on the high scale, place one lead on a ground of the ignition coil.

2. Place the second lead into one of the rearward terminals of the ignition coil primary connector.

3. The ohmmeter scale should read infinite. If not, replace the ignition coil.

4. Using the low scale, place the ohmmeter leads into each of the outer terminals of the coil connector.

5. The reading should be zero or very low. If not, replace the ignition coil.

6. Using the high scale, place one ohmmeter lead on the coil secondary terminal and the sec-

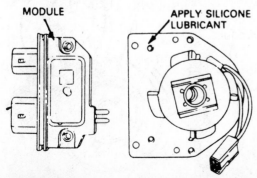

Module replacement and use of silicone lubricant, type two distributor

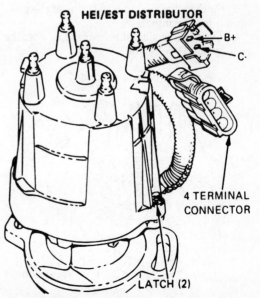

HEI/EST distributor, type three (Tang Drive) distributor

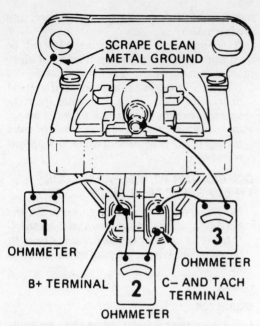

Testing the ignition coil, type three (Tang Drive) distributor

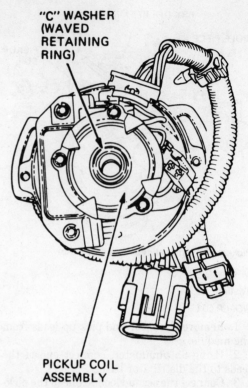

Pick-up coil removal, type three (Tang Drive) distributor

ond lead into the rearward terminal of the ignition coil primary connector.

7. The reading should not be infinite. If so, replace the ignition coil.

Testing

PICK-UP COIL

1. Remove the rotor and pick-up leads from the module.

2. Using an ohmmeter, connect one of the leads to the distributor base.

3. Connect the second lead to one of the pick-up coil lead terminals

4. The reading should be infinite. If not, the pick-up coil is defective.

NOTE: *During the ohmmeter tests, flex the leads by hand to check for intermediate opens in the wiring.*

5. Connect both ohmmeter lead to the pick-up coil terminals at the connector.

6. The reading should be of one steady value, 500-1500Ω.

7. If the reading is not within specifications, the pick-up coil must is defective.

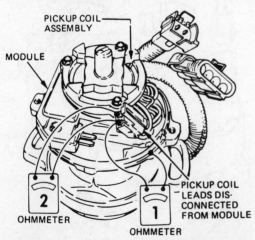

Testing the pick-up coil, type three (Tang Drive) distributor

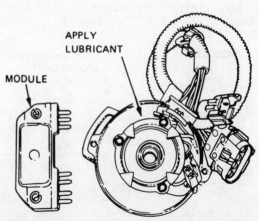

Module replacement and use of silicone lubricant, type three (Tang Drive) distributor

Testing

IGNITION MODULE

Because of the complexity of the internal circuitry of the HEI/EST module, it is recommended the module be tested with an accurate module tester.

It is imperative that silicone lubricant be used under the module when it is installed, to prevent module failure due to overheating.

NOTE: *The module can be removed without distributor disassembly. The distributor shaft and C-clip must be removed before the pick-up coil can be removed. Before removing the roll pin from the distributor tang drive to shaft, a spring must first be removed.*

GENERAL MOTORS DIRECT IGNITION SYSTEM (DIS)/ ELECTRONIC SPARK TIMING (EST)

General Information

The Direct Ignition System (DIS) does not use the conventional distributor and ignition coil. The system consists of ignition module, crankshaft sensor or combination sensor, along with the related connecting wires and Electronic Spark Timing (EST) portion of the Electronic Control Module (ECM).

The DIS system uses a "waste spark" method of spark distribution. Companion cylinders are paired and the spark occurs simultaneously in the cylinder with the piston coming up on the compression stroke and in the companion cylinder with the piston coming up on the exhaust stroke.

1. Example of firing order and companion cylinders: 1-2-3-4-5-6; 1/4, 2/5, 3/6.

2. Example of firing order and companion cylinders: 1-6-5-4-3-2; 1/4, 6/3, 5/2.

3. Example of firing order and companion cylinders: 1-3-4-2; 1/4, 2/3

NOTE: *Notice the companion cylinders in the V6 engine firing order remain the same, but the cylinder firing order sequence differs.*

The cylinder on the exhaust stroke requires very little of the available voltage to arc, so the remaining high voltage is used by the cylinder in the firing position (TDC compression). This same process is repeated when the companion cylinders reverse roles.

It is possible in an engine no-load condition, for one plug to fire, even though the spark plug lead from the same coil is disconnected from the other spark plug. The disconnected spark plug lead acts as one plate of a capacitor, with the engine being the other plate. These two capacitors plates are charged as a current surge (spark) jumps across the gap of the connected spark plug.

These plates are then discharged as the secondary energy is dissipated in an oscillating current across the gap of the spark plug still connected. Because of the direction of current flow in the primary windings and thus in the secondary windings, one spark plug will fire from the center electrode to the side electrode, while the other will fire from the side electrode to the center electrode.

These systems utilize the EST signal from the ECM, as do the convention distributor type ignition systems equipped with the EST system to control timing.

In the Direct Ignition system and while under 400 rpm, the DIS ignition module controls the spark timing through a module timing mode. Over 400 rpm, the ECM controls the spark timing through the EST mode. In the Direct Ignition system, to properly control the ignition timing, the ECM relies on the the following information from the various sensors.

1. Engine load (manifold pressure or vacuum).

2. Atmospheric (barometric) pressure.

3. Engine temperature.

4. Manifold air temperature.

5. Crankshaft position.

6. Engine speed (rpm).

Direct Ignition System Components

NOTE: *The Direct Ignition System/EST is used with TBI and Ported fuel injection systems.*

CRANKSHAFT SENSOR

A magnetic crankshaft sensor (Hall Effect switch) is used and is remotely mounted on the opposite side of the engine from the DIS module. The sensor protrudes in to the engine block, within 0.050″ of the crankshaft reluctor.

The reluctor is a special wheel cast into the crankshaft with seven slots machined into it, six of them being evenly spaced at 60° apart. A seventh slot is spaced 10° from one of the other slots and serves as a generator of a "sync-pulse". As the reluctor rotates as part of the crankshaft, the slots change the magnetic field of the sensor, creating an induced voltage pulse.

Based on the crankshaft sensor pulses, the DIS module sends reference signals to the ECM, which are used to indicate crankshaft position and engine speed. The DIS module will continue to send these reference pulses to the ECM at a rate of one per each 120° of crankshaft rotation. The ECM actvates the fuel injectors, based on the recognition of every other reference pulse, beginning at a crankshaft position 120° after piston top dead center (TDC). By

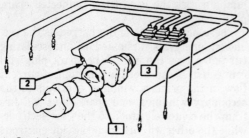

1. Crankshaft reluctor
2. Crankshaft sensor
3. Dis-assembly

Sensor to crank reluctor relationship, DIS/EST system

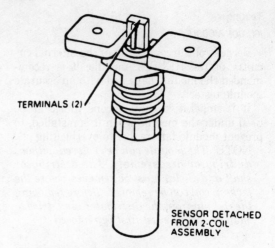

TERMINALS (2)

SENSOR DETACHED
FROM 2-COIL
ASSEMBLY

Crankshaft sensor, DIS System

comparing the time between the pulses, the DIS module can recognize the pulse representing the seventh slot (sync-pulse) which starts the calculation of ignition coil sequencing. The second crankshaft pulse following the sync-pulse signals the DIS module to fire the No.2-5 ignition coil, the fourth crankshaft pulse signals the module to fire No.3-6 ignition coil and the sixth crankshaft pulse signals the module to fire the 1-4 ignition coil.

IGNITION COILS

There are two separate coils for the four cylinder engines and three separate coils for the V6 engines, mounted to the coil/module assembly. Spark distribution is synchronized by a signal from the crankshaft sensor which the ignition module uses to trigger each coil at the proper time. Each coil provides the spark for two spark plugs.

Two types of ignition coil assemblies are used, Type I and Type II During the diagnosis of the systems, the correct type of ignition coil assembly must be identified and the diagnosis directed to that system.

Type I module/coil assembly has three twin tower ignition coils, combined into a single coil pack unit. This unit is mounted to the DIS module. ALL THREE COILS MUST BE REPLACED AS A UNIT. A separate current source through a fused circuit to the module terminal **P** is used to power the ignition coils.

Type II coil/module assembly has three separate coils that are mounted to the DIS module. EACH COIL CAN BE REPLACED SEPARATELY. A fused low current source to the module terminal **M**, provides power for the sensors, ignition coils and internal module circuitry.

DIS MODULE

The DIS module monitors the crankshaft sensor signal and based on these signals, sends a reference signal to the ECM so that correct spark and fuel injector control can be maintained during all driving conditions. During cranking, the DIS module monitors the sync-pulse to begin the ignition firing sequence. Below 400 rpm, the module controls the spark advance by triggering each of the ignition coils at a predetermined interval, based on engine speed only. Above 400 rpm, the ECM controls the spark timing (EST) and compensates for all driving conditions. The DIS module must receive a sync-pulse and then a crank signal, in that order, to enable the engine to start.

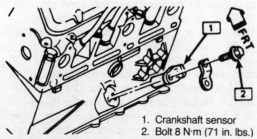

1. Crankshaft sensor
2. Bolt 8 N·m (71 in. lbs.)

Crankshaft sensor, 2.8L V6 engine

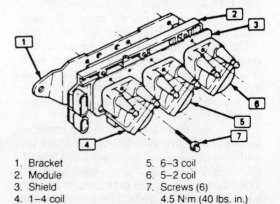

1. Bracket
2. Module
3. Shield
4. 1-4 coil
5. 6-3 coil
6. 5-2 coil
7. Screws (6)
   4.5 N·m (40 lbs. in.)

Exploded view of the DIS assembly, 2.8L V6 engine

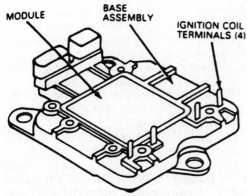

Base assembly of the four cylinder system

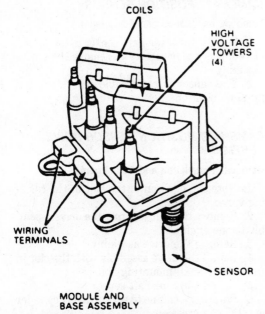

Four cylinder ignition system, DIS

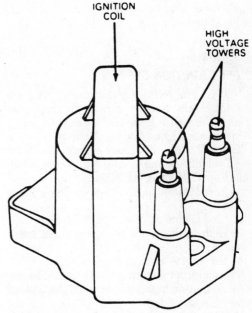

6 cylinder ignition coil removed from the assembly

The DIS module is not repairable. When a module is replaced, the remaining DIS components must be transferred to the new module.

DIRECT IGNITION ELECTRONIC SPARK TIMING (EST) CIRCUITS

This system uses the same EST to ECM circuits that the distributor type systems with EST use. The following is a brief description for the EST circuits.

DIS REFERENCE, CIRCUIT 430

The crankshaft sensor generates a signal to the ignition module, which results in a reference pulse being sent to the ECM. The ECM uses this signal to calculate crankshaft position and engine speed for injector pulse width.

NOTE: *The crankshaft sensor is mounted to the base of the DIS module on the 2.5L four cylinder engines and is mounted directly into the side of the engine block.*

REFERENCE GROUND, CIRCUIT 453

This wire is grounded through the module and insures that the ground circuit has no voltage drop between the ignition module and the ECM, which can affect performance.

BY-PASS, CIRCUIT 424

At approximately 400 rpm, the ECM applies 5 volts to this circuit to switch spark timing control from the DIS module to the ECM. An open or grounded by pass circuit will set a code 42 and result in the engine operating in a back-up ignition timing mode (module timing) at a calculated timing value. This may cause poor performance and reduced fuel economy.

ELECTRONIC SPARK TIMING (EST), CIRCUIT 423

The DIS module sends a reference signal to the ECM when the engine is cranking. While the engine is under 400 rpm, the DIS module controls the ignition timing. When the engine speed exceeds 400 rpm, the ECM applies 5 volts to the By-pass line to switch the timing to the ECM control (EST).

An open or ground in the EST circuit will result in the engine continuing to run, but in a back-up ignition timing mode (module timing mode) at a calculated timing value and the SERVICE ENGINE SOON light will not be on. If the EST fault is still present, the next time the engine is restarted, a code 42 will be set and the engine will operate in the module timing mode. This may cause poor performance and reduced fuel economy.

Diagnosis

DIRECT IGNITION SYSTEM

NOTE: *The following diagnostic aids are quick checks. Should more in-depth diagnosis of the system be needed, refer to Chilton's Electronic Engine Control Manual.*

The ECM uses information from the MAP and Coolant sensors, in addition to rpm to calculate spark advance as follows;

1. Low MAP output voltage = More spark advance.
2. Cold engine = More spark advance.
3. High MAP output voltage = Less spark advance.
4. Hot engine = Less spark advance.

Therefore, detonation could be caused by low MAP output or high resistance in the coolant sensor circuit.

Poor performance could be caused by high MAP output or low resistance in the coolant sensor circuit.

If the engine cranks but will not operate, or starts, then immediately stalls, diagnosis must be accomplished to determine if the failure is in the DIS system or the fuel system.

CHECKING EST PERFORMANCE

The ECM will set timing at a specified value when the diagnostic **TEST** terminal in the ALDL connector is grounded. To check for EST operation, run the engine at 1500 rpm with the terminal ungrounded. Then ground the **TEST** terminal. If the EST is operating, there should be a noticeable engine rpm change. A fault in the EST system will set a trouble code 42.

CODE 12

Code 12 is used during the diagnostic circuit check procedure to test the diagnostic and code display ability of the ECM. This code indicates that the ECM is not receiving the engine rpm (reference) signal. This occurs with the ignition key in the ON position and the engine not operating.

SETTING IGNITION TIMING

Because the reluctor wheel is an integral part of the crankshaft and the crankshaft sensor is mounted in a fixed position, timing adjustment is not possible.

CRANKSHAFT SENSOR

Adjustment

1. Rotate the harmonic balancer until the interrupter ring fills the sensor slot and the edge of the interrupter window is aligned with the edge of the deflector on the pedestal.
2. Adjust the sensor so that there is an equal distance on each side of the disc.
3. There should be approximately 0.025" clearance between the disc and the sensor.

NOTE: *Special tools are available for the measurement of the clearance through Kent Moore Tool Company.*

4. Tighten the retaining bolt and recheck the clearance at approximately 120° apart.
5. If the interrupter ring contacts the sensor at any point of the 360° circle, the interrupter ring has excessive runout and must be replaced.

CAMSHAFT POSITION SENSOR

Removal, Installation and Adjustment

1. If only the camshaft sensor is being replaced, it is not necessary to remove the entire assembly.
2. The sensor is replaceable separately and into one position.

CAMSHAFT POSITION SENSOR DRIVE ASSEMBLY

Removal, Installation and Adjustment

1. Note the position of the slot in the rotating vane.
2. Remove the bolt securing the drive assembly to the engine.
3. Remove the drive assembly.
4. Install the drive assembly with the slot in the vane. Install mounting bolt.
5. Install the camshaft sensor.
6. Rotate the engine to set the No. 1 cylinder at TDC compression.
7. Mark the harmonic balancer and rotate the engine to 25° after TDC.
8. Remove the plug wires from the coil assembly.
9. Using weatherpack removal tool J-28742-A, or equivalent, remove terminal **B** of the sensor 3-way connector on the module side.
10. Probe terminal **B** by installing a jumper and reconnecting the wire removed to the jumper wire.
11. Connect a voltmeter between the jumper wire and ground.
12. With the key On and the engine stopped, rotate the camshaft sensor counterclockwise until the sensor switch just closes. This is indicated by the voltage reading going from a high 5-12 volts to a low 0-2 volts. The low voltage indicates the switch is closed.
13. Tighten the retaining bolt and reinstall the wire into terminal **B**.
14. Install remaining components.

GENERAL MOTORS CORPORATION ELECTRONIC SPARK TIMING (EST) SYSTEM

GENERAL DESCRIPTION

The High Energy Ignition (HEI) system controls fuel combustion by providing the spark to ignite the compressed air/fuel mixture, in the combustion chamber, at the correct time. To provide improved engine performance, fuel economy and control of the exhaust emissions, the ECM controls distributor spark advance (timing) with the Electronic Spark Timing (EST) system.

The standard High Energy Ignition (HEI) system has a modified distributor module which is used in conjunction with the EST system. The module has seven terminals instead of the four used without EST. Two different terminal arrangements are used, depending upon the distributor used with a particular engine application.

To properly control ignition/combustion timing, the ECM needs to know the following information:

1. Crankshaft position.
2. Engine speed (rpm).
3. Engine load (manifold pressure or vacuum).
4. Atmospheric (barometric) pressure.
5. Engine temperature.
6. Transmission gear position (certain models)

The EST system consists of the distributor module, ECM and its connecting wires. The distributor has four wires from the HEI module connected to a four terminal connector, which mates with a four wire connector from the ECM.

These circuits perform the following functions:

1. Distributor reference at terminal **B**. This provides the ECM with rpm and crankshaft position information.
2. Reference ground at terminal **D**. This wire is grounded in the distributor and makes sure the ground circuit has no voltage drop, which could affect performance. If this circusit is open, it could cause poor performance.
3. By-pass at terminal **C**. At approximately 400 rpm, the ECM applies 5 volts to this circuit to switch the spark timing control from the HEI module to the ECM. An open or grounded bypass circuit will set a Code 42 and the engine will run at base timing, plus a small amount of advance built into the HEI module.
4. EST at terminal **A**. This triggers the HEI module. The ECM does not know what the actual timing is, but it does know when it gets

its reference signal. It then advances or retards the spark timing from that point. Therefore, if the base timing is set incorrectly, the entire spark curve will be incorrect.

An open circuit in the EST circuit will set a Code 42 and cause the engine to run on the HEI module timing. This will cause poor performance and poor fuel economy. A ground may set a Code 42, but the engine will not run.

The ECM uses information from the MAP or VAC and coolant sensors, in addition to rpm, in order to calculate spark advance as follows:

1. Low MAP output voltage (high VAC sensor output voltage) would require MORE spark advance.
2. Cold engine would require MORE spark advance.
3. High MAP output voltage (low VAC sensor output voltage) would require LESS spark advance.
4. Hot engine would require LESS spark advance.

RESULTS OF INCORRECT EST OPERATION

Detonation could be caused by low MAP output (high VAC sensor output), or high resistance in the coolant sensor circuit.

Poor performance could be caused by high MAP output (low VAC sensor output) or low resistance in the coolant sensor circuit.

HOW CODE 42 IS DETERMINED

When the systems is operating on the HEI module with no voltage in the by-pass line, the HEI module grounds the EST signal. The ECM expects to sense no voltage on the EST line during this condition. If it senses voltage, it sets Code 42 and will not go into the EST mode.

When the rpm for EST is reached (approximately 400 rpm), the ECM applies 5 volts to the by-pass line and the EST should no longer be grounded in the HEI module, so the EST voltage should be varying.

If the by-pass line is open, the HEI module will not switch to the EST mode, so the EST voltage will be low and Code 42 will be set.

If the EST line is grounded, the HEI module will switch to the EST, but because the line is grounded, there will be no EST signal and the engine will not operate. A Code 42 may or may not be set.

GENERAL MOTORS CORPORATION ELECTRONIC SPARK CONTROL (ESC) SYSTEM

GENERAL DESCRIPTION

The Electronic Spark Control (ESC) operates in conjunction with the Electronic Spark Timing (EST) system and modifies (retards) the spark advance when detonation occurs. The retard mode is held for approximately 20 seconds after which the spark control will again revert to the Electronic Spark Timing (EST) system. There are three basic components of the Electronic Spark Control (ESC) system.

SENSOR

The Electronic Spark Control (ESC) sensor detects the presence (or absence) and intensity of the detonation by the vibration characteristics of the engine. The output is an electrical signal that goes to the controller. A sensor failure would allow no spark retard.

DISTRIBUTOR

The distributor is an HEI/EST unit with an electronic module, modified so it can respond to the ESC controller signal. This command is delayed when detonation is occurring, thus providing the level of spark retard required. The amount of spark retard is a function of the degree of detonation.

CONTROLLER

The Electronic Spark Control (ESC) controller processes the sensor signal into a command signal to the distributor, to adjust the spark timing. The process is continuous, so that the presence of detonation is monitored and controlled. The controller is a hard wired signal processor and amplifier which operates from 6-16 volts. Controller failure would be no ignition, no retard or full retard. The controller has no memory storage.

CODE 43

Should a Code 43 be set in the ECM memory, it would indicate that the ESC system retard signal has been sensed by the ECM for too long a period of time. When voltage at terminal **L** of the ECM is low, spark timing is retarded. Normal voltage in the non-retarded mode is approximately 7.5 volts or more.

BASIC IGNITION TIMING

NOTE: *1987-88 Cavaliers, both 4- and 6-cyl. engines, have distributorless ignition systems (DIS). Because the reluctor wheel is an integral part of the crankshaft, and the crankshaft sensor is mounted in a fixed position, timing adjustment is not possible.*

Basic ignition timing is critical to the proper operation of the ESC system. Always follow the Vehicle Emission Control Information label procedures when adjusting ignition timing.

Some engines will incorporate a magnetic timing probe hole for use with special electronic timing equipment. Consult the manufacturer's instructions for the use of this electronic timing equipment.

Ignition timing is the measurement, in degrees of crankshaft rotation, of the point at which the spark plugs fire in each of the cylinders. It is measured in degrees before or after Top Dead Center (TDC) of the compression stroke.

Because it takes a fraction of a second for the spark plug to ignite the mixture in the cylinder, the spark plug must fire a little before the piston reaches TDC. Otherwise, the mixture will not completely ignited as the piston passes TDC and the full power of the explosion will not be used by the engine.

The timing measurement is given in degrees of crankshaft rotation before the piston reaches TDC (BTDC). If the setting for the ignition timing is 5° BTDC, the spark plug must fire 5° before each piston reaches TDC. This only holds true, however, when the engine is at idle speed.

As the engine speed increases, the pistons go faster. The spark plugs have to ignite the fuel even sooner if it is to be completely ignited when the piston reaches TDC.

If the ignition is set too far advanced (BTDC), the ignition and expansion of the fuel in the cylinder will occur too soon and tend to force the piston down while it is still traveling up. This causes engine ping. If the ignition spark is set too far retarded, after TDC (ATDC), the piston will have already passed TDC and started on its way down when the fuel is ignited. This will cause the piston to be forced down for only a portion of its travel. This will result in poor engine performance and lack of power.

Ignition timing for this engine should be accomplished using the averaging method in which the timing of each cylinder can be brought into closer agreement with the base timing specification.

The averaging method involves the use of a double notched crankshaft pulley. When timing the engine, the coil wire, instead of the Number 1 plug wire, should be used to trigger the timing light. The notch for the No. 1 cylinder is scribed across all three edges of the double sheave pulley. Another notch located 180° away from the No. 1 cylinder notch is scribed only across the center section of the pulley to make it distinguishable from the No. 1 cylinder notch.

Since the trigger signal for the timing light is picked up at the coil wire, each spark firing results in a flash from the timing light. A slight jiggling of the timing notch may be apparent since each cylinder firing is being displayed. Optimum timing of all cylinders is accomplished by centering the total apparent notch width about the correct timing specification.

There are three basic types of timing light available. The first is a simple neon bulb with two wire connections (one for the spark plug and one for the plug wire, connecting the light in series). This type of light is quite dim, and must be held closely to the marks to be seen, but it is quite inexpensive. The second type of light operates from the car's battery. Two alligator clips connect to the battery terminals, while a third wire connects to the spark plug with an adapter. This type of light is more expensive, but the xenon bulb provides a nice bright flash which can even be seen in sunlight. The third type replaces the battery source with 110 volt house current. Some timing lights have other functions built into them, such as dwell meters, tachometers, or remote starting switches. These are convenient, in that they reduce the tangle of wires under the hood, but may duplicate the functions of tools you already have.

Because your car has electronic ignition, you should use a timing light with an inductive pickup. This pickup simply clamps around the Number 1 spark plug wire (in this case, the coil wire), eliminating the adapter. It is not susceptible to crossfiring or false triggering, which may occur with a conventional light due to the greater voltages produced by HEI.

ADJUSTMENT

1. Refer to the instructions on the emission control sticker inside the engine compartment. Follow all instructions on the label.

2. Locate the timing marks on the crankshaft pulley and the front of the engine.

3. Clean off the marks so that you can see them. Chalk or white paint will help to make them more visible.

4. Attach a tachometer to the engine as detailed previously.

5. Disconnect the 4-terminal EST connector at the distributor so that the engine will switch to the bypass timing mode (please refer to Chapter 4 for more information).

6. Attach a timing light as per the manufacturer's instructions. Clamp the inductive pickup around the HIGH TENSION COIL WIRE (not the No. 1 spark plug wire) at the distributor. Before installing the pick-up on the wire, it will be necessary to peel back the protective plastic cover which encases the wire.

7. Loosen the distributor clamp bolt slightly so that the distributor may be rotated as necessary to adjust timing.

8. Check that all wires are clear of the fan and then start the engine. Allow the engine to reach normal operating temperature.

9. Aim the timing light at the marks. A slight jiggling of the notch on the pulley may appear due to the fact that each cylinder is being displayed as it fires. The apparent notch width cannot be reduced by a timing adjustment.

10. Center the total apparent notch width about the correct timing mark on the indicator by rotating the distributor housing. This will insure that the average cylinder timing is as close to specifications as possible. Once again, the apparent notch width cannot be reduced by timing adjustment.

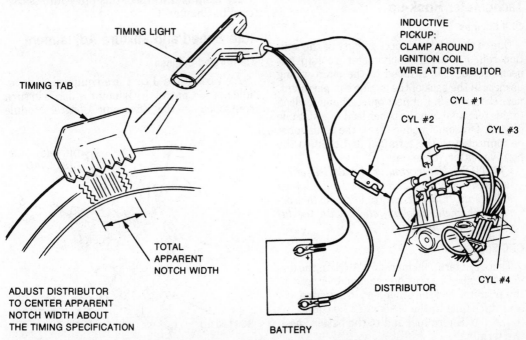

TIMING LIGHT

INDUCTIVE PICKUP: CLAMP AROUND IGNITION COIL WIRE AT DISTRIBUTOR

TIMING TAB

CYL #1

CYL #2

CYL #3

TOTAL APPARENT NOTCH WIDTH

CYL #4

ADJUST DISTRIBUTOR TO CENTER APPARENT NOTCH WIDTH ABOUT THE TIMING SPECIFICATION

DISTRIBUTOR

BATTERY

Ignition timing is accomplished using the averaging method

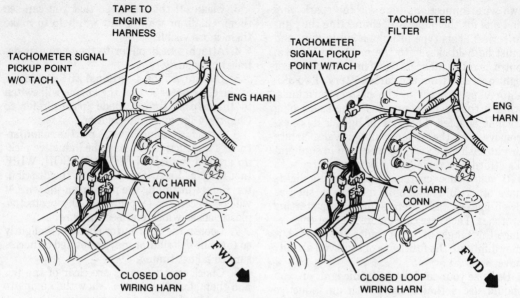

Tachometer hookup connections on the 4 cyl. OHV engines

11. Turn off the engine and tighten the distributor lock bolt. Start the engine and recheck the timing. Sometimes the distributor will move a little during the tightening process. If the ignition timing is within 1° of the correct setting, that is close enough; a tolerance of up to 2° is permitted by the manufacturer.

12. Turn off the engine and disconnect the timing light and the tachometer. Reconnect the 4-terminal EST connector.

Tachometer Hook-up

OHV Engines

Due to the relative inaccessibility of the ignition coil, a separate tachometer hookup has been provided. It is taped to the main wiring harness in the back of the engine compartment, near the firewall. Connect one tachometer lead to this terminal and the other lead to a suitable ground. On some tachometers, the leads must be connected to the terminal and then to the positive battery terminal.

CAUTION: *Never ground the TACH terminal; serious module and ignition coil damage will result. If there is any doubt as to the correct tachometer hookup, check with the tachometer manufacturer.*

OHC Engines

There is a terminal marked TACH on the distributor cap. Connect one tachometer lead to this terminal and the other lead to a ground. On some tachometer, the leads must be connected to the TACK terminal and to the battery positive terminal.

CAUTION: *Never ground the TACH termi-*

nal; serious module and ignition coil damage will result. If there is any doubt as to the correct tachometer hookup, check with the tachometer manufacturer.

Valve Adjustment

All models utilize an hydraulic valve lifter system to obtain zero lash. No adjustment is necessary. An initial adjustment is required anytime that the lifters are removed or the valve train is disturbed, this procedure is covered in Chapter 3.

Idle Speed and Mixture Adjustment

Carbureted Engines

All carbureted J-cars are equipped with an Idle Speed Control (ISC) motor which is in turn controlled by the Electronic Control Module

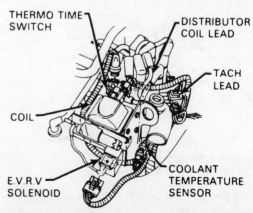

Tachometer hookup connection on the V6 engine

(ECM). All idle speeds are programmed into the ECM's memory and then relayed to the ISC motor as any given situation requires. Curb idle is pre-set at the factory and not routinely adjustable. Although curb idle is not to be adjusted under normal conditions, it can be adjusted, but only upon replacement of the ISC (for further details, refer to Chapter 5).

The idle mixture screws are concealed under staked-in plugs. Idle mixture is not considered to be a normal tune-up procedure, because of the sensitivity of emission control adjustments. Mixture adjustment requires not only the special tools with which to remove the concealing plugs, but also the addition of an artificial enrichment substance (generally propane) which must be introduced into the carburetor by means of a finely calibrated metering valve. These tools are not generally available and require a certain amount of expertise to use, therefore, mixture adjustments are purposely not covered in this book. If you suspect that your car's carburetor requires a mixture adjustment, we strongly recommend that the job be referred to a qualified service technician.

Fuel Injected Engines

The fuel injected vehicles are controlled by a computer which supplies the correct amount of fuel during all engine operating conditions; no adjustment is necessary.

Engine and Engine Overhaul

3

UNDERSTANDING THE ENGINE ELECTRICAL SYSTEM

The engine electrical system can be broken down into three separate and distinct systems: (1) the starting system; (2) the charging system; (3) the ignition system.

Battery and Starting System

The battery is the first link in the chain of mechanisms which work together to provide cranking of the automobile engine. In most modern cars, the battery is a lead-acid electrochemical device consisting of six 2 volt (2V) subsections connected in series so the unit is capable of producing approximately 12V of electrical pressure. Each subsection, or sell, consists of a series of positive and negative plates held a short distance apart in a solution of sulfuric acid and water. The two types of plates are of dissimilar metals. This causes a chemical reaction to be set up, and it is this reaction which produces current flow from the battery when its positive and negative terminals are connected to an electrical appliance such as a lamp or motor. The continued transfer of electrons would eventually convert the sulfuric acid in the electrolyte to water, and make the two plates identical in chemical composition. As electrical energy is removed from the battery, its voltage output tend to drop. Thus, measuring battery voltage and battery electrolyte composition are two ways of checking the ability of the unit to supply power. During the starting of the engine, electrical energy is removed from the battery. However, if the charging circuit is in good condition and the operating conditions are normal, the power removed from the battery will be replaced by the generator (or alternator) which will force electrons back through the battery, reversing the normal flow, and restoring the battery to its original chemical state.

The battery and starting motor are linked by very heavy electrical cables designed to minimize resistance to the flow of current. Generally, the major power supply cable that leaves the battery goes directly to the starter, while other electrical system needs are supplied by a smaller cable. During the starter operation, power flows from the battery to the starter and is grounded through the car's frame and the battery's negative ground strap.

The starting motor is a specially designed, direct current electric motor capable of producing a very great amount of power for its size. One thing that allows the motor to produce a great deal of power is its tremendous rotating speed. It drives the engine through a tiny pinion gear (attached to the starter's armature), which drives the very large flywheel ring gear at a greatly reduced speed. Another factor allowing it to produce so much power is that only intermittent operation is required of it. Thus, little allowance for air circulation is required, and the windings can be built into a very small space.

The starter solenoid is a magnetic device which employs the small current supplied by the starting switch circuit of the ignition switch. This magnetic action moves a plunger which mechanically engages the starter and electrically closes the heavy switch which connects it to the battery. The starting switch circuit consists of the starting switch contained within the ignition switch, a transmission neutral safety switch or clutch pedal switch, and the wiring necessary to connect these with the starter solenoid or relay.

A pinion, which is a small gear, is mounted to a one-way drive clutch. this clutch is splined to the starter armature shaft. When the ignition switch is moved to the start position, the solenoid plunger slides the pinion toward the flywheel ring gear via a collar and spring. If the teeth on the pinion and flywheel match properly, the pinion will engage the flywheel immediately. IF the gear teeth butt one another, the spring will be compressed and will force the gears to mesh as soon as the starter turns far enough to allow them to do so. As the solenoid plunger reaches the end of its travel, it closes the contacts that connect the battery and starter and then the engine is cranked.

As soon as the engine starts, the flywheel ring gear begins turning fast enough to drive the pinion at an extremely high rate of speed. At this point, the one-way clutch begins allowing the pinion to spin faster that the starter shaft so that the starter will not operate at excessive speed. When the ignition switch is released from the starter position, the solenoid is de-energized, and a spring contained within the solenoid assembly pulls the gear out of mesh and interrupts the current flow to the starter.

Some starters employ a separate relay, mounted away from the starter, to switch the motor and solenoid current on and off. The relay thus replaces the solenoid electrical switch, but does not eliminate the need for a solenoid mounted on the starter used to mechanically engage the starter drive gears. The relay is used to reduce the amount of current the starting switch must carry.

The Charging System

The automobile charging system provides electrical power for operation of the vehicle's ignition and starting systems and all the electrical accessories. The battery serves as an electrical surge of storage tank, storing (in chemical form) the energy originally produced by the engine driven generator. The system also provides a means of regulating generator output to protect the battery from being overcharged and to avoid excessive voltage to the accessories.

The storage battery is a chemical device incorporating parallel lead plates in a tank containing a sulfuric acid-water solution. Adjacent plates are slightly dissimilar, and the chemical reaction of the two dissimilar plates produces electrical energy when the battery is connected to a load such as the starter motor. The chemical reaction is reversible, so that when the generator is producing a voltage (electrical pressure) greater then that produced by the battery, electricity is forced into the battery, and the battery is returned to its fully charged state.

The vehicle's generator is driven mechanically, through V belts, by the engine crankshaft. It consists of two coils of fine wire, one stationary (the stator), and one movable (the rotor). The rotor may also be known as the armature and consists of fine wire wrapped around an iron core which is mounted on a shaft. The electricity which flows through the two coils of wire (provided initially by the battery in some cases) creates an intense magnetic field around both rotor and stator, and the interaction between the two fields creates voltage, allowing the generator to power the accessories and charge the battery.

There are two types of generators; the earlier is the direct current (DC) type. The current produced by the DC generator is generated in the armature and carried off the spinning armature by stationary brushes contacting the commutator. The commutator is a series of smooth metal contact plates on the end of the armature. The commutator plates, which are separated from one another by a very short gap, are connected to the armature circuits so that current will flow in one direction only in wires carrying the generator output. The generator stator consists of two stationary coils of wire which draw some of the output current of the generator to form a powerful magnetic field and create the interaction of fields which generates the voltage. The generator field is wired in series with the regulator.

Newer automobiles use alternating current generators or alternators because they are more efficient, can be rotated at higher speeds, and have fewer brush problems, In an alternator, the field rotates while all the current produced passes only through the stator windings. The brushes bear against continuous slip rings rather than a commutator. This causes the current produced to periodically reverse the direction of its flow. Diodes (electrical one-way switches) block the flow of current from traveling in the wrong direction. A series of diodes is wired together to permit the alternating flow of the stator to be converted to a pulsating, but unidirectional flow of current from traveling in the wrong direction. A series of diodes is wires together to permit the alternating flow of the stator to be converted to a pulsating, but unidirectional flow at the alternator output. The alternator's field is wires in series with the voltage regulator.

The regulator consist of several circuits. Each circuit has a core, or magnetic coil of wire, which operates a switch. Each switch is connected to ground through on or more resistors. The coil of wire responds directly to system voltage. When the voltage reaches the required level, the magnetic field created by the winding of wire closes the switch and inserts a resistance into the generator field circuit, thus reducing the output. The contacts of the switch cycle open and close many times each second to precisely control voltage.

While alternators are self-limiting as far as maximum current is concerned. DC generators employ a current regulating circuit which responds directly to the total amount of current flowing through the generator circuit rather than to the output voltage. The current regulator is similar to the voltage regulator except all system current must flow through the energizing coil on its way to the various accessories.

SAFETY PRECAUTIONS

Observing these precautions will ensure safe handling of the electrical system components, and will avoid damage to the vehicle's electrical system:

a. Be absolutely sure of the polarity of a booster battery before making connections. Connect the cables positive to positive, and negative to negative. Connect positive cables first and then make the last connection to ground on the body of the booster vehicle so that arcing cannot ignite hydrogen gas that may have accumulated near the battery. Even momentary connection of a booster battery with the polarity reversed will damage alternator diodes.

b. Disconnect both vehicle battery cables before attempting to charge a battery.

c. Never ground the alternator or generator output or battery terminal. Be cautious when using metal tools around a battery to avoid creating a short circuit between the terminals.

d. Never ground the field circuit between the alternator and regulator.

e. Never run an alternator or generator without load unless the field circuit is disconnected.

f. Never attempt to polarize an alternator.

g. Keep the regulator cover in place when taking voltage and current limiter readings.

h. Use insulated tools when adjusting the regulator.

i. Whenever DC generator-to-regulator wires have been disconnected, the generator must be repolarized. To do this with an externally grounded, light duty generator, momentarily place a jumper wires between the battery terminal and the generator terminal of the regulator. With an internally grounded heavy duty unit, disconnect the wire to the regulator field terminal and touch the regulator battery terminal with it.

ENGINE ELECTRICAL

Ignition Coil

The High Energy Ignition distributor is used on all engines. The ignition coil is either mounted to the top of the distributor cap or is externally mounted on the engine, having a secondary circuit high tension wire connecting the coil

to the distributor cap and interconnecting primary wiring as part of the engine harness.

The Direct Ignition System (DIS) does not use the conventional distributor and ignition coil. The system consists of ignition module, crankshaft sensor or combination sensor, along with the related connecting wires and Electronic Spark Timing (EST) portion of the Electronic Control Module (ECM).

TESTING

Distributor With Separate Coil
Type One

1. Disconnect the primary wiring connectors and secondary coil wire from the ignition coil.
2. Using an ohmmeter on the high scale, connect one lead to a grounding screw and the second lead to one of the primary coil terminals.
3. The reading should be infinite. If not, replace the ignition coil.
4. Using the low scale, place the ohmmeter leads on both the primary coil terminals.
5. The reading should be very low or zero. If not, replace the ignition coil.
6. Using the high scale, place one ohmmeter lead on the high tension output terminal and the other lead on a primary coil terminal.
7. The reading should NOT be infinite. If it is, replace the ignition coil.

Distributor With Separate Coil
Type Two

1. Using an ohmmeter set on the high scale, place one lead on a ground of the ignition coil.
2. Place the second lead into one of the rearward terminals of the ignition coil primary connector.
3. The ohmmeter scale should read infinite. If not, replace the ignition coil.
4. Using the low scale, place the ohmmeter leads into each of the outer terminals of the coil connector.
5. The reading should be zero or very low. If not, replace the ignition coil.
6. Using the high scale, place one ohmmeter lead on the coil secondary terminal and the second lead into the rearward terminal of the ignition coil primary connector.
7. The reading should not be infinite. If so, replace the ignition coil.

Distributor With Separate Coil
Type Three w/Tang Drive

1. Using an ohmmeter set on the high scale, place one lead on a ground of the ignition coil.
2. Place the second lead into one of the rearward terminals of the ignition coil primary connector.
3. The ohmmeter scale should read infinite. If not, replace the ignition coil.

4. Using the low scale, place the ohmmeter leads into each of the outer terminals of the coil connector.

5. The reading should be zero or very low. If not, replace the ignition coil.

6. Using the high scale, place one ohmmeter lead on the coil secondary terminal and the second lead into the rearward terminal of the ignition coil primary connector.

7. The reading should not be infinite. If so, replace the ignition coil.

Direct Ignition System (DIS)

There are two separate coils for the 4-cylinder engines and three separate coils for the V6 engines, mounted to the coil/module assembly. Spark distribution is synchronized by a signal from the crankshaft sensor which the ignition module uses to trigger each coil at the proper time. Each coil provides the spark for two spark plugs.

Two types of ignition coil assemblies are used, Type I and Type II During the diagnosis of the systems, the correct type of ignition coil assembly must be identified and the diagnosis directed to that system.

Type I module/coil assembly has three twin tower ignition coils, combined into a single coil pack unit. This unit is mounted to the DIS module. ALL THREE COILS MUST BE REPLACED AS A UNIT. A separate current source through a fused circuit to the module terminal **P** is used to power the ignition coils.

Type II coil/module assembly has three separate coils that are mounted to the DIS module. EACH COIL CAN BE REPLACED SEPARATELY. A fused low current source to the module terminal **M**, provides power for the sensors, ignition coils and internal module circuitry.

Ignition Module
DISTRIBUTOR WITH SEPARATE COIL TYPE ONE

NOTE: *This type distributor has no vacuum or centrifugal advance mechanism and has the pick-up coil mounted above the module. This distributor is used with the EST system.*

Because of the complexity of the internal circuitry of the HEI/EST module, it is recommended the module be tested with an accurate module tester.

It is imperative that silicone lubricant be used under the module when it is installed, to prevent module failure due to overheating.

NOTE: *The module and the Hall Effect switch (if used) can be removed from the distributor without disassembly. To remove the pick-up coil, the distributor shaft must be re-moved to expose a waved retaining ring (C-washer) holding the pick-up coil in place.*

DISTRIBUTOR WITH SEPARATE COIL TYPE TWO

NOTE: *This type distributor has no vacuum or centrifugal advance mechanisms and the module has two outside terminal connections for the wiring harness. This distributor is used with the EST system.*

Because of the complexity of the internal circuitry of the HEI/EST module, it is recommended the module be tested with an accurate module tester.

It is imperative that silicone lubricant be used under the module when it is installed, to prevent module failure due to overheating.

NOTE: *The module can be removed without distributor disassembly. To remove the pick-up coil, the distributor shaft must be removed. A retainer can then be removed from the top of the pole piece and the pick-up coil removed.*

DISTRIBUTOR WITH SEPARATE COIL TYPE THREE W/TANG DRIVE

NOTE: *This distributor is used with the EST system. The unit is mounted horizontally to the valve cover housing and is driven by the camshaft, through a tang on the distributor shaft.*

Because of the complexity of the internal circuitry of the HEI/EST module, it is recommended the module be tested with an accurate module tester.

It is imperative that silicone lubricant be used under the module when it is installed, to prevent module failure due to overheating.

NOTE: *The module can be removed without distributor disassembly. The distributor shaft and C-clip must be removed before the pick-up coil can be removed. Before removing the roll pin from the distributor tang drive to shaft, a spring must first be removed.*

Distributor
REMOVAL AND INSTALLATION
OHV Engines

WARNING: *On Chevrolet V6 models the distributor body is involved in the engine lubricating system. The lubricating circuit to the right bank valve train can be interrupted by misalignment of the distributor body. See Firing Order illustrations for correct distributor positioning.*

The 1987-88 Chevrolet built 4-cylinder 2.0L and V6 2.8L engines do not have a distributor. For an explanation of this type of ignition system refer to (DIS) Ignition System in Chapter 2.

1. Disconnect the negative battery cable.
2. Tag and disconnect all wires leading from the distributor cap.
3. Remove the air cleaner housing as previously detailed.
4. Remove the distributor cap.
5. Disconnect the AIR pipe-to-exhaust manifold hose at the air management valve.
6. Unscrew the rear engine lift bracket bolt and nut, lift it off the stud and then position the entire assembly out of the way to facilitate better access to the distributor.
7. Mark the position of the distributor, relative to the engine block and then scribe a mark on the distributor body indicating the initial position of the rotor.
8. Remove the holddown nut and clamp from the base of the distributor. Remove the distributor from the engine. The drive gear on the distributor shaft is helical and the shaft will rotate slightly as the distributor is removed. Note and mark the position of the rotor at this second position. Do not crank the engine while the distributor is removed.
9. To install the distributor, rotate the shaft until the rotor aligns with the second mark you made (when the shaft stopped moving). Lubricate the drive gear with clean engine oil and install the distributor into the engine. As the distributor is installed, the rotor should move to the first mark that you made. This will ensure proper timing. If the marks do not align properly, remove the distributor and try again.
10. Install the clamp and holddown nut.

NOTE: *You may wish to use a magnet attached to an extension bar to position the clamp on the stud.*

11. Installation of the remaining components is in the reverse order of removal. Check the ignition timing.

OHC Engines

1. Disconnect the battery ground.
2. Mark the spark plug wires and remove the wires and coil.
3. Matchmark the position of the rotor, distributor body and cylinder head.
4. Disconnect the wiring from the distributor.
5. Remove the two distributor holddown nuts.
6. Remove the distributor.
7. Installation is the reverse of removal. Torque the holddown nuts to 13 ft.lb. If the engine was rotated while the distributor was out, see steps 1-5 of the above procedure.

INSTALLATION IF THE ENGINE WAS DISTURBED

If the engine was cranked while the distributor was removed, you will have to place the engine on TDC of the compression stroke to obtain proper ignition timing.

1. Remove the No. 1 spark plug.
2. Place your thumb over the spark plug hole. Crank the engine slowly until compression is felt. It will be easier if you have someone rotate the engine by hand, using a wrench on the crankshaft pulley.
3. Align the timing mark on the crankshaft pulley with the 0 degree mark on the timing scale attached to the front of the engine. This places the engine at TDC of the compression stroke.

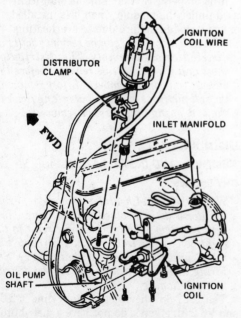

Removing the OHV 4-Cyl. distributor

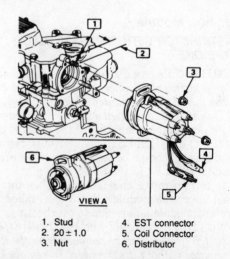

1. Stud
2. 20 ± 1.0
3. Nut
4. EST connector
5. Coil Connector
6. Distributor

Distributor mounting on OHC 4-cyl. engines

4. Turn the distributor shaft until the rotor points to the No. 1 spark plug tower on the cap.

5. Install the distributor into the engine. Be sure to align the distributor-to-engine block mark made earlier.

6. Perform Steps 10-11 of the preceding removal and installation procedure.

Alternator

The alternating current generator (alternator) supplies a continuous output of electrical energy at all engine speeds. The alternator generates electrical energy for the engine and all electrical components, and recharges the battery by supplying it with current. This unit consists of four main assemblies: two end frame assemblies, a rotor assembly, and a stator assembly. The rotor is supported in the drive end frame by a ball bearing and at the other end by a roller bearing. These bearings are lubricated during manufacture and require no maintenance. There are six diodes in the end frame assembly. Diodes are electrical check valves that change the alternating current supplied from the stator windings to a direct current (DC), delivered to the output (BAT) terminal. Three diodes are negative and are mounted flush with the end frame; the other three are positive and are mounted into a strip called a heat sink. The positive diodes are easily identified as the ones within small cavities or depressions. A capacitor, or condenser, mounted on the end frame protects the rectifier bridge and diode trio from high voltages, and suppresses radio noise. This capacitor requires no maintenance.

Two models of the SI series alternator are used on J-cars. The 10 SI and 15 SI are of similar construction; the 15 SI is slightly larger, uses different stator windings, and produces more current.

ALTERNATOR PRECAUTIONS

1. When installing a battery, make sure that the positive and negative cables are not reversed.

2. When jump-starting the car, be sure that like terminals are connected. This also applies to using a battery charger. Reversed polarity will burn out the alternator and regulator in a matter of seconds.

3. Never operate the alternator with the battery disconnected or on an otherwise uncontrolled open circuit.

4. Do not short across or ground any alternator or regulator terminals.

5. Do not try to polarize the alternator.

6. Do not apply full battery voltage to the field (brown) connector.

7. Always disconnect the battery ground cable before disconnecting the alternator lead.

8. Always disconnect the battery (negative cable first) when charging it.

9. Never subject the alternator to excessive heat or dampness. If you are steam cleaning the engine, cover the alternator.

10. Never use arc-welding equipment on the car with the alternator connected.

CHARGING SYSTEM TROUBLESHOOTING

There are many possible ways in which the charging system can malfunction. Often the source of a problem is difficult to diagnose, requiring special equipment and a good deal of experience. This is usually not the case, however, where the charging system fails completely and causes the dash board warning light to come on or the battery to become dead. To troubleshoot a complete system failure only two pieces of equipment are needed: a test light, to determine that current is reaching a certain point; and a current indicator (ammeter), to determine the direction of the current flow and its measurement in amps.

This test works under three assumptions:

1. The battery is known to be good and fully charged.

2. The alternator belt is in good condition and adjusted to the proper tension.

3. All connections in the system are clean and tight.

NOTE: *In order for the current indicator to give a valid reading, the car must be equipped with battery cables which are of the same gauge size and quality as original equipment battery cables.*

1. Turn off all electrical components on the car. Make sure the doors of the car are closed. If the car is equipped with a clock, disconnect the clock by removing the lead wire from the rear of the clock. Disconnect the positive battery cable from the battery and connect the ground wire on a test light to the disconnected positive battery cable. Touch the probe end of the test light to the positive battery post. The test light should not light. If the test light does light, there is a short or open circuit on the car.

2. Disconnect the voltage regulator wiring harness connector at the voltage regulator. Turn on the ignition key. Connect the wire on a test light to a good ground (engine bolt). Touch the probe end of a test light to the ignition wire connector into the voltage regulator wiring connector. This wire corresponds to the I terminal on the regulator. If the test light goes on, the charging system warning light circuit is complete. If the test light does not come on and the warning light on the instrument panel is on, either the resistor wire, which is parallel with the

warning light, or the wiring to the voltage regulator, is defective. If the test light does not come on and the warning light is not on, either the bulb is defective or the power supply wire form the battery through the ignition switch to the bulb has an open circuit. Connect the wiring harness to the regulator.

3. Examine the fuse link wire in the wiring harness from the starter relay to the alternator. If the insulation on the wire is cracked or split, the fuse link may be melted. Connect a test light to the fuse link by attaching the ground wire on the test light to an engine bolt and touching the probe end of the light to the bottom of the fuse link wire where it splices into the alternator output wire. If the bulb in the test light does not light, the fuse link is melted.

4. Start the engine and place a current indicator on the positive battery cable. Turn off all electrical accessories and make sure the doors are closed. If the charging system is working properly, the gauge will show a draw of less than 5 amps. If the system is not working prop-

erly, the gauge will show a draw of more than 5 amps. A charge moves the needle toward the battery, a draw moves the needle away from the battery. Turn the engine off.

5. Disconnect the wiring harness from the voltage regulator at the regulator at the regulator connector. Connect a male spade terminal (solderless connector) to each end of a jumper wire. Insert one end of the wire into the wiring harness connector which corresponds to the **A** terminal on the regulator. Insert the other end of the wire into the wiring harness connector which corresponds to the **F** terminal on the regulator. Position the connector with the jumper wire installed so that it cannot contact any metal surface under the hood. Position a current indicator gauge on the positive battery cable. Have an assistant start the engine. Observe the reading on the current indicator. Have your assistant slowly raise the speed of the engine to about 2,000 rpm or until the current indicator needle stops moving, whichever comes first. Do not run the engine for more than a short period

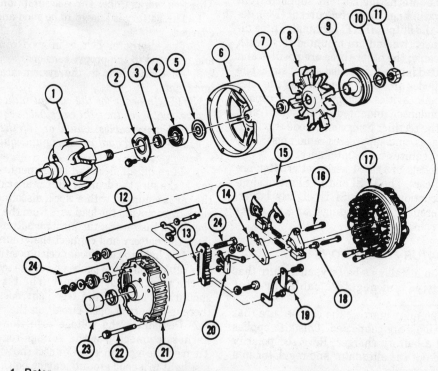

1. Rotor	9. Pulley	17. Stator
2. Front bearing retainer	10. Lockwasher	18. Insulating washer
3. Inner collar	11. Pulley nut	19. Capacitor
4. Bearing	12. Terminal assembly	20. Diode trio
5. Washer	13. Rectifier bridge	21. Rear housing
6. Front housing	14. Regulator	22. Through bolt
7. Outer collar	15. Brush assembly	23. Bearing and seal assembly
8. Fan	16. Screw	24. Terminal assembly

Exploded view of the 10SI alternator (15SI similar)

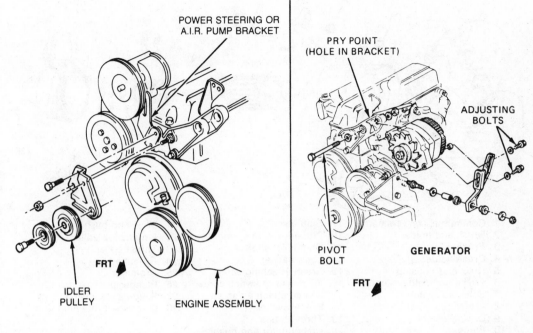

POWER STEERING OR
A.I.R. PUMP BRACKET

PRY POINT
(HOLE IN BRACKET)

ADJUSTING
BOLTS

IDLER
PULLEY

FRT

ENGINE ASSEMBLY

PIVOT
BOLT

GENERATOR

FRT

Alternator installation details

of time in this condition. If the wiring harness connector or jumper wire becomes excessively hot during this test, turn off the engine and check for a grounded wire in the regulator wiring harness. If the current indicator shows a charge of about three amps less than the output of the alternator, the alternator is working properly. If the previous tests showed a draw, the voltage regulator is defective. If the gauge does not show the proper charging rate, the alternator is defective.

REMOVAL AND INSTALLATION

1. Disconnect the negative battery cable at the battery.
   CAUTION: *Failure to disconnect the negative cable may result in injury from the positive battery lead at the alternator, and may short the alternator and regulator during the removal process.*
2. Disconnect and label the two terminal plug and the battery leads from the rear of the alternator.
3. Loosen the mounting bolts. Push the alternator inwards and slip the drive belt off the pulley.
4. Remove the mounting bolts and remove the alternator.
5. To install, place the alternator in its brackets and install the mounting bolts. Do not tighten them yet.
6. Slip the belt back over the pulley. Pull outwards on the unit and adjust the belt tension

(see Chapter 1). Tighten the mounting and adjusting bolts.
7. Install the electrical leads.
8. Install the negative battery cable.

Regulator

A solid state regulator is mounted within the alternator. All regulator components are enclosed in a solid mold. The regulator is non-adjustable and requires no maintenance.

Starter

REMOVAL AND INSTALLATION

1. Disconnect the negative battery cable at the battery.
2. Label and disconnect the solenoid wires and battery cable.
3. Remove the rear motor support bracket. Remove the air conditioning compressor support rod (if so equipped).
4. Working under the car, remove the two starter-to-engine bolts, and allow the starter to drop down. Note the location and number of any shims. Remove the starter.
5. Installation is the reverse. Tighten the mounting bolts to 25-35 ft.lb.

STARTER OVERHAUL

Drive Replacement

1. Disconnect the field coil straps from the solenoid.

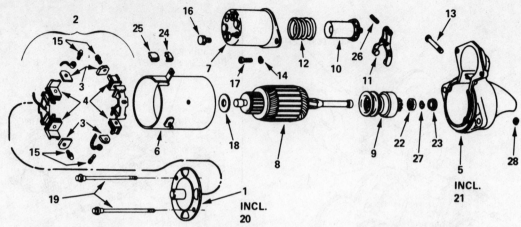

1. Commutator end frame
2. Brush and holder
3. Brush
4. Brush holder
5. Drive end housing
6. Frame and field assembly
7. Solenoid switch
8. Armature
9. Drive assembly
10. Plunger
11. Shift lever
12. Plunger return spring
13. Shift lever shaft
14. Lock washer
15. Brush attaching screw
16. Field lead to switch screw
17. Switch attaching screw
18. Brake washer
19. Through bolt
20. Commutator end bushing
21. Drive end bushing
22. Pinion stop collar
23. Thrust collar
24. Grommet
25. Grommet
26. Plunger pin
27. Pinion stop retainer ring
28. Lever shaft retaining ring

Exploded view of the 5MT starter motor

Troubleshooting Basic Charging System Problems

Problem	Cause	Solution
Noisy alternator	• Loose mountings • Loose drive pulley • Worn bearings • Brush noise • Internal circuits shorted (High pitched whine)	• Tighten mounting bolts • Tighten pulley • Replace alternator • Replace alternator • Replace alternator
Squeal when starting engine or accelerating	• Glazed or loose belt	• Replace or adjust belt
Indicator light remains on or ammeter indicates discharge (engine running)	• Broken fan belt • Broken or disconnected wires • Internal alternator problems • Defective voltage regulator	• Install belt • Repair or connect wiring • Replace alternator • Replace voltage regulator
Car light bulbs continually burn out— battery needs water continually	• Alternator/regulator overcharging	• Replace voltage regulator/alternator
Car lights flare on acceleration	• Battery low • Internal alternator/regulator problems	• Charge or replace battery • Replace alternator/regulator
Low voltage output (alternator light flickers continually or ammeter needle wanders)	• Loose or worn belt • Dirty or corroded connections • Internal alternator/regulator problems	• Replace or adjust belt • Clean or replace connections • Replace alternator or regulator

2. Remove the through-bolts, and separate the commutator end frame, field frame assembly, drive housing, and armature assembly from each other.

3. Slide the two piece thrust collar off the end of the armature shaft.

4. Slide a suitably sized metal cylinder, such as a standard half-inch pipe coupling, or an old pinion, on the shaft so that the end of the coupling or pinion butts up against the edge of the pinion retainer.

5. Support the lower end of the armature se-

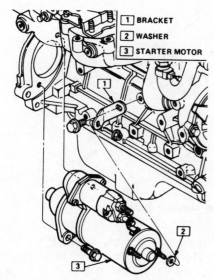

1 BRACKET
2 WASHER
3 STARTER MOTOR

Starter mounting on OHC 4-cyl. engines

curely on a soft surface, such as a wooden block, and tap the end of the coupling or pinion, driving the retainer towards the armature end of the snap ring.

6. Remove the snapring from the groove in the armature shaft with a pair of pliers. Then, slide the retainer and starter drive from the shaft.

7. To reassemble, lubricate the drive end of the armature shaft with silicone lubricant, and then slide the starter drive onto the shaft with the pinion facing outward. Slide the retainer onto the shaft with the cupped surface facing outward.

8. Again support the armature on a soft surface, with the pinion at the upper end. Center the snap ring on the top of the shaft (use a new snap ring if the original was damaged during removal). Gently place a block of wood flat on top of the snap ring so as not to move it from a centered position. Tap the wooden block with a hammer in order to force the snap ring around the shaft. Then, slide the ring down into the snap ring groove.

9. Lay the armature down flat on the surface you're working on. Slide the retainer close up on to the shaft and position it and the thrust collar next to the snap ring. Using two pairs of pliers on opposite sides of the shaft, squeeze the thrust collar and the retainer together until the snap ring is forced into the retainer.

10. Lube the drive housing bushing with a silicone lubricant. Then, install the armature and clutch assembly into the drive housing, engaging the solenoid shift lever with the clutch, and positioning the front end of armature shaft into the bushing.

11. Apply a sealing compound approved for

this application onto the drive housing; then position the field frame around the armature shaft and against the drive housing. Work slowly and carefully to prevent damaging the starter brushes.

12. Lubricate the bushing in the commutator end frame with a silicone lubricant, place the leather brake washer onto the armature shaft, and then slide the commutator end frame over the shaft and into position against the field frame. Line up the bolt holes, and then install and tighten the thru-bolts.

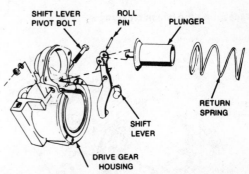

SHIFT LEVER PIVOT BOLT   ROLL PIN   PLUNGER
RETURN SPRING
SHIFT LEVER
DRIVE GEAR HOUSING

Starter shift lever and drive end housing disassembled

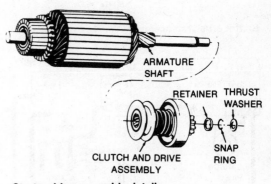

ARMATURE SHAFT
RETAINER   THRUST WASHER
SNAP RING
CLUTCH AND DRIVE ASSEMBLY

Starter drive assembly details

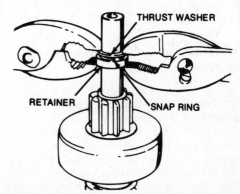

THRUST WASHER
RETAINER   SNAP RING

Starter drive retainer, thrust washer and snap ring installation

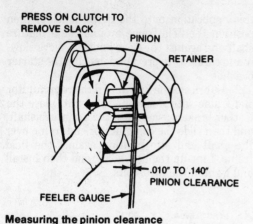

Measuring the pinion clearance

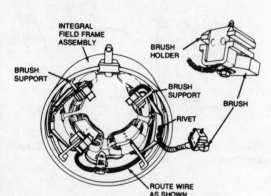

Starter brush replacement

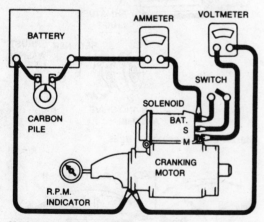

No-load test connections

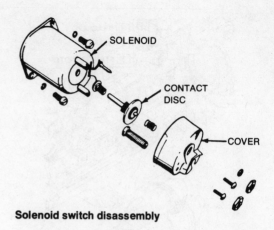

Solenoid switch disassembly

the solenoid on a test bench. If the pinion clearance is incorrect, disassemble the solenoid and the shift lever, inspect, and replace worn parts.

Brush Replacement

1. After removing the starter from the engine, disconnect the field coil from the motor solenoid terminal.
2. Remove the starter through-bolts and remove the commutator end frame and washer.
3. Remove the field frame and the armature assembly from the drive housing.
4. Remove the brush holder pivot pin which positions one insulated and one grounded brush.
5. Remove the brush springs.
6. Remove the brushes.
7. Installation is in the reverse order of removal.

Starter Solenoid Replacement

1. Remove the screw and washer from the motor connector strap terminal.
2. Remove the two screws which retain the solenoid housing to the end frame assembly.
3. Twist the solenoid clockwise to remove the flange key from the keyway slot in the housing.
4. Remove the solenoid assembly.
5. With the solenoid return spring installed on the plunger, position the solenoid body on the drive housing and turn it counterclockwise to engage the flange key in the keyway slot.
6. Install the two screws which retain the solenoid housing to the end frame.

Battery

Refer to Chapter 1 for details on battery maintenance.

REMOVAL AND INSTALLATION

1. Disconnect the negative (ground) cable first, then the positive cable. The side terminal cables are retained only by the center bolt.

13. Reconnect the field coil straps to the motor terminal of the solenoid.

NOTE: *If replacement of the starter drive fails to cure the improper engagement of the starter pinion to the flywheel, there are probably defective parts in the solenoid and/or shift lever. The best procedure would probably be to take the assembly to a shop where a pinion clearance check can be made by energizing*

CAUTION: *To avoid sparks, always disconnect the negative cable first, and connect it last.*

2. Remove the battery holddown clamp.

3. Remove the battery.

4. Before installing the battery, clean the battery terminals and the cables thoroughly.

5. Check the battery tray to be sure it is clear of any debris. If it is rusty, it should be wirebrushed clean and given a coat of anti-rust paint, or replaced.

6. Install the battery in the tray, being sure it is centered in the lip.

7. Install the holddown clamp. Tighten to 6 ft.lb., which is tight enough to hold the battery in place, but loose enough to prevent the case from cracking.

8. Connect the positive, then the negative battery cables. Installation torque for the cables is 9 ft.lb. Give the terminals a light external coat of grease after installation to retard corrosion.

WARNING: *Make absolutely sure that the battery is connected properly before you turn on the ignition switch. Reversed polarity can burn out the alternator and regulator in a matter of seconds.*

ENGINE MECHANICAL

NOTE: *J-Cars use four different 4-cylinder engines. Two are built by Chevrolet, a 1835.5cc (1.8L) 112 cid and a 1986.8cc (2.0L) 121 cid. Both of these Chevrolet-built engines are of the overhead valve configuration (OHV). That means that the camshaft is in*

Troubleshooting Basic Starting System Problems

Problem	Cause	Solution
Starter motor rotates engine slowly	• Battery charge low or battery defective	• Charge or replace battery
	• Defective circuit between battery and starter motor	• Clean and tighten, or replace cables
	• Low load current	• Bench-test starter motor. Inspect for worn brushes and weak brush springs.
	• High load current	• Bench-test starter motor. Check engine for friction, drag or coolant in cylinders. Check ring gear-to-pinion gear clearance.
Starter motor will not rotate engine	• Battery charge low or battery defective	• Charge or replace battery
	• Faulty solenoid	• Check solenoid ground. Repair or replace as necessary.
	• Damage drive pinion gear or ring gear	• Replace damaged gear(s)
	• Starter motor engagement weak	• Bench-test starter motor
	• Starter motor rotates slowly with high load current	• Inspect drive yoke pull-down and point gap, check for worn end bushings, check ring gear clearance
	• Engine seized	• Repair engine
Starter motor drive will not engage (solenoid known to be good)	• Defective contact point assembly	• Repair or replace contact point assembly
	• Inadequate contact point assembly ground	• Repair connection at ground screw
	• Defective hold-in coil	• Replace field winding assembly
Starter motor drive will not disengage	• Starter motor loose on flywheel housing	• Tighten mounting bolts
	• Worn drive end busing	• Replace bushing
	• Damaged ring gear teeth	• Replace ring gear or driveplate
	• Drive yoke return spring broken or missing	• Replace spring
Starter motor drive disengages prematurely	• Weak drive assembly thrust spring	• Replace drive mechanism
	• Hold-in coil defective	• Replace field winding assembly
Low load current	• Worn brushes	• Replace brushes
	• Weak brush springs	• Replace springs

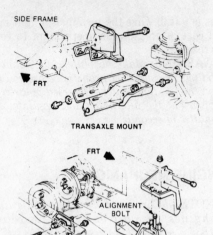

Front engine mount—1982 2.0L eng.

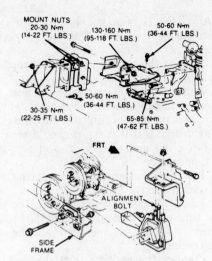

Front engine mount—1983–84 2.0L eng.

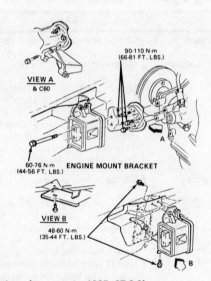

Front engine mount—1985–87 2.0L eng.

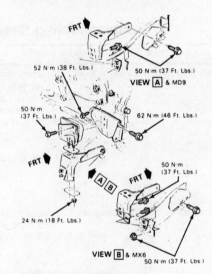

Rear engine mount—2.8L V6 eng.

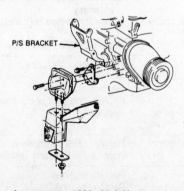

Rear engine mount—1982–85 2.0L eng.

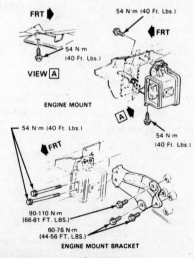

Front engine mount—2.8L V6 eng.

the block and the rest of the valve train is on top of the head. The two other engines are Pontiac (Brazil) built. The 1797.9cc (1.8L) 110 cid and the (2.0) 122 overhead cam engines (OHC). This means that the camshaft and valve components are all located in the engine head. The two Chevrolet-built engines are virtually identical in all aspects except cubic inch displacement.

The Pontiac-built engines are quite different in most respects.

In the 1985 Model year, a 2838.4cc (2.8L), 173 cid V6 engine was introduced. This engine is a high output version of the Chevy-built V6, using MFI (multi-port fuel injection).

Engine Overhaul Tips

Most engine overhaul procedures are fairly standard. In addition to specific parts replacement procedures and complete specifications for your individual engine, this chapter also is a guide to accept rebuilding procedures. Examples of standard rebuilding practice are shown and should be used along with specific details concerning your particular engine.

Competent and accurate machine shop services will ensure maximum performance, reliability and engine life.

In most instances it is more profitable for the do-it-yourself mechanic to remove, clean and inspect the component, buy the necessary parts and deliver these to a shop for actual machine work.

On the other hand, much of the rebuilding work (crankshaft, block, bearings, piston rods, and other components) is well within the scope of the do-it-yourself mechanic.

TOOLS

The tools required for an engine overhaul or parts replacement will depend on the depth of your involvement. With a few exceptions, they will be the tools found in a mechanic's tool kit (see Chapter 1). More in-depth work will require any or all of the following:

• a dial indicator (reading in thousandths) mounted on a universal base

• micrometers and telescope gauges
• jaw and screw-type pullers
• scraper
• valve spring compressor
• ring groove cleaner
• piston ring expander and compressor
• ridge reamer
• cylinder hone or glaze breaker
• Plastigage®
• engine stand

The use of most of these tools is illustrated in this chapter. Many can be rented for a one-time use from a local parts jobber or tool supply house specializing in automotive work.

Occasionally, the use of special tools is called for. See the information on Special Tools and Safety Notice in the front of this book before substituting another tool.

INSPECTION TECHNIQUES

Procedures and specifications are given in this chapter for inspecting, cleaning and assessing the wear limits of most major components. Other procedures such as Magnaflux® and Zyglo® can be used to locate material flaws and stress cracks. Magnaflux® is a magnetic process applicable only to ferrous materials. The Zyglo® process coats the material with a fluorescent dye penetrant and can be used on any material Check for suspected surface cracks can be more readily made using spot check dye. The dye is sprayed onto the suspected area, wiped off and the area sprayed with a developer. Cracks will show up brightly.

OVERHAUL TIPS

Aluminum has become extremely popular for use in engines, due to its low weight. Observe the following precautions when handling aluminum parts:

• Never hot tank aluminum parts (the caustic hot tank solution will eat the aluminum.

• Remove all aluminum parts (identification tag, etc.) from engine parts prior to the tanking.

• Always coat threads lightly with engine oil or anti-seize compounds before installation, to prevent seizure.

• Never overtorque bolts or spark plugs especially in aluminum threads.

Stripped threads in any component can be repaired using any of several commercial repair kits (Heli-Coil®, Microdot®, Keenserts®, etc.).

When assembling the engine, any parts that will be frictional contact must be prelubed to provide lubrication at initial start-up. Any product specifically formulated for this purpose can be used, but engine oil is not recommended as a prelube.

When semi-permanent (locked, but removable) installation of bolts or nuts is desired, threads should be cleaned and coated with Loctite® or other similar, commercial non-hardening sealant.

REPAIRING DAMAGED THREADS

Several methods of repairing damaged threads are available. Heli-Coil® (shown here), Keenserts® and Microdot® are among the most widely used. All involve basically the same principle — drilling out stripped threads, tapping the hole and installing a prewound insert — making welding, plugging and oversize fasteners unnecessary.

Two types of thread repair inserts are usually supplied: a standard type for most Inch Coarse, Inch Fine, Metric Course and Metric Fine thread sizes and a spark lug type to fit most spark plug port sizes. Consult the individual manufacturer's catalog to determine exact applications. Typical thread repair kits will contain a selection of prewound threaded inserts, a tap (corresponding to the outside diameter threads of the insert) and an installation tool. Spark plug inserts usually differ because they require a tap equipped with pilot threads and a combined reamer/tap section. Most manufacturers also supply blister-packed thread repair inserts separately in addition to a master kit containing a variety of taps and inserts plus installation tools.

Before effecting a repair to a threaded hole,

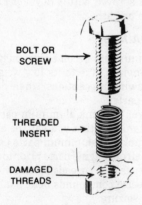

BOLT OR SCREW →

THREADED INSERT →

DAMAGED THREADS →

Damaged bolt holes can be repaired with thread repair inserts

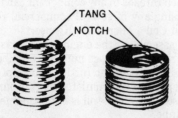

TANG

NOTCH

Standard thread repair insert (left) and spark plug thread insert (right)

Drill out the damaged threads with specified drill. Drill completely through the hole or to the bottom of a blind hole

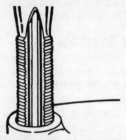

With the tap supplied, tap the hole to receive the thread insert. Keep the tap well oiled and back it out frequently to avoid clogging the threads

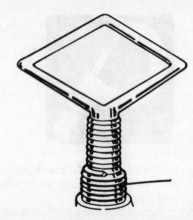

Screw the threaded insert onto the installation tool until the tang engages the slot. Screw the insert into the tapped hole until it is ¼–½ turn below the top surface. After installation break off the tang with a hammer and punch

remove any snapped, broken or damaged bolts or studs. Penetrating oil can be used to free frozen threads. The offending item can be removed with locking pliers or with a screw or stud extractor. After the hole is clear, the thread can be repaired, as shown in the series of accompanying illustrations.

Checking Engine Compression

A noticeable lack of engine power, excessive oil consumption and/or poor fuel mileage mea-

Standard Torque Specifications and Fastener Markings

In the absence of specific torques, the following chart can be used as a guide to the maximum safe torque of a particular size/grade of fastener.

- There is no torque difference for fine or coarse threads.
- Torque values are based on clean, dry threads. Reduce the value by 10% if threads are oiled prior to assembly.
- The torque required for aluminum components or fasteners is considerably less.

U.S. Bolts

SAE Grade Number	1 or 2			5			6 or 7		
Number of lines always 2 less than the grade number.									
Bolt Size (Inches)—(Thread)	Maximum Torque			Maximum Torque			Maximum Torque		
	Ft./Lbs.	Kgm	Nm	Ft./Lbs.	Kgm	Nm	Ft./Lbs.	Kgm	Nm
¼—20	5	0.7	6.8	8	1.1	10.8	10	1.4	13.5
—28	6	0.8	8.1	10	1.4	13.6			
⁵⁄₁₆—18	11	1.5	14.9	17	2.3	23.0	19	2.6	25.8
—24	13	1.8	17.6	19	2.6	25.7			
⅜—16	18	2.5	24.4	31	4.3	42.0	34	4.7	46.0
—24	20	2.75	27.1	35	4.8	47.5			
⁷⁄₁₆—14	28	3.8	37.0	49	6.8	66.4	55	7.6	74.5
—20	30	4.2	40.7	55	7.6	74.5			
½—13	39	5.4	52.8	75	10.4	101.7	85	11.75	115.2
—20	41	5.7	55.6	85	11.7	115.2			
⁹⁄₁₆—12	51	7.0	69.2	110	15.2	149.1	120	16.6	162.7
—18	55	7.6	74.5	120	16.6	162.7			
⅝—11	83	11.5	112.5	150	20.7	203.3	167	23.0	226.5
—18	95	13.1	128.8	170	23.5	230.5			
¾—10	105	14.5	142.3	270	37.3	366.0	280	38.7	379.6
—16	115	15.9	155.9	295	40.8	400.0			
⅞— 9	160	22.1	216.9	395	54.6	535.5	440	60.9	596.5
—14	175	24.2	237.2	435	60.1	589.7			
1— 8	236	32.5	318.6	590	81.6	799.9	660	91.3	894.8
—14	250	34.6	338.9	660	91.3	849.8			

Metric Bolts

Relative Strength Marking	4.6, 4.8			8.8		
Bolt Markings						
Bolt Size Thread Size x Pitch (mm)	Maximum Torque			Maximum Torque		
	Ft./Lbs.	Kgm	Nm	Ft./Lbs.	Kgm	Nm
6 x 1.0	2–3	.2–.4	3–4	3–6	.4–.8	5–8
8 x 1.25	6–8	.8–1	8–12	9–14	1.2–1.9	13–19
10 x 1.25	12–17	1.5–2.3	16–23	20–29	2.7–4.0	27–39
12 x 1.25	21–32	2.9–4.4	29–43	35–53	4.8–7.3	47–72
14 x 1.5	35–52	4.8–7.1	48–70	57–85	7.8–11.7	77–110
16 x 1.5	51–77	7.0–10.6	67–100	90–120	12.4–16.5	130–160
18 x 1.5	74–110	10.2–15.1	100–150	130–170	17.9–23.4	180–230
20 x 1.5	110–140	15.1–19.3	150–190	190–240	26.2–46.9	160–320
22 x 1.5	150–190	22.0–26.2	200–260	250–320	34.5–44.1	340–430
24 x 1.5	190–240	26.2–46.9	260–320	310–410	42.7–56.5	420–550

sured over an extended period are all indicators of internal engine war. Worn piston rings, scored or worn cylinder bores, blown head gaskets, sticking or burnt valves and worn valve seats are all possible culprits here. A check of each cylinder's compression will help you locate the problems.

As mentioned in the Tools and Equipment section of Chapter 1, a screw-in type compression gauge is more accurate that the type you simply hold against the spark plug hole, although it takes slightly longer to use. It's worth it to obtain a more accurate reading. Follow the procedures below.

1. Warm up the engine to normal operating temperature.

2. Remove all the spark plugs.

3. Disconnect the **BAT** terminal and if so equipped, the four terminal connector from the HEI distributor. On 1987 and later Cavaliers, disconnect the ECM fuse.

4. Fully open the throttle either by operating the throttle linkage by hand or by having an assistant floor the accelerator pedal.

5. Screw the compression gauge into the no. 1 spark plug hole until the fitting is snug.

WARNING: *Be careful not to crossthread the plug hole. On aluminum cylinder heads use extra care, as the threads in these heads are easily ruined.*

6. Ask an assistant to depress the accelerator pedal fully on both carbureted and fuel injected vehicles. Then, while you read the compression gauge, ask the assistant to crank the engine two or three times in short bursts using the ignition switch.

7. Read the compression gauge at the end of each series of cranks, and record the highest of these readings. Repeat this procedure for each of the engine's cylinders. Compare the highest reading of each cylinder to the compression pressure specification in the Tune-Up Specifications chart in Chapter 2. The specs in this chart are maximum values.

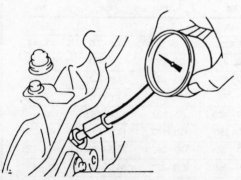

The screw-in type compression gauge is more accurate

A cylinder's compression pressure is usually acceptable if it is not less than 70% of maximum. And no cylinder should be less than 100 lbs.

8. If a cylinder is unusually low, pour a tablespoon of clean engine oil into the cylinder through the spark plug hole and repeat the compression test. If the compression comes up after adding the oil, it appears that the cylinder's piston rings or bore are damaged or worn. If the pressure remains low, the valves may not be seating properly (a valve job is needed), or the head gasket may be blown near that cylinder. If compression in any two adjacent cylinders is low, and if the addition of oil doesn't help the compression, there is leakage past the head gasket. Oil and coolant water in the combustion chamber can result from this problem. There may be evidence of water droplets on the engine dipstick when a head gasket has blown.

Engine
REMOVAL AND INSTALLATION
OHV 4-Cylinder Engines
1982-84

NOTE: *This procedure will require the use of a special powertrain alignment tool #M6X1X65.*

1. Disconnect the battery cables at the battery, negative cable first.

2. Remove the air cleaner. Drain the cooling system.

CAUTION: *When draining the coolant, keep in mind that cats and dogs are attracted by the ethylene glycol antifreeze, and are quite likely to drink any that is left in an uncovered container or in puddles on the ground. This will prove fatal in sufficient quantity. Always drain the coolant into a sealable container. Coolant should be reused unless it is contaminated or several years old.*

3. Remove the power steering pump (if so equipped) and position it out of the way. Leave the lines connected. Remove the windshield washer bottle.

4. If the car is equipped with air conditioning, remove the relay bracket at the bulkhead connector. Remove the bulkhead connector and then separate the wiring harness connections.

5. If equipped with cruise control, remove the servo bracket and position it out of the way.

6. Tag and disconnect all vacuum hoses and wires.

7. Remove the master cylinder at the vacuum booster.

8. Remove all heater and radiator hoses and position them out of the way.

Troubleshooting Engine Mechanical Problems

Problem	Cause	Solution
External oil leaks	• Fuel pump gasket broken or improperly seated	• Replace gasket
	• Cylinder head cover RTV sealant broken or improperly seated	• Replace sealant; inspect cylinder head cover sealant flange and cylinder head sealant surface for distortion and cracks
	• Oil filler cap leaking or missing	• Replace cap
	• Oil filter gasket broken or improperly seated	• Replace oil filter
	• Oil pan side gasket broken, improperly seated or opening in RTV sealant	• Replace gasket or repair opening in sealant; inspect oil pan gasket flange for distortion
	• Oil pan front oil seal broken or improperly seated	• Replace seal; inspect timing case cover and oil pan seal flange for distortion
	• Oil pan rear oil seal broken or improperly seated	• Replace seal; inspect oil pan rear oil seal flange; inspect rear main bearing cap for cracks, plugged oil return channels, or distortion in seal groove
	• Timing case cover oil seal broken or improperly seated	• Replace seal
	• Excess oil pressure because of restricted PCV valve	• Replace PCV valve
	• Oil pan drain plug loose or has stripped threads	• Repair as necessary and tighten
	• Rear oil gallery plug loose	• Use appropriate sealant on gallery plug and tighten
	• Rear camshaft plug loose or improperly seated	• Seat camshaft plug or replace and seal, as necessary
	• Distributor base gasket damaged	• Replace gasket
Excessive oil consumption	• Oil level too high	• Drain oil to specified level
	• Oil with wrong viscosity being used	• Replace with specified oil
	• PCV valve stuck closed	• Replace PCV valve
	• Valve stem oil deflectors (or seals) are damaged, missing, or incorrect type	• Replace valve stem oil deflectors
	• Valve stems or valve guides worn	• Measure stem-to-guide clearance and repair as necessary
	• Poorly fitted or missing valve cover baffles	• Replace valve cover
	• Piston rings broken or missing	• Replace broken or missing rings
	• Scuffed piston	• Replace piston
	• Incorrect piston ring gap	• Measure ring gap, repair as necessary
	• Piston rings sticking or excessively loose in grooves	• Measure ring side clearance, repair as necessary
	• Compression rings installed upside down	• Repair as necessary
	• Cylinder walls worn, scored, or glazed	• Repair as necessary
	• Piston ring gaps not properly staggered	• Repair as necessary
	• Excessive main or connecting rod bearing clearance	• Measure bearing clearance, repair as necessary
No oil pressure	• Low oil level	• Add oil to correct level
	• Oil pressure gauge, warning lamp or sending unit inaccurate	• Replace oil pressure gauge or warning lamp
	• Oil pump malfunction	• Replace oil pump
	• Oil pressure relief valve sticking	• Remove and inspect oil pressure relief valve assembly
	• Oil passages on pressure side of pump obstructed	• Inspect oil passages for obstruction

Troubleshooting Engine Mechanical Problems (cont.)

Problem	Cause	Solution
No oil pressure (cont.)	• Oil pickup screen or tube obstructed	• Inspect oil pickup for obstruction
	• Loose oil inlet tube	• Tighten or seal inlet tube
Low oil pressure	• Low oil level	• Add oil to correct level
	• Inaccurate gauge, warning lamp or sending unit	• Replace oil pressure gauge or warning lamp
	• Oil excessively thin because of dilution, poor quality, or improper grade	• Drain and refill crankcase with recommended oil
	• Excessive oil temperature	• Correct cause of overheating engine
	• Oil pressure relief spring weak or sticking	• Remove and inspect oil pressure relief valve assembly
	• Oil inlet tube and screen assembly has restriction or air leak	• Remove and inspect oil inlet tube and screen assembly. (Fill inlet tube with lacquer thinner to locate leaks.)
	• Excessive oil pump clearance	• Measure clearances
	• Excessive main, rod, or camshaft bearing clearance	• Measure bearing clearances, repair as necessary
High oil pressure	• Improper oil viscosity	• Drain and refill crankcase with correct viscosity oil
	• Oil pressure gauge or sending unit inaccurate	• Replace oil pressure gauge
	• Oil pressure relief valve sticking closed	• Remove and inspect oil pressure relief valve assembly
Main bearing noise	• Insufficient oil supply	• Inspect for low oil level and low oil pressure
	• Main bearing clearance excessive	• Measure main bearing clearance, repair as necessary
	• Bearing insert missing	• Replace missing insert
	• Crankshaft end play excessive	• Measure end play, repair as necessary
	• Improperly tightened main bearing cap bolts	• Tighten bolts with specified torque
	• Loose flywheel or drive plate	• Tighten flywheel or drive plate attaching bolts
	• Loose or damaged vibration damper	• Repair as necessary
Connecting rod bearing noise	• Insufficient oil supply	• Inspect for low oil level and low oil pressure
	• Carbon build-up on piston	• Remove carbon from piston crown
	• Bearing clearance excessive or bearing missing	• Measure clearance, repair as necessary
	• Crankshaft connecting rod journal out-of-round	• Measure journal dimensions, repair or replace as necessary
	• Misaligned connecting rod or cap	• Repair as necessary
	• Connecting rod bolts tightened improperly	• Tighten bolts with specified torque
Piston noise	• Piston-to-cylinder wall clearance excessive (scuffed piston)	• Measure clearance and examine piston
	• Cylinder walls excessively tapered or out-of-round	• Measure cylinder wall dimensions, rebore cylinder
	• Piston ring broken	• Replace all rings on piston
	• Loose or seized piston pin	• Measure piston-to-pin clearance, repair as necessary
	• Connecting rods misaligned	• Measure rod alignment, straighten or replace
	• Piston ring side clearance excessively loose or tight	• Measure ring side clearance, repair as necessary
	• Carbon build-up on piston is excessive	• Remove carbon from piston

Troubleshooting Engine Mechanical Problems (cont.)

Problem	Cause	Solution
Valve actuating component noise	• Insufficient oil supply	• Check for: (a) Low oil level (b) Low oil pressure (c) Plugged push rods (d) Wrong hydraulic tappets (e) Restricted oil gallery (f) Excessive tappet to bore clearance
	• Push rods worn or bent	• Replace worn or bent push rods
	• Rocker arms or pivots worn	• Replace worn rocker arms or pivots
	• Foreign objects or chips in hydraulic tappets	• Clean tappets
	• Excessive tappet leak-down	• Replace valve tappet
	• Tappet face worn	• Replace tappet; inspect corresponding cam lobe for wear
	• Broken or cocked valve springs	• Properly seat cocked springs; replace broken springs
	• Stem-to-guide clearance excessive	• Measure stem-to-guide clearance, repair as required
	• Valve bent	• Replace valve
	• Loose rocker arms	• Tighten bolts with specified torque
	• Valve seat runout excessive	• Regrind valve seat/valves
	• Missing valve lock	• Install valve lock
	• Push rod rubbing or contacting cylinder head	• Remove cylinder head and remove obstruction in head
	• Excessive engine oil (four-cylinder engine)	• Correct oil level

Troubleshooting the Cooling System

Problem	Cause	Solution
High temperature gauge indication—overheating	• Coolant level low	• Replenish coolant
	• Fan belt loose	• Adjust fan belt tension
	• Radiator hose(s) collapsed	• Replace hose(s)
	• Radiator airflow blocked	• Remove restriction (bug screen, fog lamps, etc.)
	• Faulty radiator cap	• Replace radiator cap
	• Ignition timing incorrect	• Adjust ignition timing
	• Idle speed low	• Adjust idle speed
	• Air trapped in cooling system	• Purge air
	• Heavy traffic driving	• Operate at fast idle in neutral intermittently to cool engine
	• Incorrect cooling system component(s) installed	• Install proper component(s)
	• Faulty thermostat	• Replace thermostat
	• Water pump shaft broken or impeller loose	• Replace water pump
	• Radiator tubes clogged	• Flush radiator
	• Cooling system clogged	• Flush system
	• Casting flash in cooling passages	• Repair or replace as necessary. Flash may be visible by removing cooling system components or removing core plugs.
	• Brakes dragging	• Repair brakes
	• Excessive engine friction	• Repair engine
	• Antifreeze concentration over 68%	• Lower antifreeze concentration percentage
	• Missing air seals	• Replace air seals
	• Faulty gauge or sending unit	• Repair or replace faulty component
	• Loss of coolant flow caused by leakage or foaming	• Repair or replace leaking component, replace coolant
	• Viscous fan drive failed	• Replace unit

Troubleshooting the Cooling System (cont.)

Problem	Cause	Solution
Low temperature indication—undercooling	• Thermostat stuck open • Faulty gauge or sending unit	• Replace thermostat • Repair or replace faulty component
Coolant loss—boilover	• Overfilled cooling system • Quick shutdown after hard (hot) run • Air in system resulting in occasional "burping" of coolant • Insufficient antifreeze allowing coolant boiling point to be too low • Antifreeze deteriorated because of age or contamination • Leaks due to loose hose clamps, loose nuts, bolts, drain plugs, faulty hoses, or defective radiator • Faulty head gasket • Cracked head, manifold, or block • Faulty radiator cap	• Reduce coolant level to proper specification • Allow engine to run at fast idle prior to shutdown • Purge system • Add antifreeze to raise boiling point • Replace coolant • Pressure test system to locate source of leak(s) then repair as necessary • Replace head gasket • Replace as necessary • Replace cap
Coolant entry into crankcase or cylinder(s)	• Faulty head gasket • Crack in head, manifold or block	• Replace head gasket • Replace as necessary
Coolant recovery system inoperative	• Coolant level low • Leak in system • Pressure cap not tight or seal missing, or leaking • Pressure cap defective • Overflow tube clogged or leaking • Recovery bottle vent restricted	• Replenish coolant to FULL mark • Pressure test to isolate leak and repair as necessary • Repair as necessary • Replace cap • Repair as necessary • Remove restriction
Noise	• Fan contacting shroud • Loose water pump impeller • Glazed fan belt • Loose fan belt • Rough surface on drive pulley • Water pump bearing worn • Belt alignment	• Reposition shroud and inspect engine mounts • Replace pump • Apply silicone or replace belt • Adjust fan belt tension • Replace pulley • Remove belt to isolate. Replace pump. • Check pulley alignment. Repair as necessary.
No coolant flow through heater core	• Restricted return inlet in water pump • Heater hose collapsed or restricted • Restricted heater core • Restricted outlet in thermostat housing • Intake manifold bypass hole in cylinder head restricted • Faulty heater control valve • Intake manifold coolant passage restricted	• Remove restriction • Remove restriction or replace hose • Remove restriction or replace core • Remove flash or restriction • Remove restriction • Replace valve • Remove restriction or replace intake manifold

NOTE: *Immediately after shutdown, the engine enters a condition known as heat soak. This is caused by the cooling system being inoperative while engine temperature is still high. If coolant temperature rises above boiling point, expansion and pressure may push some coolant out of the radiator overflow tube. If this does not occur frequently it is considered normal.*

5. Disconnect the ECM harness at the engine.

6. Disconnect and tag all necessary vacuum hoses.

7. Disconnect the radiator hoses at the engine.

8. Disconnect the heater hoses at the engine.

9. Remove the exhaust heat shield.

10. If equipped with air conditioning, remove the adjustment bolt at the motor mount.

11. Disconnect the engine wiring harness at the bulkhead.

12. Remove the windshield washer bottle.

13. Remove the alternator belt or serpentine, if so equipped.

14. Relieve the fuel system pressure as out-lined in Chapter 1 and disconnect the fuel hoses.

15. Raise the vehicle.

16. If equipped with air conditioning, remove the air conditioning brace.

17. Remove the inner fender splash shield.

18. If equipped with air conditioning, remove the air conditioning compressor.

19. Remove the flywheel splash shield.

20. Disconnect the starter wires.

21. Remove the front starter brace and starter.

22. Remove the torque converter bolts.

23. Remove the crankshaft pulley using Tool J-24420.

24. Remove the oil filter.

General Engine Specifications

Year	VIN	No. Cylinder Displacement cu. in. (liter)	Fuel System Type	Net Horsepower @ rpm	Net Torque @ rpm (ft. lbs.)	Bore x Stroke (in.)	Compression Ratio	Oil Pressure @ rpm
1982	G	4-110 (1.8)	2 bbl	88 @ 5100	100 @ 2800	3.50 x 2.91	9.0:1	45 @ 2400
	B	4-122 (2.0)	2 bbl	90 @ 5100	111 @ 2800	3.50 x 3.15	9.0:1	45 @ 2400
1983	O	4-110 (1.8)	TBI	84 @ 5200	102 @ 2800	3.34 x 3.13	8.8:1	45 @ 2400
	J	4-110 (1.8)	MFI Turbo	150 @ 5600	150 @ 2800	3.34 x 3.13	8.0:1	65 @ 2500
	P	4-122 (2.0)	TBI	86 @ 4900	100 @ 3000	3.50 x 3.15	9.3:1	68 @ 1200
	B	4-122 (2.0)	TBI	86 @ 4900	110 @ 3000	3.50 x 3.15	9.3:1	45 @ 2400
	W	6-173 (2.8)	MFI	120 @ 4800	155 @ 3600	3.50 x 2.99	8.9:1	50 @ 2400
1984	O	4-110 (1.8)	TBI	84 @ 5200	102 @ 2800	3.34 x 3.13	8.8:1	45 @ 2400
	J	4-110 (1.8)	MFI Turbo	150 @ 5600	150 @ 2800	3.34 x 3.13	8.0:1	65 @ 2500
	P	4-122 (2.0)	TBI	86 @ 4900	100 @ 3000	3.50 x 3.15	9.3:1	68 @ 1200
	W	6-173 (2.8)	MFI	120 @ 4800	155 @ 3600	3.50 x 2.99	8.9:1	50 @ 2400
1985	O	4-110 (1.8)	TBI	84 @ 5200	102 @ 2800	3.34 x 3.13	8.8:1	45 @ 2400
	J	4-110 (1.8)	MFI Turbo	150 @ 5600	150 @ 2800	3.34 x 3.13	8.0:1	65 @ 2500
	P	4-122 (2.0)	TBI	86 @ 4900	100 @ 3000	3.50 x 3.15	9.3:1	68 @ 1200
	W	6-173 (2.8)	MFI	120 @ 4800	155 @ 3600	3.50 x 2.99	8.9:1	50 @ 2400
1986	O	4-110 (1.8)	TBI	84 @ 5200	102 @ 2800	3.34 x 3.13	8.8:1	45 @ 2400
	J	4-110 (1.8)	MFI Turbo	150 @ 5600	150 @ 2800	3.34 x 3.13	8.0:1	65 @ 2500
	P	4-122 (2.0)	TBI	86 @ 4900	100 @ 3000	3.50 x 3.15	9.3:1	68 @ 1200
	W	6-173 (2.8)	MFI	120 @ 4800	155 @ 3600	3.50 x 2.99	8.9:1	50 @ 2400
1987	M	4-122 (2.0)	MFI Turbo	160 @ 5600	160 @ 2800	3.38 x 3.38	8.0:1	65 @ 2500
	1	4-122 (2.0)	TBI (HO)	90 @ 5600	108 @ 3200	3.50 x 3.15	9.0:1	63–77 @ 1200
	K	4-122 (2.0)	TBI	102 @ 5200	130 @ 2800	3.38 x 3.38	8.8:1	45 @ 2000
	W	6-173 (2.8)	MFI	120 @ 4800	155 @ 3600	3.50 x 2.99	8.9:1	50 @ 2400

Valve Specifications

Year	VIN	No. Cylinder Displacement cu. in. (liter)	Seat Angle (deg.)	Face Angle (deg.)	Spring Test Pressure (lbs.)	Spring Installed Height (in.)	Stem-to-Guide Clearance (in.)		Stem Diameter (in.)	
							Intake	Exhaust	Intake	Exhaust
1982	G	4-110 (1.8)	46	45	183 @ 1.33	1.60	0.0011–0.0026	0.0014–0.0031	0.3139–0.3144	0.3129–0.3136
	B	4-122 (2.0)	46	45	183 @ 1.33	1.60	0.0011–0.0026	0.0014–0.0031	0.3139–0.3144	0.3129–0.3136
1983	O	4-110 (1.8)	46	46	NA	NA	0.0006–0.0016	0.0012–0.0024	NA	NA
	J	4-110 (1.8)	46	46	NA	NA	0.0006–0.0016	0.0012–0.0024	NA	NA
	P	4-122 (2.0)	46	45	183 @ 1.33	1.60	0.0011–0.0026	0.0014–0.0031	0.3139–0.3144	0.3129–0.3136
	B	4-122 (2.0)	46	45	183 @ 1.33	1.60	0.0011–0.0026	0.0014–0.0031	0.3139–0.3144	0.3129–0.3136
	W	6-173 (2.8)	46	45	195 @ 1.18	1.57	0.0010–0.0027	0.0010–0.0027	NA	NA
1984	O	4-110 (1.8)	46	46	NA	NA	0.0006–0.0016	0.0012–0.0024	NA	NA
	J	4-110 (1.8)	46	46	NA	NA	0.0006–0.0016	0.0012–0.0024	NA	NA
	P	4-122 (2.0)	46	45	183 @ 1.33	1.60	0.0011–0.0026	0.0014–0.0031	0.3139–0.3144	0.3129–0.3136
	W	6-173 (2.8)	46	45	195 @ 1.18	1.57	0.0010–0.0027	0.0010–0.0027	NA	NA
1985	O	4-110 (1.8)	46	46	NA	NA	0.0006–0.0016	0.0012–0.0024	NA	NA
	J	4-110 (1.8)	46	46	NA	NA	0.0006–0.0016	0.0012–0.0024	NA	NA
	P	4-122 (2.0)	46	45	183 @ 1.33	1.60	0.0011–0.0026	0.0014–0.0031	0.3139–0.3144	0.3129–0.3136
	W	6-173 (2.8)	46	45	195 @ 1.18	1.57	0.0010–0.0027	0.0010–0.0027	NA	NA
1986	O	4-110 (1.8)	46	46	NA	NA	0.0006–0.0016	0.0012–0.0024	NA	NA
	J	4-110 (1.8)	46	46	NA	NA	0.0006–0.0016	0.0012–0.0024	NA	NA
	P	4-122 (2.0)	46	45	183 @ 1.33	1.60	0.0011–0.0026	0.0014–0.0031	0.3139–0.3144	0.3129–0.3136
	W	6-173 (2.8)	46	45	195 @ 1.18	1.57	0.0010–0.0027	0.0010–0.0027	NA	NA
1987	M	4-122 (2.0)	45	46	NA	NA	0.0006–0.0020	0.0010–0.0024	NA	NA
	1	4-122 (2.0)	46	45	183 @ 1.33	1.60	0.0011–0.0026	0.0014–0.0030	NA	NA
	K	4-122 (2.0)	45	46	NA	NA	0.0006–0.0020	0.0010–0.0024	NA	NA
	W	6-173 (2.8)	46	45	195 @ 1.18	1.57	0.0010–0.0027	0.0010–0.0027	NA	NA

NA—Not available at time of publication

Camshaft Specifications

All measurements given in inches.

Year	VIN	No. Cylinder Displacement cu. in. (liter)	Journal Diameter					Lobe Lift		Bearing Clearance	Camshaft End Play
			1	2	3	4	5	In.	Ex.		
1982	G	4-110 (1.8)	1.8677–1.8696	1.8677–1.8696	1.8677–1.8696	1.8677–1.8696	1.8677–1.8696	0.2625	0.2625	0.0010–0.0039	NA
	B	4-122 (2.0)	1.8677–1.8696	1.8677–1.8696	1.8677–1.8696	1.8677–1.8696	1.8677–1.8696	0.2600	0.2600	0.0010–0.0039	NA
1983	O	4-110 (1.8)	1.6714–1.6720	1.6812–1.6816	1.6911–1.6917	1.7009–1.7015	1.7108–1.7114	0.2409	0.2409	NA	0.016–0.064
	J	4-110 (1.8)	1.6714–1.6720	1.6812–1.6816	1.6911–1.6917	1.7009–1.7015	1.7108–1.7114	0.2409	0.2409	NA	0.016–0.064
	P	4-122 (2.0)	1.8677–1.8696	1.8677–1.8696	1.8677–1.8696	1.8677–1.8696	1.8677–1.8696	0.2600	0.2600	0.0010–0.0039	NA
	B	4-122 (2.0)	1.8677–1.8696	1.8677–1.8696	1.8677–1.8696	1.8677–1.8696	1.8677–1.8696	0.2600	0.2600	0.0010–0.0039	NA
	W	6-173 (2.8)	1.8678–1.8815	1.8678–1.8815	1.8678–1.8815	1.8678–1.8815	1.8678–1.8815	0.2626	0.2732	NA	NA
1984	O	4-110 (1.8)	1.6714–1.6720	1.6812–1.6816	1.6911–1.6917	1.7009–1.7015	1.7108–1.7114	0.2409	0.2409	NA	0.016–0.064
	J	4-110 (1.8)	1.6174–1.6720	1.6812–1.6816	1.6911–1.6917	1.7009–1.7015	1.7108–1.7114	0.2409	0.2409	NA	0.016–0.064
	P	4-122 (2.0)	1.8677–1.8696	1.8677–1.8696	1.8677–1.8696	1.8677–1.8696	1.8677–1.8696	0.2600	0.2600	0.0010–0.0039	NA
	W	6-173 (2.8)	1.8678–1.8815	1.8678–1.8815	1.8678–1.8815	1.8678–1.8815	1.8678–1.8815	0.2626	0.2732	NA	NA
1985	O	4-110 (1.8)	1.6714–1.6720	1.6812–1.6816	1.6911–1.6917	1.7009–1.7015	1.7108–1.7114	0.2409	0.2409	NA	0.016–0.064
	J	4-110 (1.8)	1.6174–1.6720	1.6812–1.6816	1.6911–1.6917	1.7009–1.7015	1.7108–1.7114	0.2409	0.2409	NA	0.016–0.064
	P	4-122 (2.0)	1.8677–1.8696	1.8677–1.8696	1.8677–1.8696	1.8677–1.8696	1.8677–1.8696	0.2600	0.2600	0.0010–0.0039	NA
	W	6-173 (2.8)	1.8678–1.8815	1.8678–1.8815	1.8678–1.8815	1.8678–1.8815	1.8678–1.8815	0.2626	0.2732	NA	NA
1986	O	4-110 (1.8)	1.6714–1.6720	1.6812–1.6816	1.6911–1.6917	1.7009–1.7015	1.7108–1.7114	0.2409	0.2409	NA	0.004–0.016
	J	4-110 (1.8)	1.6174–1.6720	1.6812–1.6816	1.6911–1.6917	1.7009–1.7015	1.7108–1.7114	0.2409	0.2409	NA	0.004–0.016
	P	4-122 (2.0)	1.8677–1.8696	1.8677–1.8696	1.8677–1.8696	1.8677–1.8696	1.8677–1.8696	0.2600	0.2600	0.0010–0.0039	NA
	W	6-173 (2.8)	1.8678–1.8815	1.8678–1.8815	1.8678–1.8815	1.8678–1.8815	1.8678–1.8815	0.2626	0.2732	NA	NA
1987	M	4-122 (2.0)	1.6714–1.6720	1.6812–1.6816	1.6911–1.6917	1.7009–1.7015	1.7008–1.7114	0.2409	0.2409	0.0008	0.016–0.064
	1	4-122 (2.0)	1.8670–1.8690	1.8670–1.8690	1.8670–1.8690	1.8670–1.8690	1.8670–1.8690	0.2600	0.2600	0.0010–0.0040	NA
	K	4-122 (2.0)	1.6714–1.6720	1.6812–1.6816	1.6911–1.6917	1.7009–1.7015	1.7108–1.7114	0.2409	0.2409	0.0008	0.016–0.064
	W	6-173 (2.8)	1.8678–1.8815	1.8678–1.8815	1.8678–1.8815	1.8678–1.8815	1.8678–1.8815	0.2626	0.2732	NA	NA

NA—Not available at time of publication

Crankshaft and Connecting Rod Specifications

All measurements are given in inches.

Year	VIN	No. Cylinder Displacement cu. in. (liter)	Crankshaft				Connecting Rod		
			Main Brg. Journal Dia.	Main Brg. Oil Clearance	Shaft End-play	Thrust on No.	Journal Diameter	Oil Clearance	Side Clearance
1982	G	4-110 (1.8)	2.4944–2.4954 ②	0.0006–0.0018 ③	0.0019–0.0071	4	1.9983–1.9993	0.0009–0.0031	0.0039–0.0240
	B	4-122 (2.0)	2.4944–2.4954 ②	0.0006–0.0018 ③	0.0019–0.0071	4	1.9983–1.9993	0.0009–0.0031	0.0039–0.0240
1983	O	4-110 (1.8)	①	0.0006–0.0016	0.0027–0.0118	3	1.9278–1.9286	0.0007–0.0024	0.0027–0.0095
	J	4-110 (1.8)	①	0.0006–0.0016	0.0027–0.0118	3	1.9278–1.9286	0.0007–0.0024	0.0027–0.0095
	P	4-122 (2.0)	2.4944–2.4954 ②	0.0006–0.0018 ③	0.0019–0.0071	4	1.9983–1.9993	0.0009–0.0031	0.0039–0.0240
	B	4-122 (2.0)	2.4944–2.4954 ②	0.0006–0.0018 ③	0.0019–0.0071	4	1.9983–1.9993	0.0009–0.0031	0.0039–0.0240
	W	6-173 (2.8)	2.6473–2.6482	0.0016–0.0033	0.0024–0.0083	3	1.9983–1.9994	0.0014–0.0037	0.0063–0.0173
1984	O	4-110 (1.8)	①	0.0006–0.0016	0.0027–0.0118	3	1.9278–1.9286	0.0007–0.0024	0.0027–0.0095
	J	4-110 (1.8)	①	0.0006–0.0016	0.0027–0.0118	3	1.9278–1.9286	0.0007–0.0024	0.0027–0.0095
	P	4-122 (2.0)	2.4944–2.4954 ②	0.0006–0.0018 ③	0.0019–0.0071	4	1.9983–1.9993	0.0009–0.0031	0.0039–0.0240
	W	6-173 (2.8)	2.6473–2.6482	0.0016–0.0033	0.0024–0.0083	3	1.9983–1.9994	0.0014–0.0037	0.0063–0.0173
1985	O	4-110 (1.8)	①	0.0006–0.0016	0.0027–0.0118	3	1.9278–1.9286	0.0007–0.0024	0.0027–0.0095
	J	4-110 (1.8)	①	0.0006–0.0016	0.0027–0.0118	3	1.9278–1.9286	0.0007–0.0024	0.0027–0.0095
	P	4-122 (2.0)	2.4944–2.4954 ②	0.0006–0.0018 ③	0.0019–0.0071	4	1.9983–1.9993	0.0009–0.0031	0.0039–0.0240
	W	6-173 (2.8)	2.6473–2.6482	0.0016–0.0033	0.0024–0.0083	3	1.9983–1.9994	0.0014–0.0037	0.0063–0.0173
1986	O	4-110 (1.8)	①	0.0006–0.0016	0.0027–0.0118	3	1.9278–1.9286	0.0007–0.0024	0.0027–0.0095
	J	4-110 (1.8)	①	0.0006–0.0016	0.0027–0.0118	3	1.9278–1.9286	0.0007–0.0024	0.0027–0.0095
	P	4-122 (2.0)	2.4944–2.4954 ②	0.0006–0.0018 ③	0.0019–0.0071	4	1.9983–1.9993	0.0009–0.0031	0.0039–0.0240
	W	6-173 (2.8)	2.6473–2.6482	0.0016–0.0033	0.0024–0.0083	3	1.9983–1.9994	0.0014–0.0037	0.0063–0.0173
1987	M	4-122 (2.0)	①	0.0006–0.0016	0.0030–0.0120	4	1.9278–1.9286	0.0007–0.0024	0.0027–0.0095
	1	4-122 (2.0)	2.4945–2.4954	0.0006–0.0019	0.0020–0.0080	4	1.9983–1.9994	0.0010–0.0031	0.0040–0.0150

Crankshaft and Connecting Rod Specifications (cont.)

All measurements are given in inches.

Year	VIN	No. Cylinder Displacement cu. in. (liter)	Crankshaft				Connecting Rod		
			Main Brg. Journal Dia.	Main Brg. Oil Clearance	Shaft End-play	Thrust on No.	Journal Diameter	Oil Clearance	Side Clearance
1987	K	4-122 (2.0)	①	0.0006– 0.0016	0.0030– 0.0120	4	1.9278– 1.9286	0.0007– 0.0024	0.0027– 0.0095
	W	6-173 (2.8)	2.6473– 2.6482	0.0016– 0.0033	0.0024– 0.0083	3	1.9983– 1.9994	0.0014– 0.0037	0.0063– 0.0173

① Bearings are identified by color:
   Brown 2.2830–2.2832;
   Green 2.2827–2.2830
② No. 5: 2.4936–2.4946
③ No. 5: 0.0014–0.0027

Piston and Ring Specifications

All measurements are given in inches.

Year	VIN	No. Cylinder Displacement cu. in. (liter)	Piston Clearance	Ring Gap			Ring Side Clearance		
				Top Compression	Bottom Compression	Oil Control	Top Compression	Bottom Compression	Oil Control
1982	G	4-110 (1.8)	0.0008– 0.0018	0.0098– 0.0197	0.0098– 0.0197	Snug	0.0012– 0.0027	0.0012– 0.0027	0.0078
	B	4-122 (2.0)	0.0008– 0.0018	0.0098– 0.0197	0.0098– 0.0197	Snug	0.0012– 0.0027	0.0012– 0.0027	0.0078
1983	O	4-110 (1.8)	0.0008 ①	0.0010– 0.0020	0.0010– 0.0020	0.0010– 0.0020	0.0020– 0.0030	0.0010– 0.0024	Snug
	J	4-110 (1.8)	0.0008 ①	0.0010– 0.0020	0.0010– 0.0020	0.0010– 0.0020	0.0020– 0.0030	0.0010– 0.0024	Snug
	P	4-122 (2.0)	0.0008– 0.0018	0.0098– 0.0197	0.0098– 0.0197	Snug	0.0012– 0.0027	0.0012– 0.0027	0.0078
	B	4-122 (2.0)	0.0008– 0.0018	0.0098– 0.0197	0.0098– 0.0197	Snug	0.0012– 0.0027	0.0012– 0.0027	0.0078
	W	6-173 (2.8)	0.0007– 0.0017	0.0098– 0.0197	0.0098– 0.0197	0.020– 0.055	0.0012– 0.0027	0.0016– 0.0037	0.0078 Max
1984	O	4-110 (1.8)	0.0008 ①	0.0010– 0.0020	0.0010– 0.0020	0.0010– 0.0020	0.0020– 0.0030	0.0010– 0.0024	Snug
	J	4-110 (1.8)	0.0008 ①	0.0010– 0.0020	0.0010– 0.0020	0.0010– 0.0020	0.0020– 0.0030	0.0010– 0.0024	Snug
	P	4-122 (2.0)	0.0007– 0.0017	0.0098– 0.0197	0.0098– 0.0197	Snug	0.0012– 0.0027	0.0012– 0.0027	0.0078
	W	6-173 (2.8)	0.0007– 0.0017	0.0098– 0.0197	0.0098– 0.0197	0.020– 0.055	0.0012– 0.0027	0.0016– 0.0037	0.0078 Max
1985	O	4-110 (1.8)	0.0008 ①	0.0010– 0.0020	0.0010– 0.0020	0.0010– 0.0020	0.0020– 0.0030	0.0010– 0.0024	Snug
	J	4-110 (1.8)	0.0008 ①	0.0010– 0.0020	0.0010– 0.0020	0.0010– 0.0020	0.0020– 0.0030	0.0010– 0.0024	Snug
	P	4-122 (2.0)	0.0007– 0.0017	0.0098– 0.0197	0.0098– 0.0197	Snug	0.0012– 0.0027	0.0012– 0.0027	0.0078
	W	6-173 (2.8)	0.0007– 0.0017	0.0098– 0.0197	0.0098– 0.0197	0.020– 0.055	0.0012– 0.0027	0.0016– 0.0037	0.0078 Max
1986	O	4-110 (1.8)	0.0008 ①	0.0010– 0.0020	0.0010– 0.0020	0.0010– 0.0020	0.0020– 0.0030	0.0010– 0.0024	Snug

Piston and Ring Specifications (cont.)

All measurements are given in inches.

Year	VIN	No. Cylinder Displacement cu. in. (liter)	Piston Clearance	Ring Gap Top Compression	Ring Gap Bottom Compression	Ring Gap Oil Control	Ring Side Clearance Top Compression	Ring Side Clearance Bottom Compression	Ring Side Clearance Oil Control
1986	J	4-110 (1.8)	0.0008 ①	0.0010– 0.0020	0.0010– 0.0020	0.0010– 0.0020	0.0020– 0.0030	0.0010– 0.0024	Snug
	P	4-122 (2.0)	0.0008– 0.0018	0.0098– 0.0197	0.0098– 0.0197	Snug	0.0012– 0.0027	0.0012– 0.0027	0.0078
	W	6-173 (2.8)	0.0007– 0.0017	0.0098– 0.0197	0.0098– 0.0197	0.020– 0.055	0.0012– 0.0027	0.0016– 0.0037	0.0078 Max
1987	M	4-122 (2.0)	0.0004– 0.0012	0.0100– 0.0200	0.0010– 0.0200	0.016– 0.055	0.0020– 0.0030	0.0010– 0.0024	0.0047
	1	4-122 (2.0)	0.0098– 0.0220	0.0100– 0.0200	0.0100– 0.0200	0.010– 0.050	0.0010– 0.0030	0.0010– 0.0030	0.0006– 0.0090
	K	4-122 (2.0)	0.0004– 0.0012	0.0100– 0.0200	0.0100– 0.0200	0.016– 0.055	0.0020– 0.0030	0.0010– 0.0024	0.0047
	W	6-173 (2.8)	0.0007– 0.0017	0.0098– 0.0197	0.0098– 0.0197	0.020– 0.055	0.0012– 0.0027	0.0016– 0.0037	0.0078 Max

① Code J: 0.0004–0.0012

25. Disconnect the engine to transmission support bracket.

26. Disconnect the right rear motor mount.

27. Disconnect the exhaust pipe at the manifold.

28. Disconnect the exhaust pipe at at the center hanger and loosen the muffler hanger.

29. Disconnect the T.V and shift cable bracket.

30. Remove the lower two bell housing bolts.

31. Lower the car.

32. Remove the right front motor mount nuts.

33. Remove the alternator and if necessary, the adjusting brace.

34. Disconnect the master cylinder from the booster, set aside and suitably support.

35. Install a lifting device.

36. Remove the right front motor mount bracket.

37. Remove the remaining upper bellhousing bolts.

38. Remove the power steering pump while lifting the engine.

39. Remove the engine.

To Install

1. Install the engine.

2. Install the power steering pump while lowering the engine.

3. Install the upper bellhousing bolts.

4. Install the right front motor mount bracket.

5. Remove the lifting device.

6. Connect the master cylinder from the booster, set aside and suitably support.

7. Install the alternator and if removed, the adjusting brace.

8. Install the right front motor mount nuts.

9. Raise the car.

10. Install the remaining two bell housing bolts.

11. Connect the T.V and shift cable bracket.

12. Connect the exhaust pipe at at the center hanger and loosen the muffler hanger.

13. Connect the exhaust pipe at the manifold.

14. Connect the right rear motor mount. If the rear engine mount bracket is removed, the following procedure should be used to ensure proper engine mount bracket locations:

 a. Loosely install the engine mount bracket.

 b. Raise the engine and transaxle.

 c. Torque the engine mount nuts and bolts to the specifications shown.

15. Connect the engine to transmission support bracket.

16. Install the oil filter.

17. RemoveInstall the crankshaft pulley using Tool J 24420.

18. Install the torque converter bolts.

19. Install the front starter brace and starter.

20. Connect the starter wires.

21. Install the flywheel splash shield.

22. If equipped with air conditioning, install the air conditioning compressor.

23. Install the inner fender splash shield.

24. If equipped with air conditioning, install the air conditioning brace.

25. Lower the vehicle.

26. Connect the fuel hoses.

Torque Specifications
All readings in ft. lbs.

Year	VIN	No. Cylinder Displacement cu. in. (liter)	Cylinder Head Bolts	Main Bearing Bolts	Rod Bearing Bolts	Crankshaft Pulley Bolts	Flywheel Bolts	Manifold		Spark Plugs
								Intake	Exhaust	
1982	G	4-110 (1.8)	65–75	63–74	34–40	66–84	45–55	20–25	22–28	15
	B	4-122 (2.0)	65–75	63–77	34–43	66–89	45–63 ②	18–25	20–30	15
1983	O	4-110 (1.8)	①	57	39	115	45	25	16	15
	J	4-110 (1.8)	①	57	39	115	45	25	16	15
	P	4-122 (2.0)	65–75	63–77	34–43	68–89	45–63 ②	18–25	20–30	15
	B	4-122 (2.0)	65–75	63–77	34–43	68–89	45–63 ②	18–25	20–30	15
	W	6-173 (2.8)	70	68	37	75	45	23	25	15
1984	O	4-110 (1.8)	①	57	39	115	45	25	16	15
	J	4-110 (1.8)	①	57	39	115	45	25	16	15
	P	4-122 (2.0)	65–75	63–77	34–43	68–89	45–63 ②	18–25	20–30	15
	W	6-173 (2.8)	70	68	37	75	45	23	25	15
1985	O	4-110 (1.8)	①	57	39	115	45	25	16	15
	J	4-110 (1.8)	①	57	39	115	45	25	16	15
	P	4-122 (2.0)	65–75	63–77	34–43	68–89	45–63 ②	18–25	34–44	7–20
	W	6-173 (2.8)	75	70	34–45	75	45	13–25	19–31	15
1986	O	4-110 (1.8)	①	57	39	115	45	25	16	15
	J	4-110 (1.8)	①	57	39	115	45	25	16	15
	P	4-122 (2.0)	73–85	63–77	34–43	68–89	45–63 ②	18–25	34–44	7–20
	W	6-173 (2.8)	75	70	34–45	75	45	13–25	19–31	15
1987	M	4-122 (2.0)	①	④	⑤	107	48	16	16	7–15
	1	4-122 (2.0)	③	63–77	34–43	68–89	45–63 ②	18–25	16–13	7–20
	K	4-122 (2.0)	①	④	⑤	107	48	16	16	7–15
	W	6-173 (2.8)	75	70	34–45	75	45	25	15–23	10–25

CAUTION: Verify the correct original equipment engine is in the vehicle by referring to the VIN engine code before torquing any bolts.

① Torque bolts to 18 ft. lb., then turn each bolt 60°, in sequence, 3 times for a 180° rotation, then run the engine to normal operating temperature and turn each bolt, in sequence, an additional 30°–50°

② Auto. Trans.: 45–59

③ Long: 73–83
   Short: 62–70

④ 44 ft. lbs. plus a 40° to 50° turn

⑤ 26 ft. lbs. plus a 40° to 45° turn

27. Install the alternator belt or serpentine belt, if so equipped.
28. Install the windshield washer bottle.
29. Connect the engine wiring harness at the bulkhead.
30. Install the exhaust heat shield.
31. Connect the heater hoses at the engine.
32. Connect the radiator hoses at the engine.
33. Connect all vacuum hoses.
34. Connect the ECM harness at the engine.
35. Connect the accelerator cable and T.V. cables.

36. Install the air cleaner.
37. Fill the cooling system.
38. Connect the battery.

OHC 4-Cylinder Engines

NOTE: *This procedure requires the use of a special tool.*
1. Remove battery cables.
2. Drain cooling system.
CAUTION: *When draining the coolant, keep in mind that cats and dogs are attracted by the ethylene glycol antifreeze, and are quite*

likely to drink any that is left in an uncovered container or in puddles on the ground. This will prove fatal in sufficient quantity. Always drain the coolant into a sealable container. Coolant should be reused unless it is contaminated or several years old.

3. Remove air cleaner.

4. Disconnect engine electrical harness at bulkhead.

5. Disconnect electrical connector at brake cylinder.

6. Remove throttle cable from bracket and E.F.I. assembly.

7. Remove vacuum hoses from E.F.I. assembly.

8. Remove power steering high pressure hose at cut-off switch.

9. Remove vacuum hoses at map sensor and canister.

10. Disconnect air conditioning relay cluster switches.

11. Remove power steering return hose at pump.

12. Disconnect ECM wire connections and feed harness through bulkhead and lay harness over engine.

13. Remove upper and lower radiator hoses from engine.

14. Remove electrical connections from temperature switch at thermostat housing.

15. Disconnect transmission shift cable at transmission.

16. Hoist car.

17. Remove speedometer cable at transmission and bracket.

18. Disconnect exhaust pipe at exhaust manifold.

19. Remove exhaust pipe from converter.

20. Remove heater hoses from heater core.

21. Remove fuel lines at flex hoses.

22. Remove transmission cooler lines at flex hoses.

23. Remove left and right front wheels.

24. Remove right hand spoiler section and splash shield.

25. Remove right and left brake calipers and support with wire.

26. Remove right and left tie rod ends.

27. Disconnect electrical connections at air conditioning compressor.

28. Remove air conditioning compressor and mounting brackets, support air conditioning compressor with wire in wheel opening.

29. Remove front suspension support attachment bolts (6 bolts each side).

30. Lower car.

31. Support front of vehicle by placing two short jackstands under core support.

32. Position front post hoist to the rear of cowl.

33. Position a 4″ x 4″ x 6′ timber on front post hoist.

34. Raise vehicle enough to remove jackstands.

35. Position a 4-wheel dolly under engine and transaxle assembly.

36. Position three (3) 4″ x 4″ x 12″ blocks under engine and transaxle assembly only, letting support rails hang free.

37. Lower vehicle onto 4-wheel dolly slightly.

38. Remove rear transaxle mount attachment bolts (2).

39. Remove left front engine mount attachment bolts (3).

40. Remove two (2) engine support to body attachment bolts behind right-hand inner axle U-joint.

41. Remove one (1) attaching bolt and nut from right-hand chassis side rail to engine mount bracket.

42. Remove six (6) strut attachment nuts.

43. Raise vehicle letting engine, transaxle and suspension resting on 4-wheel dolly.

Reverse the removal procedure for engine installation with the following exceptions.

1. With one man's assistance, position engine and transaxle assembly in chassis.

2. Install transaxle and left front mounts to side rail bolts loosely.

3. Install M6X1X65 alignment bolt in left front mount to prevent powertrain misalignment.

4. Torque transaxle mount bolts to 42 ft.lb. and left front mount bolts to 18 ft.lb.

5. Install right rear mount to body bolts and torque to 38 ft.lb.

6. Install right rear mount to chassis side rail bolt and nut torque to 38 ft.lb.

7. Place a floor jack under control arms, jack struts into position and install retaining nuts.

8. Raise vehicle.

9. Using a transmission jack or suitable lifting equipment, raise control arms and attach tie rod ends.

2.8L V6 Engine

1. Disconnect the negative battery cable. Drain the cooling system and remove the air cleaner assembly.

CAUTION: *When draining the coolant, keep in mind that cats and dogs are attracted by the ethylene glycol antifreeze, and are quite likely to drink any that is left in an uncovered container or in puddles on the ground. This will prove fatal in sufficient quantity. Always drain the coolant into a sealable container. Coolant should be reused unless it is contaminated or several years old.*

2. Remove the air flow sensor. Remove the

exhaust crossover heat shield and remove the crossover pipe.

3. Remove the serpentine belt tensioner and belt.

4. Remove the power steering pump mounting bracket. Disconnect the heater pipe at the power steering pump mounting bracket.

5. Disconnect the radiator hoses from the engine.

6. Disconnect the accelerator and throttle valve cable at the throttle valve.

7. Remove the alternator. Tag and disconnect the wiring harness at the engine.

8. Relieve the fuel pressure (see Chapter 1) and disconnect the fuel hose. Disconnect the coolant bypass and the overflow hoses at the engine.

9. Tag and remove the vacuum hoses to the engine.

10. Raise the vehicle and support it safely.

11. Remove the inner fender splash shield. Remove the harmonic balancer.

12. Remove the flywheel cover. Remove the starter bolts. Tag and disconnect the electrical connections to the starter. Remove the starter.

13. Disconnect the wires at the oil sending unit.

14. Remove the air conditioning compressor and related brackets.

15. Disconnect the exhaust pipe at the rear of the exhaust manifold.

16. Remove the flex plate-to-torque converter bolts.

17. Remove the transaxle-to-engine bolts. Remove the engine-to-rear mount frame nuts.

18. Disconnect the shift cable bracket at the transaxle. Remove the lower bell housing bolts.

19. Lower the vehicle and disconnect the heater hoses at the engine.

20. Install a suitable engine lifting device. While supporting the engine and transaxle, remove the upper bell housing bolts.

21. Remove the front mounting bolts.

22. Remove the master cylinder from the booster.

23. Remove the engine assembly from the vehicle.

To Install

1. Install the engine and remove the engine lifting device.

2. Install the master cylinder to the booster.

3. Install the front mounting bolts.

4. Install the upper bell housing bolts.

5. Connect the heater hoses at the engine.

6. Connect the shift cable bracket at the transaxle. Install the lower bell housing bolts.

7. Install the transaxle-to-engine bolts. Install the engine-to-rear mount frame nuts.

8. Install the flex plate-to-torque converter bolts.

9. Connect the exhaust pipe at the rear of the exhaust manifold.

10. Install the air conditioning compressor and related brackets.

11. Connect the wires at the oil sending unit.

12. Install the flywheel cover. Install the starter bolts. Connect the electrical connections to the starter. Install the starter.

13. Install the inner fender splash shield. Install the harmonic balancer.

14. Lower the vehicle.

15. Install the vacuum hoses to the engine.

16. Connect the fuel hose. Connect the coolant bypass and the overflow hoses at the engine.

17. Install the alternator. Connect the wiring harness at the engine.

18. Connect the accelerator and throttle valve cable at the throttle valve.

19. Connect the radiator hoses to the engine.

20. Install the power steering pump mounting bracket. Connect the heater pipe at the power steering pump mounting bracket.

21. Install the serpentine belt tensioner and belt.

22. Install the air flow sensor. Install the exhaust crossover heat shield and crossover pipe.

23. Connect the negative battery cable. Fill the cooling system and install the air cleaner assembly.

Rocker Arm Cover

REMOVAL AND INSTALLATION

1.8L, 2.0L OHV Engine

1982-86

1. Disconnect the negative battery cable.

2. Remove the air cleaner.

3. Disconnect the canister purge line and the PCV valve.

4. Disconnect the spark plug wires at the spark plugs and pull the wires away from the rocker arm cover.

5. Loosen the accelerator linkage bracket.

6. Remove the rocker arm cover bolts.

7. Remove the rocker arm cover. If the cover adheres to the cylinder head, lightly tap the end of the cover with a rubber mallet. If necessary, carefully pry until loose.

WARNING: *Do not distort the sealing flange.*

8. Clean the sealing surfaces of the head and the cover.

9. Place a ⅛″ wide bead of RTV sealant all around the rocker arm cover sealing surface.

NOTE: *When going aropund the attaching bolt holes, always flow the RTV on the inboard side of the bolt holes.*

10. Install the valve cover and torque the bolts to 8 ft.lb. while the sealant is still wet.

NOTE: AT TIME OF INSTALLATION, FLANGES MUST BE FREE OF OIL. A ⅛ BEAD OF SEALANT MUST BE APPLIED TO FLANGES AND SEALANT MUST BE WET TO TOUCH WHEN BOLTS ARE TORQUED.

NOTE: AT TIME OF INSTALLATION, FLANGES MUST BE FREE OF OIL. A 2.0-3.0 BEAD OF SEALANT MUST BE APPLIED TO FLANGES AND SEALANT MUST BE WET TO TOUCH WHEN BOLTS ARE TORQUED.

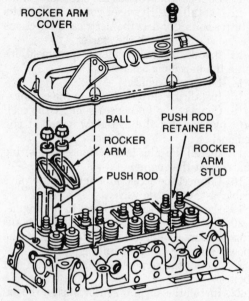

Rocker arm and cover, 1982–83 1.8, 2.0L OHV engine

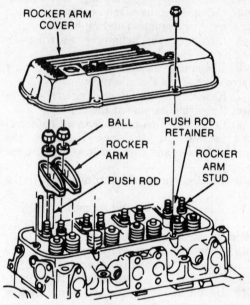

Rocker arm and cover, 1984–86 1.8, 2.0L OHV engine

WARNING: *Keep the sealant out of the bolt holes as this could cause a "Hydraulic lock" condition which could damage the head casting.*

11. Install the remaining parts and reconnect the battery cable.

1987-88

1. Disconnect the negative battery cable.
2. Disconnect the AIR hose at the TBI and air cleaner.
3. Remove the hose from the intake to the cover.
4. Remove the rocker arm cover bolts and remove the cover.
5. Clean the sealing surfaces of the head and the cover.
6. Install a new gasket, reposition the cover and torque the bolts to 8 ft.lb.
7. Install all hoses removed and connect the negative battery cable.

V6 Engine

1984-86 LEFT

1. Disconnect the negative battery cable.
2. Remove the coil at the bracket.
3. Disconnect the PCV hose.
4. Disconnect the spark plug wires at the spark plugs and pull the wires away from the rocker arm cover.
5. Loosen the accelerator linkage bracket.

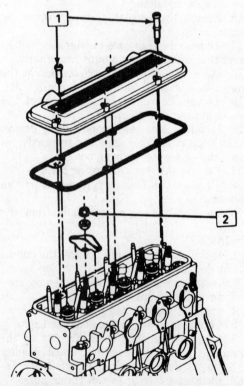

1. 6–9 ft. lbs.   2. 11–18 ft. lbs.

Rocker arm and cover, 1987, 2.0L OHV engine

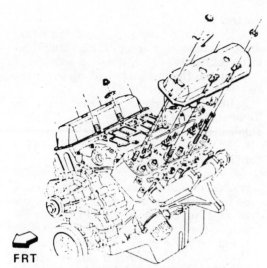

FRT

Rocker arm cover installation, 1984–86 V6 engine

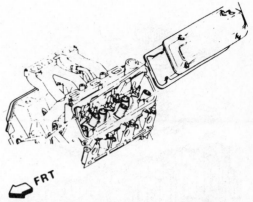

FRT

Rocker arm cover installation, 1987 V6 engine

6. Remove the rocker arm cover bolts.

7. Remove the rocker arm cover. If the cover adheres to the cylinder head, lightly tap the end of the cover with a rubber mallet. If necessary, carefully pry until loose.

WARNING: *Do not distort the sealing flange.*

8. Clean the sealing surfaces of the head and the cover.

9. Place a ⅛″ wide bead of RTV sealant at the intake manifold and the cylinder head split line.

10. Install the valve cover and torque the bolts to 90 in.lb. while the sealant is still wet.

11. Install the remaining parts and reconnect the battery cable.

1984-86 RIGHT

1. Disconnect the negative battery cable.

2. Disconnect the intake runners.

3. Remove the rocker arm cover bolts.

4. Remove the rocker arm cover. If the cover adheres to the cylinder head, lightly tap the end of the cover with a rubber mallet. If necessary, carefully pry until loose.

WARNING: *Do not distort the sealing flange.*

5. Clean the sealing surfaces of the head and the cover.

6. Place a ⅛″ wide bead of RTV sealant at the intake manifold and the cylinder head split line.

7. Install the valve cover and torque the bolts to 90 in.lb. while the sealant is still wet.

8. Install the remaining parts and reconnect the battery cable.

1987-88 LEFT

1. Disconnect the negative battery cable.

2. Remove the bracket tube at the cover.

3. Remove the plug wire cover.

4. Disconnect the heater hose at the filler neck.

5. Remove the cover bolts and remove the cover.

6. If the cover adheres to the cylinder head, lightly tap the end of the cover with a soft rubber mallet or palm of the hand.

WARNING: *Do not distort or scratch the sealing flange.*

7. Clean the sealing surfaces of the head and the cover.

8. Install a new gasket and make sure it is seated properly in the rocker cover groove.

9. Apply RTV sealant in the notch.

10. Install the rocker cover and tighten the retaining bolts to 6-9 ft.lb.

11. Install the remaining parts and reconnect the battery cable.

1987-88 RIGHT

1. Disconnect the negative battery cable.

2. Disconnect the brake booster vacuum line at the bracket.

3. Disconnect the cable bracket at the plenum.

4. Remove the vacuum line bracket at the cable bracket.

5. Disconnect the lines at the alternator brace stud.

6. Disconnect the rear alternator brace.

7. Remove the serpentine belt.

8. Disconnect the alternator and lay to one side.

9. Remove the PCV valve.

10. Loosen the alternator bracket.

11. Remove the rocker cover bolts, plug wires and rocker cover.

12. If the cover adheres to the cylinder head, lightly tap the end of the cover with a soft rubber mallet or palm of the hand.

WARNING: *Do not distort or scratch the sealing flange.*

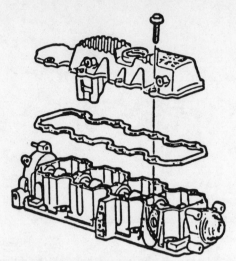

Camshaft carrier cover, OHC engine

13. Clean the sealing surfaces of the head and the cover.

14. Install a new gasket and make sure it is seated properly in the rocker cover groove.

15. Apply RTV sealant in the notch.

16. Install the rocker cover and tighten the retaining bolts to 6-9 ft.lb.

17. Install the remaining parts and reconnect the battery cable.

Camshaft Carrier Cover

REMOVAL AND INSTALLATION

OHC Engines

1. Remove the air cleaner on non-turbo models.

2. Disconnect the breather hoses.

3. Disconnect the induction tube on turbo models.

4. Remove the bolts and remove the cover.

5. Clean the sealing surfaces on the camshaft carrier and cover.

6. Reposition the cover with a new gasket and torque the retainer bolts to 6 ft.lb.

7. Install the air cleaner and breather hoses.

8. Install the induction tube on turbo models

Rocker Arms and Pushrods

REMOVAL, INSTALLATION AND ADJUSTMENT

OHV 4-Cylinder Engines

1. Remove the air cleaner. Remove the cylinder head cover.

2. Remove the rocker arm nut and ball. Lift the rocker arm off the stud. Always keep the rocker arm assemblies together and install them on the same stud. Remove the pushrods.

To install:

3. Coat the bearing surfaces of the rocker arms and the rocker arm balls with Molykote® or its equivalent.

4. Install the pushrods making sure that they seat properly in the lifter.

5. Install the rocker arms, balls and nuts. Tighten the rocker arm nuts until all lash is eliminated.

6. Adjust the valves when the lifter is on the base circle of a camshaft lobe:

a. Crank the engine until the mark on the crankshaft pulley lines up with the **O** mark on the timing tab. Make sure that the engine is in the No. 1 firing position. Place your fingers on the No. 1 rocker arms as the mark on the crank pulley comes near the **O** mark. If the valves are not moving, the engine is in the No. 1 firing position. If the valves move, the engine is in the No. 4 firing position; rotate the engine one complete revolution and it will be in the No. 1 position.

b. When the engine is in the No. 1 firing position, adjust the following valves:
- Exhaust--1,3
- Intake--1,2

c. Back the adjusting nut out until lash can be felt at the pushrod, then turn the nut until all lash is removed (this can be determined by rotating the pushrod while turning the adjusting nut). When all lash has been removed, turn the nut in 1½ additional turns, this will center the lifter plunger.

d. Crank the engine one complete revolution until the timing tab and the **O** mark are again in alignment. Now the engine is in the No. 4 firing position. Adjust the following valves:
- Exhaust--2,4
- Intake--3,4

7. Installation of the remaining components is the reverse order of removal.

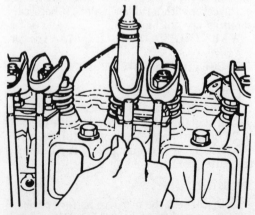

Tighten the rocker arm nut until the pushrod cannot be rotated between your fingers

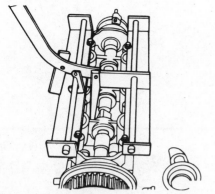

Compressing the valve spring using special tool J-33302 on OHC engines

OHC 4-Cylinder Engines

NOTE: *A special tool is required for this procedure.*

1. Remove the camshaft carrier cover.

2. Using a valve train compressing fixture, tool J-33302, depress all the lifters at once.

3. Remove the rocker arms, placing them on the workbench in the same order that they were removed.

4. Remove the hydraulic valve lash compensators keeping them in the order in which they were removed.

5. Installation is the reverse of removal. Rocker arms and compensators must be replaced in the exact same position as when they were removed.

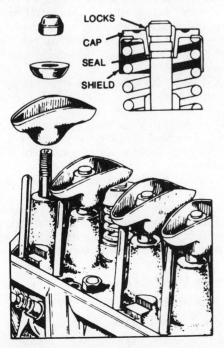

LOCKS

CAP

SEAL

SHIELD

V6-173 rocker arm, pivot and nut

6-173

NOTE: *Some engines are assembled using RTV (Room Temperature Vulcanizing) silicone sealant in place of rocker arm cover gasket. If the engine was assembled using RTV, never use a gasket when reassembling. Conversely, if the engine was assembled using a rocker arm cover gasket, never replace it with RTV.*

When using RTV, an 1/8" bead is sufficient. Always run the bead on the inside of the bolt holes.

Rocker arms are removed by removing the adjusting nut. Be sure to adjust valve lash after replacing rocker arms.

NOTE: *When replacing an exhaust rocker, move an old intake rocker arm to the exhaust rocker arm stud and install the new rocker arm on the intake stud.*

Cylinder heads use threaded rocker arm studs. If the threads in the head are damaged or stripped, the head can be retapped and a helical type insert installed.

NOTE: *If engine is equipped with the A.I.R. exhaust emission control system, the interfering components of the system must be removed. Disconnect the lines at the air injection nozzles in the exhaust manifolds.*

Thermostat

REMOVAL AND INSTALLATION

OHV 4-Cylinder Engines

The thermostat is located inside a housing on the back of the cylinder head. It is not necessary to remove the radiator hose from the thermostat housing when removing the thermostat.

1. Disconnect the negative battery cable.

2. Drain the cooling system and remove the air cleaner.

CAUTION: *When draining the coolant, keep in mind that cats and dogs are attracted by the ethylene glycol antifreeze, and are quite likely to drink any that is left in an uncovered container or in puddles on the ground. This will prove fatal in sufficient quantity. Always drain the coolant into a sealable container. Coolant should be reused unless it is contaminated or several years old.*

3. Disconnect the A.I.R. pipe at the upper check valve and the bracket at the water outlet.

4. Disconnect the electrical lead.

5. Remove the two retaining bolts from the thermostat housing and lift up the housing with the house attached. Lift out the thermostat.

6. Insert the new thermostat, spring end down. Apply a thin bead of silicone sealer to the housing mating surface and install the housing

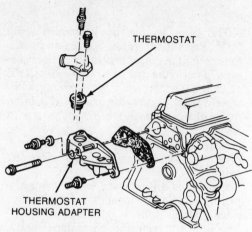

Thermostat installation details

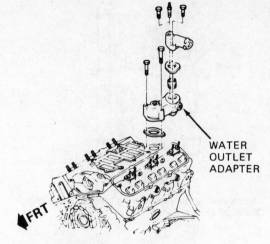

Thermostat housing, V6 engine

while the sealer is still wet. Tighten the housing retaining bolts to 6 ft.lb.

NOTE: *Poor heater output and slow warmup is often caused by a thermostat stuck in the open position; occasionally one sticks shut causing immediate overheating. Do not attempt to correct a chronic overheating condition by permanently removing the thermostat. Thermostat flow restriction is designed into the system; without it, localized overheating (due to coolant turbulence) may occur, causing expensive troubles.*

7. Installation of the remaining components is in the reverse order of removal.

OHC 4-Cylinder Engines

1. Remove the thermostat housing.
2. Grasp the handle of the thermostat and pull it from the housing.
3. Install the thermostat in the housing, pushing it down as far as it will go to make sure it's seated.

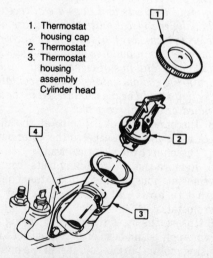

1. Thermostat housing cap
2. Thermostat
3. Thermostat housing assembly Cylinder head

OHC 4-cyl. engine thermostat mounting

4. Install the housing on the engine, using a new gasket coated with sealer.

6-173

1. Disconnect the negative battery cable.
2. Drain the cooling system.

CAUTION: *When draining the coolant, keep in mind that cats and dogs are attracted by the ethylene glycol antifreeze, and are quite likely to drink any that is left in an uncovered container or in puddles on the ground. This will prove fatal in sufficient quantity. Always drain the coolant into a sealable container. Coolant should be reused unless it is contaminated or several years old.*

3. Some models with cruise control have a vacuum modulator attached to the thermostat housing with a bracket. If your vehicle is equipped as such, remove the bracket from the housing.
4. Unbolt the water outlet from the intake manifold, remove the outlet and lift the thermostat out of the manifold.
5. Clean both of the mating surfaces and run a 1/8" wide bead of R.T.V. (room temperature vulcanizing) sealer in the groove of the water outlet.
6. Install the thermostat (spring towards engine) and bolt the water outlet into place while the R.T.V. sealer is still wet. Torque the bolts to 21 ft.lb. The remainder of the installation is the reverse of removal. Check for leaks after the car is started and correct as required.

Intake Manifold

REMOVAL AND INSTALLATION

OHV 4-Cylinder Engines

1. Disconnect the negative battery cable.
2. Remove the air cleaner. Drain the cooling system.

CAUTION: *When draining the coolant, keep in mind that cats and dogs are attracted by the ethylene glycol antifreeze, and are quite likely to drink any that is left in an uncovered container or in puddles on the ground. This will prove fatal in sufficient quantity. Always drain the coolant into a sealable container. Coolant should be reused unless it is contaminated or several years old.*

3. Tag and disconnect all necessary vacuum lines and wires. Remove the idler pulley.

4. Remove the A.I.R. drive belt. If equipped with power steering, remove the drive belt and then remove the pump with the lines attached. Position the pump out of the way.

5. Remove the A.I.R. bracket-to-intake manifold bolt. Remove the air pump pulley.

6. If equipped with power steering, remove the A.I.R. through-bolt and then the power steering adjusting bracket.

7. Loosen the lower bolt on the air pump mounting bracket so that the bracket will rotate.

8. Disconnect the fuel lines at the carburetor or TBI unit. Disconnect the carburetor or TBI linkage and then remove the carburetor or TBI unit.

CAUTION: *The fuel lines are pressurized (especially with fuel injection). Removal may cause fuel spray resulting in personal injury. Do not remove before bleeding the pressure from the fuel system. See Chapter 1 for the procedure.*

9. Lift off the Early Fuel Evaporation (EFE) heater grid.

10. Remove the distributor.

11. Remove the mounting bolts and nuts and remove the intake manifold. Make sure to disconnect the heater hose and condenser from the bottom of the intake manifold before you lift it all the way out.

12. Using a new gasket, replace the manifold, tightening the nuts and bolts to specification.

13. Installation of the remaining components is in the reverse order of removal. Adjust all

necessary drive belts and check the ignition timing.

OHC 4-Cylinder Engines
EXCEPT TURBOCHARGED

1. Remove air cleaner.

2. Drain cooling system.

CAUTION: *When draining the coolant, keep in mind that cats and dogs are attracted by the ethylene glycol antifreeze, and are quite likely to drink any that is left in an uncovered container or in puddles on the ground. This will prove fatal in sufficient quantity. Always drain the coolant into a sealable container. Coolant should be reused unless it is contaminated or several years old.*

3. Remove generator and generator bracket at camshaft carrier.

4. Remove power steering pump and lay to one side.

5. Remove power steering bracket at intake manifold.

6. Remove ignition coil.

7. Remove throttle cable from bracket at intake manifold.

8. Disconnect throttle, downshift and TV cables from EFI assembly.

9. Disconnect wire harness connectors from TBI assembly.

10. Remove vacuum brake hose at filter.

11. Disconnct the inlet and outlet fuel lines.

CAUTION: *The fuel lines are pressurized (especially with fuel injection). Removal may cause fuel spray resulting in personal injury. Do not remove before bleeding the pressure from the fuel system. See Chapter 1 for the procedure.*

12. Remove preheat water hose at water pump and intake manifold.

13. Remove S-hose from inlet tube to water pump.

14. Disconnect necessary ECM harness connectors and move ECM harness assembly for access to lower intake manifold retaining nuts.

15. Remove four (4) lower intake manifold retaining nuts and washers.

16. Remove five (5) upper intake manifold retaining nuts and washers and remove intake manifold.

17. Install the intake manifold and install the five (5) upper intake manifold retaining nuts and washers. Torque the bolts to 16 ft.lb.

18. Install the four (4) lower intake manifold retaining nuts and washers. Torque the bolts to 16 ft.lb.

19. Connect the ECM harness connectors.

20. Install the S-hose on the water pump.

21. Install the preheat water hose on the water pump and intake manifold.

22. Connect the inlet and outlet fuel lines.

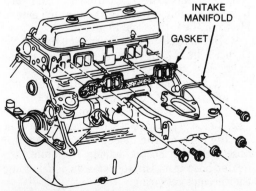

INTAKE MANIFOLD

GASKET

Intake manifold installation details

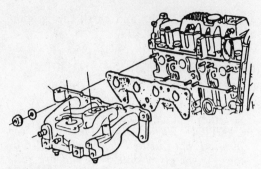

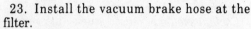

Intake manifold, OHC engine without turbocharger

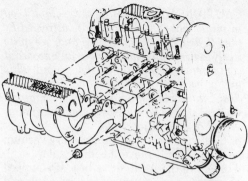

Intake manifold, OHC engine with turbocharger

23. Install the vacuum brake hose at the filter.

24. Connect the wire harness connectors at the TBI assembly.

25. Connect the throttle, downshift and TV cables at the EFI assembly.

26. Install the throttle cable on the bracket at the intake manifold.

27. Install the ignition coil.

28. Install the power steering bracket at the intake manifold.

29. Install the power steering pump.

30. Install the alternator and bracket at the camshaft carrier.

31. Fill the cooling system.

32. Install the air cleaner.

TURBOCHARGED ENGINES

1. Disconnect the induction tube and hoses.

2. Disconnect the wiring to the throttle body, M.A.P. sensor and wastegate.

3. Disconnect the PCV hose.

4. Disconnect the vacuum hose to the throttle body.

5. Disconnect the throttle cable and cruise control cable ,if so equipped.

6. Disconnect the wiring to the ignition coil.

7. Disconnect the manifold support bracket.

8. Disconnect the wiring to the fuel injectors.

9. Remove the bolt from the rear generator bracket to the generator.

10. Disconnect the fuel lines to the to the fuel rail inlet and regulator outlet.

CAUTION: *The fuel lines are pressurized (especially with fuel injection). Removal may cause fuel spray resulting in personal injury. Do not remove before bleeding the pressure from the fuel system. See Chapter 1 for the procedure.*

11. Remove the retaining nuts and washers and remove the intake manifold and gasket.

12. If installing a new manifold transfer all necessary parts from the old manifold to the new manifold.

13. Clean the mating surfaces at the cylinder head and the manifold.

14. Install the manifold with new gasket.

15. Install the retaining nuts and washers and torque to 18 ft.lb.

16. Connect the fuel lines.

17. Install the power steering and generator adjusting brackets.

18. Install the wiring to the fuel injectors.

19. Install the wiring to the ignition coil.

20. Install the wiring to the ignition coil.

21. Install the throttle cable and cruise control cable.

22. Install the vacuum hoses and PCV hoses.

23. Connect the wiring to the throttle body, M.A.P. sensor and wastegate.

24. Install the induction tube and hoses.

6-173

1. Disconnect the negative battery cable.

2. Disconnect the accelerator cable bracket at the plenum.

3. Disconnect the throttle body and the EGR pipe from the EGR valve. Remove the plenum assembly.

4. Disconnect the fuel line along the fuel rail.

5. Disconnect the serpentine drive belt. Remove the power steering pump mounting bracket.

6. Remove the heater pipe at the power steering pump bracket.

7. Tag and disconnect the wiring at the alternator and remove the alternator.

8. Disconnect the wires from the cold start injector assembly. Remove the injector assembly from the intake manifold.

9. Disconnect the idle air vacuum hose at the throttle body. Disconnect the wires at the injectors.

10. Remove the fuel rail, breather tube and the fuel runners from the engine.

11. Tag and disconnect the coil wires.

12. Remove the rocker arm covers. Drain the cooling system, the disconnect the radiator hose at the thermostat housing. Disconnect the heater hose from the thermostat housing and the thermostat wiring.

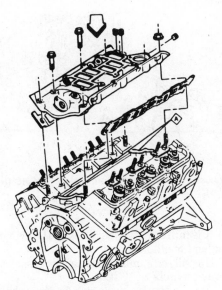

Intake manifold, 1984–86 V6 engine

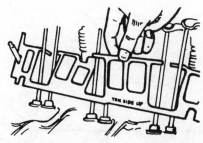

Cut the 6-173 intake manifold gasket as necessary

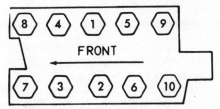

6-173 intake manifold torque sequence

CAUTION: *When draining the coolant, keep in mind that cats and dogs are attracted by the ethylene glycol antifreeze, and are quite likely to drink any that is left in an uncovered container or in puddles on the ground. This will prove fatal in sufficient quantity. Always drain the coolant into a sealable container. Coolant should be reused unless it is contaminated or several years old.*

13. Remove the distributor.

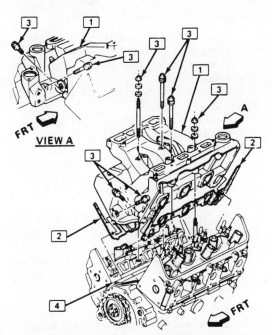

1. Intake manifold   3. 25 N·m (18 lbs. ft.)
2. Gasket   4. Sealer
Intake manifold, 1987 V6 engine

14. Remove the thermostat assembly housing.

15. Remove the intake manifold bolts and remove the intake manifold from the engine.

To install:

1. The gaskets are marked for right and left side installation; do not interchange them. Clean the sealing surface of the engine block, and apply a $\frac{3}{16}$" wide bead of silicone sealer to each ridge.

2. Install the new gaskets onto the heads. The gaskets will have to be cut slightly to fit past the center pushrods. Do not cut any more material than necessary. Hold the gaskets in place by extending the ridge bead of sealer $\frac{1}{4}$" onto the gasket ends.

3. Install the intake manifold. The area between the ridges and the manifold should be completely sealed.

4. Install the retaining bolts and nuts, and tighten in sequence to 23 ft.lb. Do not overtighten; the manifold is made from aluminum, and can be warped or cracked with excessive force.

5. The rest of installation is the reverse of removal. Adjust the ignition timing after installation, and check the coolant level after the engine has warmed up.

Exhaust Manifold

REMOVAL AND INSTALLATION

OHV 4-Cylinder Engines

1. Disconnect the negative battery cable.

2. Remove the air cleaner. Remove the exhaust manifold shield. Raise and support the front of the vehicle.

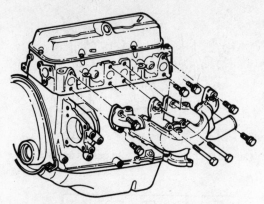

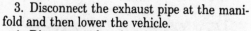

Exhaust manifold installation, 1.8, 2.0L OHV engine

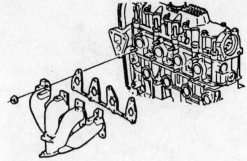

Exhaust manifold installation, 1.8L, 2.0L OHC (Non turbo)

3. Disconnect the exhaust pipe at the manifold and then lower the vehicle.

4. Disconnect the air management-to-check valve hose and remove the bracket. Disconnect the oxygen sensor lead wire.

5. Remove the alternator belt. Remove the alternator adjusting bolts, loosen the pivot bolt and pivot the alternator upward.

6. Remove the alternator brace and the A.I.R. pipes bracket bolt.

7. Unscrew the mounting bolts and remove the exhaust manifold. The manifold should be removed with the A.I.R. plumbing as an assembly. If the manifold is to be replaced, transfer the plumbing to the new one.

8. Clean the mating surfaces on the manifold and the head, position the manifold and tighten the bolts to the proper specifications.

9. Installation of the remaining components is in the reverse order of removal.

OHC 4-Cylinder Engines

EXCEPT TURBOCHARGER

1. Remove air cleaner.
2. Remove spark plug wires and retainers.
3. Remove oil dipstick tube and breather assembly.
4. Disconnect oxygen sensor wire.
5. Disconnect exhaust pipe from manifold flange.
6. Remove exhaust manifold to cylinder head attaching nuts and remove manifold and gasket.
7. Installation is the reverse of removal. Torque the bolts to 16-19 ft.lb.

WITH TURBOCHARGER

1. Remove the turbo induction tube.
2. Disconnect the spark plug wires.
3. Remove the bolts and nuts between the turbo and exhaust manifold.
4. Remove the bolts and nuts and remove the manifold and gasket.

5. Clean the mating surfaces at the cylinder head and manifold.

6. Install the manifold with a new gasket and torque the nuts to 16 ft.lb.

7. Install the turbocharger to the exhaust manifold and torque the nuts to 18 ft.lb.

8. Install the spark plug wires and the turbo induction tube.

NOTE: *Before installing a new gasket on the 1.8L MFI Turbo engine (code J), check for the location of the stamped part number on the surface. This gasket should be installed with this number toward the manifold. The gasket appears to be the same in either direction but it is not. Installing the gasket backwards will result in a leak.*

6-173

LEFT SIDE

1. Disconnect the negative battery cable.
2. Remove the air cleaner assembly.
3. Remove the air flow sensor. Remove the engine heat shield.
4. Disconnect the crossover pipe at the manifold.
5. Remove the exhaust manifold bolts.
6. Remove the exhaust manifold.

To install:

1. Clean the mating surfaces of the cylinder head and manifold. Install the manifold onto the head, and install the retaining bolts finger tight.

2. Tighten the manifold bolts in a circular pattern, working from the center to the ends, to 25 ft.lb. in two stages.

3. Connect the exhaust pipe to the manifold.

4. The remainder of installation is the reverse of removal.

RIGHT SIDE

1. Disconnect the negative battery cable.
2. Remove the air cleaner assembly.
3. Remove the air flow sensor. Remove the engine heat shield.

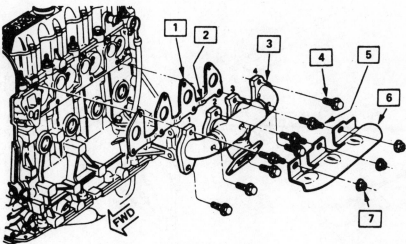

1. Gasket
2. Expansion joints
   face outward
3. Manifold asm.
4. Bolt & Lockwasher asm.
   27 N·m (20 lb. ft.)

5. Stud bolt & lockwasher
   asm. 27 N·m (20 lb.ft.)
6. Shield
7. Nut 22 N·m (16 lb. ft.)

Torque no. 2 & 3 manifold
runners prior to no. 1 & 4
runners

Exhaust manifold installation, 1.8L, 2.0L OHC (turbo)

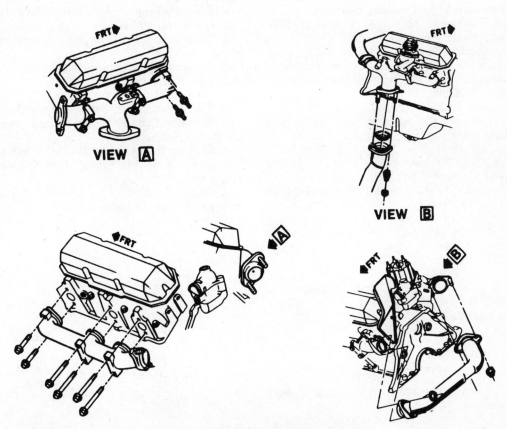

VIEW A

VIEW B

Exhaust manifold installation, 2.8L, 1984–86

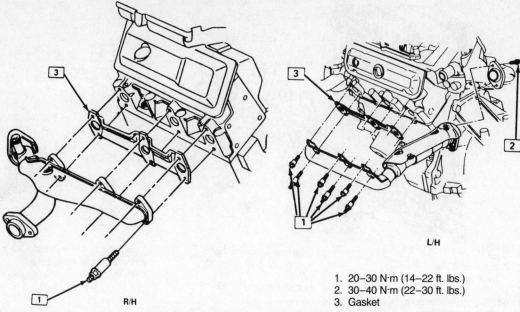

1. 20–30 N·m (14–22 ft. lbs.)
2. 30–40 N·m (22–30 ft. lbs.)
3. Gasket

Exhaust manifold installation, 2.8L, 1987

4. Disconnect the crossover pipe at the manifold.

5. Disconnect the accelerator and throttle valve cable at the throttle lever and the plenum. Move aside to gain working clearance.

6. Disconnect the power steering line at the power steering pump.

7. Remove the EGR valve assembly.

8. Raise the vehicle and support it safely.

9. Disconnect the exhaust pipe at the exhaust manifold.

10. Lower the vehicle.

11. Remove the manifold bolts and remove the exhaust manifold.

To install:

1. Clean the mating surfaces of the cylinder head and manifold. Position the manifold against the head and install the retaining bolts finger tight.

2. Tighten the bolts in a circular pattern, working from the center to the ends, to 25 ft.lb. in two stages.

3. Install the air supply system.

4. Install the spark plug wires.

5. Raise and support the car. Connect the exhaust pipe to the manifold and install new flange bolts.

Turbocharger

REMOVAL AND INSTALLATION

1. Raise the car and support it with jackstands.

2. Remove the lower fan retaining screw.

3. Disconnect the exhaust pipe.

4. Remove the rear air conditioning support bracket and loosen the remaining bolts.

5. Remove the turbo support bracket bolt to the engine.

6. Disconnect the oil drain hose at the turbo.

7. Lower the vehicle.

8. Disconnect the coolant recovery pipe and move to one side.

9. Disconnect the induction tube.

10. Disconnect the cooling fan.

11. Disconnect the oxygen sensor.

12. Disconnect the oil feed pipe at the union.

13. Disconnect the air intake duct and vacuum hose at the actuator.

14. Remove the exhaust manifold retaining nuts and remove the exhaust manifold and turbocharger.

15. Install the exhaust manifold and turbocharger. Torque the bolts to 16 ft.lb.

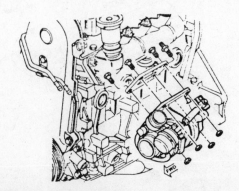

Turbocharger mounting

16. Install the exhaust manifold retaining nuts.

17. Connect the air intake duct and vacuum hose at the actuator.

18. Connect the oil feed pipe at the union.

19. Connect the oxygen sensor.

20. Connect the cooling fan.

21. Connect the induction tube.

22. Connect the coolant recovery pipe and move to one side.

23. Lower the vehicle.

24. Connect the oil drain hose at the turbo.

25. Install the turbo support bracket bolt to the engine.

26. Install the rear air conditioning support bracket.

27. Connect the exhaust pipe.

28. Install the lower fan retaining screw.

Air Conditioning Compressor

REMOVAL AND INSTALLATION

1. Discharge the air conditioning system.

NOTE: *Refer to Chapter 1 for discharging and charging of the air conditioning system and the precautions of handling refrigerant.*

2. Hoist the car and support safely. If necessary, on some models, remove the right air dam and splash shield.

3. Disconnect the electrical connection at the compressor clutch and remove the refrigerant line connection at the rear of the compressor. Cap all openings at once!

4. Remove the compressor attaching bolts and remove the compressor.

5. Installation is the reverse of removal.

Condenser

REMOVAL AND INSTALLATION

Cavalier

1982-86 4-CYLINDER ENGINE

1. Disconnect the negative battery cable.

2. Discharge the air conditioning system.

NOTE: *Refer to Chapter 1 for discharging and charging of the air conditioning system and the precautions of handling refrigerant.*

3. Remove the right upper baffle.

4. Remove the air cleaner duct from the radiator support.

5. Remove the condenser upper brackets and rubber mounts.

6. Raise the vehicle.

7. Remove the front valence.

8. Remove the upper and lower condenser lines.

9. Remove the condenser by lifting up and out of mounts, then lower between the radiator support and bumper.

1985-86 V6 ENGINE

1. Disconnect the negative battery cable.

2. Discharge the air conditioning system.

NOTE: *Refer to Chapter 1 for discharging and charging of the air conditioning system and the precautions of handling refrigerant.*

3. Drain the cooling system.

CAUTION: *When draining the coolant, keep in mind that cats and dogs are attracted by the ethylene glycol antifreeze, and are quite likely to drink any that is left in an uncovered container or in puddles on the ground. This will prove fatal in sufficient quantity. Always drain the coolant into a sealable container. Coolant should be reused unless it is contaminated or several years old.*

4. Remove the air cleaner cover.

5. Remove the hood latch assembly.

6. Disconnect the wires at the cooling fan.

7. Remove the upper radiator hose at the radiator.

8. Remove the fan and shroud.

9. Remove the lower hose at the water pump.

10. Disconnect the air conditioning lines at the condenser manifold.

11. Remove the upper radiator retainer.

12. Remove the radiator and condenser and separate the condenser from the radiator.

1987-88 ALL ENGINES

1. Disconnect the negative battery cable.

2. Discharge the air conditioning system.

NOTE: *Refer to Chapter 1 for discharging and charging of the air conditioning system and the precautions of handling refrigerant.*

3. Drain the cooling system.

CAUTION: *When draining the coolant, keep in mind that cats and dogs are attracted by the ethylene glycol antifreeze, and are quite likely to drink any that is left in an uncovered container or in puddles on the ground. This will prove fatal in sufficient quantity. Always drain the coolant into a sealable container. Coolant should be reused unless it is contaminated or several years old.*

4. Remove the air cleaner intake.

5. Remove the right upper baffle at the tie bar.

6. Remove the grille.

7. Remove the ambient temperature sensor.

8. Remove the lower front valence.

9. Disconnect the block connector at the condenser.

10. Remove the block connector bracket at the radiator.

11. Remove the condenser mounting bolts.

12. Remove the condenser by lowering between the radiator support and the bumper.

Firenza

1982-88

1. Disconnect the negative battery cable.
2. Discharge the air conditioning system.
NOTE: *Refer to Chapter 1 for discharging and charging of the air conditioning system and the precautions of handling refrigerant.*
3. Jack up the car, support safely and remove the front, left and right air dams and the lower fascia to fender bolts.
4. Disconnect the lower line at the condenser.
5. Lower the car and remove both core support to fascia filler panels, mounting brackets and hood latch.
6. Remove the headlamp bezels, upper fascia to fender bolts and pull the fascia forward.
7. Disconnect the upper condenser line. On later models disconnect the block fitting and discard the O-ring seals.
8. Remove the condenser brackets and condenser.

Cimarron

1982-86

1. Disconnect the negative battery cable.
2. Discharge the air conditioning system.
NOTE: *Refer to Chapter 1 for discharging and charging of the air conditioning system and the precautions of handling refrigerant.*
3. Jack up the car and support it safely.
4. Remove the front, left and right air dams and the lower fascia to fender bolts.
5. Disconnect the refrigerant line block fitting at the condenser.
6. Lower the car and remove both core support to fascia filler panels, mounting brackets and hood latch.
7. Remove the headlamp bezels, upper fascia to fender bolts and pull the fascia forward.
8. Remove the condenser brackets and condenser.

1987-88

1. Disconnect the negative battery cable.
2. Discharge the air conditioning system.
NOTE: *Refer to Chapter 1 for discharging and charging of the air conditioning system and the precautions of handling refrigerant.*
3. Remove the block fitting bolt and bracket to the radiator.
4. Jack up the car and support it safely.
5. Remove the lower valence panel.
6. Remove the condenser retaining bolts and the sensor connector.
7. Remove the bracket from the block fitting.
8. When installing, lubricate and install new O-rings.

J2000, 2000 and Sunbird

1982-86

1. Disconnect the negative battery cable.
2. Discharge the air conditioning system.
NOTE: *Refer to Chapter 1 for discharging and charging of the air conditioning system and the precautions of handling refrigerant.*
3. Jack up the car and support it safely.
4. Remove the front, left and right air dams and the lower fascia to fender bolts.
5. Disconnect the refrigerant line block fitting at the condenser.
6. Lower the car and remove both core support to fascia filler panels, mounting brackets and hood latch.
7. Remove the headlamp bezels, upper fascia to fender bolts and pull the fascia forward.
8. Remove the condenser brackets and condenser.

1987

1. Disconnect the negative battery cable.
2. Discharge the air conditioning system.
NOTE: *Refer to Chapter 1 for discharging and charging of the air conditioning system and the precautions of handling refrigerant.*
3. Drain the cooling system.
CAUTION: *When draining the coolant, keep in mind that cats and dogs are attracted by the ethylene glycol antifreeze, and are quite likely to drink any that is left in an uncovered container or in puddles on the ground. This will prove fatal in sufficient quantity. Always drain the coolant into a sealable container. Coolant should be reused unless it is contaminated or several years old.*
4. Disconnect the upper tie bar to header filler panels.
5. Remove the hood latch assembly.
6. Disconnect the overflow tube and air hoses at the left side.
7. Remove the overflow tube brackets.
8. Disconnect the cooling fan wires and remove the cooling fan.
9. Disconnect the upper and lower radiator hoses at the radiator.
10. Remove the radiator.
11. Disconnect the compressor discharge hose at the condenser.
12. Remove the side baffle lower and side screws and move rearward for access to the liquid hose.
13. Disconnect the liquid hose at the condenser.
14. Remove the radiator lower mounts.
15. Disconnect the electrical conduit at the front upper tie bar.
16. Remove the left headlamp bezel.
17. Disconnect the left outer headlamp connector.

18. Remove the left fender to front end panel retaining bolts and separate.

19. Remove the fog lamp sockets, if so equipped.

20. Disconnect the condenser upper mounting brackets.

21. Remove the condenser between the upper tie bar and the front end panel. Rotate 90° clockwise to remove.

Skyhawk

1982-86

1. Disconnect the negative battery cable.
2. Discharge the air conditioning system.
NOTE: *Refer to Chapter 1 for discharging and charging of the air conditioning system and the precautions of handling refrigerant.*
3. Jack up the car and support it safely.
4. Remove the front, left and right air dams and the lower fascia to fender bolts.
5. Disconnect the refrigerant line block fitting at the condenser.
6. Lower the car and remove both core support to fascia filler panels, mounting brackets and hood latch.
7. Remove the headlamp bezels, upper fascia to fender bolts and pull the fascia forward.
8. Remove the condenser brackets and condenser.

Radiator

REMOVAL AND INSTALLATION

1. Disconnect the negative battery cable.
2. Drain the cooling system.
CAUTION: *When draining the coolant, keep in mind that cats and dogs are attracted by the ethylene glycol antifreeze, and are quite likely to drink any that is left in an uncovered container or in puddles on the ground. This will prove fatal in sufficient quantity. Always drain the coolant into a sealable container. Coolant should be reused unless it is contaminated or several years old.*
3. Disconnect the electrical lead at the fan motor.
4. Remove the fan frame-to-radiator support attaching bolts and then remove the fan assembly.
5. Disconnect the upper and lower radiator hoses and the coolant recovery hose from the radiator.
6. Disconnect the transmission oil cooler lines from the radiator and wire them out of the way.
7. Remove the radiator-to-radiator support attaching bolts and clamps. Remove the radiator.
8. Place the radiator in the vehicle so that the bottom is located in the lower mounting pads. Tighten the attaching bolts and clamps.
9. Connect the transmission oil cooler lines and tighten the bolts to 20 ft.lb.
10. Installation of the remaining components is in the reverse order of removal.

Water Pump

REMOVAL AND INSTALLATION

OHV 4-Cylinder Engines

1. Disconnect the negative battery cable.
2. Drain the cooling system.
CAUTION: *When draining the coolant, keep in mind that cats and dogs are attracted by the ethylene glycol antifreeze, and are quite likely to drink any that is left in an uncovered container or in puddles on the ground. This will prove fatal in sufficient quantity. Always drain the coolant into a sealable container. Coolant should be reused unless it is contaminated or several years old.*
3. Remove all accessory drive belts or the serpentine belt.
4. Remove the alternator.
5. Unscrew the water pump pulley mounting bolts and then pull off the pulley.
6. Remove the mounting bolts and remove the water pump.
7. Place a ⅛″ wide bead of RTV sealant on the water pump sealing surface. While the sealer is still wet, install the pump and tighten the bolts to 13-18 ft.lb.
8. Installation of the remaining components is in the reverse order of removal.

OHC 4-Cylinder Engines

1. Remove the timing belt as described later.
2. Remove the timing belt rear protective covers.
3. Remove the hose from the pump.
4. Unbolt and remove the pump.
5. Installation is the reverse of removal. Torque the bolts to 19 ft.lb.

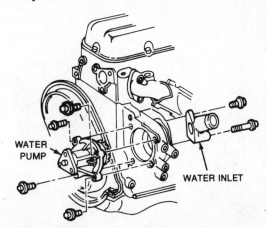

WATER PUMP

WATER INLET

Water pump installation, OHV four cyl. engine

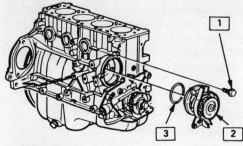

1. Bolt 28 N·m (21 lb. ft.)
2. Water pump
3. Seal ring

Water pump installation, OHC engines

6-173

1. Disconnect battery negative cable.
2. Drain cooling system.

CAUTION: *When draining the coolant, keep in mind that cats and dogs are attracted by the ethylene glycol antifreeze, and are quite likely to drink any that is left in an uncovered container or in puddles on the ground. This will prove fatal in sufficient quantity. Always drain the coolant into a sealable container. Coolant should be reused unless it is contaminated or several years old.*

3. Disconnect the serpentine belt at the water pump pulley.
4. On 1985-86 models, disconnect the wires at the air conditioning pressure cycling switch and remove the cycling switch.
5. Remove the water pump pulley.
6. Remove the pump retaining bolts and remove the water pump.
7. Clean the gasket surfaces.
8. Install the gasket and water pump.
9. Install the water pump pulley.
10. Install the air conditioning pressure cycling switch on 1985-86 models.
11. Install the serpentine belt.

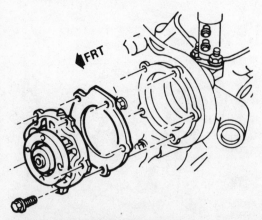

Water pump installation, V6 engines

12. Fill the cooling system.
13. Reconnect the battery, start the engine and check for leaks.

Cylinder Head

REMOVAL AND INSTALLATION

OHV 4-Cylinder Engines

NOTE: *The engine should be overnight cold before removing the cylinder head.*

1. Disconnect the negative battery cable.
2. Drain the cooling system into a clean container; the coolant can be reused if it is still good.

CAUTION: *When draining the coolant, keep in mind that cats and dogs are attracted by the ethylene glycol antifreeze, and are quite likely to drink any that is left in an uncovered container or in puddles on the ground. This will prove fatal in sufficient quantity. Always drain the coolant into a sealable container. Coolant should be reused unless it is contaminated or several years old.*

3. Remove the air cleaner. Raise and support the front of the vehicle.
4. Remove the exhaust shield. Disconnect the exhaust pipe.
5. Remove the heater hose from the intake manifold and then lower the car.
6. Unscrew the mounting bolts and remove the engine lift bracket (includes air management).
7. Remove the distributor. Disconnect the vacuum manifold at the alternator bracket.
8. Tag and disconnect the remaining vacuum lines at the intake manifold and thermostat.
9. Remove the air management pipe at the exhaust check valve.
10. Disconnect the accelerator linkage at the carburetor or T.B.I. unit and then remove the linkage bracket.
11. Tag and disconnect all necessary wires. Remove the upper radiator hose at the thermostat.
12. Remove the bolt attaching the dipstick tube and hot water bracket.
13. Remove the idler pulley. Remove the A.I.R. and power steering pump drive belts.
14. Remove the A.I.R. bracket-to-intake manifold bolt. If equipped with power steering, remove the air pump pulley, the A.I.R. through-bolt and the power steering adjusting bracket.
15. Loosen the A.I.R. mounting bracket lower bolt so that the bracket will rotate.
16. Disconnect and plug the fuel line at the carburetor.
17. Remove the alternator. Remove the alternator brace from the head and then remove the upper mounting bracket.

18. Remove the cylinder head cover. Remove the rocker arms and pushrods.

19. Remove the cylinder head bolts in the order given in the illustration. Remove the cylinder head with the carburetor or T.B.I. unit, intake and exhaust manifolds still attached.

20. To install, the gasket surfaces on both the head and the block must be clean of any foreign matter and free of any nicks or heavy scratches. Cylinder bolt threads in the block and the bolt must be clean.

21. Place a new cylinder head gasket in position over the dowel pins on the block. Carefully guide the cylinder head into position.

22. Coat the cylinder bolts with sealing compound and install them finger tight.

23. Using a torque wrench, gradually tighten the bolts in the sequence shown in the illustration to the proper specifications.

24. Install the rocker arms and pushrods.

25. Install the cylinder head cover.

26. Install the alternator brace on the head. Install the upper mounting bracket.

27. Install the alternator.

28. Connect the fuel line at the carburetor.

29. Install the A.I.R. bracket-to-intake manifold bolt. If equipped with power steering, install the air pump pulley, the A.I.R. throughbolt and the power steering adjusting bracket.

30. Install the idler pulley. Install the A.I.R. and power steering pump drive belts.

31. Install the bolt attaching the dipstick tube and hot water bracket.

32. Connect all wires.

33. Install the upper radiator hose at the thermostat.

34. Install the linkage bracket and connect the accelerator linkage at the carburetor or T.B.I.

35. Install the air management pipe at the exhaust check valve.

36. Connect the remaining vacuum lines at the intake manifold and thermostat.

37. Install the distributor.

38. Connect the vacuum manifold at the alternator bracket.

39. Install the engine lift bracket (includes air management).

40. Install the heater hose at the intake manifold.

41. Connect the exhaust pipe.

42. Install the exhaust shield.

43. Install the air cleaner.

44. Fill the cooling system.

45. Connect the negative battery cable.

OHC 4-Cylinder Engine

1. Remove air cleaner or induction tube (turbo engines).

2. Drain cooling system.

CAUTION: *When draining the coolant, keep in mind that cats and dogs are attracted by the ethylene glycol antifreeze, and are quite likely to drink any that is left in an uncovered container or in puddles on the ground. This will prove fatal in sufficient quantity. Always drain the coolant into a sealable container. Coolant should be reused unless it is contaminated or several years old.*

3. Remove generator and pivot bracket at camshaft carrier housing.

4. Disconnect power steering pump and bracket and lay to one side.

5. Disconnect ignition coil electrical connections and remove coil.

6. Disconnect spark plug wires and distributor cap and remove.

7. Remove throttle cable from bracket at intake manifold.

8. Disconnect throttle cable, downshift cable and T.V. cable from E.F.I. assembly.

9. Disconnect E.C.M. connectors from E.F.I. assembly.

10. Remove vacuum brake hose at filter.

11. Disconnect inlet and return fuel lines at flex joints.

CAUTION: *The fuel lines are pressurized (especially Turbo Engines). Removal may cause fuel spray resulting in personal injury. Do not remove before bleeding the pressure*

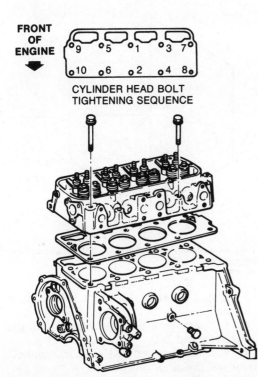

FRONT OF ENGINE

CYLINDER HEAD BOLT TIGHTENING SEQUENCE

Cylinder head bolt tightening sequence

from the fuel system. See Chapter 1 for the procedure.

12. Remove water pump bypass hose at intake manifold and water pump.

13. Disconnect ECM harness connectors at intake manifold.

14. Disconnect heater hose from intake manifold.

15. Disconnect exhaust pipe at exhaust manifold. On turbo engines, disconnect the exhaust manifold at the turbo connection.

16. Disconnect breather hose at camshaft carrier.

17. Remove upper radiator hose.

18. Disconnect engine electrical harness and wires from thermostat housing.

19. Remove timing cover.

20. Remove timing probe holder.

21. Loosen water pump retaining bolts and remove timing belt.

22. Loosen camshaft carrier and cylinder head attaching bolts a little at a time in sequence shown.

NOTE: *Camshaft carrier and cylinder head bolts should only be removed when engine is cold.*

23. Remove camshaft carrier assembly.

24. Remove cylinder head, intake manifold and exhaust manifold as an assembly.

25. Install cylinder head, intake manifold and exhaust manifold as an assembly. Torque the bolts in sequence to the values shown in the Torque Chart.

26. Install camshaft carrier assembly.

27. Tighten the camshaft carrier and cylinder head attaching bolts a little at a time in sequence shown.

28. Install timing belt.

29. Install timing probe holder.

30. Install timing cover.

31. Connect engine electrical harness and wires at thermostat housing.

32. Install upper radiator hose.

33. Connect breather hose at camshaft carrier.

34. Connect exhaust pipe at exhaust manifold. On turbo engines, connect the exhaust manifold at the turbo connection.

35. Connect heater hose at intake manifold.

36. Connect ECM harness connectors at intake manifold.

37. Install water pump bypass hose at intake manifold and water pump.

38. Connect inlet and return fuel lines at flex joints.

39. Install vacuum brake hose at filter.

40. Connect E.C.M. connectors at E.F.I. assembly.

41. Connect throttle cable, downshift cable and T.V. cable at E.F.I. assembly.

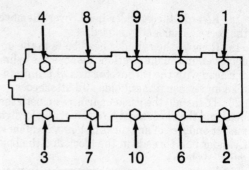

OHC 4-cyl. engine camshaft carrier and head bolt loosening sequence

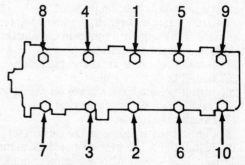

OHC 4-cyl. engine camshaft carrier and head bolt tightening sequence

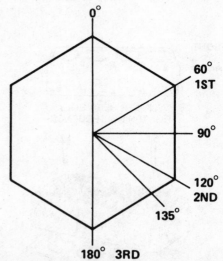

OHC 4-cyl. engine cylinder head bolt torque degree sequence

42. Install throttle cable at bracket on intake manifold.

43. Connect spark plug wires and install the distributor cap.

44. Connect ignition coil electrical connections and install coil.

45. Install power steering pump and bracket.

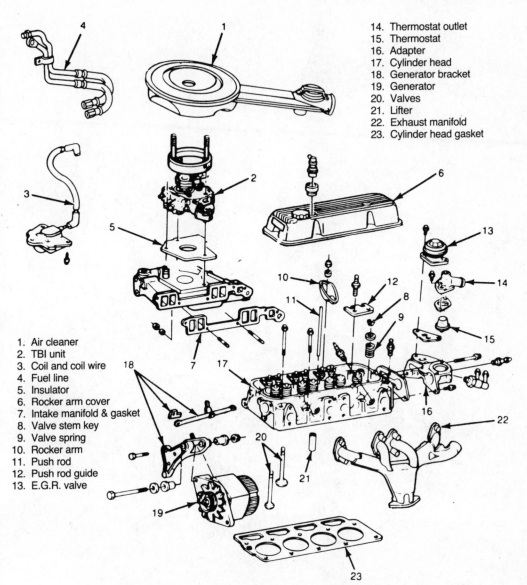

14. Thermostat outlet
15. Thermostat
16. Adapter
17. Cylinder head
18. Generator bracket
19. Generator
20. Valves
21. Lifter
22. Exhaust manifold
23. Cylinder head gasket

1. Air cleaner
2. TBI unit
3. Coil and coil wire
4. Fuel line
5. Insulator
6. Rocker arm cover
7. Intake manifold & gasket
8. Valve stem key
9. Valve spring
10. Rocker arm
11. Push rod
12. Push rod guide
13. E.G.R. valve

Disassembled view of cylinder head, 1982–86 OHV four cyl. engine

46. Install alternator and pivot bracket on camshaft carrier housing.

47. Fill cooling system.

48. Install air cleaner or induction tube (turbo engines).

6-173

LEFT SIDE

1. Raise and support the car.

2. Drain the coolant from the block and lower the car.

CAUTION: *When draining the coolant, keep in mind that cats and dogs are attracted by the ethylene glycol antifreeze, and are quite likely to drink any that is left in an uncovered* container *or in puddles on the ground. This will prove fatal in sufficient quantity. Always drain the coolant into a sealable container. Coolant should be reused unless it is contaminated or several years old.*

3. Remove the intake manifold.

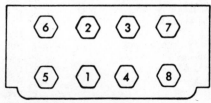

V6-173 head bolt torque sequence

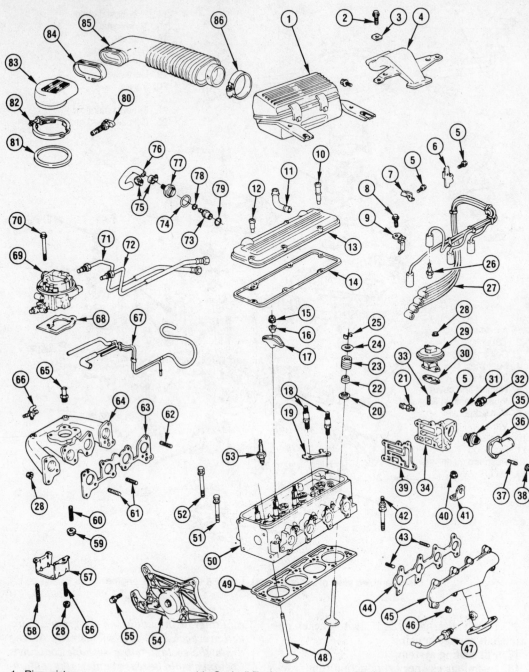

1. Ring, piston	14. Seal, oil fil tube	27. Nut, connecting rod
2. Piston, w/pin	15. Bolt, (m6 × 1 × 16)	28. Bearing, crankshaft
3. Bolt, connecting rod	16. Plug	29. Seal, crankshaft rear oil
4. Bearing, connecting rod	17. Cover, camshaft rear	30. Bolt, flywheel
5. Pin, cylinder head dowel	18. Bolt, (M6 × 1 × 13)	31. Retainer, flywheel
6. Plug, cylinder water jacket hole	19. Plug	32. Flywheel, crankshaft
7. Pin, clutch housing	20. Clamp	33. Bolt, clutch cover & pressure plate
8. Cord, engine block heater	21. Hose, coolant inlet	34. Washer, spring lock (5/16)
9. Heater, engine block	22. Bolt, (8 × 1.25 × 25)	35. Cover, plate, clutch pressure
10. Retainer	23. Inlet, coolant	36. Plate, clutch driven
11. Cap, oil fil & gage	24. Gasket, coolant inlet	37. Sealant
12. Bolt, (M8 × 1.25 × 12)	25. Plug, hex (1/4–13 × .56)	38. Bolt, crankshaft bearing cap
13. Tube, oil fil	26. Engine, partial	39. Cap, crankshaft bearing

Disassembled view of cylinder head, 1987 OHV four cyl. engine

4. Remove the exhaust crossover at the intake manifold.

5. Remove the alternator and AIR pump brackets.

6. Remove the dipstick tube.

7. Loosen the rocker arm bolts and remove the pushrods. Keep the pushrods in the same order as removed.

8. Remove the cylinder head bolts in stages and in the reverse order of the tightening sequence.

9. Remove the cylinder head. Do not pry on the head to loosen it.

10. Installation is the reverse of removal.

The words "This side Up" on the new cylinder head gasket should face upward. Coat the cylinder head bolts with sealer and on 1985-86 models torque to 70 ft.lb. in the sequence shown. On 1987-88 models, use a 12″ clicker torque wrench and torque to 33 ft.lb. then rotate the wrench an additional 90° (¼ turn) in the sequence shown. Make sure the pushrods seat in the lifter seats and adjust the valves.

RIGHT SIDE

1. Raise the car and drain the coolant from the block.

CAUTION: *When draining the coolant, keep in mind that cats and dogs are attracted by the ethylene glycol antifreeze, and are quite likely to drink any that is left in an uncovered container or in puddles on the ground. This will prove fatal in sufficient quantity. Always drain the coolant into a sealable container. Coolant should be reused unless it is contaminated or several years old.*

2. Disconnect the exhaust pipe and lower the car.

3. If equipped, remove the cruise control servo bracket.

4. Remove the air management valve and hose.

5. Remove the intake manifold.

6. Remove the exhaust crossover.

7. Loosen the rocker arm nuts and remove the pushrods. Keep the pushrods in the order in which they were removed.

8. Remove the cylinder head bolts in stages and in the reverse order of the tightening sequence.

9. Remove the cylinder head. Do not pry on the cylinder head to loosen it.

10. Installation is the reverse of removal.

The words "This side Up" on the new cylinder head gasket should face upward. Coat the cylinder head bolts with sealer and on 1985-86 models torque to 70 ft.lb. in the sequence shown. On 1987-88 models, use a 12″ clicker torque wrench and torque to 33 ft.lb. then rotate the wrench an additional 90° (¼ turn) in the sequence shown. Make sure the pushrods seat in the lifter seats and adjust the valves.

40. Sealer
41. Bolt, (M8 × 1.25 × 25)
42. Drive, oil pump
43. Shaft, distributor to oil pump
44. Retainer
45. Pump, w/screen
46. Bolt, oil pump & screen
47. Stud
48. Seal, oil pan rear
49. Pan, oil
50. Nut, (M6 × 1 × 6.5)
51. Bolt, (M6 × 1 × 13)
52. Gasket, oil pan drain screw
53. Screw, oil pan drain (M12 × 1.75)
54. Shim, starter motor
55. Motor, starter
56. Bolt, starter motor outboard (M10 × 46)
57. Bolt, starter motor inboard (M10 × 118)
58. Bolt, (M10 × 1.5 × 20)
59. Nut, (#10–24)
60. Washer, flat
61. Bracket, starter motor
62. Bolt, crankshaft pulley hub (M12 × 1.5 × 50)
63. Washer
64. Pulley, crankshaft
65. Seal, crankshaft front oil
66. Screw, hex (M6 × 1 × 30)
67. Cover, crankcase front end
68. Chain, camshaft timing
69. Sprocket, crankshaft

70. Key
71. Crankshaft, engine
72. Gasket, Water Pump
73. Pump, coolant
74. Pulley, water pump
75. Bolt, (M8 × 1.25 × 16)
76. Bolt, (M8 × 1.25 × 20)
77. Bolt, tensioner timing chain (M8 × 1.25 × 23)
78. Tensioner, timing chain
79. Bolt, hex (M12 × 1.75 × 35)
80. Washer, camshaft sprocket
81. Sprocket, camshaft
82. Screw, camshaft thrust plate
83. Plate, camshaft thrust
84. Pin, (M6 × 16)
85. Bearing, camshaft
86. Camshaft, engine
87. Switch, fuel pump
88. Valve, oil filter by-pass
89. Filter, oil (PF52)
90. Connector, oil filter adapter
91. Adapter, oil filter
92. Gasket, oil filter adapter
93. Lifter, hydraulic valve
94. Rod, push
95. Coil, w/module ignition
96. Bolt, (M8 × 1.25 × 18)
97. Stud, ignition coil
98. Sensor
99. Gasket

Disassembled view of cylinder head, 1982–86 OHV four cyl. engine

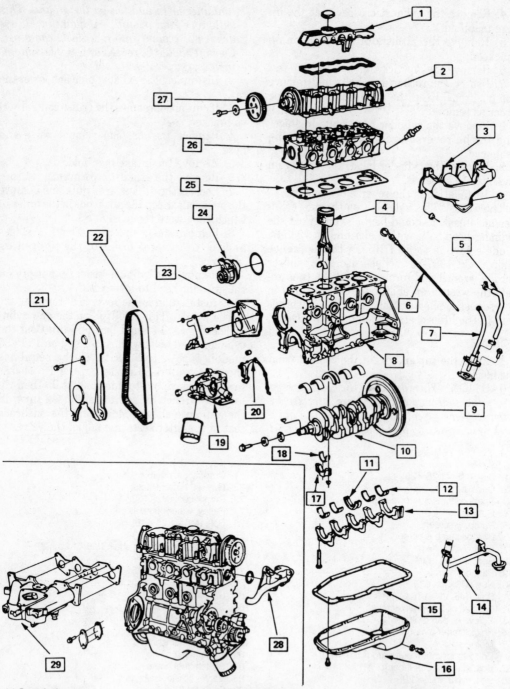

1. Camshaft cover
2. Camshaft carrier
3. Exhaust manifold (VIN code O)
4. Piston
5. Vent tube (VIN code O)
6. Oil dipstick
7. Tube
8. Cylinder block
9. Flywheel
10. Crankshaft
11. Main thrust bearing
12. Main bearings
13. Main bearing caps
14. Oil pump pickup tube
15. Gasket
16. Oil pan
17. Connecting rod cap
18. Connecting rod bearing
19. Oil pump
20. Gasket
21. Front cover
22. Timing belt
23. Rear cover
24. Water pump
25. Head gasket
26. Cylinder head
27. Camshaft sprocket
28. Water crossover
29. Intake manifold (VIN code O)

Disassembled view of the 1.8 L OHC engine assembly

RESURFACING

Cylinder Head Flatness

When the cylinder head is removed, check the flatness of the cylinder head gasket surfaces.

1. Place a straightedge across the gasket surface of the cylinder head. Using feeler gauges, determine the clearance at the center of the straightedge.

2. If warpage exceeds 0.003" (0.076mm) in a 6" (152mm) span, or 0.006" (0.152mm) over the total length, the cylinder head must be resurfaced.

3. If necessary to refinish the cylinder head gasket surface, do not plane or grind off more than 0.254mm (0.010") from the original gasket surface.

NOTE: *When milling the cylinder heads of V6 engines, the intake manifold mounting position is altered, and must be corrected by milling the manifold flange a proportionate amount. Consult an experienced machinist about this.*

CLEANING AND INSPECTION

1. Clean all carbon from the combustion chambers and valve ports.

2. Thoroughly clean the valve guides.

3. Clean all carbon and sludge from the pushrods, rocker arms and pushrod guides.

4. Clean the valve stems and heads on a buffing wheel.

5. Clean the carbon deposits from the head gasket mating surface.

6. Inspect the cylinder head for cracks in the exhaust ports, combustion chambers or external cracks to the water jacket.

7. Inspect the valves for burned heads, cracked faces or damaged stems.

8. Measure the valve stem clearance as follows:

    a. Clamp a dial indicator on ones side of the cylinder head. Locate the indicator so that movement of the valve stem from side to side (crosswise to the head) will cause direct movement of the indicator stem. The indicator stem must contact the side of the valve stem just above the guide.

    b. Drop the valve head 1.5mm off the valve seat.

    c. Move the stem of the valve from side to side, using light pressure to obtain a clearance reading. If the clearance exceeds specifications, it will be necessary to ream the valve guides for oversize valves. Service valves are available in standard, 0.089mm, 0.394mm and 0.775mm O.S. sizes.

NOTE: *If valve guides must be reamed this service is available at most machine shops.*

9. Check the valve spring tension with tool J-8056, spring tester. Springs should be compressed to the specified height and checked against the specifications chart. Springs should be replaced if not within (10 lbs. of the specified load (without dampers).

10. Inspect the rocker arms studs for wear or damage.

NOTE: *If a dial indicator is not available to you, take your cylinder head to a qualified machine shop for inspection*

Valves and Springs

REMOVAL AND INSTALLATION

1. Block the head on its side, or install a pair of head-holding brackets made especially for valve removal.

2. Use a socket slightly larger than the valve stem and keepers, place the socket over the valve stem and gently hit the socket with a plastic hammer to break loose any varnish buildup.

3. Remove the valve keepers, retainer, spring shield and valve spring using a valve spring compressor (the locking C-clamp type is the easiest kind to use).

4. Put the parts in a separate container numbered for the cylinder being worked on; do not mix them with other parts removed.

5. Remove and discard the valve stem oil seals. A new seal will be used at assembly time.

6. Remove the valves from the cylinder head and place them, in order, through numbered holes punched in a stiff piece of cardboard or wood valve holding stick.

NOTE: *The exhaust valve stems, on some engines, are equipped with small metal caps. Take care not to lose the caps. Make sure to reinstall them at assembly time. Replace any caps that are worn.*

7. Use an electric drill and rotary wire brush to clean the intake and exhaust valve ports, combustion chamber and valve seats. In some cases, the carbon will need to be chipped away. Use a blunt pointed drift for carbon chipping. Be careful around the valve seat areas.

8. Use a wire valve guide cleaning brush and safe solvent to clean the valve guides.

9. Clean the valves with a revolving wires brush. Heavy carbon deposits may be removed with the blunt drift.

NOTE: *When using a wire brush to clean carbon on the valve ports, valves etc., be sure that the deposits are actually removed, rather than burnished.*

10. Wash and clean all valve springs, keepers, retaining caps etc., in safe solvent.

11. Clean the head with a brush and some safe solvent and wipe dry.

12. Check the head for cracks. Cracks in the cylinder head usually start around an exhaust

1. Camshaft cover
2. Camshaft cover gasket
3. Camshaft carrier
4. Cylinder head
5. Cylinder head gasket
6. Front cover backing
7. Camshaft sprocket
8. Timing belt
9. Front cover
10. Water pump
11. Crankshaft gear
12. Oil pump gasket
13. Oil pump
14. Oil filter
15. Oil pan gasket
16. Oil scraper
17. Oil pan

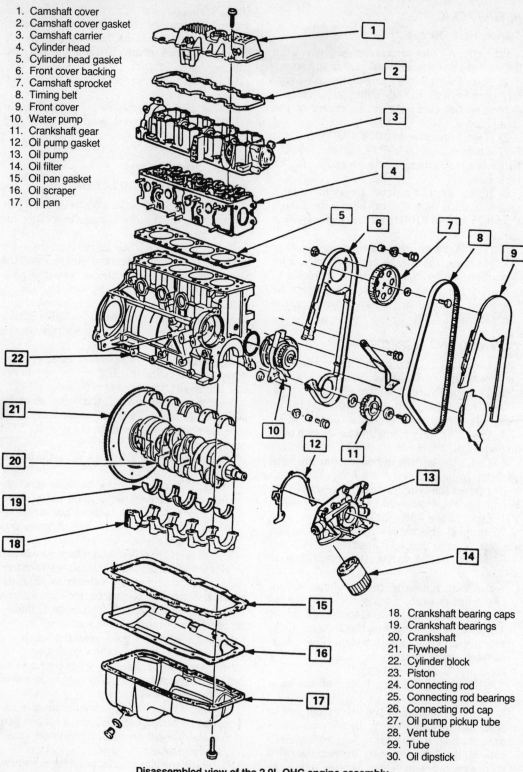

18. Crankshaft bearing caps
19. Crankshaft bearings
20. Crankshaft
21. Flywheel
22. Cylinder block
23. Piston
24. Connecting rod
25. Connecting rod bearings
26. Connecting rod cap
27. Oil pump pickup tube
28. Vent tube
29. Tube
30. Oil dipstick

Disassembled view of the 2.0L OHC engine assembly

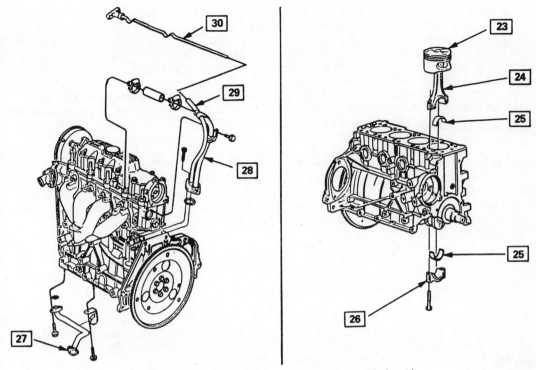

Disassembled view of the 2.0L OHC engine assembly (cont.)

valve seat because it is the hottest part of the combustion chamber. If a crack is suspected but cannot be detected visually have the area checked with dye penetrant or other method by the machine shop.

13. After all cylinder head parts are reasonably clean, check the valve stem-to-guide clear-

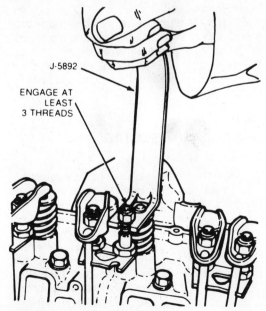

J-5892

ENGAGE AT LEAST 3 THREADS

Valve spring compressing tool

ance. If a dial indicator is not on hand, a visual inspection can give you a fairly good idea if the guide, valve stem or both are worn.

14. Insert the valve into the guide until slight away from the valve seat. Wiggle the valve sideways. A small amount of wobble is normal, excessive wobble means a worn guide or valve stem. If a dial indicator is on hand, mount the indicator so that the stem of the valve is at 90° to the valve stem, as close to the valve guide as possible. Move the valve off the seat, and measure the valve guide-to-stem clearance by rocking the stem back and forth to actuate the dial indicator. Measure the valve stem using a micrometer and compare to specifications to determine whether stem or guide wear is causing excessive clearance.

15. The valve guide, if worn, must be repaired before the valve seats can be resurfaced. Ford supplies valves with oversize stems to fit valve guides that are reamed to oversize for repair. The machine shop will be able to handle the guide reaming for you. In some cases, if the guide is not too badly worn, knurling may be all that is required.

16. Reface, or have the valves and valve seats refaced. The valve seats should be a true 45° angle. Remove only enough material to clean up any pits or grooves. Be sure the valve seat is not too wide or narrow. Use a 60° grinding wheel to remove material from the bottom of the seat for

raising and a 30° grinding wheel to remove material from the top of the seat to narrow.

17. After the valves are refaced by machine, hand lap them to the valve seat. Clean the grinding compound off and check the position of face-to-seat contact. Contact should be close to the center of the valve face. If contact is close to the top edge of the valve, narrow the seat; if too close to the bottom edge, raise the seat.

18. Valves should be refaced to a true angle of 44°. Remove only enough metal to clean up the valve face or to correct runout. If the edge of a valve head, after machining, is $\frac{1}{32}''$ (0.8mm) or less replace the valve. The tip of the valve stem should also be dressed on the valve grinding machine, however, do not remove more than 0.010″ (0.254mm).

19. After all valve and valve seats have been machined, check the remaining valve train parts (springs, retainers, keepers, etc.) for wear. Check the valve springs for straightness and tension.

20. Install the valves in the cylinder head and metal caps.

21. Install new valve stem oil seals.

22. Install the valve keepers, retainer, spring shield and valve spring using a valve spring compressor (the locking C-clamp type is the easiest kind to use).

23. Check the valve spring installed height, shim or replace as necessary.

CHECKING VALVE SPRINGS

Place the valve spring on a flat surface next to a carpenter's square. Measure the height of the spring, and rotate the spring against the edge of the square to measure distortion. If the spring height varies (by comparison) by more than $\frac{1}{16}''$ (1.6mm) or if the distortion exceeds $\frac{1}{16}''$ (1.6mm), replace the spring.

Have the valve springs tested for spring pressure at the installed and compressed (installed height minus valve lift) height using a valve spring tester. Springs should be within one pound, plus or minus each other. Replace springs as necessary.

VALVE SPRING INSTALLED HEIGHT

After installing the valve spring, measure the distance between the spring mounting pad and the lower edge of the spring retainer. Compare the measurement to specifications. If the installed height is incorrect, add shim washers between the spring mounting pad and the spring. Use only washers designed for valve springs, available at most parts houses.

Check the installed height of the valve springs, using a narrow thin scale. On the OHV 4-cylinder engine, measure from the top of the spring seat to the bottom of the cap.

On the V6 engine measure from the top of the spring damper "feet" to the bottom inside of the oil shedder for exhaust and from the top of the spring shim to the bottom of the valve cap for the intake. If this is found to exceed the specified height, install an additional valve spring seat shim approximately 0.7mm thick.

NOTE: *At no time should the valve spring be shimmed to give an installed height under the minimum specified.*

VALVE STEM OIL SEALS

When installing valve stem oil seals, ensure that a small amount of oil is able to pass the seal to lubricate the valve stems and guide walls, otherwise, excessive wear will occur.

On the V6 engine, check each valve stem oil seal by placing the valve stem leak detector tool J-23994, over the end of the valve stem and against the cap. Operate the vacuum pump and make sure no air leaks past the seal.

VALVE SEATS

If the valve seat is damaged or burnt and cannot be serviced by refacing, it may be possible to have the seat machined and an insert installed. Consult an automotive machine shop for their advice.

VALVE GUIDES

Worn valve guides can, in most cases, be reamed to accept a valve with an oversized stem. Valve guides that are not excessively worn or distorted may, in some cases, be knurled rather than reamed. However, if the valve stem is worn reaming for an oversized valve stem is the answer since a new valve would be required.

Knurling is a process in which metal is displaced and raised, thereby reducing clearance. Knurling also produces excellent oil control. The possibility of knurling instead of reaming the valve guides should be discussed with a machinist.

Oil Pan

REMOVAL AND INSTALLATION

OHV 4-Cylinder Engines

1. Disconnect the negative battery cable.

2. Drain the crankcase. Raise and support the front of the vehicle.

CAUTION: *The EPA warns that prolonged contact with used engine oil may cause a number of skin disorders, including cancer! You should make every effort to minimize your exposure to used engine oil. Protective gloves should be worn when changing the oil. Wash your hands and any other exposed skin areas as soon as possible after exposure to*

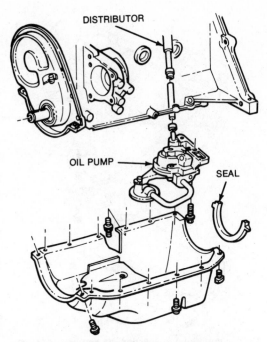

Oil pan installation, OHV four cyl.—1982–86

used engine oil. Soap and water, or waterless hand cleaner should be used.

3. Remove the air conditioning brace if so equipped.

4. Remove the exhaust shield and disconnect the exhaust pipe at the manifold.

5. Remove the starter motor and position it out of the way.

6. Remove the flywheel cover.

7. Remove the four right support bolts. Lower the support slightly to gain clearance for oil pan removal.

8. On cars equipped with automatic transmission, remove the oil filter and extension.

9. Remove the oil pan bolts and remove the oil pan.

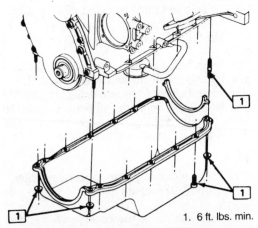

1. 6 ft. lbs. min.

Oil pan installation, OHV four cyl.—1987

NOTE: *Prior to oil pan installation, check that the sealing surfaces on the pan, cylinder block and front cover are clean and free of oil. If installing the old pan, be sure that all old RTV has been removed.*

7. Apply a ⅛″ wide bead of RTV sealant to the oil pan sealing surface. Use a new oil pan rear seal, apply a thin coat of RTV sealer on the ends down to the ears, install the pan against the case and install bolts. Tighten the bolts to 9-13 ft.lb.

8. On cars equipped with automatic transmission, replace the oil filter adapter seal and replace the oil filter adapter.

9. Install the remaining components is in the reverse order of removal.

OHC 4-Cylinder Engines

1. Raise and support the car safely.
2. Remove right front wheel.
3. Remove right hand splash shield.
4. Position jackstands at jacking points.
5. Drain engine oil.

CAUTION: *The EPA warns that prolonged contact with used engine oil may cause a number of skin disorders, including cancer! You should make every effort to minimize your exposure to used engine oil. Protective gloves should be worn when changing the oil. Wash your hands and any other exposed skin areas as soon as possible after exposure to used engine oil. Soap and water, or waterless hand cleaner should be used.*

6. If necessary on some models, remove lower air conditioning bracket strut rod attachment bolt and swing aside.

7. Remove exhaust pipe to manifold attachment bolts. On turbo models, disconnect the exhaust pipe at the wastegate.

8. Remove flywheel dust cover.

9. Remove oil pan bolts and remove the oil pan.

10. Clean the sealing surfaces, install the oil pan with a new gasket and apply RTV as shown

Oil pan installation, 1.8L OHC engine.

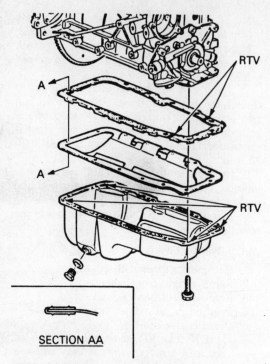

SECTION AA

Oil pan installation, 2.0L OHC engine

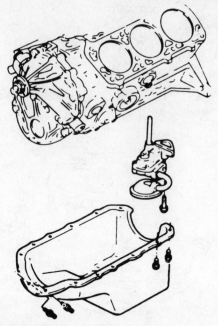

Oil pan and pump installation, V6 engine—1984–86

in the illustration. Install the bolts to the oil pan with Loctite® on the threads. Torque the pan bolts to 48 in.lb.

6-173

1. Disconnect the battery ground.
2. Raise and support the car on jackstands.
3. Drain the oil.

CAUTION: *The EPA warns that prolonged contact with used engine oil may cause a number of skin disorders, including cancer! You should make every effort to minimize your exposure to used engine oil. Protective gloves should be worn when changing the oil. Wash your hands and any other exposed skin areas as soon as possible after exposure to used engine oil. Soap and water, or waterless hand cleaner should be used.*

4. Remove the bellhousing cover.
5. Remove the starter.
6. Remove the oil pan bolts and remove the oil pan.
7. Intallation is the reverse of removal. On 1985-86 models, the pan is installed using RTV gasket material in place of a gasket. Make sure that the sealing surfaces are free of old RTV material. Use a 1/8″ bead of RTV material on the pan sealing flange. On 1987-88 models the pan is installed using a gasket. Torque the M8 × 1.25 × 14.0 pan bolts to 15-30 ft.lb. and the M6 × 1 × 16.0 pan bolts to 6-15 ft.lb.

Oil Pump

REMOVAL AND INSTALLATION

OHV 4-Cylinder Engines

1. Remove the engine oil pan.
2. Remove the pump attaching bolts and carefully lower the pump.
3. Install in reverse order. Installation torque is 26-38 ft.lb.

OHC 4-Cylinder Engines

1. Remove the crankshaft sprocket.
2. Remove the timing belt rear covers.
3. Disconnect the oil pressure switch wires.
4. Remove the oil pan.
5. Remove the oil filter.
6. Unbolt and remove the oil pick-up tube.
7. Unbolt and remove the oil pump.
8. On the 2.0L engine, pry out the front oil seal.
9. Installation is the reverse of removal. Use new gaskets in all instances. On the 2.0L engine, install a new front seal using tool J33083 Seal Installer. Torque the oil pump bolts to 60 in.lb. Torque the oil pan bolts to 48 in.lb., and the oil pick-up tube bolts to 60 in.lb.

6-173

1. Remove the oil pan as described earlier.
2. Unbolt and remove the oil pump and pickup.
3. Installation is the reverse of removal. Torque to 20-31 ft.lb.

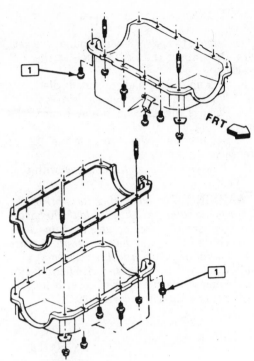

1. 20–30 N·m (15–22 ft. lbs.)
   All 8–12 N·m (6–9 ft. lbs.)

Oil pan installation, V6 engine—1987

Timing Belt/Chain Front Cover
REMOVAL AND INSTALLATION
OHV 4-Cylinder Engine

NOTE: *The following procedure requires the use of a special tool.*

1. Remove the engine drive belts (1982-86) or the serpentine belt and tensioner (1987-88).

2. Although not absolutely necessary, removal of the right front inner fender splash shield will facilitate access to the front cover.

3. Unscrew the center bolt from the crankshaft pulley and slide the pulley and hub from the crankshaft.

4. Remove the alternator lower bracket.

5. Remove the oil pan-to-front cover bolts.

6. Remove the front cover-to-block bolts and then remove the front cover. If the front cover is difficult to remove, use a plastic mallet.

7. The surfaces of the block and front cover must be clean and free of oil. on 1982-86 models, apply a ⅛" wide bead of RTV sealant to the cover. The sealant must be wet to the touch when the bolts are torqued down. On 1987-88 models a gasket is used. Torque the bolts to 6-9 ft.lb.

NOTE: *When applying RTV sealant to the front cover, be sure to keep it out of the bolt holes.*

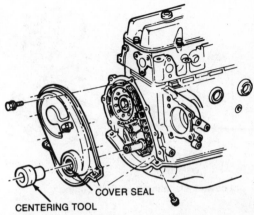

Front cover installation; a centering tool can aid in positioning

8. Position the front cover on the block using a centering tool (J-23042) and tighten the screws.

9. Installation of the remaining components is in the reverse order of removal.

1.8L OHC Engine

1. Remove the generator pivot bolts.

2. Remove the power steering belt.

3. Remove the two upper timing belt cover bolts.

4. Disconnect the canister purge hose.

5. Raise the car and support it safely.

6. Remove the right front wheel.

7. Remove the splash shield.

8. Remove the two lower timing cover bolts.

9. Lower the car and remove the timing belt cover.

10. Reverse the above procedure to install.

2.0L OHC Engine

1. Remove the belt, tensioner bolt and tensioner.

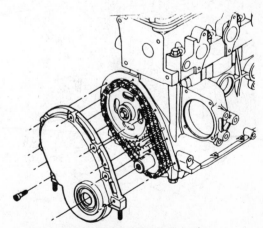

Front cover installation, 1987 OHV engine

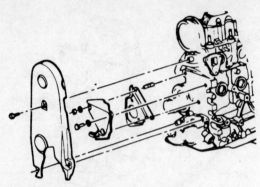

Front cover installation, 1.8L OHC engine

2. Unsnap the cover (upper first).

3. To install, snap the cover (lower first).

4. Install the tensioner and bolt then the serpentine belt.

6-173

1. Disconnect the battery ground cable.

2. Drain the cooling system.

CAUTION: *When draining the coolant, keep in mind that cats and dogs are attracted by the ethylene glycol antifreeze, and are quite likely to drink any that is left in an uncovered container or in puddles on the ground. This will prove fatal in sufficient quantity. Always drain the coolant into a sealable container. Coolant should be reused unless it is contaminated or several years old.*

3. Disconnect the MAP sensor and the EGR solenoid.

4. Remove the coolant recovery tank.

5. Remove the serpentine belt adjustment pulley.

6. Remove the alternator and disconnect the electrical wires.

7. Remove the power steering pump bracket.

8. Disconnect the heater pipe at the P/S bracket.

9. Jack up the car and support it safely.

10. Remove the inner splash shield.

11. Remove the air conditioning compressor belt.

12. Remove the flywheel cover at the transaxle.

13. Remove the harmonic balancer with tool J-23523-1.

WARNING: *The outer ring (weight) of the harmonic balancer is bonded to the hub with rubber. Breakage may occur if the balancer is hammered back onto the crankshaft. A press or special installation tool is necessary.*

14. Remove the serpentine belt idler pulley.

15. Remove the pan to front cover bolts.

16. Remove the lower cover bolts.

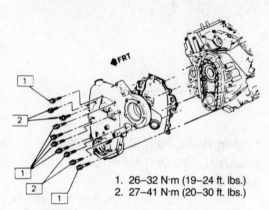

1. 26–32 N·m (19–24 ft. lbs.)
2. 27–41 N·m (20–30 ft. lbs.)

Front cover installation, V6 engine, 1984–86

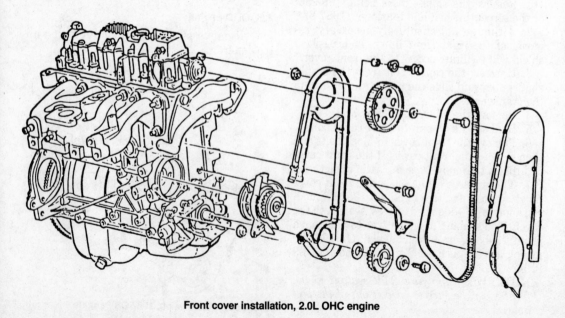

Front cover installation, 2.0L OHC engine

17. Lower the vehicle.
18. Disconnect the radiator hose at the water pump.
19. Remove the heater pipe at the goose neck.
20. Disconnect the bypass and overflow hoses.
21. Disconnect the canister purge hose.
22. Remove the upper front cover bolts and remove the front cover.

To install

1. Clean all the gasket mounting surfaces on the front cover and block and place a new gas-ket to the front cover sealing surface. Apply a continuous ⅛″ wide bead of sealer (1052357 or equivalent) to the oil pan sealing surface of the front cover.

2. Place the front cover on the engine and in-stall the upper front cover bolts.

3. Raise the vehicle and support it safely.

4. Install the lower cover bolts.

5. Install the oil pan to cover screws.

6. Install the serpentine belt idler pulley.

7. Install the harmonic balancer. (See the Harmonic Balancer Removal and Installation procedure.)

8. Install the flywheel cover on the transaxle.

9. Install the air conditioning compressor belt.

10. Install the inner splash shield.

11. Lower the vehicle and install the remain-der of the parts in the reverse order of removal.

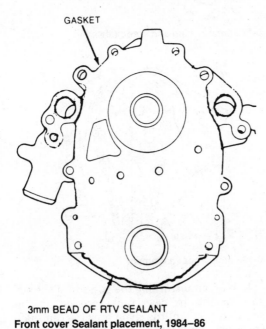

GASKET

3mm BEAD OF RTV SEALANT
Front cover Sealant placement, 1984–86

1. Front cover
2. Gasket
3. 18–36 N·m (13–26 ft. lbs.)
4. 27–48 N·m (20–35 ft. lbs.)
5. Sealer #1052080 or equivalent

Front cover installation, V6 engine, 1987

Timing Cover Oil Seal
REPLACEMENT
OHV 4-Cylinder and V6 Engines Only

The oil seal can be replaced with the cover ei-ther on or off the engine. If the cover is on the engine, remove the crankshaft pulley and hub first. Pry out the seal using a large screwdriver, being careful not to distort the seal mating sur-face. Install the new seal so that the open side or helical side is towards the engine. Press it into place with a seal driver made for the pur-pose. Chevrolet recommends a tool, J-35468 Seal Centering Tool. Install the hub if removed.

Timing Chain and Sprockets
REMOVAL AND INSTALLATION
OHV 4-Cylinder Engines

1. Remove the front cover as previously detailed.

2. Place the No. 1 piston at TDC of the com-pression stroke so that the marks on the cam-shaft and crankshaft sprockets are in align-ment (see illustration).

3. Loosen the timing chain tensioner nut as far as possible without actually removing it.

4. Remove the camshaft sprocket bolts and remove the sprocket and chain together. If the sprocket does not slide from the camshaft easi-ly, a light blow with a soft mallet at the lower edge of the sprocket will dislodge it.

5. Use a gear puller (J-2288-8-20) and re-move the crankshaft sprocket.

6. Press the crankshaft sprocket back onto the crankshaft.

7. Install the timing chain over the camshaft sprocket and then around the crankshaft sprocket. Make sure that the marks on the two

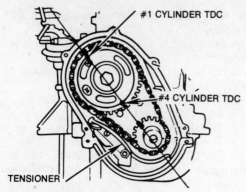

Timing mark alignment

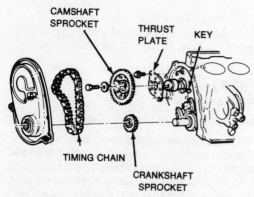

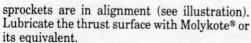

Front cover installation, 1982–86 OHC

6-173 timing chain and sprockets

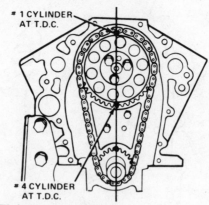

6-173 timing gear alignment

sprockets are in alignment (see illustration). Lubricate the thrust surface with Molykote® or its equivalent.

8. Align the dowel in the camshaft with the dowel hole in the sprocket and then install the sprocket onto the camshaft. Use the mounting bolts to draw the sprocket onto the camshaft and then tighten to 66-88 ft.lb.

9. Lubricate the timing chain with clean engine oil. Tighten the chain tensioner.

10. Installation of the remaining components is in the reverse order of removal.

6-173

1. Remove the front cover.

2. Place the No. 1 piston at TDC and the stamped timing marks on both sprockets are closest to one another and in line between the shaft centers (No. 4 firing position).

3. Take out the three bolts that hold the camshaft sprocket to the camshaft. This sprocket is a light press fit on the camshaft and will come off readily. If the sprocket does not come off easily, a light blow on the lower edge of the sprocket with a plastic mallet should dislodge the sprocket. The chain comes off with the camshaft sprocket. A gear puller will be required to remove the crankshaft sprocket.

4. Without disturbing the position of the engine, mount the new crank sprocket on the shaft, then mount the chain over the camshaft sprocket. Arrange the camshaft sprocket in such a way that the timing marks will line up between the shaft centers and the camshaft locating dowel will enter the dowel hole in the cam sprocket.

5. Place the cam sprocket, with its chain mounted over it, in position on the front of the camshaft and pull up with the three bolts that hold it to the camshaft.

6. Lubricate the timing chain with oil.

7. After the sprockets are in place, turn the engine two full revolutions to make certain that the timing marks are in correct alignment between the shaft centers.

Timing Belt

REMOVAL AND INSTALLATION

OHC Engine Only

NOTE: *The following procedure requires the use of a special tool.*

1. Remove the timing belt front cover.

2. Rotate the crankshaft so that the timing mark on the crankshaft pulley lines up with the

Belt Size	19mm
INITIAL ADJUSTMENT	
New Belt	22 lbs.
Used Belt	18 lbs.
CHECKING VALUE	
New Belt	18–27 lbs.
Used Belt	13–22 lbs.

1. Tension gauge J-26486
2. Adjustment tool J-33039

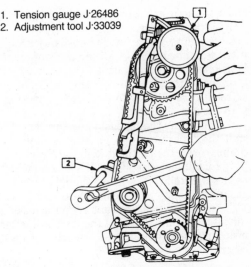

Timing belt tension adjustment on OHC 4-cyl. engines

10 degree BTDC mark on the indicator scale. The mark on the camshaft sprocket must line up with mark on the camshaft carrier.

3. Remove the crankshaft pulley as previously described.

4. Remove timing probe holder.

5. Loosen the water pump retaining bolts and rotate the water pump to loosen the timing belt.

6. Remove the timing belt.

7. Install timing belt on sprockets.

8. Install the crankshaft pulley.

9. Check if the mark on the camshaft sprocket lines up with mark on the camshaft carrier. The timing mark on the crankshaft pulley should line up at 10 degrees BTDC on the indicator scale.

WARNING: *Do not turn the camshaft. Use only the crankshaft nut to turn. Turning the nut on the camshaft directly can damage the camshaft bearings.*

10. Rotate the water pump clockwise using Tool J-33039 until all slack is removed from the belt. Slightly tighten the water pump retaining bolts.

11. Install Tool J-26486 between the water pump and camshaft sprockets so that the pointer is midway between the sprockets.

12. If the tension is incorrect, loosen the water pump and rotate it using Tool J-33039 until the proper tension is obtained.

13. Fully torque the water pump retaining bolts to 18 ft.lb. taking care not to further rotate the water pump.

14. Install timing probe holder. Torque nuts to 19 ft.lb.

15. Install the timing belt front cover and torque the attaching bolts to 5 ft.lb.

16. Install and adjust the generator and power steering belt. Refill the cooling system, if necessary.

Timing Belt Rear Cover
REMOVAL AND INSTALLATION
OHC Engines Only

1. Remove the timing belt from the crankshaft sprocket as previously outlined.

2. Remove the timing belt rear covers attaching bolts and the rear covers.

3. Install the rear covers and torque the attaching bolts to 19 ft.lb.

4. Install the timing belt and adjust as previously outlined.

Camshaft
REMOVAL AND INSTALLATION
OHV 4-Cylinder Engines

1. Remove the engine.

2. Remove the cylinder head cover, pivot the rocker arms to the sides, and remove the pushrods, keeping them in order. Remove the valve lifters, keeping them in order. There are special tools which make lifter removal easier.

3. Remove the front cover.

4. Remove the distributor.

5. Remove the fuel pump and its pushrod.

6. Remove the timing chain and sprocket as described earlier in this chapter.

7. Carefully pull the camshaft from the

Camshaft sprocket removal on OHC 4-cyl. engines

block, being sure that the camshaft lobes do not contact the bearings.

8. To install, lubricate the camshaft journals with clean engine oil. Lubricate the lobes with Molykote® or the equivalent.

9. Install the camshaft into the engine, being extremely careful not to contact the bearings with the cam lobes.

10. Install the timing chain and sprocket. Install the fuel pump and pushrod. Install the timing cover. Install the distributor.

11. Install the valve lifters. If a new camshaft has been installed, new lifters should be used to ensure durability of the cam lobes.

12. Install the pushrods and rocker arms and the intake manifold. Adjust the valve lash after installing the engine. Install the cylinder head cover.

OHC Engines

NOTE: *The following procedure requires the use of a special tool.*

1. Remove camshaft carrier cover.

2. Using valve train compressing Fixture J-33302, which holds the valves in place, compress valve springs and remove rocker arms.

3. Remove timing belt front cover.

4. Remove timing belt as previously outlined.

5. Remove camshaft sprocket as previously outlined.

6. Remove distributor.

7. Remove camshaft thrust plate from rear of camshaft carrier.

8. Slide camshaft rearward and remove it from the carrier.

9. Install a new camshaft carrier front oil seal using Tool J-33085.

10. Place camshaft in the carrier.

WARNING: *Take care not to damage the carrier front oil seal when installing the camshaft.*

11. Install camshaft thrust plate retaining bolts. Torque bolts to 70 in.lb.

12. Check camshaft end play, which should be within 0.016-0.064mm.

13. Install distributor.

14. Install camshaft sprocket as previously described.

15. Install timing belt as previously described.

16. Install timing belt front cover.

17. Using valve train compressing fixture J-33302, compress valve springs and replace rocker arms.

18. Install camshaft carrier cover as previously described.

6-173

Follow the 6-173 engine removal procedure then remove the camshaft as follows:

1. Remove intake manifold, valve lifters and timing chain cover as described in this section. If the car is equipped with air conditioning, unbolt the condenser and move it aside without disconnecting any lines.

2. Remove fuel pump and pump pushrod.

3. Remove camshaft sprocket bolts, sprocket and timing chain. A light blow to the lower edge of a tight sprocket should free it (use a plastic mallet).

4. Install two bolts in cam bolt holes and pull cam from block.

5. To install, reverse removal procedure aligning the sprocket timing marks.

Camshaft Carrier
REMOVAL AND INSTALLATION
OHC Engines Only

NOTE: *Whenever the camshaft carrier bolts are loosened, it is necessary to replace the cylinder head gasket. To do this, see the previous instructions under Cylinder Head Removal and Installation.*

1. Disconnect the positive crankcase ventilation hose from the camshaft carrier.

2. Remove the distributor.

3. Remove the camshaft sprocket as previously outlined.

4. Loosen the camshaft carrier and cylinder head attaching bolts a little at a time in the sequence shown in the Cylinder Head Removal and Installation procedure.

NOTE: *Camshaft carrier and cylinder head bolts should be loosened only when the engine is cold.*

5. Remove the camshaft carrier.

6. Remove the camshaft thrust plate from the rear of the camshaft carrier.

7. Slide the camshaft rearward and remove it from the carrier.

8. Remove the carrier front oil seal.

9. Install a new carrier front oil seal using Tool J-33085.

10. Place the camshaft in the carrier.

WARNING: *Take care not to damage the carrier front oil seal when installing the camshaft.*

11. Install the camshaft thrust plate and the retaining bolts. Torque the bolts to 70 in.lb.

12. Check camshaft end-play which should be within 0.04-0.16mm.

13. Clean the sealing surfaces on cylinder head and carrier. Apply a continuous 3mm bead of RTV sealer.

14. Install the camshaft carrier on the cylinder head.

15. Install the camshaft carrier and cylinder head attaching bolts.

16. Torque the bolts a little at a time in the

proper sequence, to 18 ft.lb. Then turn each bolt 60 degrees clockwise in the proper sequence for three times until a 180 degree rotation is obtained, or equivalent to ½ turn. After remainder of installation is completed (with the exception of brackets that attach to carrier), start engine and let it run until thermostat opens. Torque all bolts an additional 30° to 50° in the proper sequence.

17. Install the camshaft sprocket as outlined below.

18. Install the distributor.

19. Connect the positive crankcase ventilation hose to the camshaft carrier.

Camshaft Sprocket

REMOVAL AND INSTALLATION

OHC Engines Only

1. Remove the timing belt front cover.

2. Align the mark on camshaft sprocket with mark on camshaft carrier.

3. Remove timing probe holder.

4. Loosen the water pump retaining bolts and remove the timing belt from the camshaft sprocket.

5. Remove the camshaft carrier cover as previously outlined.

6. Hold the camshaft with a open-end wrench. For this purpose a hexagonal is provided in the camshaft. Remove the camshaft sprocket retaining bolt and washer and then the sprocket.

7. Install the camshaft sprocket and align marks on camshaft sprocket and camshaft carrier.

8. Hold the camshaft with a hexagonal open-end wrench. Install the sprocket washer and retaining bolt. Torque to 34 ft.lb.

9. Install the camshaft carrier cover as previously outlined.

10. Install the timing belt on sprockets and adjust as previously outlined.

11. Install timing probe holder. Torque nuts to 19 ft.lb.

12. Install timing belt front cover.

Crankshaft Sprocket

REMOVAL AND INSTALLATION

OHC Engines Only

1. Remove the timing belt from the crankshaft sprocket as previously described.

2. Remove the crankshaft sprocket to crankshaft attaching bolt and the thrust washer.

3. Remove the sprocket.

4. Position the sprocket over the key on end of crankshaft.

5. Install the thrust washer and the attach-

ing bolt. Torque to 115 ft.lb. (through 1983), 107 ft.lb. plus a 45° rotation (1984-88).

6. Install the timing belt and adjust as previously described.

Pistons and Connecting Rod

REMOVAL

1. Remove the engine assembly from the car, see Engine Removal and Installation.

2. Remove the intake manifold, cylinder head or heads.

3. Remove the oil pan.

4. Remove the oil pump assembly.

5. Stamp the cylinder number on the machined surfaces of the bolt bosses of the connecting rod and cap for identification when reinstalling. If the pistons are to be removed from the connecting rod, mark the cylinder number on the piston with a silver pencil or quick drying paint for proper cylinder identification and cap to rod location. The V6-173 is numbered 1-3-5 on the right bank, 2-4-6 on the left bank.

6. Examine the cylinder bore above the ring travel. If a ridge exists, remove the ridge with a ridge reamer before attempting to remove the piston and rod assembly.

7. Remove the rod bearing cap and bearing.

8. Install a guide hose over threads of rod bolts. This is to prevent damage to bearing journal and rod bolt threads.

9. Remove the rod and piston assembly through the top of the cylinder bore.

10. Remove any other rod and piston assemblies in the same manner.

CLEANING AND INSPECTION

Connecting Rods

Wash connecting rods in cleaning solvent and dry with compressed air. Check for twisted or bent rods and inspect for nicks or cracks. Replace connecting rods that are damaged.

Pistons

Clean varnish from piston skirts and pins with a cleaning solvent. DO NOT WIRE BRUSH ANY PART OF THE PISTON. Clean the ring grooves with a groove cleaner and make sure oil ring holes and slots are clean.

Inspect the piston for cracked ring lands, skirts or pin bosses, wavy or worn ring lands, scuffed or damaged skirts, eroded areas at top of the piston. Replace pistons that are damaged or show signs of excessive wear.

Inspect the grooves for nicks or burrs that might cause the rings to hang up.

Measure piston skirt (across center line of piston pin) and check piston clearance.

PISTON PIN REMOVAL AND INSTALLATION

Use care at all times when handling and servicing connecting rods and pistons. To prevent possible damage to these units, do not clamp rod or piston in vise since they may become distorted. Do not allow pistons to strike against one another, against hard objects or bench surfaces, since distortion of piston contour or nicks in the soft aluminum material may result.

1. Remove piston rings using suitable piston ring remover.

2. Install guide bushing of piston pin removing and installing tool.

3. Install piston and connecting rod assembly on support and place assembly in an arbor

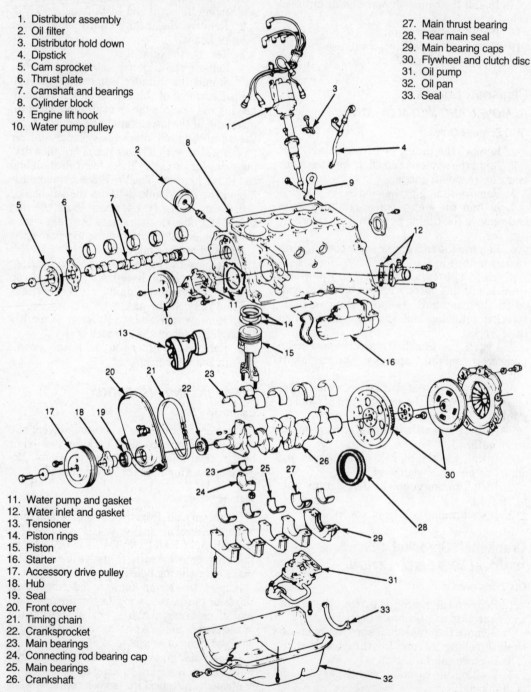

1. Distributor assembly
2. Oil filter
3. Distributor hold down
4. Dipstick
5. Cam sprocket
6. Thrust plate
7. Camshaft and bearings
8. Cylinder block
9. Engine lift hook
10. Water pump pulley
11. Water pump and gasket
12. Water inlet and gasket
13. Tensioner
14. Piston rings
15. Piston
16. Starter
17. Accessory drive pulley
18. Hub
19. Seal
20. Front cover
21. Timing chain
22. Cranksprocket
23. Main bearings
24. Connecting rod bearing cap
25. Main bearings
26. Crankshaft
27. Main thrust bearing
28. Rear main seal
29. Main bearing caps
30. Flywheel and clutch disc
31. Oil pump
32. Oil pan
33. Seal

Cylinder block assembly, OHV engine—1982–86

press. Press pin out of connecting rod, using the appropriate piston pin tool.

MEASURING THE OLD PISTONS

Check used piston to cylinder bore clearance as follows:

1. Measure the cylinder bore diameter with a telescope gauge.

2. Measure the piston diameter. When measuring piston for size or taper, measurement must be made with the piston pin removed.

3. Subtract piston diameter from cylinder bore diameter to determine piston-to-bore clearance.

4. Compare piston-to-bore clearance obtained with those clearances recommended. Determine if piston-to-bore clearance is in acceptable range.

5. When measuring taper, the largest reading must be at the bottom of the skirt.

SELECTING NEW PISTONS

1. If the used piston is not acceptable, check service piston sizes and determine if a new piston can be selected. Service pistons are available in standard, high limit and standard 0.254mm oversize.

2. If the cylinder bore must be reconditioned, measure the new piston diameter, then hone cylinder bore to obtain preferable clearance.

3. Select new piston and mark piston to identify the cylinder for which it was fitted. On some cars oversize pistons may be found. These pistons will be 0.254mm oversize.

CYLINDER HONING

1. When cylinders are being honed, follow the manufacturer's recommendations for the use of the hone.

2. Occasionally during the honing operation, the cylinder bore should be thoroughly cleaned and the selected piston checked for correct fit.

3. When finish honing a cylinder bore, the hone should be moved up and down at a sufficient speed to obtain very fine uniform surface finish marks in a cross hatch pattern of approximately 45 to 65 degrees included angle. The finish marks should be clean but not sharp, free from imbedded particles and torn or folded metal.

4. Permanently mark the piston for the cylinder to which it has been fitted and proceed to hone the remaining cylinders.

WARNING: *Handle pistons with care. Do not attempt to force pistons through cylinders until the cylinders have been honed to correct size. Pistons can be distorted through careless handling.*

5. Thoroughly clean the bores with hot water and detergent. Scrub well with a stiff bristle brush and rinse thoroughly with hot water. It is extremely essential that a good cleaning operation be performed. If any of the abrasive material is allowed to remain in the cylinder bores, it will rapidly wear the new rings and cylinder bores. The bores should be swabbed several times with light engine oil and a clean cloth and then wiped with a clean dry cloth. CYLINDERS SHOULD NOT BE CLEANED WITH KEROSENE OR GASOLINE. Clean the remainder of the cylinder block to remove the excess material spread during the honing operation.

CHECKING CYLINDER BORE

Cylinder bore size can be measured with inside micrometers or a cylinder gauge. The most wear will occur at the top of the ring travel.

Reconditioned cylinder bores should be held to not more than 0.025mm out-of-round and 0.025mm taper.

If the cylinder bores are smooth, the cylinder walls should not be deglazed. If the cylinder walls are scored, the walls may have to be honed before installing new rings. It is important that reconditioned cylinder bores be thoroughly washed with a soap and water solution to remove all traces of abrasive material to eliminate premature wear.

Piston Rings

The pistons have three rings (two compression rings and one oil ring). The oil ring consists of two rails and an expander. Pistons do not have oil drain holes behind the rings.

RING TOLERANCES

When installing new rings, ring gap and side clearance should be check as as follows:

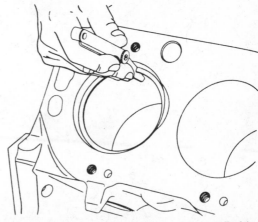

Check the ring end gap with the ring installed in its cylinder

PISTON RING AND RAIL GAP

Each ring and rail gap must be measured with the ring or rail positioned squarely and at the bottom of the ring-travel area of the bore.

SIDE CLEARANCE

Each ring must be checked for side clearance in its respective piston groove by inserting a feeler gauge between the ring and its upper

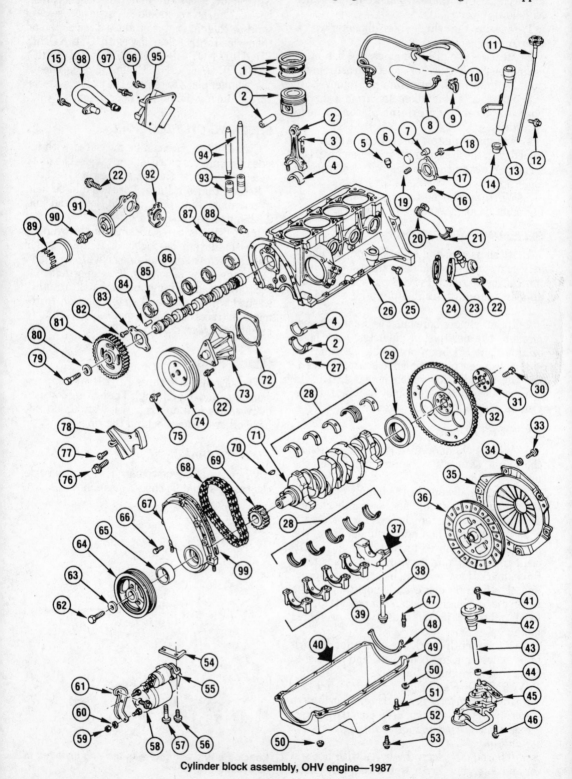

Cylinder block assembly, OHV engine—1987

land. The piston grooves must be cleaned before checking ring for side clearance. See PISTON RING CLEARANCE specifications at the end of this section for ring side clearance specifications. To check oil ring side clearance, the oil rings must be installed on the piston.

RING INSTALLATION

For service ring specifications and detailed installation productions, refer to the instructions furnished with the parts package.

CONNECTING ROD BEARINGS

Removal, Inspection, Installation

If you have already removed the connecting rod and piston assemblies from the engine, follow only steps 3-7 of the following procedure.

The connecting rod bearings are designed to have a slight projection above the rod and cap faces to insure a positive contact. The bearings can be replaced with removing the rod and piston assembly from the engine.

1. Ring, piston
2. Piston, w/pin
3. Bolt, connecting rod
4. Bearing, connecting rod
5. Pin, cylinder head dowel
6. Plug, cylinder water jacket hole
7. Pin, clutch housing
8. Cord, engine block heater
9. Heater, engine block
10. Retainer
11. Cap, oil fil & gage
12. Bolt, (M8 × 1.25 × 12)
13. Tube, oil fil
14. Seal, oil fil tube
15. Bolt, (m6 × 1 × 16)
16. Plug
17. Cover, camshaft rear
18. Bolt, (M6 × 1 × 13)
19. Plug
20. Clamp
21. Hose, coolant inlet
22. Bolt, (8 × 1.25 × 25)
23. Inlet, coolant
24. Gasket, coolant inlet
25. Plug, hex (¼–18 × .56)
26. Engine, partial
27. Nut, connecting rod
28. Bearing, crankshaft
29. Seal, crankshaft rear oil
30. Bolt, flywheel
31. Retainer, flywheel
32. Flywheel, crankshaft
33. Bolt, clutch cover & pressure plate
34. Washer, spring lock (⁵⁄₁₆)
35. Cover, plate, clutch pressure
36. Plate, clutch driven
37. Sealant
38. Bolt, crankshaft bearing cap
39. Cap, crankshaft bearing
40. Sealer
41. Bolt, (M8 × 1.25 × 25)
42. Drive, oil pump
43. Shaft, distributor to oil pump
44. Retainer
45. Pump, w/screen
46. Bolt, oil pump & screen
47. Stud
48. Seal, oil pan rear
49. Pan, oil
50. Nut, (M6 × 1 × 6.5)
51. Bolt, (M6 × 1 × 13)
52. Gasket, oil pan drain screw
53. Screw, oil pan drain (M12 × 1.75)
54. Shim, starter motor
55. Motor, starter
56. Bolt, starter motor outboard (M10 × 46)
57. Bolt, starter motor inboard (M10 × 118)
58. Bolt, (M10 × 1.5 × 20)
59. Nut, (#10–24)
60. Washer, flat
61. Bracket, starter motor
62. Bolt, crankshaft pulley hub (M12 × 1.5 × 50)
63. Washer
64. Pulley, crankshaft
65. Seal, crankshaft front oil
66. Screw, hex (M6 × 1 × 30)
67. Cover, crankcase front end
68. Chain, camshaft timing
69. Sprocket, crankshaft
70. Key
71. Crankshaft, engine
72. Gasket, Water Pump
73. Pump, coolant
74. Pulley, water pump
75. Bolt, (M8 × 1.25 × 16)
76. Bolt, (M8 × 1.25 × 20)
77. Bolt, tensioner timing chain (M8 × 1.25 × 23)
78. Tensioner, timing chain
79. Bolt, hex (M12 × 1.75 × 35)
80. Washer, camshaft sprocket
81. Sprocket, camshaft
82. Screw, camshaft thrust plate
83. Plate, camshaft thrust
84. Pin, (M6 × 16)
85. Bearing, camshaft
86. Camshaft, engine
87. Switch, fuel pump
88. Valve, oil filter by-pass
89. Filter, oil (PF52)
90. Connector, oil filter adapter
91. Adapter, oil filter
92. Gasket, oil filter adapter
93. Lifter, hydraulic valve
94. Rod, push
95. Coil, w/module ignition
96. Bolt, (M8 × 1.25 × 18)
97. Stud, ignition coil
98. Sensor
99. Gasket

Cylinder block assembly, OHV engine—1987

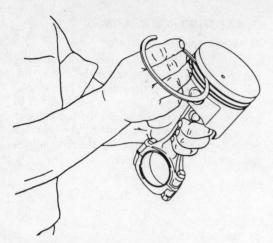

Checking the ring side clearance

1. Remove the oil pan, see Oil Pan. It may be necessary to remove the oil pump to provide access to rear connecting rod bearings.

2. With the connecting rod journal at the bottom, stamp the cylinder number on the machined surfaces of connecting rod and cap for identification when reinstalling, then remove caps.

3. Inspect journals for roughness and wear. Slight roughness may be removed with a fine grit polishing cloth saturated with engine oil. Burrs may be removed with a fine oil stone by moving the stone on the journal circumference.

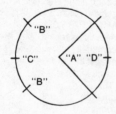

ENGINE LEFT   ENGINE FRONT ENGINE RIGHT

"A" OIL RING SPACER GAP
(Tang in Hole or Slot within Arc)

"B" OIL RING RAIL GAPS

"C" 2ND COMPRESSION RING GAP

"D" TOP COMPRESSION RING GAP

Ring gap locations

WARNING: *Do not move the stone back and forth across the journal. If the journals are scored or ridged, the crankshaft must be replaced.*

4. The connecting rod journals should be checked for out-of-round and correct size with a micrometer.

NOTE: *Crankshaft rod journals will normally be standard size. If any undersized crankshafts are used, all will be 0.254mm undersize and 0.254mm will be stamped on the number 4 counterweight.*

If plastic gauging material is to be used:

5. Clean oil from the journal bearing cap, connecting rod and outer and inner surface of the bearing inserts. Position insert so that tang is properly aligned with notch in rod and cap.

6. Place a piece of plastic gauging material in the center of lower bearing shell.

7. Remove bearing cap and determine bearing clearances by comparing the width of the flattened plastic gauging material at its widest point with the graduation on the container. The number within the graduation on the envelope indicates the clearance in thousandths of an inch or millimeters. If this clearance is excessive, replace the bearing and recheck clearance with plastic gauging material. Lubricate bearing with engine oil before installation. Repeat Steps 2 through 7 on remaining connecting rod bearings. All rods must be connected to their journals when rotating the crankshaft to prevent engine damage.

PISTON AND CONNECTING ROD
Assembly And Installation

1. Install connecting rod bolt guide hose over rod bolt threads.

2. Apply engine oil to the rings and piston, then install piston ring compressing tool on the piston.

3. Install the assembly in its respective cylinder bore (arrow of the piston towards the front of the engine).

NOTE: *On the OHC engine, code M, the piston must be marked during disassembly.*

4. Lubricate the crankshaft journal with engine oil and install connecting rod bearing and cap, with bearing index tang in rod and cap on same side. On the OHC engines the identification numbers must be on the same side and facing the water pump.

NOTE: *When more than one rod and piston assembly is being installed, the connecting rod cap attaching nuts should only be tightened enough to keep each rod in position until all have been installed. This will aid installation of remaining piston assemblies.*

5. Torque rod bolt nuts to specification.

6. Install all other removed parts.

7. Install the engine in the car, see Engine Removal and Installation.

Crankshaft

REMOVAL

1. Remove the engine assembly as previously outlined.

2. Remove the engine front cover.

3. Remove the timing chain and sprockets.

4. Remove the oil pan.

5. Remove the oil pump.

6. Stamp the cylinder number on the machined surfaces of the bolt bosses of the connecting rods and caps for identification when reinstalling. If the pistons are to be removed from the connecting rod, mark cylinder number on piston with a silver pencil or quick-drying paint for proper cylinder identification and cap to rod location.

7. Remove the connecting rod caps and install thread protectors.

8. Mark the main bearing caps so that they can be installed in their original positions.

9. Remove all the main bearing caps.

10. Note position of keyway in crankshaft so it can be installed in the same position.

11. Lift crankshaft out of block. Rods will pivot to the center of the engine when the crankshaft is removed.

12. Remove both halves of the rear main oil seal.

INSTALLATION

1. Measure the crankshaft journals with a micrometer to determine the correct size rod and main bearings to be used. Whenever a new or reconditioned crankshaft is installed, new connecting rod bearings and main bearings should be installed. See Main Bearings and Rod Bearings.

2. Clean all oil passages in the block (and crankshaft if it is being reused).

NOTE: *A new rear main seal should be installed anytime the crankshaft is removed or replaced.*

3. Install sufficient oil pan bolts in the block to align with the connecting rod bolts. Use rubber bands between the bolts to position the connecting rods as required. Connecting rod position can be adjusted by increasing the tension on the rubber bands with additional turns around the pan bolts or thread protectors.

4. Position the upper half of main bearings in the block and lubricate with engine oil.

5. Position crankshaft keyway in the same position as removed and lower into block. The connecting rods will follow the crank pins into the correct position as the crankshaft is lowered.

6. Lubricate the thrust fllanges with 1050169 Lubricant or equivalent. Install caps with lower half of bearings lubricated with engine oil. Lubricate cap bolts with engine oil and install, but do not tighten.

7. With a block of wood, bump shaft in each direction to align thrust flanges of main bearing. After bumping shaft in each direction, wedge the shaft to the front and hold it while torquing the thrust bearing cap bolts.

WARNING: *In order to prevent the possibility of cylinder block and/or main bearing cap damage, the main bearing caps are to be tapped into their cylinder block cavity using a brass or leather mallet before attaching bolts are installed. Do not use attaching bolts to pull main bearing caps into their seats. Failure to observe this information may damage the cylinder block or a bearing cap.*

8. Torque all main bearing caps to specification.

9. Remove the connecting rod bolt thread protectors and lubricate the connecting rod bearings with engine oil.

10. Install the connecting rod bearing caps in their original position. Torque the nuts to specification.

11. Complete the installation by reversing the removal steps.

Main Bearings

CHECKING BEARING CLEARANCE

1. Remove bearing cap and wipe oil from crankshaft journal and outer and inner surfaces of bearing shell.

2. Place a piece of plastic gauging material in the center of bearing.

3. Use a floor jack or other means to hold crankshaft against upper bearing shell. This is necessary to obtain accurate clearance readings when using plastic gauging material.

4. Reinstall bearing cap and bearing. Place engine oil on cap bolts and install Torque bolts to specification.

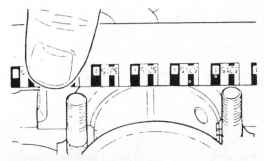

Measuring bearing clearance

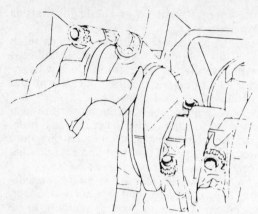

Measuring crankshaft end play

Measuring connecting rod side clearance (Double rod journal)

5. Remove bearing cap and determine bearing clearance by comparing the width of the flattened plastic gauging material at its widest point with graduations on the gauging material container. The number within the graduation on the envelope indicates the clearance in millimeters or thousandths of an inch. If the clearance is greater than allowed, REPLACE BOTH BEARING SHELLS AS A SET. Recheck clearance after replacing shells. Refer to Main Bearing Replacement.

REPLACEMENT

Main bearing clearances must be corrected by the use of selective upper and lower shells. UNDER NO CIRCUMSTANCES should the use of shims behind the shells to compensate for wear be attempted. To install main bearing shells, proceed as follows:

1. Remove the oil pan as outlined elsewhere

Measuring connecting rod side clearance (single rod journal)

in this Chapter. On some models, the oil pump may also have to be removed.

2. Loosen all main bearing caps.

3. Remove bearing cap and remove lower shell.

4. Insert a flattened cotter pin or roll out pin in the oil passage hole in the crankshaft, then rotate the crankshaft in the direction opposite to cranking rotation. The pin will contact the upper shell and roll it out.

5. The main bearing journals should be checked for roughness and wear. Slight roughness may be removed with a fine grit polishing cloth saturated with engine oil. Burrs may be removed with a fine oil stone. If the journals are scored or ridged, the crankshaft must be replaced.

The journals can be measured for out-of-round with the crankshaft installed by using a crankshaft caliper and inside micrometer or a main bearing micrometer. The upper bearing shell must be removed when measuring the crankshaft journals. Maximum out-of-round of the crankshaft journals must not exceed 0.037mm.

6. Clean crankshaft journals and bearing caps thoroughly before installing new main bearings.

7. Apply special lubricant, No. 1050169 or equivalent, to the thrust flanges of bearing shells.

8. Place new upper shell on crankshaft journal with locating tang in correct position and rotate shaft to turn it into place using cotter pin or roll out pin as during removal.

9. Place new bearing shell in bearing cap.

10. Install a new oil seal in the rear main bearing cap and block.

11. Lubricate the removed or replaced main bearings with engine oil. Lubricate the thrust surface with lubricant 1050169 or equivalent.

12. Lubricate the main bearing cap bolts with engine oil.

WARNING: *In order to prevent the possibility of cylinder block and/or main bearing cap damage, the main bearing caps are to be tapped into their cylinder block cavity using a brass or leather mallet before attaching bolts are installed. Do not use attaching bolts to pull main bearing caps into their seats. Failure to observe this information may damage the cylinder block or a bearing cap.*

13. Torque the main bearing cap bolts to 107 ft.lb.

Flywheel/Flex Plate and Ring Gear

NOTE: *Flex plate is the term for a flywheel mated with an automatic transmission.*

REMOVAL AND INSTALLATION

All Engines

NOTE: *The ring gear is replaceable only on engines mated with a manual transmission. Engines with automatic transmissions have ring gears which are welded to the flex plate.*

1. Remove the transmission and transfer case.

2. Remove the clutch, if equipped, or torque converter from the flywheel. The flywheel bolts should be loosened a little at a time in a cross pattern to avoid warping the flywheel. On cars with manual transmissions, replace the pilot bearing in the end of the crankshaft if removing the flywheel.

3. The flywheel should be checked for cracks and glazing. It can be resurfaced by a machine shop.

4. If the ring gear is to be replaced, drill a hole in the gear between two teeth, being careful not to contact the flywheel surface. Using a cold chisel at this point, crack the ring gear and remove it.

5. Polish the inner surface of the new ring gear and heat it in an oven to about 600°F (316°C). Quickly place the ring gear on the flywheel and tap it into place, making sure that it is fully seated.

WARNING: *Never heat the ring gear past 800°F (426°C), or the tempering will be destroyed.*

6. Position the flywheel on the end of the crankshaft. Torque the bolts a little at a time, in a cross pattern, to the torque figure shown in the Torque Specifications Chart.

7. Install the clutch or torque converter.

8. Install the transmission and transfer case.

Rear Main Oil Seal

REMOVAL AND INSTALLATION

OHV 4-Cylinder Engines

1982-84 (TWO PIECE SEAL)

1. Remove the oil pan and pump.

2. Remove the rear main bearing cap.

3. Gently pack the upper seal into the groove approximately ¼" on each side.

4. Measure the amount the seal was driven in on one side and add $\frac{1}{16}$". Cut this length from the old lower cap seal. Be sure to get a sharp cut. Repeat for the other side.

5. Place the piece of cut seal into the groove and pack the seal into the block. Do this for each side.

6. Install a piece of Plastigage® or the equivalent on the bearing journal. Install the rear cap and tighten to 75 ft.lb. Remove the cap and check the gauge for bearing clearance. If out of specification, the ends of the seal may be frayed or not flush, preventing the cap from proper seating. Correct as required.

7. Clean the journal, and apply a thin film of sealer to the mating surfaces of the cap and tighten to 70 ft.lb. Install the pan and pump.

NOTE: *Some 1982 1.8L engines (Code G), experience a rear main seal oil leak. To cor-*

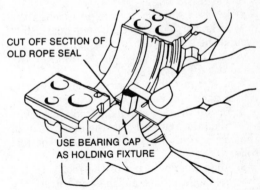

CUT OFF SECTION OF OLD ROPE SEAL

USE BEARING CAP AS HOLDING FIXTURE

Use the bearing cap to hold the old lower seal while you cut it

COATED AREA INDICATED WITH #1052357 SEALER OR EQUIVALENT.

SEALER

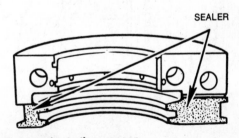

Apply sealer to the rear cap

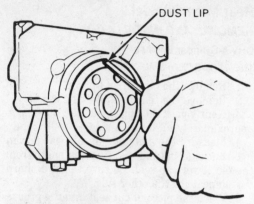

Removing the old one piece seal, 1985–87

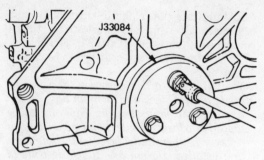

Installation of the one piece seal, 1985–87

rect this condition a new crankshaft part No. 14086053 and a one piece rear main seal kit part No. 14081761 has been released for service. The one piece seal kit contains an installation tool, rear main seal, and an instruction sheet.

1985-88 (ONE PIECE SEAL)

1. Jack up the engine and support it safely.
2. Remove the transmission as outlined in Chapter 7.
3. Remove the flywheel.
NOTE: *Now is the time to confirm that the rear seal is leaking.*
4. Insert a suitable pry tool in through the dust lip and pry out the seal by moving the tool around the seal until it is removed.
WARNING: *Use care not to damage the crankshaft seal surface with a pry tool.*
5. Before installing, lubricate the seal bore to seal surface with engine oil.
6. Install the new seal using tool J-34686.
7. Slide the new seal over the mandrel until the dust lip bottoms squarely against the tool collar.
8. Align the dowel pin of the tool with the dowel pin hole in the crankshaft and attach the

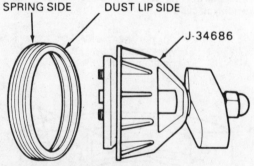

SEAL BORE TO SEAL SURFACE TO BE LUBRICATED WITH ENGINE OIL BEFORE ASSEMBLY

One piece seal installation tool, 1985–87

tool to the crankshaft. Tighten the attaching screws to 2-5 ft.lb.
9. Tighten the T-handle of the tool to push the seal into the bore. Continue until the tool collar is flush against the block.
10. Loosen the T-handle completely. Remove the attaching screws and the tool.
NOTE: *Check to see that the seal is squarely seated in the bore.*
11. Install the flywheel and transmission.
12. Start the engine and check for leaks.

OHC 4-Cylinder Engines

1982-84

NOTE: *The following procedure requires the use of special tools.*
1. Remove engine as previously outlined.
2. Remove flywheel dust cover.
3. Remove flexplate to torque converter attachment bolts on automatic vehicles.
4. Remove bellhousing bolts and separate engine from transaxle assembly.
5. Remove flexplate on automatic transaxle vehicles.
6. Remove pressure plate, clutch disc and flywheel on manual transaxle vehicles.
7. Using a screwdriver or suitable tool, remove rear main oil seal.
8. Clean cylinder block and crankshaft sealing surface.
9. Inspect crankshaft for nicks, scratches, etc.
10. Coat seal and engine mating surfaces with engine oil.
11. Position seal on Protector (J-33084-2) and place onto crankshaft flywheel flange.
12. Install Seal Installer (J-33084) on crankshaft flywheel flange, starting the three (3) bolts EVENLY in a rotational sequence until the seal bottoms in the block.
13. For remainder of installation reverse steps 6 through 1 of removal procedure.

1985-88

NOTE: *The rear main bearing oil seal is a one piece unit and can be replaced without removing the oil pan or the crankshaft.*

1. Remove the transaxle assembly as outlined in Chapter 7.

2. Remove the flywheel retaining bolts and remove the flywheel.

3. If equipped with manual transaxle, remove the pressure plate and disc.

4. Pry out the rear main seal.

5. Clean the block and crankcase to seal mating surfaces.

6. Position the rear main seal to the block and press evenly into place using tool J33084. Lubricate the outside of the seal to aid assembly.

7. Install the flywheel and torque the bolts to 44 ft.lb.

8. Install the pressure plate and disc, if equipped with manual transaxle.

9. Install the transaxle assembly as outlined in Chapter 7.

6-173

1985-88

1. Support the engine with J-28467 engine support or equivalent.

2. Remove the transmission as outlined in Chapter 7.

3. Remove the flywheel.

NOTE: *Now is the time to confirm that the rear seal is leaking.*

4. Insert a suitable pry tool in through the dust lip and pry out the seal by moving the tool around the seal until it is removed.

WARNING: *Use care not to damage the crankshaft seal surface with a pry tool.*

5. Before installing, lubricate the seal bore to seal surface with engine oil.

6. Install the new seal using tool J-34686.

7. Slide the new seal over the mandrel until the dust lip bottoms squarely against the tool collar.

8. Align the dowel pin of the tool with the dowel pin hole in the crankshaft and attach the tool to the crankshaft. Tighten the attaching screws to 2-5 ft.lb.

9. Tighten the T-handle of the tool to push the seal into the bore. Continue until the tool collar is flush against the block.

10. Loosen the T-handle completely. Remove the attaching screws and the tool.

NOTE: *Check to see that the seal is squarely seated in the bore.*

11. Install the flywheel and transmission.

12. Start the engine and check for leaks.

Exhaust System

Safety Precautions

For a number of reasons, exhaust system work can be the most dangerous type of work you can do on your car. Always observe the following precautions:

● Support the car extra securely. Not only will you often be working directly under it, but you'll frequently be using a lot of force, say, heavy hammer blows, to dislodge rusted parts. This can cause a car that's improperly supported to shift and possibly fall.

● Wear goggles. Exhaust system parts are always rusty. Metal chips can be dislodged, even when you're only turning rusted bolts. Attempting to pry pipes apart with a chisel makes the chips fly even more frequently.

● If you're using a cutting torch, keep it a great distance from either the fuel tank or lines. Stop what you're doing and feel the temperature of the fuel bearing pipes on the tank frequently. Even slight heat can expand and/or vaporize fuel, resulting in accumulated vapor, or even a liquid leak, near your torch.

● Watch where your hammer blows fall and make sure you hit squarely. You could easily tap a brake or fuel line when you hit an exhaust system part with a glancing blow. Inspect all lines and hoses in the area where you've been working.

CAUTION: *Be very careful when working on or near the catalytic converter. External temperatures can reach 1,500°F (816°C) and more, causing severe burns. Removal or installation should be performed only on a cold exhaust system.*

Special Tools

A number of special exhaust system tools can be rented from auto supply houses or local stores that rent special equipment. A common one is a tail pipe expander, designed to enable you to join pipes of identical diameter.

It may also be quite helpful to use solvents designed to loosen rusted bolts or flanges. Soaking rusted parts the night before you do the job can speed the work of freeing rusted parts considerably. Remember that these solvents are often flammable. Apply only to parts after they are cool!

COMPONENT REPLACEMENT

System components may be welded or clamped together. The system consists of a head pipe, catalytic converter, intermediate pipe, muffler and tail pipe, in that order from the engine to the back of the car.

The head pipe is bolted to the exhaust manifold, except on turbocharged engines, in which case it is bolted to the turbocharger outlet elbow. Various hangers suspend the system from the floor pan. When assembling exhaust system parts, the relative clearances around all system parts is extremely critical. See the accompanying illustration and observe all clearances during assembly. In the event that the system is welded, the various parts will have to be cut apart for removal. In these cases, the cut parts may not be reused. To cut the parts, a hacksaw is the best choice. An oxy-acetylene cutting torch may be faster but the sparks are DANGEROUS near the fuel tank, and, at the very least, accidents could happen, resulting in damage to other under-car parts, not to mention yourself!

The following replacement steps relate to clamped parts:

1. Raise and support the car on jackstands. It's much easier on you if you can get the car up on 4 stands. Some pipes need lots of clearance for removal and installation. If the system has been in the car for a long time, spray the clamped joints with a rust dissolving solutions such as WD-40(RG) or Liquid Wrench (RG), and let it set according to the instructions on the can.

2. Remove the nuts from the U-bolts; don't be surprised if the U-bolts break while removing the nuts. Age and rust account for this. Besides, you shouldn't reuse old U-bolts. When unbolting the headpipe from the exhaust manifold, make sure that the bolts are free before trying to remove them. If you snap a stud in the exhaust manifold, the stud will have to be removed with a bolt extractor, which often necessitates the removal of the manifold itself. On J-cars, the headpipe uses a necked collar for sealing purposes at the manifold, eliminating the need for a gasket. On turbocharged engines, however, a gasket is used at the joint between the headpipe and the turbocharger outlet.

3. After the clamps are removed from the joints, first twist the parts at the joints to break loose rust and scale, then pull the components apart with a twisting motion. If the parts twist freely but won't pull apart, check the joint. The clamp may have been installed so tightly that it has caused a slight crushing of the joint. In this event, the best thing to do is secure a chisel designed for the purpose and, using the chisel and a hammer, peel back the female pipe end until the parts are freed.

4. Once the parts are freed, check the condition of the pipes which you had intended keeping. If their condition is at all in doubt, replace them too. You went to a lot of work to get one or more components out. You don't want to have

to go through that again in the near future. If you are retaining a pipe, check the pipe end. If it was crushed by a clamp, it can be restored to its original diameter using a pipe expander, which can be rented at most good auto parts stores. Check, also, the condition of the exhaust system hangers. If ANY deterioration is noted, replace them. Oh, and one note about parts: use only parts designed for your car. Don't use fits-all parts or flex pipes. The fits-all parts never fit and the flex pipes don't last very long.

5. When installing the new parts, coat the pipe ends with exhaust system lubricant. It makes fitting the parts much easier. It's also a good idea to assemble all the parts in position before clamping them. This will ensure a good fit, detect any problems and allow you to check all clearances between the parts and surrounding frame and floor members. See the accompanying illustrations for the proper clearances.

6. When you are satisfied with all fits and clearances, install the clamps. The headpipe-to-manifold nuts should be torqued to 20 ft.lb. If the studs were rusty, wire-brush them clean and spray them with WD-40® or Liquid Wrench®. This will ensure a proper torque reading. Position the clamps on the slip points as illustrated. The slits in the female pipe ends should be under the U-bolts, not under the clamp end. Tighten the U-bolt nuts securely, without crushing the pipe. The pipe fit should be tight, so that you can't swivel the pipe by hand. Don't forget: always use new clamps. When the system is tight, recheck all clearances. Start the engine and check the joints for leaks. A leak can be felt by hand. MAKE CERTAIN THAT THE CAR IS SECURE ON THE JACKSTANDS BEFORE GETTING UNDER IT WITH THE ENGINE RUNNING!! If any leaks are detected, tighten the clamp until the leak stops. If the pipe starts to deform before the leak stops, reposition the clamp and tighten it. If that still doesn't stop the leak, it may be that you don't have enough overlap on the pipe fit. Shut off the engine and try pushing the pipe together further. Be careful; the pipe gets hot quickly.

7. When everything is tight and secure, lower the car and take it for a road test. Make sure there are no unusual sounds or vibration. Most new pipes are coated with a preservative, so the system will be pretty smelly for a day or two while the coating burns off.

Emission Controls

4

EMISSION CONTROLS

There are three sources of automotive pollutants: crankcase fumes, exhaust gases, and gasoline evaporation. The pollutants formed from these substances fall into three categories: unburnt hydrocarbons (HC), carbon monoxide (CO), and oxides of nitrogen (NOx). The equipment that is used to limit these pollutants is commonly called emission control equipment.

Positive Crankcase Ventilation System

All J-cars are equipped with a positive crankcase ventilation (PCV) system to control crankcase blow-by vapors. The system functions as follows:

When the engine is running, a small portion of the gases which are formed in the combustion chamber leak by the piston rings and enter the crankcase. Since these gases are under pressure, they tend to escape from the crankcase and enter the atmosphere. If these gases are allowed to remain in the crankcase for any period of time, they contaminate the engine oil and cause sludge to build up in the crankcase. If the gases are allowed to escape into the atmosphere, they pollute the air with unburned hydrocarbons. The job of the crankcase emission control equipment is to recycle these gases back into the engine combustion chamber where they are reburned.

The crankcase (blow-by gases are recycled in the following way: as the engine is running, clean, filtered air is drawn through the air filter and into the crankcase. As the air passes through the crankcase, it picks up the combustion gases and carries them out of the crankcase, through the oil separator, through the PCV valve, and into the induction system. As they enter the intake manifold, they are drawn into the combustion chamber where they are reburned.

The most critical component in the system is the PCV valve. This valve controls the amount of gases which are recycled into the combustion chamber. At low engine speeds, the valve is partially closed, limiting the flow of gases into the intake manifold. As engine speed increases, the valve opens to admit greater quantities of gases into the intake manifold. If the valve should become blocked or plugged, the gases will be prevented from escaping from the crankcase by the normal route. Since these gases are under pressure, they will find their own way out of the crankcase. This alternate route is usually a weak oil seal or gasket in the engine. As the gas escapes by the gasket, it also creates an oil leak. Besides causing oil leaks, a clogged PCV valve also allows these gases to remain in the crankcase for an extended period of time, promoting the formation of sludge in the engine.

SERVICE

Inspect the PCV system hose and connections at each tune-up and replace any deteriorated hoses. Check the PCV valve at every tune-up and replace it at 30,000 mile intervals. Replacement procedures are in Chapter 1.

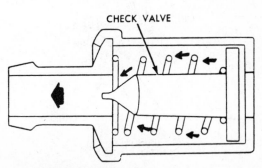

CHECK VALVE

Cross section of a PCV valve

Evaporative Emission Control System

The basic Evaporative Emission Control System (EEC) used on all J-cars is the carbon canister storage method. The system is used to reduce emissions of fuel vapors from the car's fuel system. Evaporated fuel vapors are stored for burning during combustion rather than being vented into the atmosphere when the engine is not running. To accomplish this, the fuel tank and the carburetor float bowl are vented through a vapor canister containing activated charcoal. The system utilizes a sealed fuel tank with a dome that collects fuel vapors and allows them to pass on into a line connected with the vapor canister. In addition, the vapors that form above the float chamber in the carburetor also pass into a line connected with the canister. The canister absorbs these vapors in a bed of activated charcoal and retains them until the canister is purged or cleared by air drawn through the filter at its bottom. The absorbing occurs when the car is not running, while the purging or cleaning occurs when the car is running. The amount of vapor being drawn into the engine at any given time is too small to have an effect on either fuel economy or engine performance.

The Electronic Control Module (ECM) controls the vacuum to the canister purge valve by using an electrically operated solenoid valve. When the system is in the Open Loop mode, the solenoid valve is energized and blocks all vacuum to the canister purge valve. When the system is in the Closed Loop mode, the solenoid

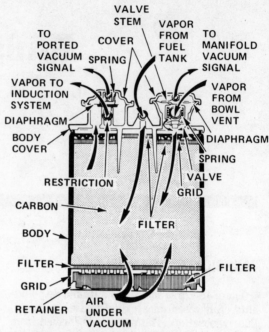

Cross section of the vapor canister

valve is de-energized and vacuum is then supplied to operate the purge valve. This releases the fuel vapors, collected in the canister, into the induction system.

It is extremely important that only vapors be transferred to the engine. To avoid the possibility of liquid fuel being drawn into the system, the following features are included as part of the total system:

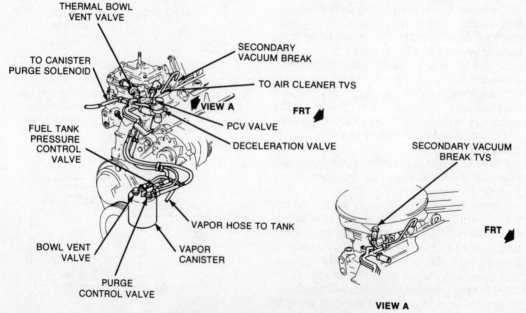

Evaporative emission control system

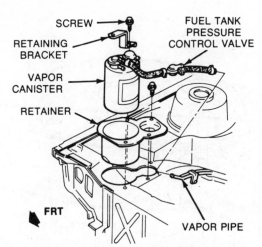

SCREW
RETAINING BRACKET
VAPOR CANISTER
RETAINER
FUEL TANK PRESSURE CONTROL VALVE
FRT
VAPOR PIPE

Vapor canister removal and installation details

• A fuel tank overfill protector is provided to assure adequate room for expansion of liquid fuel volume with temperature changes.

• A one point fuel tank venting system is provided on all models to assure that the tank will be vented under any normal car attitude. This is accomplished by the use of a domed tank.

• A pressure-vacuum relief valve is located in the fuel cap.

VAPOR CANISTER REMOVAL AND INSTALLATION

1. Loosen the screw holding the canister retaining bracket.
2. If equipped with air conditioning, loosen the attachments holding the accumulator and pipe assembly.
3. Rotate the canister retaining bracket and remove the canister.
4. Tag and disconnect the hoses leading from the canister.
5. Installation is in the reverse order of removal.

FILTER REPLACEMENT

1. Remove the vapor canister.
2. Pull the filter out from the bottom of the canister.
3. Install a new filter and then replace the canister.

Exhaust Emission Controls

Exhaust emission control systems constitute the largest body of emission control devices installed on the J-car. Included in this category are: Thermostatic Air Cleaner (THERMAC); Air Management System; Early Fuel Evaporation System (EFE); Exhaust Gas Recirculation (EGR); Computer Command Control System (CCC); Deceleration Valve; Mixture Control So-

lenoid (M/C); Throttle Position Sensor (TPS); Idle Speed Control (ISC); Electronic Spark Timing (EST); Transmission Converter Clutch (TCC); Catalytic Converter and the Oxygen Sensor System. A brief description of each system and any applicable service procedures follows.

Thermostatic Air Cleaner (THERMAC)

All engines use the THERMAC system. This system is designed to warm the air entering the carburetor when underhood temperatures are low, and to maintain a controlled air temperature into the carburetor at all times. By allowing preheated air to enter the carburetor, the amount of time the choke is on is reduced, resulting in better fuel economy and lower emissions. Engine warm-up time is also reduced.

The THERMAC system is composed of the air cleaner body, a filter, sensor unit, vacuum diaphragm, damper door, and associated hoses and connections. Heat radiating from the exhaust manifold is trapped by a heat stove and is ducted to the air cleaner to supply heated air to the carburetor. A movable door in the air cleaner case snorkel allows air to be drawn in from the heat stove (cold operation). The door position is controlled by the vacuum motor, which receives intake manifold vacuum as modulated by the temperature sensor.

SYSTEM CHECKS

1. Check the vacuum hoses for leaks, kinks, breaks, or improper connections and correct any defects.
2. With the engine off, check the position of the damper door within the snorkel. A mirror can be used to make this job easier. The damper door should be open to admit outside air.
3. Apply at least 7 in.Hg of vacuum to the damper diaphragm unit. The door should close. If it doesn't, check the diaphragm linkage for binding and correct hookup.
4. With the vacuum still applied and the door closed, clamp the tube to trap the vacuum. If the door doesn't remain closed, there is a leak in the diaphragm assembly.

Air Management System

The AIR management system, is used to provide additional oxygen to continue the combustion process after the exhaust gases leave the combustion chamber. Air is injected into either the exhaust port(s), the exhaust manifold(s) or the catalytic converter by an engine driven air pump. The system is in operation at all times and will bypass air only momentarily during deceleration and at high speeds. The bypass func-

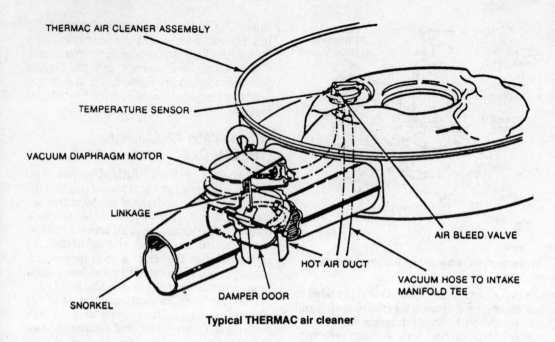

THERMAC AIR CLEANER ASSEMBLY

TEMPERATURE SENSOR

VACUUM DIAPHRAGM MOTOR

LINKAGE

AIR BLEED VALVE

HOT AIR DUCT

VACUUM HOSE TO INTAKE MANIFOLD TEE

SNORKEL

DAMPER DOOR

Typical THERMAC air cleaner

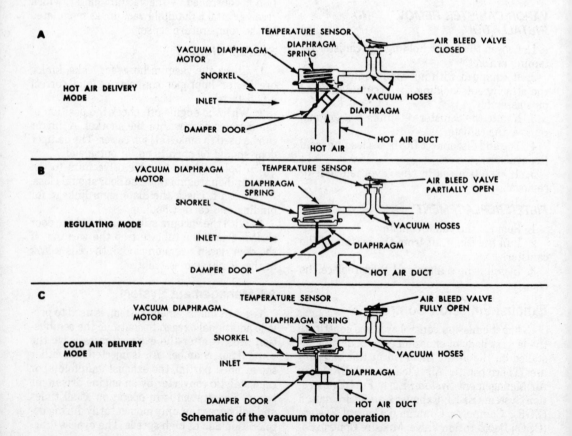

A

TEMPERATURE SENSOR

DIAPHRAGM SPRING

AIR BLEED VALVE CLOSED

VACUUM DIAPHRAGM MOTOR

SNORKEL

HOT AIR DELIVERY MODE

INLET

VACUUM HOSES

DIAPHRAGM

DAMPER DOOR

HOT AIR DUCT

HOT AIR

B

VACUUM DIAPHRAGM MOTOR

TEMPERATURE SENSOR

DIAPHRAGM SPRING

AIR BLEED VALVE PARTIALLY OPEN

SNORKEL

REGULATING MODE

INLET

VACUUM HOSES

DIAPHRAGM

DAMPER DOOR

HOT AIR DUCT

C

TEMPERATURE SENSOR

AIR BLEED VALVE FULLY OPEN

VACUUM DIAPHRAGM MOTOR

DIAPHRAGM SPRING

SNORKEL

COLD AIR DELIVERY MODE

INLET

VACUUM HOSES

DIAPHRAGM

DAMPER DOOR

HOT AIR DUCT

Schematic of the vacuum motor operation

tion is performed by the Air Management Valve, while the check valve protects the air pump by preventing any backflow of exhaust gases.

The AIR management system helps reduce HC and CO content in the exhaust gases by injecting air into the exhaust ports during cold engine operation. This air injection also helps the catalytic converter to reach the proper temperature quicker during warmup. When the engine is warm (Closed Loop), the AIR system injects air into the beds of a three-way converter to lower the HC and the CO content in the exhaust.

The Air Management system utilizes the following components:

1. An engine driven AIR pump
2. AIR management valves (Air Control, Air Switching)
3. Air flow and control hoses
4. Check valves
5. A dual-bed, three-way catalytic converter

The belt driven, vane-type air pump is located at the front of the engine and supplies clean air to the AIR system for purposes already stated. When the engine is cold, the Electronic Control Module (ECM) energizes an AIR control solenoid. This allows air to flow to the AIR switching valve. The AIR switching valve is then energized to direct air to the exhaust ports.

When the engine is warm, the ECM de-energizes the AIR switching valve, thus directing the air between the beds of the catalytic converter. This provides additional oxygen for the oxidizing catalyst in the second bed to decrease HC and CO, while at the same time keeping oxygen levels low in the first bed, enabling the reducing catalyst to effectively decrease the levels of NOx.

If the AIR control valve detects a rapid increase in manifold vacuum (deceleration), certain operating modes (wide open throttle, etc.) or if the ECM self-diagnostic system detects any problem in the system, air is diverted to the air cleaner or directly into the atmosphere.

The primary purpose of the ECM's divert mode is to prevent backfiring. Throttle closure at the beginning of deceleration will temporarily create air/fuel mixtures which are too rich to burn completely. These mixtures become burnable when they reach the exhaust if combined with the injection air. The next firing of the engine will ignite this mixture causing an exhaust backfire. Momentary diverting of the injection air from the exhaust prevents this.

The AIR management system check valves and hoses should be checked periodically for any leaks, cracks or deterioration.

REMOVAL AND INSTALLATION

Air Pump

1. Remove the AIR management valves and/or adapter at the pump.
2. Loosen the air pump adjustment bolt and remove the drive belt.
3. Unscrew the pump mounting bolts and then remove the pump pulley.
4. Unscrew the pump mounting bolts and then remove the pump.

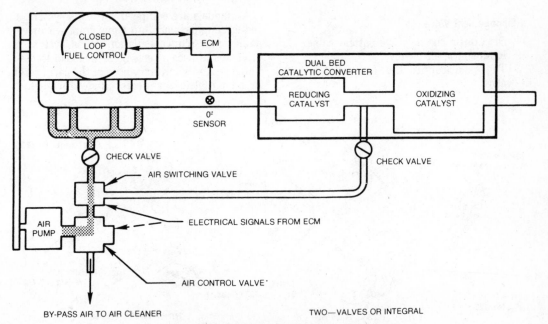

Air management system operation—cold engine

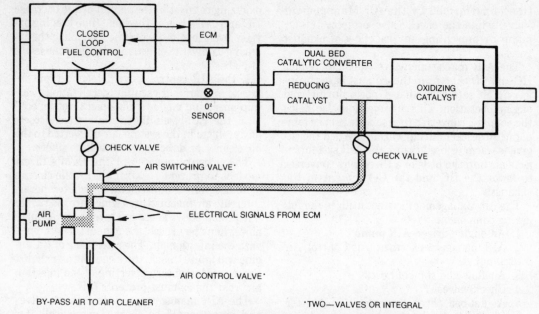

Air management system operation—warm engine

5. Installation is in the reverse order of removal. Be sure to adjust the drive belt tension after installing it.

Check Valve

1. Release the clamp and disconnect the air hoses from the valve.
2. Unscrew the check valve from the air injection pipe.
3. Installation is in the reverse order of removal.

Air Management Valve

1. Disconnect the negative battery cable.
2. Remove the air cleaner.
3. Tag and disconnect the vacuum hose from the valve.

4. Tag and disconnect the air outlet hoses from the valve.
5. Bend back the lock tabs and then remove the bolts holding the elbow to the valve.
6. Tag and disconnect any electrical connections at the valve and then remove the valve from the elbow.
7. Installation is in the reverse order of removal.

Early Fuel Evaporation (EFE)

All models are equipped with this system to reduce engine warm-up time, improve driveability and reduce emissions. The system is electric and uses a ceramic heater grid located underneath the primary bore of the carburetor as part of the carburetor insulator/gasket.

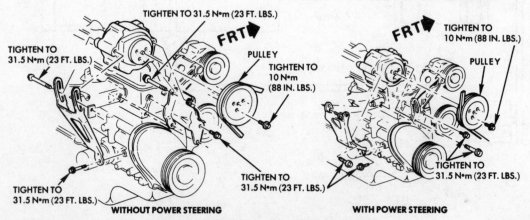

Air pump removal and installation details

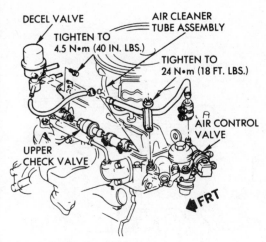

Upper check valve and hoses

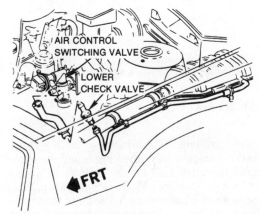

Lower check valve and hoses

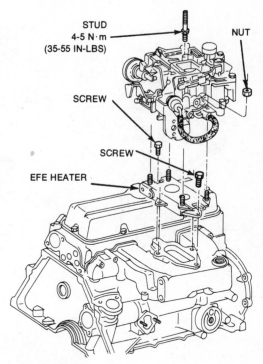

EFE heater grid

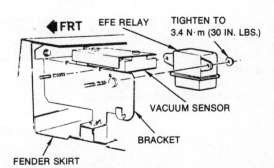

Heater relay installation details

When the ignition switch is turned on and the engine coolant temperature is low, voltage is applied to the EFE relay by the ECM. The EFE relay in turn energizes the heater grid. When the coolant temperature increases, the ECM de-energizes the relay which will then shut off the EFE heater.

REMOVAL AND INSTALLATION

1. Remove the air cleaner and disconnect the negative battery cable.
2. Disconnect all electrical, vacuum and fuel connections from the carburetor.
3. Disconnect the EFE heater electrical lead.
4. Remove the carburetor as detailed later in this chapter.
5. Lift off the EFE heater grid.
6. Installation is in the reverse order of removal.

EFE HEATER RELAY REPLACEMENT

1. Disconnect the negative battery cable.
2. Remove the retaining bracket on the right fender skirt.

3. Tag and disconnect all electrical connections.
4. Unscrew the retaining bolts and remove the relay.
5. Installation is in the reverse order of removal.

Exhaust Gas Recirculation (EGR)

All models are equipped with this system, which consists of a metering valve, a vacuum line to the carburetor or intake manifold, and cast-in exhaust passages in the intake manifold. The EGR valve is controlled by vacuum, and opens and closes in response to the vacuum signals to admit exhaust gases into the air/fuel mixture. The exhaust gases lower peak combus-

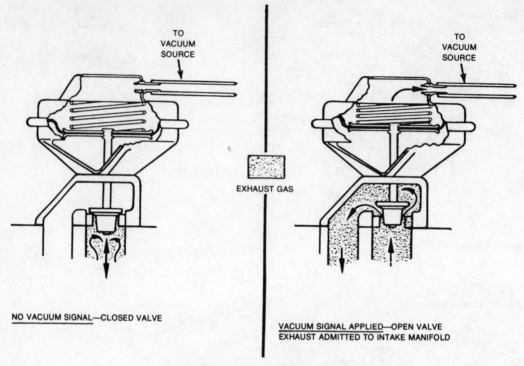

Vacuum modulated EGR valve

tion temperatures, reducing the formation of NOx. The valve is closed at idle and wide open throttle, but is open between the two extreme positions.

There are actually two types of EGR systems: Vacuum Modulated and Exhaust Back Pres-

sure Modulated. The principle of both systems is the same; the only difference is in the method used to control how far the EGR valve opens.

In the Vacuum Modulated system, the amount of exhaust gas admitted into the intake manifold depends on a ported vacuum signal. A

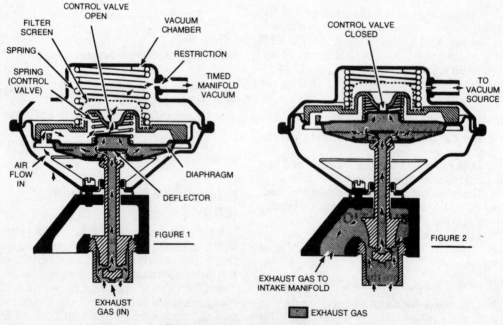

Exhaust gas modulated EGR valve

ported vacuum signal is one taken from the carburetor above the throttle plates; thus, the vacuum signal (amount of vacuum) is dependent on how far the throttle plates are opened. When the throttle is closed (idle or deceleration) there is no vacuum signal. Thus, the EGR valve is closed, and no exhaust gas enters the intake manifold. As the throttle is opened, a vacuum is produced, which opens the EGR valve, admitting exhaust gas into the intake manifold.

In the Exhaust Back Pressure Modulated system, a transducer is installed in the EGR valve body. The vacuum is still ported vacuum, but the transducer uses exhaust gas pressure to control an air bleed within the valve to modify this vacuum signal.

SYSTEM CHECKS

1. Check to see if the EGR valve diaphragm moves freely. Use your finger to reach up under the valve and push on the diaphragm. If it doesn't move freely, the valve should be replaced. The use of a mirror will aid the inspection process.

CAUTION: *If the engine is hot, wear a glove to protect your hand.*

2. Install a vacuum gauge into the vacuum line between the EGR valve and the carburetor. Start the engine and allow it to reach operating temperature.

3. With the car in either Park or Neutral, increase the engine speed until at least 5 in.Hg is showing on the gauge.

4. Remove the vacuum hose from the EGR valve. The diaphragm should move downward (valve closed). The engine speed should increase.

5. Install the vacuum hose and watch for the EGR valve to open (diaphragm moving upward). The engine speed should decrease to its former level, indicating exhaust recirculation.

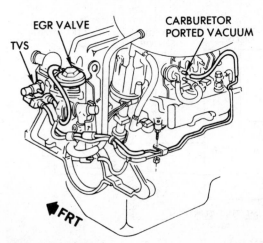

EGR system layout

6. If the diaphragm doesn't move:

a. Check engine vacuum; it should be at least 5 in. Hg with the throttle open and engine running.

b. Check to see that the engine is at normal operating temperature.

c. Check for vacuum at the EGR hose. If no vacuum is present, check the hose for leaks, breaks, kinks, improper connections, etc., and replace as necessary.

If the diaphragm moves, but the engine speed doesn't change, check the EGR passages in the intake manifold for blockage.

REMOVAL AND INSTALLATION

1. Disconnect the vacuum hose.

2. Remove the bolts or nuts holding the EGR valve to the engine.

3. Remove the valve.

4. Clean the mounting surfaces before replacing the valve. Install the valve onto the manifold, using a new gasket. Be sure to install the spacer, if used. Connect the vacuum hose and check the valve operation.

Computer Command Control System (CCC)

The Computer Command Control System (CCC) is an electronically controlled exhaust emission system that can monitor and control a large number of interrelated emission control systems. It can monitor up to 15 various engine/vehicle operating conditions and then use this information to control as many as 9 engine related systems. The system is thereby making constant adjustments to maintain good vehicle performance under all normal driving conditions while at the same time allowing the catalytic converter to effectively control the emissions of HC, CO and NOx.

In addition, the system has a built in diagnostic system that recognizes and identifies possible operational problems and alerts the driver through a "Check Engine" light in the instrument panel. The light will remain on until the problem is corrected. The system also has built in back-up systems that in most cases of an operational problem will allow for the continued operation of the vehicle in a near normal manner until the repairs can be made.

The CCC system has some components in common with the old G.M. C-4 system, although they are not interchangeable. These components include the Electronic Control Module (ECM), which controls many more functions than does its predecessor, an oxygen sensor system, an electronically controlled variable-mixture carburetor, a three-way catalytic converter, throttle position and coolant sensors, a Barometric Pressure Sensor (BARO), a Manifold Absolute Pressure Sensor (MAP) and a "Check Engine" light in the instrument panel.

Components unique to the CCC system include the Air Injection Reaction (AIR) management system, a charcoal canister purge solenoid, EGR valve controls, a vehicle speed sensor (in the instrument panel), a transmission converter clutch solenoid (only on models with automatic transmission), idle speed control and Electronic Spark Timing (EST).

The ECM, in addition to monitoring sensors and sending out a control signal to the carburetors, also controls the following components or sub-systems: charcoal canister purge control, the AIR system, idle speed, automatic transmission converter lockup, distributor ignition timing, and EGR valve, and the air conditioner converter clutch.

The EGR valve control solenoid is activated by the ECM in a fashion similar to that of the charcoal canister purge solenoid described earlier in this chapter. When the engine is cold, the ECM energizes the solenoid, which blocks the vacuum signal to the EGR valve. When the engine is warm, the ECM de-energizes the solenoid and the vacuum signal is allowed to reach and then activate the EGR valve.

The idle speed control adjusts the idle speed to all particular engine load conditions and will lower the idle under no-load or low-load conditions in order to conserve fuel.

BASIC TROUBLESHOOTING

NOTE: *The following explains how to activate the Trouble Code signal light in the instrument cluster. This is not a full fledged CCC system troubleshooting and isolation procedure.*

Before suspecting the CCC system, or any of its components as being faulty, check the ignition system (distributor, timing, spark plugs and wires). Check the engine compression, the

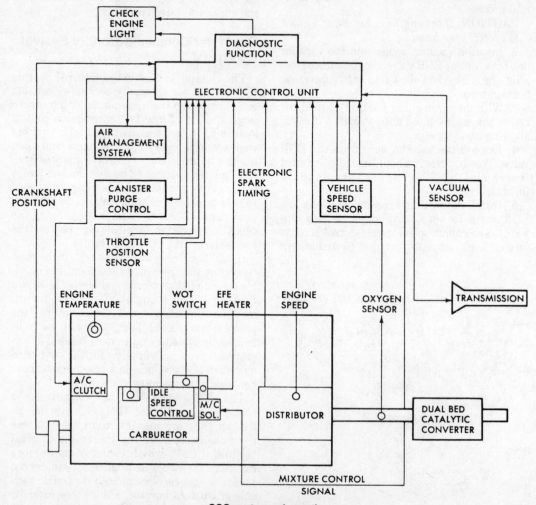

CCC system schematic

air cleaner and any of the emission control components that are not controlled by the ECM. Also check the intake manifold, the vacuum hoses and hose connectors for any leaks. Check the carburetor mounting bolts for tightness.

The following symptoms could indicate a possible problem area with the CCC system:

1. Detonation
2. Stalling or rough idling when the engine is cold
3. Stalling or rough idling when the engine is hot
4. Missing
5. Hesitation
6. Surging
7. Poor gasoline mileage
8. Sluggish or spongy performance
9. Hard starting when engine is cold
10. Hard starting when the engine is hot
11. Objectionable exhaust odors
12. Engine cuts out
13. Improper idle speed

As a bulb and system check, the "Check Engine" light will come on when the ignition switch is turned to the **ON** position but the engine is not started.

The "Check Engine" light will also produce the trouble code/codes by a series of flashes which translate as follows: When the diagnostic test terminal under the instrument panel is grounded, with the ignition in the **ON** position and the engine not running, the "Check Engine" light will flash once, pause, and then flash twice in rapid succession. This is a Code 12, which indicates that the diagnostic system is working. After a long pause, the Code 12 will repeat itself two more times. This whole cycle will then repeat itself until the engine is started or the ignition switch is turned **OFF**.

When the engine is started, the "Check Engine" light will remain on for a few seconds and then turn off. If the "Check Engine" light remains on, the self-diagnostic system has detected a problem. If the test terminal is then grounded, the trouble code will flash (3) three times. If more than one problem is found to be in existence, each trouble code will flash (3) three times and then change to the next one. Trouble codes will flash in numerical order (lowest code number to highest). The trouble

Trouble Code Identification Chart

NOTE: *Always ground the test terminal AFTER the engine is running.*

Trouble Code	Refers To:
12	No reference pulses to the ECM. This is not stored in the memory and will only flash when the fault is present (not to be confused with the Code 12 discussed earlier).
13	Oxygen sensor circuit. The engine must run for at least 5 min. before this code will set.
14	Shortened coolant circuit. The engine must run at least 2 min. before this code will set.
15	Open coolant sensor circuit. The engine must run at least 5 min. before this code will set.
21	Throttle position sensor circuit. The engine must run up to 25 sec., below 800 rpm, before this code will set.
23	Open or grounded carburetor solenoid circuit.
24	Vehicle Speed Sensor (VSS) circuit. The engine must run for at least 5 min. at road speed for this code to set.
32	Altitude Compensator circuit.
34	Vacuum sensor circuit. The engine must run up to 5 min., below 800 rpm, before this code will set.
35	Idle speed control switch circuit shorted. Over ½ throttle for at least 2 sec.
41	No distributor reference pulses to the ECM at specified engine vacuum. This code will store in memory.
42	Electronic Spark Timing (EST) bypass circuit grounded.
44	Lean oxygen sensor indication. The engine must run at least 5 min., in closed loop, at part throttle and road load for this code to set.
45	Rich system indication. The engine must run at least 5 min., in closed loop, at part throttle and road load for this code to set.
44&45	(at same time) Faulty oxygen sensor circuit.
51	Faulty calibration unit (PROM) or installation. It takes 30 sec. for this code to set.
54	Shorted M/C solenoid circuit and/or faulty ECM.
55	Grounded Vref (terminal 21), faulty oxygen sensor or ECM.

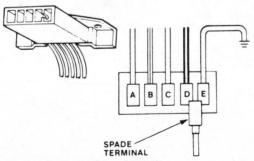

SPADE
TERMINAL

Test terminal and ground location

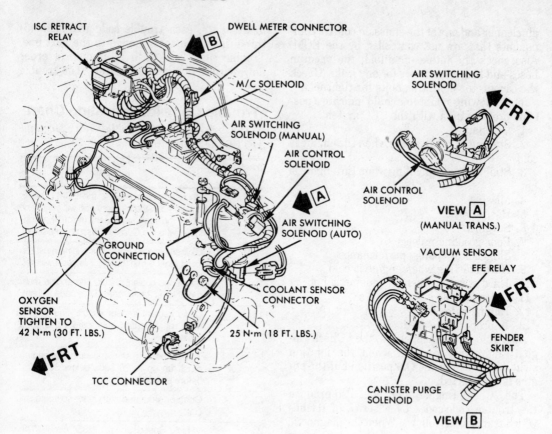

ISC RETRACT RELAY

DWELL METER CONNECTOR

M/C SOLENOID

AIR SWITCHING SOLENOID (MANUAL)

AIR CONTROL SOLENOID

AIR SWITCHING SOLENOID (AUTO)

GROUND CONNECTION

OXYGEN SENSOR TIGHTEN TO 42 N·m (30 FT. LBS.)

25 N·m (18 FT. LBS.)

COOLANT SENSOR CONNECTOR

FRT

TCC CONNECTOR

AIR SWITCHING SOLENOID

FRT

AIR CONTROL SOLENOID

VIEW A
(MANUAL TRANS.)

VACUUM SENSOR

EFE RELAY

FRT

FENDER SKIRT

CANISTER PURGE SOLENOID

VIEW B

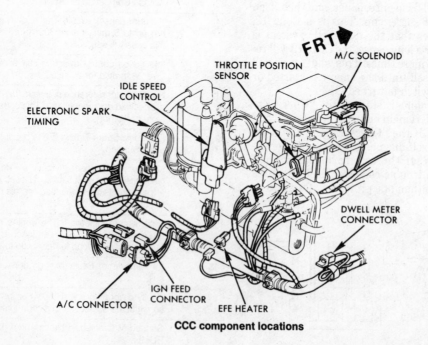

FRT

M/C SOLENOID

THROTTLE POSITION SENSOR

IDLE SPEED CONTROL

ELECTRONIC SPARK TIMING

DWELL METER CONNECTOR

A/C CONNECTOR

IGN FEED CONNECTOR

EFE HEATER

CCC component locations

code series will repeat themselves for as long as the test terminal remains grounded.

A trouble code indicates a problem with a given circuit. For example, trouble code 14 indicates a problem in the cooling sensor circuit. This includes the coolant sensor, its electrical harness and the Electronic Control Module (ECM).

Since the self-diagnostic system cannot diagnose every possible fault in the system, the absence of a trouble code does not necessarily mean that the system is trouble-free. To determine whether or not a problem with the system exists that does not activate a trouble code, a system performance check must be made. This job should be left to a qualified service technician.

In the case of an intermittent fault in the system, the "Check Engine" light will go out when the fault goes away, but the trouble code will remain in the memory of the ECM. Therefore, if a trouble code can be obtained even though the "Check Engine" light is not on, it must still be evaluated. It must be determined if the fault is intermittent or if the engine must be operating under certain conditions (acceleration, deceleration, etc.) before the "Check Engine" light will come on. In some cases, certain trouble codes will not be recorded in the ECM until the engine has been operated at part throttle for at least 5 to 18 minutes.

On the CCC system, a trouble code will be stored until the terminal **R** at the ECM has been disconnected from the battery for at least 10 seconds.

ACTIVATING THE TROUBLE CODE

On the CCC system, locate the test terminal under the instrument panel (see illustration). Use a jumper wire and ground only the lead.

NOTE: *Ground the test terminal according to the instructions given previously in the Basic Troubleshooting section.*

Deceleration Valve

The purpose of the deceleration valve is to prevent backfiring in the exhaust system during deceleration. The normal position of the valve is closed. When deceleration causes a sudden vacuum increase in the vacuum signal lines, the pressure differential on the diaphragm will overcome the closing force of the spring, opening the valve and bleeding air into the intake manifold.

Air trapped in the chamber above the vacuum diaphragm will bleed at a calibrated rate through the delay valve portion of the integral check and delay valve, reducing the vacuum acting on the diaphragm. When the vacuum

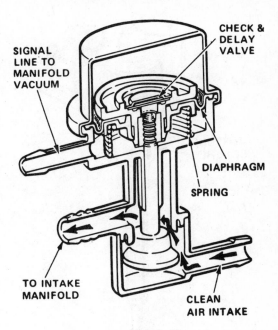

Cross section of the deceleration valve

load on the diaphragm and the spring load equalize, the valve assembly will close, shutting off the air flow into the intake manifold.

The check valve portion of the check and delay valve provides quick balancing of chamber pressure when a sudden decrease in vacuum is caused by acceleration rather than deceleration.

Mixture Control Solenoid (M/C)

The fuel flow through the carburetor idle main metering circuits is controlled by a mixture control (M/C) solenoid located in the carburetor. The M/C solenoid changes the air/fuel mixture to the engine by controlling the fuel flow through the carburetor. The ECM controls the solenoid by providing a ground. When the solenoid is energized, the fuel flow through the carburetor is reduced, providing a leaner mixture. When the ECM removes the ground, the solenoid is de-energized, increasing the fuel flow and providing a richer mixture. The M/C solenoid is energized and de-energized at a rate of 10 times per second.

Throttle Position Sensor (TPS)

The throttle position sensor is mounted in the carburetor body and is used to supply throttle position information to the ECM. The ECM memory stores an average of operating condi-

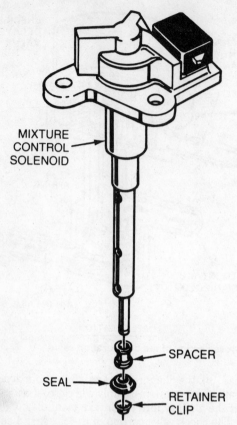

The mixture control (M/C) solenoid is located in the carburetor

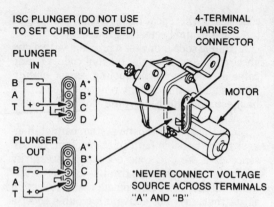

*NEVER CONNECT VOLTAGE SOURCE ACROSS TERMINALS "A" AND "B"

The idle speed control motor (ISC) is mounted on the carburetor

tions with the ideal air/fuel ratios for each of those conditions. When the ECM receives a signal that indicates throttle position change, it immediately shifts to the last remembered set of operating conditions that resulted in an ideal air/fuel ratio control. The memory is continually being updated during normal operations.

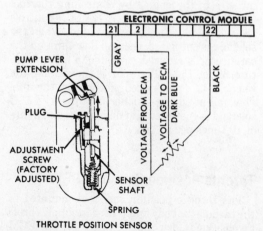

Throttle position sensor

Idle Speed Control (ISC)

The idle speed control does just what its name implies-it controls the idle. The ISC is used to maintain low engine speeds while at the same time preventing stalling due to engine load changes. The system consists of a motor assembly mounted on the carburetor which moves the throttle lever so as to open or close the throttle blades.

The whole operation is controlled by the ECM. The ECM monitors engine load to determine the proper idle speed. To prevent stalling, it monitors the air conditioning compressor switch, the transmission, the park/neutral switch and the ISC throttle switch. The ECM processes all this information and then uses it to control the ISC motor which in turn will vary the idle speed as necessary.

Electronic Spark Timing (EST)

All models use EST. The EST distributor, as described in an earlier chapter, contains no vacuum or centrifugal advance mechanism and uses a seven terminal HEI module. It has four wires going to a four terminal connector in addition to the connectors normally found on HEI distributors. A reference pulse, indicating engine rpm is sent to the ECM. The ECM determines the proper spark advance for the engine operating conditions and then sends an EST pulse back to the distributor.

Under most normal operating conditions, the ECM will control the spark advance. However, under certain operating conditions such as cranking or when setting base timing, the distributor is capable of operating without ECM control. This condition is called BYPASS and is determined by the BYPASS lead which runs from the ECM to the distributor. When the BYPASS lead is at the proper voltage (5), the ECM will control the spark. If the lead is grounded or open circuited, the HEI module itself will control the spark. Disconnecting the 4-terminal EST connector will also cause the engine to operate in the BYPASS mode.

Transmission Converter Clutch (TCC)

All models with an automatic transmission use TCC. The ECM controls the converter by means of a solenoid mounted in the transmission. When the vehicle speed reaches a certain level, the ECM energizes the solenoid and allows the torque converter to mechanically couple the transmission to the engine. When the operating conditions indicate that the transmission should operate as a normal fluid coupled transmission, the ECM will de-energize the solenoid. Depressing the brake will also return the transmission to normal automatic operation.

Catalytic Converter

The catalytic converter is a muffler-like container built into the exhaust system to aid in the reduction of exhaust emissions. The catalyst element consists of individual pellets or a honeycomb monolithic substrate coated with a noble metal such as platinum, palladium, rhodium or a combination. When the exhaust gases come into contact with the catalyst, a chemical reaction occurs which will reduce the pollutants into harmless substances like water and carbon dioxide.

There are essentially two types of catalytic converters: an oxidizing type and a three-way type. The oxidizing type requires the addition of oxygen to spur the catalyst into reducing the engine's HC and CO emissions into H_2O and CO_2. The oxidizing catalytic converter, while effectively reducing HC and CO emissions, does little, if anything in the way of reducing NOx

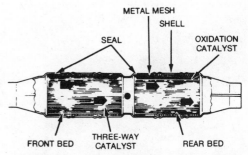

Cutaway view of the typical three-way catalytic converter

emissions. Thus, the three-way catalytic converter.

The three-way converter, unlike the oxidizing type, is capable of reducing HC, CO and NOx emissions; all at the same time. In theory, it seems impossible to reduce all three pollutants in one system since the reduction of HC and CO requires the addition of oxygen, while the reduction of NOx calls for the removal of oxygen. In actuality, the three-way system really can reduce all three pollutants, but only if the amount of oxygen in the exhaust system is precisely controlled. Due to this precise oxygen control requirement, the three-way converter system is used only in conjunction with an oxygen sensor system.

There are no service procedures required for the catalytic converter, although the converter body should be inspected occasionally for damage.

PRECAUTIONS

1. Use only unleaded fuel.
2. Avoid prolonged idling; the engine should run no longer than 20 min. at curb idle and no longer than 10 min. at fast idle.
3. Do not disconnect any of the spark plug leads while the engine is running.
4. Make engine compression checks as quickly as possible.

CATALYST TESTING

At the present time there is no known way to reliably test catalytic converter operation in the field. The only reliable test is a 12 hour and 40 min. soak test (CVS) which must be done in a laboratory.

An infrared HC/CO tester is not sensitive enough to measure the higher tailpipe emissions from a failing converter. Thus, a bad converter may allow enough emissions to escape so that the car is no longer in compliance with Federal or state standards, but will still not cause the needle on a tester to move off zero.

The chemical reactions which occur inside a catalytic converter generate a great deal of heat. Most converter problems can be traced to

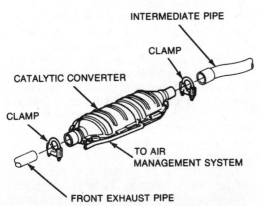

The catalytic converter is upstream of the muffler

Oxygen sensor

fuel or ignition system problems which cause unusually high emissions. As a result of the increased intensity of the chemical reactions, the converter literally burns itself up.

A completely failed converter might cause a tester to show a slight reading. As a result, it is occasionally possible to detect one of these.

As long as you avoid severe overheating and the use of leaded fuels it is reasonably safe to assume that the converter is working properly. If you are in doubt, take the car to a diagnostic center that has a tester.

Oxygen Sensor

An oxygen sensor is used on all models. The sensor protrudes into the exhaust stream and monitors the oxygen content of the exhaust gases. The difference between the oxygen content of the exhaust gases and that of the outside air generates a voltage signal to the ECM. The ECM monitors this voltage and, depending upon the value of the signal received, issues a command to adjust for a rich or a lean condition.

No attempt should ever be made to measure the voltage output of the sensor. The current drain of any conventional voltmeter would be such that it would permanently damage the sensor. No jumpers, test leads or any other electrical connections should ever be made to the sensor. Use these tools ONLY on the ECM side of the wiring harness connector AFTER disconnecting it from the sensor.

REMOVAL AND INSTALLATION

The oxygen sensor must be replaced every 30,000 miles (48,000 km.). The sensor may be difficult to remove when the engine temperature is below 120°F (49°C). Excessive removal force may damage the threads in the exhaust manifold or pipe; follow the removal procedure carefully.

1. Locate the oxygen sensor. It protrudes from the center of the exhaust manifold at the front of the engine compartment (it looks somewhat like a spark plug).

2. Disconnect the electrical connector from the oxygen sensor.

3. Spray a commercial heat riser solvent onto the sensor threads and allow it to soak in for at least five minutes.

4. Carefully unscrew and remove the sensor.

5. To install, first coat the new sensor's threads with G.M. anti-seize compound No. 5613695 or the equivalent. This is not a conventional anti-seize paste. The use of a regular compound may electrically insulate the sensor, rendering it inoperative. You must coat the threads with an electrically conductive anti-seize compound.

6. Installation torque is 30 ft.lb. (42 Nm.). Do not overtighten.

7. Reconnect the electrical connector. Be careful not to damage the electrical pigtail. Check the sensor boot for proper fit and installation.

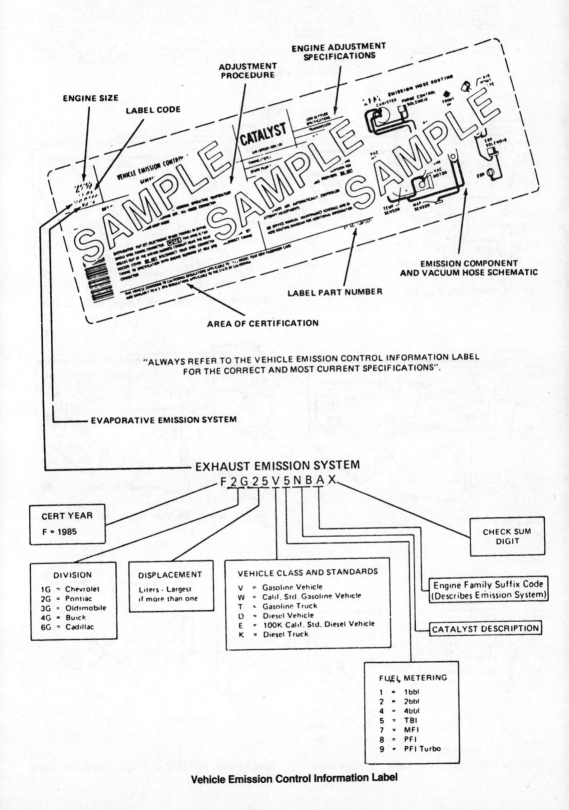

Vehicle Emission Control Information Label

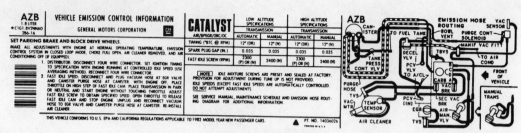

1982 1.8L VIN B, 2 BB1

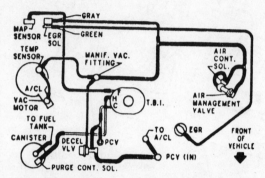

1983 2.0L VIN P, TBI, Man. Trans., w/AMV-Federal

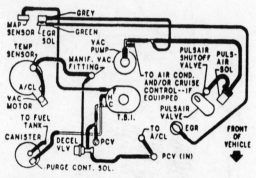

1983 2.0L VIN P, TBI, Man. Trans., w/cruise cont.—All

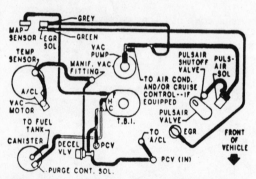

1983 2.0L VIN P, TBI, Auto. Trans., wo/cruise cont.—All

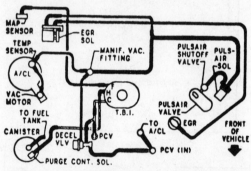

1983 2.0L VIN P, TBI, Man. Trans., wo/cruise cont.—All

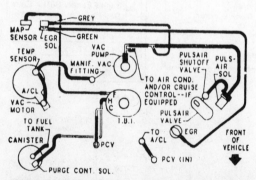

1983 2.0L VIN P, TBI, Auto. Trans., w/cruise cont.—All

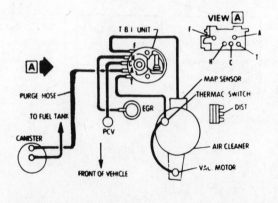

1984 1.8L VIN O, TBI, Man. & Auto Trans., wo/cruise cont.—Calif.

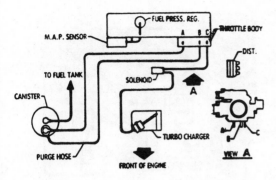

1984 1.8L VIN J, TBI Turbo, Man. & Auto. Trans.—Federal

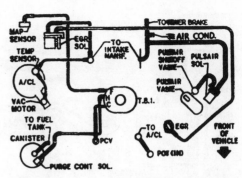

1984 2.0L VIN P, TBI, Man. & Auto. Trans.—Calif.

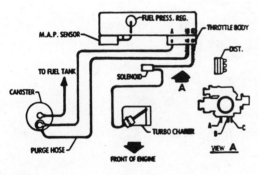

FAY

1984 1.8L VIN J, TBI Turbo, Man. & Auto. Trans.—Calif.

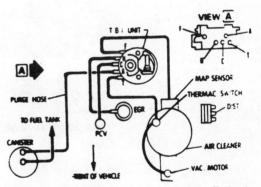

1984 1.8L VIN O, TBI, Man. & Auto. Trans.—Federal

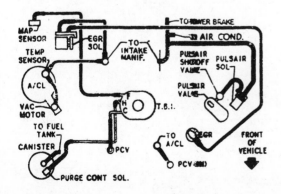

1984 2.0L VIN P, TBI, Man. & Auto. Trans.—Federal

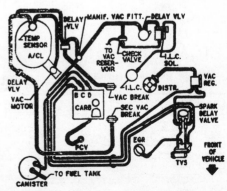

1984 2.0L VIN P, 2 BB1, Man. Trans.—Canada

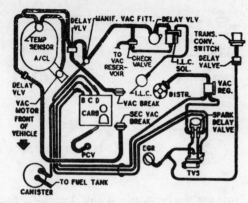

1984 2.0L VIN P, 2 BB1, Man. Trans.—Canada

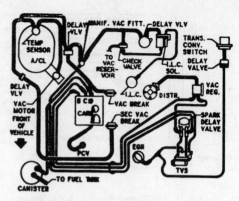

1984 2.0L VIN P, 2 BB1, Man. Trans.—Canada

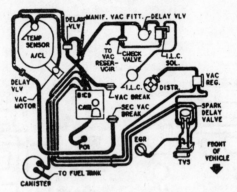

1984 2.0L VIN P, 2 BB1, Auto. Trans.—Canada

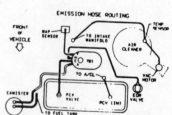

1985 2.0L VIN P, Cavalier—Federal

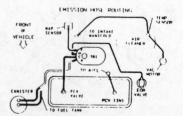

1985 2.0L VIN P, Cavalier—Calif.

1985-4 CYL-2.0L VIN P CAVALIER—CALIFORNIA

1985 2.0L VIN P, Cavalier—Canada

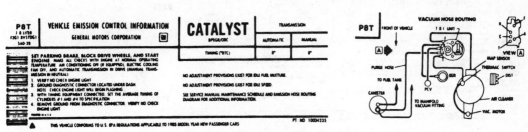

1985 1.8L Vin O, Pont. 2000—Federal

1985-4 CYL-1.8L VIN O PONT 2000—FEDERAL

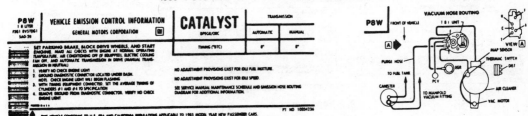

1985 1.8L Vin O, Pont. 2000—California

1985-4 CYL-1.8L VIN O PONT 2000—CALIFORNIA

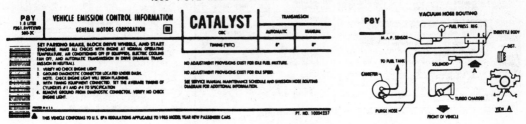

1985 1.8L Vin J, Pont. 2000—California

1985-4 CYL-1.8L VIN J PONT 2000 TURBO—CALIFORNIA

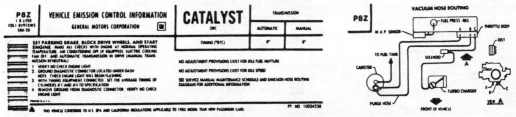

1985 1.8L Vin J, Pont. 2000 Turbo—California

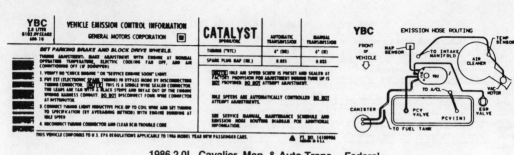

1986 2.0L, Cavalier, Man. & Auto Trans.—Federal

1986 2.0L, Cavalier, Man. & Auto Trans.—Calif.

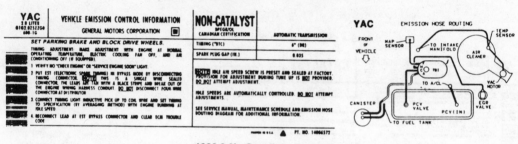

1986 2.8L, Cavalier—Canada

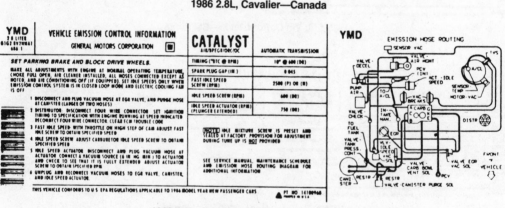

1986 2.8L, Cavalier—Auto. Trans.—Federal

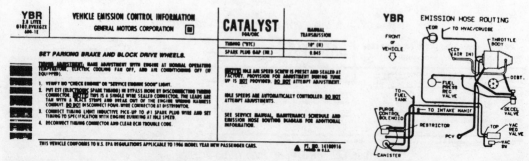

1986 2.8L, Cavalier—Man. Trans. (MG2, MG6)—Federal

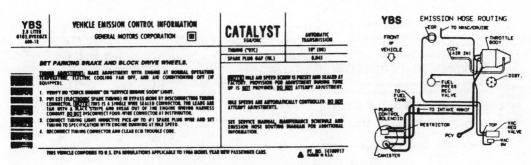

1986 2.8L, Cavalier—Auto. Trans. (MD9)—Federal

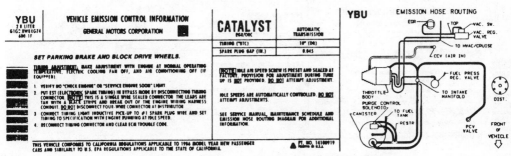

1986 2.8L, Cavalier—Auto. Trans. (MD9, ME9)—Calif.

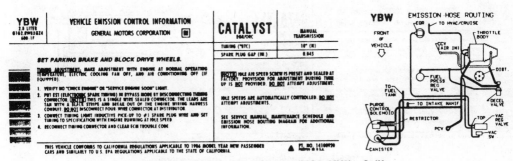

1986 2.8L, Cavalier—Man. Trans.—(MG2, MX6)—Calif.

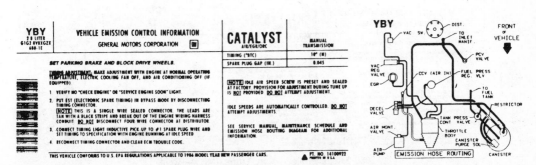

1986 2.8L, Cavalier—Man. Trans. (MB1)—Federal

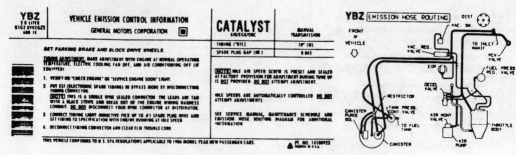

1986 2.8L, Cavalier—Man. Trans.—Federal

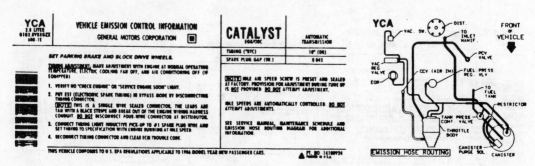

1986 2.8L, Cavalier—Auto. Trans. (MD8)—Federal

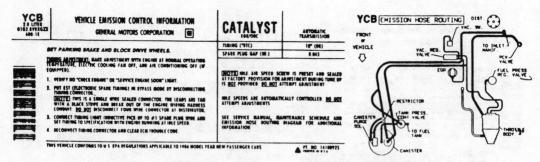

1986 2.8L, Cavalier—Auto. Trans.—Federal

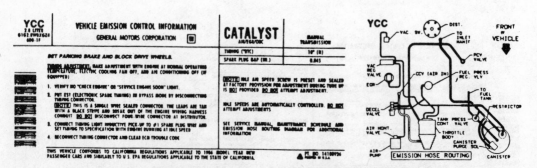

1986 2.8L, Cavalier—Man. Trans. (MB1)—Calif.

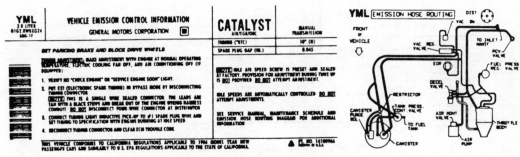

1986 2.8L, Cavalier—Man. Trans.—Calif.

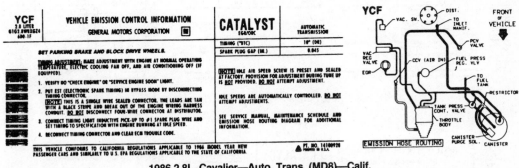

1986 2.8L, Cavalier—Auto. Trans. (MD8)—Calif.

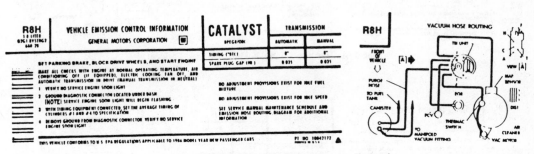

1986 1.8L, Pontiac—Auto. & Man. Trans.—Federal

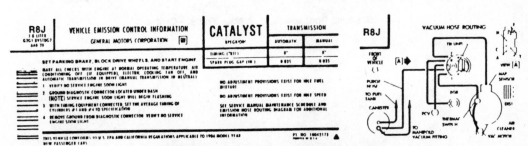

1986 1.8L, Pontiac—Auto. & Man. Trans.—Calif.

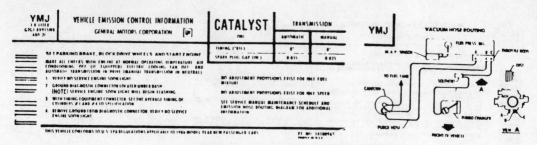

1986 1.8L, Pontiac—Auto. & Man. Trans.—Federal

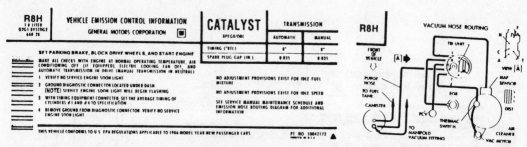

1986 1.8L, Pontiac—Auto. & Man. Trans.—Calif.

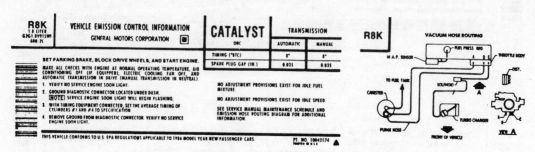

1986 1.8L, Pontiac—Auto. & Man. Trans.—Federal

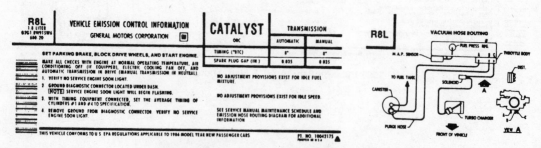

1986 1.8L, Pontiac—Auto. & Man. Trans.—Calif.

Fuel System

5

GENERAL FUEL SYSTEM COMPONENTS

Carbureted Engine Fuel Pumps

A mechanical fuel pump is used on the J-cars. It is of the diaphragm-type and because of the design is serviced by replacement only. No adjustments or repairs are possible. The pump is operated by an eccentric on the camshaft.

TESTING THE FUEL PUMP

To determine if the pump is in good condition, tests for both volume and pressure should be performed. The tests are made with the pump installed, and the engine at normal operating temperature and idle speed. Never replace a fuel pump without first performing these simple tests.

Be sure that the fuel filter has been changed at the specified interval, If in doubt, install a new filter Test

1. Disconnect the fuel line at the carburetor and connect a fuel pump pressure gauge. Fill the carburetor float bowl with gasoline.

2. Start the engine and check the pressure with the engine at idle. If the pump has a vapor return hose, squeeze it off so that an accurate reading can be obtained. Pressure should not be below 4.5 psi.

3. If the pressure is incorrect, replace the pump. If it is ok, go on to the volume test.

Volume Test

4. Disconnect the pressure gauge. Run the fuel line into a graduated container.

5. Run the engine at idle until one pint of gasoline has been pumped. One pint should be delivered in 30 seconds or less. There is normally enough fuel in the carburetor float bowl to perform this test, but refill it if necessary.

6. If the delivery rate is below the minimum,

check the lines for restrictions or leaks, then replace the pump.

REMOVAL AND INSTALLATION

The fuel pump is located at the center rear of the engine.

1. Disconnect the negative cable at the battery. Raise and support the car.

2. Disconnect the inlet hose from the pump. Disconnect the vapor return hose, if equipped.

3. Loosen the fuel line at the carburetor, then disconnect the outlet pipe from the pump.

4. Remove the two mounting bolts and remove the pump from the engine.

5. To install, place a new gasket on the pump and install the pump on the engine. Tighten the two mounting bolts alternately and evenly.

6. Install the pump outlet pipe. This is easier if the pipe is disconnected from the carburetor. Tighten the fitting while backing up the pump nut with another wrench. Install the pipe at the carburetor.

7. Install the inlet and vapor hoses. Lower the car, connect the negative battery cable, start the engine, and check for leaks.

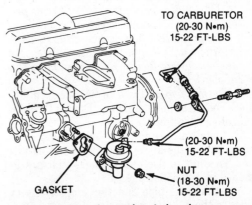

TO CARBURETOR
(20-30 N•m)
15-22 FT-LBS

(20-30 N•m)
15-22 FT-LBS

NUT
(18-30 N•m)
15-22 FT-LBS

GASKET

Fuel pump installation, carbureted engines

Fuel Injected Engine Fuel Pumps

The electric fuel pump is attached to the fuel sending unit. The pump used on the 1.8L and 2.0L OHV engine with throttle body injection is a low pressure pump that ranges from 4-13 psi.

The fuel pump used on the 2.8L V6 engine with port fuel injection is a higher pressure pump.

FUEL PUMP FLOW TEST

1. Test the fuel pump by connecting a hose from the EFI fuel feed line at the engine to a suitable unbreakable container. Apply battery voltage to the fuel pump test terminal (terminal **G** of the ALCL).

2. The fuel pump should supply ½ pint or more in 15 seconds.

3. If the flow is below minimum, chewck for fuel restriction. If there is no restriction, check the pump pressure.

FUEL SYSTEM PRESSURE TEST

1.8L, 2.0L OHV engines

1. Attach one adapter (J-29658-82) to gauge J-29658. To the other end of the gage, attach adapter J-29658-85.

2. Release the fuel system pressure.
CAUTION: *To reduce the risk of fire or personal injury, it is necessary to relieve the fuel system pressure before servicing the fuel system. Refer to Fuel System Pressure Release in the appropriate fuel injection system in this chapter.*

3. Disconnect the fuel feed hose at the engine to body connection.

4. Install the fuel pressure gage.

5. Start the engine and note the reading on the gauge. The pressure should be 9-13 psi.

6. Remove the gauge and reconnect the hose to the pipe. Start the engine and check for leaks.

1.8L, 2.0L OHC engines (TBI)

1. Release the fuel system pressure.
CAUTION: *To reduce the risk of fire or personal injury, it is necessary to relieve the fuel system pressure before servicing the fuel system. Refer to Fuel System Pressure Release in the appropriate fuel injection system in this chapter.*

2. Obtain two sections of ⅜" steel tubing. Each should be about 10" long. Double flare one end of each section.

3. Install a flare nut on each section. Connect each of the above sections of tubing into the flare nut to flre nut adapters that are included in J-29658 gauge.

4. Attach the pipe and the adapter assemblies to the J-29658 gauge.

5. Jack up the car and support it safely.

6. Disconnect the front fuel feed hose from the fuel pipe on the body.

7. Install a 10" length of ⅜" fuel hose on the fuel pipe on the body. Attach the other end of the hose onto one of the sections of the pipe mentioned in Step 2. Secure the hose connections with clamps.

8. Start the engine and check for leaks.

9. Observe the fuel pressure reading. It should be 9-13 psi.

10. Depressurize the fuel system and remove the gauge with adapters. Reconnect the fuel feed hose to the pipe and torque the clamp to 15 in.lb.

11. Lower the car, start the engine and check for fuel leaks.

1.8L, 2.0L OHC (Port Injection)

The pump will deliver fuel to the fuel rail and injectors, then to the pressure regulator, where the system pressure is controlled to about 35-38 psi. Excess fuel is then returned to the fuel tank.

When the engine is stopped, the engine can be turned **ON** by applying battery voltage to the test terminal located in the engine compartment.

1. Wrap a towel around the fuel pressure connector to absorb any small amount of fuel leakage that may occur while installing the gage J-34730-1. Pressure should not leak down after the fuel pump is shut **OFF**.

2. When the engine is idling, the manifold pressure is low (high vacuum) and is applied to the fuel regulator diaphragm. This will offset the spring and lower the fuel pressure to 25-30 psi. This idle pressure will vary somewhat depending on the barometric pressure, however the pressure idling should be less indicating pressure regulator control.

3. Pressure that continues to fall is caused by one of the following:

• In-tank fuel pumnp check valve not holding
• Pump coupling hose or pulsator leaking
• Fuel pressure regulator valve leaking
• Injector(s) sticking open
NOTE: *A injector sticking open can best be determined by checking for a fouled or saturated spark plug(s).*

2.8L V6 engine (Multi-Port Injection)

When the ignition switch is turned **ON**, the Electronic Control Module (ECM) will turn **ON** the in-tank fuel pump. It will remain **ON** as long as the engine is cranking or running, and the ECM is recieving references pulses. If there are no reference pulses, the ECM will shut

OFF the fuel pump within 2 seconds after ignition **ON** or engine stops.

The pump will deliver fuel to the fuel rail and injectors, then to the pressure regulator, where the system pressure is controlled to about 34-47 psi. Excess fuel is then returned to the fuel tank.

1. Wrap a towel around the fuel pressure connector to absorb any small amount of fuel leakage that may occur while installing the gage.

2. The ignition should be off for at least 10 seconds and the air conditioning **OFF**.

3. With the ignition **ON** the fuel pump should run for about 2 seconds. The ignition **ON** fuel pump pressure should be 40.5-47 psi. This pressure is controlled by the spring pressure within the regulator assembly.

4. When the engine is idling, the manifold pressure is low (high vacuum) and is applied to the fuel regulator diaphragm. This will offset the spring and lower the fuel pressure. This idle pressure will vary somewhat depending on the barometric pressure, however the pressure idling should be less indicating pressure regulator control.

5. Pressure that continues to fall is caused by one of the following:

- In-tank fuel pumnp check valve not holding
- Pump coupling hose or pulsator leaking
- Fuel pressure regulator valve leaking
- Injector(s) sticking open

NOTE: *A injector sticking open can best be determined by checking for a fouled or saturated spark plug(s).*

REMOVAL AND INSTALLATION

1. Release the fuel system pressure.

CAUTION: *To reduce the risk of fire or personal injury, it is necessary to relieve the fuel system pressure before servicing the fuel system. Refer to Fuel System Pressure Release in the appropriate fuel injection system in this chapter.*

2. Disconnect the negative battery cable.

3. Jack up the car and support it safely.

4. Remove the fuel tank.

5. Remove the fuel lever sending unit and pump assembly by turning the cam lock ring counterclockwise. Lift the assembly from the fuel tank and remove the fuel pump from the fuel level sending unit.

6. Pull the fuel pump up into the attaching hose or pulsator while pulling outward away from the bottom support. After the pump is clear of the bottom support, pull the pump assembly out of the rubber connector or pulsator for removal.

7. To install, push the pump into the attaching hose.

8. Install the fuel level sending unit and pump assembly into the tank assembly. Use new O-ring during reassembly.

WARNING: *Be careful not to fold over or twist the strainer when installing the sending unit as it will restrict fuel flow. Also, be careful the strainer does not block full travel of the float arm.*

9. Install the cam lock over the assembly and lock by turning clockwise.

10. Install the fuel tank.

Fuel Tank

REMOVAL AND INSTALLATION

1. Disconnect the negative cable at the battery. Raise and support the car.

2. Drain the tank. There is no drain plug; remaining fuel in the tank must be siphoned through the fuel feed line (the line to the fuel pump), because of the restrictor in the filler neck.

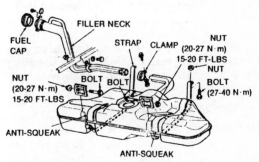

Fuel tank removal and installation details

3. Disconnect the hose and the vapor return hose from the level sending unit fittings.

4. Remove the ground wire screw.

5. Unplug the level sending unit electrical connector.

6. Disconnect the vent hose.

7. Unbolt the support straps, and lower and remove the tank. Installation is the reverse of removal.

CARBURETED FUEL SYSTEM

Carburetor

The Rochester E2SE is used on all 1982 J-cars. It is a two barrel, two stage carburetor of downdraft design used in conjunction with the Computer Command Control system of fuel control. The carburetor has special design fea-

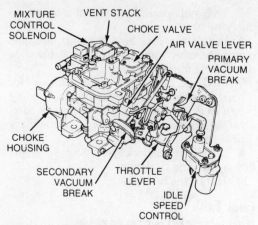

MIXTURE CONTROL SOLENOID

VENT STACK

CHOKE VALVE

AIR VALVE LEVER

PRIMARY VACUUM BREAK

CHOKE HOUSING

SECONDARY VACUUM BREAK

THROTTLE LEVER

IDLE SPEED CONTROL

Rochester E2SE carburetor

tures for optimum air/fuel mixture control during all ranges of engine operation.

MODEL IDENTIFICATION

General Motors Rochester carburetors are identified by their model code. The first number indicates the number of barrels, while one of the last letters indicates the type of choke used. These are V for the manifold mounted choke coil, C for the choke coil mounted in the carburetor body, and E for electric choke, also mounted on the carburetor. Model codes ending in A indicate an altitude-compensation carburetor.

REMOVAL AND INSTALLATION

1. Remove the air cleaner and gasket.
2. Disconnect the fuel pipe and all vacuum lines.
3. Tag and disconnect all electrical connections.
4. Disconnect the downshift cable.

5. If equipped with cruise control, disconnect the linkage.
6. Unscrew the carburetor mounting bolts and remove the carburetor.
7. Before installing the carburetor, fill the float bowl with gasoline to reduce the battery strain and the possibility of backfiring when the engine is started again.
8. Inspect the EFE heater for damage. Be sure that the throttle body and EFE mating surfaces are clean.
9. Install the carburetor and tighten the nuts alternately to the proper specifications.
10. Installation of the remaining components is in the reverse order of removal.

OVERHAUL

Efficient carburetion depends greatly on careful cleaning and inspection during overhaul, since dirt, gum, water, or varnish in or on the carburetor parts are often responsible for poor performance.

Overhaul your carburetor in a clean, dust-free area. Carefully disassemble the carburetor, referring often to the exploded views and directions packaged with the rebuilding kit. Keep all similar and look-alike parts segregated during disassembly and cleaning to avoid accidental interchange during assembly. Make a note of all jet sizes.

When the carburetor is disassembled, wash all parts (except diaphragms, electric choke units, pump plunger, and any other plastic, leather, fiber, or rubber parts) in clean carburetor solvent. Do not leave parts in the solvent any longer than is necessary to sufficiently loosen the deposits. Excessive cleaning may remove the special finish from the float bowl and choke valve bodies, leaving these parts unfit for service. Rinse all parts in clean solvent and blow

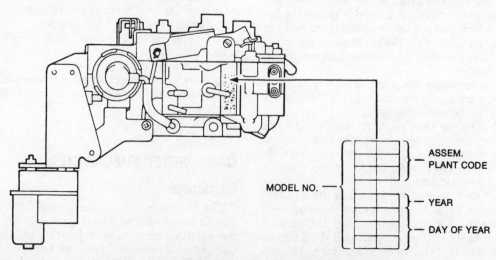

MODEL NO. —

ASSEM. PLANT CODE

YEAR

DAY OF YEAR

The carburetor identification number is stamped on the float bowl

them dry with compressed air or allow them to air dry. Wipe clean all cork, plastic, leather, and fiber parts with a clean, lint-free cloth.

Blow out all passages and jets with compressed air and be sure that there are no restrictions or blockages. Never use wire or similar tools to clean jets, fuel passages, or air bleeds. Clean all jets and valves separately to avoid accidental interchange.

Check all parts for wear or damage. If wear or damage is found, replace the defective parts. Especially check the following:

1. Check the float needle and seat for wear. If wear is found, replace the complete assembly.

2. Check the float hinge pin for wear and the float(s) for dents or distortion. Replace the float if fuel has leaked into it.

3. Check the throttle and choke shaft bores for wear or an out-of-round condition. Damage or wear to the throttle arm, shaft, or shaft bore will often require replacement of the throttle body. These parts require a close tolerance of fit; wear may allow air leakage, which could affect starting and idling.

NOTE: *Throttle shafts and bushings are not included in overhaul kits. They can be purchased separately.*

4. Inspect the idle mixture adjusting needles for burrs or grooves. Any such condition requires replacement of the needle, since you will not be able to obtain a satisfactory idle.

5. Test the accelerator pump check valves. They should pass air one way but not the other. Test for proper seating by blowing and sucking on the valve. Replace the valve check ball and spring as necessary. If the valve is satisfactory, wash the valve parts again to remove breath moisture.

6. Check the bowl cover for warped surfaces with a straightedge.

7. Closely inspect the accelerator pump plunger for wear and damage, replacing as necessary.

8. After the carburetor is assembled, check the choke valve for freedom of operation.

Carburetor overhaul kits are recommended for each overhaul. These kits contain all gaskets and new parts to replace those which deteriorate most rapidly. Failure to replace all parts supplied with the kit (especially gaskets) can result in poor performance later.

Some carburetor manufacturers supply overhaul kits for three basic types: minor repair; major repair; and gasket kits. Basically, the contain the following:

Minor Repair Kits:
- All gaskets
- Float needle valve
- All diagrams
- Spring for the pump diaphragm

Major Repair Kits:
- All jets and gaskets
- All diaphragms
- Float needle valve
- Pump ball valve
- Float
- Complete intermediate rod
- Intermediate pump lever
- Some cover hold-down screws and washers

Gasket Kits:
- All gaskets

After cleaning and checking all components, reassemble the carburetor, using new parts and referring to the exploded view. When reassembling, make sure that all screws and jets are tight in their seats, but do not overtighten as the tips will be distorted. Tighten all screws gradually, in rotation. Do not tighten needle valves into their seats; uneven jetting will result. Always use new gaskets. Be sure to adjust the float level when reassembling.

PRELIMINARY CHECKS

The following should be observed before attempting any adjustments.

1. Thoroughly warm the engine. If the engine is cold, be sure that it reaches operating temperature.

2. Check the torque of all carburetor mounting nuts and assembly screws. Also check the intake manifold-to-cylinder head bolts. If air is leaking at any of these points, any attempts at adjustment will inevitably lead to frustration.

3. Check the manifold heat control valve (if used) to be sure that it is free.

4. Check and adjust the choke as necessary.

5. Adjust the idle speed and mixture. If the mixture screws are capped, don't adjust them unless all other causes of rough idle have been eliminated. If any adjustments are performed that might possibly change the idle speed or mixture, adjust the idle and mixture again when you are finished.

Before you make any carburetor adjustments make sure that the engine is in tune. Many problems which are thought to be carburetor-related can be traced to an engine which is simply out-of-tune. Any trouble in these areas will have symptoms like those of carburetor problems.

FLOAT ADJUSTMENT

1. Remove the air horn from the throttle body.

2. Use your fingers to hold the retainer in place, and to push the float down into light contact with the needle.

3. Measure the distance from the toe of the float (furthest from the hinge) to the top of the carburetor (gasket removed).

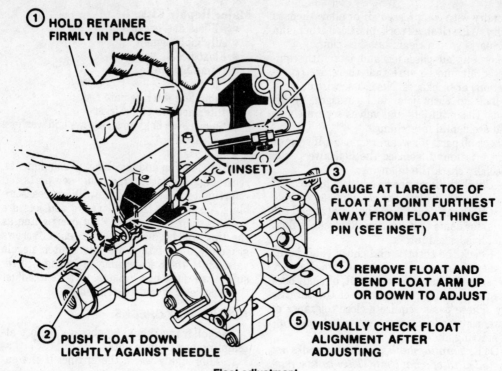

① **HOLD RETAINER FIRMLY IN PLACE**

(INSET)

③ **GAUGE AT LARGE TOE OF FLOAT AT POINT FURTHEST AWAY FROM FLOAT HINGE PIN (SEE INSET)**

④ **REMOVE FLOAT AND BEND FLOAT ARM UP OR DOWN TO ADJUST**

⑤ **VISUALLY CHECK FLOAT ALIGNMENT AFTER ADJUSTING**

② **PUSH FLOAT DOWN LIGHTLY AGAINST NEEDLE**

Float adjustment

4. To adjust, remove the float and gently bend the arm to specification. After adjustment, check the float alignment in the chamber.

PUMP ADJUSTMENT

E2SE carburetors have a non-adjustable pump lever. No adjustments are either necessary or possible.

FAST IDLE ADJUSTMENT

1. Set the ignition timing and curb idle speed, and disconnect and plug hoses as directed on the emission control decal.
2. Place the fast idle screw on the highest step of the cam.
3. Start the engine and adjust the engine speed to specification with the fast idle screw.

CHOKE COIL LEVER ADJUSTMENT

1. Remove the three retaining screws and remove the choke cover and coil. On models with a riveted choke cover, drill out the three rivets and remove the cover and choke coil.
NOTE: *A choke stat cover retainer kit is required for reassembly.*
2. Place the fast idle screw on the high step of the cam.
3. Close the choke by pushing in on the intermediate choke lever.
4. Insert a drill or gauge of the specified size into the hole in the choke housing. The choke lever in the housing should be up against the side of the gauge.
5. If the lever does not just touch the gauge, bend the intermediate choke rod to adjust.

FAST IDLE CAM (CHOKE ROD) ADJUSTMENT

NOTE: *A special angle gauge should be used. If it is not available, an inch measurement can be made.*
1. Adjust the choke coil lever and fast idle first.
2. Rotate the degree scale until it is zeroed.
3. Close the choke and install the degree scale onto the choke plate. Center the leveling bubble.
4. Rotate the scale so that the specified degree is opposite the scale pointer.
5. Place the fast idle screw on the second step of the cam (against the high step). Close the choke by pushing in the intermediate lever.
6. Bend the fast idle cam rod at the U to adjust the angle to specifications.

AIR VALVE ROD ADJUSTMENT

1. Seat the vacuum diaphragm with an outside vacuum source. Tape over the purge bleed hole if present.
2. Close the air valve.
3. Insert the specified gauge between the rod and the end of the slot in the plunger.
4. Bend the rod to adjust the clearance.

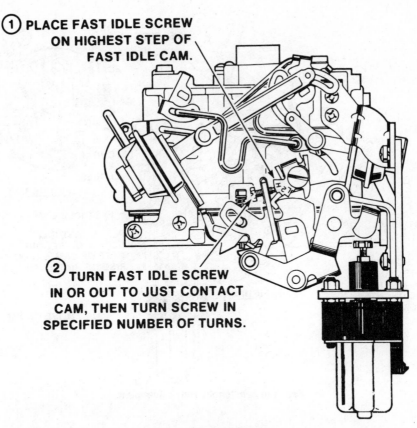

① PLACE FAST IDLE SCREW ON HIGHEST STEP OF FAST IDLE CAM.

② TURN FAST IDLE SCREW IN OR OUT TO JUST CONTACT CAM, THEN TURN SCREW IN SPECIFIED NUMBER OF TURNS.

Fast idle adjustment

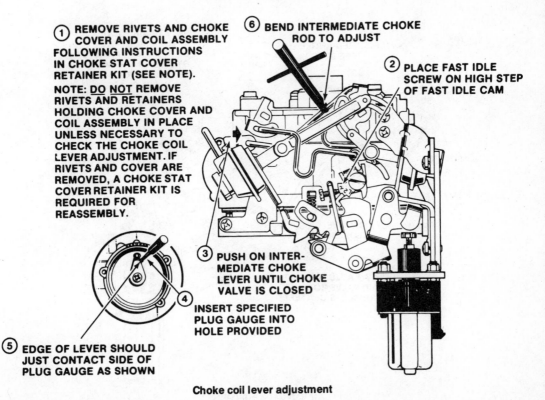

① REMOVE RIVETS AND CHOKE COVER AND COIL ASSEMBLY FOLLOWING INSTRUCTIONS IN CHOKE STAT COVER RETAINER KIT (SEE NOTE).

NOTE: DO NOT REMOVE RIVETS AND RETAINERS HOLDING CHOKE COVER AND COIL ASSEMBLY IN PLACE UNLESS NECESSARY TO CHECK THE CHOKE COIL LEVER ADJUSTMENT. IF RIVETS AND COVER ARE REMOVED, A CHOKE STAT COVER RETAINER KIT IS REQUIRED FOR REASSEMBLY.

⑥ BEND INTERMEDIATE CHOKE ROD TO ADJUST

② PLACE FAST IDLE SCREW ON HIGH STEP OF FAST IDLE CAM

③ PUSH ON INTERMEDIATE CHOKE LEVER UNTIL CHOKE VALVE IS CLOSED

④ INSERT SPECIFIED PLUG GAUGE INTO HOLE PROVIDED

⑤ EDGE OF LEVER SHOULD JUST CONTACT SIDE OF PLUG GAUGE AS SHOWN

Choke coil lever adjustment

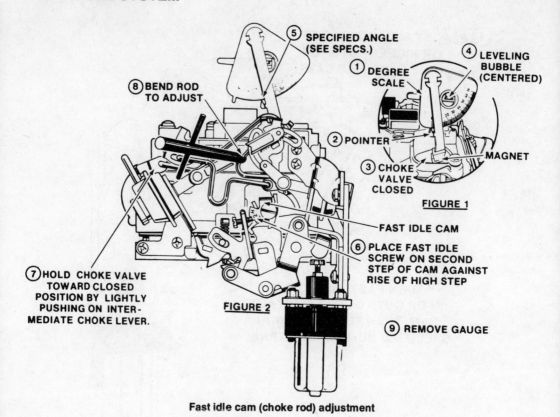

⑤ SPECIFIED ANGLE (SEE SPECS.)

⑧ BEND ROD TO ADJUST

① DEGREE SCALE

④ LEVELING BUBBLE (CENTERED)

② POINTER

③ CHOKE VALVE CLOSED

MAGNET

FIGURE 1

FAST IDLE CAM

⑥ PLACE FAST IDLE SCREW ON SECOND STEP OF CAM AGAINST RISE OF HIGH STEP

⑦ HOLD CHOKE VALVE TOWARD CLOSED POSITION BY LIGHTLY PUSHING ON INTERMEDIATE CHOKE LEVER.

FIGURE 2

⑨ REMOVE GAUGE

Fast idle cam (choke rod) adjustment

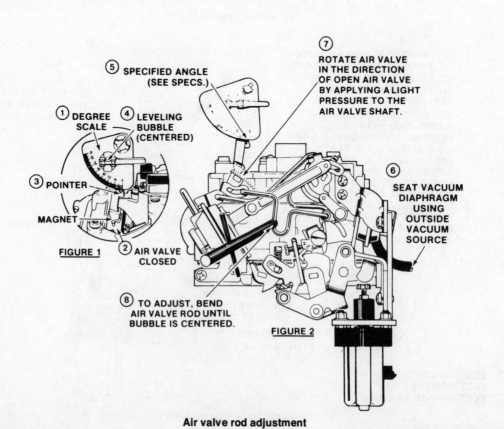

⑤ SPECIFIED ANGLE (SEE SPECS.)

⑦ ROTATE AIR VALVE IN THE DIRECTION OF OPEN AIR VALVE BY APPLYING A LIGHT PRESSURE TO THE AIR VALVE SHAFT.

① DEGREE SCALE

④ LEVELING BUBBLE (CENTERED)

③ POINTER

MAGNET

FIGURE 1

② AIR VALVE CLOSED

⑥ SEAT VACUUM DIAPHRAGM USING OUTSIDE VACUUM SOURCE

⑧ TO ADJUST, BEND AIR VALVE ROD UNTIL BUBBLE IS CENTERED.

FIGURE 2

Air valve rod adjustment

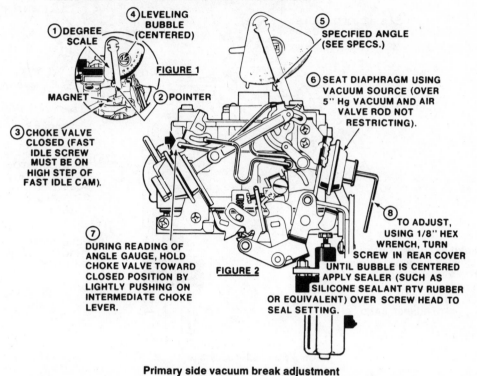

NOTE: PRIOR TO ADJUSTMENT, REMOVE VACUUM BREAK FROM CARBURETOR. PLACE BRACKET IN VICE AND, USING SAFETY PRECAUTIONS, GRIND OFF ADJUSTMENT SCREW CAP. REINSTALL VACUUM BREAK.

④ LEVELING BUBBLE (CENTERED)

① DEGREE SCALE

⑤ SPECIFIED ANGLE (SEE SPECS.)

FIGURE 1

MAGNET

② POINTER

⑥ SEAT DIAPHRAGM USING VACUUM SOURCE (OVER 5" Hg VACUUM AND AIR VALVE ROD NOT RESTRICTING).

③ CHOKE VALVE CLOSED (FAST IDLE SCREW MUST BE ON HIGH STEP OF FAST IDLE CAM).

⑧ TO ADJUST, USING 1/8" HEX WRENCH, TURN SCREW IN REAR COVER UNTIL BUBBLE IS CENTERED APPLY SEALER (SUCH AS SILICONE SEALANT RTV RUBBER OR EQUIVALENT) OVER SCREW HEAD TO SEAL SETTING.

⑦ DURING READING OF ANGLE GAUGE, HOLD CHOKE VALVE TOWARD CLOSED POSITION BY LIGHTLY PUSHING ON INTERMEDIATE CHOKE LEVER.

FIGURE 2

Primary side vacuum break adjustment

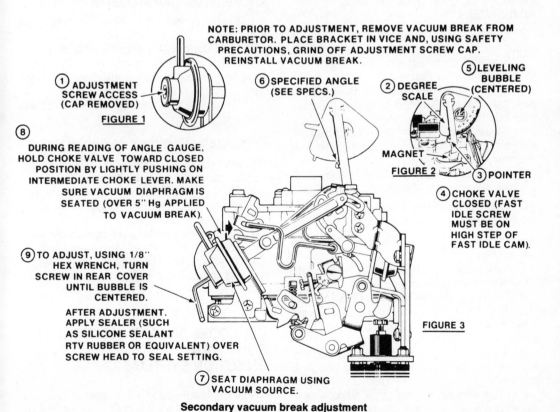

NOTE: PRIOR TO ADJUSTMENT, REMOVE VACUUM BREAK FROM CARBURETOR. PLACE BRACKET IN VICE AND, USING SAFETY PRECAUTIONS, GRIND OFF ADJUSTMENT SCREW CAP. REINSTALL VACUUM BREAK.

① ADJUSTMENT SCREW ACCESS (CAP REMOVED)

FIGURE 1

⑥ SPECIFIED ANGLE (SEE SPECS.)

② DEGREE SCALE

⑤ LEVELING BUBBLE (CENTERED)

MAGNET

FIGURE 2

③ POINTER

④ CHOKE VALVE CLOSED (FAST IDLE SCREW MUST BE ON HIGH STEP OF FAST IDLE CAM).

⑧ DURING READING OF ANGLE GAUGE, HOLD CHOKE VALVE TOWARD CLOSED POSITION BY LIGHTLY PUSHING ON INTERMEDIATE CHOKE LEVER. MAKE SURE VACUUM DIAPHRAGM IS SEATED (OVER 5" Hg APPLIED TO VACUUM BREAK).

⑨ TO ADJUST, USING 1/8" HEX WRENCH, TURN SCREW IN REAR COVER UNTIL BUBBLE IS CENTERED.

AFTER ADJUSTMENT. APPLY SEALER (SUCH AS SILICONE SEALANT RTV RUBBER OR EQUIVALENT) OVER SCREW HEAD TO SEAL SETTING.

FIGURE 3

⑦ SEAT DIAPHRAGM USING VACUUM SOURCE.

Secondary vacuum break adjustment

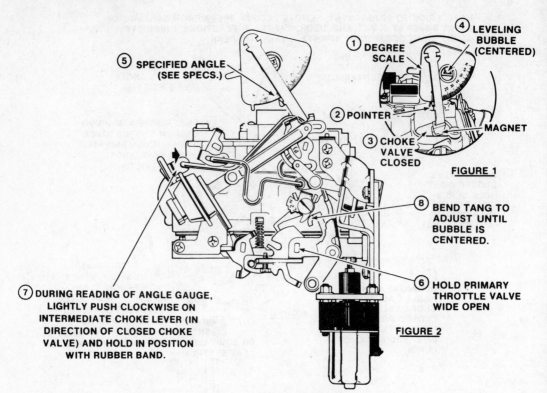

① DEGREE SCALE

④ LEVELING BUBBLE (CENTERED)

⑤ SPECIFIED ANGLE (SEE SPECS.)

② POINTER

③ CHOKE VALVE CLOSED

MAGNET

FIGURE 1

⑧ BEND TANG TO ADJUST UNTIL BUBBLE IS CENTERED.

⑦ DURING READING OF ANGLE GAUGE, LIGHTLY PUSH CLOCKWISE ON INTERMEDIATE CHOKE LEVER (IN DIRECTION OF CLOSED CHOKE VALVE) AND HOLD IN POSITION WITH RUBBER BAND.

⑥ HOLD PRIMARY THROTTLE VALVE WIDE OPEN

FIGURE 2

Choke unloader adjustment

PRIMARY SIDE VACUUM BREAK ADJUSTMENT

1. Follow Steps 1-4 of the Fast Idle Cam Adjustment.
2. Seat the choke vacuum diaphragm with an outside vacuum source.
3. Push in on the intermediate choke lever to close the choke valve, and hold closed during adjustment.
4. Adjust by using a ⅛" hex wrench to turn the screw in the rear cover until the bubble is centered.
5. After adjusting, apply RTV silicone sealant over the screw to seal the setting.

SECONDARY VACUUM BREAK ADJUSTMENT

1. Follow Steps 1-4 of the Fast Idle Cam Adjustment.
2. Seat the choke vacuum diaphragm with an outside vacuum source.
3. Push in on the intermediate choke lever to close the choke valve, and hold closed during adjustment. Make sure the plunger spring is compressed and seated, if present.
4. Adjust by using a ⅛" hex wrench to turn the screw in the rear cover until the bubble is centered.
5. After adjusting, apply RTV silicone sealant over the screw to seal the setting.

CHOKE UNLOADER ADJUSTMENT

1. Follow Steps 1-4 of the Fast Idle Cam Adjustment.
2. Hold the primary throttle wide open.
3. If the engine is warm, close the choke valve by pushing in on the intermediate choke lever.
4. Bend the unloader tang until the bubble is centered.

SECONDARY LOCKOUT ADJUSTMENT

1. Pull the choke wide open by pushing out on the intermediate choke lever.
2. Open the throttle until the end of the secondary actuating lever is opposite the toe of the lockout lever.
3. Gauge clearance between the lockout lever and secondary lever should be as specified.
4. To adjust, bend the lockout lever where it contacts the fast idle cam.

GM MODEL 300 AND 500 THROTTLE BODY (TBI) INJECTION SYSTEMS

The single bore, Model 300 throttle body unit used on the 1983-86 1.8L OHC engine and the

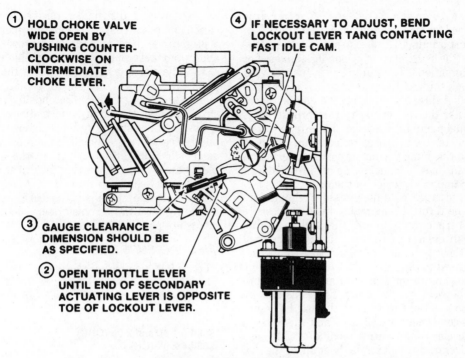

① HOLD CHOKE VALVE WIDE OPEN BY PUSHING COUNTER-CLOCKWISE ON INTERMEDIATE CHOKE LEVER.

④ IF NECESSARY TO ADJUST, BEND LOCKOUT LEVER TANG CONTACTING FAST IDLE CAM.

③ GAUGE CLEARANCE - DIMENSION SHOULD BE AS SPECIFIED.

② OPEN THROTTLE LEVER UNTIL END OF SECONDARY ACTUATING LEVER IS OPPOSITE TOE OF LOCKOUT LEVER.

Secondary lockout adjustment

Model 500 throttle body unit used on the 1983-86 2.0L OHV engine are similar systems.

In these throttle body systems, a single fuel injector mounted at the top of the throttle body sprays fuel down through the throttle valve and into the intake manifold. The throttle body resembles a carburetor in appearance but does away with much of the carburetor's complexity (choke system and linkage, power valves, accelerator pump, jets, fuel circuits, etc.), replacing these with the electrically operated fuel injector.

The injector is actually a solenoid which when activated lifts a pintle valve off its seat, allowing the pressurized (10 psi) fuel behind the valve to spray out. The nozzle of the injector is designed to atomize the fuel for complete air/fuel mixture.

The activating signal for the injector originates with the Electronic Control Module (ECM), which monitors engine temperature, throttle position, vehicle speed and several other engine-related conditions then continuously updates injector opening times in relation to the information given by these sensors.

The throttle body is also equipped with an idle air control valve. When the valve opens it allows air to bypass the throttle, which provides the additional air required to idle at elevated speed when the engine is cold. The idle air control motor also compensates for accessory loads and changing engine friction during break-in. The idle speed control valve is controlled by the ECM.

Fuel pressure for the system is provided by an in-tank fuel pump. The pump is a two-stage

E2SE Carburetor Specifications

Year	Carburetor Identification	Float Level (in.)	Fast Idle (rpm)	Choke Coil Lever (in.)	Fast Idle Cam (deg.)	Air Valve Rod (deg.)	Primary Vacuum Break (deg/in.)	Choke Setting (notches)	Secondary Vacuum Break (deg/in.)	Choke Unloader (deg/in.)	Secondary Lockout (in.)
1982	17081600	5/16	①	.085	24	1	20/.110	①	27/.157	35/.220	.012
	17081601	5/16	①	.085	24	1	20/.110	①	27/.157	35/.220	.012
	17081607	5/16	①	.085	24	1	20/.110	①	27/.157	35/.220	.012
	17081700	5/16	①	.085	24	1	20/.110	①	27/.157	35/.220	.012
	17081701	5/16	①	.085	24	1	20/.110	①	27/.157	35/.220	.012

① See underhood emissions sticker

turbine designed powered by a DC motor. It is designed for smooth, quiet operation, high flow and fast priming. The design of the fuel inlet reduces the possibility of vapor lock under hot fuel conditions. The pump sends fuel forward through the fuel line to a stainless steel high-flow fuel filter mounted on the engine. From the filter the fuel moves to the throttle body. The fuel pump inlet is located in a reservoir in the fuel tank which insures a constant supply of fuel to the pump during hard cornering and on steep inclines. The fuel pump is controlled by a fuel pump relay, which in turn receives its signal from the ECM. A fuel pressure regulator inside the throttle body maintains fuel pressure at 10 psi and routes unused fuel back to the fuel tank through a fuel return line. On the dual throttle body system, a fuel pressure compensator is used on the second throttle body assembly to compensate for a momentary fuel pressure drop between the two units. This constant circulation of fuel through the throttle body prevents component overheating and vapor lock.

The electronic control module (ECM), also called a micro-computer, is the brain of the fuel injection system. After receiving input from various sensing elements in the system the ECM commands the fuel injector, idle air control motor, EST distributor, torque converter clutch and other engine actuators to operate in a pre-programmed manner to improve driveability and fuel economy while controlling emissions. The sensing elements update the computer every tenth of a second for general information and every 12.5 milliseconds for critical emissions and driveability information.

The ECM has limited system diagnostic capability. If certain system malfunctions occur, the diagnostic Check Engine light in the instrument panel will light, alerting the driver to the need for service.

Since both idle speed and mixture are controlled by the ECM on this system, no adjustments are possible or necessary.

FUEL PRESSURE RELEASE

CAUTION: *To reduce the risk of fire or personal injury, it is necessary to relieve the fuel system pressure before servicing the fuel system.*

1983-86 1.8L and 2.0L (OHC)
1983-84 2.0L (OHV)

1. Remove the fuel pump fuse from the fuse block.

2. Crank the engine. The engine will run un-

1. Fuel meter assembly
2. Gasket—fuel meter body
3. Screw & washer assy—attach. (3)
4. Fuel injector kit
5. Filter—fuel injector nozzle
6. Seal—small "O" ring
7. Seal—large "O" ring
8. Back-up washer—fuel injector
9. Gasket—fuel meter cover
10. Dust seal—press, regulator
11. Gasket—fuel meter outlet
12. Screw & washer assy—long (3)
13. Screw & washer assy—short (2)
14. Nut—fuel inlet
15. Gasket—fuel inlet nut
16. Nut—fuel outlet
17. Gasket—fuel outlet nut
18. Fuel meter body assembly
19. Throttle body assembly
20. Screw—idle stop
21. Spring—idle stop screw
22. Lever—TPS
23. Screw—TPS lever attaching
24. Sensor—throttle position kit
25. Retainer—TPS (2)
26. Screw—TPS attaching (2)
27. Washer—TPS screw (2)
28. Idle air control valve
29. Gasket—control valve to T.B.
30. Gasket—flange mounting

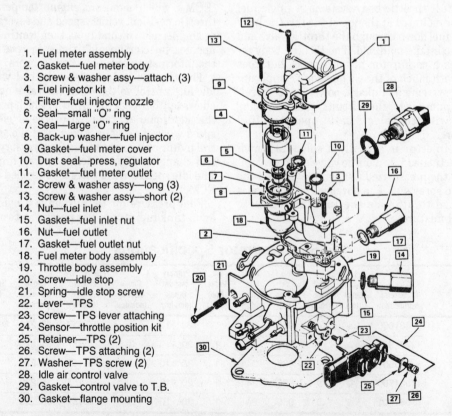

Exploded view of the GM Model 500 throttle body injection unit, Model 6300 similar

CHILTON'S
FUEL ECONOMY
& TUNE-UP TIPS

Tune-up • Spark Plug Diagnosis • Emission Controls

Fuel System • Cooling System • Tires and Wheels

General Maintenance

CHILTON'S FUEL ECONOMY & TUNE-UP TIPS

Fuel economy is important to everyone, no matter what kind of vehicle you drive. The maintenance-minded motorist can save both money and fuel using these tips and the periodic maintenance and tune-up procedures in this Repair and Tune-Up Guide.

There are more than 130,000,000 cars and trucks registered for private use in the United States. Each travels an average of 10-12,000 miles per year, and, and in total they consume close to 70 billion gallons of fuel each year. This represents nearly ⅔ of the oil imported by the United States each year. The Federal government's goal is to reduce consumption 10% by 1985. A variety of methods are either already in use or under serious consideration, and they all affect you driving and the cars you will drive. In addition to "down-sizing", the auto industry is using or investigating the use of electronic fuel delivery, electronic engine controls and alternative engines for use in smaller and lighter vehicles, among other alternatives to meet the federally mandated Corporate Average Fuel Economy (CAFE) of 27.5 mpg by 1985. The government, for its part, is considering rationing, mandatory driving curtailments and tax increases on motor vehicle fuel in an effort to reduce consumption. The government's goal of a 10% reduction could be realized — and further government regulation avoided — if every private vehicle could use just 1 less gallon of fuel per week.

How Much Can You Save?

Tests have proven that almost anyone can make at least a 10% reduction in fuel consumption through regular maintenance and tune-ups. When a major manufacturer of spark plugs sur-

TUNE-UP

1. Check the cylinder compression to be sure the engine will really benefit from a tune-up and that it is capable of producing good fuel economy. A tune-up will be wasted on an engine in poor mechanical condition.

2. Replace spark plugs regularly. New spark plugs alone can increase fuel economy 3%.

3. Be sure the spark plugs are the correct type (heat range) for your vehicle. See the Tune-Up Specifications.

Heat range refers to the spark plug's ability to conduct heat away from the firing end. It must conduct the heat away in an even pattern to avoid becoming a source of pre-ignition, yet it must also operate hot enough to burn off conductive deposits that could cause misfiring.

The heat range is usually indicated by a number on the spark plug, part of the manufacturer's designation for each individual spark plug. The numbers in bold-face indicate the heat range in each manufacturer's identification system.

Manufacturer	Typical Designation
AC	R **45** TS
Bosch (old)	WA **145** T30
Bosch (new)	HR **8** Y
Champion	RBL **15** Y
Fram/Autolite	4**15**
Mopar	P-**62** PR
Motorcraft	BRF-**42**
NGK	BP **5** ES-15
Nippondenso	W **16** EP
Prestolite	14GR **5** 2A

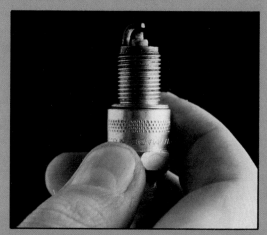

Periodically, check the spark plugs to be sure they are firing efficiently. They are excellent indicators of the internal condition of your engine.

On AC, Bosch (new), Champion, Fram/Autolite, Mopar, Motorcraft and Prestolite, a higher number indicates a hotter plug. On Bosch (old), NGK and Nippondenso, a higher number indicates a colder plug.

4. Make sure the spark plugs are properly gapped. See the Tune-Up Specifications in this book.

5. Be sure the spark plugs are firing efficiently. The illustrations on the next 2 pages show you how to "read" the firing end of the spark plug.

6. Check the ignition timing and set it to specifications. Tests show that almost all cars have incorrect ignition timing by more than 2°.

veyed over 6,000 cars nationwide, they found that a tune-up, on cars that needed one, increased fuel economy over 11%. Replacing worn plugs alone, accounted for a 3% increase. The same test also revealed that 8 out of every 10 vehicles will have some maintenance deficiency that will directly affect fuel economy, emissions or performance. Most of this mileage-robbing neglect could be prevented with regular maintenance.

Modern engines require that all of the functioning systems operate properly for maximum efficiency. A malfunction anywhere wastes fuel. You can keep your vehicle running as efficiently and economically as possible, by being aware of your vehicle's operating and performance characteristics. If your vehicle suddenly develops performance or fuel economy problems it could be due to one or more of the following:

PROBLEM	POSSIBLE CAUSE
Engine Idles Rough	Ignition timing, idle mixture, vacuum leak or something amiss in the emission control system.
Hesitates on Acceleration	Dirty carburetor or fuel filter, improper accelerator pump setting, ignition timing or fouled spark plugs.
Starts Hard or Fails to Start	Worn spark plugs, improperly set automatic choke, ice (or water) in fuel system.
Stalls Frequently	Automatic choke improperly adjusted and possible dirty air filter or fuel filter.
Performs Sluggishly	Worn spark plugs, dirty fuel or air filter, ignition timing or automatic choke out of adjustment.

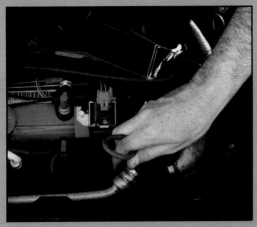

Check spark plug wires on conventional point type ignition for cracks by bending them in a loop around your finger.

Be sure that spark plug wires leading to adjacent cylinders do not run too close together. (Photo courtesy Champion Spark Plug Co.)

7. If your vehicle does not have electronic ignition, check the points, rotor and cap as specified.

8. Check the spark plug wires (used with conventional point-type ignitions) for cracks and burned or broken insulation by bending them in a loop around your finger. Cracked wires decrease fuel efficiency by failing to deliver full voltage to the spark plugs. One misfiring spark plug can cost you as much as 2 mpg.

9. Check the routing of the plug wires. Misfiring can be the result of spark plug leads to adjacent cylinders running parallel to each other and too close together. One wire tends to pick up voltage from the other causing it to fire "out of time".

10. Check all electrical and ignition circuits for voltage drop and resistance.

11. Check the distributor mechanical and/or vacuum advance mechanisms for proper functioning. The vacuum advance can be checked by twisting the distributor plate in the opposite direction of rotation. It should spring back when released.

12. Check and adjust the valve clearance on engines with mechanical lifters. The clearance should be slightly loose rather than too tight.

SPARK PLUG DIAGNOSIS

Normal

APPEARANCE: This plug is typical of one operating normally. The insulator nose varies from a light tan to grayish color with slight electrode wear. The presence of slight deposits is normal on used plugs and will have no adverse effect on engine performance. The spark plug heat range is correct for the engine and the engine is running normally.

CAUSE: Properly running engine.

RECOMMENDATION: Before reinstalling this plug, the electrodes should be cleaned and filed square. Set the gap to specifications. If the plug has been in service for more than 10-12,000 miles, the entire set should probably be replaced with a fresh set of the same heat range.

Oil Deposits

APPEARANCE: The firing end of the plug is covered with a wet, oily coating.

CAUSE: The problem is poor oil control. On high mileage engines, oil is leaking past the rings or valve guides into the combustion chamber. A common cause is also a plugged PCV valve, and a ruptured fuel pump diaphragm can also cause this condition. Oil fouled plugs such as these are often found in new or recently overhauled engines, before normal oil control is achieved, and can be cleaned and reinstalled.

RECOMMENDATION: A hotter spark plug may temporarily relieve the problem, but the engine is probably in need of work.

Incorrect Heat Range

APPEARANCE: The effects of high temperature on a spark plug are indicated by clean white, often blistered insulator. This can also be accompanied by excessive wear of the electrode, and the absence of deposits.

CAUSE: Check for the correct spark plug heat range. A plug which is too hot for the engine can result in overheating. A car operated mostly at high speeds can require a colder plug. Also check ignition timing, cooling system level, fuel mixture and leaking intake manifold.

RECOMMENDATION: If all ignition and engine adjustments are known to be correct, and no other malfunction exists, install spark plugs one heat range colder.

Photos Courtesy Fram Corporation

Carbon Deposits

APPEARANCE: Carbon fouling is easily identified by the presence of dry, soft, black, sooty deposits.

CAUSE: Changing the heat range can often lead to carbon fouling, as can prolonged slow, stop-and-start driving. If the heat range is correct, carbon fouling can be attributed to a rich fuel mixture, sticking choke, clogged air cleaner, worn breaker points, retarded timing or low compression. If only one or two plugs are carbon fouled, check for corroded or cracked wires on the affected plugs. Also look for cracks in the distributor cap between the towers of affected cylinders.

RECOMMENDATION: After the problem is corrected, these plugs can be cleaned and reinstalled if not worn severely.

MMT Fouled

APPEARANCE: Spark plugs fouled by MMT (Methycyclopentadienyl Maganese Tricarbonyl) have reddish, rusty appearance on the insulator and side electrode.

CAUSE: MMT is an anti-knock additive in gasoline used to replace lead. During the combustion process, the MMT leaves a reddish deposit on the insulator and side electrode.

RECOMMENDATION: No engine malfunction is indicated and the deposits will not affect plug performance any more than lead deposits (see Ash Deposits). MMT fouled plugs can be cleaned, regapped and reinstalled.

High Speed Glazing

APPEARANCE: Glazing appears as shiny coating on the plug, either yellow or tan in color.

CAUSE: During hard, fast acceleration, plug temperatures rise suddenly. Deposits from normal combustion have no chance to fluff-off; instead, they melt on the insulator forming an electrically conductive coating which causes misfiring.

RECOMMENDATION: Glazed plugs are not easily cleaned. They should be replaced with a fresh set of plugs of the correct heat range. If the condition recurs, using plugs with a heat range one step colder may cure the problem.

Ash (Lead) Deposits

APPEARANCE: Ash deposits are characterized by light brown or white colored deposits crusted on the side or center electrodes. In some cases it may give the plug a rusty appearance.

CAUSE: Ash deposits are normally derived from oil or fuel additives burned during normal combustion. Normally they are harmless, though excessive amounts can cause misfiring. If deposits are excessive in short mileage, the valve guides may be worn.

RECOMMENDATION: Ash-fouled plugs can be cleaned, gapped and reinstalled.

Detonation

APPEARANCE: Detonation is usually characterized by a broken plug insulator.

CAUSE: A portion of the fuel charge will begin to burn spontaneously, from the increased heat following ignition. The explosion that results applies extreme pressure to engine components, frequently damaging spark plugs and pistons.

Detonation can result by over-advanced ignition timing, inferior gasoline (low octane) lean air/fuel mixture, poor carburetion, engine lugging or an increase in compression ratio due to combustion chamber deposits or engine modification.

RECOMMENDATION: Replace the plugs after correcting the problem.

EMISSION CONTROLS

13. Be aware of the general condition of the emission control system. It contributes to reduced pollution and should be serviced regularly to maintain efficient engine operation.

14. Check all vacuum lines for dried, cracked or brittle conditions. Something as simple as a leaking vacuum hose can cause poor performance and loss of economy.

15. Avoid tampering with the emission control system. Attempting to improve fuel econ-

FUEL SYSTEM

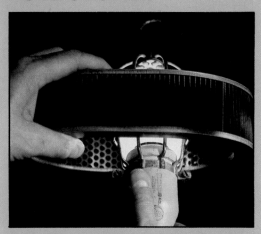

Check the air filter with a light behind it. If you can see light through the filter it can be reused.

Extremely clogged filters should be discarded and replaced with a new one.

18. Replace the air filter regularly. A dirty air filter richens the air/fuel mixture and can increase fuel consumption as much as 10%. Tests show that 1/3 of all vehicles have air filters in need of replacement.

19. Replace the fuel filter at least as often as recommended.

20. Set the idle speed and carburetor mixture to specifications.

21. Check the automatic choke. A sticking or malfunctioning choke wastes gas.

22. During the summer months, adjust the automatic choke for a leaner mixture which will produce faster engine warm-ups.

COOLING SYSTEM

29. Be sure all accessory drive belts are in good condition. Check for cracks or wear.

30. Adjust all accessory drive belts to proper tension.

31. Check all hoses for swollen areas, worn spots, or loose clamps.

32. Check coolant level in the radiator or expansion tank.

33. Be sure the thermostat is operating properly. A stuck thermostat delays engine warm-up and a cold engine uses nearly twice as much fuel as a warm engine.

34. Drain and replace the engine coolant at least as often as recommended. Rust and scale

TIRES & WHEELS

38. Check the tire pressure often with a pencil type gauge. Tests by a major tire manufacturer show that 90% of all vehicles have at least 1 tire improperly inflated. Better mileage can be achieved by over-inflating tires, but never exceed the maximum inflation pressure on the side of the tire.

39. If possible, install radial tires. Radial tires deliver as much as 1/2 mpg more than bias belted tires.

40. Avoid installing super-wide tires. They only create extra rolling resistance and decrease fuel mileage. Stick to the manufacturer's recommendations.

41. Have the wheels properly balanced.

omy by tampering with emission controls is more likely to worsen fuel economy than improve it. Emission control changes on modern engines are not readily reversible.

16. Clean (or replace) the EGR valve and lines as recommended.

17. Be sure that all vacuum lines and hoses are reconnected properly after working under the hood. An unconnected or misrouted vacuum line can wreak havoc with engine performance.

23. Check for fuel leaks at the carburetor, fuel pump, fuel lines and fuel tank. Be sure all lines and connections are tight.

24. Periodically check the tightness of the carburetor and intake manifold attaching nuts and bolts. These are a common place for vacuum leaks to occur.

25. Clean the carburetor periodically and lubricate the linkage.

26. The condition of the tailpipe can be an excellent indicator of proper engine combustion. After a long drive at highway speeds, the inside of the tailpipe should be a light grey in color. Black or soot on the insides indicates an overly rich mixture.

27. Check the fuel pump pressure. The fuel pump may be supplying more fuel than the engine needs.

28. Use the proper grade of gasoline for your engine. Don't try to compensate for knocking or "pinging" by advancing the ignition timing. This practice will only increase plug temperature and the chances of detonation or pre-ignition with relatively little performance gain.

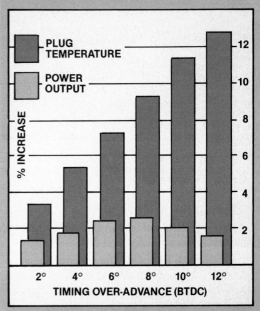

Increasing ignition timing past the specified setting results in a drastic increase in spark plug temperature with increased chance of detonation or preignition. Performance increase is considerably less. (Photo courtesy Champion Spark Plug Co.)

that form in the engine should be flushed out to allow the engine to operate at peak efficiency.

35. Clean the radiator of debris that can decrease cooling efficiency.

36. Install a flex-type or electric cooling fan, if you don't have a clutch type fan. Flex fans use curved plastic blades to push more air at low speeds when more cooling is needed; at high speeds the blades flatten out for less resistance. Electric fans only run when the engine temperature reaches a predetermined level.

37. Check the radiator cap for a worn or cracked gasket. If the cap does not seal properly, the cooling system will not function properly.

42. Be sure the front end is correctly aligned. A misaligned front end actually has wheels going in differed directions. The increased drag can reduce fuel economy by .3 mpg.

43. Correctly adjust the wheel bearings. Wheel bearings that are adjusted too tight increase rolling resistance.

Check tire pressures regularly with a reliable pocket type gauge. Be sure to check the pressure on a cold tire.

GENERAL MAINTENANCE

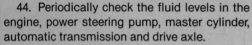

Check the fluid levels (particularly engine oil) on a regular basis. Be sure to check the oil for grit, water or other contamination.

A vacuum gauge is another excellent indicator of internal engine condition and can also be installed in the dash as a mileage indicator.

44. Periodically check the fluid levels in the engine, power steering pump, master cylinder, automatic transmission and drive axle.

45. Change the oil at the recommended interval and change the filter at every oil change. Dirty oil is thick and causes extra friction between moving parts, cutting efficiency and increasing wear. A worn engine requires more frequent tune-ups and gets progressively worse fuel economy. In general, use the lightest viscosity oil for the driving conditions you will encounter.

46. Use the recommended viscosity fluids in the transmission and axle.

47. Be sure the battery is fully charged for fast starts. A slow starting engine wastes fuel.

48. Be sure battery terminals are clean and tight.

49. Check the battery electrolyte level and add distilled water if necessary.

50. Check the exhaust system for crushed pipes, blockages and leaks.

51. Adjust the brakes. Dragging brakes or brakes that are not releasing create increased drag on the engine.

52. Install a vacuum gauge or miles-per-gallon gauge. These gauges visually indicate engine vacuum in the intake manifold. High vacuum = good mileage and low vacuum = poorer mileage. The gauge can also be an excellent indicator of internal engine conditions.

53. Be sure the clutch is properly adjusted. A slipping clutch wastes fuel.

54. Check and periodically lubricate the heat control valve in the exhaust manifold. A sticking or inoperative valve prevents engine warm-up and wastes gas.

55. Keep accurate records to check fuel economy over a period of time. A sudden drop in fuel economy may signal a need for tune-up or other maintenance.

til it runs out of fuel. Crank the engine again for 3 seconds making sure it is out of fuel.

3. Turn the ignition off and replace the fuse.

1985-86 2.0L (OHV)

The TBI injection systems used on the 1985-86 engines contain a constant bleed feature in the pressure regulator that relieves pressure any time the engine is turned off. Therefore, no special relieve procedure is required, however, a small amount of fuel may be released when the fuel line is disconnected.

CAUTION: *To reduce the chance of personal injury, cover the fuel line with cloth to collect the fuel and then place the cloth in an approved container.*

FUEL SYSTEM PRESSURE TEST

CAUTION: *To reduce the risk of fire and personal injury, it is necessary to relieve the fuel system pressure before servicing fuel system components (Refer to the appropriate procedure above).*

1. Remove the air cleaner. Plug the thermal vacuum port on the throttle body.

2. Remove the fuel line between the throttle body and filter.

3. Install a fuel pressure gauge between the throttle body and fuel filter. The gauge should be able to register at least 15 psi.

4. Start the car. The pressure reading should be 9-13 psi.

5. Depressurize the system and remove the gauge.

6. Assemble the system.

TOOLS

The system does not require special tools for diagnosis. A tachometer, test light, ohmmeter, digital voltmeter with 10 megohms impedance, vacuum pump, vacuum gauge and jumper wires are required for diagnosis. A test light or voltmeter must be used when specified in the procedures.

Idle Air Control Assembly
REMOVAL AND INSTALLATION

1. Remove the air cleaner.

2. Disconnect the electrical connection from the idle air control assembly.

3. Using a 1¼" wrench, remove the idle air control assembly from the throttle body.

WARNING: *Before installing a new assembly, measure the distance that the conical valve is extended. This measurement should be made from motor housing to end of cone. It should be greater than 1⅛". If the cone is extended too far damage to the motor may result.*

There are two different types of IAC assem-

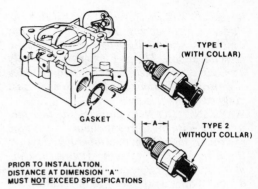

PRIOR TO INSTALLATION,
DISTANCE AT DIMENSION "A"
MUST NOT EXCEED SPECIFICATIONS

Idle air control valve installation

blies that could be used on your car. Identify the replacement IAC assembly as either being type I (having a collar at the electric terminal) or Type II (without a collar). If the meassured demension is greater than 1⅛", the distance must be reduced as follows:

a. TYPE I: Insert firm pressure on the conical valve to extract it. A slight side to side movement may be helpfull.

b. TYPE II: Compress the retaining spring from the conical valve inward with a clockwise motion. Return the spring to the original position with the straight portion of the spring end aligned with the flat portion of the valve.

4. Install the new idle air control valve to the throttle body with a new gasket and tighten to 13 ft.lb.

5. Install the electrical connection to the valve.

6. Install the air cleaner.

NOTE: *When the vehicle is operated at normal engine temperature at approximately 30 MPH, the ECM causes the valve pintle to seat in the throttle body.*

Fuel Pressure (Regulator/Compensator)
REMOVAL AND INSTALLATION

CAUTION: *To reduce the risk of fire and personal injury, it is necessary to relieve the fuel system pressure before servicing fuel system components (Refer to the appropriate procedure above).*

1. Remove air cleaner.

2. Disconnect electrical connector to injector by squeezing on two tabs and pulling straight up.

3. Remove five screws securing fuel meter cover to fuel meter body. Notice location of two short screws during removal.

CAUTION: *Do not remove the four screws securing the pressure regulator to the fuel me-*

ter cover. *The fuel pressure regulator includes a large spring under heavy tension which, if accidentally released, could cause personal injury. The fuel meter cover is only serviced as a complete assembly and includes the fuel pressure regulator preset and plugged at the factory.*
WARNING: *DO NOT immerse the fuel meter cover (with pressure regulator) in any type of cleaner. Immersion in cleaner will damage the internal fuel pressure regulator diaphragms and gaskets.*
4. Installation is the reverse of removal.

Throttle Position Sensor
CHECK

Model 300

1. Remove air cleaner.
2. Disconnect T.P.S. harness from T.P.S.
3. Using three jumper wires connect T.P.S. harness to T.P.S.
4. With ignition **ON**, engine stopped, use a digital voltmeter to measure voltage between terminals B and C.
5. Voltage should read 0.450-1.250 volts.
NOTE: *The TPS on this model is not adjustable.*

Model 500

Throttle position sensor adjustment should be checked after minimum air adjustment is completed.
1. Remove air cleaner.
2. Disconnect T.P.S. harness from T.P.S.
3. Using three jumper wires connect T.P.S. harness to T.P.S.
4. With ignition **ON**, engine stopped, use a digital voltmeter to measure voltage between terminals B and C.
5. Voltage should read 0.525volts ± 0.075 volts.
6. Adjust T.P.S. if required.
7. With ignition **OFF**, remove jumpers and connect T.P.S. harness to T.P.S.
8. Install air cleaner.

Throttle Position Sensor
ADJUSTMENT

Model 500

1. After installing TPS to throttle body, install throttle body unit to engine.
2. Remove EGR valve and heat shield from engine.
3. Using three six inch jumpers, connect TPS harness to TPS.
4. With ignition **ON**, engine stopped, use a

digital voltmeter to measure voltage between TPS terminals B and C.
5. Loosen two TPS attaching screws and rotate throttle position sensor to obtain a voltage reading of 0.525volts ± 0.075 volts.
6. With ignition **OFF**, remove jumpers and reconnect TPS harness to TPS.
7. Install EGR valve and heat shield to engine, using new gasket as necessary.
8. Install air cleaner gasket and air cleaner to throttle body unit.

REMOVAL AND INSTALLATION

The throttle position sensor (TPS) is an electrical unit and must not be immersed in any type of liquid solvent or cleaner. The TPS is factory adjusted and the retaining screws are spot welded in place to retain the critical setting. With these considerations, it is possible to clean the throttle body assembly without removing the TPS if care is used. Should TPS replacement be required however, proceed using the following steps:
1. Invert throttle body and place on a clean, flat surface.
2. Using a $5/16''$ drill bit, drill completely through two (2) TPS screw access holes in base of throttle body to be sure of removing the spot welds holding TPS screws in place.
3. Remove the two TPS attaching screws, lockwashers, and retainers. Then, remove TPS sensor from throttle body. DISCARD SCREWS. New screws are supplied in service kits.
4. If necessary, remove screw holding Throttle Position Sensor actuator lever to end of throttle shaft.
5. Remove the Idle Air Control assembly and gasket from the throttle body.
WARNING: *DO NOT immerse the idle air control motor in any type of cleaner and it should always be removed before throttle body cleaning. Immersion in cleaner will damage the IAC assembly. It is replaced only as a complete assembly.*
Further disassembly of the throttle body is not required for cleaning purposes. The throttle valve screws are permanently staked in place and should not be removed. The throttle body is serviced as a complete assembly.

ASSEMBLY

1. Place throttle body assembly on holding fixture to avoid damaging throttle valve.
2. Using a new sealing gasket, install idle air control motor in throttle body. Tighten motor securely.
WARNING: *DO NOT overtighten to prevent damage to valve.*

3. If removed, install throttle position sensor actuator lever by aligning flats on lever with flats on end of shaft. Install retaining screw and tighten securely.

NOTE: *Install throttle position sensor after completion of assembly of the throttle body unit. Use thread locking compound supplied in service kit on attaching screws.*

Fuel Injector

REMOVAL AND INSTALLATION

1. Remove the air cleaner.

2. Disconnect injector electrical connector by squeezing two tabs together and pulling straight up.

WARNING: *Use care in removing to prevent damage to the electrical connector pins on top of the injector, injector fuel filter and nozzle. The fuel injector is only serviced as a complete assembly. Do not immerse it in any type of cleaner.*

3. Remove the fuel meter cover.

4. Using a small awl, gently pry up on the injector evenly and carefully remove it.

5. Installation is the reverse of removal, with the following recommendations.

Use Dexron®II transmission fluid to lubricate all O-rings. Install the steel backup washer in the recess of the fuel meter body. Then, install the O-ring directly above backup washer, pressing the O-ring into the recess.

WARNING: *Do not attempt to reverse this procedure and install backup washer and O-ring after injector is located in the cavity. To do so will prevent seating of the O-ring in the recess.*

Fuel Meter Cover

REMOVAL AND INSTALLATION

1. Remove the five fuel meter cover screws and lockwashers holding the cover on the fuel meter body.

2. Lift off fuel meter cover (with fuel pressure regulator assembly).

3. Remove the fuel meter cover gaskets.

CAUTION: *Do not remove the four screws securing the pressure regulator to the fuel meter cover. The fuel pressure regulator includes a large spring under heavy tension which, if accidentally released, could cause personal injury. The fuel meter cover is only serviced as a complete assembly and includes the fuel pressure regulator preset and plugged at the factory.*

WARNING: *Do not immerse the fuel meter cover (with pressure regulator) in any type of cleaner. Immersion in cleaner will damage*

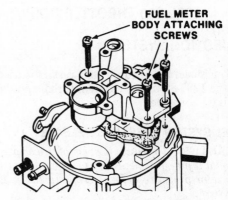

FUEL METER BODY ATTACHING SCREWS

Removing the fuel meter body assembly

the internal fuel pressure regulator diaphragms and gaskets.

4. Remove the sealing ring (dust seal from the fuel meter body).

5. Installation is the reverse of removal.

Fuel Meter Body

REMOVAL AND INSTALLATION

1. Remove the fuel inlet and outlet nuts and gaskets from fuel meter body.

2. Remove three screws and lockwashers. Remove fuel meter body from throttle body assembly.

NOTE: *The air cleaner stud must have been removed previously.*

3. Remove fuel meter body insulator gasket.

4. Installation is the reverse of removal.

Throttle Body

REMOVAL AND INSTALLATION

1. Disconnect the battery cables at the battery.

2. Remove the air cleaner assembly, noting the connection points of the vacuum lines.

3. Disconnect the electrical connectors at the injector, idle air control motor, and throttle position sensor.

4. Disconnect the vacuum lines from the TBI unit, noting the connection points. During installation, refer to the underhood emission control information decal for vacuum line routing information.

5. Disconnect the throttle and cruise control (if so equipped) cables at the TBI unit.

6. Disconnect the fuel return line.

7. Disconnect the fuel feed line.

8. Unbolt and remove the TBI unit.

9. Installation is the reverse of the previous steps. Torque the TBI bolts to 120-168 inch lbs. during installation.

GM MODEL 700 THROTTLE BODY (TBI) INJECTION SYSTEM

The Model 700 throttle body system is used on the 1987-88 2.0L OHC (non-turbo) and the 2.0L OHV engines.

FUEL SYSTEM PRESSURE RELEASE

CAUTION: *To reduce the risk of fire or personal injury, it is necessary to relieve the fuel system pressure before servicing the fuel system.*

The TBI Model 700 used on these engines contains no constant bleed feature to relieve pressure as the 1985-86 models therefore, the following procedure must be followed:

1. Place the transmission selector in Park (Neutral on manual transmissions), set the parking brake and block the drive wheels.

2. Disconnect the fuel pump at the rear body conncector.

CAUTION: *A small amount of fuel may be released after the fuel line is disconnected. To reduce the chance of personal injury, cover the fuel line with cloth to collectthe fuel and then place the cloth in an approved container.*

3. Start the engine and allow it to run a few seconds until it stops for lack of fuel.

4. Engage the starter for three seconds to dissipate fuel pressure in the lines. The fuel connections are now safe for servicing.

5. When pressure is relieved and servicing is complete, reconnect the fuel pump at the rear body connector.

Injector

REPLACEMENT

WARNING: *When removing the injectors, be careful not to damage the electrical connector pins (on top of the injector), the injector fuel filter and the nozzle. The fuel injector is serviced as a complete assembly ONLY. The injector is an electrical component and should not be immersed in any kind of cleaner.*

1. Remove the air cleaner.

CAUTION: *To reduce the risk of fire and personal injury, it is necessary to relieve the fuel system pressure before servicing fuel system components (Refer to the appropriate procedure above).*

2. Disconnect the electrical connector to the fuel injector.

3. Remove the injector retainer screw and retainer.

4. Using a fulcrum, place a suitable tool under the ridge opposite the connector end and carefully pry the injector out.

5. Remove the upper and lower O-rings from the injector and in the fuel injector cavity and discard.

WARNING: *Be sure to replace the injector with an identical part. Injectors from other models can fit in the Model 700, but are calibrated for different flow rates. There is a part number located on the top of the injector*

6. Inspect the filter for evidence of contamination.

7. Lubricate the new upper and lower O-rings with automatic transmission fluid and place them on the injector. Make sur the upper O-ring is in the groove and the lower one is flush up against the filter.

8. Install the injector assembly by pushing it straight into the fuel injector cavity.

NOTE: *Make sure the electrical connector end on the injector is facing in the general direction to the cut-out in the fuel meter body for the wire grommet.*

9. Install the injector retainer, using appropriate thread locking compound on the retainer attaching screw. Tighten to 27 in.lb.

10. With the engine off and the ignition on, check for fuel leaks

Pressure Regulator Assembly

REPLACEMENT

WARNING: *To prevent leaks, the pressure regulator diaphragm assembly must be replaced whenever the cover is removed.*

CAUTION: *To reduce the risk of fire and personal injury, it is necessary to relieve the fuel system pressure before servicing fuel system components (Refer to the appropriate procedure above).*

1. Remove the air cleaner and gasket and discard the gasket.

2. Remove the four pressure regulator attaching screws, while keeping the pressure regulator compressed.

CAUTION: *The pressure regulator contains a large spring under heavy compression. Use care when removing the screws to prevent personal injury.*

3. Remove the pressure regulator cover assembly.

4. Remove the spring seat.

5. Remove the pressure regulator diaphragm assembly.

6. Install the pressure regulator diaphragm assembly, making sure it is seated in the groove in the fuel meter body.

7. Install the regulator spring seat and spring into the cover assembly.

8. Install the cover assembly over the diaphragm, while aligning the mounting holes.

9. While maintaining pressure on the regulator spring, install the four screw assemblies that have been coated with appropriate thread locking compound. Tighten the screws to 22 in.lb.

10. With the engine off and the ignition on, check for fuel leaks.

11. Install the air cleaner and a new gasket.

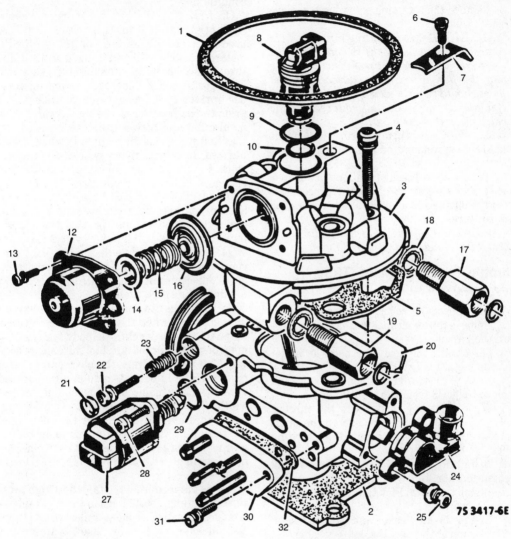

1. Gasket—air filter
2. Gasket—flange
3. Fuel meter assembly
4. Screw & washer assembly—fuel meter body attaching
5. Gasket—fuel meter body to throttle body
6. Screw—injector retainer
7. Retainer—injector
8. Fuel injector
9. O-ring—fuel injector—upper
10. O-ring—fuel injector—lower
11. Filter—injector
12. Pressure regulator cover assembly
13. Screw—pressure regulator attaching
14. Seat—spring
15. Spring—pressure regulator
16. Pressure regulator diaphragm assembly
17. Nut—fuel inlet
18. Seal—fuel nut
19. Nut—fuel outlet
20. Throttle body assembly
21. Plug—idle stop screw
22. Screw & washer assembly—idle stop
23. Spring—idle stop screw
24. Sensor—throttle position (TPS)
25. Screw & washer assembly—TPS attaching
26. Screw—TPS
27. Idle air control valve (IACV)
28. Screw—IACV attaching
29. O-ring—IACV
30. Tube module assembly
31. Screw—manifold assembly
32. Gasket—tubes manifold

Exploded view of the GM Model 700 throttle body injection unit

Idle Air Control Valve
REPLACEMENT

1. Remove the air cleaner.
2. Disconnect the electrical connector from the idle air control valve.
3. Remove the retaining screws and remove the IAC valve.

WARNING: *Before installing a new idle air control valve, measure the distance that the valve extends (from the tip of the valve pintle and the flange mounting surface. The distance should be no greater than 1⅛" (28mm). If it extends too far, damage will occur to the valve when it is installed.*

4. To adjust, exert firm pressure, with slight side to side movement, on the pintle to retract it.
5. To complete the installation, use a new gasket and reverse the removal procedures. Start the engine and allow it to reach operating temperature.

NOTE: *The ECM will reset the idle speed when the vehicle is driven at 30 mph.*

Throttle Position Sensor (TPS)
REPLACEMENT

1. Disconnect the negative battery cable.
2. Remove the air cleaner and gasket and discard the gasket.
3. Disconnect the rear alternator braacket and the metal PCV tube.
4. Remove the two TPS attaching screws and remove the TPS from the throttle body.
5. When installing, make sure the throttle body is closed and install the TPS on the shaft. Rotate counterclockwise to align the mounting holes.
6. Install the two TPS attaching screws and tighten to 18 in.lb.
7. Install the metal PCV tube and the rear alternator bracket.
8. Install the air cleaner and new gasket.
9. Reconnect the negative battery cable.

GENERAL MOTORS MULTI-PORT (MFI) AND SEQUENTIAL (SFI) FUEL INJECTION SYSTEMS

General Information

On 1984 and later 2.8 V6 engines, a new multi-port fuel injection (MFI) system is available. The MFI system is controlled by an electronic control module (ECM) which monitors engine operations and generates output signals to provide the correct air/fuel mixture, ignition timing and engine idle speed control. Input to the control unit is provided by an oxygen sensor, coolant temperature sensor, detonation sensor, hot film air mass sensor and throttle position sensor. The ECM also receives information concerning engine rpm, road speed, transmission gear position, power steering and air conditioning.

On 1.8L, 2.0L OHC, turbocharged models, a sequential port fuel injection system (SFI) is used for more precise fuel control. With SFI, metered fuel is timed and injected sequentially through six Bosch injectors into individual cylinder ports. Each cylinder receives one injection per working cycle (every two revolutions), just prior to the opening of the intake valve. The main difference between the two types of fuel injection systems is the manner in which fuel is injected. In the multiport system, all injectors work simultaneously, injecting half the fuel charge each engine revolution. The control units are different for SFI and MFI systems, but most other components are similar. In addition, the SFI system incorporates a new Computer Controlled Coil Ignition system that uses an electronic coil module that replaces the conventional distributor and coil used on most engines. An electronic spark control (ESC) is used to adjust the spark timing.

Both systems use Bosch injectors, one at each intake port, rather than the single injectior found on the earlier throttle body system. The injectors are mounted on a fuel rail and are activated by a signal from the electronic control module. The injector is a solenoid-operated valve which remains open depending on the width of the electronic pulses (length of the signal) from the ECM; the longer the open time, the more fuel is injected. In this manner, the air/fuel mixture can be precisely controlled for maximum performance with minimum emissions.

Fuel is pumped from the tank by a high pressure fuel pump, located inside the fuel tank. It is a positive displacement roller vane pump. The impeller serves as a vapor separator and pre-charges the high pressure assembly. A pressure regulator maintains 28-36 psi (28-50 psi on turbocharged engines) in the fuel line to the injectors and the excess fuel is fed back to the tank. On MFI systems, a fuel accumulator is used to dampen the hydraulic line hammer in the system created when all injectors open simultaneously.

The Mass Air Flow Sensor is used to measure the mass of air that is drawn into the engine cylinders. It is located just ahead of the air throttle in the intake system and consists of a heated film which measures the mass of air, rather than just the volume. A resistor is used to measure the temperature of the incoming air and the air mass sensor maintains the temperature of the film at 75° above ambient temperature. As the ambient (outside) air temperature rises, more energy is required to maintain the heated film at the higher temperature and the control unit uses this difference in required energy to calculate the mass of the incoming air. The control unit uses this information to determine the duration of fuel injection pulse, timing and EGR.

The throttle body incorporates an idle air control (IAC) that provides for a bypass channel through which air can flow. It consists of an orifice and pintle which is controlled by the ECM through a stepper motor. The IAC provides air flow for idle and allows additional air during cold start until the engine reaches operating temperature. As the engine temperature rises, the opening through which air passes is slowly closed.

The throttle position sensor (TPS) provides the control unit with information on throttle position, in order to determine injector pulse width and hence correct mixture. The TPS is connected to the throttle shaft on the throttle body and consists of a potentiometer with one end connected to a 5 volt source from the ECM and the other to ground. A third wire is connected to the ECM to measure the voltage output from the TPS which changes as the throttle valve angle is changed (accelerator pedal moves). At the closed throttle position, the output is low (approximately 0.4 volts); as the throttle valve opens, the output increases to a maximum 5 volts at wide open throttle (WOT). The TPS can be misadjusted open, shorted, or loose and if it is out of adjustment, the idle quality or WOT performance may be poor. A loose TPS can cause intermittent bursts of fuel from the injectors and an unstable idle because the ECM thinks the throttle is moving. This should cause a trouble code to be set. Once a trouble code is set, the ECM will use a preset value for TPS and some vehicle performance may return. A small amount of engine coolant is routed through the throttle assembly to prevent freezing inside the throttle bore during cold operation.

CHECK ENGINE LIGHTS

The Check Engine light on the instrument panel is used as a warning lamp to tell the driver that a problem has occured in the electronic engine control system. When the self-diagnosis mode is activated by grounding the test terminal of the diagnostic connector, the check engine light will flash stored trouble codes to help isolate system problems. The electronic control module (ECM) has a memory that knows what certain engine sensors should be under certain conditions. If a sensor reading is not what the

ECM thinks it should be, the control unit will illuminate the check engine light and store a trouble code in its memory. The trouble code indicates what circuit the problem is in, each circuit consisting of a sensor, the wiring harness and connectors to it and the ECM.

The Assembly Line Communications Link (ALCL) is a diagnostic connector located in the passenger compartment, usually under the left side of the instrument panel. It has terminals which are used in the assembly plant to check that the engine is operating properly before shipment. Terminal B is the diagnostic test terminal and Terminal A is the ground. By connecting the two terminals together with a jumper wire, the diagnostic mode is activated and the control unit will begin to flash trouble codes using the check engine light.

NOTE: *Some models have a Service Engine Soon light instead of a Check Engine display.*

When the test terminal is grounded with the key ON and the engine stopped, the ECM will display code 12 to show that the system is working. The ECM will usually display code 12 three times, then start to display any stored trouble codes. If no trouble codes are stored, the ECM will continue to display code 12 until the test terminal is disconnected. Each trouble code will be flashed three times, then code 12 will display again. The ECM will also energize all controlled relays and solenoids when in the diagnostic mode to check function.

When the test terminal is grounded with the engine running, it will cause the ECM to enter the Field Service Mode. In this mode, the service engine soon light will indicate whether the system is in Open or Closed loop operation. In open loop, the light will flash 2½ times per second; in closed loop, the light will flash once per second. In closed loop, the light will stay out most of the time if the system is too lean and will stay on most of the time if the system is too rich.

NOTE: *The vehicle may be driven in the Field Service mode and system evaluated at any steady road speed. This mode is useful in diagnosing driveability problems where the system is rich or lean too long.*

Trouble codes should be cleared after service is completed. To clear the trouble code memory, disconnect the battery for at least 10 seconds. This may be accomplished by disconnecting the ECM harness from the positive battery pigtail or by removing the ECM fuse.

WARNING: *The ignition switch must be OFF when disconnecting or reconnecting power to the ECM. The vehicle should be driven after the ECM memory is cleared to allow the system to readjust itself. The vehicle should be driven at part throttle under mod-*

GM Port Injection Trouble Codes

Trouble Codes	Circuit
12	Normal operation
13	Oxygen sensor
14	Coolant sensor (low voltage)
15	Coolant sensor (high voltage)
21	Throttle position sensor (high voltage)
22	Throttle position sensor (low voltage)
24	Speed sensor
32	EGR vacuum control
33	Mass air flow sensor
34	Mass air flow sensor
42	Electronic spark timing
43	Electronic spark control
44	Lean exhaust
45	Rich exhaust
51	PROM failure

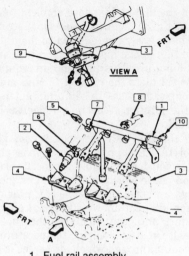

1. Fuel rail assembly
2. Injector
3. Intake manifold
4. Injector housing assembly
5. Injector retaining clip
6. Injector retaining groove
7. Injector cup flange
8. Injector control harness
9. Pressure regulator
10. Fuel pressure test point

Exploded view of the fuel rail and injector assembly, 1.8L, 2.0L OHC

erate acceleration with the engine at normal operating temperature. A change in performance should be noted initially, but normal performance should return quickly.

FUEL PRESSURE RELEASE

To reduce the risk of fire or personal injury, it is necessary to relieve the fuel system pressure before servicing the fuel system.

1. Connect a J 34730-1 fuel gage or equivalent to the fuel pressure valve. Wrap a shop towel around the fitting while connecting the gage to avoid spillage.

2. Install a bleed hose into an approved container and open the valve to bleed the system pressure.

FUEL SYSTEM PRESSURE TEST

When the ignition switch is turned ON, the in-tank fuel pump is energized for as long as the engine is cranking or running and the control unit is receiving signals from the HEI distributor. If there are no reference pulses, the control unit will shut off the fuel pump within two seconds. The pump will deliver fuel to the fuel rail and injectors, then the pressure regulator where the system pressure is controlled to maintain 30-35 psi (1984-86 OHC), 30-40 psi (1987-88 OHC), 40.5-47 psi (1984-88 2.8L V6).

1. Connect pressure gauge J-34370-1, or equivalent, to fuel pressure test point on the fuel rail. Wrap a rag around the pressure tap to absorb any leakage that may occur when installing the gauge.

2. Turn the ignition ON and check that pump pressure is 34-40 psi. This pressure is controlled by spring pressure within the regulator assembly.

3. Start the engine and allow it to idle. The fuel pressure should drop to 28-32 psi due to the lower manifold pressure.

NOTE: *The idle pressure will vary somewhat depending on barometric pressure. Check for a drop in pressure indicating regulator control, rather than specific values.*

4. On turbocharged models, use a low pressure air pump to apply air pressure to the regulator to simulate turbocharger boost pressure. Boost pressure should increase fuel pressure one pound for every pound of boost. Again, look for changes rather than specific pressures. The maximum fuel pressure should not exceed 46 psi.

5. If the fuel pressure drops, check the operation of the check valve, the pump coupling connection, fuel pressure regulator valve and the injectors. A restricted fuel line or filter may also cause a pressure drop. To check the fuel pump output, restrict the fuel return line and run 12 volts to the pump. The fuel pressure should rise

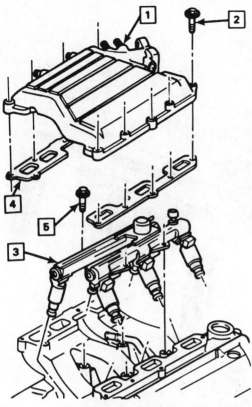

1. Plenum
2. Bolt (9) 21 N·m (16 ft lbs)
3. Fuel rail asm
4. Gasket
5. Bolt (4) 25 N·m (19 ft lbs)

Fuel rail and injectors, 1984–86 2.8L V6 engine

to approximately 75 psi with the return line restricted.

Fuel Injectors
REMOVAL AND INSTALLATION
1.8L, 2.0L OHC Engines

WARNING: *Use care in removing the fuel injectors to prevent damage to the electrical connector pins on the injector and the nozzle. The fuel injector is serviced as a complete assembly only and should not be immersed in any kind of cleaner.*

1. Relieve fuel system pressure.
2. Remove the injector electrical connections.
3. Remove the fuel rail.
4. Separate the injector from the fuel rail.
5. Installation is the reverse of removal. Replace the O-rings when installing injectors into intake manifold.

2.8L V6 Engines
1984-86

Each port injector is located and held in position by a retainer clip that must be rotated to release and/or lock the injector in place.

1. Rotate the injector retaining clip(s) the the unlocked position.
2. Remove the port injectors.
3. Install new O-ring seals and lubricate with engine oil.
4. Position the injectors to the fuel rail and pressure regulator assembly.
5. Rotate the injector retaining clips to the locking position.

1987-88

1. Remove and support the fuel rail.
2. Remove the injector retaining clip by spreading the open end of the clip slightly and removing from the rail.
3. Remove the injector(s).
4. Remove the O-rings from both ends of the injectors.
5. Install new O-ring seals and lubricate with engine oil.
6. Place new injector retaining clips on the injector assembly. Position the open end of the clip so it is facing the injector electrical connector.
7. Install the injector assembly(ies) into the fuel rail socket(s). Push in far enough to engage the retainer clip with machined slots on the socket.

Fuel Pressure Regulator
REMOVAL AND INSTALLATION
1.8L, 2.0L OHC Engines

CAUTION: *To reduce the risk of fire or personal injury, it is necessary to relieve the fuel system pressure before servicing the fuel system.*

1. Relieve fuel system pressure.
2. Remove pressure regulator from fuel rail. Place a rag around the base of the regulator to catch any spilled fuel.
3. Installation is the reverse of removal.

2.8L V6 engine
1984-86

The pressure regulator is factory adjusted and is not serviceable. Do not attempt to remove the regulator from the fuel rail.

1987-88

1. Remove and support the fuel rail.
2. Remove the fuel inlet and outlet fittings and gaskets.
3. Remove the pressure regulator bracket attaching screws and mounting bracket.

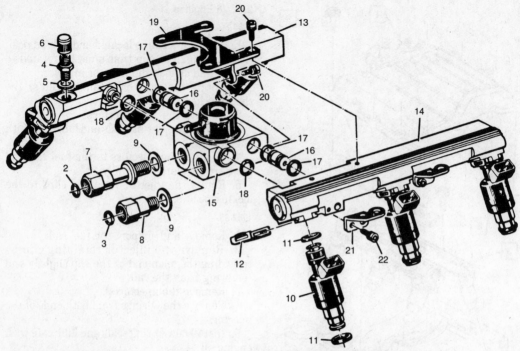

2. O-ring—fuel inlet line
3. O-ring—fuel return line
4. Fuel pressure connection assembly
5. Seal—fuel pressure connection
6. Cap—fuel pressure connection
7. Fitting—fuel inlet
8. Fitting—fuel outlet
9. Gasket—fuel fitting
10. MPFI multec injector assembly
11. Seal—O-ring—injector
12. Clip—injector retainer
13. Fuel rail & plug assembly—left hand
14. Fuel rail & plug assembly—right hand
15. Pressure regulator assembly
16. Connector—base to rail
17. Seal—O-ring—connector
18. O-ring—fuel return
19. Bracket—pressure regulator mounting
20. Screw assembly—pressure regulator bracket attaching
21. Bracket—rail mounting
22. Screw assembly—bracket attaching

Exploded view of the fuel rail assembly, 1984–86 2.8L V6 engine

4. Remove the right and left hand fuel rail assemblies from the pressure regulator assembly.

5. Remove the base to rail connectors from the regulator or rails.

6. Disassemble connector O-rings from the base to rail connectors.

7. Remove the fuel return O-ring from the fuel rails.

8. Lubricate new fuel return O-rings with engine oil and install on the fuel rails.

9. Lubricate new connector O-rings with engine oil and install to the base to rail connectors.

10. Install the base to rail connectors in the regulator assembly.

11. Install the right and left hand fuel rail assemblies to the pressure regulator assembly.

12. Install the pressure regulator mounting bracket with the attaching screws. Tighten the screws to 28 in.lb.

13. Install new fuel inlet and outlet fitting gaskets and tighten the fittings to 20 in.lb.

Fuel Rail Assembly

REMOVAL AND INSTALLATION

1.8L, 2.0L OHC Engines

Refer to the illustration for fuel rail removal on these models.

2.8L V6 Engine

1984-86

1. Disconnect the negative battery cable.
CAUTION: *To reduce the risk of fire or personal injury, it is necessary to relieve the fuel system pressure before servicing the fuel system.*

2. Relieve fuel system pressure. Refer to the procedure above.

3. Remove the intake manifold plenum.

   a. Disconnect the vacuum lines.

   b. Remove the EGR-to-plenum nuts.

   c. Remove the two throttle body bolts.

   d. Remove the throttle cable to bracket bolts.

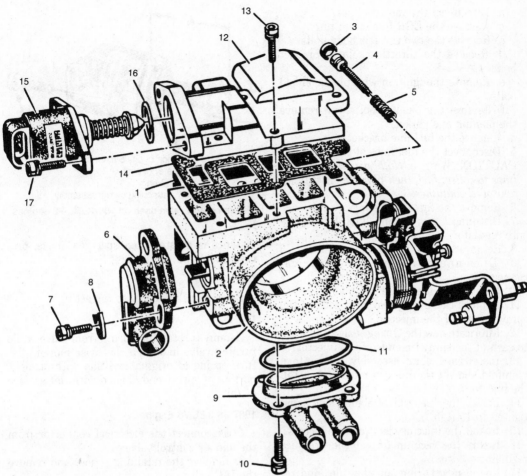

1. Gasket—flange
2. Throttle body assembly
3. Plug—idle stop screw
4. Screw assembly—idle stop
5. Spring—idle stop screw assembly
6. Sensor—throttle position (TPS)
7. Screw assembly—TPS attaching
8. Retainer—TPS attaching screw
9. Cover—coolant cavity
10. Screw assembly—coolant cover attaching
11. O-ring—coolant cover to throttle body
12. Idle air/vacuum signal housing assembly
13. Screw assembly—idle air/vacuum signal assembly
14. Gasket—idle air/vacuum signal assembly
15. Valve assembly—idle air control (IAC)
16. O-ring—idle air control valve
17. Screw assembly—idle air control valve attaching

Throttle body assembly used on the 1987 2.8L, V6 engines

e. Remove the plenum bolts and remove the plenum and gasket.

4. Remove the cold start valve and tube assembly.

5. Remove the retaining nut from the stud for the fuel lines at the head.

6. Disconnect the fuel lines at the rail.

7. Disconnect the vacuum line at the regulator.

8. Remove the rail retaining bolts.

9. Disconnect the injector electrical connectors.

10. Remove the fuel rail assembly.

11. To install use new injector O-rings and lubricate with engine oil.

12. Reverse the removal procedure.

1987-88

1. Disconnect the negative battery cable.
CAUTION: *To reduce the risk of fire or personal injury, it is necessary to relieve the fuel system pressure before servicing the fuel system.*

2. Relieve fuel system pressure. Refer to the procedure above.

3. Remove the intake manifold plenum.

a. Disconnect the vacuum lines.

b. Remove the EGR-to-plenum nuts.

c. Remove the two throttle body bolts.

d. Remove the throttle cable to bracket bolts.

e. Remove the ignition wire plastic shield bolts.

f. Remove the plenum bolts and remove the plenum and gasket.

4. Remove the fuel line bracket bolt.

5. Disconnect the fuel lines at the rail.

CAUTION: *Wrap a cloth around the fuel lines to collect fuel, then place the fuel in an approved container.*

6. Remove the fuel line O-rings.

7. Disconnect the vacuum line at the pressure regulator.

8. Remove the four rail retaining bolts.

9. Disconnect the injector electrical connectors.

10. Remove the fuel rail assembly.

11. Remove the O-ring seal from each of the spray tip end of the injector.

12. Lubricate new the O-ring seals and install to each of the spray tip ends of the injector.

13. Install the fuel rail assembly in the intake manifold and tilt the rail assembly and install the injectors.

14. Install the fuel rail attaching bolts and tighten to 19 ft.lb.

15. Install the injector electrical connectors.

16. Install the vacuum line at the pressure regulator.

17. Install new O-rings on the inlet and return fuel lines.

18. Use a back-up wrench and install the fuel inlet and outlet fittings.

19. Connect the negative battery cable.

Idle Air Control Valve

REMOVAL AND INSTALLATION

All Except 1987-88 2.8L V6 Engine

1. Remove electrical connector from idle air control valve.

2. Remove the idle air control valve using a suitable wrench.

3. Installation is the reverse of removal. Before installing the idle air control valve, measure the distance that the valve is extended. Measurement should be made from the motor housing to the end of the cone. The distance should not exceed 1⅛", or damage to the valve may occur when installed. Use a new gasket and turn the ignition on then off again to allow the ECM to reset the idle air control valve.

Identify replacement IAC valve as being either Type 1 (with collar at electric terminal end) or Type 2 (without collar). If measuring

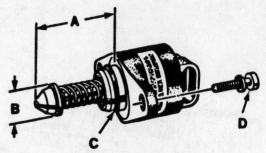

A. Distance of pintle extension
B. Diameter of pintle
C. IACV O-ring
D. IACV attaching screw assembly

Idle air control valve used on 1987 2.8L, V6 engines

distance is greater than specified above, proceed as follows:

TYPE 1

Press on valve firmly to retract it.

TYPE 2

Compress retaining spring from valve while turning valve in with a clockwise motion. Return spring to original position with straight portion of spring end aligned with flat surface of valve.

1987-88 2.8L V6 Engine

1. Disconnect the electrical connector from the idle air control valve.

3. Remove the retaining screws and remove the IAC valve.

WARNING: *Before installing a new idle air control valve, measure the distance that the*

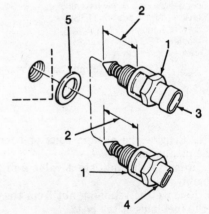

1. Idle air control valve
2. Less than 1⅛ inch (28 mm)
3. Type 1 (with collar)
4. Type 2 (without collar)
5. Gasket

Idle air control valves used on all except 1987 2.8L, V6 engines

valve extends (from the tip of the valve pintle and the flange mounting surface.The distance should be no greater than 28mm. If it extends too far, damage will occur to the valve when it is installed.

4. To adjust, exert firm pressure, with slight side to side movement, on the pintle to retract it.

5. To complete the installation, use a new seal lubricated with engine oil and install the IAC assembly. Tighten the screws to 30 in.lb. Install the electrical connector. Start the engine and allow it to reach operating temperature.

NOTE: *The ECM will reset whenever the engine is started and then shut off.*

Oxygen Sensor
REMOVAL AND INSTALLATION

WARNING: *The oxygen sensor uses a permanently attached pigtail and connector. This pigtail should not be removed from the oxygen sensor. Damage or removal of the pigtail or connector could affect proper operation of the oxygen sensor.*

The oxygen sensor is installed in the exhaust manifold and is removed in the same manner as a spark plug. The sensor may be difficult to remove when the engine temperature is below 120°F (48°C) and excessive force may damage threads in the exhaust manifold or exhaust pipe. Exercise care when handling the oxygen sensor; the electrical connector and louvered end must be kept free of grease, dirt, or other contaminants. Avoid using cleaning solvents of any kind and don't drop or roughly handle the sensor. A special anti-seize compound is used on the oxygen sensor threads when installing and care should be used NOT to get compound on the sensor itself. Disconnect the negative battery cable when servicing the oxygen sensor and torque to 30 ft.lb. when installing.

Electronic Control Module (ECM)
REMOVAL AND INSTALLATION

The electronic control module (ECM) is located under the instrument panel. To allow one model of ECM to be used on different models, a device called a calibrator or PRCM (Programmable Read Only Memory) is installed inside the ECM which contains information on the vehicle weight, engine, transmission, axle ratio, etc. The PROM is specific to the exact model and replacement part numbers must be checked carefully to make sure the correct PROM is being installed during service. Replacement ECM units (called Controllers) are supplied WITHOUT a PROM. The PROM from the old ECM must be carefully removed and installed in the replacement unit during service. Another device called a CALPAK is used to allow fuel delivery if other parts of the ECM are damaged (the Limp Home mode). The CALPAK is similiar in appearance to the PROM and is located in the same place in the ECM, under an access cover. Like the PROM, the CALPAK must be removed and transferred to the new ECM unit being installed.

NOTE: *If the diagnosis indicates a faulty ECM unit, the PROM should be checked to see if they are the correct parts. Trouble code 51 indicates that the PROM is installed incorrectly. When replacing the production ECM with a new part, it is important to transfer the Broadcast code and production ECM number to the new part label. Do not record on the ECM cover.*

CAUTION: *The ignition must be OFF whenever disconnecting or connecting the ECM electrical harness. It is possible to install a PROM backwards during service. Exercise care when replacing the PROM that it is installed correctly, or the PROM will be destroyed when the ignition is switched ON.*

To remove the ECM, first disconnect the battery. Remove the wiring harness and mounting hardware, then remove the ECM from the passenger compartment. The PROM and CALPAK are located under the access cover on the top of the control unit. Using the rocker type PROM removal tool, or equivalent, engage one end of the PROM carrier with the hook end of the tool. Press on the vertical bar end of the tool and rock the engaged end of the PROM carrier up as far as possible. Engage the opposite end of the PROM carrier in the same manner and rock this end up as far as possible. Repeat this process until the PROM carrier and PROM are free of the socket. The PROM carrier should only be removed with the removal tool or damage to the PROM or PROM socket may occur.

Chassis Electrical

UNDERSTANDING AND TROUBLESHOOTING ELECTRICAL SYSTEMS

With the rate at which both import and domestic manufacturers are incorporating electronic control systems into their production lines, it won't be long before every new vehicle is equipped with one or more on-board computer. These electronic components (with no moving parts) should theoretically last the life of the vehicle, provided nothing external happens to damage the circuits or memory chips.

While it is true that electronic components should never wear out, in the real world malfunctions do occur. It is also true that any computer-based system is extremely sensitive to electrical voltages and cannot tolerate careless or haphazard testing or service procedures. An inexperienced individual can literally do major damage looking for a minor problem by using the wrong kind of test equipment or connecting test leads or connectors with the ignition switch ON. When selecting test equipment, make sure the manufacturers instructions state that the tester is compatible with whatever type of electronic control system is being serviced. Read all instructions carefully and double check all test points before installing probes or making any test connections.

The following section outlines basic diagnosis techniques for dealing with computerized automotive control systems. Along with a general explanation of the various types of test equipment available to aid in servicing modern electronic automotive systems, basic repair techniques for wiring harnesses and connectors is given. Read the basic information before attempting any repairs or testing on any computerized system, to provide the background of information necessary to avoid the most common and obvious mistakes that can cost both time and money. Although the replacement and test-ing procedures are simple in themselves, the systems are not, and unless one has a thorough understanding of all components and their function within a particular computerized control system, the logical test sequence these systems demand cannot be followed. Minor malfunctions can make a big difference, so it is important to know how each component affects the operation of the overall electronic system to find the ultimate cause of a problem without replacing good components unnecessarily. It is not enough to use the correct test equipment; the test equipment must be used correctly.

Safety Precautions

CAUTION: *Whenever working on or around any computer based microprocessor control system, always observe these general precautions to prevent the possibility of personal injury or damage to electronic components.*

• Never install or remove battery cables with the key ON or the engine running. Jumper cables should be connected with the key OFF to avoid power surges that can damage electronic control units. Engines equipped with computer controlled systems should avoid both giving and getting jump starts due to the possibility of serious damage to components from arcing in the engine compartment when connections are made with the ignition ON.

• Always remove the battery cables before charging the battery. Never use a high output charger on an installed battery or attempt to use any type of "hot shot" (24 volt) starting aid.

• Exercise care when inserting test probes into connectors to insure good connections without damaging the connector or spreading the pins. Always probe connectors from the rear (wire) side, NOT the pin side, to avoid accidental shorting of terminals during test procedures.

• Never remove or attach wiring harness

connectors with the ignition switch ON, especially to an electronic control unit.

• Do not drop any components during service procedures and never apply 12 volts directly to any component (like a solenoid or relay) unless instructed specifically to do so. Some component electrical windings are designed to safely handle only 4 or 5 volts and can be destroyed in seconds if 12 volts are applied directly to the connector.

• Remove the electronic control unit if the vehicle is to be placed in an environment where temperatures exceed approximately 176°F (80°C), such as a paint spray booth or when arc or gas welding near the control unit location in the car.

ORGANIZED TROUBLESHOOTING

When diagnosing a specific problem, organized troubleshooting is a must. The complexity of a modern automobile demands that you approach any problem in a logical, organized manner. There are certain troubleshooting techniques that are standard:

1. Establish when the problem occurs. Does the problem appear only under certain conditions? Were there any noises, odors, or other unusual symptoms?

2. Isolate the problem area. To do this, make some simple tests and observations; then eliminate the systems that are working properly. Check for obvious problems such as broken wires, dirty connections or split or disconnected vacuum hoses. Always check the obvious before assuming something complicated is the cause.

3. Test for problems systematically to determine the cause once the problem area is isolated. Are all the components functioning properly? Is there power going to electrical switches and motors? Is there vacuum at vacuum switches and/or actuators? Is there a mechanical problem such as bent linkage or loose mounting screws? Doing careful, systematic checks will often turn up most causes on the first inspection without wasting time checking components that have little or no relationship to the problem.

4. Test all repairs after the work is done to make sure that the problem is fixed. Some causes can be traced to more than one component, so a careful verification of repair work is important to pick up additional malfunctions that may cause a problem to reappear or a different problem to arise. A blown fuse, for example, is a simple problem that may require more than another fuse to repair. If you don't look for a problem that caused a fuse to blow, for example, a shorted wire may go undetected.

Experience has shown that most problems tend to be the result of a fairly simple and obvious cause, such as loose or corroded connectors or air leaks in the intake system; making careful inspection of components during testing essential to quick and accurate troubleshooting. Special, hand held computerized testers designed specifically for diagnosing the system are available from a variety of aftermarket sources, as well as from the vehicle manufacturer, but care should be taken that any test equipment being used is designed to diagnose that particular computer controlled system accurately without damaging the control unit (ECU) or components being tested.

NOTE: *Pinpointing the exact cause of trouble in an electrical system can sometimes only be accomplished by the use of special test equipment. The following describes commonly used test equipment and explains how to put it to best use in diagnosis. In addition to the information covered below, the manufacturer's instructions booklet provided with the tester should be read and clearly understood before attempting any test procedures.*

TEST EQUIPMENT

Jumper Wires

Jumper wires are simple, yet extremely valuable, pieces of test equipment. Jumper wires are merely wires that are used to bypass sections of a circuit. The simplest type of jumper wire is merely a length of multistrand wire with an alligator clip at each end. Jumper wires are usually fabricated from lengths of standard automotive wire and whatever type of connector (alligator clip, spade connector or pin connector) that is required for the particular vehicle being tested. The well equipped tool box will have several different styles of jumper wires in several different lengths. Some jumper wires are made with three or more terminals coming from a common splice for special purpose testing. In cramped, hard-to-reach areas it is advisable to have insulated boots over the jumper wire terminals in order to prevent accidental grounding, sparks, and possible fire, especially when testing fuel system components.

Jumper wires are used primarily to locate open electrical circuits, on either the ground (-) side of the circuit or on the hot (+) side. If an electrical component fails to operate, connect the jumper wire between the component and a good ground. If the component operates only with the jumper installed, the ground circuit is open. If the ground circuit is good, but the component does not operate, the circuit between the power feed and component is open. You can sometimes connect the jumper wire directly from the battery to the hot terminal of the component, but first make sure the component uses 12 volts in operation. Some electrical components, such as fuel injectors, are designed to operate on about 4 volts and running 12 volts directly to the injector terminals can burn out the wiring. By inserting an inline fuseholder between a set of test leads, a fused jumper wire can be used for bypassing open circuits. Use a 5 amp fuse to provide protection against voltage spikes. When in doubt, use a voltmeter to check the voltage input to the component and measure how much voltage is being applied normally. By moving the jumper wire successively back from the lamp toward the power source, you can isolate the area of the circuit where the open is located. When the component stops functioning, or the power is cut off, the open is in the segment of wire between the jumper and the point previously tested.

CAUTION: *Never use jumpers made from wire that is of lighter gauge than used in the circuit under test. If the jumper wire is of too small gauge, it may overheat and possibly melt. Never use jumpers to bypass high resistance loads (such as motors) in a circuit. Bypassing resistances, in effect, creates a short circuit which may, in turn, cause damage and fire. Never use a jumper for anything other than temporary bypassing of components in a circuit.*

12 Volt Test Light

The 12 volt test light is used to check circuits and components while electrical current is flowing through them. It is used for voltage and ground tests. Twelve volt test lights come in different styles but all have three main parts; a ground clip, a probe, and a light. The most commonly used 12 volt test lights have pick-type probes. To use a 12 volt test light, connect the ground clip to a good ground and probe wherever necessary with the pick. The pick should be sharp so that it can penetrate wire insulation to make contact with the wire, without making a large hole in the insulation. The wrap-around light is handy in hard to reach areas or where it is difficult to support a wire to push a probe pick into it. To use the wrap around light, hook the wire to probed with the hook and pull the trigger. A small pick will be forced through the wire insulation into the wire core.

CAUTION: *Do not use a test light to probe electronic ignition spark plug or coil wires. Never use a pick-type test light to probe wiring on computer controlled systems unless specifically instructed to do so. Any wire insulation that is pierced by the test light probe should be taped and sealed with silicone after testing.*

Like the jumper wire, the 12 volt test light is used to isolate opens in circuits. But, whereas the jumper wire is used to bypass the open to operate the load, the 12 volt test light is used to locate the presence of voltage in a circuit. If the test light glows, you know that there is power up to that point; if the 12 volt test light does not glow when its probe is inserted into the wire or connector, you know that there is an open circuit (no power). Move the test light in successive steps back toward the power source until the light in the handle does glow. When it does glow, the open is between the probe and point previously probed.

NOTE: *The test light does not detect that 12 volts (or any particular amount of voltage) is present; it only detects that some voltage is present. It is advisable before using the test light to touch its terminals across the battery posts to make sure the light is operating properly.*

Self-Powered Test Light

The self-powered test light usually contains a 1.5 volt penlight battery. One type of self-powered test light is similar in design to the 12 volt test light. This type has both the battery and the light in the handle and pick-type probe tip. The second type has the light toward the open tip, so that the light illuminates the contact point. The self-powered test light is dual purpose piece of test equipment. It can be used to test for either open or short circuits when power is isolated from the circuit (continuity test). A powered test light should not be used on any computer controlled system or component unless specifically instructed to do so. Many engine sensors can be destroyed by even this small amount of voltage applied directly to the terminals.

Open Circuit Testing

To use the self-powered test light to check for open circuits, first isolate the circuit from the vehicle's 12 volt power source by disconnecting the battery or wiring harness connector. Connect the test light ground clip to a good ground and probe sections of the circuit sequentially with the test light. (start from either end of the circuit). If the light is out, the open is between the probe and the circuit ground. If the light is on, the open is between the probe and end of the circuit toward the power source.

Short Circuit Testing

By isolating the circuit both from power and from ground, and using a self-powered test light, you can check for shorts to ground in the circuit. Isolate the circuit from power and ground. Connect the test light ground clip to a good ground and probe any easy-to-reach test point in the circuit. If the light comes on, there is a short somewhere in the circuit. To isolate the short, probe a test point at either end of the isolated circuit (the light should be on). Leave the test light probe connected and open connectors, switches, remove parts, etc., sequentially, until the light goes out. When the light goes out, the short is between the last circuit component opened and the previous circuit opened.

NOTE: *The 1.5 volt battery in the test light does not provide much current. A weak battery may not provide enough power to illuminate the test light even when a complete circuit is made (especially if there are high resistances in the circuit). Always make sure that the test battery is strong. To check the battery, briefly touch the ground clip to the probe; if the light glows brightly the battery is strong enough for testing. Never use a self-powered test light to perform checks for opens or shorts when power is applied to the electrical system under test. The 12 volt vehicle power will quickly burn out the 1.5 volt light bulb in the test light.*

Voltmeter

A voltmeter is used to measure voltage at any point in a circuit, or to measure the voltage drop across any part of a circuit. It can also be used to check continuity in a wire or circuit by indicating current flow from one end to the other. Voltmeters usually have various scales on the meter dial and a selector switch to allow the selection of different voltages. The voltmeter has a positive and a negative lead. To avoid damage to the meter, always connect the negative lead to the negative (-) side of circuit (to ground or nearest the ground side of the circuit) and connect the positive lead to the positive (+) side of the circuit (to the power source or the nearest power source). Note that the negative voltmeter lead will always be black and that the positive voltmeter will always be some color other than black (usually red). Depending on how the voltmeter is connected into the circuit, it has several uses.

A voltmeter can be connected either in parallel or in series with a circuit and it has a very high resistance to current flow. When connected in parallel, only a small amount of current will flow through the voltmeter current path; the rest will flow through the normal circuit current path and the circuit will work normally. When the voltmeter is connected in series with a circuit, only a small amount of current can flow through the circuit. The circuit will not work properly, but the voltmeter reading will show if the circuit is complete or not.

Available Voltage Measurement

Set the voltmeter selector switch to the 20V position and connect the meter negative lead to the negative post of the battery. Connect the positive meter lead to the positive post of the battery and turn the ignition switch ON to provide a load. Read the voltage on the meter or digital display. A well charged battery should register over 12 volts. If the meter reads below 11.5 volts, the battery power may be insufficient to operate the electrical system properly. This test determines voltage available from the battery and should be the first step in any electrical trouble diagnosis procedure. Many electrical problems, especially on computer controlled systems, can be caused by a low state of charge in the battery. Excessive corrosion at the battery cable terminals can cause a poor contact that will prevent proper charging and full battery current flow.

Normal battery voltage is 12 volts when fully charged. When the battery is supplying current to one or more circuits it is said to be "under load". When everything is off the electrical system is under a "no-load" condition. A fully charged battery may show about 12.5 volts at no load; will drop to 12 volts under medium load; and will drop even lower under heavy load. If the battery is partially discharged the voltage decrease under heavy load may be excessive, even though the battery shows 12 volts or more at no load. When allowed to discharge further, the battery's available voltage under load will decrease more severely. For this reason, it is important that the battery be fully charged during all testing procedures to avoid errors in diagnosis and incorrect test results.

Voltage Drop

When current flows through a resistance, the voltage beyond the resistance is reduced (the larger the current, the greater the reduction in voltage). When no current is flowing, there is no voltage drop because there is no current flow. All points in the circuit which are connected to the power source are at the same voltage as the power source. The total voltage drop always equals the total source voltage. In a long circuit with many connectors, a series of small, unwanted voltage drops due to corrosion at the connectors can add up to a total loss of voltage which impairs the operation of the normal loads in the circuit.

INDIRECT COMPUTATION OF VOLTAGE DROPS

1. Set the voltmeter selector switch to the 20 volt position.
2. Connect the meter negative lead to a good ground.
3. Probe all resistances in the circuit with the positive meter lead.
4. Operate the circuit in all modes and observe the voltage readings.

DIRECT MEASUREMENT OF VOLTAGE DROPS

1. Set the voltmeter switch to the 20 volt position.

2. Connect the voltmeter negative lead to the ground side of the resistance load to be measured.

3. Connect the positive lead to the positive side of the resistance or load to be measured.

4. Read the voltage drop directly on the 20 volt scale.

Too high a voltage indicates too high a resistance. If, for example, a blower motor runs too slowly, you can determine if there is too high a resistance in the resistor pack. By taking voltage drop readings in all parts of the circuit, you can isolate the problem. Too low a voltage drop indicates too low a resistance. If, for example, a blower motor runs too fast in the MED and/or LOW position, the problem can be isolated in the resistor pack by taking voltage drop readings in all parts of the circuit to locate a possibly shorted resistor. The maximum allowable voltage drop under load is critical, especially if there is more than one high resistance problem in a circuit because all voltage drops are cumulative. A small drop is normal due to the resistance of the conductors.

HIGH RESISTANCE TESTING

1. Set the voltmeter selector switch to the 4 volt position.

2. Connect the voltmeter positive lead to the positive post of the battery.

3. Turn on the headlights and heater blower to provide a load.

4. Probe various points in the circuit with the negative voltmeter lead.

5. Read the voltage drop on the 4 volt scale. Some average maximum allowable voltage drops are:

FUSE PANEL – 7 volts
IGNITION SWITCH – 5volts
HEADLIGHT SWITCH – 7 volts
IGNITION COIL (+) – 5 volts
ANY OTHER LOAD – 1.3 volts
NOTE: *Voltage drops are all measured while a load is operating; without current flow, there will be no voltage drop.*

Ohmmeter

The ohmmeter is designed to read resistance (ohms) in a circuit or component. Although there are several different styles of ohmmeters, all will usually have a selector switch which permits the measurement of different ranges of resistance (usually the selector switch allows the multiplication of the meter reading by 10, 100, 1000, and 10,000). A calibration knob allows the meter to be set at zero for accurate mea-

surement. Since all ohmmeters are powered by an internal battery (usually 9 volts), the ohmmeter can be used as a self-powered test light. When the ohmmeter is connected, current from the ohmmeter flows through the circuit or component being tested. Since the ohmmeter's internal resistance and voltage are known values, the amount of current flow through the meter depends on the resistance of the circuit or component being tested.

The ohmmeter can be used to perform continuity test for opens or shorts (either by observation of the meter needle or as a self-powered test light), and to read actual resistance in a circuit. It should be noted that the ohmmeter is used to check the resistance of a component or wire while there is no voltage applied to the circuit. Current flow from an outside voltage source (such as the vehicle battery) can damage the ohmmeter, so the circuit or component should be isolated from the vehicle electrical system before any testing is done. Since the ohmmeter uses its own voltage source, either lead can be connected to any test point.

NOTE: *When checking diodes or other solid state components, the ohmmeter leads can only be connected one way in order to measure current flow in a single direction. Make sure the positive (+) and negative (-) terminal connections are as described in the test procedures to verify the one-way diode operation.*

In using the meter for making continuity checks, do not be concerned with the actual resistance readings. Zero resistance, or any resistance readings, indicate continuity in the circuit. Infinite resistance indicates an open in the circuit. A high resistance reading where there should be none indicates a problem in the circuit. Checks for short circuits are made in the same manner as checks for open circuits except that the circuit must be isolated from both power and normal ground. Infinite resistance indicates no continuity to ground, while zero resistance indicates a dead short to ground.

RESISTANCE MEASUREMENT

The batteries in an ohmmeter will weaken with age and temperature, so the ohmmeter must be calibrated or "zeroed" before taking measurements. To zero the meter, place the selector switch in its lowest range and touch the two ohmmeter leads together. Turn the calibration knob until the meter needle is exactly on zero.

NOTE: *All analog (needle) type ohmmeters must be zeroed before use, but some digital ohmmeter models are automatically calibrated when the switch is turned on. Self-cali-*

brating digital ohmmeters do not have an adjusting knob, but its a good idea to check for a zero readout before use by touching the leads together. All computer controlled systems require the use of a digital ohmmeter with at least 10 meagohms impedance for testing. Before any test procedures are attempted, make sure the ohmmeter used is compatible with the electrical system or damage to the onboard computer could result.

To measure resistance, first isolate the circuit from the vehicle power source by disconnecting the battery cables or the harness connector. Make sure the key is OFF when disconnecting any components or the battery. Where necessary, also isolate at least one side of the circuit to be checked to avoid reading parallel resistances. Parallel circuit resistances will always give a lower reading than the actual resistance of either of the branches. When measuring the resistance of parallel circuits, the total resistance will always be lower than the smallest resistance in the circuit. Connect the meter leads to both sides of the circuit (wire or component) and read the actual measured ohms on the meter scale. Make sure the selector switch is set to the proper ohm scale for the circuit being tested to avoid misreading the ohmmeter test value.

CAUTION: *Never use an ohmmeter with power applied to the circuit. Like the self-powered test light, the ohmmeter is designed to operate on its own power supply. The normal 12 volt automotive electrical system current could damage the meter.*

Ammeters

An ammeter measures the amount of current flowing through a circuit in units called amperes or amps. Amperes are units of electron flow which indicate how fast the electrons are flowing through the circuit. Since Ohms Law dictates that current flow in a circuit is equal to the circuit voltage divided by the total circuit resistance, increasing voltage also increases the current level (amps). Likewise, any decrease in resistance will increase the amount of amps in a circuit. At normal operating voltage, most circuits have a characteristic amount of amperes, called "current draw" which can be measured using an ammeter. By referring to a specified current draw rating, measuring the amperes, and comparing the two values, one can determine what is happening within the circuit to aid in diagnosis. An open circuit, for example, will not allow any current to flow so the ammeter reading will be zero. More current flows through a heavily loaded circuit or when the charging system is operating.

An ammeter is always connected in series with the circuit being tested. All of the current that normally flows through the circuit must also flow through the ammeter; if there is any other path for the current to follow, the ammeter reading will not be accurate. The ammeter itself has very little resistance to current flow and therefore will not affect the circuit, but it will measure current draw only when the circuit is closed and electricity is flowing. Excessive current draw can blow fuses and drain the battery, while a reduced current draw can cause motors to run slowly, lights to dim and other components to not operate properly. The ammeter can help diagnose these conditions by locating the cause of the high or low reading.

Multimeters

Different combinations of test meters can be built into a single unit designed for specific tests. Some of the more common combination test devices are known as Volt/Amp testers, Tach/Dwell meters, or Digital Multimeters. The Volt/Amp tester is used for charging system, starting system or battery tests and consists of a voltmeter, an ammeter and a variable resistance carbon pile. The voltmeter will usually have at least two ranges for use with 6, 12 and 24 volt systems. The ammeter also has more than one range for testing various levels of battery loads and starter current draw and the carbon pile can be adjusted to offer different amounts of resistance. The Volt/Amp tester has heavy leads to carry large amounts of current and many later models have an inductive ammeter pickup that clamps around the wire to simplify test connections. On some models, the ammeter also has a zero-center scale to allow testing of charging and starting systems without switching leads or polarity. A digital multimeter is a voltmeter, ammeter and ohmmeter combined in an instrument which gives a digital readout. These are often used when testing solid state circuits because of their high input impedance (usually 10 megohms or more).

The tach/dwell meter combines a tachometer and a dwell (cam angle) meter and is a specialized kind of voltmeter. The tachometer scale is marked to show engine speed in rpm and the dwell scale is marked to show degrees of distributor shaft rotation. In most electronic ignition systems, dwell is determined by the control unit, but the dwell meter can also be used to check the duty cycle (operation) of some electronic engine control systems. Some tach/dwell meters are powered by an internal battery, while others take their power from the car battery in use. The battery powered testers usually require calibration much like an ohmmeter before testing.

Special Test Equipment

A variety of diagnostic tools are available to help troubleshoot and repair computerized engine control systems. The most sophisticated of these devices are the console type engine analyzers that usually occupy a garage service bay, but there are several types of aftermarket electronic testers available that will allow quick circuit tests of the engine control system by plugging directly into a special connector located in the engine compartment or under the dashboard. Several tool and equipment manufacturers offer simple, hand held testers that measure various circuit voltage levels on command to check all system components for proper operation. Although these testers usually cost about $300-$500, consider that the average computer control unit (or ECM) can cost just as much and the money saved by not replacing perfectly good sensors or components in an attempt to correct a problem could justify the purchase price of a special diagnostic tester the first time it's used.

These computerized testers can allow quick and easy test measurements while the engine is operating or while the car is being driven. In addition, the on-board computer memory can be read to access any stored trouble codes; in effect allowing the computer to tell you where it hurts and aid trouble diagnosis by pinpointing exactly which circuit or component is malfunctioning. In the same manner, repairs can be tested to make sure the problem has been corrected. The biggest advantage these special testers have is their relatively easy hookups that minimize or eliminate the chances of making the wrong connections and getting false voltage readings or damaging the computer accidentally.

NOTE: *It should be remembered that these testers check voltage levels in circuits; they don't detect mechanical problems or failed components if the circuit voltage falls within the preprogrammed limits stored in the tester PROM unit. Also, most of the hand held testes are designed to work only on one or two systems made by a specific manufacturer.*

A variety of aftermarket testers are available to help diagnose different computerized control systems. Owatonna Tool Company (OTC), for example, markets a device called the OTC Monitor which plugs directly into the assembly line diagnostic link (ALDL). The OTC tester makes diagnosis a simple matter of pressing the correct buttons and, by changing the internal PROM or inserting a different diagnosis cartridge, it will work on any model from full size to subcompact, over a wide range of years. An adapter is supplied with the tester to allow connection to all types of ALDL links, regardless of the number of pin terminals used. By inserting an updated PROM into the OTC tester, it can be easily updated to diagnose any new modifications of computerized control systems.

Wiring Harnesses

The average automobile contains about ½ mile of wiring, with hundreds of individual connections. To protect the many wires from damage and to keep them from becoming a confusing tangle, they are organized into bundles, enclosed in plastic or taped together and called wire harnesses. Different wiring harnesses serve different parts of the vehicle. Individual wires are color coded to help trace them through a harness where sections are hidden from view.

A loose or corroded connection or a replacement wire that is too small for the circuit will add extra resistance and an additional voltage drop to the circuit. A ten percent voltage drop can result in slow or erratic motor operation, for example, even though the circuit is complete. Automotive wiring or circuit conductors can be in any one of three forms:

1. Single strand wire
2. Multistrand wire
3. Printed circuitry

Single strand wire has a solid metal core and is usually used inside such components as alternators, motors, relays and other devices. Multistrand wire has a core made of many small strands of wire twisted together into a single conductor. Most of the wiring in an automotive electrical system is made up of multistrand wire, either as a single conductor or grouped together in a harness. All wiring is color coded on the insulator, either as a solid color or as a colored wire with an identification stripe. A printed circuit is a thin film of copper or other conductor that is printed on an insulator backing. Occasionally, a printed circuit is sandwiched between two sheets of plastic for more protection and flexibility. A complete printed circuit, consisting of conductors, insulating material and connectors for lamps or other components is called a printed circuit board. Printed circuitry is used in place of individual wires or harnesses in places where space is limited, such as behind instrument panels.

Wire Gauge

Since computer controlled automotive electrical systems are very sensitive to changes in resistance, the selection of properly sized wires is critical when systems are repaired. The wire gauge number is an expression of the cross section area of the conductor. The most common system for expressing wire size is the American Wire Gauge (AWG) system.

Wire cross section area is measured in circular mils. A mil is $\frac{1}{1000}$" (0.001"); a circular mil is the area of a circle one mil in diameter. For example, a conductor ¼" in diameter is 0.250 in. or 250 mils. The circular mil cross section area of the wire is 250 squared (250^2)or 62,500 circular mils. Imported car models usually use metric wire gauge designations, which is simply the cross section area of the conductor in square millimeters (mm^2).

Gauge numbers are assigned to conductors of various cross section areas. As gauge number increases, area decreases and the conductor becomes smaller. A 5 gauge conductor is smaller than a 1 gauge conductor and a 10 gauge is smaller than a 5 gauge. As the cross section area of a conductor decreases, resistance increases and so does the gauge number. A conductor with a higher gauge number will carry less current than a conductor with a lower gauge number.

NOTE: *Gauge wire size refers to the size of the conductor, not the size of the complete wire. It is possible to have two wires of the same gauge with different diameters because one may have thicker insulation than the other.*

12 volt automotive electrical systems generally use 10, 12, 14, 16 and 18 gauge wire. Main power distribution circuits and larger accessories usually use 10 and 12 gauge wire. Battery cables are usually 4 or 6 gauge, although 1 and 2 gauge wires are occasionally used. Wire length must also be considered when making repairs to a circuit. As conductor length increases, so does resistance. An 18 gauge wire, for example, can carry a 10 amp load for 10 feet without excessive voltage drop; however if a 15 foot wire is required for the same 10 amp load, it must be a 16 gauge wire.

An electrical schematic shows the electrical current paths when a circuit is operating properly. It is essential to understand how a circuit works before trying to figure out why it doesn't. Schematics break the entire electrical system down into individual circuits and show only one particular circuit. In a schematic, no attempt is made to represent wiring and components as they physically appear on the vehicle; switches and other components are shown as simply as possible. Face views of harness connectors show the cavity or terminal locations in all multi-pin connectors to help locate test points.

If you need to backprobe a connector while it is on the component, the order of the terminals must be mentally reversed. The wire color code can help in this situation, as well as a keyway, lock tab or other reference mark.

NOTE: *Wiring diagrams are not included in this book. As trucks have become more complex and available with longer option lists, wiring diagrams have grown in size and complexity. It has become almost impossible to provide a readable reproduction of a wiring diagram in a book this size. Information on ordering wiring diagrams from the vehicle manufacturer can be found in the owner's manual.*

WIRING REPAIR

Soldering is a quick, efficient method of joining metals permanently. Everyone who has the occasion to make wiring repairs should know how to solder. Electrical connections that are soldered are far less likely to come apart and will conduct electricity much better than connections that are only "pig-tailed" together. The most popular (and preferred) method of soldering is with an electrical soldering gun. Soldering irons are available in many sizes and wattage ratings. Irons with higher wattage ratings deliver higher temperatures and recover lost heat faster. A small soldering iron rated for no more than 50 watts is recommended, especially on electrical systems where excess heat can damage the components being soldered.

There are three ingredients necessary for successful soldering; proper flux, good solder and sufficient heat. A soldering flux is necessary to clean the metal of tarnish, prepare it for soldering and to enable the solder to spread into tiny crevices. When soldering, always use a resin flux or resin core solder which is non-corrosive and will not attract moisture once the job is finished. Other types of flux (acid core) will leave a residue that will attract moisture and cause the wires to corrode. Tin is a unique metal with a low melting point. In a molten state, it dissolves and alloys easily with many metals. Solder is made by mixing tin with lead. The most common proportions are 40/60, 50/50 and 60/40, with the percentage of tin listed first. Low priced solders usually contain less tin, making them very difficult for a beginner to use because more heat is required to melt the solder. A common solder is 40/60 which is well suited for all-around general use, but 60/40 melts easier, has more tin for a better joint and is preferred for electrical work.

Soldering Techniques

Successful soldering requires that the metals to be joined be heated to a temperature that will melt the solder – usually 360-460°F (182-238°C). Contrary to popular belief, the purpose of the soldering iron is not to melt the solder itself, but to heat the parts being soldered to a temperature high enough to melt the solder when it is touched to the work. Melting flux-cored solder on the soldering iron will usually destroy the effectiveness of the flux.

NOTE: *Soldering tips are made of copper for good heat conductivity, but must be "tinned" regularly for quick transference of heat to the project and to prevent the solder from sticking to the iron. To "tin" the iron, simply heat it and touch the flux-cored solder to the tip; the solder will flow over the hot tip. Wipe the excess off with a clean rag, but be careful as the iron will be hot.*

After some use, the tip may become pitted. If so, simply dress the tip smooth with a smooth file and "tin" the tip again. An old saying holds that "metals well cleaned are half soldered." Flux-cored solder will remove oxides but rust, bits of insulation and oil or grease must be removed with a wire brush or emery cloth. For maximum strength in soldered parts, the joint must start off clean and tight. Weak joints will result in gaps too wide for the solder to bridge.

If a separate soldering flux is used, it should be brushed or swabbed on only those areas that are to be soldered. Most solders contain a core of flux and separate fluxing is unnecessary. Hold the work to be soldered firmly. It is best to solder on a wooden board, because a metal vise will only rob the piece to be soldered of heat and make it difficult to melt the solder. Hold the soldering tip with the broadest face against the work to be soldered. Apply solder under the tip close to the work, using enough solder to give a heavy film between the iron and the piece being soldered, while moving slowly and making sure the solder melts properly. Keep the work level or the solder will run to the lowest part and favor the thicker parts, because these require more heat to melt the solder. If the soldering tip overheats (the solder coating on the face of the tip burns up), it should be retinned. Once the soldering is completed, let the soldered joint stand until cool. Tape and seal all soldered wire splices after the repair has cooled.

Wire Harness and Connectors

The on-board computer (ECM) wire harness electrically connects the control unit to the various solenoids, switches and sensors used by the control system. Most connectors in the engine compartment or otherwise exposed to the elements are protected against moisture and dirt which could create oxidation and deposits on the terminals. This protection is important because of the very low voltage and current levels used by the computer and sensors. All connectors have a lock which secures the male and female terminals together, with a secondary lock holding the seal and terminal into the connec-

tor. Both terminal locks must be released when disconnecting ECM connectors.

These special connectors are weather-proof and all repairs require the use of a special terminal and the tool required to service it. This tool is used to remove the pin and sleeve terminals. If removal is attempted with an ordinary pick, there is a good chance that the terminal will be bent or deformed. Unlike standard blade type terminals, these terminals cannot be straightened once they are bent. Make certain that the connectors are properly seated and all of the sealing rings in place when connecting leads. On some models, a hinge-type flap provides a backup or secondary locking feature for the terminals. Most secondary locks are used to improve the connector reliability by retaining the terminals if the small terminal lock tangs are not positioned properly.

Molded-on connectors require complete replacement of the connection. This means splicing a new connector assembly into the harness. All splices in on-board computer systems should be soldered to insure proper contact. Use care when probing the connections or replacing terminals in them as it is possible to short between opposite terminals. If this happens to the wrong terminal pair, it is possible to damage certain components. Always use jumper wires between connectors for circuit checking and never probe through weather-proof seals.

Open circuits are often difficult to locate by sight because corrosion or terminal misalignment are hidden by the connectors. Merely wiggling a connector on a sensor or in the wiring harness may correct the open circuit condition. This should always be considered when an open circuit or a failed sensor is indicated. Intermittent problems may also be caused by oxidized or loose connections. When using a circuit tester for diagnosis, always probe connections from the wire side. Be careful not to damage sealed connectors with test probes.

All wiring harnesses should be replaced with identical parts, using the same gauge wire and connectors. When signal wires are spliced into a harness, use wire with high temperature insulation only. With the low voltage and current levels found in the system, it is important that the best possible connection at all wire splices be made by soldering the splices together. It is seldom necessary to replace a complete harness. If replacement is necessary, pay close attention to insure proper harness routing. Secure the harness with suitable plastic wire clamps to prevent vibrations from causing the harness to wear in spots or contact any hot components.

NOTE: *Weatherproof connectors cannot be*

replaced with standard connectors. Instructions are provided with replacement connector and terminal packages. Some wire harnesses have mounting indicators (usually pieces of colored tape) to mark where the harness is to be secured.

In making wiring repairs, it's important that you always replace damaged wires with wires that are the same gauge as the wire being replaced. The heavier the wire, the smaller the gauge number. Wires are color-coded to aid in identification and whenever possible the same color coded wire should be used for replacement. A wire stripping and crimping tool is necessary to install solderless terminal connectors. Test all crimps by pulling on the wires; it should not be possible to pull the wires out of a good crimp.

Wires which are open, exposed or otherwise damaged are repaired by simple splicing. Where possible, if the wiring harness is accessible and the damaged place in the wire can be located, it is best to open the harness and check for all possible damage. In an inaccessible harness, the wire must be bypassed with a new insert, usually taped to the outside of the old harness.

When replacing fusible links, be sure to use fusible link wire, NOT ordinary automotive wire. Make sure the fusible segment is of the same gauge and construction as the one being replaced and double the stripped end when crimping the terminal connector for a good contact. The melted (open) fusible link segment of the wiring harness should be cut off as close to the harness as possible, then a new segment spliced in as described. In the case of a damaged fusible link that feeds two harness wires, the harness connections should be replaced with two fusible link wires so that each circuit will have its own separate protection.

NOTE: *Most of the problems caused in the wiring harness are due to bad ground connections. Always check all vehicle ground connections for corrosion or looseness before performing any power feed checks to eliminate the chance of a bad ground affecting the circuit.*

Repairing Hard Shell Connectors

Unlike molded connectors, the terminal contacts in hard shell connectors can be replaced. Weatherproof hard-shell connectors with the leads molded into the shell have non-replaceable terminal ends. Replacement usually involves the use of a special terminal removal tool that depress the locking tangs (barbs) on the connector terminal and allow the connector to be removed from the rear of the shell. The connector shell should be replaced if it shows any

evidence of burning, melting, cracks, or breaks. Replace individual terminals that are burnt, corroded, distorted or loose.

NOTE: *The insulation crimp must be tight to prevent the insulation from sliding back on the wire when the wire is pulled. The insulation must be visibly compressed under the crimp tabs, and the ends of the crimp should be turned in for a firm grip on the insulation.*

The wire crimp must be made with all wire strands inside the crimp. The terminal must be fully compressed on the wire strands with the ends of the crimp tabs turned in to make a firm grip on the wire. Check all connections with an ohmmeter to insure a good contact. There should be no measurable resistance between the wire and the terminal when connected.

Mechanical Test Equipment

Vacuum Gauge

Most gauges are graduated in inches of mercury (in.Hg), although a device called a manometer reads vacuum in inches of water (in. H_2O). The normal vacuum reading usually varies between 18 and 22 in.Hg at sea level. To test engine vacuum, the vacuum gauge must be connected to a source of manifold vacuum. Many engines have a plug in the intake manifold which can be removed and replaced with an adapter fitting. Connect the vacuum gauge to the fitting with a suitable rubber hose or, if no manifold plug is available, connect the vacuum gauge to any device using manifold vacuum, such as EGR valves, etc. The vacuum gauge can be used to determine if enough vacuum is reaching a component to allow its actuation.

Hand Vacuum Pump

Small, hand-held vacuum pumps come in a variety of designs. Most have a built-in vacuum gauge and allow the component to be tested without removing it from the vehicle. Operate the pump lever or plunger to apply the correct amount of vacuum required for the test specified in the diagnosis routines. The level of vacuum in inches of Mercury (in.Hg) is indicated on the pump gauge. For some testing, an additional vacuum gauge may be necessary.

Intake manifold vacuum is used to operate various systems and devices on late model vehicles. To correctly diagnose and solve problems in vacuum control systems, a vacuum source is necessary for testing. In some cases, vacuum can be taken from the intake manifold when the engine is running, but vacuum is normally provided by a hand vacuum pump. These hand vacuum pumps have a built-in vacuum gauge that allow testing while the device is still at-

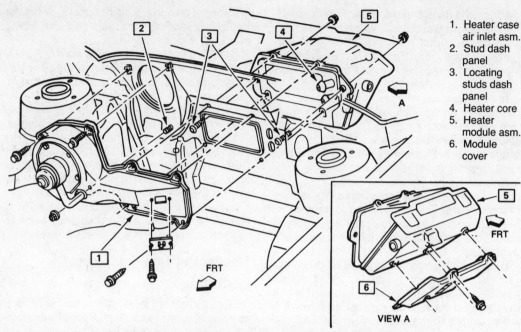

1. Heater case air inlet asm.
2. Stud dash panel
3. Locating studs dash panel
4. Heater core
5. Heater module asm.
6. Module cover

VIEW A

Heater assembly on models without air conditioning

tached to the component. For some tests, an additional vacuum gauge may be necessary.

HEATER AND AIR CONDITIONING

Blower Motor

REMOVAL AND INSTALLATION

1. Disconnect the negative battery cable.
2. Disconnect the electrical connections at the blower motor and blower resistor.
3. Remove the plastic water shield from the right side of the cowl.
4. Remove the blower motor retaining screws and then pull the blower motor and cage out.
5. Hold the blower motor cage and remove the cage retaining nut from the blower motor shaft.
6. Remove the blower motor and cage.
7. Installation is the reverse of removal.

Heater Core

REMOVAL AND INSTALLATION

Cars Without Air Conditioning

1. Disconnect the negative battery cable and drain the cooling system.
   CAUTION: *When draining the coolant, keep in mind that cats and dogs are attracted by the ethylene glycol antifreeze, and are quite likely to drink any that is left in an uncovered container or in puddles on the ground. This*
will prove fatal in sufficient quantity. Always drain the coolant into a sealable container. Coolant should be reused unless it is contaminated or several years old.
2. Remove the heater inlet and outlet hoses from the heater core.
3. Remove the heater outlet deflector.
4. Remove the retaining screws and then remove the heater core cover.
5. Remove the heater core retaining straps and then remove the heater core.
6. Installation is the reverse of removal.

Cars With Air Conditioning

1. Disconnect the negative battery cable and drain the cooling system.
   CAUTION: *When draining the coolant, keep in mind that cats and dogs are attracted by the ethylene glycol antifreeze, and are quite likely to drink any that is left in an uncovered container or in puddles on the ground. This will prove fatal in sufficient quantity. Always drain the coolant into a sealable container. Coolant should be reused unless it is contaminated or several years old.*
2. Raise and support the front of the vehicle.
3. Disconnect the drain tube from the heater case.
4. Remove the heater hoses from the heater core.
5. Lower the car. Remove the right and left hush panels, the steering column trim cover, the heater outlet duct and the glove box.
6. Remove the heater core cover. Be sure to

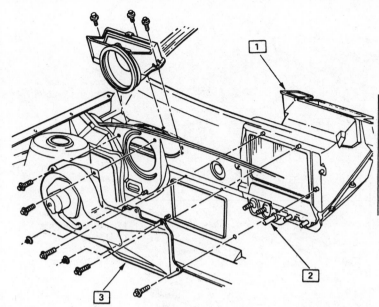

1. Heater & evaporator
2. Drain tube
3. Blower assembly

NOTICE: WHEN REMOVING THE HEATER & EVAPORATOR ASSEMBLY, PULL ASSEMBLY STRAIGHT TOWARD INTERIOR OF CAR UNTIL PLASTIC DRAIN TUBE CLEARS COWL. IF ASSEMBLY IS TILTED IN ANY DIRECTION BEFORE THE TUBE CLEARS THE COWL, THE TUBE MAY BREAK.

Heater assembly on models with air conditioning

pull the cover straight to the rear so as not to damage the drain tube.

7. Remove the heater core clamps and then remove the core.

8. Reverse the above procedure to install, charge the A/C system (refer to Chapter 1), and fill the cooling system.

Evaporator Core
REMOVAL AND INSTALLATION

1. Disconnect the negative battery cable and discharge the A/C system.
   NOTE: *Refer to Chapter 1 for Discharging, Charging and Evacuation of the A/C systems*
2. Jack up the car and support it safely.
3. On the 1987-88 Sunbird, remove the bolts to the transaxle support (automatic only).
4. On the 1987-88 Firenza, disconnect the rear lateral transaxle strut mount, if equipped.
5. Disconnect the heater hoses and evaporator lines at the heater core and evaporator core.
6. Remove the drain tube.
7. Remove the right hand and left hand hush panels, steering column trim cover, heater outlet duct and glove box.
8. Remove the heater core cover by pulling straight rearward on the cover to avoid breaking the drain tube.
9. Remove the heater core clamps and remove the heater core.
10. Remove the screws holding the defroster vacuum actuator to the module case.
11. Remove the evaporator cover and remove the evaporator core.

12. To install, reposition the core and install the cover.
13. Install the screws holding the defroster vacuum actuator to the module case.
14. Install the heater core clamps and cover.
15. Install the right hand and left hand hush panels, steering column trim cover, heater outlet duct and glove box.
16. Install the drain tube.
17. Connect the heater hoses and evaporator lines at the heater core and evaporator core.
18. On the 1987-88 Firenza, connect the rear lateral transaxle strut mount, if equipped.
19. On the 1987-88 Sunbird, install the bolts to the transaxle support (automatic only).
20. Lower the car and charge the A/C system (refer to Chapter 1), and fill the cooling system.

Radio
REMOVAL AND INSTALLATION

WARNING: *Do not operate the radio with the speaker leads disconnected. Operating the radio without an electrical load will damage the output transistors.*

1. Disconnect the negative battery cable.
2. Remove the instrument panel trim plate.
3. Check the right side of the radio to determine whether a nut or a stud is used for side retention.
4. If a nut is used, remove the hush panel and then loosen the nut from below on cars without air conditioning. On cars with air conditioning, remove the hush panel, the A/C duct and the A/C control head for access to the nut. Do not remove the nut; loosen it just enough to

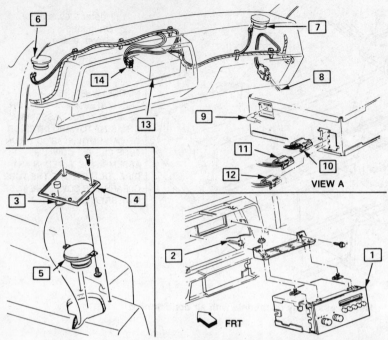

1. Radio
2. Screw on side of radio fits here
3. Retainer
4. Grille
5. Speaker
6. Frt speaker assembly
7. Frt speaker assembly
8. Rear speaker wire
9. Antenna
10. Rear speakers
11. Front speakers
12. I.P. harness
13. Receiver asm.
14. I.P. harness

VIEW A

FRT

Typical radio removal and installation details

pull the radio out. If a rubber stud is used, go on to Step 5.

5. Remove the two radio bracket-to-instrument panel attaching screws. Pull the radio forward far enough to disconnect the wiring and antenna and then remove the radio.

6. Installation is the reverse of removal.

WINDSHIELD WIPERS

Blade and Arm

REPLACEMENT

Wiper blade replacement procedures are detailed in Chapter 1.

NOTE: *Removal of the wiper arms requires the use of a special tool, G.M. J8966 or its equivalent. Versions of this tool are generally available in auto parts stores.*

1. Insert the tool under the wiper arm and lever the arm off the shaft.

2. Disconnect the washer hose from the arm (if so equipped). Remove the arm.

3. Installation is the reverse of removal.

The proper park position is at the top of the blackout line on the glass. If the wiper arms and blades were in the proper position prior to removal, adjustment should not be required.

ADJUSTMENT

The only adjustment for the wiper arms is to remove an arm from the transmission shaft, ro-

Remove the wiper arm with the special tool

tate the arm the required distance and direction and then install the arm back in position so it is in line with the blackout line on the glass. The wiper motor must be in the park position.

The correct blade-out wipe position on the driver's side is 28mm from the tip of the blade to the left windshield pillar moulding. The correct blade-down wipe position on the passenger side of the car is in line with the blackout line at the bottom of the glass.

Linkage

REMOVAL AND INSTALLATION

1. Remove the wiper arms.
2. Remove the shroud top vent grille.
3. Loosen (but do not remove) the drive link-to-crank arm attaching nuts.

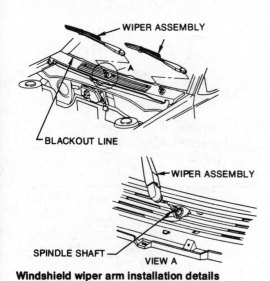

Windshield wiper arm installation details

4. Unscrew the linkage-to-cowl panel retaining screws and remove the linkage.

5. Installation is the reverse of removal.

Wiper Motor

REMOVAL AND INSTALLATION

1. Loosen (but do not remove) the drive link-to-crank arm attaching nuts and detach the drive link from the motor crank arm.

2. Tag and disconnect all electrical leads from the wiper motor.

3. Unscrew the mounting bolts, rotate the motor up and outward and remove it.

4. Guide the crank arm through the opening

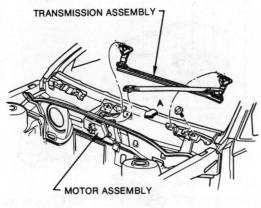

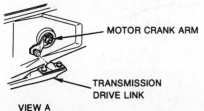

VIEW A

Wiper motor and transmission (linkage) assembly

in the body and then tighten the mounting bolts to 4-6 ft. lbs.

5. Install the drive link to the crank arm with the motor in the park position.

6. Installation of the remaining components is the reverse of removal.

Rear Window Wiper Motor

REMOVAL AND INSTALLATION

Station Wagon

1. Turn the ignition switch OFF.

2. Pull the wiper arm from the pivot shaft.

3. Remove the pivot shaft nut and spacers.

4. Open the tailgate and remove the inner trim panel.

5. Remove the license plate housing.

6. Disconnect the license plate light wiring.

7. Disconnect the wiper motor wiring.

8. Remove the linkage arm locking clip, pry off the arm and remove the linkage.

9. Remove the motor and bracket attaching screws and remove the motor.

10. Installation is the reverse of removal.

INSTRUMENTS AND SWITCHES

Instrument Cluster

REMOVAL AND INSTALLATION

1. Disconnect the negative battery cable.

2. Remove the right and left hush panels and the steering column trim cover.

3. Disconnect the vent panels from the bottom of the panel (if so equipped).

4. Remove the glove box. Disconnect the temperature and mode control cables on cars without air conditioning. On cars with air conditioning, remove the lower A/C duct.

5. Remove the three steering column retaining bolts (two at the instrument panel pad and one at the cowl) and lower the steering column.

6. Remove the lower right hand trim plate. Disconnect the cigar lighter and accessory switches.

7. Pull the heater or A/C control head out far enough to disconnect any wiring or vacuum harnesses, then remove the head.

8. Disconnect the front end and engine harnesses from the bulkhead connector in the engine compartment and then remove the bulkhead connector from the cowl (2 screws).

9. Loosen the set screw and remove the hood release handle. Unscrew the retaining nut and pull the hood release cable loose.

10. Unscrew the four upper instrument panel retaining screws (in the defroster duct openings).

11. Unscrew the two lower corner instrument

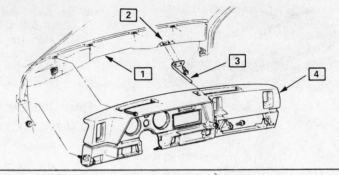

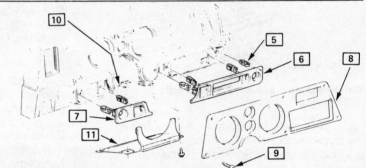

1. Dash panel
2. Weld nuts
3. Center reinf.
4. Pad asm.
5. Snap-in clips
6. R.H. lower I.P. trim plate
7. L.H. lower I.P. trim plate
8. I.P. trim plate
9. Torx screw
10. Hush panel
11. Steering column trim cover

Instrument panel and trim plate removal and installation details

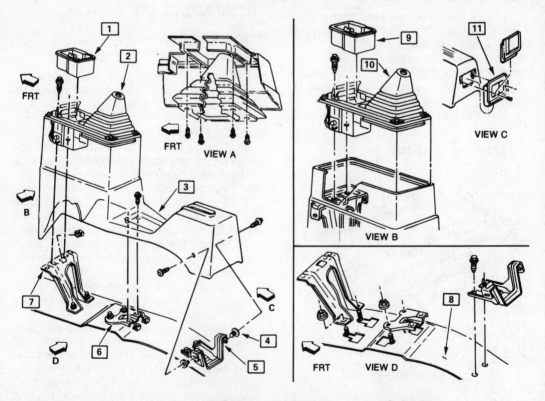

1. Ash tray
2. Boot
3. Console asm.
4. Push-in nut
5. Rear mounting bracket
6. Center mounting bracket
7. Front mounting bracket
8. Floor panel
9. Ash tray
10. Trimplate
11. Rear ash tray
    assembly

Center console removal and installation details—manual transaxle

panel retaining nuts. Remove the screw to the instrument panel brace from the left side of the glove box opening.

12. Pull the instrument panel out far enough to disconnect the ignition, the headlight dimmer switch and the turn signal switch. Tag and disconnect all other wiring and vacuum lines.

13. Remove the instrument panel with the wiring harness intact.

To install:

14. Install the instrument panel and wiring harness intact.

15. Connect the ignition, the headlight dimmer switch and the turn signal switch. Connect all other wiring and vacuum lines.

16. Install the two lower corner instrument panel retaining nuts. Install the screw to the instrument panel brace on the left side of the glove box opening.

17. Install the four upper instrument panel retaining screws (in the defroster duct openings).

18. Install the hood release handle.

19. Install the bulkhead connector from the cowl (2 screws). Connect the front end and engine harnesses at the bulkhead connector in the engine compartment.

20. Install the control head.

21. Install the lower right hand trim plate. Connect the cigar lighter and accessory switches.

22. Install the three steering column retaining bolts (two at the instrument panel pad and one at the cowl).

23. Connect the temperature and mode control cables on cars without air conditioning.

24. On cars with air conditioning.

25. Install the lower A/C duct.

26. Install the glove box.

27. Connect the vent panels at the bottom of the panel (if so equipped).

28. Install the right and left hush panels and the steering column trim cover.

29. Connect the negative battery cable.

Center Console

REMOVAL AND INSTALLATION

Manual Transmission

1. Place the gear selector in Neutral and apply the parking brake.

2. Lift the ashtray out of the console and then remove the two screws in the opening.

3. Loosen the set screw underneath the shifter knob and remove the knob.

4. Remove the screw under the parking brake handle. Remove the two screws at the rear of the console and lift it off.

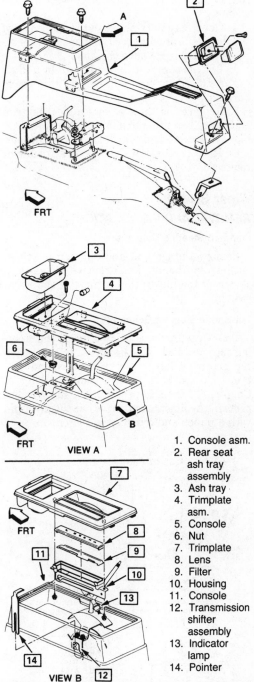

1. Console asm.
2. Rear seat ash tray assembly
3. Ash tray
4. Trimplate asm.
5. Console
6. Nut
7. Trimplate
8. Lens
9. Filter
10. Housing
11. Console
12. Transmission shifter assembly
13. Indicator lamp
14. Pointer

Center console removal and installation details—automatic transaxle

5. Installation is in the reverse order of removal.

Automatic Transmission

1. Place the gear selector in Neutral and apply the parking brake.

2. Lift out the ashtray from the front of the

console and remove the two screws from the opening.

3. Gently pry the emblem out of the center of the shift knob and remove the snap ring that secures the knob. Remove the knob.

4. Lift the trim plate assembly out by pulling the front end up first. Disconnect the wiring harness.

5. Remove the three screws under the trim plate and then lift out the rear ashtray and remove the screw under it. Remove the console.

6. Installation is in the reverse order of removal.

Wiper Switch
REMOVAL AND INSTALLATION
Standard Steering Columns

Remove the ignition and dimmer switch as outlined in Chapter 7 and remove the parts as shown in the illustration to remove the wiper switch.

Adjustable Steering Columns

The wiper switch is located inside the steering column cover. To gain access to the switch the steering wheel, turn signal switch and ignition lock will have to be removed. (Refer to Chapter 7 for these procedures). Remove the parts in the illustration, drive out the pivot pin with a punch and remove the switch.

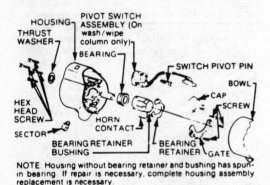

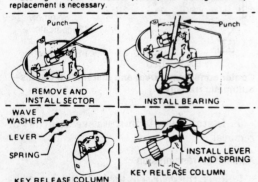

Wiper switch and related parts, standard steering column

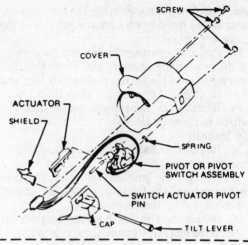

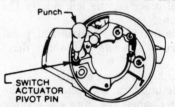

Wiper switch and related parts, adjustable steering column

Headlight Switch
REMOVAL AND INSTALLATION

1. Disconnect the negative battery cable.

2. Pull the knob out fully, remove the knob from the rod by depressing the retaining clip from the underside the knob.

3. Remove the trimplate.

4. Remove the switch by removing the nut, rotating the switch 180°, then tilting forward and and pulling out. Disconnect the wire harness.

5. Reverse the above to install.

Clock
REMOVAL AND INSTALLATION

The clock is part of the radio. If the clock is found to be defective the radio will have to be removed and sent to an authorized facility for clock repair.

Speedometer Cable
REPLACEMENT

1. Reach behind the instrument cluster and push the speedometer cable casing toward the speedometer while depressing the retaining spring on the back of the instrument cluster case. Once the retaining spring has released, hold it in while pulling outward on the casing to disconnect the casing from the speedometer.

NOTE: *Removal of the steering column trim*

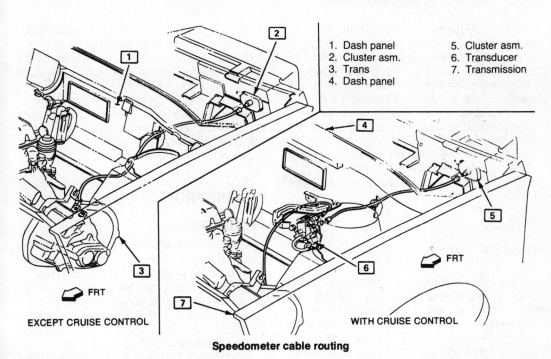

1. Dash panel
2. Cluster asm.
3. Trans
4. Dash panel
5. Cluster asm.
6. Transducer
7. Transmission

EXCEPT CRUISE CONTROL

WITH CRUISE CONTROL

Speedometer cable routing

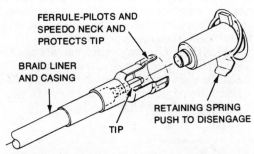

FERRULE-PILOTS AND SPEEDO NECK AND PROTECTS TIP

BRAID LINER AND CASING

TIP

RETAINING SPRING PUSH TO DISENGAGE

Speedometer cable disengagement at the speedometer

plate and/or the speedometer cluster may provide better access to the cable.

2. Remove the cable casing sealing plug from the dash panel. Then, pull the casing down from behind the dash and remove the cable.

3. If the cable is broken and cannot be entirely removed from the top, support the car securely, and then unscrew the cable casing connector at the transmission. Pull the bottom part of the cable out, and then screw the connector back onto the transmission.

4. Lubricate the new cable. Insert it into the casing until it bottoms. Push inward while rotating it until the square portion at the bottom engages with the coupling in the transmission, permitting the cable to move in another inch or so. Then, reconnect the cable casing to the speedometer and install the sealing plug into the dash panel.

Ignition Switch

The ignition switch removal and installation procedure is given in Chapter 7, under steering, because the steering wheel must be removed for access to the ignition switch.

LIGHTING

Headlights

REMOVAL AND INSTALLATION

1. Remove the headlamp trim panel (grille panel) attaching screws.
   NOTE: *The trim panel retaining screws on the Cavalier are under the hood, on top of the front support (see illustration).*

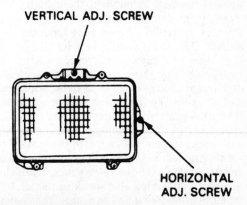

VERTICAL ADJ. SCREW

HORIZONTAL ADJ. SCREW

Headlight aiming screw location

2. Remove the four headlamp bulb retaining screws. These are the screws which hold the retaining ring for the bulb to the front of the car. Do not touch the two headlamp aiming screws, at the top and side of the retaining ring, or the headlamp aim will have to be readjusted.

3. Pull the bulb and ring forward and separate them. Unplug the electrical connector from the rear of the bulb.

4. Plug the new bulb into the electrical connector. Install the bulb into the retaining ring and install the ring and bulb. Install the trim panel.

TRAILER WIRING

Wiring the car for towing is fairly easy. There are a number of good wiring kits available and these should be used, rather than trying to design your own. All trailers will need brake lights and turn signals as well as tail lights and side marker lights. Most states require extra marker lights for overly wide trailers. Also, most states have recently required back-up lights for trailers, and most trailer manufacturers have been building trailers with back-up lights for several years.

Additionally, some Class I, most Class II and just about all Class III trailers will have electric brakes.

Add to this number an accessories wire, to operate trailer internal equipment or to charge the trailer's battery, and you can have as many as seven wires in the harness.

Determine the equipment on your trailer and buy the wiring kit necessary. The kit will contain all the wires needed, plus a plug adapter set which included the female plug, mounted on the bumper or hitch, and the male plug, wired into, or plugged into the trailer harness.

When installing the kit, follow the manufacturer's instructions. The color coding of the wires is standard throughout the industry.

One point to note, some domestic vehicles, and most imported vehicles, have separate turn signals. On most domestic vehicles, the brake lights and rear turn signals operate with the same bulb. For those vehicles with separate turn signals, you can purchase an isolation unit so that the brake lights won't blink whenever the turn signals are operated, or, you can go to your local electronics supply house and buy four diodes to wire in series with the brake and turn signal bulbs. Diodes will isolate the brake and turn signals. The choice is yours. The isolation units are simple and quick to install, but far more expensive than the diodes. The diodes, however, require more work to install properly,

since they require the cutting of each bulb's wire and soldering in place of the diode.

One final point, the best kits are those with a spring loaded cover on the vehicle mounted socket. This cover prevents dirt and moisture from corroding the terminals. Never let the vehicle socket hang loosely. Always mount it securely to the bumper or hitch.

NOTE: *For more information on towing a trailer please refer to Chapter 1.*

CIRCUIT PROTECTION

Fusible Links

A fusible link is a protective device used in an electrical circuit. When the current increases beyond a certain amperage, the fusible metal of the wire link melts, thus breaking the electrical circuit and preventing further damage to other components and wiring. Whenever a fusible link is melted because of a short circuit, correct the cause before installing a new one.

To replace a fusible link, cut off the burned link beyond the original splice. Replace the link with a new one of the same rating. If the splice has two wires, two repair links are required, one for each wire. Connect the new fusible link to the wires, then crimp securely.

WARNING: *Use only replacements of the same electrical capacity as the original, available from your dealer. Replacements of a different electrical value will not provide adequate system protection.*

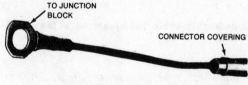

Fusible links before and after a short circuit

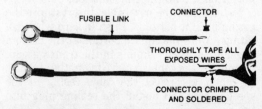

New fusible links are spliced to the wire

Fuses

Fuses protect all the major electrical systems in the car. In case of an electrical overload, the fuse melts, breaking the circuit and stopping the flow of electricity.

If a fuse blows, the cause should be investigated and corrected before the installation of a new fuse. This, however, is easier to say than to do. Because each fuse protects a limited number of components, your job is narrowed down somewhat. Begin your investigation by looking for obvious fraying, loose connections, breaks in insulation, etc. Use the techniques outlined at the beginning of this chapter. Electrical

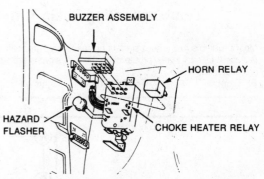

The convenience center is on the left side kick panel, under the dashboard

problems are almost always a real headache to solve, but if you are patient and persistent, and approach the problem logically (that is, don't start replacing electrical components randomly), you will eventually find the solution.

The amperage of each fuse and the circuit it protects are marked on the fusebox, which is located under the left side (driver's side) of the instrument panel and pulls down for easy.

Circuit Breakers

The headlights are protected by a circuit breaker in the headlamp switch. If the circuit breaker trips, the headlights will either flash on and off, or stay off altogether. The circuit breaker resets automatically after the overload is removed.

The windshield wipers are also protected by a circuit breaker. If the motor overheats, the circuit breaker will trip, remaining off until the motor cools or the overload is removed. One common cause of overheating is operation of the wipers in heavy snow.

The circuit breakers for the power door locks and power windows are located in the fuse box.

Flashers

The hazard flasher is located in the convenience center', under the dash, on the left side kick panel. The horn relay and the buzzer assembly may be found here also. The turn signal flasher is installed in a clamp attached to the base of the steering column support inside the car. In all cases, replacement is made by unplugging the old unit and plugging in a new one.

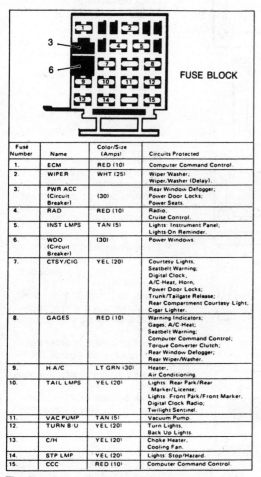

FUSE BLOCK

Fuse Number	Name	Color/Size (Amps)	Circuits Protected
1.	ECM	RED (10)	Computer Command Control.
2.	WIPER	WHT (25)	Wiper Washer; Wiper Washer (Delay).
3.	PWR ACC (Circuit Breaker)	(30)	Rear Window Defogger; Power Door Locks; Power Seats.
4.	RAD	RED (10)	Radio. Cruise Control.
5.	INST LMPS	TAN (5)	Lights: Instrument Panel; Lights-On Reminder.
6.	WDO (Circuit Breaker)	(30)	Power Windows.
7.	CTSY/CIG	YEL (20)	Courtesy Lights; Seatbelt Warning; Digital Clock; A/C-Heat, Horn; Power Door Locks; Trunk/Tailgate Release; Rear Compartment Courtesy Light; Cigar Lighter.
8.	GAGES	RED (10)	Warning Indicators; Gages; A/C-Heat; Seatbelt Warning; Computer Command Control; Torque Converter Clutch; Rear Window Defogger; Rear Wiper/Washer.
9.	H-A/C	LT GRN (30)	Heater; Air Conditioning.
10.	TAIL LMPS	YEL (20)	Lights: Rear Park/Rear Marker/License; Lights: Front Park/Front Marker; Digital Clock Radio; Twilight Sentinel.
11.	VAC PUMP	TAN (5)	Vacuum Pump.
12.	TURN B U	YEL (20)	Turn Lights; Back Up Lights.
13.	C/H	YEL (20)	Choke Heater; Cooling Fan.
14.	STP LMP	YEL (20)	Lights: Stop/Hazard.
15.	CCC	RED (10)	Computer Command Control.

The fuse box is under the left side of the instrument panel

Troubleshooting Basic Turn Signal and Flasher Problems

Most problems in the turn signals or flasher system, can be reduced to defective flashers or bulbs, which are easily replaced. Occasionally, problems in the turn signals are traced to the switch in the steering column, which will require professional service.

F = Front   R = Rear   ● = Lights off   o = Lights on

Problem		Solution
Turn signals light, but do not flash		• Replace the flasher
No turn signals light on either side		• Check the fuse. Replace if defective. • Check the flasher by substitution • Check for open circuit, short circuit or poor ground
Both turn signals on one side don't work		• Check for bad bulbs • Check for bad ground in both housings
One turn signal light on one side doesn't work		• Check and/or replace bulb • Check for corrosion in socket. Clean contacts. • Check for poor ground at socket
Turn signal flashes too fast or too slow		• Check any bulb on the side flashing too fast. A heavy-duty bulb is probably installed in place of a regular bulb. • Check the bulb flashing too slow. A standard bulb was probably installed in place of a heavy-duty bulb. • Check for loose connections or corrosion at the bulb socket
Indicator lights don't work in either direction		• Check if the turn signals are working • Check the dash indicator lights • Check the flasher by substitution
One indicator light doesn't light		• On systems with 1 dash indicator: See if the lights work on the same side. Often the filaments have been reversed in systems combining stoplights with taillights and turn signals. Check the flasher by substitution • On systems with 2 indicators: Check the bulbs on the same side Check the indicator light bulb Check the flasher by substitution

Troubleshooting Basic Lighting Problems

Problem	Cause	Solution
Lights		
One or more lights don't work, but others do	• Defective bulb(s) • Blown fuse(s) • Dirty fuse clips or light sockets • Poor ground circuit	• Replace bulb(s) • Replace fuse(s) • Clean connections • Run ground wire from light socket housing to car frame
Lights burn out quickly	• Incorrect voltage regulator setting or defective regulator • Poor battery/alternator connections	• Replace voltage regulator • Check battery/alternator connections
Lights go dim	• Low/discharged battery • Alternator not charging • Corroded sockets or connections • Low voltage output	• Check battery • Check drive belt tension; repair or replace alternator • Clean bulb and socket contacts and connections • Replace voltage regulator
Lights flicker	• Loose connection • Poor ground • Circuit breaker operating (short circuit)	• Tighten all connections • Run ground wire from light housing to car frame • Check connections and look for bare wires
Lights "flare"—Some flare is normal on acceleration—if excessive, see "Lights Burn Out Quickly"	• High voltage setting	• Replace voltage regulator
Lights glare—approaching drivers are blinded	• Lights adjusted too high • Rear springs or shocks sagging • Rear tires soft	• Have headlights aimed • Check rear springs/shocks • Check/correct rear tire pressure
Turn Signals		
Turn signals don't work in either direction	• Blown fuse • Defective flasher • Loose connection	• Replace fuse • Replace flasher • Check/tighten all connections
Right (or left) turn signal only won't work	• Bulb burned out • Right (or left) indicator bulb burned out • Short circuit	• Replace bulb • Check/replace indicator bulb • Check/repair wiring
Flasher rate too slow or too fast	• Incorrect wattage bulb • Incorrect flasher	• Flasher bulb • Replace flasher (use a variable load flasher if you pull a trailer)
Indicator lights do not flash (burn steadily)	• Burned out bulb • Defective flasher	• Replace bulb • Replace flasher
Indicator lights do not light at all	• Burned out indicator bulb • Defective flasher	• Replace indicator bulb • Replace flasher

Troubleshooting Basic Dash Gauge Problems

Problem	Cause	Solution
Coolant Temperature Gauge		
Gauge reads erratically or not at all	• Loose or dirty connections • Defective sending unit • Defective gauge	• Clean/tighten connections • Bi-metal gauge: remove the wire from the sending unit. Ground the wire for an instant. If the gauge registers, replace the sending unit. • Magnetic gauge: disconnect the wire at the sending unit. With ignition ON gauge should register COLD. Ground the wire; gauge should register HOT.
Ammeter Gauge—Turn Headlights ON (do not start engine). Note reaction		
Ammeter shows charge Ammeter shows discharge Ammeter does not move	• Connections reversed on gauge • Ammeter is OK • Loose connections or faulty wiring • Defective gauge	• Reinstall connections • Nothing • Check/correct wiring • Replace gauge
Oil Pressure Gauge		
Gauge does not register or is inaccurate	• On mechanical gauge, Bourdon tube may be bent or kinked • Low oil pressure • Defective gauge • Defective wiring • Defective sending unit	• Check tube for kinks or bends preventing oil from reaching the gauge • Remove sending unit. Idle the engine briefly. If no oil flows from sending unit hole, problem is in engine. • Remove the wire from the sending unit and ground it for an instant with the ignition ON. A good gauge will go to the top of the scale. • Check the wiring to the gauge. If it's OK and the gauge doesn't register when grounded, replace the gauge. • If the wiring is OK and the gauge functions when grounded, replace the sending unit
All Gauges		
All gauges do not operate	• Blown fuse • Defective instrument regulator	• Replace fuse • Replace instrument voltage regulator
All gauges read low or erratically	• Defective or dirty instrument voltage regulator	• Clean contacts or replace
All gauges pegged	• Loss of ground between instrument voltage regulator and car • Defective instrument regulator	• Check ground • Replace regulator
Warning Lights		
Light(s) do not come on when ignition is ON, but engine is not started	• Defective bulb • Defective wire • Defective sending unit	• Replace bulb • Check wire from light to sending unit • Disconnect the wire from the sending unit and ground it. Replace the sending unit if the light comes on with the ignition ON.
Light comes on with engine running	• Problem in individual system • Defective sending unit	• Check system • Check sending unit (see above)

Troubleshooting the Heater

Problem	Cause	Solution
Blower motor will not turn at any speed	• Blown fuse • Loose connection • Defective ground • Faulty switch • Faulty motor • Faulty resistor	• Replace fuse • Inspect and tighten • Clean and tighten • Replace switch • Replace motor • Replace resistor
Blower motor turns at one speed only	• Faulty switch • Faulty resistor	• Replace switch • Replace resistor
Blower motor turns but does not circulate air	• Intake blocked • Fan not secured to the motor shaft	• Clean intake • Tighten security
Heater will not heat	• Coolant does not reach proper temperature • Heater core blocked internally • Heater core air-bound • Blend-air door not in proper position	• Check and replace thermostat if necessary • Flush or replace core if necessary • Purge air from core • Adjust cable
Heater will not defrost	• Control cable adjustment incorrect • Defroster hose damaged	• Adjust control cable • Replace defroster hose

Troubleshooting Basic Windshield Wiper Problems

Problem	Cause	Solution
Electric Wipers		
Wipers do not operate— Wiper motor heats up or hums	• Internal motor defect • Bent or damaged linkage • Arms improperly installed on linking pivots	• Replace motor • Repair or replace linkage • Position linkage in park and reinstall wiper arms
Wipers do not operate— No current to motor	• Fuse or circuit breaker blown • Loose, open or broken wiring • Defective switch • Defective or corroded terminals • No ground circuit for motor or switch	• Replace fuse or circuit breaker • Repair wiring and connections • Replace switch • Replace or clean terminals • Repair ground circuits
Wipers do not operate— Motor runs	• Linkage disconnected or broken	• Connect wiper linkage or replace broken linkage
Vacuum Wipers		
Wipers do not operate	• Control switch or cable inoperative • Loss of engine vacuum to wiper motor (broken hoses, low engine vacuum, defective vacuum/fuel pump) • Linkage broken or disconnected • Defective wiper motor	• Repair or replace switch or cable • Check vacuum lines, engine vacuum and fuel pump • Repair linkage • Replace wiper motor
Wipers stop on engine acceleration	• Leaking vacuum hoses • Dry windshield • Oversize wiper blades • Defective vacuum/fuel pump	• Repair or replace hoses • Wet windshield with washers • Replace with proper size wiper blades • Replace pump

Drive Train

7

UNDERSTANDING THE MANUAL TRANSMISSION

Because of the way an internal combustion engine breathes, it can produce torque, or twisting force, only within a narrow speed range. Most modern, overhead valve engines must turn at about 2,500 rpm to produce their peak torque. By 4,500 rpm they are producing so little torque that continued increases in engine speed produce no power increases.

The torque peak on overhead camshaft engines is, generally, much higher, but much narrower.

The manual transmission and clutch are employed to vary the relationship between engine speed and the speed of the wheels so that adequate engine power can be produced under all circumstances. The clutch allows engine torque to be applied to the transmission input shaft gradually, due to mechanical slippage. The car can, consequently, be started smoothly from a full stop.

The transmission changes the ratio between the rotating speeds of the engine and the wheels by the use of gears. 4-speed or 5-speed transmissions are most common. The lower gears allow full engine power to be applied to the wheels during acceleration at low speeds.

The clutch drive plate is a thin disc, the center of which is splined to the transmission input shaft. Both sides of the disc are covered with a layer of material which is similar to brake lining and which is capable of allowing slippage without roughness or excessive noise.

The clutch cover is bolted to the engine flywheel and incorporates a diaphragm spring which provides the pressure to engage the clutch. The cover also houses the pressure plate. The driven disc is sandwiched between the pressure plate and the smooth surface of the flywheel when the clutch pedal is released,

thus forcing it to turn at the same speed as the engine crankshaft.

The transmission contains a mainshaft which passes all the way through the transmission, from the clutch to the halfshafts. This shaft is separated at one point, so that front and rear portions can turn at different speeds.

Power is transmitted by a countershaft in the lower gears and reverse. The gears of the countershaft mesh with gears on the mainshaft, allowing power to be carried from one to the other. All the countershaft gears are integral with that shaft, while several of the mainshaft gears can either rotate independently of the shaft or be locked to it. Shifting from one gear to the next causes one of the gears to be freed from rotating with the shaft and locks another to it. Gears are locked and unlocked by internal dog clutches which slide between the center of the gear and the shaft. The forward gears usually employ synchronizers; friction members which smoothly bring gear and shaft to the same speed before the toothed dog clutches are engaged.

The clutch is operating properly if:

1. It will stall the engine when released with the vehicle held stationary.

2. The shift lever can be moved freely between 1st and reverse gears when the vehicle is stationary and the clutch disengaged.

A clutch pedal free-play adjustment is incorporated in the linkage. If there is about 1-2″ (25-50mm) of motion before the pedal begins to release the clutch, it is adjusted properly. Inadequate free-play wears all parts of the clutch releasing mechanisms and may cause slippage. Excessive free-play may cause inadequate release and hard shifting of gears.

Some clutches use a hydraulic system in place of mechanical linkage. If the clutch fails to release, fill the clutch master cylinder with fluid to the proper level and pump the clutch pedal to fill the system with fluid. Bleed the system in the same way as a brake system. If leaks are located, tighten loose connections or overhaul the master or slave cylinder as necessary.

Front wheel drive cars do not have conventional rear axles or drive shafts. Instead, power is transmitted from the engine to a transaxle, or a combination of transmission and drive axle, in one unit. Both the transmission and drive axle accomplish the same function as their counterparts in a front engine/rear drive axle design. The difference is in the location of the components.

In place of a conventional driveshaft, a front-wheel-drive design uses two driveshafts, sometimes called halfshafts, which couple the drive axle portion of the transaxle to the wheels. Universal joints or constant velocity joints are used just as they would in a rear-wheel drive design.

Manual Transaxle

REMOVAL AND INSTALLATION

NOTE: *On 1982-=84 models, whenever the transaxle mount is removed, the alignment bolt M6 × 1 × 65 must be installed in the right front engine mount to prevent power train misalignment*

1. Disconnect the negative battery cable.
2. Install an engine holding bar so that one end is supported on the cowl tray over the wiper motor and the other end rests on the radiator support. Use padding and be careful not to damage the paint or body work with the bar. Attach a lifting hook to the engine lift ring and to the bar and raise the engine enough to take the pressure off the motor mounts.

NOTE: *If a lifting bar and hook is not available, a chain hoist can be used, however, during the procedure the vehicle must be raised, at which time the chain hoist must be adjusted to keep tension on the engine/transaxle assembly.*

3. Remove the heater hose clamp at the transaxle mount bracket. Disconnect the electrical connector and remove the horn assembly on 4 cyl models.
4. Remove the transaxle mount attaching bolts. Discard the bolts attaching the mount to the side frame: New bolts must be used at installation.
5. On 1982-84 models, disconnect the clutch cable from the clutch release lever. On 1985-87 models, disconnect the clutch slave cylinder from the transaxle support bracket and lay aside. Remove the transaxle mount bracket attaching bolts and nuts.
6. On V6 engines remove the following:
   a. Remove the air intake duct from the air cleaner.
   b. Remove the left fender brace.
   c. Disconnect the M.A.T. sensor lead at the air cleaner.
   d. Disconnect the mass air flow sensor lead.
   e. Remove the PCV pipe retaining clamp from the air intake duct.
   f. Remove the clamp retaining the air intake duct to the throttle body.
   g. Remove the Mass Air Flow Sensor mounting boltRemove the air cleaner bracket mounting bolts at the battery tray.
   h. Remove the air cleaner, mass air flow sensor and air intake duct as an assembly.
   i. Remove the heat shield at the crossover pipe and remove the crossover pipe.
6. Disconnect the shift cables and retaining clips at the transaxle. Disconnect the ground cables at the transaxle mounting stud.
7. Remove the four upper transaxle-to-engine mounting bolts.
8. Raise the vehicle and support it on stands. Remove the left front wheel.
9. Remove the left front inner splash shield. Remove the transaxle strut and bracket.
10. Remove the clutch housing cover bolts.
11. Disconnect the speedometer cable at the transaxle.

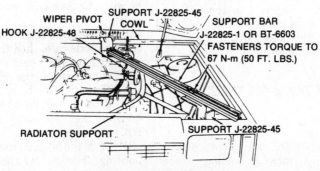

WIPER PIVOT
HOOK J-22825-48
SUPPORT J-22825-45
COWL
SUPPORT BAR
J-22825-1 OR BT-6603
FASTENERS TORQUE TO
67 N-m (50 FT. LBS.)
RADIATOR SUPPORT
SUPPORT J-22825-45

Install an engine holding bar

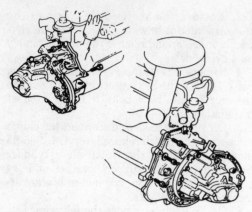

Engine-to-transaxle bolts

12. Disconnect the stabilizer bar at the left suspension support and control arm.

13. Disconnect the ball joint from the steering knuckle.

14. Remove the left suspension support attaching bolts and remove the support and control arm as an assembly.

15. Install boot portectors and disengage the drive axles at the transaxle. Remove the left side shaft from the transaxle.

16. Position a jack under the transaxle case, remove the lower two transaxle-to-engine mounting bolts and remove the transaxle by sliding it towards the driver's side, away from the engine. Carefully lower the jack, guiding the right shaft out the transaxle.

17. When installing the transaxle, guide the right drive axle into its bore as the transaxle is being raised. The right drive axle CANNOT be readily installed after the transaxle is connected to the engine. Tighten the transaxle-to-engine mounting bolts to 55 ft. lbs. Tighten the suspension support-to-body attaching bolts to 75 ft. lbs. and the clutch housing cover bolts to 10 ft. lbs. Using new bolts, install and tighten the transaxle mount-to-side frame to 40 ft. lbs. When installing the bolts attaching the mount-to-transaxle bracket on the 1982-84 models, check the alignment bolt at the engine mount. If excessive effort is required to remove the alignment bolt, realign the powertrain components and tighten the bolts to 40 ft. lbs., and then remove the alignment bolt.

5-SPEED (ISUZU, 76mm) OVERHAUL

Transaxle Case

DISASSEMBLY

1. Remove the clutch release bearing. Attach the transaxle to the transaxle holding fixture tool No. J-33366.

2. Remove the 7 rear cover bolts and the cover.

3. Remove the control box assembly together with the four bolts from the case.

4. Shift the transaxle into gear, then remove the 5th speed drive and the driven gear retaining nuts from the input and the output shaft. Shift the transaxle back into Neutral and aligning the detents on the shift rails.

5. Remove the detent spring retaining bolts for the 1st-2nd, the 3rd-4th and the Reverse-5th speeds. Remove the detent springs and the detent balls. Remove the Reverse detent spring retaining bolts, the spring and the detent.

6. Place the 5th speed synchronizer in Neutral, then remove the roll pin from the 5th gear shift fork and the 5th gear synchronizer hub, the sleeve, the roller bearing and the gear. Remove the shift fork as an assembly from the output shaft. Remove the 5th speed gear from the input shaft.

7. Remove the Torx® bolts from the bearing retainer, then the bearing retainer and the shims from the input and the output shafts.

8. Remove the Reverse idler shaft-to-case bolt.

9. Using tools No. J-22888 and J-22888-30, remove the output shaft collar and the thrust washer.

10. Remove the transaxle case-to-clutch housing bolts and separate the cases.

11. Remove the Reverse idler gear and the Reverse idler shaft.

12. Lift the 5th gear shaft. With the detent aligned facing the same way, remove the 5th and the Reverse shafts at the same time.

13. Using a punch and a hammer, remove the roll pin from the 1-2 shift fork. Slide the shaft upward to clear the housing, then remove the fork and the shaft from the case.

14. Remove the cotter pin, then remove the pin and the Reverse shift lever.

15. Remove the input and the output shafts with the 3-4 shift fork and the shaft as an assembly.

16. Remove the differential case assembly.

17. Remove the Reverse shift bracket together with the four bolts and the three interlock pins.

18. Remove the rear bearing outer race from the transaxle case, then the input shaft race.

19. Remove the outer races from the input shaft front bearing, the output shaft front and the differential side bearings.

20. Remove the input shaft seal from the housing, then the clutch shaft seal only when replacement is required.

21. Drive the bushing toward the inside of the housing, then remove the fork assembly only when replacing the clutch fork assembly.

ASSEMBLY

Before reassembly, attach the clutch housing to the transaxle holding fixture (if removed).

1. Install the input shaft seal.

2. Install the front outer bearing races for the input shaft, the output shaft and the differential into the clutch housing. Press the input, the output and the differential races into the housing.

3. Apply grease to the three interlock pins and install them on the clutch housing.

4. Install the Reverse shift bracket on the clutch housing. Use the 3rd-4th shift rod to align the bracket to the housing. Install and torque the retaining bolts. Make sure the rod operates smoothly after installation.

5. Install the differential assembly first, then the input and the output shaft with the 3rd-4th shift fork and the shaft together as an assembly into the clutch housing.

NOTE: *Make sure the interlock pin is in the 3rd-4th shifter shaft before installing.*

6. The 3rd-4th shift shaft is installed into the raised collar of the Reverse shift lever bracket.

7. Install the 1-2 shift fork onto the synchronizer sleeve and insert the shifter shaft into the Reverse shift lever bracket. Align the hole in the fork with the shaft and install the roll pin.

8. Install the Reverse lever on the shift bracket.

9. Install the Reverse and the 5th gear shifter shaft; engage the Reverse shaft with the Reverse shift lever at the same time.

NOTE: *Make sure the interlock pin is in the 5th gear shifter shaft before installing.*

10. Install the Reverse idler shaft with the gear into the clutch housing.

NOTE: *Make sure the Reverse lever is engaged in the gear collar.*

1. CLUTCH AND DIFF. HOUSING
2. CLUTCH SHAFT BUSHING
3. INPUT SHAFT OIL SEAL
4. DRIVE SHAFT OIL SEAL
5. STRAIGHT KNOCK PIN
6. TRANSAXLE CASE
7. DRAIN PLUG
8. GASKET
9. MAGNET
10. BEARING RETAINER
11. REAR COVER
12. GASKET
13. INPUT SHAFT
14. INPUT SHAFT FRONT BEARING
15. 3RD GEAR ASSEMBLY
16. 3RD/4TH SYNCHRONIZER ASM.
17. SYNCHRONIZER SLEEVE
18. CLUTCH HUB
19. INSERT
20. INSERT SPRING
21. 3RD/4TH BLOCKER RING
22. 4TH GEAR ASSEMBLY
23. 3RD NEEDLE BEARING
24. 4TH NEEDLE BEARING
25. 4TH COLLAR
26. 4TH GEAR THRUST WASHER
27. INPUT SHAFT REAR BEARING
28. 5TH GEAR
29. INPUT SHAFT END NUT
30. OUTPUT SHAFT
31. OUTPUT SHAFT FRONT BEARING
32. 1ST GEAR ASSEMBLY
33. 1ST/2ND SYNCHRONIZER ASSEMBLY
34. REVERSE GEAR
35. CLUTCH HUB
36. INSERT
37. INSERT SPRING
38. 1ST/2ND BLOCKER RING
39. 2ND GEAR ASSEMBLY
40. 1ST NEEDLE BEARING
41. 2ND NEEDLE BEARING
42. 2ND COLLAR
43. 3RD/4TH OUTPUT GEAR
44. KEY
45. OUTPUT SHAFT REAR BEARING
46. INPUT SHAFT BEARING SHIM
47. OUTPUT SHAFT BEARING SHIM
48. 5TH GEAR THRUST WASHER
49. 5TH NEEDLE BEARING
50. 5TH COLLAR
51. 5TH GEAR ASSEMBLY
52. 5TH SYNCHRONIZER ASSEMBLY
53. SYNCHRONIZER SLEEVE
54. CLUTCH HUB
55. INSERT
56. INSERT SPRING
57. 5TH BLOCKER RING
58. INSERT STOPPER PLATE
59. OUTPUT SHAFT END NUT
60. REVERSE IDLER GEAR ASM.
61. REVERSE IDLER SHAFT
62. STRAIGHT PIN
63. REVERSE IDLER SHAFT BOLT
64. GASKET
65. CLUTCH FORK SHAFT ASM.
66. CLUTCH RELEASE BEARING
67. RELEASE BEARING SPRING
68. CLUTCH SHAFT BUSHING
69. CLUTCH SHAFT SEAL
70. CLUTCH PRESSURE PLATE ASM.
71. CLUTCH DISK ASSEMBLY

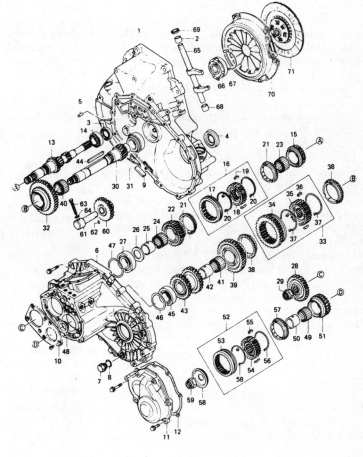

Disassembled view of the 5-speed, Isuzu (76mm) transmission

11. Using tool No. J-33373, measure and determine the shim size.

a. Position the outer bearing races on the input, the output and the differential bearings. Position the shim selection gauges on the bearing races. The three gauges are identified: Input, Output and Differential.

b. Place the 7 spacers (provided with the tool No. J-33373) evenly around the clutch housing perimeter.

c. Install the bearing and the shim retainer on the transaxle case. Torque the bolts to 11-16 ft. lbs.

d. Carefully position the transaxle case over the gauges and on the spacers. Install the bolts (provided in the tool kit) and tighten the bolts alternately until the case is seated on the spacers, then torque the bolts to 10 ft. lbs.

e. Rotate each gauge to seat the bearings. Rotate the differential case through three revolutions in each direction.

f. With the three gauges compressed, measure the gap between the outer sleeve and the base pad using the available shim sizes. Use the largest shim that can be placed into the gap and drawn through without binding; this will be the correct shim for the bearing being measured.

g. When each of the three shims selected, remove the transaxle case, the spacers and the three gauges.

12. Position the shim selected for the input, the output and the differential into the bearing race bores in the transaxle case.

13. Using tool No. J-24256-A, J-8092 and an arbor press, install the rear input shaft bearing race; press the bearing until it is seated in its bore.

14. Using tool No. J-33370, J-8092 and an arbor press, install the rear output shaft bearing; press the bearing until it is seated in its bore.

15. Using tool No. J-8611-01, J-8092 and an arbor press, install the rear differential case bearing race; press the bearing until it is seated in its bore.

16. Apply a ⅛" bead of Loctite® 514 to the mating surfaces of the clutch housing and the transaxle case.

17. Be sure the magnet is installed in the transaxle case.

18. Install the case on the clutch housing and the Reverse idle shaft bolt into the case, then torque the bolt to 22-33 ft. lbs.

19. Install the 14 case bolts and torque them to 22-33 ft. lbs. (in a diagonal sequence).

20. Install the drive axle seals.

21. Install the thrust washer and the collar to the output shaft.

22. Install the 5th gear to the input shaft. Install the needle bearing, the 5th gear, the blocking ring, the hub/sleeve assembly (with the shift fork in its groove) and the backing plate on the output shaft. Align the shift fork on the shifter shaft and install the roll pin.

23. Install the Reverse detent balls and the springs, then the 1st-2nd, the 3rd-4th and the 5th speed gears. Install the bolts and torque to 15-21 ft. lbs.

24. Apply Loctite® 262 to the input and the output shaft threads. Install new retaining nuts and torque to 87-101 ft. lbs.; stake the nuts after reaching the final torque.

25. Install the gasket and the control box assembly on the transaxle case, then torque the bolts to 11-16 ft. lbs.

NOTE: *Make sure the transaxle shifts properly before installing the rear cover.*

26. Install the gasket and the rear cover with the 7 bolts, then torque the bolts to 11-16 ft. lbs.

27. Install the clutch fork assembly (if removed). Using tool No. J-28412, install the bushing into the upper hole. Install the oil seal. Before installing the bushing, apply grease to both the interior and the exterior.

28. Install the clutch release bearing.

Input Shaft

DISASSEMBLY

1. Using tool No. J-22912-01 and an arbor press, remove the front bearing.

2. Pull out the rear bearing 4th gear, the 3rd-4th synchronizer assembly and 3rd gear as an assembly.

NOTE: *This procedure requires a arbor press and tool No. J-22912-01.*

3. Remove the outer parts from, the input shaft.

Output Shaft

DISASSEMBLY

1. Using tool No. J-22227-A and an arbor press, remove the front bearing.

2. Using tool No. J-22912-01 and an arbor press, remove the rear bearing and the 3rd-4th gear as an assembly.

3. Remove the key, the 2nd gear, the needle bearing and the blocking ring.

4. Using an arbor press, remove the collar, the Reverse gear assembly and the 1st gear as an assembly.

5-SPEED (MUNCIE) OVERHAUL

Axle Shaft Seal

REPLACEMENT

NOTE: *To perform this procedure, you will need a seal installer backed up by a driver handle. Use GM Part Nos. J-26938 and J-8092 or the equivalent.*

1. Disconnect the negative battery cable. Remove the axle from the car as described in the appropriate car section.

2. Carefully pry the old axle seal out of the transaxle.

3. Put the new seal onto the seal installer and then assemble the driver handle to the installer's outer end. Drive the seal in, being care-

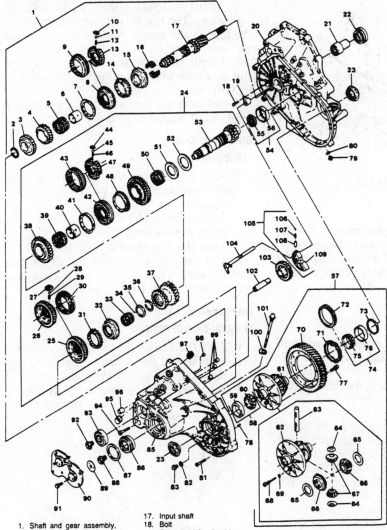

47. 1st/2nd synchronizer hub
48. 1st gear synchronizer blocking ring
49. 1st speed output gear
50. 1st speed output bearing
51. Thrust bearing
52. Thrust washer
53. Output shaft
54. Output shaft support bearing
55. Output bearing
56. Output bearing race
57. Differential and gear assembly
58. Differential bearing assembly
59. Differential bearing race
60. Differential bearing
61. Differential case assembly
62. Differential case
63. Differential cross pin
64. Pinion gear thrust washer
65. Side gear thrust washer
66. Differential side gear
67. Differential pinion gear
68. Pinion gear shaft bolt
69. Lockwasher
70. Differential ring gear
71. Speedometer output gear (mechanical speedometers)
72. Speedometer output gear (electronic speedometers)
73. Differential shim
74. Differential bearing assembly
75. Differential bearing
76. Differential bearing race
77. Differential ring gear bolt
78. Pin (2)
79. Oil drain plug
80. Washer
81. Transmission case bolt
82. Washer
83. Level check plug
84. (no designation)
85. Transmission case
86. Output gear bearing
87. Output gear shim
88. Output gear bearing retainer
89. Oil slinger washer
90. Transmission case end plate
91. Output gear bearing
92. Input gear retainer retainer
93. Input gear bearing
94. Reverse idler bolt
95. Detent lever bushing
96. Sliding sleeve bushing
97. Shift shaft needle bearing
98. Reverse shift rail bushing
99. Shift rail bushing (3)
100. Fluid level indicator washer
101. Fluid level indicator
102. Reverse idler shaft
103. Reverse idler gear
104. Reverse idler gear shift rail
105. Reverse idler gear bracket assembly
106. Reverse idler gear ball retaining bracket
107. Reverse idler gear spring bracket
108. Reverse idler gear detent bracket sleeve
109. Reverse idler gear bracket

1. Shaft and gear assembly, input cluster
2. Snap ring
3. Fifth speed input gear
4. Fourth speed input gear
5. Bearing cage
6. Needle race
7. Synchronizer ring blocker, fourth speed
8. Synchronizer assembly, fourth speed
9. Synchronizer sleeve, third and fourth speeds
10. Synchronizer key, third and fourth speeds
11. Synchronizer ball, third/fourth speeds (3)
12. Synchronizer spring, third/fourth speeds
13. Clutch hub, third/fourth speed synchronizer
14. Synchronizer ring, blocker, 3rd speed
15. Third speed input gear
16. Bearing cage (2)

17. Input shaft
18. Bolt
19. Reverse shift rail guide
20. Differential and clutch housing
21. Input shaft bearing and sleeve assembly
22. Clutch release bearing assembly
23. Drive axle oil seal
24. Output cluster shaft and gear assembly
25. Reverse output gear/5th speed synchronizer assembly
26. Reverse gear
27. 3rd gear synchronizer key (3)
28. 5th speed synchronizer ball (3)
29. 5th speed synchronizer spring
30. 5th speed synchronizer sleeve
31. 5th gear synchronizer blocking ring

32. 5th speed output gear
33. 5th speed output bearing
34. Thrust washer positioner ball
35. Thrust washer
36. Snap ring
37. 3rd/4th speed cluster gear
38. 2nd speed output gear
39. 2nd speed output bearing
40. 2nd speed output bearing race
41. 2nd speed synchronizer blocking ring
42. 1st/2nd gear synchronizer assembly
43. 1st/2nd speed synchronizer sleeve
44. 1st/2nd speed synchronizer key
45. 1st/2nd speed synchronizer ball
46. 1st/2nd speed synchronizer spring

Disassembled view of the 5-speed, Muncie transmission

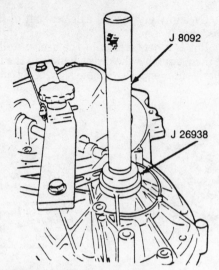

J 8092

J 26938

**Replacing an axle seal on the GM
Muncie 5-speed transaxle**

ful to keep the handle perpendicular to the seal
aperture so that it will be located squarely.

4. Install the driveshaft as described in the
car section. Recheck the fluid level and, if necessary, refill the axle with fluid.

Clutch Shaft and Bushing

REPLACEMENT

NOTE: *To perform this procedure, you will
need the following GM parts or their
equivalent: Bushing remover/installer J-
36037; bushing remover J-36032; bushing
installer J-36033; a slide hammer J-23907;
and a drive handle J-36190.*

CAUTION: *Whenever removing the clutch
lever assembly, FIRST disconnect the clutch
master cylinder pushrod at the clutch pedal.
FAILURE TO DO THIS MAY RESULT IN
PERMANENT DAMAGE TO THE SLAVE
CYLINDER, if the clutch pedal is depressed
while the lever is disconnected.*

1. Remove the transaxle from the car as described in the appropriate car section.

2. Remove the clutch release lever from the
end of the clutch shaft. Then, pull out the
clutch shaft seal.

3. Drive the upper clutch shaft bushing into
the transaxle housing with a hammer and the
bushing remover/installer. Then, turn the
clutch shaft slightly for clearance and remove it
from the clutch housing.

4. Install the bushing remover and slide
hammer, engaging the second step on the bushing remover below the bushing and then tight-
en the screw to expand the legs and force the
bushing out of its position in the housing.
Then, remove the bushing and tools.

5. Install the lower bushing by slipping it

onto the end of tool 36033 or equivalent. Slide
the tool and new bushing through the upper
bushing bore and down into the lower bore, and
then use the slide hammer to force the bushing
fully into the bore.

6. Install the clutch shaft.

7. Install the upper bushing with J-36037 or
equivalent. Tap the busing into the bore until
the line on the tool is flush with the housing
surface.

8. Install the dust seal. Then, install the
clutch release lever, torquing the through bolt
to 37 ft. lbs.

9. Reinstall the transaxle. Check the fluid
level and, if necessary, add fluid.

Shift Shaft Seal

REPLACEMENT

NOTE: *To perform this procedure, you will
need a seal installer GM tool No. J-35823 or
equivalent.*

1. Loosen the pinch bolt on the shift shaft lever. Then, remove the lever from the shaft.

2. Slide the cylindrical seal off the shaft.

3. Use the seal installer to install the seal
onto the shaft. Then, install the pinch bolts and
torque the through bolt/nut to 20 ft. lbs.

Disassembly of Transaxle

EXTERNAL LINKAGE REMOVAL

CAUTION: *The shift shaft must NOT turn
during the next step, or the transmission may
be damaged.*

1. Fit a large wrench onto the shift lever to
keep it from turning; then, unscrew the nut located at the top of the shift shaft.

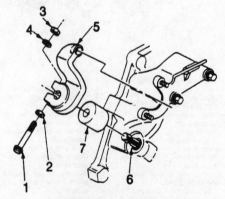

1. Shift lever through bolt
2. Washer
3. Through bolt attaching nut
4. Washer
5. Shift lever
6. Shift shaft
7. Shift shaft seal

**Replacing the shift shaft seal on the GM
Muncie 5-Speed**

2. Remove the washer, lever, pivot pin, and pivot.

3. Remove the pin and then the collar located just below the shift lever.

4. Remove the bolts that hold the shift lever bracket to the transaxle case and then remove the bracket.

5. Unscrew and remove the fluid level indicator and then the washer underneath it.

6. Remove the electronic speedometer signal unit, the retainer mounting bolt, and the retainer.

SHIFT RAIL DETENT AND CLUTCH AND DIFFERENTIAL HOUSING DISASSEMBLY

1. Remove the clutch throwout bearing. Puncture the detent holder cover near its center and then use an awl or similar tool to pry it off.

2. Earlier models only have an interlock plate. If the transaxle has this piece, remove the two interlock plate mounting bolts and then remove the interlock plate.

3. Remove the detent holder, springs (4), and interlock pins (2).

4. Remove the four detent balls.

5. Remove the reverse shift rail bushing by prying it loose via the two slots using small prying instruments.

SHIFT SHAFT DETENT COMPONENTS AND TRANSMISSION HOUSING DISASSEMBLY

1. Remove the snapring which retains the shift shaft cover and then remove the cover.

2. Remove the screw which retains the 5th/reverse bias outer spring seat and then remove the spring seat itself. Then, remove the bias spring and inner spring seat.

SEPARATING THE TRANSMISSION CASE AND CLUTCH HOUSING

1. Remove the 15 transmission case retaining bolts. Then separate the clutch housing from the transmisson case.

2. Lift the differential gear assembly (complete with roller bearings on both sides) out of the transmission case.

3. Remove the magnet from the transmission case.

4. Remove the bearing from the upper end of the output shaft.

REMOVAL OF SHIFT SHAFT COMPONENTS

1. Place a rag or other means of catching the shift shaft pin underneath he shift shaft, and then use a thin object and a hammer to tap the shift shaft pin out of the shaft.

2. Remove the shift shaft, catching the four rollers and two shift shaft pins as you remove it. Then, remove the 1st/2nd bias spring.

3. Remove the shift lever and reverse lever from the case.

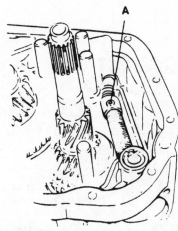

A. Shift shaft pin
Remove the shift lever pin ("A")

REMOVAL OF GEAR CLUSTER SUPPORT COMPONENTS

NOTE: *Removal of the output cluster gear retainer requires a special hex socket, J36031 or equivalent.*

1. First, push downward on the 3rd/4th shift rail to engage 4th gear. Then, do the same for the reverse shift rail to engage reverse.

2. Remove the nine retaining bolts from the transmission end plate. Then remove the end plate.

3. Remove and retain the selective shim from the groove in the housing on the output shaft side.

4. Remove the oil shield located in the center of the same area of the housing; then unscrew and remove the output gear cluster retainer, turning it *clockwise* in order to do so.

5. Remove the input gear cluster retainer using the same tool (rotation is normal). Then, shift both shift rails back to neutral.

REMOVAL OF GEAR CLUSTERS

NOTE: *To perform this procedure, you'll need: a hydraulic press, a gear cluster and transmission case assembly and disassembly pallet, Tool No. J-36182-1 or equivalent; two disassembly adapters J-36282-2 or equivalent, and a J-36185 gear cluster remover.*

1. Slide the adapters onto the two pegs on either side of the press. Position the pallet and adapters in the press. Then, position the transaxle case and gear cluster assembly onto the pallet and adapters. Make sure the pilots at the ends of the shift rails and input and output shafts align with the corresponding holes in the fixture.

2. Position the gear cluster remover on top of the shaft support bearings and pilot surfaces.

3. Locate the ram of the press squarely on

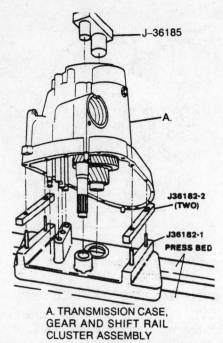

A. TRANSMISSION CASE,
GEAR AND SHIFT RAIL
CLUSTER ASSEMBLY

**Separating the transmission case from
the gearshift rail clusters**

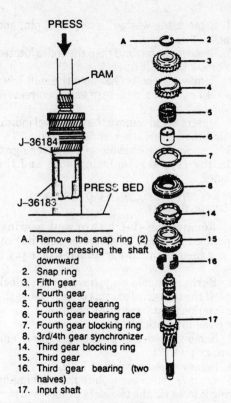

A. Remove the snap ring (2)
   before pressing the shaft
   downward
2. Snap ring
3. Fifth gear
4. Fourth gear
5. Fourth gear bearing
6. Fourth gear bearing race
7. Fourth gear blocking ring
8. 3rd/4th gear synchronizer
14. Third gear blocking ring
15. Third gear
16. Third gear bearing (two
    halves)
17. Input shaft

Disassembling the input shaft

top of the gear cluster remover. Then, press the
shafts and gear clusters out of the transaxle
case.

REMOVAL OF SHIFT RAILS

4. Remove the transmission case from the
press. Remove the 1-2 shift rail assembly.
Then, remove the lock pin from the assembly.

5. Remove the 3-4 rail assembly. Remove the
5th gear rail assembly. Finally, remove the reverse rail assembly.

6. Remove the shift gate. Disengage and then
remove the shift gate roller.

DISASSEMBLY AND INSPECTION

NOTE: *You'll need an oven that will produce
250° F. and hold gear assemblies or the gear
cluster and other small parts to reassemble
the unit. You'll also need hot tap water to heat
the speedometer gear prior to assembly. To
disassemble and reassemble the input shaft,
you'll need a hydraulic press, a J-22912-01
gear remover/installer, a press tube J-36183
or equivalent and a reducer J-36184 for the
input/output shaft gears. Use a heavy
assembly lubricant, part No. 1052931 or
equivalent to pre-lube parts during assembly
for protection until the gearbox lubricates
itself and is broken in.*

INPUT SHAFT DISASSEMBLY AND ASSEMBLY

NOTE: *Before disassembly, carefully
identify and label the blocker rings for 3rd*

*and 4th gears, as they are easily confused
during assembly.*

1. Remove the snapring from the top of the
shaft. Position the shaft with the snapring
groove upward and the lower end inserted into
the press tube and reducer. Center the top of
the shaft under the press ram. Press the shaft
downward and out of the gears and associated
parts. Remove the gear, bearing, race, two
blocking rings, and the synchronizer assembly
and associated gear.

2. Remove the 3rd gear bearing.

3. Clean all parts in a safe solvent and air dry
them. Then inspect as follows:

   a. Inspect the shaft for spline wear or
cracks and replace it if any are visible.

   b. Inspect the gear teeth for scuffing,
nicks, burrs, or breaks and replace gears that
show such defects.

   c. Inspect the bearings by rotating them
slowly and checking for roughness in rotation, burrs or pits, and replace as necessary.

   d. Inspect the bearing races and shaft
bearing surfaces for scoring, wear, or overheating and replace parts as necessary.

   e. Inspect the snapring for nicks, distortion, or wear and replace if any of these conditions exist.

   f. See the head below referring to "Synchronizer Disassembly and Inspection". In-

spect the synchronizer as described there, and replace defective parts.

g. Very slight defects in all parts except bearings can sometimes be removed with a soft stone or crocus cloth. It is permissible to clean up and re-use parts in this manner if only a small amount of metal must be removed.

4. Heat the 5th gear assembly and bearing race for 10 minutes in an oven preheated to 250° F.

5. Prelube all parts on wear surfaces as the assembly proceeds. While the gear is heating, assemble the two 3rd gear bearings and then the 3rd gear to the shaft. Install the 3rd gear with the cone upward. Then, install the blocking ring.

6. Assemble the shaft into the press tube and reducer and position the remover/installer so that the two, small diameter permanent gears near the bottom of the shaft straddle the in-

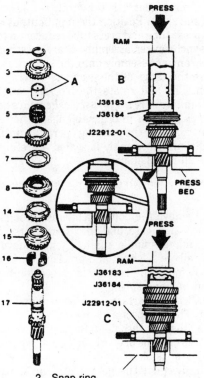

2. Snap ring
3. 5th gear
4. 4th gear
5. 4th gear bearing
6. 4th gear bearing race
7. 4th gear synchro blocking ring
8. 3rd/4th gear synchronizer
14. 3rd gear blocking ring
15. 3rd gear
16. 3rd gear bearing
17. Input shaft

Input shaft assembly

staller. Position the assembly onto the press so that the shaft protrudes down through the hole in the press bed.

7. Install the two 3rd gear bearings, 3rd gear (with the cone upward) and synchronizer blocking ring onto the shaft. Position the synchronizer onto the top of the shaft with the side marked "3rd gear" and the small outside diameter groove of the sleeve toward the 3rd gear. Position the gear installer on top of the synchronizer unit. Start the press operation cautiously and watch the position of the synchronizer. Stop the press before the synchronizer unit tangs touch those on the gears. Then, lift the 3rd gear blocking ring and 3rd gear so that their tangs fit into the tangs on the synchronizer. Then, press the synchronizer on until it is seated. Carefully remove any shavings that may have been created during the pressing operation.

8. Install the bearing race (preheated) and the bearing. Install the 4th gear blocking ring.

9. Install the 4th gear, cone downward.

10. Install the shaft assembly into the press tube and reducer and position the assembly squarely on the press. Install the 5th gear (preheated) on top, flat side down. Press the gear into position and install the ssnapring.

OUTPUT SHAFT DISASSEMBLY AND ASSEMBLY

NOTE: *To perform this procedure, you will need: a press of at least 15 tons capacity; an input/output shaft gear remover/installer J-22912-01 or equivalent; a J-36183 or equivalent input/output shaft gears press tube; a J-36184 input/output shaft press tube installer; and an oven that will produce 250° F. and hold gear assemblies or the gear cluster and other small parts. Before proceeding with disassembly, identify and label the blocking rings for 5th, 2nd, and 1st gears. They must be reinstalled in the correct positions. Use a heavy assembly lubricant, part No. 1052931 or equivalent to pre-lube parts during assembly for protection until the gearbox lubricates itself and is broken in.*

1. Install the gear remover/installer and shaft assembly into the press. The remover/installer has a tang which must locate in the shifting fork groove of the reverse/5th gear synchronizer assembly. The remover/installer rests on the press bed.

2. Press the shaft downward so the reverse/5th gear synchronizer assembly is pressed off the top. Then, remove the shaft from the press and remove: the blocker ring, 5th speed gear, 5th gear bearing, thrust washer, and thrust washer positioner ball.

3. Using snapring pliers, open and then work the snapring off the shaft.

4. Install the shaft in the press, supported via the lower side of the 1st speed gear by the input/output shaft gears press tube, resting on the press bed. Use the press ram, resting against the top of the shaft, to force the shaft downward (this will require at least 15 tons pressure) and force the 1st gear and parts above it off the shaft. Separate the following parts from the shaft: 2nd gear, bearing, bearing race, 1-2 synchronizer, blocking rings, 3-4 gear cluster, 1st gear, bearing, caged thrust bearing, and thrust washer.

5. Clean all parts in a safe solvent and air dry them. Then inspect as follows:

a. Inspect the shaft for spline wear or cracks and replace it if any are visible.

b. Inspect the gear teeth for scuffing, nicks, burrs, or breaks and replace gears that show such defects.

c. Inspect the bearings by rotating them slowly and checking for roughness in rotation, burrs or pits, and replace as necessary.

d. Inspect the bearing races and shaft bearing surfaces for scoring, wear, or overheating and replace parts as necessary.

e. Inspect the snapring for nicks, distortion, or wear and replace if any of these conditions exist.

f. See the head below referring to "Synchronizer Disassembly and Inspection". Inspect the synchronizer as described there, and replace defective parts.

g. Very slight defects in all parts except bearings can sometimes be removed with a soft stone or crocus cloth. It is permissible to clean up and re-use parts in this manner if only a small amount of metal must be removed.

6. Put the 2nd gear bearing race, and the 3rd-4th gear cluster in an oven at 250° F. The race requires at least 10 minutes preheating before assembly and the gear cluster at least 20 minutes preheating.

7. Install the thrust washer onto the shaft, *chamfer downward.* Then, install the caged thrust bearing, *needles downward.*

8. Install the 1st gear bearing. Then, install the 1st gear, cone upward. Install the 1st gear blocking ring.

9. Position the shaft into the press with the bottom protruding through the press bed. Locate the 1-2 synchronizer assembly on top of the shaft, with the side marked "1st" and the smaller outside diameter groove on the sleeve facing 1st gear. Use the J-36183 or equivalent input/output shaft gears press tube and the J-36184 input/output shaft press tube installer. Start pressing the synchronizer assembly onto the shaft, but stop before the tangs of the gear and synchronizer touch. Lift and rotate the blocking ring and gear *making sure the thrust washer stays downward in position* in order to engage the tangs. Then, continue the pressing operation until the synchronizer assembly is seated. Carefully remove all metal shavings.

10. Install the 2nd gear bearing race (preheated), 2nd gear bearing, and 2nd gear with the cone downward .

11. Position the preheated 3rd-4th gear cluster onto the shaft. Make sure the larger outside diameter gear is below the smaller one. Use the press and press tube reducer to press the cluster into position.

12. Install the snapring with ssnapring pliers. Then, install the thrust washer positoning ball, holding it in position with petroleum jelly. Install the thrust washer, aligning the slot in it with the ball.

13. Install the 5th gear bearing and then install the 5th gear, with the cone upward. Install the 5th gear blocking ring.

14. Position the shaft in the press. Position the reverse gear/5th synchronizer assembly onto the shaft. Position the input/output shaft gear press tube and press tube reducer on top of the synchronizer assembly. Start pressing the synchronizer assembly onto the shaft, but stop before the tangs of the gear and synchronizer touch. Lift and rotate the blocking ring and gear *making sure the thrust washer stays downward in position* in order to engage the tangs. Then, continue the pressing operation until the synchronizer assembly is seated. Carefully remove all metal shavings.

DISASSEMBLY AND ASSEMBLY OF THE REVERSE IDLER GEAR

1. Remove the bolt which runs through the transmission case and into the reverse idler gear sliding spindle shaft. Then, remove the shift rail, gear, shaft, and bracket.

2. Remove the reverse idler gear shift rail, detent ball and spring.

3. Clean all parts in a safe solvent and air dry them. Then inspect as follows:

a. Inspect the shaft for scoring, wear or cracks or signs of overheating and replace it if any are visible.

b. Inspect the gear teeth for scuffing, nicks, burrs, or breaks and replace gears that show such defects.

c. Inspect the bushing inside the gear, checking for scores, burrs, out-of-roundness, or overheating, and replace as necessary.

d. Very slight defects in all parts except bearings can sometimes be removed with a soft stone or crocus cloth. It is permissible to clean up and re-use parts in this manner if only a small amount of metal must be removed.

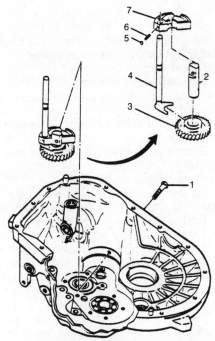

1. Bolt (torque to 16 ft. lbs.)
2. Sliding spindle shaft
3. Reverse idler gear
4. Reverse shift idler gear rail
5. Detent ball
6. Detent spring
7. Reverse idler gear bracket

Disassembly of the reverse idler gear components

4. Assemble all parts as described in the following steps, lubricating wear surfaces with a lubricant designed to protect the parts till they become lubricated by normal gearbox operation such as GM part No. 1052931.

5. Install the detent spring and ball into the reverse idler bracket.

6. Install the shift rail into the reverse idler gear bracket. Then, install the reverse idler gear onto the shaft with the slot in the gear facing the threaded hole in the shaft.

7. Install the entire assembly into the transaxle. Then, install the fastening bolt and torque it to 16 ft. lbs.

DISASSEMBLY AND ASSEMBLY OF THE TRANSMISSION CASE

NOTE: *To perform this procedure, you will need the following special tools or equivalent: J-8092 universal driver handle; J23907 slide hammer and adapter set; J-36027 shift shaft bearing remover; J-36029 shift rail bushing remover and installer; J-36032 clutch shaft inner bushing and reverse shift rail remover; J-36034 sliding sleeve bushing remover and installer; J-36039 shift detent lever bushing remover and installer; J-36181 differential*

bearing cup remover; J-36190 universal driver handle. Throughout this disassembly procedure, note that it is not necessary to remove bushings or bearings as a matter of routine. Inspect the bearing or bushing and the mating surface of the corresponding shaft. Inspect bushings for scores, burrs, out-of-round wear, or bluing (from overheating). Remove the bearing or bushing and replace it and the corresponding part only if there is evidence of damage or it is clear that the part is worn out.

1. Remove the snapring and plug from the rear of the sliding sleeve bore. Then, remove the screw-in spring retainer, the spring, and the sliding sleeve. Remove (if necessary) the sliding sleeve bushing with J-36034 and J-36190 or equivalent.

2. Remove the detent lever. If its wear surface is scored or worn, also remove the bushing it rides in with J-36039 and J-36190 or equivalent.

3. Pry out the shift shaft seal with a small, flat-bladeed screwdriver.

4. If necessary, remove the shift shaft bearing with J-36027 and J-36190 or equivalent.

5. Remove the axle shaft seal. As necessary, remove the outer race for the differential carrier support bearing with J-36181 and J-8092. Then, remove the three shift rail plugs from the transmission case.

6. (As necessary) remove the input shaft support bearing. Remove the output shaft support bearing.

7. Remove (as necessary) the three shift rail bushings with J-36029 and J-31690. Use the small end of the J-36029-2 adapter in the bushing.

8. As necessary, remove the reverse shift rail bushing with J-36032 and J-23907. Remove the stud that screws into the top of one of the shift rail bushing bores.

9. Inspect the case as follows:

a. Inspect the bearing race bores for wear, scratches, or grooves.

b. Inspect the gear teeth for scuffing, nicks, burrs, or breaks and replace gears that show such defects.

c. Inspect the bushings for scoring, burrs or pits, out-of-round or evidence of overheating (bluing) and replace as necessary.

d. Inspect the case for cracks, the threaded openings in the case for damaged threads, and the mounting faces for nicks, burrs, or scratches. Replace the case if it is cracked. Clean up damaged damaged threads with a used tap of the correct size (a brand-new tap will cut oversize threads).

e. Very slight defects in all parts except bearings can sometimes be removed with a soft stone or crocus cloth. It is permissible to clean up and re-use parts in this manner if only a small amount of metal must be removed.

NOTE: *The following special tools or equivalent designs from other sources are required to reassemble the case:*
J-26938 differential seal and race installer; J-35823 shift shaft seal installer; J-36209 shift rail bushing remover/intaller; J-36034 sliding sleeve bushing remover/installer; J-36039 shift detent lever remover/installer; J-36189 shift shaft bearing installer; J-26190 universal driver handle.

1. If it has been removed, install the shift shaft bearing with J-36189 and J-36190. Install the shift shaft seal with J-35823.

2. If it they been removed, install the three shift rail bushings. In doing this, install the bearings on the J-36029-2 adapter and retain them with the J-36029-1.

3. If it has been removed, install the reverse rail bushing with J-36030 and J-36190.

4. Install the differential carrier support outer bearing race with J-26938.

5. Install the axle seals with J-26938.

6. Install the three shift rail plugs into the case, screwing them in just until they are even with the surface of the case.

7. If it has been removed, install the detent lever bushing with J-36039 and J-36190. Then, install the detent lever.

8. If it has been removed, install the sliding sleeve bushing with J-36034 and J-36190.

9. Install the sliding sleeve bushing with J-36034 and J-36190. Then, install the sliding sleeve, spring, and retaining screw, torquing the retaining screw to 32 ft. lbs.

10. Install the plug into the sliding sleeve bore, and then install the snapring, flat side up.

11. Install the stud with the chamfer outward, torqing to 15 ft. lbs.

NOTE: *To perform this procedure you will need the following special tools or equivalent designs from other sources: a hydraulic press; a J-8092 universal driver handle; J-23907 slide hammer and adapter set; J-35824 input bearing assembly remover and installer; J-36029 shift rail bushing remover/installer; J-36032 clutch shaft inner bushing/reverse shift rail remover; J-36037 clutch shaft upper bushing remover/installer; J-36038 output shaft race bearing remover; J-36181 differential; bearing cup remover. Throughout this disassembly procedure, note that it is not necessary to remove bushings or bearings as a matter of routine. Inspect the bearing or bushing and the mating surface of the corresponding shaft. Inspect bushings for*

scores, burrs, out-of-round wear, or bluing (from overheating). Remove the bearing or bushing and replace it and the corresponding part only if there is evidence of damage or it is clear that the part is worn out.

1. Remove the two axle bearing race retainer bolts and the retainer. Remove the race with J-36038 and J-23907.

2. Remove the bolts, washers, spacer, and interlock plate.

3. Remove its mounting bolt and the reverse rail guide.

4. Remove the rear axle seal.

5. Remove the differential bearing race and selective shim pack with J-36181 and J-8092.

6. With a small screwdriver, pry out the clutch shaft seal.

7. Remove the upper bushing for the outer end of the clutch shaft with J-36037. Then, remove the clutch shaft itself. Remove the inner clutch shaft bushing with the J-36032 and J-23907.

8. Place the assembly in a hydraulic press. Fit the J-35824 into the end of the bearing sleeve assembly. Then, press the sleeve out of the case via the outer end of the special tool.

9. Remove the shift rail bushings by inserting the small end of the J-36029-2 adapter into each bushing.

10. Remove the drain plug and washer. Remove the breather assembly.

11. Inspect the assembly as follows:

   a. Clean all parts in solvent and allow them to dry.

   b. Inspect the housing bearing race bore for wear, scratches or grooves.

   c. Inspect the case for cracks, damaged threads, or nicks, burrs, or scratches in the mounting faces.

   d. Replace the case if there are any cracks. Very slight defects can sometimes be removed with a soft stone or crocus cloth. It is permissible to clean up and re-use the case in this manner if only a small amount of metal must be removed.

NOTE: *The following tools are required to reassemble the case: a hydraulic press; a J-8092 universal drive handle; a J-23423-A differential/ output shaft bearing cup installer; a J-35824 input bearing assembly remover/installer; a J-36029 shift rail bushing installer; a J-36033 chutch shaft inner bushing installer; a J-36037 chutch shaft upper bushing remover/installer; a J-36190 universal driver handle; and Loctite 242® or equivalent. Do not install the differential bearing race and axle seal until sater, when the bearing is shimmed for proper preload.*

1. Install the drain plug with a new washer, and torque it to 18 ft. lbs.

2. As necessary, install new shift rail bushings. Use tools J-36029 and J-36190, placing the bushing on the J-36029-2 adapter and retaining them between the -1 and -2 sections of the tool. *Make sure the bushings do not protrude into the transmission case side of the clutch housing* .

3. Coat the outside diameter with a small amount of Loctite 242® or equivalent. *Make sure the Oil seepage hole faces DOWNWARD inside the clutch housing.* Then, install a new bearing sleeve assembly with a hydraulic press and J-35842.

4. As necessary, install a new inner clutch shaft bushing with J-36033 amd J-36190. Then, install the clutch shaft.

5. As necessary, install a new outer clutch shaft bushing with J-36037. Make sure the bushing is positioned so that the outer end is flush with the bottom of the seal bore.

6. Install a new clutch shaft seal.

7. Install a new reverse rail guide with the short side going into its bore, and then install the retaining bolt, torquing to 15 ft. lbs.

8. Install a new output shaft bearing race, with J-J-23423-A and J-8092, *aligning cutouts in the race with the slots in the case* .

9. Install the output shaft retainer and bolts, torquing to 15 ft. lbs.

10. Coat the retaining bolts with Loctite 242® or equivalent and install the interlock plate, spacers, washers, and retaining bolts, torquing to 15 ft. lbs. Install the breather assembly.

SYNCHRONIZER DISASSEMBLY, INSPECTION, AND ASSEMBLY

1. Wrap each unit tightly in a shop rag to retain parts. Press the center hub of each unit through the sleeve to disassemble.

2. Clean all parts with solvent and then allow them to air dry. Inspect each unit as follows:

a. Inspect all hub and ring teeth for excess wear, scuffing, nicks, burrs, or actual breakage and replace defective parts.

b. Check symchronizer keys for either wear or distortion and replace those which are found to be defective.

c. Check the detent balls and retaining springs for distortion, cracks or wear. Replace defective parts.

d. Very slight defects in all parts except bearings can sometimes be removed with a soft stone or crocus cloth. It is permissible to clean up and re-use parts in this manner if only a small amount of metal must be removed.

1. Assemble the 1st/2nd and 3rd/4th synchonizer assemblies as follows:

a. Position the synchronizer sleeve with the smaller outside diameter groove upward.

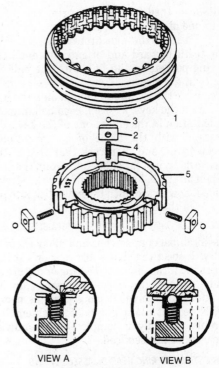

VIEW A   VIEW B

1. 1st/2nd synchronizer sleeve
2. 1st/2nd synchronizer key (3)
3. 1st/2nd synchronizer detent ball (3)
4. 1st/2nd synchronizer spring (3)
5. 1st/2nd synchronizer hub

Disassembly of the 1–2 synchronizer unit

Position the hub with the side marked "1st" upward on the 1st/2nd synchronizer and the side marked "3rd" upward on the 3rd/4th synchronizer. Turn the sleeve so that the ball detents in the sleeve will correspond with the ball and spring pockets in the hub. Then, slide the sleeve onto the hub.

b. Insert each spring into its corresponding key. Lift the sleeve just enough to provide clearance and then install each of these assemblies into the sleeve/hub assembly with the bevel cut on the key facing the sleeve. Slip each ball into the hole in the end of the key, depress it with a flat-bladed screwdriver and rock the sleeve downward and over the ball to retain it. When all three spring, key, and ball assemblies are installed, slide the sleeve downward until the balls click into position in the detents inside the sleeve.

2. Assemble the 5th synchronizer assembly as follows:

a. Position the gear with the integral synchronizer hub upward. Insert each detent spring into the indentation in the rear of one of the semi-circular keys. Position each key with the semi-circle downward and the teeth outward. Insert each key/spring assembly into one of the slots in the integral hub.

b. Position the synchronizer sleeve with the teeth upward and oriented to align the spring pockets in the hub with the ball detents in the sleeve.

c. Slide the sleeve far enough onto the hub to retain the keys. Position each ball into the indentation in the end of one of the keys, depress it with the blade of a conventional screwdriver, and then rock that area of the sleeve down just far enough to retain the ball. When all the balls are retained by the sleeve, slide it downward until the balls click into position in the detents.

INSPECTION OF SHIFT RAIL AND FORK ASSEMBLIES

Clean all parts in solvent and allow them to air dry. Inspect the shafts for wear or scoring. Inspect the forks for wear, scoring or distortion (bends). Inspect the levers for wear or distortion such as bending. Replace parts as necessary. Note that the major rail/fork assemblies are replacable only as complete units--individual parts are not serviced.

DIFFERENTIAL AND RING GEAR DISASSEMBLY AND ASSEMBLY

NOTE: *To perform this procedure, you will need the following GM special tools or equivalent designs from other sources: J-2241-11 or J-23598 side bearing puller adapter; J-22888 bearing remover; (2) J-22888-35 bearing remover leg.*

1. Remove the ten ring gear bolts and then separate the ring gear from the differential carrier assembly.

2. Remove the differential bearings with the bearing remover and the side bearing puller adapter.

3. Remove the speedometer cable or sending unit drive gear (it cannot be removed without breaking it).

4. Remove the bolt and washer that retain the cross-differential pin. Slide the pin out and then remove the two side differential gears and the two differential pinion gears, each with its own washer.

5. Inspect the differential components as follows:

a. Clean all parts in solvent and allow them to air dry.

b. Inspect gears for scuffed, nicked, burred, or broken teeth.

c. Inspect the carrier for distortion, out-of-round bores, and scoring and replace it if any of these conditions is present.

d. Inspect the differential bearings for roughness of rotation, burrs, or pits.

e. Inspect the two sets of two thrust washers for wear, scuffing, nicks, or burrs.

f. Very slight defects can sometimes be removed with a soft stone or crocus cloth. It is permissible to clean up and re-use parts in this manner if only a small amount of metal must be removed. Clean up or, if necessary, replace defective parts.

NOTE: *To assemble the differential and ring gear, you will need the following special tools or equivalent designs from other than GM sources: a hydraulic press; a J-22919 differential inner bearing installer; hot tap water to heat the mechanical speedometer drive gear; a 250° F. oven to heat the electronic type of speedometer drive gear. Supply both new bolts (10) for attaching the ring gear to the differential carrier and a new speedometer drive gear before beginning work. Note also that if the transmission or clutch and differential case, differential carrier, or differential bearing assemblies have been replaced, new selective shims must be installed to provide proper bearing preload, according to "Selecting and Installing New Differential Selective Shims" below.*

6. If the transaxle uses a mechanical speedometer drive gear (which is made of nylon), preheat it in hot tap water for five minutes. If it uses an electronic speedometer drive gear (made of steel), preheat it in an oven at 250° F. for 120 minutes before installing it. Install the drive gear. Allow it to cool before proceeding.

7. Install the two differential bearings, using the press and the Inner Bearing Installer so the bearings will not be damaged.

8. Install the side differential gears and their two thrust washers. Install the pinion gears and their two washers onto the cross-differential pin. Install the pin and its retaining capscrew with its lockwasher. Torque the capscrew to 84 inch lbs.

9. Install the ring gear onto the differential carrier with the chamfer on the inside diameter facing the carrier. Install the 10 new mounting bolts, and torque them to 61 ft. lbs. If the parts mentioned in the note above have been replaced, perform "Selecting and Installing New Differential Selective Shims" below.

SELECTING AND INSTALLING NEW DIFFERENTIAL SELECTIVE SHIMS

NOTE: *To perform this procedure, you will need the following GM special tools or equivalent designs from other sources: J-8092 universal drive handle; J-26935 shim selection set; J-26938 and J-8092 axle seal and bearing race installer.*

1. Install the seven spacers (J-26935-13) into the inner side of the transmission case and slide the long attaching bolts through from the outside.

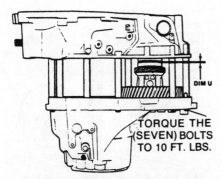

View of the differential assembled for measurement of the selective shim. Use bolts of measurement/type M8 x 1.25-6G 6.3 in. long.

TORQUE THE (SEVEN) BOLTS TO 10 FT. LBS.

SHIM PART NO.	DIM U mm (IN.)	COLOR	STRIPES
14082132	0.30 (0.012)	ORANGE	1
14082133	0.35 (0.014)	ORANGE	2
14082134	0.40 (0.016)	ORANGE	3
14082135	0.45 (0.018)	ORANGE	4
14082136	0.50 (0.020)	YELLOW	1
14082137	0.55 (0.022)	YELLOW	2
14082138	0.60 (0.024)	YELLOW	3
14082139	0.65 (0.026)	YELLOW	4
14082140	0.70 (0.028)	WHITE	1
14082141	0.75 (0.030)	WHITE	2
14082142	0.80 (0.031)	WHITE	3
14082143	0.85 (0.033)	WHITE	4
14082144	0.90 (0.035)	GREEN	1
14082145	0.95 (0.037)	GREEN	2
14082146	1.00 (0.039)	GREEN	3
14082147	1.05 (0.041)	GREEN	4
14082148	1.10 (0.043)	BLUE	1
14082149	1.15 (0.045)	BLUE	2
14082150	1.20 (0.047)	BLUE	3
14082151	1.25 (0.049)	BLUE	4
14082152	1.30 (0.051)	RED	1

2. Install the bearing race directly over the differential bearing on the clutch and differential housing side even though it will eventually be mounted in the clutch and differential housing. Then, install the J-26935-3 spacer over the bearing cup.

3. Bolt the clutch and differential housing over the spacers and torque the long though-bolts to 10 ft. lbs. Then, measure the width of the slot in the spacer (dimension "U") with a feeler gauge. Use gauges of the dimensions for "U" shown in the chart. Use the largest gauge that does not bind in the slot. When you have determined the proper dimension, read down the list of dimensions and pick the one two sizes larger.

4. Remove the through bolts, separate the case halves, and remove the spacers. Install the selected shim of the proper size into the bore in the clutch and differential housing case.

5. Install the bearing race with the bearing race and axle seal installer. Install the axle seal with the same special tools.

Assembly of The Transaxle

ASSEMBLY OF THE GEARSHIFT RAILS AND SUPPORT COMPONENTS

NOTE: *To perform this procedure, you will need a hydraulic press, a J-35824 or equivalent output/input shaft support bearing installer, a J-36031 or equivalent*

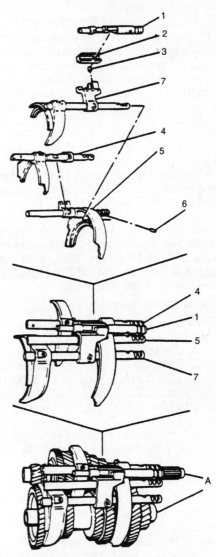

A. Gear cluster and shift rail assembly
1. Reverse rail
2. Shift gate
3. Roller
4. 3rd/4th rail
5. 1st/2nd rail
6. Interlock pin
7. 5th rail

Assembly of the gear shift forks and rails

retainer bolt hex socket, and a J-36182-1 or equivalent gear cluster a transmission case assembly/disassembly pallet, and petroleum jelly.

1. Position the input and output shafts next to each other with corresponding gears in normal mesh. Then install the following parts:

   a. The 1-2 shift rail

   b. Install the lock pin in the end of the 1-2 shift rail, using petroleum jelly to retain it.

   c. The 3-4 shift rail.

   d. The 5th shift rail.

   e. The Reverse shift rail.

   f. The shift gate and disengage roller.

2. Position the entire gear cluster and shift rail assembly onto the assembly/disassembly pallet, aligning the shift rail and shaft pilots with the corresponding holes in the fixture.

3. Install the transmission case over the shafts, aligning the bearing bores with the shaft pilots. Install a new output shaft bearing, using the output shaft support bearing installer and the press. Install a new input shaft bearing in the same way.

4. Slide the shift rails so as to engage both 4th and reverse gears. Then, check that the output and input shaft bearings are still fully seated in the case.

5. Install new ouput and input shaft bearing retainers with the retainer bolt hex socket, torquing both to 50 ft. lbs. Then, shift both forks back to Neutral position. Turn the transmission case over and support it.

ASSEMBLY OF THE SHIFT SHAFT

1. Install the reverse shift lever. Install the forward shift lever and bias spring.

2. Assemble the four shift shaft rollers and two shift shaft pins into the shift shaft, using petroleum jelly to retain them in place. Then, slide the shift shaft assembly into the gearbox by gently tapping it with a light hammer, aligning the hole in the shaft with the hole in the shift lever. Install the shift lever retaining pin so its ends are even with the surface of the shift lever.

ASSEMBLY OF THE CLUTCH AND DIFFERENTIAL HOUSING

NOTE: *You will need a sealant equivalent to GM Part No. 1052942 to perform this procedure.*

1. Apply the sealant mentioned above to the outside of the bolt hole pattern in the flange of the gear case.

2. Position the differential assembly into the case. Then, install the output shaft bearing to the upper end of the output shaft, turning it so the small inside diameter of the bearing cage faces the clutch housing.

3. Install the magnet into the case.

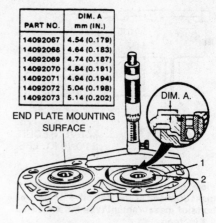

PART NO.	DIM. A mm (IN.)
14092067	4.54 (0.179)
14092068	4.64 (0.183)
14092069	4.74 (0.187)
14092070	4.84 (0.191)
14092071	4.94 (0.194)
14092072	5.04 (0.198)
14092073	5.14 (0.202)

1. Output shaft support bearing
2. Bearing retainer (torque to 50 ft. lbs.)

Selecting the shim for the output shaft support bearing

4. Install the clutch housing onto the transmission case, and install the attaching bolts, torquing them to 15 ft. lbs.

SELECTING AND INSTALLING NEW OUTPUT SHAFT SUPPORT BEARING SELECTIVE SHIMS

NOTE: *To perform this procedure, you will need a J-2600-19 metric dial depth gauge or equivalent, an ordinary michrometer, and a sealer such as 1052942.*

1. First, inspect the output bearing to be sure the it is fully seated in its bore. Make sure the associated bearing retainer is properly torqued, breaking loose the bolts and retorquing, if necessary.

2. Use the depth dial gauge to measure the distance between the end plate mounting surface and outer race of the output shaft bearing. The arms of the gauge rest on the mounting surface and the actuating pin of the dial gauge rests on the race. Consult the chart and select the shim dimension ("A") closest to the gauge reading. Slip the shim into position.

3. Subtract the thickness of the shim (as shown in the chart) from the gauge reading found in the step above. Make sure the result does not exceed 0.03mm or, if shim thickness exceeds the measurement (so you get a minus value), the difference is not greater than 0.03mm. In other words, the upper surface of the shim can be as much as 0.03mm above or 0.03mm below the end plate mounting surface. If necessary, change the shim to the next thinner one to correct a dimension more than 0.03mm above the mounting surface; change it to the next thicker one to correct a dimension more than 0.03mm below the mounting surface.

INSTALLING THE TRANSMISSION CASE END PLATE

4. Install the oil slinger onto the upper surface of the bearing. Apply the sealer mentioned in the note above to the bolt hole pattern for the outside end plate. Then, install the end plate and the nine bolts, and torque the bolts to 15 ft. lbs.

INSTALLING THE SHIFT RAIL DETENT INTO THE CLUTCH AND DIFFERENTIAL HOUSING

1. Fill the breather hole in the case with petroleum jelly. Position the shift rails in neutral position in order to expose all the interlock notches. Position the reverse shift rail so that the detent ball sits in the notch on the rail and, at the same time, on the reverse bushing.

2. Install the reverse shift rail bushing. Then, install the four detent balls into the notches in the shift rails and retain them with petroleum jelly.

3. Install the two interlock pins and four springs into the bores of the detent holder.

4. Install the assembled detent holder. Work the balls into the spring pockets, using a small screwdriver. Pry the reverse rail upward to permit its detent ball to enter the spring pocket.

5. Now, use the screwdriver to gently pry the holder into a position which will cause the bolt holes to align with the threads in the detent holder assembly. On earlier models install the interlock plate.

6. If the transaxle uses the interlock plate, make sure the 3-4 shift rail protrudes fully through the center of the lock plate and that the 1-2 shift rail protrudes fully through the aperture in the outer edge. If the 1-2 rail does not protrude fully, the entire shift mechanism will be locked up when the unit is assembled. Then,

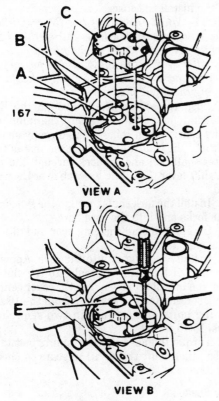

A. Reverse shift rail notch positioned so that the detent ball rests on the bushing ("167")
B. Retain all detent balls ("171") as shown in View A, with petroleum jelly
C. Assembled detent holder ("169"), shown in view A
D. Position the detent balls into the spring pockets, using a small screwdriver as shown in View B
E. Pry the reverse rail ("A") upward to allow its detent ball to enter the spring pocket, as shown in View B

Installing the detent holder

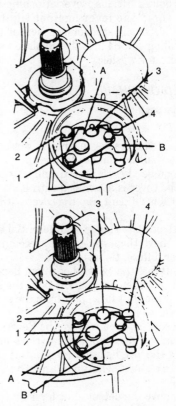

A. Interlock plate (used on early models only)
B. Detent holder assembly
1. Reverse shift rail
2. 3–4 shift rail
3. 1–2 shift rail
4. 5th gear shift rail

Checking the position of the shift rail detents

install the interlock plate or holder mounting bolts and torque them to 84 inch lbs.

7. Install the protective cover by tapping it until it is seated in its bore in the transaxle case.

8. Apply a high temperature grease to its inside bore, and then install the clutch throwout bearing.

INSTALLING THE SHIFT SHAFT DETENT COMPONENTS INTO THE TRANSMISSION HOUSING

1. Install the inner spring seat followed by the 5th/Reverse bias spring. Hold this spring in position while installing the outer spring seat and then starting the fastening screw. Torque the screw to 84 inch lbs.

2. Install the protective cover so that its retaining ring is past the snapring groove and then install the snapring.

INSTALLING THE TRANSAXLE EXTERNALLY MOUNTED LINKAGE

1. Install the external linkage in reverse order of removal. Observe the following torques: bracket bolts 17 ft. lbs.; lever attaching nut 61 ft. lbs. (hold the lever against tightening torque); electronic speedometer sensor assembly retaining bolt 84 inch lbs. Replace the fluid level indicator washer.

4-SPEED OVERHAUL

Transaxle Case

DISASSEMBLY

1. Place the transaxle onto a work stand, with the shaft assemblies facing up.

2. Remove the 15 clutch housing-to-case bolts. The cover is assembled with RTV sealer, if removal is difficult, rap the cover with a soft hammer.

3. Lift out the ring gear/differential assembly and move them aside; this procedure does not cover differential overhaul.

4. Shift into the Neutral position. Bend back the lock tab, then remove the bolt, the shifter shaft and the shift fork shaft from the synchronizer forks.

5. Disengage, then remove the Reverse shift fork from the guide pin and interlock bracket. Unscrew the lock bolt and remove the Reverse idler gear shaft, the gear and the spacer assembly.

6. Remove the detent shift lever and the interlock assembly, leaving the shift forks engaged with the synchronizers.

7. Lift the input and the output shafts from the case as an assembly.

NOTE: *When removing the shafts, mark the location and the position of the shift forks, then remove them from the shafts.*

ASSEMBLY

1. Place the input and the output shafts together on the workbench. Install the shift forks onto the shafts, then carefully lower them into the case as an assembly.

2. Place the interlock bracket onto a dummy shaft (make sure the bracket engages the shift fork fingers), then place the detent shift lever into the interlock.

3. Install the shifter shaft through the interlock bracket and the detent shift lever (do not push through any farther). Install the Reverse shift fork onto the dummy shaft and engage the fork with the interlock bracket.

4. Install the Reverse idler gear, the shaft and the install the spacer.

NOTE: *When installing the Reverse idler shaft, make sure the long end of the shaft points upward; the large chamfered ends of the idler gear teeth should also be facing up. The flat on the Reverse idler shaft should be facing the input shaft.*

5. Push the shifter shaft through the Reverse shift fork until it fits into the inhibitor spring spacer, then remove the dummy shaft. Shift into the Neutral position, then install the shifter shaft bolt and the lock through the detent shift lever. Bend the lock tab over the bolt head.

6. Install the fork shaft through the synchronizer forks and into the case bore.

7. Carefully install the ring gear and differential case assembly.

8. Install the magnet into the case. Apply a thin bead of RTV silicone sealer to the clutch cover and install the cover. Tap the cover gently with a soft hammer to seat it. Install the 15 attaching bolts and torque (in two sequence steps) to 16 ft. lbs.

9. Torque the idler shaft retaining bolt to 7 ft. lbs., then shift through the gears to check operation.

Input Shaft

DISASSEMBLY

1. Install the support plates under the 4th gear, then press the gear and the left hand bearing from the shaft.

2. Remove the brass blocking ring and the 3rd-4th synchronizer ssnapring.

3. Install the support plates behind the 3rd gear, then press the 3rd gear and the synchronizer from the shaft. Press the right hand bearing from the shaft.

ASSEMBLY

1. Using a long piece of pipe or GM tool No. J-28406, press the right hand bearing onto the shaft.

2. Place the 3rd gear onto the shaft; it should

have its synchronizer portion facing up towards the 3rd-4th synchronizer. Install the brass blocking ring onto the gear, then press the 3rd-4th gear synchronizer into place.

3. Using a piece of pipe, which will contact the synchronizer hub near the shaft, install the snapring with the beveled edges away from the synchronizer.

CAUTION: *When installing the snapring, do not press on the outside of the hub.*

4. Install the brass blocking ring. Press the 4th gear onto the shaft with its synchronizer portion facing the synchronizer, then press the left hand bearing into place.

Output Shaft
DISASSEMBLY

1. Install the support plates behind the 4th gear. Use a rod or a pilot which will fit the through the left hand bearing to press off the bearing and the 4th gear.

2. Remove the 3rd gear snapring, then slide the 1st-2nd synchronizer into 1st position. Support the 2nd with the plates, then press the 2nd and the 3rd gear off the output shaft.

3. Remove the brass blocking ring and the 1st-2nd synchronizer ssnapring.

4. Use the press plates to support the 1st gear, then press the gear and the synchronizer from the shaft. Press the right hand bearing from the shaft.

5. Pry out the synchronizer springs, being careful not to distort them. Scribe a mark across the hub and the sleeve, then separate the hub, the sleeve and the three keys, mark their locations.

6. Replace the parts as necessary. Assemble the hub and the sleeve according to the scribed marks. The extruded lip on the hub faces away from the shift fork groove in the sleeve.

7. Install one retaining spring, then carefully pull it away from the key positions (one at a time) and install the keys. The spring must be caught on the keys. Install the other spring on the other side in the same way, but be sure the open segment is in a different position (staggered) relative to the opening in the first spring installed.

ASSEMBLY

1. Press the right hand bearing into place. Install the 1st gear and its brass blocking ring onto the shaft, then (using a long pipe) press the 1st-2nd synchronizer into position.

NOTE: *When pressing the hub onto the shaft; do not press on the outer edges of the hub or the sleeve.*

2. Install the snapring and the brass blocking ring over the synchronizer.

3. Place the 2nd gear onto the shaft. Press

the 3rd gear into place (with its hub away from the 2nd gear); press on the gear close to the shaft-do not press on its outer edges. Install the 3rd gear snapring.

4. Press the 4th gear into place, with its hub facing the 3rd gear. Press the left hand bearing into place.

Case
OVERHAUL

1. Remove the Reverse inhibitor fitting from the outside of the case, then the spring, the pilot and the spacer from the inside.

2. Using a bearing puller, remove the input and the output shaft bearing cups, then slip out the oil slingers.

3. Check the interlock bracket, the Reverse shift fork guide pins and the case magnet for wear or damage. Clean the sealant from the case.

NOTE: *The preload shims must be selected before final assembly.*

4. Install the three left hand bearing cups, then the input shaft, the output shaft and the differential assemblies into position in the case. Install the three right hand bearing cups onto their bearings.

5. Place the GM gauge tools No. J-26935-2 on the input bearing, J-26935-4 on the output bearing and J-26935-3 on the differential bearing.

NOTE: *When installing the gauge tools, make sure they fit smoothly and completely over the bearings.*

6. Install the metal oil shield retainer over the tool No. J-26935-4 on the output shaft.

7. Install the spacers supplied with the spacer kit around the perimeter of the transaxle case. Carefully install the clutch cover over the gauges and spacers. Install the long bolts provided, then torque evenly and in rotation to 10 ft. lbs.

8. Rotate each gauge to seat the bearings. Rotate the differential case through three revolutions in each direction.

NOTE: *The gap between the outer sleeve and the base pad is the correct thickness for the preload shim at each location. The largest shim which can be placed in the gap and drawn through without binding is the correct one for the assembly.*

9. Remove the clutch cover, the spacers and the gauges. Place the selected shims in their respective bores in the clutch cover and add the metal shield, then install the bearing cups.

SHIFT LINKAGE ADJUSTMENT

4-Speed

1. Disconnect the negative battery cable.
2. Place the transaxle in 1st gear, then loos-

en the shift cable attaching nuts **E** at the transaxle lever **D** and **F**.

3. Remove the console trim plate and remove the shifter boot and retainer.

4. With the shift lever in the 1st gear position (pulled to the left and held against the stop) insert a yke clip to hold the lever hard against the reverse lockout stop as shown in view **D**. Install a No. 22 ($^5/_{32}$″) drill bit into the alignment hole at the side of the shifter assembly as shown in view **C**.

5. Remove the lash from the transaxle by rotating the upright select lever (lever D) while tightening the cable attaching pin nut **E**.

6. Tighten nut **E** on letter **F**.

7. Remove the drill bit and yoke at the shifter assembly, install the shifter boot and retainer and connect the negative battery cable.

8. Connect the negative batery cable.

9. Install the shifter boot and trim plate.

10. Road test the vehicle to check for good gate feel during shifting. Fine tune the adjustment as necessary.

5-Speed

1. Disconnect the negative battery cable.

2. Place the transaxle in 3rd gear. Remove the lock pin **H** and reinstall with the tapered end down. This will lock the transaxle in 3rd gear.

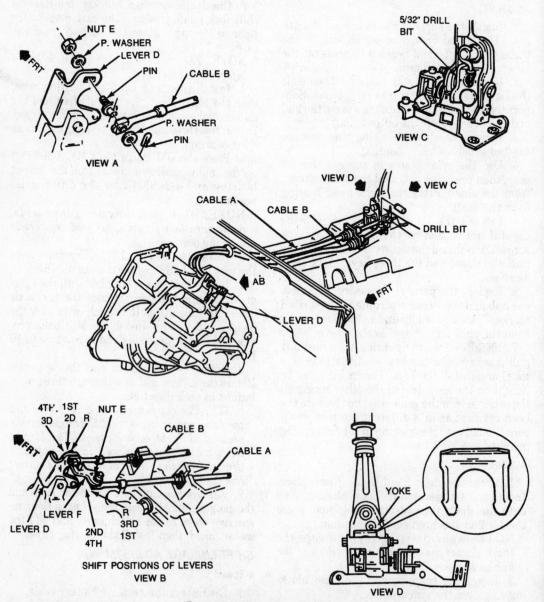

SHIFT POSITIONS OF LEVERS
VIEW B

Four speed shift cable adjustment

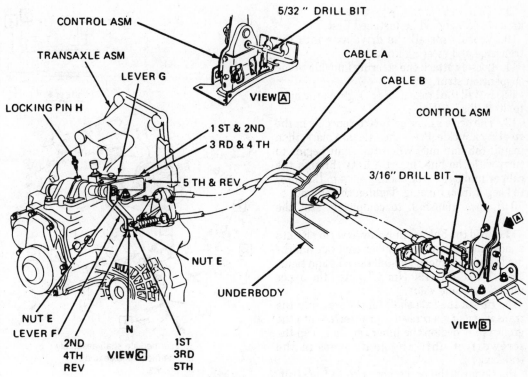

CONTROL ASM

TRANSAXLE ASM

LEVER G

LOCKING PIN H

5/32 " DRILL BIT

VIEW Ⓐ

CABLE A

CABLE B

CONTROL ASM

1 ST & 2ND

3 RD & 4 TH

5 TH & REV

3/16" DRILL BIT

NUT E

UNDERBODY

VIEW Ⓑ

NUT E
LEVER F

N

2ND   1ST
4TH   VIEWⒸ   3RD
REV   5TH

Five speed shift cable adjustment

3. Loosen the shift cable attaching nuts **E** at the transaxle lever **G** and **F**.

4. Remove the console trim plate and remove the shifter boot. Remove the console.

5. Install a No. 22 ($^5/_{32}$") drill bit into the alignment hole at the side of the shifter assembly as shown in view **A**.

6. Align the hole in select lever (view B) with the slot in the shifter plate and install a $^3/_{16}$" drill bit.

7. Tighten nut **E** at levers **G** and **F**.

8. Remove the drill bits from the alignment holes at the shifter. Remove lockpin **H**.

9. Install the console, shifter boot and retainer and connect the negative battery cable.

10. Road test the vehicle to check for good gate feel during shifting. Fine tune the adjustment as necessary.

Drive Axles

The J-cars use unequal-length halfshafts, with specific application for automatic and manual transaxle use. All halfshafts except the left-hand inboard joint of the automatic transaxle incorporate a male spline; the shafts interlock with the transaxle gears through the use of barrel-type snaprings. The left-hand inboard shaft on the automatic transaxle uses a female spline which installs over a stub shaft protrud-

ing from the transaxle. Four constant velocity joints are used, two on each shaft. The inner joints are of the double offset design; the outer joints are Rzeppa-type.

REMOVAL AND INSTALLATION

1982-86

1. Remove the hub nut.

2. Raise the front of the car. Remove the wheel and tire.

3. Install an axle shaft boot seal protector, G.M. special tool No. J-28712 or the equivalent, onto the seal.

4. Disconnect the brake hose clip from the MacPherson strut, but do not disconnect the hose from the caliper. Remove the brake caliper from the spindle, and hang the caliper out of the way by a length of wire. Do not allow the caliper to hang by the brake hose.

5. Mark the camber alignment cam bolt for reassembly. Remove the cam bolt and the upper attaching bolt from the strut and spindle.

6. Pull the steering knuckle assembly from the strut bracket.

7. Using G.M. special tool J-28468 or the equivalent, remove the axle shaft from the transaxle.

8. Using G.M. special tool J-28733 or the equivalent spindle remover, remove the axle shaft from the hub and bearing assembly.

9. If a new drive axle is to be installed, a new knuckle seal should be installed first.

10. Loosely install the drive axle into the transaxle and steering knuckle.

11. Loosely attach the steering knuckle to the suspension strut.

12. Install the brake caliper. Tighten the bolts to 30 ft. lbs. (40Nm.).

13. The drive axle is an interference fit in the steering knuckle. Press the axle into place, then install the hub nut. When the shaft begins to turn with the hub, insert a drift through the caliper into one of the cooling slots in the rotor to keep it from turning. Tighten the hub nut to 70 ft. lbs. (100Nm.). to completely seat the shaft.

14. Load the hub assembly by lowering it onto a jackstand. Align the camber cam bolt marks made during removal, install the bolt and tighten to 140 ft. lbs. (190 Nm.). Tighten the upper nut to the same value.

15. Install the axle shaft all the way into the transaxle using a screwdriver inserted into the groove provided on the inner retainer. Tap the screwdriver until the shaft seats in the transaxle.

16. Connect the brake hose clip to the strut. Install the tire and wheel, lower the car, and tighten the hub nut to 225 ft. lbs. (305 Nm.).

1987-88

1. Raise the car and suitably support.
2. Remove the wheel assembly.
3. Insert a drift into the into the caliper and rotor to prevent the rotor from turning.
4. Remove the shaft nut and washer.
5. Remove the caliper from the steering knuckle and suspend the caliper assembly with a wire.
6. Remove the rotor from the hub and bearing assembly.
7. Disconnect the stabilizer shaft from the control arm.
8. Remove the ball joint from the steering knuckle.
9. Remove the drive axle from the transaxle. Remove the driveaxle from the hub and bearing assembly using tool J-28733.
10. Install the drive axle into the hub and bearing assembly and the transaxle.
11. Install the lower ball joint to the steering knuckle.
12. Install the stabilizer shaft to the control arm.
13. Install the rotor to the hub and bearing assembly.
14. Install the caliper to the steering knuckle.
15. Install a washer and a new shaft nut.
16. 3.
Insert a drift into the into the caliper and ro-

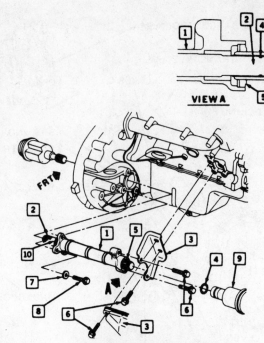

1. Intermediate shaft assembly
2. Intermediate axle shaft
3. Bracket
4. Axle shaft retaining ring
5. Lip seal
6. Bolt 50 N·m (37 lbs. ft.)
7. Washer
8. Bolt 25 N·m (18 lbs. ft.)
9. Right drive axle
10. "O" ring seal

Intermediate shaft assembly, 2.8 V6 engine

tor to prevent the rotor from turning and torque to 191 ft. lbs.

17. seat the drive axle into the transaxle by placing a screwdriver into the groove on the joint housing and tapping until seated.

18. Verify that the drive axle is seated into the transaxle by grasping on the housing and pulling outward.

19. Install the wheel assembly.

20. Lower the car

Intermediate shaft
REMOVAL AND INSTALLATION
1987-88 V6 and Turbo Models

1. Raise the car and suitably support.
2. Remove the wheel assembly.
3. Drain the transaxle.
4. On the V6 engine, install the modified outer seal protector J-34754.
5. Remove the stabilizer shaft from the right control arm.
6. Remove the right ball joint from the knuckle.

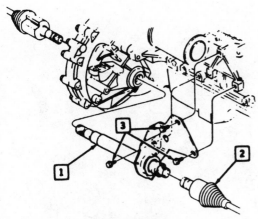

1. Intermediate shaft
2. Right axle shaft
3. Bolt 47 N·m (35 lbs. ft.)

Intermediate shaft assembly, Turbo engine

7. Disconnect the drive axle from the intermediate axle shaft.

8. On the turbo models, disconnect the detonation sensor and connection.

9. On the turbo models, remove the power steering pump brace.

10. On the V6 engine, remove the two housing to bracket bolts.

11. On the V6 engine, remove the bottom bracket to engine bolt and loosen the top bolt, rotate the bracket out of the way.

12. Remove the 3 bolts holding the housing to the transaxle.

13. To install, place the intermediate shaft into position and lkock the intermediate axle shaft into the transaxle.

14. Install the 3 bolts holding the housing to the transaxle and tighten to 18 ft. lbs.

15. On the V6 engine rotate the bracket into position and install the bottom bolt, tighten both bolts to 37 ft. lbs.

16. On the V6 engine, Install the two housing to bracket bolts and tighten to 37 ft. lbs.

17. On the turbo models, install the power steering pump brace.

18. On the turbo models, connect the detonation sensor.

19. Coat the splines with chassis grease.

20. Connect the drive axle to the intermediate axle shaft.

21. Connect the right ball joint to the knuckle.

22. Install the stabilizer shaft to the right control arm.

23. On the V6 engine, remove the modified outer seal protector J-34754.

24. Install the wheel.

25. Lower the car and fill the transaxle with the proper fluid.

CONSTANT VELOCITY JOINT OVERHAUL
Outer Joint

1. Remove the axle shaft.

2. Cut off the seal retaining clamp. Using a brass drift and a hammer, lightly tap the seal retainer from the outside toward the inside of the shaft to remove from the joint.

3. Use a pair of snapring pliers to spread the retaining ring apart. Pull the axle shaft from the joint.

4. Using a brass drift and a hammer, lightly tap on the inner race cage until it has tilted sufficiently to remove one of the balls. Remove the other balls in the same manner.

5. Pivot the cage 90° and, with the cage ball windows aligned with the outer joint windows, lift out the cage and the inner race.

6. The inner race can be removed from the cage by pivoting it 90° and lifting out. Clean all parts thoroughly and inspect for wear.

7. To install, put a light coat of the grease provided in the rebuilding kit onto the ball grooves of the inner race and outer joint. Install the parts in the reverse order of removal. To install the seal retainer, install the axle shaft assembly into an arbor press. Support the seal retainer on blocks, and press the axle shaft down until the seal retainer seats on the outer joint. When assembling, apply half the grease provided in the rebuilding kit to the joint; fill the seal (boot) with the rest of the grease.

Inner Joint

1. The joint seal is removed in the same manner as the outer joint seal. Follow Steps 1-3 of the outer joint procedure.

2. To disassemble the inner joint, remove the ball retaining ring from the joint. Pull the cage and inner race from the joint. The balls will come out with the race.

3. Center the inner race lobes in the cage windows, pivot the race 90°, and lift the race from the cage.

4. Assembly of the joint is the reverse. The inner joint seal retainer must be pressed onto the joint. See Step 7 of the outer joint procedure.

CLUTCH

Understanding the Clutch

The purpose of the clutch is to disconnect and connect engine power from the transmission. A car at rest requires a lot of engine torque to get all that weight moving. An internal combustion engine does not develop a high starting torque (unlike steam engines), so it must be allowed to

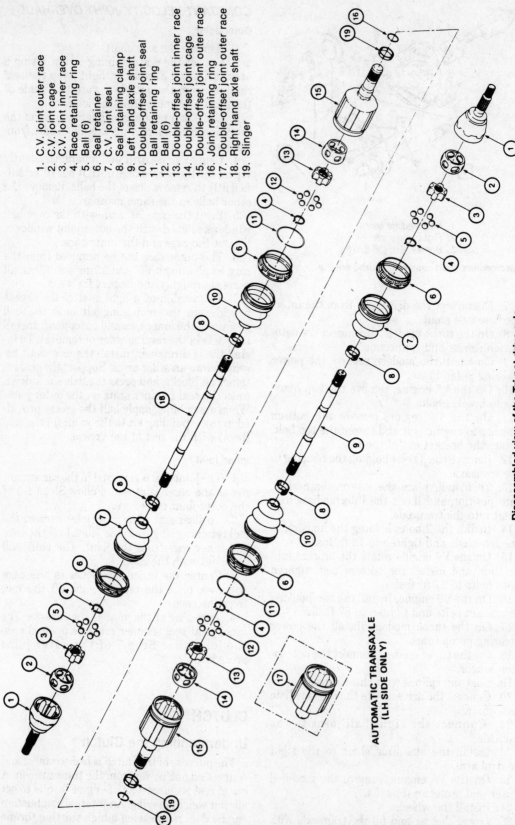

1. C.V. joint outer race
2. C.V. joint cage
3. C.V. joint inner race
4. Race retaining ring
5. Ball (6)
6. Seal retainer
7. C.V. joint seal
8. Seal retaining clamp
9. Left hand axle shaft
10. Double-offset joint seal
11. Ball retaining ring
12. Ball (6)
13. Double-offset joint inner race
14. Double-offset joint cage
15. Double-offset joint outer race
16. Joint retaining ring
17. Double-offset joint outer race
18. Right hand axle shaft
19. Slinger

AUTOMATIC TRANSAXLE
(LH SIDE ONLY)

Disassembled view of the Tri-pot drive axle

operate without any load until it builds up enough torque to move the car. Torque increases with engine rpm. The clutch allows the engine to build up torque by physically disconnecting the engine from the transmission, re-

lieving the engine of any load or resistance. The transfer of engine power to the transmission (the load) must be smooth and gradual; if it weren't, drive line components would wear out or break quickly. This gradual power transfer is

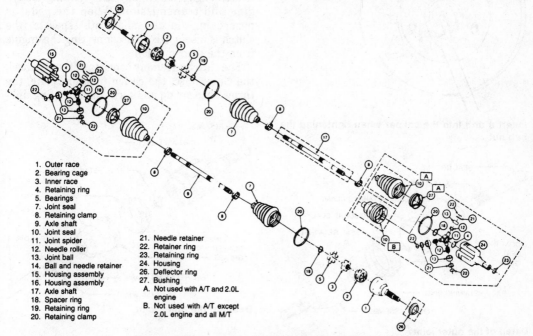

1. Outer race
2. Bearing cage
3. Inner race
4. Retaining ring
5. Bearings
7. Joint seal
8. Retaining clamp
9. Axle shaft
10. Joint seal
11. Joint spider
12. Needle roller
13. Joint ball
14. Ball and needle retainer
15. Housing assembly
16. Housing assembly
17. Axle shaft
18. Spacer ring
19. Retaining ring
20. Retaining clamp

21. Needle retainer
22. Retainer ring
23. Retaining ring
24. Housing
25. Deflector ring
27. Bushing
A. Not used with A/T and 2.0L engine
B. Not used with A/T except 2.0L engine and all M/T

Disassembled view of the Double Offset Design drive axle

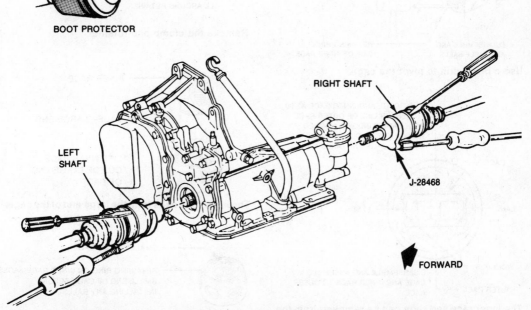

J-28712

BOOT PROTECTOR

RIGHT SHAFT

LEFT SHAFT

J-28468

FORWARD

Halfshaft removal; the special tools are attached to slide hammers in this diagram

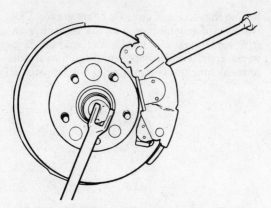

Insert a drift into the caliper when tightening the hub nut

made possible by gradually releasing the clutch pedal. The clutch disc and pressure plate are the connecting link between the engine and transmission. When the clutch pedal is released, the disc and plate contact each other (clutch engagement), physically joining the engine and transmission. When the pedal is pushed in, the disc and plate separate (the clutch is disengaged), disconnecting the engine from the transmission.

The clutch assembly consists of the flywheel, the clutch disc, the clutch pressure plate, the throwout bearing and fork, the actuating link-

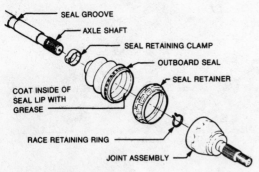

Detail of the outer joint

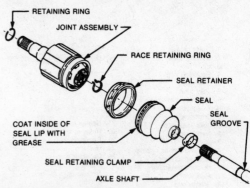

Detail of the inner joint

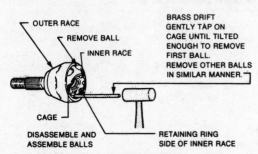

Use a brass drift to pivot the cage

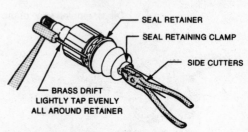

Remove the clamp and retainer

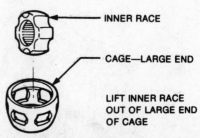

The inner race exits from the large end of the cage

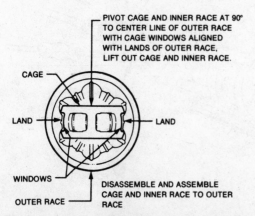

The inner race and cage can be removed from the outer race when pivoted 90°

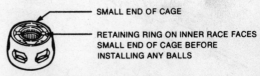

Inner race installed in the cage

age and the pedal. The flywheel and clutch pressure plate (driving members) are connected to the engine crankshaft and rotate with it. The clutch disc is located between the flywheel and pressure plate, and splined to the transmission shaft. A driving member is one that is attached to the engine and transfers engine power to a driven member (clutch disc) on the transmission shaft. A driving member (pressure plate) rotates (drives) a driven member (clutch disc) on contact and, in so doing, turns the transmission shaft. There is a circular diaphragm spring within the pressure plate cover (transmission side). In a relaxed state (when the clutch pedal is fully released), this spring is convex; that is, it is dished outward toward the transmission. Pushing in the clutch pedal actuates an attached linkage rod. Connected to the other end of this rod is the throwout bearing fork. The throwout bearing is attached to the fork. When the clutch pedal is depressed, the clutch linkage pushes the fork and bearing forward to contact the diaphragm spring of the pressure plate. The outer edges of the spring are secured to the pressure plate and are pivoted on rings so that when the center of the spring is compressed by the throwout bearing, the outer edges bow outward and, by so doing, pull the pressure plate in the same direction - away from the clutch disc. This action separates the disc from the plate, disengaging the clutch and allowing the transmission to be shifted into another gear. A coil type clutch return spring attached to the clutch pedal arm permits full release of the pedal. Releasing the pedal pulls the throwout bearing away from the diaphragm spring resulting in a reversal of spring position. As bearing pressure is gradually released from the spring center, the outer edges of the spring bow outward, pushing the pressure plate into closer contact with the clutch disc. As the disc and plate move closer together, friction between the two increases and slippage is reduced until, when full spring pressure is applied (by fully releasing the pedal), The speed of the disc and plate are the same. This stops all slipping, creating a direct connection between the plate and disc which results in the transfer of power from the engine to the transmission. The clutch disc is now rotating with the pressure plate at engine speed and, because it is splined to the transmission shaft, the shaft now turns at the same engine speed. Understanding clutch operation can be rather difficult at first; if you're still confused after reading this, consider the following analogy. The action of the diaphragm spring can be compared to that of an oil can bottom. The bottom of an oil can is shaped very much like the clutch diaphragm spring and pushing in on the can bottom and then releasing it produces a similar ef-

fect. As mentioned earlier, the clutch pedal return spring permits full release of the pedal and reduces linkage slack due to wear. As the linkage wears, clutch free-pedal travel will increase and free-travel will decrease as the clutch wears. Free-travel is actually throwout bearing lash.

The diaphragm spring type clutches used are available in two different designs: flat diaphragm springs or bent spring. The bent fingers are bent back to create a centrifugal boost ensuring quick re-engagement at higher engine speeds. This design enables pressure plate load to increase as the clutch disc wears and makes low pedal effort possible even with a heavy-duty clutch. The throwout bearing used with the bent finger design is 1¼" long and is shorter than the bearing used with the flat finger design. These bearings are not interchangeable. If the longer bearing is used with the bent finger clutch, free-pedal travel will not exist. This results in clutch slippage and rapid wear.

The transmission varies the gear ratio between the engine and drive wheels. It can be shifted to change engine speed as driving conditions and loads change. The transmission allows disengaging and reversing power from the engine to the wheels.

ADJUSTMENT

The J-cars have a self-adjusting clutch mechanism located on the clutch pedal, eliminating the need for periodic free play adjustments. The self-adjusting mechanism should be inspected periodically as follows:

1. Depress the clutch pedal and look for the pawl on the self-adjusting mechanism to firmly engage the teeth on the ratchet.
2. Release the clutch. The pawl should be lifted off of the teeth by the metal stop on the bracket.

Neutral Start Switch

1982-84

A neutral start switch is located on the clutch pedal assembly; the switch prevents the engine from starting unless the clutch is depressed. If the switch is faulty, it can be unbolted and replaced without removing the pedal assembly from the car. No adjustments for the switch are provided.

Neutral Start/Back-Up Light Switch Replacement

1985-88

1. Remove the console.
2. Disconnect the wiring, then replace the switch at the side of the shifter.

Driven Disc and Pressure Plate

REMOVAL AND INSTALLATION

1. Remove the transaxle.

2. Mark the pressure plate assembly and the flywheel so that they can be assembled in the same position. They were balanced as an assembly at the factory.

3. Loosen the attaching bolts one turn at a time until spring tension is relieved.

4. Support the pressure plate and remove the bolts. Remove the pressure plate and clutch disc. Do not disassemble the pressure plate assembly; replace it if defective.

5. Inspect the flywheel, clutch disc, pressure plate, throwout bearing and the clutch fork and

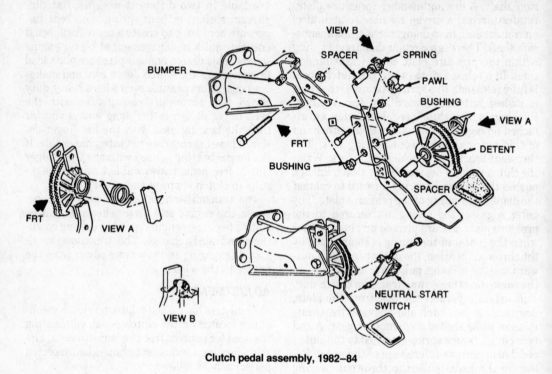

Clutch pedal assembly, 1982–84

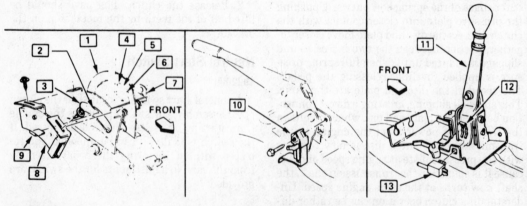

1. Detent plate
2. Tang hole
3. Tang slot
4. "Neutral" notch
5. R
6. P
7. Transmission control shifter
8. Neutral start and back-up lamp switch
9. Carrier tang
10. Park brake switch
11. Transmission shifter
12. Retaining clip
13. Back-up lamp switch

Console mounted switches, 1985–87

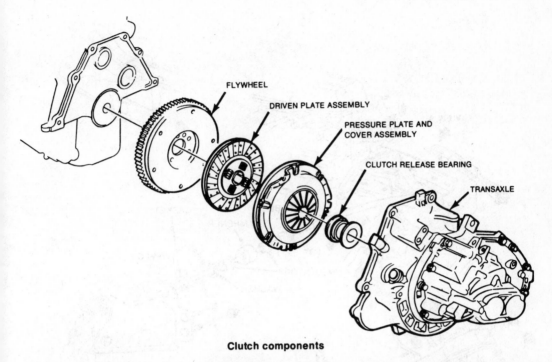

FLYWHEEL

DRIVEN PLATE ASSEMBLY

PRESSURE PLATE AND
COVER ASSEMBLY

CLUTCH RELEASE BEARING

TRANSAXLE

Clutch components

pivot shaft assembly for wear. Replace the parts as required. If the flywheel shows any signs of overheating, or if it is badly grooved or scored, it should be refaced or replaced.

6. Clean the pressure plate and flywheel mating surfaces thoroughly. Position the clutch disc and pressure plate into the installed position, and support with a dummy shaft or clutch aligning tool. The clutch plate is assembled with the damper springs offset toward the transaxle. One side of the factory supplied clutch disc is stamped "Flywheel Side".

7. Install the pressure plate-to-flywheel bolts. Tighten them gradually in a criss-cross pattern.

8. Lubricate the outside groove and the inside recess of the release bearing with high temperature grease. Wipe off any excess. Install the release bearing.

9. Install the transaxle.

Clutch Cable
REPLACEMENT
1982-84

1. Press the clutch pedal up against the bumper stop so as to release the pawl from the detent. Disconnect the clutch cable from the release lever at the transaxle assembly. Be careful that the cable does not snap back toward the rear of the car as this could damage the detent in the adjusting mechanism.

2. Remove the hush panel from inside the car.

3. Disconnect the clutch cable from the detent end tangs. Lift the locking pawl away from the detent and then pull the cable forward between the detent and the pawl.

4. Remove the windshield washer bottle.

5. From the engine side of the cowl, pull the clutch cable out to disengage it from the clutch pedal mounting bracket. The insulators, dampener and washers may separate from the cable in the process.

6. Disconnect the cable from the transaxle mounting bracket and remove it.

7. Install the cable into both insulators, damper and washer. Lubricate the rear insulator with tire mounting lube or the like to ease installation into the pedal mounting bracket.

8. From inside the car, attach the end of the cable to the detent. Be sure to route the cable underneath the pawl and into the detent cable groove.

9. Press the clutch pedal up against the bumper stop to release the pawl from the detent. Install the other end of the cable at the release lever and the transaxle mount bracket.

10. Install the hush panel and the windshield washer bottle.

11. Check the clutch operation and adjust as detailed earlier in this chapter.

Clutch Hydraulic System
REMOVAL AND INSTALLATION

NOTE: *The clutch hydraulic system is used on 1985 and later models and is serviced as a*

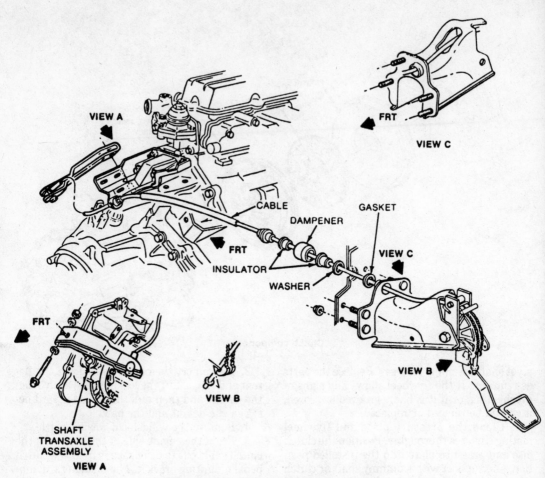

VIEW A

FRT

VIEW C

CABLE

GASKET

DAMPENER

FRT

VIEW C

INSULATOR

WASHER

VIEW B

FRT

VIEW B

SHAFT
TRANSAXLE
ASSEMBLY

VIEW A

Clutch cable and bracket assembly, 1982–84

complete unit. It has been bled of air and filled with fluid. Individual components of the system are not available separately.

2.0L Engine

1. Disconnect the negative battery cable.
2. Remove the hush panel from inside the vehicle.
3. Disconnect the clutch master cylinder push rod from the clutch pedal.
4. Remove the clutch master cylinder retaining nuts at the front of the dash.
5. Remove the slave cylinder retaining nuts at the transaxle.
6. Remove the hydraulic system as a unit from the vehicle.
7. Install the new slave cylinder to the transmission support bracket aligning the push rod into the pocket on the clutch fork outer lever. Tighten the retaining nuts evenly to prevent damage to the slave cylinder. Tighten to 14-20 ft. lbs.
NOTE: *Do not remove the plastic push rod*

retainer from the slave cylinder. The straps *will break on the first clutch pedal application.*
8. Position the clutch master cylinder to the front of the dash. Install the retaining nuts and tighten the nuts evenly to prevent damage to the master cylinder. Tighten to 15-25 ft. lbs.
9. Remove the pedal restrictor from the push rod. Lube the push rod bushing on the clutch pedal. Connect the push rod to the clutch pedal and install the retaining clip.
10. If equipped with cruise control, check the switch adjustment at the pedal bracket.
WARNING: *When adjusting the cruise control switch, do not exert an upward force on the clutch pedal pad of more than 20 lbs. or damage to the master cylinder push rod retaining ring can result.*
11. Install the hush panel.
12. Press the clutch pedal down several times. This will break the plastic retaining straps on the slave cylinder push rod. Do not remove the plastic button on the end of the push rod.
13. Connect the negative battery cable.

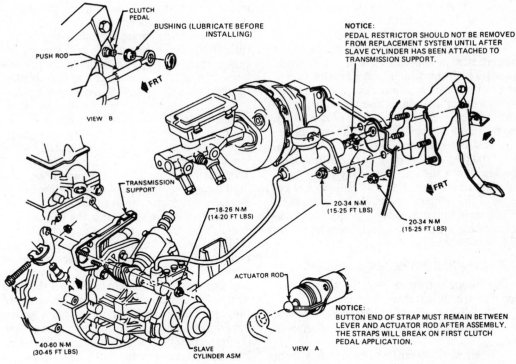

CLUTCH
PEDAL
BUSHING (LUBRICATE BEFORE
INSTALLING)

PUSH ROD

FRT

VIEW B

NOTICE:
PEDAL RESTRICTOR SHOULD NOT BE REMOVED
FROM REPLACEMENT SYSTEM UNTIL AFTER
SLAVE CYLINDER HAS BEEN ATTACHED TO
TRANSMISSION SUPPORT.

TRANSMISSION
SUPPORT

18-26 N·M
(14-20 FT LBS)

20-34 N·M
(15-25 FT LBS)

20-34 N·M
(15-25 FT LBS)

FRT

ACTUATOR ROD

40-60 N·M
(30-45 FT LBS)

SLAVE
CYLINDER ASM

VIEW A

NOTICE:
BUTTON END OF STRAP MUST REMAIN BETWEEN
LEVER AND ACTUATOR ROD AFTER ASSEMBLY.
THE STRAPS WILL BREAK ON FIRST CLUTCH
PEDAL APPLICATION.

Clutch hydraulic system, 1985–87

2.8L V6 Engine

1. Disconnect the negative battery cable.
2. Remove the air cleaner, mass air flow sensor and the air intake duct as an assembly.
3. Disconnect the electrical lead at the washer bottle. Remove the attaching bolts and washer bottle from the vehicle.
4. If equipped with cruise control, remove the mounting bracket retaining nuts from the strut tower.
5. Remove the hush panel from inside the vehicle.
6. Disconnect the clutch ms5ster cylinder push rod from the clutch pedal.
7. Remove the clutch master cylinder retaining nuts at the front of the dash.
8. Remove the slave cylinder retaining nuts at the transaxle.
9. Remove the hydraulic system as a unit from the vehicle.
10. Install the new slave cylinder to the transmission support bracket aligning the push rod into the pocket on the clutch fork outer lever. Tighten the retaining nuts evenly to prevent damage to the slave cylinder. Tighten to 14-20 ft. lbs.

NOTE: *Do not remove the plastic push rod retainer from the slave cylinder. The straps will break on the first clutch pedal application.*

11. Position the clutch master cylinder to the front of the dash. Install the retaining nuts and tighten the nuts evenly to prevent damage to the master cylinder. Tighten to 15-25 ft. lbs.
12. Remove the pedal restrictor from the push rod. Lube the push rod bushing on the clutch pedal. Connect the push rod to the clutch pedal and install the retaining clip.
13. If equipped with cruise control, check the switch adjustment at the pedal bracket.

WARNING: *When adjusting the cruise control switch, do not exert an upward force on the clutch pedal pad of more than 20 lbs. or damage to the master cylinder push rod retaining ring can result.*

14. Install the hush panel.
15. Press the clutch pedal down several times. This will break the plastic retaining straps on the slave cylinder push rod. Do not remove the plastic button on the end of the push rod.
16. Install the air cleaner, mass air flow sensor and the air intake duct as an assembly.
17. Connect the negative battery cable.

AUTOMATIC TRANSAXLE

Understanding Automatic Transmissions

The automatic transmission allows engine torque and power to be transmitted to the drive wheels within a narrow range of engine operating speeds. The transmission will allow the engine to turn fast enough to produce plenty of power and torque at very low speeds, while keeping it at a sensible rpm at high vehicle speeds. The transmission performs this job entirely without driver assistance. The transmission uses a light fluid as the medium for the transmission of power. This fluid also works in the operation of various hydraulic control circuits and as a lubricant. Because the transmission fluid performs all of these three functions, trouble within the unit can easily travel from one part to another. For this reason, and because of the complexity and unusual operating principles of the transmission, a very sound understanding of the basic principles of operation will simplify troubleshooting.

THE TORQUE CONVERTER

The torque converter replaces the conventional clutch. It has three functions:

1. It allows the engine to idle with the vehicle at a standstill, even with the transmission in gear.

2. It allows the transmission to shift from range to range smoothly, without requiring that the driver close the throttle during the shift.

3. It multiplies engine torque to an increasing extent as vehicle speed drops and throttle opening is increased. This has the effect of making the transmission more responsive and reduces the amount of shifting required.

The torque converter is a metal case which is shaped like a sphere that has been flattened on opposite sides. It is bolted to the rear end of the engine's crankshaft. Generally, the entire metal case rotates at engine speed and serves as the engine's flywheel.

The case contains three sets of blades. One set is attached directly to the case. This set forms the torus or pump. Another set is directly connected to the output shaft, and forms the turbine. The third set is mounted on a hub which, in turn, is mounted on a stationary shaft through a one-way clutch. This third set is known as the stator.

A pump, which is driven by the converter hub at engine speed, keeps the torque converter full of transmission fluid at all times. Fluid flows continuously through the unit to provide cooling.

Under low speed acceleration, the torque converter functions as follows:

The torus is turning faster than the turbine. It picks up fluid at the center of the converter and, through centrifugal force, slings it outward. Since the outer edge of the converter moves faster than the portions at the center, the fluid picks up speed.

The fluid then enters the outer edge of the turbine blades. It then travels back toward the center of the converter case along the turbine blades. In impinging upon the turbine blades, the fluid loses the energy picked up in the torus.

If the fluid were now to immediately be returned directly into the torus, both halves of the converter would have to turn at approximately the same speed at all times, and torque input and output would both be the same.

In flowing through the torus and turbine, the fluid picks up two types of flow, or flow in two separate directions. It flows through the turbine blades, and it spins with the engine. The stator, whose blades are stationary when the vehicle is being accelerated at low speeds, converts one type of flow into another. Instead of allowing the fluid to flow straight back into the torus, the stator's curved blades turn the fluid almost 90° toward the direction of rotation of the engine. Thus the fluid does not flow as fast toward the torus, but is already spinning when the torus picks it up. This has the effect of allowing the torus to turn much faster than the turbine. This difference in speed may be compared to the difference in speed between the smaller and larger gears in any gear train. The result is that engine power output is higher, and engine torque is multiplied.

As the speed of the turbine increases, the fluid spins faster and faster in the direction of engine rotation. As a result, the ability of the stator to redirect the fluid flow is reduced. Under cruising conditions, the stator is eventually forced to rotate on its one-way clutch in the direction of engine rotation. Under these conditions, the torque converter begins to behave almost like a solid shaft, with the torus and turbine speeds being almost equal.

THE PLANETARY GEARBOX

The ability of the torque converter to multiply engine torque is limited. Also, the unit tends to be more efficient when the turbine is rotating at relatively high speeds. Therefore, a planetary gearbox is used to carry the power output of the turbine to the halfshafts.

Planetary gears function very similarly to conventional transmission gears. However, their construction is different in that three elements make up one gear system, and, in that all three elements are different from one another. The three elements are: an outer gear that is shaped like a hoop, with teeth cut into the inner surface; a sun gear, mounted on a shaft and located at the very center of the outer gear; and a set of three planet gears, held by pins in a ring-

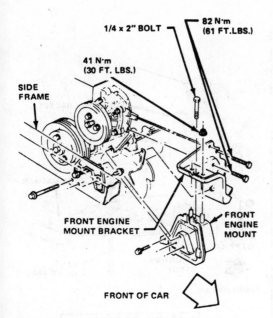

1/4 x 2" BOLT

82 N·m
(61 FT.LBS.)

41 N·m
(30 FT. LBS.)

SIDE
FRAME

FRONT ENGINE
MOUNT BRACKET

FRONT
ENGINE
MOUNT

FRONT OF CAR

Securing the front engine mount

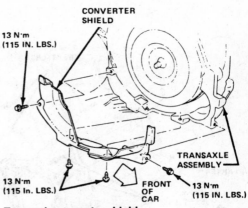

CONVERTER
SHIELD

13 N·m
(115 IN. LBS.)

TRANSAXLE
ASSEMBLY

13 N·m
(115 In. LBS.)

FRONT
OF
CAR

13 N·m
(115 IN. LBS.)

Transaxle converter shield

like planet carrier, meshing with both the sun gear and the outer gear. Either the outer gear or the sun gear may be held stationary, providing more than one possible torque multiplication factor for each set of gears. Also, if all three gears are forced to rotate at the same speed, the gearset forms, in effect, a solid shaft.

Most modern automatics use the planetary

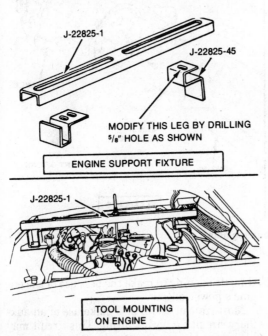

J-22825-1

J-22825-45

MODIFY THIS LEG BY DRILLING
5/8" HOLE AS SHOWN

ENGINE SUPPORT FIXTURE

J-22825-1

TOOL MOUNTING
ON ENGINE

You must hold the engine with the engine support bar

gears to provide either a single reduction ratio of about 1.8:1, or two reduction gears: a low of about 2.5:1, and an intermediate of about 1.5:1. Bands and clutches are used to hold various portions of the gearsets to the transmission case or to the shaft on which they are mounted. Shifting is accomplished, then, by changing the portion of each planetary gearset which is held to the transmission case or to the shaft.

THE SERVOS AND ACCUMULATORS

The servos are hydraulic pistons and cylinders. They resemble the hydraulic actuators used on many familiar machines, such as bulldozers. Hydraulic fluid enters the cylinder, under pressure, and forces the piston to move to engage the band or clutches.

The accumulators are used to cushion the engagement of the servos. The transmission fluid must pass through the accumulator on the way to the servo. The accumulator housing contains a thin piston which is sprung away from the discharge passage of the accumulator. When fluid passes through the accumulator on the way to the servo, it must move the piston against spring pressure, and this action smooths out the action of the servo.

THE HYDRAULIC CONTROL SYSTEM

The hydraulic pressure used to operate the servos comes from the main transmission oil pump. This fluid is channeled to the various servos through the shift valves. There is generally a manual shift valve which is operated by the transmission selector lever and an automatic shift valve for each automatic upshift the transmission provides: i.e., 2-speed automatics have a low/high shift valve, while 3-speeds have a 1-2 valve, and a 2-3 valve.

There are two pressures which effect the operation of these valves. One is the governor pressure which is affected by vehicle speed. The

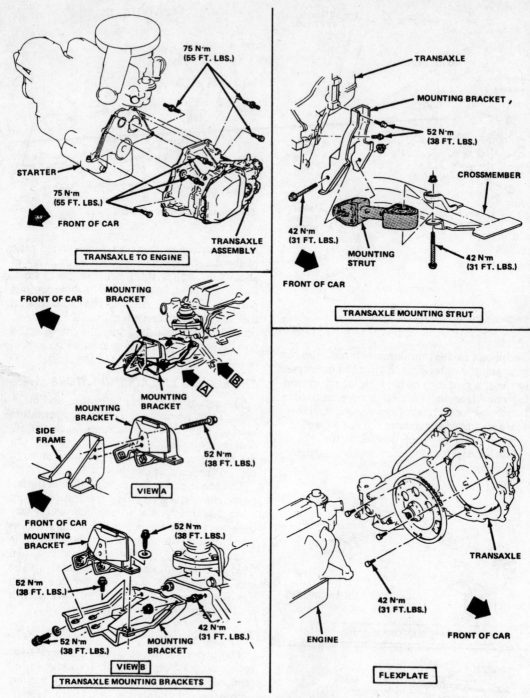

75 N·m (55 FT. LBS.)

STARTER

75 N·m (55 FT. LBS.)

FRONT OF CAR

TRANSAXLE ASSEMBLY

TRANSAXLE TO ENGINE

TRANSAXLE

MOUNTING BRACKET

52 N·m (38 FT. LBS.)

CROSSMEMBER

42 N·m (31 FT. LBS.)

MOUNTING STRUT

42 N·m (31 FT. LBS.)

FRONT OF CAR

TRANSAXLE MOUNTING STRUT

FRONT OF CAR

MOUNTING BRACKET

MOUNTING BRACKET

MOUNTING BRACKET

SIDE FRAME

52 N·m (38 FT. LBS.)

VIEW A

FRONT OF CAR

MOUNTING BRACKET

52 N·m (38 FT. LBS.)

52 N·m (38 FT. LBS.)

52 N·m (38 FT. LBS.)

MOUNTING BRACKET

42 N·m (31 FT. LBS.)

VIEW B

TRANSAXLE MOUNTING BRACKETS

TRANSAXLE

42 N·m (31 FT.LBS.)

ENGINE

FRONT OF CAR

FLEXPLATE

Transaxle mounting points

other is the modulator pressure which is affected by intake manifold vacuum or throttle position. Governor pressure rises with an increase in vehicle speed, and modulator pressure rises as the throttle is opened wider. By responding to these two pressures, the shift valves cause the upshift points to be delayed with increased

throttle opening to make the best use of the engine's power output.

Most transmissions also make use of an auxiliary circuit for downshifting. This circuit may be actuated by the throttle linkage or the vacuum line which actuates the modulator, or by a cable or solenoid. It applies pressure to a special downshift surface on the shift valve or valves.

The transmission modulator also governs the line pressure, used to actuate the servos. In this way, the clutches and bands will be actuated with a force matching the torque output of the engine.

Identification

All of the J-cars use the Turbo Hydra-Matic 125C automatic transaxle as optional equipment. This is a fully automatic unit of conventional design, incorporating a four element hydraulic torque converter, a compound planetary gear set, and a dual sprocket and drive link assembly. The sprockets and drive link (Hy-Vo chain) connect the torque converter assembly to the transmission gears. The transaxle also incorporates the differential assembly, which is of conventional design. Power is transmitted from the transmission to the final drive and differential assembly through helical cut gears.

No overhaul procedures are given in this book because of the complexity of the transaxle. Transaxle removal and installation, adjustment, and halfshaft removal, installation, and overhaul procedures are covered.

Adjustments

The neutral start switch and throttle valve are self-adjusting. The transaxle has only one band, with no provision for periodic adjustment. Pan removal, fluid and filter changes are covered in Chapter 1.

Transmission

REMOVAL AND INSTALLATION

1. Disconnect the negative battery cable where it attaches to the transaxle.
2. On the 1982-84 models, insert a ¼ x 2" bolt into the hole in the right front motor mount to prevent any mislocation during the transaxle removal.
3. On 4-cylinder engines, remove the air cleaner.
4. On V6 engines remove the following:
   a. Remove the air intake duct from the air cleaner.
   b. Remove the left fender brace.
   c. Disconnect the M.A.T. sensor lead at the air cleaner.
   d. Disconnect the mass air flow sensor lead.
   e. Remove the PCV pipe retaining clamp from the air intake duct.
   f. Remove the clamp retaining the air intake duct to the throttle body.
   g. Remove the Mass Air Flow Sensor mounting bolt. Remove the air cleaner bracket mounting bolts at the battery tray.
   h. Remove the air cleaner, mass air flow sensor and air intake duct as an assembly.
   i. Remove the heat shield at the crossover pipe and remove the crossover pipe.
5. Disconnect the T.V. cable at the throttle body.
6. Unscrew the bolt securing the T.V. cable to the transaxle. Pull up on the cable cover at the transaxle until the cable can be seen. Disconnect the cable from the transaxle rod.
7. Remove the wiring harness retaining bolt at the top of the transaxle.
8. Remove the hose from the air management valve and then pull the wiring harness up and out of the way.
9. Install an engine support bar as shown in the illustration. Raise the engine just enough to take the pressure off the motor mounts.
   CAUTION: *The engine support bar must be located in the center of the cowl and the bolts must be tightened before attempting to support the engine.*
10. Remove the transaxle mount and bracket assembly. It may be necessary to raise the engine slightly to aid in removal.
11. Disconnect the shift control linkage from the transaxle.
12. Remove the top transaxle-to-engine mounting bolts. Loosen, but do not remove, the transaxle-to-engine bolt nearest to the starter.
13. Unlock the steering column. Raise and support the front of the car. Remove the front wheels.
14. Pull out the cotter pin and loosen the castellated ball joint nut until the ball joint separates from the control arm. Repeat on the other side of the car.
15. Disconnect the stabilizer bar from the left lower control arm.
16. Remove the six bolts that secure the left front suspension support assembly.
17. Install drive axle seal protectors and connect an axle shaft removal tool (J-28468) to a slide hammer (J-23907).
18. Position the tool behind the axle shaft cones and then pull the cones out and away from the transaxle. Remove the axle shafts and plug the transaxle bores to reduce fluid leakage.
19. Remove the nut that secures the transaxle control cable bracket to the transaxle, then remove the engine-to-transaxle stud.
20. Disconnect the speedometer cable at the transaxle.
21. Disconnect the transaxle strut (stabilizer) at the transaxle.
22. Remove the four retaining screws and remove the torque converter shield.
23. Scribe a mark for on the flywheel for reas-

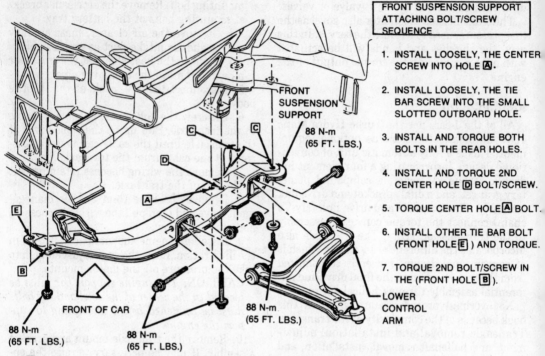

FRONT SUSPENSION SUPPORT
ATTACHING BOLT/SCREW
SEQUENCE

1. INSTALL LOOSELY, THE CENTER SCREW INTO HOLE Ⓐ.

2. INSTALL LOOSELY, THE TIE BAR SCREW INTO THE SMALL SLOTTED OUTBOARD HOLE.

3. INSTALL AND TORQUE BOTH BOLTS IN THE REAR HOLES.

4. INSTALL AND TORQUE 2ND CENTER HOLE Ⓓ BOLT/SCREW.

5. TORQUE CENTER HOLE Ⓐ BOLT.

6. INSTALL OTHER TIE BAR BOLT (FRONT HOLE Ⓔ) AND TORQUE.

7. TORQUE 2ND BOLT/SCREW IN THE (FRONT HOLE Ⓑ).

The front suspension support must be attached in this sequence

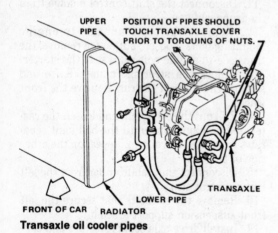

Transaxle oil cooler pipes

sembly and remove the three bolts securing the torque converter to the flex plate.

24. Disconnect and plug the oil cooler lines at the transaxle. Remove the starter.

25. Remove the screws that hold the brake and fuel line brackets to the left side of the underbody. This will allow the lines to be moved slightly for clearance during transaxle removal.

26. Remove the bolt that was loosened in Step 12.

27. Remove the transaxle to the left.

28. To install, position the transaxle in the car.

29. Place a small amount of light grease on the torque converter pilot hub.

30. Make sure to properly seat the torque convertor in the oil pump.

31. Guide the right drive axle shaft into its bore as the transaxle is being raised. The right transaxle cannot be installed AFTER the transaxle is connected to the engine.

32. Lower the transaxle to the engine bolts and remove the transaxle jack.

33. Install the transaxle to engine support bracket.

34. Install the transaxle cooler lines.

35. Position the LH axle into the transaxle.

36. Install the torque converter to flywheel bolts torque to 46 ft. lbs. Retorque the first bolt afetr all three have been tightened.

37. Install the transaxle converter shield.

38. When installing the front suspension support assembly you must follow the tightening sequence shown in the illustration at the end of Chapter 7.

39. The remainder of the installation is the reverse of removal with the following precautions.

 a. Check the suspension alignment.

 b. Check the transaxle fluid level.

Halfshaft

REMOVAL, INSTALLATION AND OVERHAUL

The procedures for the automatic transaxle half-shafts are the same as those outlined earlier for the manual transaxle.

Suspension and Steering

8

FRONT SUSPENSION

The J-cars use MacPherson strut front suspension designs. A MacPherson strut combines the functions of a shock absorber and an upper suspension member (upper arm) into one unit. The strut is surrounded by a coil spring, which provides normal front suspension functions.

The strut bolts to the body shell at its upper end, and to the steering knuckle at the lower end. The strut pivots with the steering knuckle by means of a sealed mounting assembly at the upper end which contains a preloaded, non-adjustable bearing.

The steering knuckle is connected to the chassis at the lower end by a conventional lower control arm, and pivots in the arm in a preloaded ball joint of standard design. The knuckle is fastened to the ball joint stud by means of a castellated nut and cotter pin.

Advantages of the MacPherson strut design, aside from its relative simplicity, include reduced weight and friction, minimal intrusion into the engine and passenger compartments, and ease of service.

Springs and Shock Absorbers
TESTING

The function of the shock absorber is to dampen harsh spring movement and provide a means of dissipating the motion of the wheels so that the shocks encountered by the wheels are not totally transmitted to the body and, therefore, to you and your passengers. As the wheel moves up and down, the shock absorber shortens and lengthens, thereby imposing a restraint on movement by its hydraulic action.

A good way to see if your shock absorbers are functioning correctly is to push one corner of the car until it is moving up and down for almost the full suspension travel, then release it and watch its recovery. If the car bounces slightly about one more time and then comes to a rest, the shock is alright. If the car continues to bounce excessively, the shocks will probably require replacement.

MacPherson Struts
REMOVAL AND INSTALLATION

The struts retain the springs under tremendous pressure even when removed from the car. For these reasons, several expensive special tools and substantial specialized knowledge are required to safely and effectively work on these parts. We recommend that if spring or shock absorber repair work is required, you remove the strut or struts involved and take them to a repair facility which is fully equipped and familiar with the car.

1. Working under the hood, pry off the shock cover and then unscrew the upper strut-to-body nuts.

2. Loosen the wheel nuts, raise and support the car and then remove the wheel and tire.

3. Install a drive axle protective cover (J28712).

4. Use a two-armed puller and press the tie rod out of the strut bracket.

5. Remove both strut-to-steering knuckle bolts and carefully lift out the strut.

6. Installation is in the reverse order of removal. Torque the upper strut to body nuts to 20 ft.lbs. Be sure that the flat sides of the strut-to-knuckle bolt heads are horizontal (see illustration) and torque to 133 ft. lbs.

STRUT MODIFICATION

This modification is made only if a camber adjustment is anticipated.

1. Place the strut in a vise. This step is not absolutely necessary; filing can be accom-

Troubleshooting Basic Steering and Suspension Problems

Problem	Cause	Solution
Hard steering (steering wheel is hard to turn)	• Low or uneven tire pressure • Loose power steering pump drive belt • Low or incorrect power steering fluid • Incorrect front end alignment • Defective power steering pump • Bent or poorly lubricated front end parts	• Inflate tires to correct pressure • Adjust belt • Add fluid as necessary • Have front end alignment checked/adjusted • Check pump • Lubricate and/or replace defective parts
Loose steering (too much play in the steering wheel)	• Loose wheel bearings • Loose or worn steering linkage • Faulty shocks • Worn ball joints	• Adjust wheel bearings • Replace worn parts • Replace shocks • Replace ball joints
Car veers or wanders (car pulls to one side with hands off the steering wheel)	• Incorrect tire pressure • Improper front end alignment • Loose wheel bearings • Loose or bent front end components • Faulty shocks	• Inflate tires to correct pressure • Have front end alignment checked/adjusted • Adjust wheel bearings • Replace worn components • Replace shocks
Wheel oscillation or vibration transmitted through steering wheel	• Improper tire pressures • Tires out of balance • Loose wheel bearings • Improper front end alignment • Worn or bent front end components	• Inflate tires to correct pressure • Have tires balanced • Adjust wheel bearings • Have front end alignment checked/adjusted • Replace worn parts
Uneven tire wear	• Incorrect tire pressure • Front end out of alignment • Tires out of balance	• Inflate tires to correct pressure • Have front end alignment checked/adjusted • Have tires balanced

plished by disconnecting the strut from the steering knuckle.

2. File the holes in the outer flanges so as to enlarge the bottom holes until they match the slots already in the inner flanges.

3. Camber adjustment procedures are detailed later in this chapter.

Coil Springs

REMOVAL AND INSTALLATION

CAUTION: *The coil springs are retained under considerable pressure. They can exert enough force to cause serious injury. Exercise extreme caution when disassembling the strut for coil spring removal.*

This procedure requires the use of a spring compressor and several other special tools. It cannot be performed without them. If you do not have access to these tools, DO NOT attempt to disassemble the strut.

1. Remove the strut assembly.

2. Clamp the spring compressor (J26584) in a vise. Position the strut assembly in the bottom adapter of the compresser and install the special tool J26584-86 (see illustration). Be sure that the adapter captures the strut and that the locating pins are engaged.

3. Rotate the strut assembly so that the top mounting assembly lip aligns with the compressor support notch. Insert two top adapters (J26584-88) between the top mounting assembly and the top spring seat. Position the adapters so that the split lines are in the 3 o'clock and 9 o'clock positions.

4. Using a 1″ socket, turn the screw on top of the compressor clockwise until the top support flange contacts the adapters. Continue turning the screw until the coil spring is compressed approximately ½″ (4 complete turns). Never bottom the spring or the strut damper rod.

5. Unscrew the nut from the strut damper shaft and then lift off the top mounting assembly.

6. Turn the compressor adjusting screw counterclockwise until the spring tension has been relieved. Remove the adapters and then remove the coil spring.

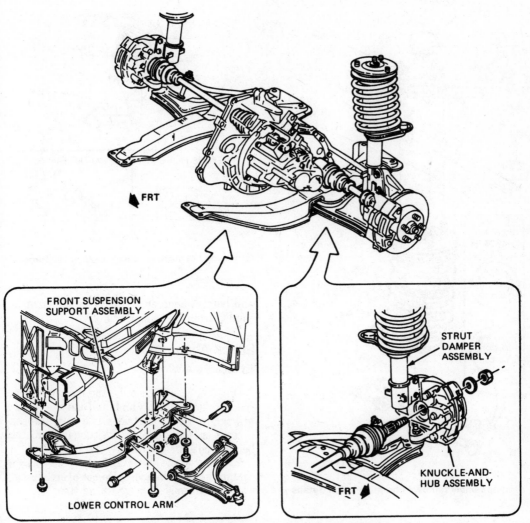

The J-cars use MacPherson strut front suspension

7. To install, clamp the strut compressor body J 26584 in a vise.

8. Position the strut assembly in the bottom adapter of the compresser and install the special tool J26584-86 (see illustration). Be sure that the adapter captures the strut and that the locating pins are engaged.

9. Position the spring on the strut. Make sure the spring is properly seated on the bottom of the spring plate.

10. Install the spring strut seat assembly on top of the spring.

11. Place BOTH J 26584-88 top adapters over the spring seat assemblies.

12. Turn the compressor forcing the screw until the compressor top support just contacts the top adapters (do not compress the spring at this time).

13. Install long extension with a socket to fit the hex on the damper shaft through the top of the spring seat. Use the extension to guide the components during reassembly.

WARNING: *NEVER place a hard tool such as pliers or screwdriver against the polished surface of the damper shaft. The shaft can be held up with your fingers or an extension in order to prevent it from receding into the strut assembly while the spring is being compressed.*

14. Compress the screw by turning the screw clockwise until approximately 1½" of damper shaft extends through the top spring plate.

WARNING: *Do not compress the spring until it bottoms.*

15. Remove the extension and socket, position the top mounting assembly over the damper shaft and install the nut. Tighten to 68 ft. lbs.

16. Turn the forcing screw counterclockwise to back off support, remove the top adapters

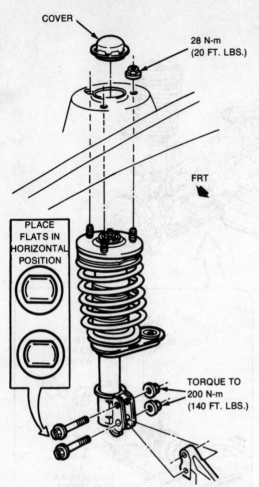

COVER

28 N·m (20 FT. LBS.)

FRT

PLACE FLATS IN HORIZONTAL POSITION

TORQUE TO 200 N·m (140 FT. LBS.)

Strut assembly removal and installation details

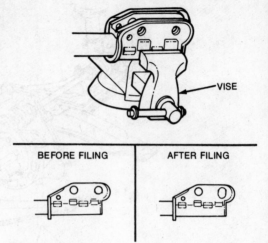

VISE

BEFORE FILING	AFTER FILING

Modifying the strut mounting holes for camber adjustment

and bottom adapter and remove the strut assembly from the compressor.

Shock Absorbers

REMOVAL AND INSTALLATION

On 1982-83 models only, the internal piston rod, cylinder assembly and fluid can be replaced utilizing a service cartridge and nut. Internal threads are located inside the tube immediately below a cut line groove.

1. Remove the strut and the coil springs. Clamp the strut in a vise. Do not overtighten it as this will cause damage to the strut tube.

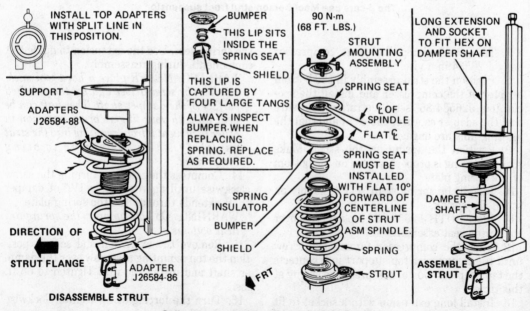

INSTALL TOP ADAPTERS WITH SPLIT LINE IN THIS POSITION.

SUPPORT

ADAPTERS J26584-88

DIRECTION OF STRUT FLANGE

ADAPTER J26584-86

DISASSEMBLE STRUT

BUMPER

THIS LIP SITS INSIDE THE SPRING SEAT

SHIELD

THIS LIP IS CAPTURED BY FOUR LARGE TANGS

ALWAYS INSPECT BUMPER WHEN REPLACING SPRING. REPLACE AS REQUIRED.

SPRING INSULATOR

BUMPER

SHIELD

FRT

90 N·m (68 FT. LBS.)

STRUT MOUNTING ASSEMBLY

SPRING SEAT

$\mathcal{C}$ OF SPINDLE

FLAT $\mathcal{C}$

SPRING SEAT MUST BE INSTALLED WITH FLAT 10° FORWARD OF CENTERLINE OF STRUT ASM SPINDLE.

SPRING

STRUT

LONG EXTENSION AND SOCKET TO FIT HEX ON DAMPER SHAFT

DAMPER SHAFT

ASSEMBLE STRUT

Coil spring removal and installation details

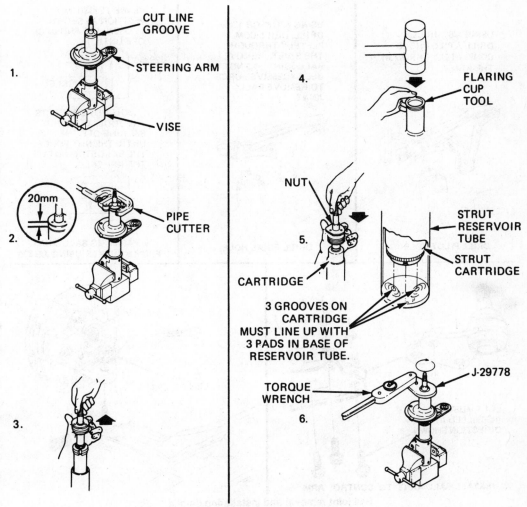

Replacing the strut cartridge

2. Locate the cut line groove just below the top edge of the strut tube. It is imperative that the groove be accurately located as any mislocation will cause inner thread damage. Using pipe cutters, cut around the groove until the tube is completely cut through.

3. Remove and discard the end cap, the cylinder and the piston rod assembly. Remove the strut assembly from the vise and pour out the old fluid.

4. Reclamp the strut in the vise. A flaring cup tool is included in the replacement cartridge kit to flare and deburr the edge that was cut on the strut tube. Place the flaring cup on the open edge of the tube and strike it with a mallet until its flat outer surface rests on the top edge of the tube. Remove the cup and discard it.

5. Try the new nut to make sure that it threads properly. If not, use the flaring cup again until it does.

6. Place the new strut cartridge into the tube. Turn the cartridge until it settles into the indentations at the base of the tube. Place the nut over the cartridge.

7. Tighten the nut to 140-170 ft. lbs. (190-230 Nm). Pull the piston rod up and down to check for proper operation.

8. Installation of the remaining components is in the reverse order of removal.

Ball Joints
INSPECTION

1. Raise and support the front of the car and let the suspension hang free.

2. Grasp the wheel at the top and the bottom and shake it in an in-and-out motion. Check for any horizontal movement of the steering knuckle relative to the lower control arm. Replace the ball joint if such movement is noted.

3. If the ball stud is disconnected from the

USING 1/8" DRILL, DRILL A PILOT HOLE COMPLETELY THROUGH THE RIVET.

DRILL PILOT HOLE

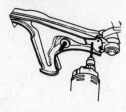

USING A 1/2" OR 13mm DRILL, DRILL COMPLETELY THROUGH THE RIVET. REMOVE BALL JOINT. DO NOT USE EXCESSIVE FORCE TO REMOVE BALL JOINT.

DRILL FINAL HOLE

PLACE J 29330 INTO POSITION AS SHOWN. LOOSEN NUT AND BACK OFF UNTIL . . .

J29330   KNUCKLE

. . . THE NUT CONTACTS THE TOOL. CONTINUE BACKING OFF THE NUT UNTIL THE NUT FORCES THE BALL STUD OUT OF THE KNUCKLE.

SEPARATING BALL JOINT FROM KNUCKLE USING J29330

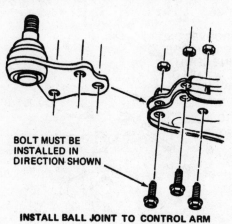

BOLT MUST BE INSTALLED IN DIRECTION SHOWN

INSTALL BALL JOINT TO CONTROL ARM

75 N·m (55 FT. LBS.)

FRT

Ball joint removal and installation details

steering knuckle and any looseness is detected, or if the ball stud can be twisted in its socket using finger pressure, replace the ball joint.

REMOVAL AND INSTALLATION

Only one ball joint is used in each lower arm. The MacPherson strut design does not use an upper ball joint.

1. Loosen the wheel nuts, raise the car, and remove the wheel.
2. Use a 1/8" drill bit to drill a hole through the center of each of the three ball joint rivets.
3. Use a 1/2" drill bit to drill completely through the rivet.
4. Use a hammer and punch to remove the rivets. Drive them out from the bottom.
5. Use the special tool J29330 or a ball joint removal tool to separate the ball joint from the steering knuckle (see illustration). Don't forget to remove the cotter pin.
6. Disconnect the stabilizer bar from the lower control arm. Remove the ball joint.

7. Install the new ball joint into the control arm with the three bolts supplied as shown and torque to 50 ft. lbs. Installation of the remaining components is in the reverse order of removal. Tighten the castellated nut on the ball joint to 55 ft. lbs. and use a new cotter pin. Check the toe setting and adjust as necessary.

Stabilizer Bar

REMOVAL AND INSTALLATION

1. Safely raise the car and allow the front lower control arms to hang free.
2. Remove the left front wheel and tire.
3. Disconnect the stabilizer shaft from the control arms.
4. Disconnect the stabilizer shaft from the support assemblies.
5. Loosen the front bolts and remove the bolts from the rear and center of the support assemblies.

6. When installing the stabilizer, loosely assemble all components while insuring that the stabilizer is centered, side to side.

Control Arm
REMOVAL AND INSTALLATION

1. Raise and support the front of the car. Remove the wheel.

2. Disconnect the stabilizer bar from the control arm and/or support.

3. Separate the ball joint from the steering knuckle as previously detailed.

4. Remove the two control arm-to-support bolts and remove the control arm.

5. If control arm support bar removal is necessary, unscrew the six mounting bolts and remove the support.

6. Installation is in the reverse order of removal. Tighten the control arm support rail bolts in the sequence shown. Check the toe and adjust as necessary.

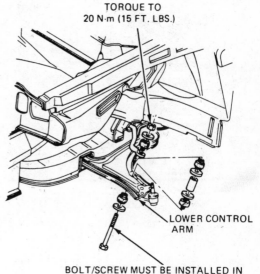

TORQUE TO
20 N·m (15 FT. LBS.)

LOWER CONTROL ARM

BOLT/SCREW MUST BE INSTALLED IN DIRECTION SHOWN.
OBTAIN TORQUE BY RUNNING NUT TO UNTHREADED PORTION OF BOLT/SCREW.

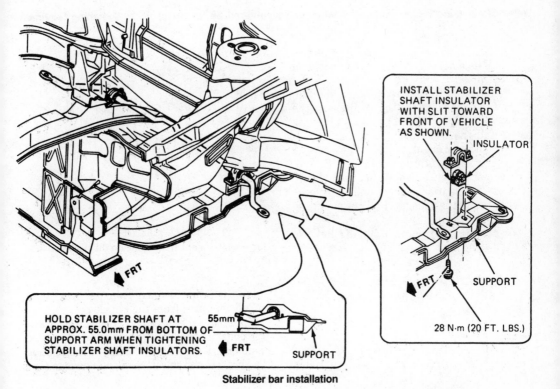

INSTALL STABILIZER SHAFT INSULATOR WITH SLIT TOWARD FRONT OF VEHICLE AS SHOWN.

INSULATOR

FRT

SUPPORT

28 N·m (20 FT. LBS.)

HOLD STABILIZER SHAFT AT APPROX. 55.0mm FROM BOTTOM OF SUPPORT ARM WHEN TIGHTENING STABILIZER SHAFT INSULATORS.

55mm

FRT

SUPPORT

Stabilizer bar installation

Wheel Bearings

The front wheel bearings are sealed, non-adjustable units which require no periodic attention. They are bolted to the steering knuckle by means of an integral flange.

Front Hub, Knuckle And Bearing
REMOVAL AND INSTSALLATION

WARNING: *You will need a special tool to pull the bearing free of the halfshaft (drive axle), G.M. tool no. J-28733 or the equivalent.*

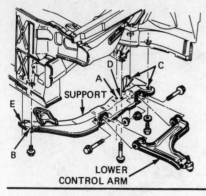

FRONT SUSP SUPPORT ASM ATTACHING BOLT/SCREW SEQUENCE

1. LOOSELY INSTALL CENTER BOLT INTO HOLE (A).
2. LOOSELY INSTALL TIE BAR BOLT INTO OUTBOARD HOLE (B).
3. INSTALL BOTH REAR BOLTS INTO HOLES (C) TORQUE REAR BOLTS.
4. INSTALL BOLT INTO CENTER HOLE(D), THEN TORQUE.
5. TORQUE BOLT IN HOLE (A).
6. INSTALL BOLT INTO FRONT HOLE (E), THEN TORQUE.
7. TORQUE BOLT IN HOLE (B).

SUPPORT-TO-BODY BOLTS . . . . .90 N·m (63 FT. LBS.)
LCA PIVOT BOLTS . . . . .95 N·m (67 FT. LBS.)

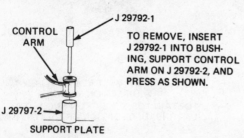

TO REMOVE, INSERT J 29792-1 INTO BUSHING, SUPPORT CONTROL ARM ON J 29792-2, AND PRESS AS SHOWN.

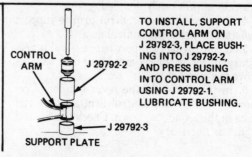

TO INSTALL, SUPPORT CONTROL ARM ON J 29792-3, PLACE BUSHING INTO J 29792-2, AND PRESS BUSING INTO CONTROL ARM USING J 29792-1. LUBRICATE BUSHING.

When installing the front suspension (control arm) support rail, be sure to follow the tightening sequence

You should also use a halfshaft boot protector, G.M. tool no. J-28712 or the equivalent to protect the parts from damage.

1. Remove the wheel cover, loosen the hub nut, and raise and support the car. Remove the front wheel.
2. Install the boot cover, G.M. part no. J-28712 or the equivalent.
3. Remove and discard the hub nut. Be sure to use a new one on assembly, not the old one.
4. Remove the brake caliper and rotor:

   a. Remove the allen head caliper mounting bolts.

   b. Remove the caliper from the knuckle and suspend from a length of wire. Do not al-

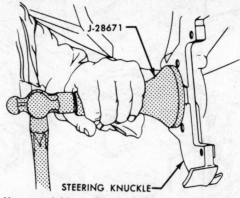

Use a seal driver when installing the new seal into the knuckle

low the caliper to hang from the brake hose. Pull the rotor from the knuckle.

5. Remove the three hub and bearing attaching bolts. If the old bearing is to be reused, match mark the bolts and holes for installation. The brake rotor splash shield will have to come off, too.
6. Attach a puller, G.M. part no. J-28733 or the equivalent, and remove the bearing. If corrosion is present, make sure the bearing is loose in the knuckle before using the puller.
7. Clean the mating surfaces of all dirt and corrosion. Check the knuckle bore and knuckle seal for damage. If a new bearing is to be installed, remove the old knuckle seal and install a new one. Grease the lips of the new seal before

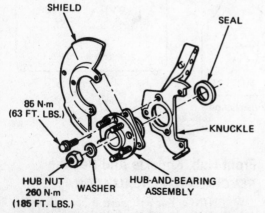

Exploded view of the hub and bearing attachment to the steering knuckle

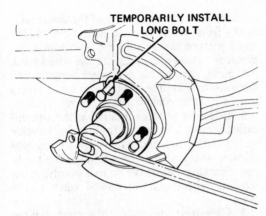

TEMPORARILY INSTALL LONG BOLT

Insert a bolt into the rotor when installing the hub nut

installation; install with a seal driver made for the purpose, G.M. tool no. J-28671 or the equivalent.

8. Push the bearing onto the halfshaft. Install a new washer and hub nut.

9. Tighten the new hub nut on the halfshaft until the bearing is seated. If the rotor and hub start to rotate as the hub nut is tightened, insert a long bolt through the cut-out in the hub assembly to prevent rotation. Do not apply full torque to the hub nut at this time. Just seat the bearing.

10. Install the brake shield and the bearing retaining bolts. Tighten the bolts evenly to 63 ft. lbs. (85 Nm).

11. Install the caliper and rotor. Be sure that the caliper hose isn't twisted. Install the caliper bolts and tighten to 21-35 ft. lbs. (28-47 Nm.).

12. Install the wheel. Lower the car. Tighten the hub nut to 185 ft. lbs. (260 Nm.).

Front End Alignment

The toe setting is the only adjustment normally required on a J-car. However, in special circumstances, such as damage due to road hazard, collision, etc., camber may be adjusted after modifying the strut as detailed earlier in this chapter. Caster is not adjustable.

CAMBER

Camber is the inward or outward tilt from the vertical, measured in degrees, of the front wheels at the top. An onward tilt gives the wheel positive camber; an inward tilt is called negative camber. Proper camber is critical to assure even tire wear.

1. Modify the suspension strut as detailed earlier.

2. Loosen the strut-to-knuckle bolts just enough to allow movement between the strut and the knuckle.

3. Grasp the top of the tire and move it in or out until the proper specification is obtained.

4. Tighten both bolts just enough to hold the adjustment. Remove the wheels and tighten the bolts to the proper specifications.

5. Replace the wheels.

TOE

Toe is the amount, measured in a fraction of a millimeter, that the wheels are closer together at one end than the other. Toe-in means that the front wheels are closer together at the front

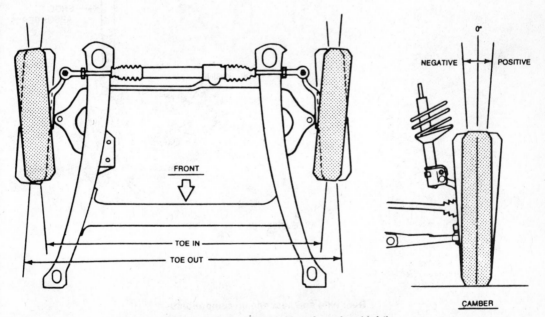

Wheel alignment: toe (left) and camber (right)

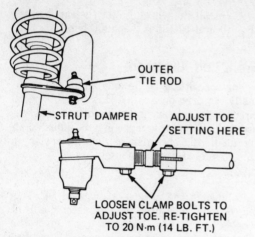

Toe adjustment is made at the tie rods

distance between the centers of the tire treads, at the front of the tire and at the rear. If the tread pattern makes this impossible, you can measure between the edges of the wheel rims, but make sure to move the car forward and measure in a couple of places to avoid errors caused by bent rims or wheel runout.

2. If the measurement is not within specifications, loosen the nuts at the steering knuckle end of the tie rod, and remove the tie rod boot clamps. Rotate the tie rods to align the toe to specifications. Rotate the tie rods evenly, or the steering wheel will be crooked when you're done.

3. When the adjustment is correct, tighten the nuts to 14 ft. lbs. (20 Nm.). Adjust the boots and tighten the clamps.

than the rear; toe-out means the rear of the front wheels are closer together than the front. J-cars are designed to have a slight amount of toe-out.

Toe is adjusted by turning the tie rods. It must be checked after camber has been adjusted, but it can be adjusted without disturbing the camber setting. You can make this adjustment without special equipment if you make very careful measurements. The wheels must be straight ahead.

1. Toe can be determined by measuring the

REAR SUSPENSION

J-cars have a semi-independent rear suspension system which consists of an axle with trailing arms and a twisting cross beam, two coil springs and two shock absorbers. The axle assembly attaches to the body through a rubber bushing located at the front of each control arm. A stabilizer bar is available as an option.

Two coil springs are used, each being retained between a seat in the underbody and one

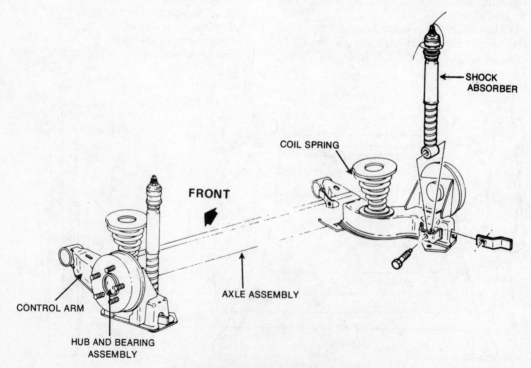

Rear axle and suspension components

on the control arm. A rubber cushion is used to isolate the coil spring upper end from the underbody seat, while the lower end sits on a combination bumper and spring insulator.

The double acting shock absorbers are filled with a calibrated amount of fluid and sealed during production. They are non-adjustable, non-refillable and cannot be disassembled.

A single unit hub and bearing assembly is bolted to both ends of the rear axle assembly; it is a sealed unit and must be replaced as one if found to be defective.

Shock Absorbers
TESTING

Visually inspect the shock absorber. If there is evidence of leakage and the shock absorber is covered with oil, the shock is defective and should be replaced.

If there is no sign of excessive leakage (a small amount of weeping is normal) bounce the car at one corner by pressing down on the fender or bumper and releasing. When you have the

Wheel Alignment

Year	Model	Caster Range (deg.)	Caster Preferred Setting (deg.)	Camber Range (deg.)	Camber Preferred Setting (deg.)	Toe-in (in.)	Steering Axis Inclination (deg.)
1982	Cavalier	NA	NA	$1/16$–$1\,1/16$	$9/16$	$1/4$–0 ①	—
	2000	NA	NA	$1/16$–$1\,1/16$	$9/16$	$1/4$–0 ①	—
	Firenza	NA	NA	$1/16$–$1\,1/16$	$9/16$	$1/4$–0 ①	—
	Skyhawk	NA	NA	$1/16$–$1\,1/16$	$9/16$	$1/4$–0 ①	—
	Cimarron	NA	NA	$1/16$–$1\,1/16$	$9/16$	$1/4$–0 ①	—
1983	Cavalier	NA	NA	$7/32$–$1\,7/32$	$23/32$	$5/16$–$1/16$ ①	—
	2000	NA	NA	$7/32$–$1\,7/32$	$23/32$	$5/16$–$1/16$ ①	—
	Firenza	NA	NA	$7/32$–$1\,7/32$	$23/32$	$5/16$–$1/16$ ①	—
	Skyhawk	NA	NA	$7/32$–$1\,7/32$	$23/32$	$5/16$–$1/16$ ①	—
	Cimarron	NA	NA	$7/32$–$1\,7/32$	$23/32$	$5/16$–$1/16$ ①	—
1984	Cavalier	NA	NA	$3/16$–$1\,3/16$	$11/16$	$1/4$–0 ①	—
	200 Sunbird	NA	NA	$3/16$–$1\,3/16$	$11/16$	$1/4$–0 ①	—
	Firenza	NA	NA	$3/16$–$1\,3/16$	$11/16$	$1/4$–0 ①	—
	Skyhawk	NA	NA	$3/16$–$1\,3/16$	$11/16$	$1/4$–0 ①	—
	Cimarron	NA	NA	$3/16$–$1\,3/16$	$11/16$	$1/4$–0 ①	—
1985	Cavalier	NA	NA	$3/16$–$1\,3/16$	$11/16$	$1/4$–0 ①	—
	2000 Sunbird	NA	NA	$3/16$–$1\,3/16$	$11/16$	$1/4$–0 ①	—
	Skyhawk	NA	NA	$3/16$–$1\,3/16$	$11/16$	$1/4$–0 ①	—
	Cimarron	NA	NA	$3/16$–$1\,3/16$	$11/16$	$1/4$–0 ①	—
1986	Cavalier	NA	NA	$3/16$–$1\,3/16$	$11/16$	$1/4$–0 ①	—
	2000 Sunbird	NA	NA	$3/16$–$1\,3/16$	$11/16$	$1/4$–0 ①	—
	Skyhawk	NA	NA	$3/16$–$1\,3/16$	$11/16$	$1/4$–0 ①	—
	Cimarron	NA	NA	$3/16$–$1\,3/16$	$11/16$	$1/4$–0 ①	—
1987	Cavalier	NA	NA	$3/16$–$1\,3/16$	$11/16$	$1/4$–0 ①	—
	2000 Sunbird	NA	NA	$3/16$–$1\,3/16$	$11/16$	$1/4$–0 ①	—
	Skyhawk	NA	NA	$3/16$–$1\,3/16$	$11/16$	$1/4$–0 ①	—
	Cimarron	NA	NA	$3/16$–$1\,3/16$	$11/16$	$1/4$–0 ①	—

NA—Not adjustable
① Preferred setting: $1/8$ out

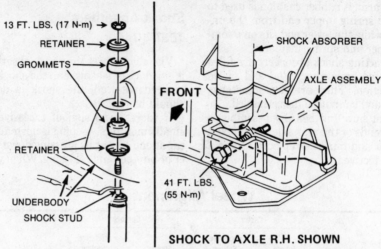

13 FT. LBS. (17 N-m)
RETAINER
GROMMETS
RETAINER
UNDERBODY
SHOCK STUD

FRONT

SHOCK ABSORBER
AXLE ASSEMBLY
41 FT. LBS. (55 N-m)

SHOCK TO AXLE R.H. SHOWN

Shock absorber mounting details; top (left) and bottom (right)

car bouncing as much as you can, release the fender or bumper. The car should stop bouncing after the first rebound. If the bouncing continues past the center point of the bounce more than once, the shock absorbers are worn and should be replaced.

REMOVAL AND INSTALLATION

1. Open the hatch or trunk lid, remove the trim cover if present, and remove the upper shock absorber nut.
2. Raise and support the car at a convenient working height if you desire. It is not necessary to remove the weight of the car from the shock absorbers, however, so you can leave the car on the ground if you prefer.
3. Remove the lower attaching bolt and remove the shock.
4. If new shock absorbers are being installed, repeatedly compress them while inverted and extend them in their normal upright position. This will purge them of air.

5. Install the shocks in the reverse order of removal. Tighten the lower mount nut and bolt to 55 ft. lbs. (41 Nm.), the upper to 13 ft. lbs. (17 Nm.).

Springs

REMOVAL AND INSTALLATION

CAUTION: *The coil springs are under a considerable amount of tension. Be very careful when removing or installing them; they can exert enough force to cause very serious injuries.*

1. Raise and support the car on a hoist. Do not use a twin-post hoist. The swing arc of the axle may cause it to slip from the hoist when the bolts are removed. If a suitable hoist is not available, raise and support the car on jackstands, and use a jack under the axle.
2. Support the axle with a jack that can be raised and lowered.
3. Remove the brake hose attaching brackets

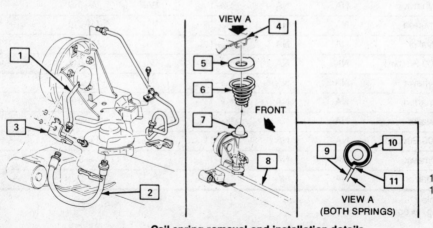

1. Center brake pipe
2. Brake hose
3. Brake pipe bracket
4. Underbody
5. Spring insulator
6. Spring
7. Compression bumper
8. Axle asm.
9. 15mm max. (.594")
10. Spring
11. Spring stop part of spring seat

VIEW A
FRONT
VIEW A (BOTH SPRINGS)

Coil spring removal and installation details

(right and left), allowing the hoses to hang freely. Do not disconnect the hoses.

4. Remove both shock absorber lower attaching bolts from the axle.

5. Lower the axle. Remove the coil spring and insulator.

6. To install, position the spring and insulator on the axle. The leg on the upper coil of the spring must be parallel to the axle, facing the lefthand side of the car.

7. Install the shock absorber bolts. Tighten to 41 ft. lbs. (55 Nm.). Install the brake line brackets. Tighten to 8 ft. lbs. (11 Nm.).

Rear Hub and Bearing
REMOVAL AND INSTALLATION

1. Loosen the wheel lug nuts. Raise and support the car and remove the wheel.

2. Remove the brake drum. Removal procedures are covered in the next chapter, if needed. WARNING: *Do not hammer on the brake drum to remove; damage to the bearing will result.*

3. Remove the four hub and bearing retaining bolts and remove the assembly from the axle. The top rear attaching bolt will not clear the brake shoe when removing the hub and bearing assembly. Partially remove the hub and bearing assembly prior to removing this bolt.

4. Installation is the reverse. Hub and bearing bolt torque is 39 ft. lbs. (52 Nm.).

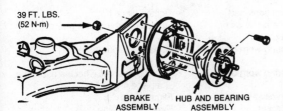

39 FT. LBS. (52 N-m)

BRAKE ASSEMBLY   HUB AND BEARING ASSEMBLY

Rear hub and bearing assembly

Stabilizer Bar
REMOVAL AND INSTALLATION

1. Raise the vehicle and support the body with jackstands.

2. Remove the nuts and bolts at both the axle and control arm attachments and remove the control arm and remove the bracket, insulator and stabilizer bar.

3. Install the U-bolts, upper clamp, spacer and insulators in the trailing axle. Position the stabilizer bar in the insulators and loosely install the lower clamp and nuts.

4. Attach the end of the stabilizer bar to the control arms and torque all nuts to 13. ft. lbs.

5. Torque the axle attaching nut to 10 ft. lbs.
6. Lower the vehicle.

Rear Axle/Control Arm

The control arms and axle are are one unit. The axle structure itself maintains the gometrical relationship of the wheels relitive to the body. The axle assembly attaches to the underbody through a rubber bushing located at the front of each control arm. Each control arm bolts to underbody brackets.

REMOVAL AND INSTALLATION

1. Raise the vehicle and support the with jackstands under the control arms.

2. Remove the stabilizer bar from the axle assembly.

3. Remove the wheel and tire assembly and brake drum. WARNING: *Do not hammer on the brake drum as damage to the bearing could result.*

4. Remove the shock absorber lower attaching bolts and paddle nuts at the axle and disconnect the shocks from the control arm.

5. Disconnect the parking brake cable from the axle assembly.

6. Disconnect the brake line at the brackets from the axle assembly.

7. Lower the rear axle and remove the coil springs and insulators.

8. Remove the control arm bolts from the underbody bracket and lower the axle.

9. Remove the hub attaching bolts and remove the hub, bearing and backing plate assembly.

10. Install the hub, bearing and backing plate assembly. Hold the nuts and tighten the attaching bolts to 39 ft. lbs.

11. Install the stabilizer bar to the axle assembly.

12. Place the axle assembly on a transmission jack and raise into position. Attach the control arms to the underbody bracket with bolts and nuts. Do not torque the bolts at this time. It wiil be necessary to torque the bolt the bolt of the control arm at standing height.

13. Install the brake line connections to the axle assembly.

14. Attach the brake cable to the rear axle assembly.

15. Position the coil springs and insulators in seats and raise the rera axle.

16. The end of the upper coil on the springs must be parallel to the axle assembly and seated in the pocket.

17. Install the shock absorber lower attachment bolts and paddle nuts to the rear axle and torque the bolts to 41 ft. lbs.

18. Install the parking brake cable to the guide hook and adjust as necessary.

Troubleshooting the Steering Column

Problem	Cause	Solution
Will not lock	· Lockbolt spring broken or defective	· Replace lock bolt spring
High effort (required to turn ignition key and lock cylinder)	· Lock cylinder defective · Ignition switch defective · Rack preload spring broken or deformed · Burr on lock sector, lock rack, housing, support or remote rod coupling · Bent sector shaft · Defective lock rack · Remote rod bent, deformed · Ignition switch mounting bracket bent · Distorted coupling slot in lock rack (tilt column)	· Replace lock cylinder · Replace ignition switch · Replace preload spring · Remove burr · Replace shaft · Replace lock rack · Replace rod · Straighten or replace · Replace lock rack
Will stick in "start"	· Remote rod deformed · Ignition switch mounting bracket bent	· Straighten or replace · Straighten or replace
Key cannot be removed in "off-lock"	· Ignition switch is not adjusted correctly · Defective lock cylinder	· Adjust switch · Replace lock cylinder
Lock cylinder can be removed without depressing retainer	· Lock cylinder with defective retainer · Burr over retainer slot in housing cover or on cylinder retainer	· Replace lock cylinder · Remove burr
High effort on lock cylinder between "off" and "off-lock"	· Distorted lock rack · Burr on tang of shift gate (automatic column) · Gearshift linkage not adjusted	· Replace lock rack · Remove burr · Adjust linkage
Noise in column	· One click when in "off-lock" position and the steering wheel is moved (all except automatic column) · Coupling bolts not tightened · Lack of grease on bearings or bearing surfaces · Upper shaft bearing worn or broken · Lower shaft bearing worn or broken · Column not correctly aligned · Coupling pulled apart · Broken coupling lower joint · Steering shaft snap ring not seated · Shroud loose on shift bowl. Housing loose on jacket—will be noticed with ignition in "off-lock" and when torque is applied to steering wheel.	· Normal—lock bolt is seating · Tighten pinch bolts · Lubricate with chassis grease · Replace bearing assembly · Replace bearing. Check shaft and replace if scored. · Align column · Replace coupling · Repair or replace joint and align column · Replace ring. Check for proper seating in groove. · Position shroud over lugs on shift bowl. Tighten mounting screws.
High steering shaft effort	· Column misaligned · Defective upper or lower bearing · Tight steering shaft universal joint · Flash on I.D. of shift tube at plastic joint (tilt column only) · Upper or lower bearing seized	· Align column · Replace as required · Repair or replace · Replace shift tube · Replace bearings
Lash in mounted column assembly	· Column mounting bracket bolts loose · Broken weld nuts on column jacket · Column capsule bracket sheared	· Tighten bolts · Replace column jacket · Replace bracket assembly

Troubleshooting the Steering Column (cont.)

Problem	Cause	Solution
Lash in mounted column assembly (cont.)	· Column bracket to column jacket mounting bolts loose	· Tighten to specified torque
	· Loose lock shoes in housing (tilt column only)	· Replace shoes
	· Loose pivot pins (tilt column only)	· Replace pivot pins and support
	· Loose lock shoe pin (tilt column only)	· Replace pin and housing
	· Loose support screws (tilt column only)	· Tighten screws
Housing loose (tilt column only)	· Excessive clearance between holes in support or housing and pivot pin diameters	· Replace pivot pins and support
	· Housing support-screws loose	· Tighten screws
Steering wheel loose—every other tilt position (tilt column only)	· Loose fit between lock shoe and lock shoe pivot pin	· Replace lock shoes and pivot pin
Steering column not locking in any tilt position (tilt column only)	· Lock shoe seized on pivot pin	· Replace lock shoes and pin
	· Lock shoe grooves have burrs or are filled with foreign material	· Clean or replace lock shoes
	· Lock shoe springs weak or broken	· Replace springs
Noise when tilting column (tilt column only)	· Upper tilt bumpers worn	· Replace tilt bumper
	· Tilt spring rubbing in housing	· Lubricate with chassis grease
One click when in "off-lock" position and the steering wheel is moved	· Seating of lock bolt	· None. Click is normal characteristic sound produced by lock bolt as it seats.
High shift effort (automatic and tilt column only)	· Column not correctly aligned	· Align column
	· Lower bearing not aligned correctly	· Assemble correctly
	· Lack of grease on seal or lower bearing areas	· Lubricate with chassis grease
Improper transmission shifting—automatic and tilt column only	· Sheared shift tube joint	· Replace shift tube
	· Improper transmission gearshift linkage adjustment	· Adjust linkage
	· Loose lower shift lever	· Replace shift tube

Troubleshooting the Ignition Switch

Problem	Cause	Solution
Ignition switch electrically inoperative	· Loose or defective switch connector	· Tighten or replace connector
	· Feed wire open (fusible link)	· Repair or replace
	· Defective ignition switch	· Replace ignition switch
Engine will not crank	· Ignition switch not adjusted properly	· Adjust switch
Ignition switch wil not actuate mechanically	· Defective ignition switch	· Replace switch
	· Defective lock sector	· Replace lock sector
	· Defective remote rod	· Replace remote rod
Ignition switch cannot be adjusted correctly	· Remote rod deformed	· Repair, straighten or replace

Troubleshooting the Turn Signal Switch

Problem	Cause	Solution
Turn signal will not cancel	• Loose switch mounting screws • Switch or anchor bosses broken • Broken, missing or out of position detent, or cancelling spring	• Tighten screws • Replace switch • Reposition springs or replace switch as required
Turn signal difficult to operate	• Turn signal lever loose • Switch yoke broken or distorted • Loose or misplaced springs • Foreign parts and/or materials in switch • Switch mounted loosely	• Tighten mounting screws • Replace switch • Reposition springs or replace switch • Remove foreign parts and/or material • Tighten mounting screws
Turn signal will not indicate lane change	• Broken lane change pressure pad or spring hanger • Broken, missing or misplaced lane change spring • Jammed wires	• Replace switch • Replace or reposition as required • Loosen mounting screws, reposition wires and retighten screws
Turn signal will not stay in turn position	• Foreign material or loose parts impeding movement of switch yoke • Defective switch	• Remove material and/or parts • Replace switch
Hazard switch cannot be pulled out	• Foreign material between hazard support cancelling leg and yoke	• Remove foreign material. No foreign material impeding function of hazard switch—replace turn signal switch.
No turn signal lights	• Inoperative turn signal flasher • Defective or blown fuse • Loose chassis to column harness connector • Disconnect column to chassis connector. Connect new switch to chassis and operate switch by hand. If vehicle lights now operate normally, signal switch is inoperative • If vehicle lights do not operate, check chassis wiring for opens, grounds, etc.	• Replace turn signal flasher • Replace fuse • Connect securely • Replace signal switch • Repair chassis wiring as required
Instrument panel turn indicator lights on but not flashing	• Burned out or damaged front or rear turn signal bulb • If vehicle lights do not operate, check light sockets for high resistance connections, the chassis wiring for opens, grounds, etc. • Inoperative flasher • Loose chassis to column harness connection • Inoperative turn signal switch • To determine if turn signal switch is defective, substitute new switch into circuit and operate switch by hand. If the vehicle's lights operate normally, signal switch is inoperative.	• Replace bulb • Repair chassis wiring as required • Replace flasher • Connect securely • Replace turn signal switch • Replace turn signal switch
Stop light not on when turn indicated	• Loose column to chassis connection • Disconnect column to chassis connector. Connect new switch into system without removing old.	• Connect securely • Replace signal switch

Troubleshooting the Turn Signal Switch (cont.)

Problem	Cause	Solution
Stop light not on when turn indicated (cont.)	Operate switch by hand. If brake lights work with switch in the turn position, signal switch is defective.	
	• If brake lights do not work, check connector to stop light sockets for grounds, opens, etc.	• Repair connector to stop light circuits using service manual as guide
Turn indicator panel lights not flashing	• Burned out bulbs	• Replace bulbs
	• High resistance to ground at bulb socket	• Replace socket
	• Opens, ground in wiring harness from front turn signal bulb socket to indicator lights	• Locate and repair as required
Turn signal lights flash very slowly	• High resistance ground at light sockets	• Repair high resistance grounds at light sockets
	• Incorrect capacity turn signal flasher or bulb	• Replace turn signal flasher or bulb
	• If flashing rate is still extremely slow, check chassis wiring harness from the connector to light sockets for high resistance	• Locate and repair as required
	• Loose chassis to column harness connection	• Connect securely
	• Disconnect column to chassis connector. Connect new switch into system without removing old. Operate switch by hand. If flashing occurs at normal rate, the signal switch is defective.	• Replace turn signal switch
Hazard signal lights will not flash— turn signal functions normally	• Blow fuse	• Replace fuse
	• Inoperative hazard warning flasher	• Replace hazard warning flasher in fuse panel
	• Loose chassis-to-column harness connection	• Conect securely
	• Disconnect column to chassis connector. Connect new switch into system without removing old. Depress the hazard warning lights. If they now work normally, turn signal switch is defective.	• Replace turn signal switch
	• If lights do not flash, check wiring harness "K" lead for open between hazard flasher and connector. If open, fuse block is defective	• Repair or replace brown wire or connector as required

19. Install the brake drums and wheel and tire assemblies. Torque the lug nuts to 103 ft. lbs.

20. Bleed the brake system and lower the car.

STEERING

All J-cars are equipped with, as standard equippment, (except Cimarron), a Saginaw manual rack and pinion steering gear. The pinion is supported by and turns in a sealed ball bearing at the top and a pressed-in roller bear-

ing at the bottom. The rack moves in bushings pressed into each end of the rack housing.

Wear compensation occurs through the action of an adjuster spring which forces the rack against the pinion teeth. This adjuster eliminates the need for periodic pinion preload adjustments. Preload is adjustable only at overhaul.

The inner tie rod assemblies are bolted to the front of the rack. A special bushing is used, allowing both rocking and rotating motion of the tie rods. Any service other than replacement of the outer tie rods or the boots requires removal of the unit from the car.

Troubleshooting the Manual Steering Gear

Problem	Cause	Solution
Hard or erratic steering	• Incorrect tire pressure	• Inflate tires to recommended pressures
	• Insufficient or incorrect lubrication	• Lubricate as required (refer to Maintenance Section)
	• Suspension, or steering linkage parts damaged or misaligned	• Repair or replace parts as necessary
	• Improper front wheel alignment	• Adjust incorrect wheel alignment angles
	• Incorrect steering gear adjustment	• Adjust steering gear
	• Sagging springs	• Replace springs
Play or looseness in steering	• Steering wheel loose	• Inspect shaft spines and repair as necessary. Tighten attaching nut and stake in place.
	• Steering linkage or attaching parts loose or worn	• Tighten, adjust, or replace faulty components
	• Pitman arm loose	• Inspect shaft splines and repair as necessary. Tighten attaching nut and stake in place
	• Steering gear attaching bolts loose	• Tighten bolts
	• Loose or worn wheel bearings	• Adjust or replace bearings
	• Steering gear adjustment incorrect or parts badly worn	• Adjust gear or replace defective parts
Wheel shimmy or tramp	• Improper tire pressure	• Inflate tires to recommended pressures
	• Wheels, tires, or brake rotors out-of-balance or out-of-round	• Inspect and replace or balance parts
	• Inoperative, worn, or loose shock absorbers or mounting parts	• Repair or replace shocks or mountings
	• Loose or worn steering or suspension parts	• Tighten or replace as necessary
	• Loose or worn wheel bearings	• Adjust or replace bearings
	• Incorrect steering gear adjustments	• Adjust steering gear
	• Incorrect front wheel alignment	• Correct front wheel alignment
Tire wear	• Improper tire pressure	• Inflate tires to recommended pressures
	• Failure to rotate tires	• Rotate tires
	• Brakes grabbing	• Adjust or repair brakes
	• Incorrect front wheel alignment	• Align incorrect angles
	• Broken or damaged steering and suspension parts	• Repair or replace defective parts
	• Wheel runout	• Replace faulty wheel
	• Excessive speed on turns	• Make driver aware of conditions
Vehicle leads to one side	• Improper tire pressures	• Inflate tires to recommended pressures
	• Front tires with uneven tread depth, wear pattern, or different cord design (i.e., one bias ply and one belted or radial tire on front wheels)	• Install tires of same cord construction and reasonably even tread depth, design, and wear pattern
	• Incorrect front wheel alignment	• Align incorrect angles
	• Brakes dragging	• Adjust or repair brakes
	• Pulling due to uneven tire construction	• Replace faulty tire

Troubleshooting the Power Steering Gear

Problem	Cause	Solution
Hissing noise in steering gear	• There is some noise in all power steering systems. One of the most common is a hissing sound most evident at standstill parking. There is no relationship between this noise and performance of the steering. Hiss may be expected when steering wheel is at end of travel or when slowly turning at standstill.	• Slight hiss is normal and in no way affects steering. Do not replace valve unless hiss is extremely objectionable. A replacement valve will also exhibit slight noise and is not always a cure. Investigate clearance around flexible coupling rivets. Be sure steering shaft and gear are aligned so flexible coupling rotates in a flat plane and is not distorted as shaft rotates. Any metal-to-metal contacts through flexible coupling will transmit valve hiss into passenger compartment through the steering column.
Rattle or chuckle noise in steering gear	• Gear loose on frame • Steering linkage looseness • Pressure hose touching other parts of car • Loose pitman shaft over center adjustment **NOTE:** A slight rattle may occur on turns because of increased clearance off the "high point." This is normal and clearance must not be reduced below specified limits to eliminate this slight rattle. • Loose pitman arm	• Check gear-to-frame mounting screws. Tighten screws to 88 N·m (65 foot pounds) torque. • Check linkage pivot points for wear. Replace if necessary. • Adjust hose position. Do not bend tubing by hand. • Adjust to specifications • Tighten pitman arm nut to specifications
Squawk noise in steering gear when turning or recovering from a turn	• Damper O-ring on valve spool cut	• Replace damper O-ring
Poor return of steering wheel to center	• Tires not properly inflated • Lack of lubrication in linkage and ball joints • Lower coupling flange rubbing against steering gear adjuster plug • Steering gear to column misalignment • Improper front wheel alignment • Steering linkage binding • Ball joints binding • Steering wheel rubbing against housing • Tight or frozen steering shaft bearings • Sticking or plugged valve spool • Steering gear adjustments over specifications • Kink in return hose	• Inflate to specified pressure • Lube linkage and ball joints • Loosen pinch bolt and assemble properly • Align steering column • Check and adjust as necessary • Replace pivots • Replace ball joints • Align housing • Replace bearings • Remove and clean or replace valve • Check adjustment with gear out of car. Adjust as required. • Replace hose
Car leads to one side or the other (keep in mind road condition and wind. Test car in both directions on flat road)	• Front end misaligned • Unbalanced steering gear valve **NOTE:** If this is cause, steering effort will be very light in direction of lead and normal or heavier in opposite direction	• Adjust to specifications • Replace valve

Troubleshooting the Power Steering Gear (cont.)

Problem	Cause	Solution
Momentary increase in effort when turning wheel fast to right or left	• Low oil level • Pump belt slipping • High internal leakage	• Add power steering fluid as required • Tighten or replace belt • Check pump pressure. (See pressure test)
Steering wheel surges or jerks when turning with engine running especially during parking	• Low oil level • Loose pump belt • Steering linkage hitting engine oil pan at full turn • Insufficient pump pressure • Pump flow control valve sticking	• Fill as required • Adjust tension to specification • Correct clearance • Check pump pressure. (See pressure test). Replace relief valve if defective. • Inspect for varnish or damage, replace if necessary
Excessive wheel kickback or loose steering	• Air in system • Steering gear loose on frame • Steering linkage joints worn enough to be loose • Worn poppet valve • Loose thrust bearing preload adjustment • Excessive overcenter lash	• Add oil to pump reservoir and bleed by operating steering. Check hose connectors for proper torque and adjust as required. • Tighten attaching screws to specified torque • Replace loose pivots • Replace poppet valve • Adjust to specification with gear out of vehicle • Adjust to specification with gear out of car
Hard steering or lack of assist	• Loose pump belt • Low oil level **NOTE:** Low oil level will also result in excessive pump noise • Steering gear to column misalignment • Lower coupling flange rubbing against steering gear adjuster plug • Tires not properly inflated	• Adjust belt tension to specification • Fill to proper level. If excessively low, check all lines and joints for evidence of external leakage. Tighten loose connectors. • Align steering column • Loosen pinch bolt and assemble properly • Inflate to recommended pressure
Foamy milky power steering fluid, low fluid level and possible low pressure	• Air in the fluid, and loss of fluid due to internal pump leakage causing overflow	• Check for leak and correct. Bleed system. Extremely cold temperatures will cause system aeration should the oil level be low. If oil level is correct and pump still foams, remove pump from vehicle and separate reservoir from housing. Check welsh plug and housing for cracks. If plug is loose or housing is cracked, replace housing.
Low pressure due to steering pump	• Flow control valve stuck or inoperative • Pressure plate not flat against cam ring	• Remove burrs or dirt or replace. Flush system. • Correct
Low pressure due to steering gear	• Pressure loss in cylinder due to worn piston ring or badly worn housing bore • Leakage at valve rings, valve body-to-worm seal	• Remove gear from car for disassembly and inspection of ring and housing bore • Remove gear from car for disassembly and replace seals

Troubleshooting the Power Steering Pump

Problem	Cause	Solution
Chirp noise in steering pump	• Loose belt	• Adjust belt tension to specification
Belt squeal (particularly noticeable at full wheel travel and stand still parking)	• Loose belt	• Adjust belt tension to specification
Growl noise in steering pump	• Excessive back pressure in hoses or steering gear caused by restriction	• Locate restriction and correct. Replace part if necessary.
Growl noise in steering pump (particularly noticeable at stand still parking)	• Scored pressure plates, thrust plate or rotor • Extreme wear of cam ring	• Replace parts and flush system • Replace parts
Groan noise in steering pump	• Low oil level • Air in the oil. Poor pressure hose connection.	• Fill reservoir to proper level • Tighten connector to specified torque. Bleed system by operating steering from right to left—full turn.
Rattle noise in steering pump	• Vanes not installed properly • Vanes sticking in rotor slots	• Install properly • Free up by removing burrs, varnish, or dirt
Swish noise in steering pump	• Defective flow control valve	• Replace part
Whine noise in steering pump	• Pump shaft bearing scored	• Replace housing and shaft. Flush system.
Hard steering or lack of assist	• Loose pump belt • Low oil level in reservoir NOTE: Low oil level will also result in excessive pump noise • Steering gear to column misalignment • Lower coupling flange rubbing against steering gear adjuster plug • Tires not properly inflated	• Adjust belt tension to specification • Fill to proper level. If excessively low, check all lines and joints for evidence of external leakage. Tighten loose connectors. • Align steering column • Loosen pinch bolt and assemble properly • Inflate to recommended pressure
Foaming milky power steering fluid, low fluid level and possible low pressure	• Air in the fluid, and loss of fluid due to internal pump leakage causing overflow	• Check for leaks and correct. Bleed system. Extremely cold temperatures will cause system aeriation should the oil level be low. If oil level is correct and pump still foams, remove pump from vehicle and separate reservoir from body. Check welsh plug and body for cracks. If plug is loose or body is cracked, replace body.
Low pump pressure	• Flow control valve stuck or inoperative • Pressure plate not flat against cam ring	• Remove burrs or dirt or replace. Flush system. • Correct
Momentary increase in effort when turning wheel fast to right or left	• Low oil level in pump • Pump belt slipping • High internal leakage	• Add power steering fluid as required • Tighten or replace belt • Check pump pressure. (See pressure test)
Steering wheel surges or jerks when turning with engine running especially during parking	• Low oil level • Loose pump belt • Steering linkage hitting engine oil pan at full turn • Insufficient pump pressure	• Fill as required • Adjust tension to specification • Correct clearance • Check pump pressure. (See pressure test). Replace flow control valve if defective.

Troubleshooting the Power Steering Pump (cont.)

Problem	Cause	Solution
Steering wheel surges or jerks when turning with engine running especially during parking (cont.)	• Sticking flow control valve	• Inspect for varnish or damage, replace if necessary
Excessive wheel kickback or loose steering	• Air in system	• Add oil to pump reservoir and bleed by operating steering. Check hose connectors for proper torque and adjust as required.
Low pump pressure	• Extreme wear of cam ring • Scored pressure plate, thrust plate, or rotor • Vanes not installed properly • Vanes sticking in rotor slots • Cracked or broken thrust or pressure plate	• Replace parts. Flush system. • Replace parts. Flush system. • Install properly • Freeup by removing burrs, varnish, or dirt • Replace part

The power steering gear is an integral unit and shares most features with the manual gear. A rotary control valve directs the hydraulic fluid to either side of the rack piston. The integral rack piston is attached to the rack and converts the hydraulic pressure into left or right lenear motion. A vane-type constant displacement pump with integral reservoir provides hydraulic pressure. No in-car adjustments are necessary or possible on the system, except for periodic belt tension checks and adjustments for the pump. See Chapter One for belt tension adjustments.

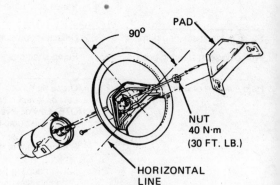

Standard steering wheel removal

Steering Wheel

REMOVAL AND INSTALLATION

Standard Wheel

1. Disconnect the negative cable at the battery.
2. Pull the pad from the wheel. The horn lead is attached to the pad at one end; the other end of the pad has a wire with a spade connector. The horn lead is disconnected by pushing and turning; the spade connector is simply unplugged.
3. Remove the retainer under the pad (if so equipped).
4. Remove the steering shaft nut.
5. There should be alignment marks already present on the wheel and shaft. If not, matchmark the parts.
6. Remove the wheel with a puller.
7. Install the wheel on the shaft, aligning the matchmarks. Install the shaft nut and tighten to 30 ft. lbs. (40 Nm.).
8. Install the retainer.
9. Plug in the spade connector, and push and

turn the horn lead to connect. Install the pad. Connect the negative battery cable.

Sport Wheel

1. Disconnect the negative cable at the battery.
2. Pry the center cap from the wheel.
3. Remove the retainer (if so equipped).
4. Remove the shaft nut.
5. If the wheel and shaft do not have factory

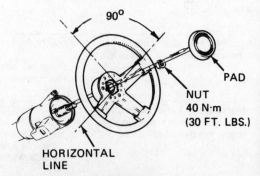

Sport steering wheel removal

installed alignment marks, matchmark the parts before removal of the wheel.

6. Install a puller and remove the wheel. A horn spring, eyelet and insulator are underneath; don't lose the parts.

7. Install the spring, eyelet and insulator into the tower on the column.

8. Align the matchmarks and install the wheel onto the shaft. Install the retaining nut and tighten to 30 ft. lbs. (40 Nm.).

9. Install the retainer. Install the center cap. Connect the negative battery cable.

Turn Signal Switch
REMOVAL AND INSTALLATION

1. Remove the steering wheel. Remove the trim cover.

2. Pry the cover from the steering column.

3. Position a U-shaped lockplate compressing tool on the end of the steering shaft and compress the lock plate by turning the shaft nut clockwise. Pry the wire snapring out of the shaft groove.

4. Remove the tool and lift the lockplate off the shaft.

5. Slip the cancelling cam, upper bearing preload spring, and thrust washer off the shaft.

6. Remove the turn signal lever. Remove the hazard flasher button retaining screw and remove the button, spring and knob.

7. Pull the switch connector out of the mast jacket and tape the upper part to facilitate switch removal. Attach a long piece of wire to the turn signal switch connector. When installing the turn signal switch, feed this wire through the column first, and then use this wire to pull the switch connector into position. On tilt wheels, place the turn signal and shifter housing in low position and remove the harness cover.

8. Remove the three switch mounting screws. Remove the switch by pulling it straight up while guiding the wiring harness cover through the column.

9. Install the replacement switch by working the connector and cover down through the housing and under the bracket. On tilt models, the connector is worked down through the housing, under the bracket, and then the cover is installed on the harness.

10. Install the switch mounting screws and the connector on the mast jacket bracket. Install the column-to-dash trim plate.

11. Install the flasher knob and the turn signal lever.

12. With the turn signal lever in neutral and the flasher knob out, slide the thrust washer, upper bearing preload spring, and cancelling cam onto the shaft.

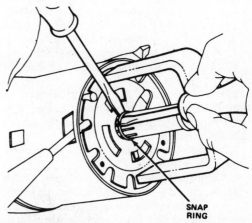

Depress the lock plate and remove the snap ring

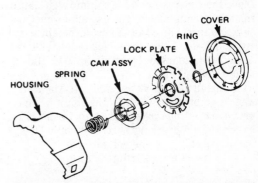

Remove these parts to get at the turn signal switch

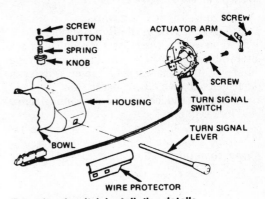

Turn signal switch installation details

13. Position the lock plate on the shaft and press it down until a new snapring can be inserted in the shaft groove. Always use a new snapring when assembling.

14. Install the cover and the steering wheel.

Ignition Switch
REMOVAL AND INSTALLATION

The switch is located inside the channel section of the brake pedal support and is complely inaccessible without first lowering the steering column. The switch is actuated by a rod and rack assembly. A gear on the end of the lock cylinder engages the toothed upper end of the rod.

1. Lower the steering column; be sure to properly support it.

2. Put the switch in the **Off-Unlocked** position. With the cylinder removed, the rod is in **Off-Unlocked** position when it is in the next to the uppermost detent.

3. Remove the two switch screws and remove the switch assembly.

4. Before installing, move the new switch slider (standard columns with automatic transmission) to the extreme left position. Move the switch slider (stanadrd columns with manual transmission) to the extreme left position. Move the slider (adjustable columns with automatic transmission) to the extreme right position and then move the slider one detent to the left (off lock). Move the slider (adjustable columns with manual transmission) to the extreme right position.

5. Install the activating rod into the switch and assemble the switch on the column. Tighten the mounting screws. Use only the specified screws, since overlength screws could impair the collapsibility of the column.

6. Reinstall the steering column.

Ignition Lock Cylinder

REMOVAL AND INSTALLATION

1. Remove the steering wheel.

2. Turn the lock to the Run position.

3. Remove the lock plate, turn signal switch or combination switch, and the key warning buzzer switch. The warning buzzer switch can be fished out with a bent paper clip.

4. Remove the lock cylinder retaining screw and lock cylinder.

WARNING: *If the screw is dropped on removal, it could fall into the column, requiring complete disassembly to retrieve the screw.*

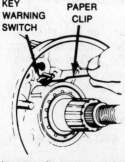

Remove the key warning buzzer switch with a paper clip

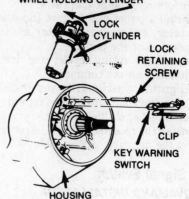

Lock cylinder installation

5. Rotate the cylinder clockwise to align the cylinder key with the keyway in the housing.

6. Push the lock all the way in.

7. Install the screw. Tighten to 15 in. lbs.

8. The rest of installation is the reverse of removal. Turn the lock to Run to install the key warning buzzer switch, which is simply pushed down into place.

Steering Column

REMOVAL AND INSTALLATION

WARNING: *Once the steering column is removed from the car, the column is extremely susceptible to damage. Dropping the column assembly on its end could collapse the steering shaft or loosen the plastic injections which maintain column rigidity. Leaning on the column assembly could cause the jacket to bend or deform. Under no conditions should the end of the shaft be hammered upon. Any of the above damage could impair the column's collapsible design.*

1. Disconnect the battery ground cable.

2. Remove the left instrument panel sound insulator.

3. Remove the left instrument panel trim pad and steering column trim collar.

4. Remove the horn contact pad, (only if column is to be disassembled).

5. Remove the steering wheel, (only if column is to be disassembled).

6. Disconnect the steering shaft to intermediate shaft connection.

7. Remove the column bracket support bolts and column bracket support nut.

8. Disconnect any electrical connections.

9. Remove the steering column.

10. Insert the steering shaft into the flexible coupling and raise the coupling into position.

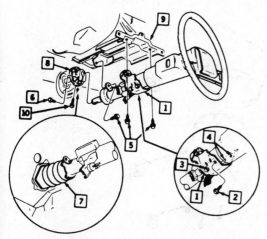

1. Upper support
2. Bolt—install first—27 N·m (20 lbs. ft.)
3. Bolt—install second—27 N·m (20 lbs. ft.)
4. Bolt—install these bolts last—27 N·m (20 lbs. ft.)
5. Bolt—27 N·m (20 lbs. ft.)
6. Upper pinch bolt—46 N·m (34 lbs. ft.)
7. Seal
8. Coupling
9. Instrument panel bracket
10. Lower pinch bolt—40 N·m (29 lbs. ft.)

Steering column mounting

11. Loosely install the three steering column attaching bolts.
12. Center the steering shaft within the steering column jacket bushing and tighten the lower attaching bolt. This can be done by moving the steering column jacket jacket assembly up and down or side to side until the steering shaft is centered.
13. Tighten the two upper attaching bolts and torqque to 20 ft. lbs.
14. Install the flexible coupling pinch bolt and torque to 34 ft. lbs.
15. Turn the steering wheel from stop to stop and observe if the steering shaft binds or rubs against the column bushing. Re-center the steering shaft if necessary.
16. Pull the seal assembly up over the end of the column bushing until the seal locks into place.
17. Install the sound insulator.
18. Connect the battery cable.

Tie Rod Ends

REMOVAL AND INSTALLATION

1. Loosen both pinch bolts at the outer tie rod.
2. Remove the tie rod end from the strut assembly using a suitable removal tool.
3. Unscrew the outer tie rod end from the tie rod adjuster, counting the number of revolutions required before they are disconnected.

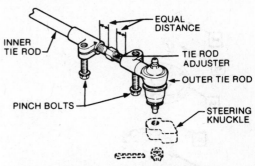

Tie rod end removal and installation details

4. Install the new tie rod end, screwing it on the same number of revolutions as counted in Step 3. When the tie rod end is installed, the tie rod adjuster must be centered between the tie rod and the tie rod end, with an equal number of threads exposed on both sides of the adjuster nut. Tighten the pinch bolts to 20 ft. lbs.
5. Install the tie rod end to the strut assembly and tighten to 50 ft. lbs. If the cotter pin cannot be installed, tighten the nut up to $\frac{1}{16}$" further. Never back off the nut to align the holes for the cotter pin.
6. Have the front end alignment adjusted.

Power Steering Pump

REMOVAL AND INSTALLATION

1. Disconnect the negative battery cable.
2. Disconnect the vent hole at the carburetor.
3. Loosen the adjusting bolt and pivot bolt on the pump, then remove the pump's drive belt.
4. Remove the three pump-to-bracket bolts and remove the adjusting bolt.
5. Remove the high pressure fitting from the pump.
6. Disconnect the reservoir-to-pump hose from the pump.
7. Remove the pump.
8. Installation is in the reverse order of removal. Torque the installation bolts to 23 ft. lbs. Adjust the belt tension and bleed the system.

BELT ADJUSTMENT

The belt tension on most components is adjusted by moving the component (power steering pump) within the range of the slotted bracket. Check the belt tension every 12 months or 10,000 miles. Push in on the drive belt about midway between the crankshaft pulley and the driven component. If the belt deflects more than $\frac{9}{16}$" or less than ⅜", adjustment is required.

1. Loosen the adjustment nut and bolt in the slotted bracket. Slightly loosen the pivot bolt.

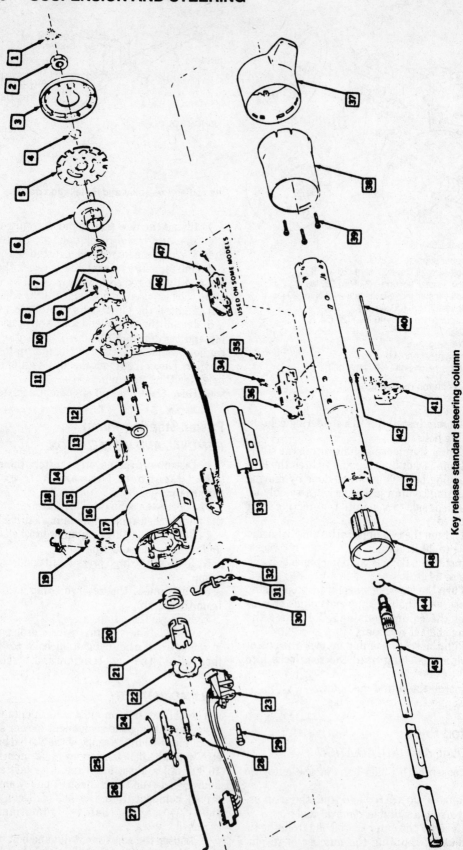

Key release standard steering column

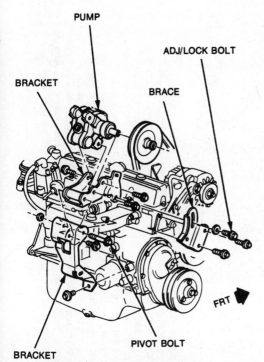

PUMP

ADJ/LOCK BOLT

BRACKET

BRACE

FRT

PIVOT BOLT

BRACKET

Power steering pump removal details

2. Pull (don't pry) the component outward to increase tension. Push inward to reduce tension. Tighten the adjusting nut and bolt and the pivot bolt.

3. Recheck the drive belt tension and readjust if necessary.

SYSTEM BLEEDING

1. Raise the front of the vehicle and support safely. This will minimize steering effort. Fill the power steering pump reservoir with Dexron®II.

2. With the engine off, keep the reservoir full as someone turns the steering wheel from lock to lock several times. Stop with the steering system at one lock.

3. Pull the high tension lead out of the coil. Continue to keep the reservoir full while cranking the engine for 30 seconds at a time (with a one minute rest in between), until fluid level remains constant.

4. Turn the steering wheel to the opposite lock and repeat Step 3.

5. Reconnect the high tension lead, start the engine and allow it to idle. Turn the wheel from lock to lock several times. Note the level of the fluid.

6. Lower the vehicle to the ground. Note the fluid level. Repeat Step 5, stopping with the wheel at the centered position.

7. The fluid level should not have risen more than 0.2″. If it has, repeat Step 6 until the level does not rise appreciably.

Rack and Pinion Unit

REMOVAL AND INSTALLATION

1. From the driver's side, remove the sound insulator.

2. From under the instrument panel, pull the seal assembly down from the steering column and remove the upper pinch bolt from the flexible coupling.

3. Remove the air cleaner and the windshield washer jar.

4. On power steering models: disconnect the pressure line from the steering gear and re-

1. Retainer
2. Hexagon jam nut
3. Shaft lock cover
4. Retaining ring
5. Steering shaft lock
6. Turn signal cancelling cam assy
7. Upper bearing spring
8. Binding head cross recess screw
9. Round washer head screw
10. Switch actuator arm assy
11. Turn signal switch assy
12. Hex washer head tapping screw
13. Thrust washer
14. Buzzer switch assy
15. Buzzer switch retaining clip
16. Lock retaining screw
17. Steering column housing
18. Switch actuator sector assy
19. Steering column lock cylinder set
20. Bearing assy
21. Bearing retaining bushing
22. Upper bearing retainer
23. Pivot & switch assy
24. Spring & bolt assy

25. Rack preload spring
26. Switch actuator rack
27. Switch actuator rod
28. Spring thrust washer
29. Switch actuator pivot pin
30. Wave washer
31. Key release lever
32. Key release spring
33. Wiring protector
34. Dimmer and ignition switch mounting stud
35. Washer head screw
36. Ignition switch assy
37. Floor shift bowl
38. Shift bowl shroud
39. Binding head cross recess screw
40. Dimmer switch actuator rod
41. Dimmer switch assy
42. Hexagon nut
43. Steering column jacket assy
44. Retaining ring
45. Steering shaft assy
46. Hex washer head tapping screw
47. Flat head screw
48. Steering column jacket bushing

Key release standard steering column

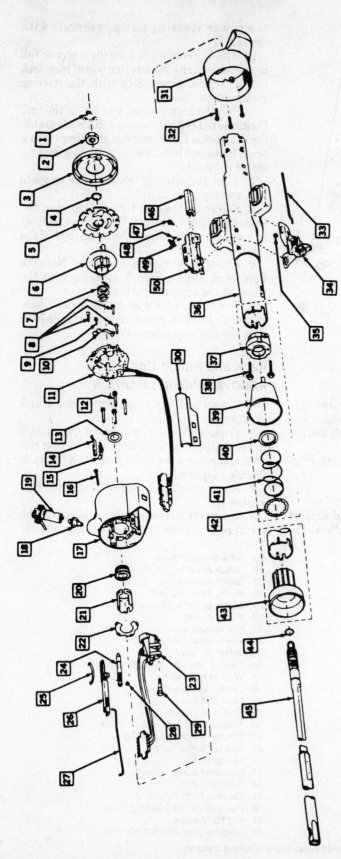

Park lock standard steering column

1. Retainer
2. Hexagon jam nut
3. Shaft lock cover
4. Retaining ring
5. Steering shaft lock
6. Turn signal cancelling cam asm
7. Upper bearing spring
8. Binding head cross recess screw
9. Round washer head screw
10. Switch actuator arm asm
11. Turn signal switch asm
12. Hex washer head tapping screw
13. Thrust washer
14. Buzzer switch asm
15. Buzzer switch retaining clip
16. Lock retaining screw
17. Steering column housing
18. Switch actuator sector
19. Steering column lock cylinder set
20. Bearing asm
21. Bearing retaining bushing
22. Upper bearing retainer
23. Pivot & switch asm
24. Lock bolt
25. Rack preload spring
26. Switch actuator rack
27. Switch actuator rod
28. Spring thrust washer
29. Switch actuator pivot pin
30. Wiring protector
31. Floor shift bowl
32. Binding hd cross recess screw
33. Dimmer switch actuator rod
34. Dimmer switch asm
35. Hexagon nut
36. Steering column jacket asm
37. Adapter & bearing asm
38. Hex washer head tapping screw
39. Bearing retainer
40. Lower bearing seat
41. Lower bearing spring
42. Lower spring retainer
43. Strg. column jacket bushing
44. Retaining ring
45. Steering shaft asm
46. Ign. switch housing asm
47. Washer head screw
48. Pan hd screw
49. Dimr & ign sw mounting stud
50. Ignition switch asm

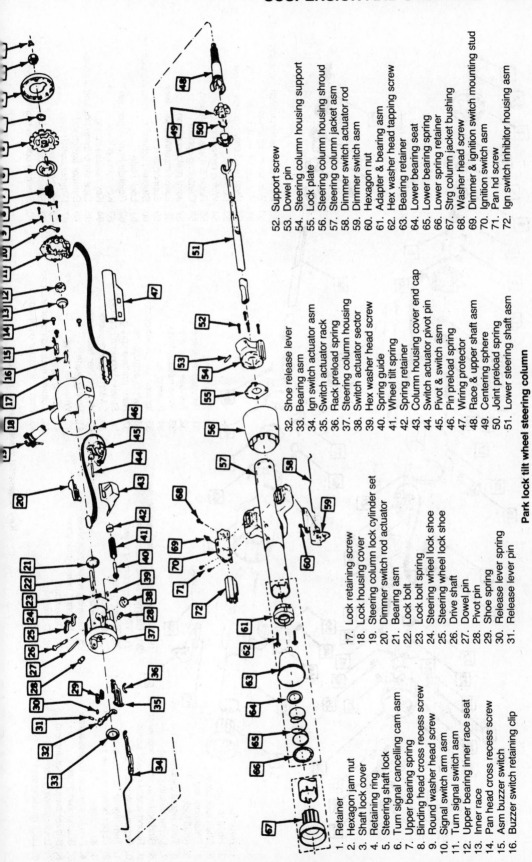

Park lock tilt wheel steering column

1. Retainer
2. Hexagon jam nut
3. Shaft lock cover
4. Retaining ring
5. Steering shaft lock
6. Turn signal cancelling cam asm
7. Upper bearing spring
8. Binding head cross recess screw
9. Round washer head screw
10. Signal switch arm asm
11. Turn signal switch asm
12. Upper bearing inner race seat
13. Inner race
14. Pan head cross recess screw
15. Asm buzzer switch
16. Buzzer switch retaining clip

17. Lock retaining screw
18. Lock housing cover
19. Steering column lock cylinder set
20. Dimmer switch rod actuator
21. Bearing asm
22. Lock bolt
23. Lock bolt spring
24. Steering wheel lock shoe
25. Steering wheel lock shoe
26. Drive shaft
27. Dowel pin
28. Pivot pin
29. Shoe spring
30. Release lever spring
31. Release lever pin

32. Shoe release lever
33. Bearing asm
34. Ign switch actuator asm
35. Switch actuator rack
36. Rack preload spring
37. Steering column housing
38. Switch actuator sector
39. Hex washer head screw
40. Spring guide
41. Wheel tilt spring
42. Spring retainer
43. Column housing cover end cap
44. Switch actuator pivot pin
45. Pivot & switch asm
46. Pin preload spring
47. Wiring protector
48. Race & upper shaft asm
49. Centering sphere
50. Joint preload spring
51. Lower steering shaft asm

52. Support screw
53. Dowel pin
54. Steering column housing support
55. Lock plate
56. Steering column housing shroud
57. Steering column jacket asm
58. Dimmer switch actuator rod
59. Dimmer switch asm
60. Hexagon nut
61. Adapter & bearing asm
62. Hex washer head tapping screw
63. Bearing retainer
64. Lower bearing seat
65. Lower bearing spring
66. Lower spring retainer
67. Strg column jacket bushing
68. Washer head screw
69. Dimmer & ignition switch mounting stud
70. Ignition switch asm
71. Pan hd screw
72. Ign switch inhibitor housing asm

Key release tilt wheel steering column

1. Retainer
2. Hexagon jam nut
3. Shaft lock cover
4. Retaining ring
5. Shaft lock
6. Turn signal cancelling cam assy
7. Upper bearing spring
8. Binding head cross recess screw
9. Round washer head screw
10. Signal switch arm assy
11. Turn signal switch assy
12. Upper bearing inner race seat
13. Inner race
14. Pan head cross recess screw
15. Buzzer switch assy
16. Buzzer switch retaining clip
17. Lock retaining screw
18. Lock housing cover

19. Steering column lock cylinder set
20. Dimmer switch rod actuator
21. Tilt lever opening shield
22. Bearing assy
23. Lock bolt
24. Lock bolt spring
25. Steering wheel lock shoe
26. Steering wheel lock shoe
27. Drive shaft
28. Dowel pin
29. Pivot pin

30. Shoe spring
31. Release lever spring
32. Release lever pin
33. Shoe release lever
34. Bearing assy
35. Ignition switch actuator assy
36. Switch actuator rack
37. Rack preload spring
38. Steering column housing
39. Switch actuator sector
40. Hex washer head screw
41. Spring guide
42. Wheel tilt spring
43. Spring retainer
44. Column housing cover end cap
45. Switch actuator pivot pin

46. Pivot & switch assy
47. Pin preload spring
48. Ignition switch assy

49. Dimmer & ignition switch mounting stud
50. Washer head screw
51. Shroud retaining plate
52. Oval head cross recess screw
53. Dowel pin
54. Wiring protector
55. Race & upper shaft assy
56. Centering sphere
57. Joint preload spring
58. Lower steering shaft assy
59. Support screw
60. Steering column housing support
61. Lock plate
62. Release lever finger pad
63. Key release lever
64. Key release spring
65. Steering column housing shroud
66. Dimmer switch rod
67. Dimmer switch assy
68. Hexagon nut
69. Steering column jacket assy.
70. Steering column jacket bushing

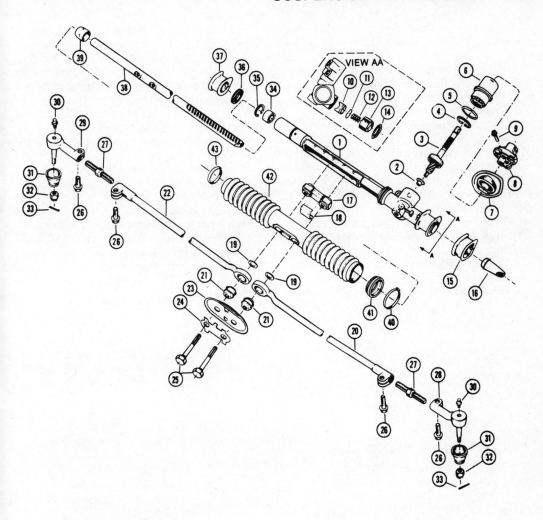

VIEW AA

1—HOUSING, RACK & PINION
2—BEARING ASSY, ROLLER
3—PINION ASSY, BEARING
4—RING, RETAINING
5—DUST SEAL, VISCOUS DAMPER
6—DAMPER ASSY, VISCOUS STRG.
7—SEAL, DASH
8—COUPLING ASSY, FLANGE & STRG.
9—BOLT, PINCH
10—BEARING, RACK
11—SEAL, O-RING
12—SPRING, ADJUSTER
13—PLUG, ADJUSTER
14—NUT, ADJUSTER PLUG LOCK
15—GROMMET, MOUNTING (LH)
16—COVER, HOUSING END
17—GUIDE, RACK
18—GUIDE, BEARING
19—WASHER, CENTER HSG COVER
20—ROD, INNER TIE (LH)
21—BUSHING, INNER PIVOT
22—ROD, INNER TIE (RH)
23—PLATE, BOLT SUPPORT
24—PLATE, LOCK
25—BOLT, INNER TIE ROD

26—BOLT, PINCH
27—ADJUSTER, TIE ROD
28—ROD ASSY, OUTER TIE (LH)
29—ROD ASSY, OUTER TIE (RH)
30—FITTING, LUBRICATION
31—SEAL, TIE ROD
32—NUT, HEX SLOTTED
33—PIN, COTTER
34—BUSHING, RACK
35—RING, INTERNAL RETAINING
36—BUSHING, BOOT RETAINING
37—GROMMET, MOUNTING (RH)
38—RACK, STEERING
39—COVER, HOUSING END
40—CLAMP, BOOT
41—BUSHING, BOOT RETAINING
42—BOOT, RACK & PINION
43—CLAMP, BOOT

Exploded view of the manual rack and pinion steering gear (power similiar)

move the screw securing the pressure line bracket to the cowl. Move the pressure line aside.

5. Raise and support the car on jackstands.

6. Remove both front wheels.

7. Disconnect both tie rods from the struts.

8. Lower the car.

9. Remove the right side rack mounting clamp.

10. Remove the left side rack mounting clamp.

11. Move the gear forward slightly. On power steering models, disconnect the fluid return pipe from the gear.

12. Remove the lower pinch bolt from the flexible coupling and separate the rack from the coupling.

13. Remove the dash seal from the rack assembly.

14. Raise and support the car on jackstands.

15. Remove the splash shield from the inner, left fender.

16. Turn the left knuckle and hub assembly to the full left turn position and remove the rack and pinion assembly through the access hole on the left fender.

17. Installation is the reverse of removal while noting the following points:

a. If the mounting studs backed out during removal, it will be necessary to re-position them prior to rack installation. Double-nut the stud so that it can be torqued to 15 ft. lb.

b. It will be good to have a helper inside the car to guide the flexible coupling onto the stub shaft and onto the steering column.

c. Torque the coupling to stub shaft to 37 ft. lbs. and the coupling to column to 30 ft. lbs. The mounting clamps should be torqued to 28 ft. lb. The tie rod nuts should be torqued to 35 ft. lb.

UNDERSTANDING THE BRAKE SYSTEM

Hydraulic System

A hydraulic system is used to actuate the brakes. The system transports the power required to force the frictional surfaces of the braking system together from the pedal to the individual braking units at each wheel. A hydraulic system is used for three reasons. First, fluid under pressure can be carried to all parts of the automobile by small hoses, some of which are flexible, without taking up a significant amount of room or posing routing problems. Second, liquid is noncompressible; a hydraulic system can transport force without modifying or reducing that force. Third, a great mechanical advantage can be given to the brake pedal end of the system, and the foot pressure required to actuate the brakes can be reduced by making the surface area of the master cylinder pistons smaller than that of any of the pistons in the wheel cylinders or calipers.

The master cylinder consists of a fluid reservoir and a double cylinder and piston assembly. Double type master cylinders are designed to separate the front and rear braking systems hydraulically in case of a leak.

Steel lines carry the brake fluid to a point on the vehicle's frame near each of the vehicle's wheels. The fluid is then carried to the slave cylinders by flexible tubes in order to allow for suspension and steering movements.

In drum brake systems, the slave cylinders are called wheel cylinders. Each wheel cylinder contains two pistons, one at either end, which push outward in opposite directions. In disc brake systems, the slave cylinders are part of the calipers. One or four cylinders are used to force the brake pads against the disc, but all cylinders contain one piston only. All slave cylinder pistons employ some type of seal, usually made of rubber, to minimize the leakage of fluid around the piston. A rubber dust boot seals the outer end of the cylinder against dust and dirt. The boot fits around the outer end of the piston on disc brake calipers, and around the brake actuating rod on wheel cylinders.

The hydraulic system operates as follows: When at rest, the entire system, from the pistons in the master cylinder to those in the wheel cylinders or calipers, is full of brake fluid. Upon application of the brake pedal, fluid trapped in front of the master cylinder pistons is forced through the lines to the slave cylinders. Here, it forces the pistons outward, in the case of drum brakes, and inward toward the disc, in the case of disc brakes. The motion of the pistons is opposed by return springs mounted outside the cylinders in drum brakes, and by internal springs or spring seals in disc brakes.

Upon release of the brake pedal, a spring located inside the master cylinder immediately returns the master cylinder pistons to the normal position. The pistons contain check valves and the master cylinder has compensating ports drilled in it. These are uncovered as the pistons reach their normal position. The piston check valves allow fluid to flow toward the wheel cylinders or calipers as the pistons withdraw. Then, as the return springs force the brake pads or shoes into the released position, the excess fluid returns to the master cylinder fluid reservoir through the compensation ports. It is during the time the pedal is in the released position that any fluid that has leaked out of the system will be replaced through the compensating ports.

Dual circuit master cylinders employ two pistons, located one behind the other, in the same cylinder. The primary piston is actuated directly by mechanical linkage from the brake pedal. The secondary piston is actuated by fluid trapped between the two pistons. If a leak develops in front of the secondary piston, it moves forward until it bottoms against the front of the master cylinder, and the fluid trapped between the pistons will operate the rear brakes. If the rear brakes develop a leak, the primary piston will move forward until direct contact with the secondary piston takes place, and it will force the secondary piston to actuate the front brakes. In either case, the brake pedal moves farther when the brakes are applied, and less braking power is available.

All dual-circuit systems use a distributor switch to warn the driver when only half of the brake system is operational. This switch is located in a valve body which is mounted on the master cylinder. A hydraulic piston receives pressure from both circuits, each circuit's pressure being applied to one end of the piston. When the pressures are in balance, the piston remains stationary. When one circuit has a leak, however, the greater pressure in that circuit during application of the brakes will push the piston to one side, closing the distributor switch and activating the brake warning light.

In disc brake systems, this valve body also contains a metering valve and, in some cases, a proportioning valve. The metering valve keeps pressure from traveling to the disc brakes on the front wheels until the brake shoes on the rear wheels have contacted the drums, ensuring that the front brakes will never be used alone. The proportioning valve throttles the pressure to the rear brakes so as to avoid rear wheel lock-up during very hard braking.

These valves may be tested by removing the lines to the front and rear brake systems and installing special brake pressure testing gauges. Front and rear system pressures are then compared as the pedal is gradually depressed. Specifications vary with the manufacturer and design of the brake system.

Brake system warning lights may be tested by depressing the brake pedal and holding it while opening one of the wheel cylinder bleeder screws. If this does not cause the light to go on, substitute a new lamp, make continuity checks, and, finally, replace the switch as necessary.

The hydraulic system may be checked for leaks by applying pressure to the pedal gradually and steadily. If the pedal sinks very slowly to the floor, the system has a leak. This is not to be confused with a springy or spongy feel due to the compression of air within the lines. If the system leaks, there will be a gradual change in the position of the pedal with a constant pressure.

Check for leaks along all lines and at wheel cylinders. If no external leaks are apparent, the problem is inside the master cylinder.

Disc Brakes

Instead of the traditional expanding brakes that press outward against a circular drum, disc brake systems utilize a cast iron disc with brake pads positioned on either side of it. Braking effect is achieved in a manner similar to the way you would squeeze a spinning phonograph record between your fingers. The disc (rotor) is a one-piece casting with cooling fins between the two braking surfaces. This enables air to circulate between the braking surfaces making them less sensitive to heat buildup and more resistant to fade. Dirt and water do not affect braking action since contaminants are thrown off by the centrifugal action of the rotor or scraped off by the pads. Also, the equal clamping action of the two brake pads tends to ensure uniform, straightline stops. All disc brakes are inherently self-adjusting.

Drum Brakes

Drum brakes employ two brake shoes mounted on a stationary backing plate. These shoes are positioned inside a circular cast iron drum which rotates with the wheel assembly. The shoes are held in place by springs; this allows them to slide toward the drums (when they are applied) while keeping the linings and drums in alignment. The shoes are actuated by a wheel cylinder which is mounted at the top of the backing plate. When the brakes are applied, hydraulic pressure forces the wheel cylinder's two actuating links outward. Since these links bear directly against the top of the brake shoes, the tops of the shoes are then forced outward against the inner side of the drum. This action forces the bottoms of the two shoes to contact the brake drum by rotating the entire assembly slightly (known as servo action). When pressure within the wheel cylinder is relaxed, return springs pull the shoes back away from the drum.

The drum brakes are designed to self-adjust during application when the car is moving in reverse. This motion causes both shoes to rotate very slightly with the drum, rocking an adjusting lever, thereby causing rotation of the adjusting screw by means of an actuating lever.

Power Brake Boosters

Power brakes operate just as standard brake systems except in the actuation of the master cylinder pistons. A vacuum diaphragm is located on the front of the master cylinder and assists the driver in applying the brakes, reducing both the effort and travel he must put into moving the brake pedal.

The vacuum diaphragm housing is connected to the intake manifold by a vacuum hose. A check valve is placed at the point where the hose enters the diaphragm housing, so that during periods of low manifold vacuum brake assist vacuum will not be lost.

Depressing the brake pedal closes off the vacuum source and allows atmospheric pressure to enter on one side of the diaphragm. This causes the master cylinder pistons to move and apply the brakes. When the brake pedal is released, vacuum is applied to both sides of the diaphragm, and return spings return the diaphragm and master cylinder pistons to the released position. If the vacuum fails, the brake pedal rod will butt against the end of the master cylinder actuating rod, and direct mechanical application will occur as the pedal is depressed.

The hydraulic and mechanical problems that apply to conventional brake systems also apply to power brakes, and should be checked for if the following tests do not reveal the problem.

Test for a system vacuum leak as described below:

1. Operate the engine at idle with the transaxle in Neutral without touching the brake pedal for at least one minute.

2. Turn off the engine, and wait one minute.

3. Test for the presence of assist vacuum by depressing the brake pedal and releasing it several times. Light application will produce less and less pedal travel, if vacuum was present. If there is no vacuum, air is leaking into the system somewhere.

4. Test for system operation as follows:

    a. Pump the brake pedal (with engine off) until the supply vacuum is entirely gone.

    b. Put a light, steady pressure on the pedal.

    c. Start the engine, and operate it at idle with the transaxle in Neutral. If the system is operating, the brake pedal should fall toward the floor if constant pressure is maintained on the pedal.

Power brake systems may be tested for hydraulic leaks just as ordinary systems are tested, except that the engine should be idling with the transaxle in Neutral throughout the test.

BRAKE SYSTEM

The J-cars have a diagonally split hydraulic system. This differs from conventional practice in that the left front and right rear brakes are on one hydraulic circuit, and the right front and left rear are on the other.

A diagonally split system necessitates the use of a special master cylinder design. The J-car master cylinder incorporates the functions of a standard tandem master cylinder, plus a warning light switch and proportioning valves (4-cyl-inder engines only). On the V6 models the proportioning valve and the brake pressure differential warning switch is located to the left frame rail below the master cylinder. Additionally, the master cylinder is designed with a quick take-up feature which provides a large volume of fluid to the brakes at low pressure when the brakes are initially applied. The low pressure fluid acts to quickly fill the large displacement requirements of the system.

The front disc brakes are single piston sliding caliper units. Fluid pressure acts equally against the piston and the bottom of the piston bore in the caliper. This forces the piston outward until the pad contacts the rotor. The force on the caliper bore forces the caliper to slide over, carrying the other pad into contact with the other side of the rotor. The disc brakes are self-adjusting.

Rear drum brakes are conventional duo-servo units. A dual piston wheel cylinder, mounted to the top of the backing plate, actuates both brake shoes. Wheel cylinder force to the shoes is supplemented by the tendency of the shoes to wrap into the drum (servo action). An actuating link, pivot and lever serve to automatically engage the adjuster as the brakes are applied when the car is moving in reverse. Provisions for manual adjustment are also provided. The rear brakes also serve as the parking brakes; linkage is mechanical.

Vacuum boost is a standard. The booster is a conventional tandem vacuum unit.

ADJUSTMENT

Disc Brakes

The front disc brakes are inherently self-adjusting. No adjustments are either necessary or possible.

Drum Brakes

The drum brakes are designed to self-adjust when applied with the car moving in reverse. However, they can also be adjusted manually. This manual adjustment should also be performed whenever the linings are replaced.

1. Use a punch to knock out the stamped area on the brake drum. If this is done with the drum installed on the car, the drum must then be removed to clean out all metal pieces. After adjustments are complete, obtain a hole cover from your dealer (Part no. 4874119 or the equivalent) to prevent entry of dirt and water into the brakes.

2. Use an awl, a screwdriver, or an adjusting tool especially made for the purpose to turn the brake adjusting screw star wheel. Expand the shoes until the drum can just barely be turned by hand.

3. Back off the adjusting screw 30 notches. If the shoes still are dragging lightly, back off the adjusting screw one or two additional notches. If the brakes still drag, the parking brake adjustment is incorrect or the parking brake is applied. Fix and start over.

4. Install the hole cover into the drum.

5. Check the parking brake adjustment.

On some models, no marked area or stamped area is present on the drum. In this case, a hole must be drilled in the backing plate:

1. All backing plates have two round flat areas in the lower half through which the parking brake cable is installed. Drill a ½″ hole into the round flat area on the backing plate opposite the parking brake cable. This will allow access to the star wheel.

2. After drilling the hole, remove the drum and remove all metal particles. Install a hole plug (Part no. 4874119 or the equivalent) to prevent the entry of water or dirt.

HYDRAULIC SYSTEM

Master Cylinder

REMOVAL AND INSTALLATION

1. Unplug the electrical connector from the master cylinder.

2. Place a number of cloths or a container under the master cylinder to catch the brake fluid. Disconnect the brake tubes from the master cylinder; use a flare nut wrench if one is available. Tape over open ends of the tubes.

Warning: *Brake fluid eats paint. Wipe up any spilled fluid immediately, then flush the area with clear water.*

3. Remove the two nuts attaching the master cylinder to the booster or firewall.

4. Remove the master cylinder.

5. To install, attach the master cylinder to the booster with the nuts. Torque to 22-30 ft. lbs. (30-45 Nm.).

6. Remove the tape from the lines and connect to the master cylinder. Torque to 10-15 ft. lbs. (13-20 Nm.). Connect the electrical lead.

7. Bleed the brakes.

OVERHAUL

This is a tedious, time-consuming job. You can save yourself a lot of trouble by buying a rebuilt master cylinder from your dealer or parts supply house. The small difference in price between a rebuilding kit and a rebuilt part usually makes it more economical, in terms of time and work, to buy the rebuilt part.

1. Remove the master cylinder.

2. Remove the reservoir cover and drain the fluid.

3. Unbolt the proportioners and failure warning switch from the side of the master cylinder body. Discard the O-rings found under the proportioners. Use new ones on installation. There may or may not be an O-ring under the original equipment failure warning switch. If there is, discard it. In either case, use an O-ring upon assembly.

4. Clamp the master cylinder body in a vise, taking care not to crush it. Depress the primary piston with a wooden dowel and remove the lock ring with a pair of snapring pliers.

5. The primary and secondary pistons can be removed by applying compressed air into one of the outlets at the end of the cylinder and plugging the other three outlets. The primary piston must be replaced as an assembly if the seals are bad. The secondary piston seals are replaceable. Install these new seals with the lips facing outwards.

6. Inspect the bore for corrosion. If any corrosion is evident, the master cylinder body must be replaced. Do not attempt to polish the bore with crocus cloth, sandpaper, or anything else. The body is aluminum; polishing the bore won't work.

7. To remove the failure warning switch piston assembly, remove the allen head plug from the end of the bore and withdraw the assembly with a pair of needlenose pliers. The switch piston assembly seals are replaceable.

8. The reservoir can be removed from the master cylinder body if necessary. Clamp the body in a vise by its mounting flange. Use a prey bar to remove the reservoir. If the reservoir is removed, remove the reservoir grommets and discard them. The quick takeup valves under the grommets are accessible after the retaining snaprings are removed. Use snapring pliers; no other tool will work.

9. Clean all parts in denatured alcohol and allow to air dry. Do not use anything else to clean, and do not wipe dry with a rag, which will leave bits of lint behind. Inspect all parts for corrosion or wear. Generally, it is best to replace all rubber parts whenever the master cylinder is disassembled, and replace any metal part which shows any sign whatsoever of wear or corrosion.

10. Lubricate all parts with clean brake fluid before assembly.

11. Install the quick take-up valves into the master cylinder body and secure with the snaprings. Make sure the snaprings are properly seated in their grooves. Lubricate the new reservoir grommets with clean brake fluid and press them into the master cylinder.

12. Install the reservoir into the grommets by placing the reservoir on its lid and pressing the master cylinder body down onto it with a rocking motion.

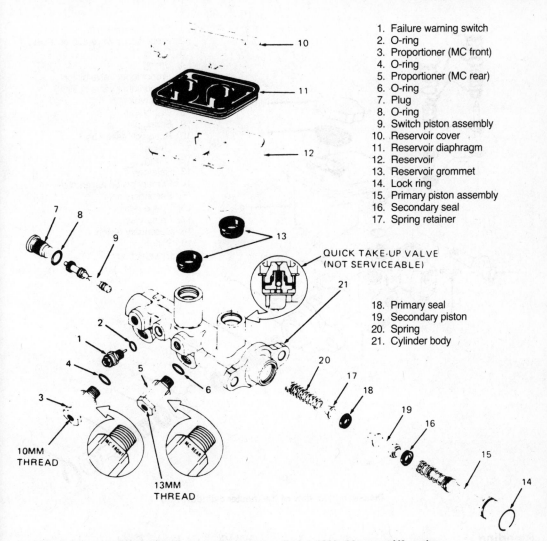

1. Failure warning switch
2. O-ring
3. Proportioner (MC front)
4. O-ring
5. Proportioner (MC rear)
6. O-ring
7. Plug
8. O-ring
9. Switch piston assembly
10. Reservoir cover
11. Reservoir diaphragm
12. Reservoir
13. Reservoir grommet
14. Lock ring
15. Primary piston assembly
16. Secondary seal
17. Spring retainer

QUICK TAKE-UP VALVE
(NOT SERVICEABLE)

18. Primary seal
19. Secondary piston
20. Spring
21. Cylinder body

10MM THREAD

13MM THREAD

Disassembled view of the master cylinder, 1982–86 except V6 engine

13. Lubricate the switch piston assembly with clean brake fluid. Install new O-rings and retainers on the piston. Install the piston assembly into the master cylinder and secure with the plug, using a new O-ring on the plug. Torque is 40-140 in. lbs. (5-16 Nm.).

14. Assemble the new secondary piston seals onto the piston. Lubricate the parts with clean brake fluid, then install the spring, spring retainer and secondary piston into the cylinder. Install the primary piston, depress, and install the lock ring.

15. Install new O-rings on the proportioners and the failure warning switch. Install the proportioners and torque to 18-30 ft. lbs. (25-40 Nm.). Install the failure warning switch and torque to 15-50 in. lbs. (2-6 Nm.).

16. Clamp the master cylinder body upright into a vise by one of the mounting flanges. Fill the reservoir with fresh brake fluid. Pump the piston with a dowel until fluid squirts from the outlet ports. Continue pumping until the expelled fluid is free of air bubbles.

17. Install the master cylinder, and bleed the brakes. Check the brake system for proper operation. Do not move the car until a hard brake pedal is obtained and the brake system has been thoroughly checked for soundness.

Proportioning Valves and Failure Warning Switch

These parts are installed in the master cylinder body on all models except the V6 engine. On these models the proportioning valve and the brake pressure differential warning switch is located to the left frame rail below the master cylinder. Refer to the master cylinder overhaul for replacement instructions for the four cylinder models.

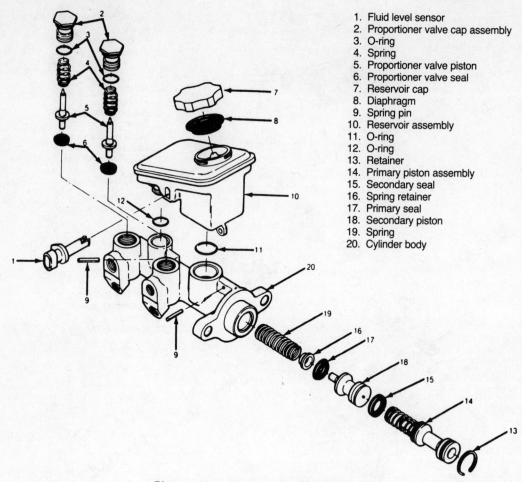

1. Fluid level sensor
2. Proportioner valve cap assembly
3. O-ring
4. Spring
5. Proportioner valve piston
6. Proportioner valve seal
7. Reservoir cap
8. Diaphragm
9. Spring pin
10. Reservoir assembly
11. O-ring
12. O-ring
13. Retainer
14. Primary piston assembly
15. Secondary seal
16. Spring retainer
17. Primary seal
18. Secondary piston
19. Spring
20. Cylinder body

Disassembled view of the master cylinder, 1987

Bleeding

The purpose of bleeding the brakes is to expel air trapped in the hydraulic system. The system must be bled whenever the pedal feels spongy, indicating that compressible air has entered the system. It must also be bled whenever the system has been opened or repaired. You will need a helper for this job.

CAUTION: *Never reuse brake fluid which has been bled from the brake system.*

1. The sequence for bleeding is right rear, left front, left rear and right front. If the car has power brakes, remove the vacuum by applying the brakes several times. Do not run the engine while bleeding the brakes.

2. Clean all the bleeder screws. You may want to give each one a shot of penetrating solvent to loosen it up; seizure is a common problem with bleeder screws, which then break off, sometimes requiring replacement of the part to which they are attached.

3. Fill the master cylinder with DOT 3 brake fluid.

WARNING: *Brake fluid absorbs moisture from the air. Don't leave the master cylinder or the fluid container uncovered any longer than necessary. Be careful handling the fluid; it eats paint.*

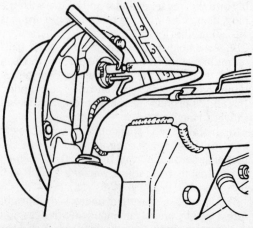

Bleeding the brakes

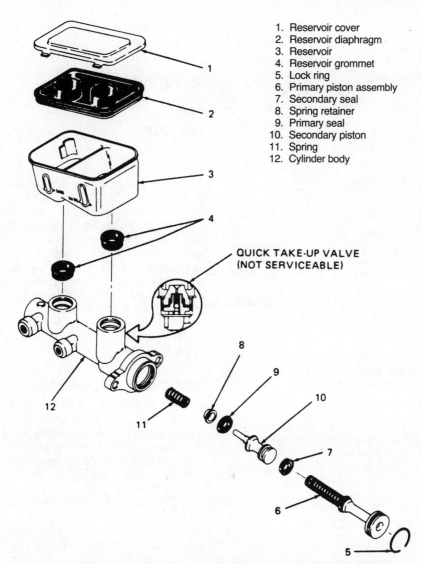

1. Reservoir cover
2. Reservoir diaphragm
3. Reservoir
4. Reservoir grommet
5. Lock ring
6. Primary piston assembly
7. Secondary seal
8. Spring retainer
9. Primary seal
10. Secondary piston
11. Spring
12. Cylinder body

QUICK TAKE-UP VALVE
(NOT SERVICEABLE)

Disassembled view of the master cylinder, 1984–86 V6 engine

Check the level of the fluid often when bleeding, and refill the reservoirs as necessary. Don't let them run dry, or you will have to repeat the process.

4. Attach a length of clear vinyl tubing to the bleeder screw on the wheel cylinder. Insert the other end of the tube into a clear, clean jar half filled with brake fluid.

5. Have your assistant slowly depress the brake pedal. As this is done, open the bleeder screw 1/3-1/2 of a turn, and allow the fluid to run through the tube. Then close the bleeder screw before the pedal reaches the end of its travel. Have your assistant slowly release the pedal. Repeat this process until no air bubbles appear in the expelled fluid.

6. Repeat the procedure on the other three

brakes, checking the level of fluid in the master cylinder reservoir often.

After you're done, there should be no sponginess in the brake pedal feel. If there is, either there is still air in the line, in which case the process should be repeated, or there is a leak somewhere, which of course must be corrected before the car is moved.

Vacuum Booster
REMOVAL AND INSTALLATION

1. Remove the master cylinder from the booster. It is not necessary to disconnect the lines from the master cylinder. Just move the cylinder aside.

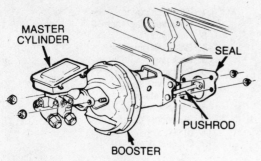

Vacuum booster mounting

2. Disconnect the vacuum booster pushrod from the brake pedal inside the car. It is retained by a bolt. A spring washer lives under the bolt head, and a flat washer goes on the other side of the pushrod eye, next to the pedal arm.

3. Remove the four attaching nuts from inside the car. Remove the booster.

4. Install the booster on the firewall. Tighten the mounting nuts to 22-33 ft. lbs. (30-45 Nm.).

5. Connect the pushrod to the brake pedal.

6. Install the master cylinder. Mounting torque is 22-33 ft. lbs. (30-45 Nm).

OVERHAUL

This job is not difficult, but requires a number of special tools which are expensive, especially if they're to be used only once. Generally, it's better to buy a new or rebuilt vacuum booster and install it yourself.

Brake Hose

REMOVAL AND INSTALLATION

Front

1. Raise and support the car safely.
2. Remove the tire and wheel .
3. Clean the dirt from both hose end fittings.
4. Remove the brake pipe from the hose.
5. Remove the brake hose from the caliper and discard the two copper gaskets on either side of the fitting block.
6. Install the hose using new copper gaskets.
7. Check that the hose doesn't rub in extreme left and right turn conditions.
8. Fill and maintain the brake fluid level in the reservoir and bleed the brake system.

Rear

1. Raise and support the car safely.
2. Clean the dirt from both hose end fittings.
3. With the aid of a backup wrench, disconnect the brake pipe fitting on both ends of the brake hose.
4. Remove the retaining clips from both ends.
5. After installing the hose fill and maintain

the brake fluid level in the reservoir and bleed the brake system.

FRONT DISC BRAKES

Pads

INSPECTION

The pad thickness should be inspected every time that the tires are removed for rotation. The outer pad an be checked by looking in at each end, which is the point at which the highest rate of wear occurs. The inner pad can be checked by looking down through the inspection hole in the top of the caliper. If the thickness of the pad is worn to within $\frac{1}{32}$" of the rivet at either end of the pad, all the pads should be replaced. This is the factory recommended measurement; your state's automobile inspection laws may not agree with this.

NOTE: *Always replace all pads on both front wheels at the same time. Failure to do so will result in uneven braking action and premature wear.*

REMOVAL AND INSTALLATION

CAUTION: *Brake shoes contain asbestos, which has been determined to be a cancer causing agent. Never clean the brake surfaces with compressed air! Avoid inhaling any dust from any brake surface! When cleaning brake surfaces, use a commercially available brake cleaning fluid.*

1. Siphon ⅔ of the brake fluid from the master cylinder reservoir. Loosen the wheel lug nuts and raise the car. Remove the wheel.

2. Position a C-clamp across the caliper so

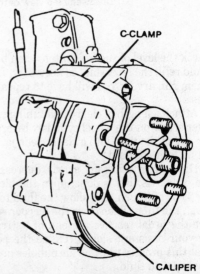

Install a C-clamp to retract the disc brake pads

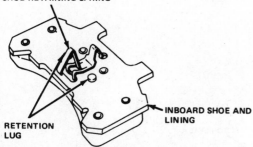

Install the retaining spring on the inboard pad

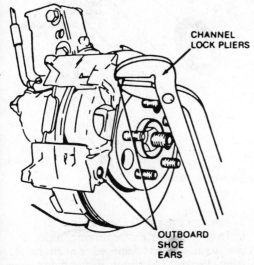

Bend the outboard pad ears into place with a large pair of slip-joint pliers

that it presses on the pads and tighten it until the caliper piston bottoms in its bore.

NOTE: *If you haven't removed some brake fluid from the master cylinder, it will overflow when the piston is retracted.*

3. Remove the C-clamp.

4. Remove the allen head caliper mounting bolts. Inspect the bolts for corrosion, and replace as necessary.

5. Remove the caliper from the steering knuckle and suspend it from the body of the car with a length of wire. Do not allow the caliper to hang by its hose.

6. Remove the pad retaining springs and remove the pads from the caliper.

7. Remove the plastic sleeves and the rubber bushings from the mounting bolt holes.

8. Install new sleeves and bushings. Lubricate the sleeves with a light coating of silicone grease before installation. These parts must always be replaced when the pads are replaced. The parts are usually included in the pad replacement kits.

NOTE: *On 1987-88 models the mounting bolt and sleeve comes as an assembly. Lubricate in the same manner.*

9. Install the outboard pad into the caliper.

10. Install the retainer spring on the inboard pad. A new spring should be included in the pad replacement.

11. Install the new inboard pad into the caliper. The retention lugs fit into the piston.

12. Use a large pair of slip joint pliers to bend the outer pad ears down over the caliper.

13. Install the caliper onto the steering knuckle. Tighten the mounting bolts to 21-35 ft. lbs. (28-47 Nm.). Install the wheel and lower the car. Fill the master cylinder to its proper level with fresh brake fluid meeting DOT 3 specifications. Since the brake hose wasn't disconnected, it isn't really necessary to bleed the brakes, although most mechanics do this as a matter of course.

Caliper

REMOVAL AND INSTALLATION

CAUTION: *Brake shoes contain asbestos, which has been determined to be a cancer causing agent. Never clean the brake surfaces with compressed air! Avoid inhaling any dust from any brake surface! When cleaning brake surfaces, use a commercially available brake cleaning fluid.*

1. Follow Steps 1, 2 and 3 of the pad replacement procedure.

2. Before removing the caliper mounting bolts, remove the bolt holding the brake hose to the caliper.

3. Remove the allen head caliper mounting bolts. Inspect them for corrosion and replace them if necessary.

4. With the pads installed as outlined in pad replacement, install the caliper and mounting bolts and torque to 21-35 ft. lbs. (28-47 Nm.). The brake hose fitting should be tightened to 18-30 ft. lbs. (24-40 Nm.).

OVERHAUL

1. Remove the caliper.

2. Remove the pads.

3. Place some cloths or a slat of wood in front of the piston. Remove the piston by applying compressed air to the fluid inlet fitting. Use just enough air pressure to ease the piston from the bore.

CAUTION: *Do not try to catch the piston with your fingers, which can result in serious injury.*

4. Remove the piston boot with a screwdriver, working carefully so that the piston bore is not scratched.

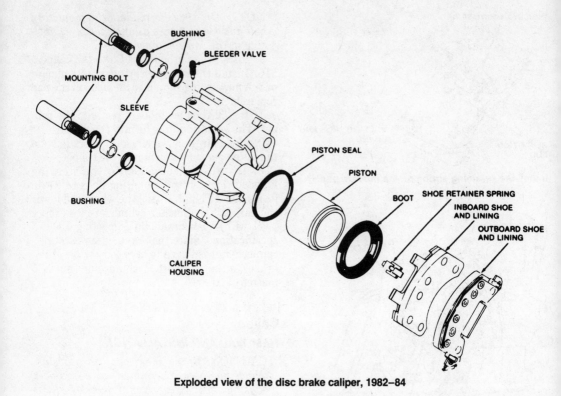

Exploded view of the disc brake caliper, 1982–84

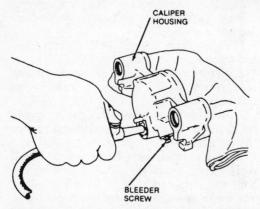

Use air pressure to remove the piston from the bore

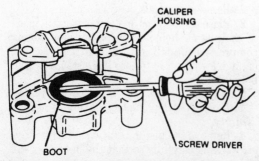

Remove the piston boot with a screwdriver

5. Remove the bleeder screw.

6. Inspect the piston for scoring, nicks, corrosion, wear, etc., and damaged or worn chrome plating. Replace the piston if any defects are found.

7. Remove the piston seal from the caliper bore groove using a piece of pointed wood or plastic. Do not use a screwdriver, which will damage the bore. Inspect the caliper bore for nicks, corrosion, and so on. Very light wear can be cleaned up with crocus cloth. Use finger pressure to rub the crocus cloth around the circumference of the bore; do not slide it in and out. More extensive wear or corrosion warrants replacement of the part.

8. Clean any parts which are to be reused in denatured alcohol. Dry them with compressed air or allow to air dry. Don't wipe the parts dry with a cloth, which will leave behind bits of lint.

9. Lubricate the new seal, provided in the repair kit, with clean brake fluid. Install the seal in its groove, making sure it is fully seated and not twisted.

10. Install the new dust boot on the piston. Lubricate the bore of the caliper with clean brake fluid and insert the piston into its bore. Position the boot in the caliper housing and seat with a seal driver of the appropriate size, or G.M. tool no. J-29077.

11. Install the bleeder screw, tightening to 80-140 in. lbs. (9-16 Nm.). Do not overtighten.

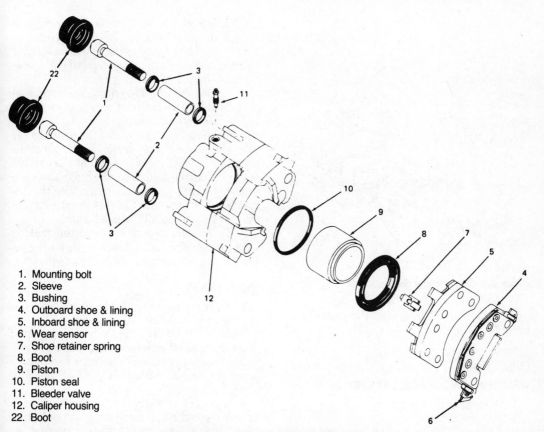

1. Mounting bolt
2. Sleeve
3. Bushing
4. Outboard shoe & lining
5. Inboard shoe & lining
6. Wear sensor
7. Shoe retainer spring
8. Boot
9. Piston
10. Piston seal
11. Bleeder valve
12. Caliper housing
22. Boot

Exploded view of the disc brake caliper, 1985–86

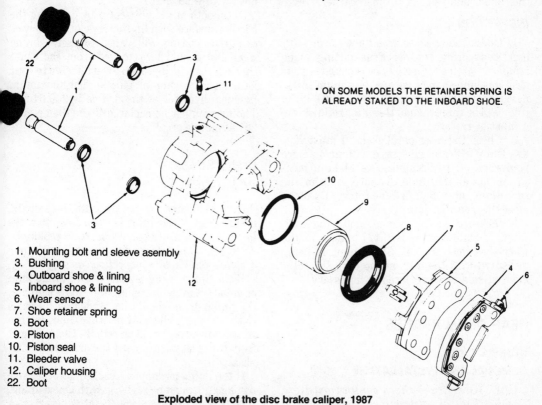

* ON SOME MODELS THE RETAINER SPRING IS
ALREADY STAKED TO THE INBOARD SHOE.

1. Mounting bolt and sleeve asembly
3. Bushing
4. Outboard shoe & lining
5. Inboard shoe & lining
6. Wear sensor
7. Shoe retainer spring
8. Boot
9. Piston
10. Piston seal
11. Bleeder valve
12. Caliper housing
22. Boot

Exploded view of the disc brake caliper, 1987

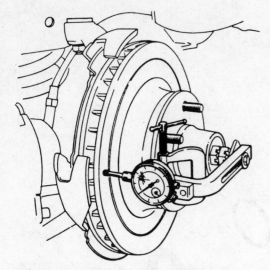

Check the runout with a dial indicator

12. Install the pads, install the caliper, and bleed the brakes.

Disc (Rotor)

REMOVAL AND INSTALLATION

1. Remove the caliper.
2. Remove the rotor.
3. To install, reposition the rotor and install the caliper and pads as outlined earlier.

INSPECTION

1. Check the rotor surface for wear or scoring. Deep scoring, grooves or rust pitting can be removed by refacing, a job to be referred to your local machine shop or garage. Minimum thickness is stamped on the rotor (21.08 mm). If the rotor will be thinner than this after refinishing, it must be replaced.
2. Check the rotor parallelism; it must vary less thn 0.013 mm measured at four or more points around the circumference. Make all measurements at the same distance in from the edge of the rotor. Refinish the rotor if it fails to meet this specification.
3. Measure the disc runout with a dial indicator. If runout exceeds 0.127 mm, and the wheel bearings are OK (if runnout is being measured with the disc on the car), the rotor must be refaced or replaced as necessary.

REAR DRUM BRAKES

Brake Drums

REMOVAL AND INSTALLATION

CAUTION: *Brake shoes contain asbestos, which has been determined to be a cancer causing agent. Never clean the brake surfaces with compressed air! Avoid inhaling any dust from any brake surface! When cleaning brake surfaces, use a commercially available brake cleaning fluid.*

1. Loosen the wheel lug nuts. Raise and support the car. Mark the relationship of the wheel to the axle and remove the wheel.
2. Mark the relationship of the drum to the axle and remove the drum. If it cannot be slipped off easily, check to see that the parking brake is fully released. If so, the brake shoes are probably locked against the drum. See the Adjustment section earlier in this chapter for details on how to back off the adjuster.
3. To install, reposition the drum making sure to align the matchmarks made during removal. Lug nut torque is 102 ft. lbs. (140 Nm.).

INSPECTION

1. After removing the brake drum, wipe out the accumulated dust with a damp cloth.
CAUTION: *Do not blow the brake dust out of the drums with compressed air or lungpower. Brake linings contain asbestos, a known cancer causing substance. Dispose of the cloth used to clean the parts after use.*
2. Inspect the drums for cracks, deep grooves, roughness, scoring, or out-of-roundness. Replace any drum which is cracked; do not try to weld it up.
3. Smooth any slight scores by polishing the friction surface with fine emery cloth. Heavy or extensive scoring will cause excessive lining wear and should be removed from the drum through resurfacing, a job to be referred to your local machine shop or garage. The maximum finished diameter of the drums is 200.64mm. The drum must be replaced if the diameter is 201.40mm or greater.

Brake Shoes
INSPECTION

After removing the brake drum, inspect the brake shoes. If the lining is worn down to within $1/32''$ of a rivet, the shoes must be replaced.
NOTE: *This figure may disagree with your state's automobile inspection laws.*
If the brake lining is soaked with brake fluid or grease, it must be replaced. If this is the case, the brake drum should be sanded with crocus cloth to remove all traces of brake fluid, and the wheel cylinders should be rebuilt. Clean all grit from the friction surface of the drum before replacing it.
If the lining is chipped, cracked, or otherwise damaged, it must be replaced with a new lining.
NOTE: *Always replace the brake linings in*

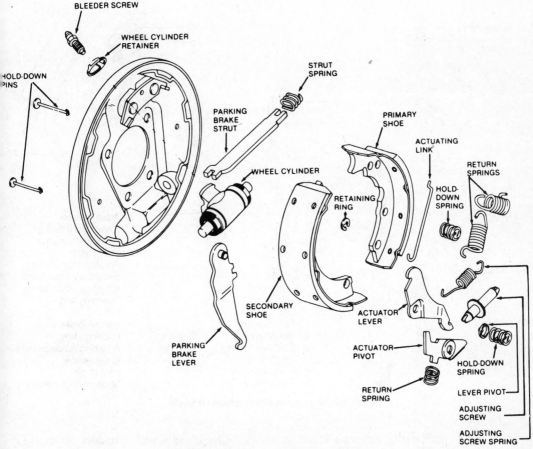

Exploded view of the drum brakes, 1982–84

sets of two on both ends of the axle. Never re-place just one shoe, or both shoes on one side.

Check the condition of the shoes, retracting springs, and holddown springs for signs of over-heating. If the shoes or springs have a slight blue color, this indicates overheating and re-placement of the shoes and springs is recom-mended. The wheel cylinders should be rebuilt as a precaution against future problems.

REMOVAL AND INSTALLATION

CAUTION: *Brake shoes contain asbestos, which has been determined to be a cancer causing agent. Never clean the brake surfaces with compressed air! Avoid inhaling any dust from any brake surface! When cleaning brake surfaces, use a commercially available brake cleaning fluid.*

1. Loosen the lug nuts on the wheel to be ser-viced, raise and support the car, and remove the wheel and brake drum.

NOTE: *It is not really necessary to remove the hub and wheel bearing assembly from the axle, but it does make the job easier. If you can*

work with the hub and bearing assembly in place, skip down to Step 3.

2. Remove the four hub and bearing assem-bly retaining bolts and remove the assembly from the axle.

3. Remove the return springs from the shoes with a pair of needle nose pliers. There are also special brake spring pliers for this job.

4. Remove the hold down springs by gripping them with a pair of pliers, then pressing down and turning 90 degrees. There are special tools to grab and turn these parts, but pliers work fairly well.

5. Remove the shoe holddown pins from be-hind the brake backing plate. They will simply slide out once the holddown spring tension is relieved.

6. Lift up the actuator lever for the self-ad-justing mechanism and remove the actuating link. Remove the actuator lever, pivot, and the pivot return spring.

7. Spread the shoes apart to clear the wheel cylinder pistons and remove the parking brake strut and spring.

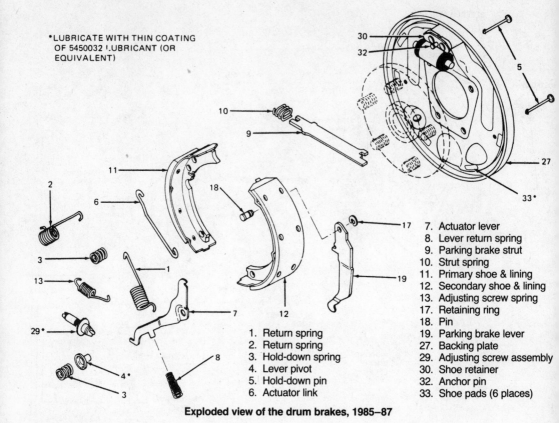

*LUBRICATE WITH THIN COATING
OF 5450032 LUBRICANT (OR
EQUIVALENT)

1. Return spring
2. Return spring
3. Hold-down spring
4. Lever pivot
5. Hold-down pin
6. Actuator link

7. Actuator lever
8. Lever return spring
9. Parking brake strut
10. Strut spring
11. Primary shoe & lining
12. Secondary shoe & lining
13. Adjusting screw spring
17. Retaining ring
18. Pin
19. Parking brake lever
27. Backing plate
29. Adjusting screw assembly
30. Shoe retainer
32. Anchor pin
33. Shoe pads (6 places)

Exploded view of the drum brakes, 1985–87

8. If the hub and bearing assembly is still in place, spread the shoes far enough apart to clear it.

9. Disconnect the parking brake cable from the lever. Remove the shoes, still connected by their adjusting screw spring, from the car.

10. With the shoes removed, note the position of the adjusting spring and remove the spring and adjusting screw.

11. Remove the C-clip from the parking brake lever and remove the lever from the secondary shoe.

12. Use a damp cloth to remove all dirt and dust from the backing plate and brake parts. See the warning about brake dust in the drum removal procedure.

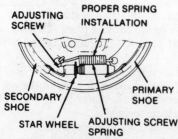

Proper spring installation is with the coils over the adjuster, not the star wheel

13. Check the wheel cylinders by carefully pulling the lower edges of the wheel cylinder boots away from the cylinders. If there is excessive leakage, the inside of the cylinder will be moist with fluid. If leakage exists, a wheel cylinder overhaul is in order. Do not delay, because brake failure could result.

NOTE: *A small amount of fluid will be present to act as a lubricant for the wheel cylinder pistons. Fluid spilling from the boot center hole, after the piston is removed, indicates cup leakage and the necessity for cylinder overhaul.*

14. Check the backing plate attaching bolts to make sure that they are tight. Use fine emery cloth to clean all rust and dirt from the shoe contact surfaces on the plate.

15. Lubricate the fulcrum end of the parking brake lever with brake grease specially made for the purpose. Install the lever on the secondary shoe and secure with C-clip.

16. Install the adjusting screw and spring on the shoes, connecting them together. The coils of the spring must not be over the star wheel on the adjuster. The left and right hand springs are not interchangeable. Do not mix them up.

17. Lubricate the shoe contact surfaces on the backing plate with the brake grease. Be certain when you are using this stuff that none of it ac-

tually gets on the linings or drums. Apply the same grease to the point where the parking brake cable contacts the plate. Use the grease sparingly.

18. Spread the shoe assemblies apart and connect the parking brake cable. Install the shoes on the backing plate, engaging the shoes at the top temporarily with the wheel cylinder pistons. Make sure that the star wheel on the adjuster is lined up with the adjusting hole in the backing plate, if the hole is back there.

19. Spread the shoes apart slightly and install the parking brake strut and spring. Make sure that the end of the strut without the spring engages the parking brake lever. The end with the spring engages the primary shoe (the one with the shorter lining).

20. Install the actuator pivot, lever and return spring. Install the actuating link in the shoe retainer. Lift up the actuator lever and hook the link into the lever.

21. Install the holddown pins through the back of the plate, install the lever pivots and holddown springs. Install the shoe return springs with a pair of pliers. Be very careful not to stretch or otherwise distort these springs.

22. Take a look at everything. Make sure the linings are in the right place, the self-adjusting mechanism is correctly installed, and the parking brake parts are all hooked up. If in doubt, remove the other wheel and take a look at that one for comparison.

23. Measure the width of the linings, then measure the inside width of the drum. Adjust the linings by means of the adjuster so that the drum will fit onto the linings.

24. Install the hub and bearing assembly onto the axle if removed. Tighten the retaining bolts to 35 ft. lbs. (55 Nm.).

25. Install the drum and wheel. Adjust the brakes using the procedure given earlier in this chapter. Be sure to install a rubber hole cover in the knock-out hole after the adjustment is complete. Adjust the parking brake.

26. Lower the car and check the pedal for any sponginess or lack of a hard feel. Check the braking action and the parking brake. The brakes must not be applied severely immediately after installation. They should be used moderately for the first 200 miles of city driving or 1000 miles of highway driving, to allow the linings to conform to the shape of the drum.

Wheel Cylinders

REMOVAL AND INSTALLATION

CAUTION: *Brake shoes contain asbestos, which has been determined to be a cancer causing agent. Never clean the brake surfaces with compressed air! Avoid inhaling any*

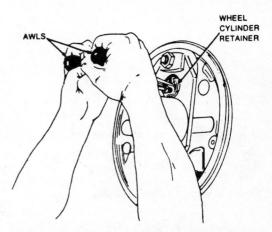

Remove the wheel cylinder retainer from the backing plate with a pair of awls or punches

dust from any brake surface! When cleaning brake surfaces, use a commercially available brake cleaning fluid.

1. Loosen the wheel lug nuts, raise and support the car, and remove the wheel. Remove the drum and brake shoes. Leave the hub and wheel bearing assembly in place.

2. Remove any dirt from around the brake line fitting. Disconnect the brake line.

3. Remove the wheel cylinder retainer by using two awls or punches with a tip diameter of ⅛" or less. Insert the awls or punches into the access slots between the wheel cylinder pilot and retainer locking tabs. Bend both tabs away simultaneously. Remove the wheel cylinder from the backing plate.

4. To install, position the wheel cylinder against the backing plate and hold it in place

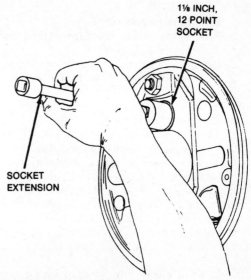

Installing a new retainer

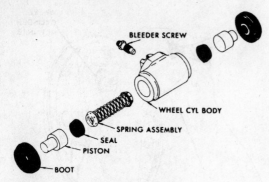

BLEEDER SCREW

WHEEL CYL BODY

SPRING ASSEMBLY

SEAL

PISTON

BOOT

Exploded view of a wheel cylinder

with a wooden block between the wheel cylinder and the hub and bearing assembly.

5. Install a new retainer over the wheel cylinder abutment on the rear of the backing plate by pressing it into place with a 1⅛″ 12-point socket and an extension.

6. Install a new bleeder screw into the wheel cylinder. Install the brake line and tighten to 10-15 ft. lbs. (13-20 Nm.).

7. The rest of installation is the reverse of removal. After the drum is installed, bleed the brakes using the procedure outlined earlier in this chapter.

OVERHAUL

As is the case with master cylinders, overhaul kits are available for the wheel cylinders. And, as is the case with master cylinders, it is usually more profitable to simply buy new or rebuilt wheel cylinders rather than rebuilding them. When rebuilding wheel cylinders, avoid getting any contaminants in the system. Always install new high quality brake fluid; the use of improper fluid will swell and deteriorate the rubber parts.

1. Remove the wheel cylinders.

2. Remove the rubber boots from the cylinder ends. Discard the boots.

3. Remove and discard the pistons and cups.

4. Wash the cylinder and metal parts in denatured alcohol.

WARNING: *Never use mineral based solvents to clean the brake parts.*

5. Allow the parts to air dry and inspect the cylinder bore for corrosion or wear. Light corrosion can be cleaned up with crocus cloth; use finger pressure and rotate the cloth around the circumference of the bore. Do not move the cloth in and out. Any deep corrosion or pitting or wear warrants replacement of the parts.

6. Rinse the parts and allow to dry. Do not dry with a rag, which will leave bits of lint behind.

7. Lubricate the cylinder bore with clean brake fluid. Insert the spring assembly.

8. Install new cups. Do not lubricate prior to assembly.

9. Install the new pistons.

10. Press the new boots onto the cylinders by hand. Do not lubricate prior to assembly.

11. Install the wheel cylinders. Bleed the brakes after installation of the drum.

PARKING BRAKE

ADJUSTMENT

1. Raise and support the car with both rear wheels off the ground.

2. Pull the parking brake lever exactly two ratchet clicks.

3. Loosen the equalizer locknut, then tighten the adjusting nut until the left rear wheel can just be turned backward using two hands, but is locked in forward rotation.

4. Tighten the locknut.

5. Release the parking brake. Rotate the rear wheels; there should be no drag.

6. Lower the car.

Cable

REMOVAL AND INSTALLATION

Front Cable

1. Place the gear selector in Neutral and apply the parking brake.

2. Remove the center console as detailed in Chapter 6.

3. Disconnect the parking brake cable from the lever.

4. Remove the cable retaining nut and the bracket securing the front cable to the floor panel.

5. Raise the car and loosen the equalizer nut.

6. Loosen the catalytic converter shield and then remove the parking brake cable from the body.

7. Disconnect the cable from the equalizer and then remove the cable from the guide and the underbody clips.

8. Position the cable to the equalizer, guide and underbody clips.

9. Install the parking brake cable to the body and tighten the catalytic converter shield.

10. Tighten the equalizer nut.

11. Install the cable retaining nut and the bracket securing the front cable to the floor panel.

12. Connect the parking brake cable to the lever.

13. Install the center console as detailed in Chapter 6.

14. Adjust the cable.

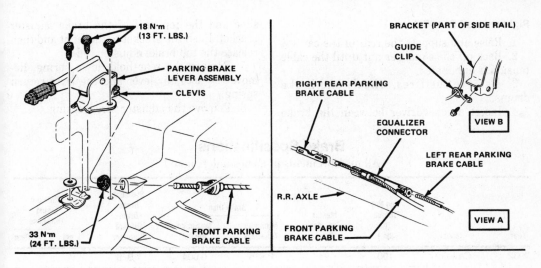

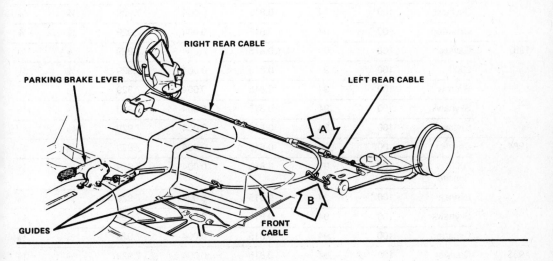

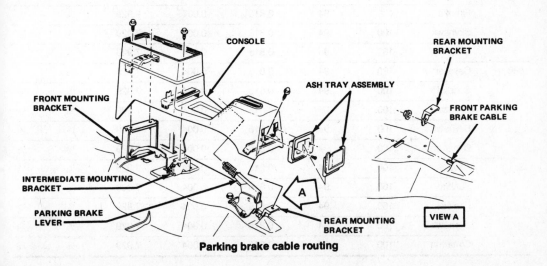

Parking brake cable routing

Right and Left Rear Cables

1. Raise and support the rear of the car.
2. Back off the equalizer nut until the cable tension is eliminated.
3. Remove the tires, wheels and brake drums.
4. Insert a screwdriver between the brake shoe and the top part of the brake adjuster bracket. Push the bracket to the front and then release the top brake adjuster rod.
5. Remove the rear hold down spring. Remove the actuator lever and the lever return spring.
6. Remove the adjuster screw spring.

Brake Specifications
All measurements in inches unless noted

| Year | Model | Lug Nut Torque (ft. lbs.) | Master Cylinder Bore | Brake Disc | | Standard Brake Drum Discard Diameter | Minimum Lining Thickness | |
				Minimum Thickness	Maximum Runout		Front	Rear
1982	Cavalier	100	.94	0.815	0.004	7.929	1/8	1/8
	2000	100	.94	0.815	0.004	7.929	1/8	1/8
	Firenza	100	.94	0.815	0.004	7.929	1/8	1/8
	Skyhawk	100	.94	0.815	0.004	7.929	1/8	1/8
	Cimarron	100	.94	0.815	0.004	7.929	1/8	1/8
1983	Cavalier	100	.94	0.815	0.004	7.929	1/8	1/8
	2000	100	.94	0.815	0.004	7.929	1/8	1/8
	Firenza	100	.94	0.815	0.004	7.929	1/8	1/8
	Skyhawk	100	.94	0.815	0.004	7.929	1/8	1/8
	Cimarron	100	.94	0.815	0.004	7.929	1/8	1/8
1984	Cavalier	100	.94	0.815	0.004	7.929	1/8	1/8
	2000 Sunbird	100	.94	0.815	0.004	7.929	1/8	1/8
	Firenza	100	.94	0.815	0.004	7.929	1/8	1/8
	Skyhawk	100	.94	0.815	0.004	7.929	1/8	1/8
	Cimarron	100	.94	0.815	0.004	7.929	1/8	1/8
1985	Cavalier	100	.94	0.815	0.004	7.929	1/8	1/8
	2000 Sunbird	100	.94	0.815	0.004	7.929	1/8	1/8
	Firenza	100	.94	0.815	0.004	7.929	1/8	1/8
	Skyhawk	100	.94	0.815	0.004	7.929	1/8	1/8
	Cimarron	100	.94	0.815	0.004	7.929	1/8	1/8
1986	Cavalier	100	.94	0.815	0.004	7.929	1/8	1/8
	Sunbird	100	.94	0.815	0.004	7.929	1/8	1/8
	Firenza	100	.94	0.815	0.004	7.929	1/8	1/8
	Skyhawk	100	.94	0.815	0.004	7.929	1/8	1/8
	Cimarron	100	.94	0.815	0.004	7.929	1/8	1/8
1987	Cavalier	100	.94	0.815	0.004	7.929	1/8	1/8
	Sunbird	100	.94	0.815	0.004	7.929	1/8	1/8
	Firenza	100	.94	0.815	0.004	7.929	1/8	1/8
	Skyhawk	100	.94	0.815	0.004	7.929	1/8	1/8
	Cimarron	100	.94	0.815	0.004	7.929	1/8	1/8

7. Remove the top rear brake shoe return spring.

8. Unhook the parking brake cable from the parking brake lever.

9. Depress the conduit fitting retaining tangs and then remove the conduit fitting from the backing plate.

10. Remove the cable end button from the connector.

11. Depress the conduit fitting retaining tangs and remove the conduit fitting from the axle bracket.

12. Install the conduit fitting to the axle bracket.

13. Install the cable end button to the connector.

14. Install the conduit fitting to the backing plate.

15. Hook the parking brake cable to the parking brake lever.

16. Install the top rear brake shoe return spring.

17. Install the adjuster screw spring.

18. Install the rear hold down spring. Install the actuator lever and the lever return spring.

19. Install the top brake adjuster rod.

20. Install the tires, wheels and brake drums.

21. Adjust the cable.

Body

10

EXTERIOR

Doors

REMOVAL

1. On doors equipped with power operated components proceed as folllows:

  a. Remove the door trim panel, insulator pad (if so equipped), and the inner panel water deflector.

  b. Disconnect the wiring components inside the door.

  c. Remove the rubber conduit from the door, then remove the wiring harness from the door through the conduit access hole.

2. Tape the area (on the door pillar and body pillar) above the lower hinge with fabric tape.

CAUTION: *Before performing the following step, cover the spring with a towel to prevent the spring from flying out and possibly causing personal injury.*

3. Insert a suitable, long, flat bladed tool under the pivot point of the hold-open link and over top of the spring. The tool should be positioned so as not to apply pressure to the hold-open link. Cover the spring with a shop cloth and lift the tool to disengage the spring. The spring can also be removed by using tool J-28625, or equivalent, door hinge spring compressor tool. The tool is stamped right side and left side. For all the J-cars the tool stamped, "left side" is used to service the right side hinge spring. The tool stamped, "right side" is used to service the left hand hinge spring.

  a. Install the two jaws of the tool over the spring. The jaw with the slots slides over spring at the hold-open link. The jaw with the hole fits over the spring at the bubble on the door hinge pillar.

  b. Install the bolt to the jaws of the tool and tighten to compress the spring.

  c. Remove the tool and spring from the door hinge assembly. Do not remove the spring from the tool.

4. When removing the hinge pin, save the "barrel" clips as follows:

  a. Using two, suitable, flat bladed tools, spread the clip enough to move the clip above the recess toward the pointed end of the pin.

  b. As the pin is removed, the clip will ride the shank of the pin and fall free.

  c. Reinstall the clips onto the pins before installing the door.

5. With the aid of a helper to support the door, remove the lower hinge pin, using a soft headed hammer and locking type pliers. The helper can aid in removing the hinge pin by raising and lowering the rear of the door.

6. Insert the bolt into the hole of the lower hinge to maintain door attachment during upper hinge pin removal.

7. Remove the upper hinge pin in the same manner as the lower. Remove the bolt from the lower hinge and remove the door from the body.

INSTALLATION

NOTE: *Before installing the door, replace the hinge pin clips or reuse the old clips as explained in the removal procedure.*

1. With the aid of a helper, position the door and insert a bolt in the lower hinge hole.

2. The upper hinge pin is inserted with the pointed end up. The lower hinge pin is inserted with the pointed end down. With the door in the full open position, install the upper hinge pin using locking-type pliers and a soft headed hammer. Use a drift punch and hammer to complete pin installation.

3. Remove the screw from the lower hinge and install the lower hinge pin. The use of the special tool J-28625 or equivalent is the recommended method for installing the hinge spring.

WARNING: *If the spring is installed before installing the upper hinge pin, damage to the hinge bushings may result!*

4. If the spring was removed using a long, flat bladed tool, install the spring as follows:

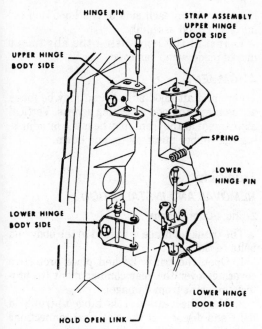

Front door hinge system

a. Place the spring in tool J-28625 or equivalent.

b. Place the tool and spring in a bench vise.

c. Compress the tool in a vise and install the bolt until the spring is fully compressed.

d. Remove the tool with the compressed spring from the vise and install in the proper position in the door lower hinge. The slot in

the jaw of the tool fits over the hold-open link. The hole in the other jaw fits over the bubble.

e. Remove the bolt from the tool to install the spring.

f. Remove the tool from the door hinge. (The tool will fall out in three pieces). Cycle the door to check spring operation.

5. If tool J-28625 or equivalent was used to remove the spring, follow Steps d, e, and f above to install the spring.

6. Remove the tape from the door and body pillars.

7. On the doors with power operated components, install all previously removed parts.

ADJUSTMENTS

The front door hinges are made of steel and are welded to the door and bolted to the body hinge pillars. No adjustment provisions are used in this type of door system.

Hood

REMOVAL AND INSTALLATION

1. Raise the hood and install protective coverings over the fender areas to prevent damage to the painted surfaces and mouldings.

2. Mark the position of the hinge on the hood to aid alignment during installation.

3. While supporting the hood, preferably with the aid of an assistant, remove the hinge to

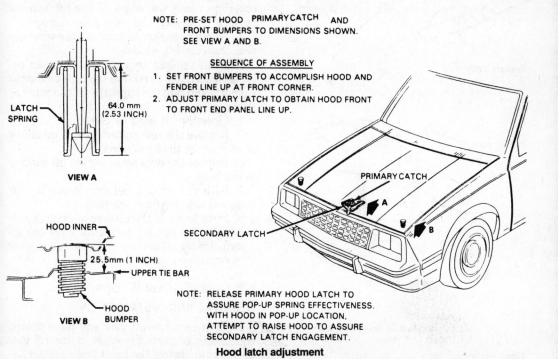

NOTE: PRE-SET HOOD PRIMARY CATCH AND
FRONT BUMPERS TO DIMENSIONS SHOWN.
SEE VIEW A AND B.

SEQUENCE OF ASSEMBLY
1. SET FRONT BUMPERS TO ACCOMPLISH HOOD AND FENDER LINE UP AT FRONT CORNER.
2. ADJUST PRIMARY LATCH TO OBTAIN HOOD FRONT TO FRONT END PANEL LINE UP.

LATCH SPRING

64.0 mm (2.53 INCH)

VIEW A

HOOD INNER

25.5mm (1 INCH)

UPPER TIE BAR

HOOD BUMPER

VIEW B

PRIMARY CATCH

SECONDARY LATCH

NOTE: RELEASE PRIMARY HOOD LATCH TO ASSURE POP-UP SPRING EFFECTIVENESS. WITH HOOD IN POP-UP LOCATION, ATTEMPT TO RAISE HOOD TO ASSURE SECONDARY LATCH ENGAGEMENT.

Hood latch adjustment

1	HOOD ASM
2	INSULATOR
3	RETAINER

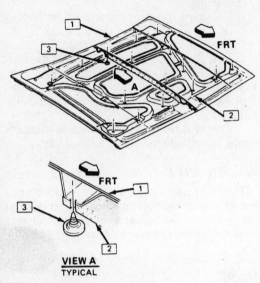

VIEW A
TYPICAL

Hood assembly

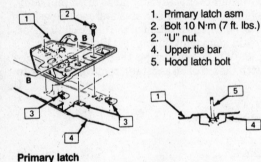

1. Primary latch asm
2. Bolt 10 N·m (7 ft. lbs.)
2. "U" nut
4. Upper tie bar
5. Hood latch bolt

Primary latch

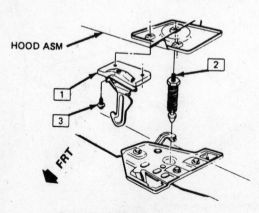

1. Secondary latch
2. Bolt & spring asm 20 N·m (15 ft. lbs.)
3. Bolt 10 N·m (7 ft. lbs.)

Hood secondary latch

hood screws on each side of the hood and remove the hood assembly.

4. Install the hood using the alignment marks made when removed.

ALIGMMENT

Fore and aft hood adjustment may be made at the hinge to hood attaching screws. Vertical adjustment at the front may be made by adjusting the rubber bumpers up and down.

Trunk Lid

REMOVAL AND INSTALLATION

2- and 4-Door Sedans

The trunk lid hinge is welded to the body and bolts to the lid.

1. Open the trunk lid and place protective coverings over the rear compartment (to protect the paint from damage).

2. Mark the location of the hinge-to-trunk lid bolts and disconnect the electrical connections and wiring from the lid (if equipped).

3. Using an assistant (to support the lid), remove the hinge-to-lid bolts and the lid from the vehicle.

4. To install, reverse the removal procedures. Adjust the position of the trunk lid to the body.

Hatchback Assembly

REMOVAL AND INSTALLATION

1. Prop open the lid and place protective coverings along the edges of the lift window opening (to protect the paint from damage).

2. Where necessary, disconnect the wire harness from the lift window.

3. While a helper supports the lid, use an awl or flat bladed tool to remove the clips on the gas supports and pull the supports off the retainer studs.

4. Close the lift window assembly.

5. Remove the rear upper garnish moulding at the rear of the headlining.

6. Remove the nuts retaining the lift window to the body.

7. With the aid of a helper, remove the lift window assembly from the body.

8. Installation is the reverse of removal.

NOTE: *The gas support assemblies are attached to the lid and the body and are secured by retaining clips and/or bolts.*

Lift Gate (Station Wagon)

REMOVAL AND INSTALLATION

1. Prop open the lift gate and place protective coverings along the edges of the lift gate opening (to protect the paint from damage).

CHILTON'S
AUTO BODY
REPAIR TIPS

Tools and Materials • Step-by-Step Illustrated Procedures
How To Repair Dents, Scratches and Rust Holes
Spray Painting and Refinishing Tips

With a little practice, basic body repair procedures can be mastered by any do-it-yourself mechanic. The step-by-step repairs shown here can be applied to almost any type of auto body repair.

TOOLS & MATERIALS

You may already have basic tools, such as hammers and electric drills. Other tools unique to body repair — body hammers, grinding attachments, sanding blocks, dent puller, half-round plastic file and plastic spreaders — are relatively inexpensive and can be obtained wherever auto parts or auto body repair parts are sold. Portable air compressors and paint spray guns can be purchased or rented.

Auto Body Repair Kits

The best and most often used products are available to the do-it-yourselfer in kit form, from major manufacturers of auto body repair products. The same manufacturers also merchandise the individual products for use by pros.

Kits are available to make a wide variety of repairs, including holes, dents and scratches and fiberglass, and offer the advantage of buying the materials you'll need for the job. There is little waste or chance of materials going bad from not being used. Many kits may also contain basic body-working tools such as body files, sanding blocks and spreaders. Check the contents of the kit before buying your tools.

BODY REPAIR TIPS

Safety

Many of the products associated with auto body repair and refinishing contain toxic chemicals. Read all labels before opening containers and store them in a safe place and manner.

• Wear eye protection (safety goggles) when using power tools or when performing any operation that involves the removal of any type of material.

• Wear lung protection (disposable mask or respirator) when grinding, sanding or painting.

Sanding

1 Sand off paint before using a dent puller. When using a non-adhesive sanding disc, cover the back of the disc with an overlapping layer or two of masking tape and trim the edges. The disc will last considerably longer.

2 Use the circular motion of the sanding disc to grind *into* the edge of the repair. Grinding or sanding away from the jagged edge will only tear the sandpaper.

3 Use the palm of your hand flat on the panel to detect high and low spots. Do not use your fingertips. Slide your hand slowly back and forth.

WORKING WITH BODY FILLER

Mixing The Filler

Cleanliness and proper mixing and application are extremely important. Use a clean piece of plastic or glass or a disposable artist's palette to mix body filler.

1 Allow plenty of time and follow directions. No useful purpose will be served by adding more hardener to make it cure (set-up) faster. Less hardener means more curing time, but the mixture dries harder; more hardener means less curing time but a softer mixture.

2 Both the hardener and the filler should be thoroughly kneaded or stirred before mixing. Hardener should be a solid paste and dispense like thin toothpaste. Body filler should be smooth, and free of lumps or thick spots.

Getting the proper amount of hardener in the filler is the trickiest part of preparing the filler. Use the same amount of hardener in cold or warm weather. For contour filler (thick coats), a bead of hardener twice the diameter of the filler is about right. There's about a 5% margin on either side, but, if in doubt use less hardener.

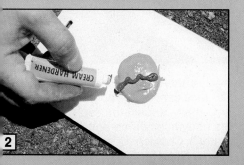

3 Mix the body filler and hardener by wiping across the mixing surface, picking the mixture up and wiping it again. Colder weather requires longer mixing times. Do not mix in a circular motion; this will trap air bubbles which will become holes in the cured filler.

Applying The Filler

1 For best results, filler should not be applied over 1/4″ thick.

Apply the filler in several coats. Build it up to above the level of the repair surface so that it can be sanded or grated down.

The first coat of filler must be pressed on with a firm wiping motion.

Apply the filler in one direction only. Working the filler back and forth will either pull it off the metal or trap air bubbles.

REPAIRING DENTS

Before you start, take a few minutes to study the damaged area. Try to visualize the shape of the panel before it was damaged. If the damage is on the left fender, look at the right fender and use it as a guide. If there is access to the panel from behind, you can reshape it with a body hammer. If not, you'll have to use a dent puller. Go slowly and work the metal a little at a time. Get the panel as straight as possible before applying filler.

1 This dent is typical of one that can be pulled out or hammered out from behind. Remove the headlight cover, headlight assembly and turn signal housing.

2 Drill a series of holes ½ the size of the end of the dent puller along the stress line. Make some trial pulls and assess the results. If necessary, drill more holes and try again. Do not hurry.

3 If possible, use a body hammer and block to shape the metal back to its original contours. Get the metal back as close to its original shape as possible. Don't depend on body filler to fill dents.

4 Using an 80-grit grinding disc on an electric drill, grind the paint from the surrounding area down to bare metal. Use a new grinding pad to prevent heat buildup that will warp metal.

5 The area should look like this when you're finished grinding. Knock the drill holes in and tape over small openings to keep plastic filler out.

6 Mix the body filler (see Body Repair Tips). Spread the body filler evenly over the entire area (see Body Repair Tips). Be sure to cover the area completely.

7 Let the body filler dry until the surface can just be scratched with your fingernail. Knock the high spots from the body filler with a body file ("Cheesegrater"). Check frequently with the palm of your hand for high and low spots.

8 Check to be sure that trim pieces that will be installed later will fit exactly. Sand the area with 40-grit paper.

9 If you wind up with low spots, you may have to apply another layer of filler.

10 Knock the high spots off with 40-grit paper. When you are satisfied with the contours of the repair, apply a thin coat of filler to cover pin holes and scratches.

11 Block sand the area with 40-grit paper to a smooth finish. Pay particular attention to body lines and ridges that must be well-defined.

12 Sand the area with 400 paper and then finish with a scuff pad. The finished repair is ready for priming and painting (see Painting Tips).

Materials and photos courtesy of Ritt Jones Auto Body, Prospect Park, PA.

REPAIRING RUST HOLES

There are many ways to repair rust holes. The fiberglass cloth kit shown here is one of the most cost efficient for the owner because it provides a strong repair that resists cracking and moisture and is relatively easy to use. It can be used on large and small holes (with or without backing) and can be applied over contoured areas. Remember, however, that short of replacing an entire panel, no repair is a guarantee that the rust will not return.

1 Remove any trim that will be in the way. Clean away all loose debris. Cut away all the rusted metal. But be sure to leave enough metal to retain the contour or body shape.

2 Grind away all traces of rust with a 24-grit grinding disc. Be sure to grind back 3-4 inches from the edge of the hole down to bare metal and be sure all traces of paint, primer and rust are removed.

3 Block sand the area with 80 or 100 grit sandpaper to get a clear, shiny surface and feathered paint edge. Tap the edges of the hole inward with a ball peen hammer.

4 If you are going to use release film, cut a piece about 2-3" larger than the area you have sanded. Place the film over the repair and mark the sanded area on the film. Avoid any unnecessary wrinkling of the film.

5 Cut 2 pieces of fiberglass matte to match the shape of the repair. One piece should be about 1" smaller than the sanded area and the second piece should be 1" smaller than the first. Mix enough filler and hardener to saturate the fiberglass material (see Body Repair Tips).

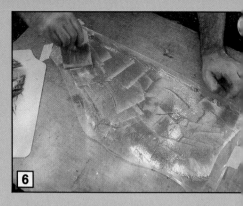

6 Lay the release sheet on a flat surface and spread an even layer of filler, large enough to cover the repair. Lay the smaller piece of fiberglass cloth in the center of the sheet and spread another layer of filler over the fiberglass cloth. Repeat the operation for the larger piece of cloth.

7 Place the repair material over the repair area, with the release film facing outward. Use a spreader and work from the center outward to smooth the material, following the body contours. Be sure to remove all air bubbles.

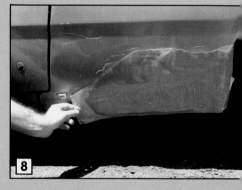

8 Wait until the repair has dried tack free and peel off the release sheet. The ideal working temperature is 60°-90° F. Cooler or warmer temperatures or high humidity may require additional curing time. Wait longer, if in doubt.

12 Block sand the topcoat smooth with finishing sandpaper (200 grit), and 400 grit. The repair is ready for masking, priming and painting (see Painting Tips).

Materials and photos courtesy Marson Corporation, Chelsea, Massachusetts

Sand and feather-edge the entire area. The initial sanding can be done with a sanding disc on an electric drill if care is used. Finish the sanding with a block sander. Low spots can be filled with body filler; this may require several applications.

10 When the filler can just be scratched with a fingernail, knock the high spots down with a body file and smooth the entire area with 80-grit. Feather the filled areas into the surrounding areas.

When the area is sanded smooth, mix some topcoat and hardener and apply it directly with a spreader. This will give a smooth finish and prevent the glass matte from showing through the paint.

PAINTING TIPS

Preparation

1 SANDING — Use a 400 or 600 grit wet or dry sandpaper. Wet-sand the area with a 1/4 sheet of sandpaper soaked in clean water. Keep the paper wet while sanding. Sand the area until the repaired area tapers into the original finish.

2 CLEANING — Wash the area to be painted thoroughly with water and a clean rag. Rinse it thoroughly and wipe the surface dry until you're sure it's completely free of dirt, dust, fingerprints, wax, detergent or other foreign matter.

3 MASKING — Protect any areas you don't want to overspray by covering them with masking tape and newspaper. Be careful not get fingerprints on the area to be painted.

4 PRIMING — All exposed metal should be primed before painting. Primer protects the metal and provides an excellent surface for paint adhesion. When the primer is dry, wet-sand the area again with 600 grit wet-sandpaper. Clean the area again after sanding.

Painting Techniques

Paint applied from either a spray gun or a spray can (for small areas) will provide good results. Experiment on an old piece of metal to get the right combination before you begin painting.

SPRAYING VISCOSITY (SPRAY GUN ONLY) — Paint should be thinned to spraying viscosity according to the directions on the can. Use only the recommended thinner or reducer and the same amount of reduction regardless of temperature.

AIR PRESSURE (SPRAY GUN ONLY) — This is extremely important. Be sure you are using the proper recommended pressure.

TEMPERATURE — The surface to be painted should be approximately the same temperature as the surrounding air. Applying warm paint to a cold surface, or vice versa, will completely upset the paint characteristics.

THICKNESS — Spray with smooth strokes. In general, the thicker the coat of paint, the longer the drying time. Apply several thin coats about 30 seconds apart. The paint should remain wet long enough to flow out and no longer; heavier coats will only produce sags or wrinkles. Spray a light (fog) coat, followed by heavier color coats.

DISTANCE — The ideal spraying distance is 8"-12" from the gun or can to the surface. Shorter distances will produce ripples, while greater distances will result in orange peel, dry film and poor color match and loss of material due to overspray.

OVERLAPPING — The gun or can should be kept at right angles to the surface at all times. Work to a wet edge at an even speed, using a 50% overlap and direct the center of the spray at the lower or nearest edge of the previous stroke.

RUBBING OUT (BLENDING) FRESH PAINT — Let the paint dry thoroughly. Runs or imperfections can be sanded out, primed and repainted.

Don't be in too big a hurry to remove the masking. This only produces paint ridges. When the finish has dried for at least a week, apply a small amount of fine grade rubbing compound with a clean, wet cloth. Use lots of water and blend the new paint with the surrounding area.

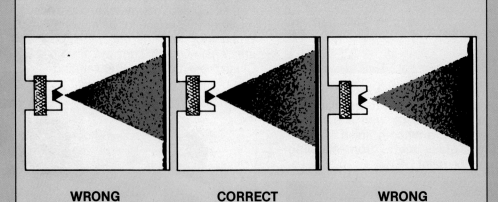

WRONG	CORRECT	WRONG
Thin coat. Stroke too fast, not enough overlap, gun too far away.	Medium coat. Proper distance, good stroke, proper overlap.	Heavy coat. Stroke too slow, too much overlap, gun too close.

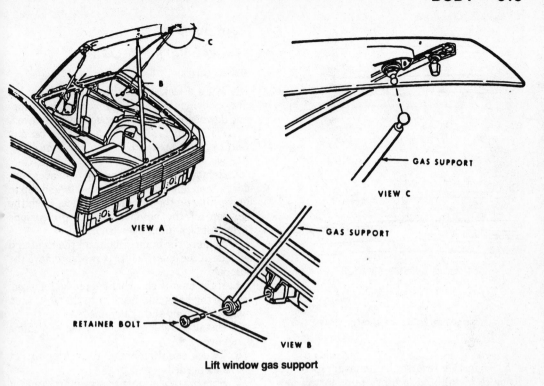

Lift window gas support

2. Where necessary, disconnect the wire harness from the lift gate.

3. While a helper supports the lid, use an awl or flat bladed tool to remove the clips on the gas supports and pull the supports off the retainer studs.

4. Use a $3/16''$ diameter rod to remove the hinge pins from the hinges. Place the end of the rod against the pointed end of the hinge pin; then strike the rod firmly to shear the retaining clip tabs and drive the pin through the hinge. Repeat the same thing on the opposite side hinge and with the aid of a helper remove the lift gate from the body.

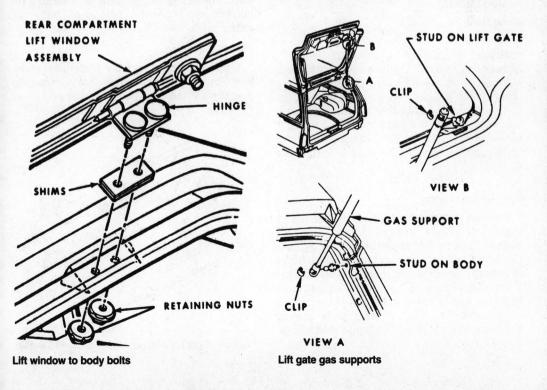

Lift window to body bolts

Lift gate gas supports

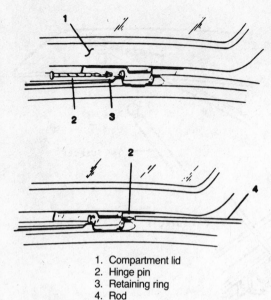

1. Compartment lid
2. Hinge pin
3. Retaining ring
4. Rod

Lift gate, hinge pin, right side shown

5. To install, reverse the removal procedure. Prior to installing the hinge pins, install new retaining clips in the notches provide in the hinge pins. Position the retaining clips so that the tabs point toward the head of the pin.

NOTE: *The gas support assemblies are attached to the lid and the body and are secured by retaining clips and/or bolts.*

ADJUSTMENTS

Trunk Lid

Fore and aft adjustment of the lid assembly is controlled by the hinge to lid attaching bolts. To adjust the lid, loosen the hinge to lid attaching bolts and shift the lid to the desired position, then tighten the bolts. To increase opening assist, use tool J-211412-1 or equivalent and move the torque rods one step toward the rear of the vehicle. To decrease opening assist, move the torque rods one step toward the front of the vehicle.

Hatchback Assembly

The rear compartment lift window assembly (hatchback) height, fore and aft and side adjustments are controlled at the hinge to body location. This area of the body has oversize hinge attaching holes in addition to the hinge to body shims. Adjustment at the hinge location must be made at the lower panel by adjusting the rubber bumpers. The retaining bolts holding the hinge to body should be tightened to 15-20 ft. lbs.

Front Bumpers

REMOVAL AND INSTALLATION

1982-83 Cavalier

1. Place a jack under the front bumper before removing the bolts to prevent it from dropping down when the bumper bolts are removed.

NOTE: *Do not rotate the energy absorber any more than needed to align the mounting holes.*

2. Remove the (1) bolt end cap to header panel right and left side. Remove the (2) end cap to fender nuts on the right and left side. Push the end cap off the bumper (plastic protrusions through holes in bumper bar).

3. Remove the bumper bolts on the right and left side at the energy absorbers and remove the bumper.

4. If the energy absorbers are to be replaced, remove the bolts and nuts from the unit, then remove the unit and the shims.

5. Install the energy and absorber and shims if removed.

6. Check the dimension and add/subtract shims as needed.

7. Support the bumper to prevent rotation of the energy absorbers.

8. Install the bolts at the bumper to energy absorber brackets, and end cap to fender and front end panel nuts.

9. If adjustment is required to align bumper, loosen the energy absorber mounting bolts and position as required (holes are slotted). Adjustment side to side can be made by loosening the bumper bracket bolts. Torque all bolts and nuts.

1984-87 Cavalier

1. Place a jack under the front bumper before removing the bolts to prevent it from dropping down when the bumper bolts are removed.

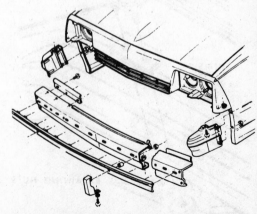

Front bumper bar and rub strips, 1982–83 Cavalier

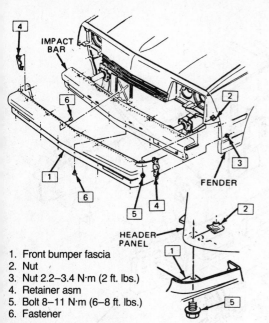

1. Front bumper fascia
2. Nut
3. Nut 2.2–3.4 N·m (2 ft. lbs.)
4. Retainer asm
5. Bolt 8–11 N·m (6–8 ft. lbs.)
6. Fastener

Front bumper assembly, 1984–87 Cavalier

NOTE: *Do not rotate the energy absorber any more than needed to align the mounting holes.*

2. Remove the right and left fascia to header panel bolts.

3. Remove the fascia to fender nuts in the right and left side.

4. Remove the bumper bolts on the right and left side at the energy absorbers and remove the bumper.

5. If the energy absorbers are to be replaced, remove the bolts and nuts from the unit, then remove the unit and the shims.

6. Install the energy absorber and shims if removed.

7. Check the dimension and add/subtract shims as needed.

8. Support the bumper to prevent rotation of the energy absorbers.

9. Install the bolts at the bumper to energy absorber brackets, and fascia to fender nuts, and fascia to fender panel bolts.

10. If adjustment is required to align bumper, loosen the energy absorber mounting bolts and position as required (holes are slotted). Adjustment side to side can be made by loosening the bumper bracket bolts. Torque all bolts and nuts.

2000

1982-87

1. Remove the front end panel (fascia).

2. Remove the bumper bar/energy absorber assembly from the body.

3. If the energy absorber must be replaced, drill out the pop rivets and install a new absorber with nuts, bolts and locking washers.

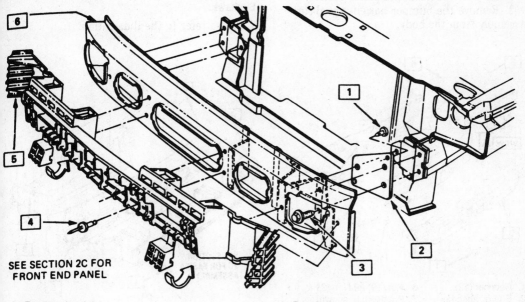

SEE SECTION 2C FOR FRONT END PANEL

1. Retainer (push in)
2. Reinforcement
3. 27 N·m (20 lb. ft.)

4. Pop rivet
5. Energy absorber pop rivet to bar
6. Bar

Front bumper bar and energy absorber, 1982–87 Sunbird (Non-GT)

1. Absorber
2. Bar assembly
3. 20–34 N·m (15–25 lb. ft.)
4. Rivet (10)
5. Fascia
6. Notch

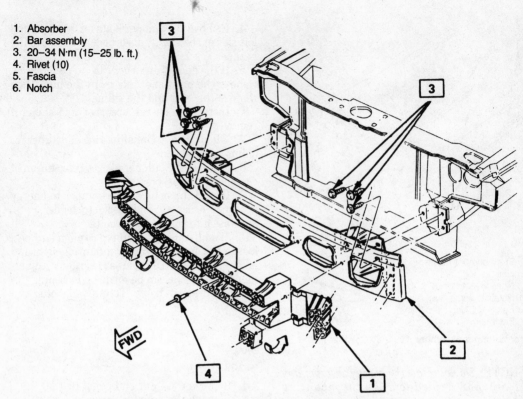

Front bumper bar and energy absorber, 1982–87 Sunbird (GT)

Firenza

1982-87

1. Remove the front end panel (fascia).
2. Remove the bumper bar/energy absorber assembly from the body.

3. If the energy absorber must be replaced, drill out the pop rivets and install a new absorber with nuts, bolts and locking washers.

Skyhawk

Please refer to the illustration.

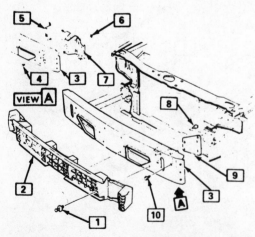

1. Retainer (12)
2. Energy absorber
3. Impact bar
4. Bolt (18)
5. Reinforcement (2)
6. Nut (18) 29 N·m (21 lb. ft.)
7. Bracket (l.h. shown)
8. Retainer (4)
9. Reinforcement
10. Bolt/screw 29 N·m (21 lb. ft.)

Front bumper bar and energy absorber, 1982–87 Firenza

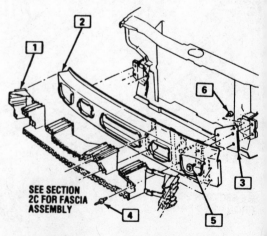

1. Energy absorber
2. Bar assembly
3. Reinforcement (2)
4. Rivet (10)
5. Bolt (6) 27 N·m (20 lb. ft.)
6. Retainer (4)

Front bumper assembly, 1984 Skyhawk shown, other years similar

Cimarron

1. Place a jack under the front bumper before removing the bolts to prevent it from dropping down when the bumper bolts are removed.
NOTE: *Do not rotate the energy absorber any more than needed to align the mounting holes.*

2. Remove the bumper extensions.

3. Remove the four nuts each side securing the bumper to the energy absorber unit.

4. Installation is the reverse of removal.

1. Impact bar
2. Impact bar outer reinforcement rh & lh
3. Bolt (12)
4. Impact bar upper reinforcement
5. Impact bar lower reinforcement
6. Self-tapping screw (2)
7. Bumper guard rh & lh
8. Bumper guard rub strip (2)
9. Bumper guard reinforcement rh & lh
10. Spacer (2)
11. Fascia retainer rh & lh
12. Fascia retainer (2)
13. Retainer (8)
14. Retainer (4)
15. Fascia support rh & lh

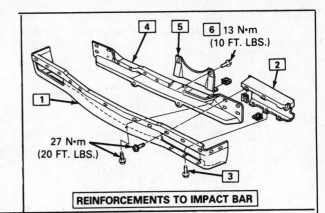

REINFORCEMENTS TO IMPACT BAR

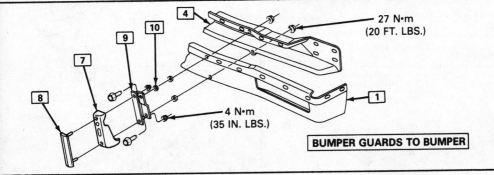

BUMPER GUARDS TO BUMPER

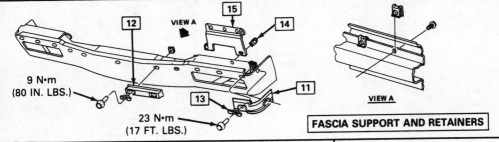

FASCIA SUPPORT AND RETAINERS

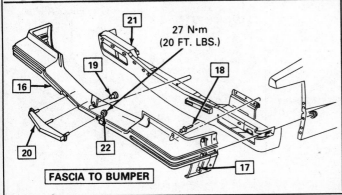

FASCIA TO BUMPER

16. Fascia
17. Fascia retainer rh & lh
18. Plastic retainer (6)
19. Fascia retainer
20. Fascia rub strip
21. Bumper assembly
22. Nuts (3)

Front bumper assembly, 1985 Cimarron

Rear Bumpers
REMOVAL AND INSTALLATION
1982-83

1. Place a jack under the rear bumper before removing the bolts to prevent it from dropping down when the bumper bolts are removed.

NOTE: *Do not rotate the energy absorber any more than needed to align the mounting holes.*

2. Remove the end cap to fender (2) nuts and (1) bolt on the right and left side. Push the end cap off the bumper (plastic protrusions through holes in bumper bar).

3. Remove the bumper bolts on the right and left side at the energy absorbers and remove the bumper.

4. If the energy absorbers are to be replaced, remove the bolts and nuts from the unit, then remove the unit and the shims.

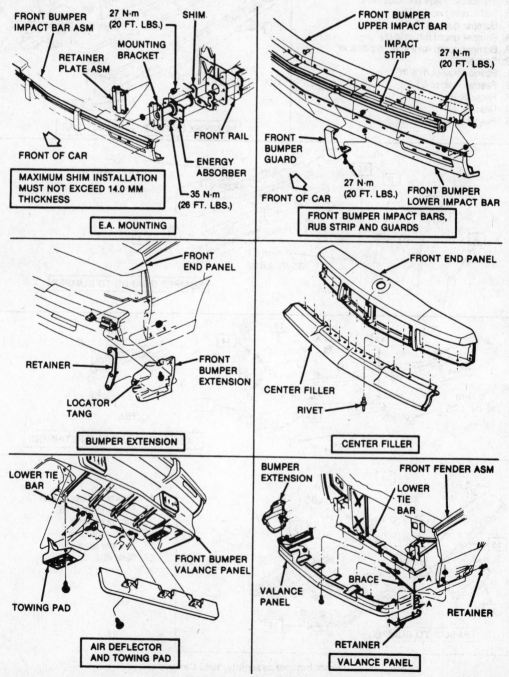

Front bumper assembly, 1987 Cimarron

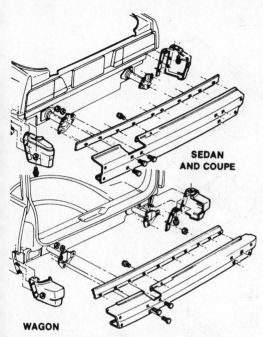

Rear bumper bar assemblies, 1982–83 Cavalier

5. Install the energy and absorber and shims if removed.

6. Check the dimension and add/subtract shims as needed.

7. Support the bumper to prevent rotation of the energy absorbers.

8. Install the bolts at the bumper to energy absorber brackets, and end cap to fender nuts and bolts.

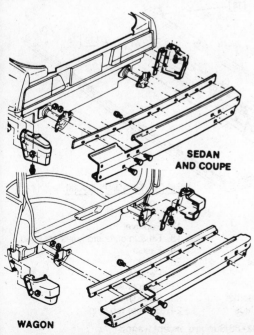

Rear bumper bar assemblies, 1984–87 Cavalier

9. If adjustment is required to align bumper, loosen the energy absorber mounting bolts and position as required (holes are slotted). Adjustment side to side can be made by loosening the bumper bracket bolts. Torque all bolts and nuts.

1984-87

1. Place a jack under the rear bumper before removing the bolts to prevent it from dropping down when the bumper bolts are removed.

NOTE: *Do not rotate the energy absorber any more than needed to align the mounting holes.*

2. Remove the bumper bolts on the right and left side and remove the bumper.

3. If the energy absorbers are to be replaced, remove the bolts and nuts from the unit, then remove the unit and the shims.

4. Install the energy absorber and shims if removed.

5. Check the dimension and add/subtract shims as needed.

6. Support the bumper to prevent rotation of the energy absorbers.

7. Install the bolts at the bumper to energy absorber brackets, and end cap to fender nuts and bolts.

8. If adjustment is required to align bumper, loosen the energy absorber mounting bolts and position as required (holes are slotted). Adjustment side to side can be made by loosening the bumper bracket bolts. Torque all bolts and nuts.

Grille

REMOVAL AND INSTALLATION

NOTE: *The following procedure includes removal of the front end panel.*

1982-87 Cavalier

1. Open the hood.

2. Remove the headlamp bezel screws (2 each).

3. Remove the (1) bolt at each fender to front end panel at the upper corner near the headlamp.

4. Disconnect the turn signal lamp socket and head lamp wiring.

5. Remove the (1) screw at each turn signal housing and remove the housings.

6. Remove the (1) bolt from the panel to radiator support located below the turn signal housing area.

7. Remove the (1) nut at the panel to the inner fender.

8. Remove the (2) nuts attaching the bumper end cap to the panel at each side.

9. Remove the (3) bolts at the baffles located at the radiator support.

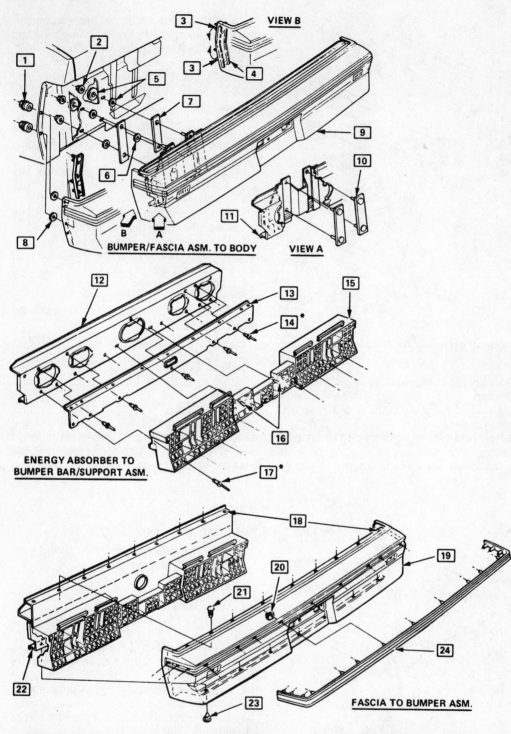

Rear bumper bar assemblies, 1982–83 Sunbird except wagon

1. 6 N·m (4.5 lb. ft.)
2. 27 N·m (20 lb. ft.)
3. Bend tabs toward center as shown
4. Retainer
5. Washers (top attachments only)
6. Retainer
7. Shim
8. Washer
9. Fascia
10. Plate
11. Bar asm.
12. Bumper bar
13. Support
14. Pop rivet
15. Energy absorber
16. Locating studs
17. Pop rivet
18. Rh & lh outboard holes not used
19. Fascia
20. U-nut
21. Retainer
22. Bumper asm.
23. Retainer
24. Bumper rub strip

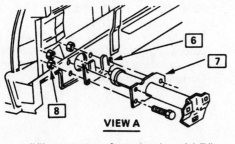

1. 29 N·m (21 lb. ft.)
2. Extension (material: urethane)
3. Filler
4. Bar
5. Bumper rub strip
6. Shim (as req.)
7. Hydraulic energy absorber
8. 27 N·m (20 lb. ft.)

VIEW A

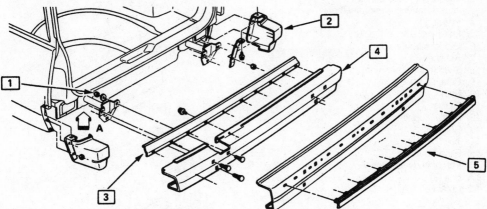

Rear bumper bar assemblies, 1982–83 Sunbird wagon

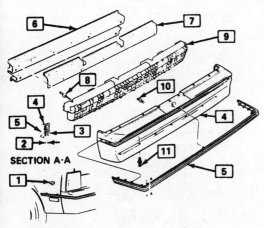

1. Nut (4)	7. Support
2. 3mm max. compression	8. Rivet (7)
3. Nut	9. Energy absorber
4. Fascia	10. Retainer (7)
5. Molding	11. Retainer (9)
6. Impact bar	

SECTION A-A

Rear bumper bar assemblies, 1982–87 Firenza except wagon

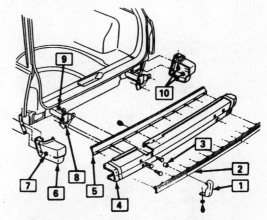

1. Guard assembly r&l	6. Bumper extension r&l
2. Rub strip assembly	7. 6 N·m (4 lb. ft.)
3. Spacer	8. Energy absorber
4. Bumper bar assembly	9. 29 N·m (21 lb. ft.)
5. Filler	10. 6 N·m (4 lb. ft.)

Rear bumper bar assemblies, 1984 Skyhawk wagon

Outside Remote Mirrors

With the remote control door outside mirror, the remote control mirror cable must be disengaged from the door trim assembly on the standard trim styles to permit trim panel removal.

On custom trim styles the remote control mirror cable must be disengaged from the upper trim panel and the upper trim panel must be removed to permit lower trim panel removal.

10. Transfer the headlamps and grille.
11. Installation is the reverse of removal.

Sunbird, Cimarron, Skyhawk, Firenza

On these models please refer to the illustrations

REMOVAL AND INSTALLATION

1. Remove the door trim panel as described in this chapter. On standard trim styles, peel back the insulator and water deflector to gain access to the mirror cable.

Refer to the illustrations for both custom trim and standard trim.

NOTE: *The mirror glass face may be replaced by placing a piece of tape over the glass then breaking the mirror face. Adhesive back mirror faces are available.*

1. Impact bar
2. Impact bar reinforcement
3. Impact bar upper reinforcement
4. Plate (2)
5. Energy absorber rh & lh
6. Impact bar seal (2)
7. Retainer (8)
8. Shim (max. 3 per side)
9. Retainer (2)
10. Body
11. Fascia
12. Fascia support
13. Retainer (8)
14. Bolt (10)
15. Fascia bumper (2)
16. Part of body assembly
17. Bolt (9)
18. Retainer (3)

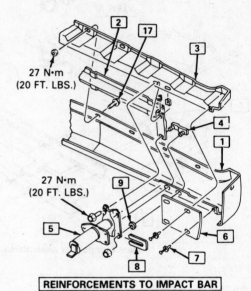

REINFORCEMENTS TO IMPACT BAR

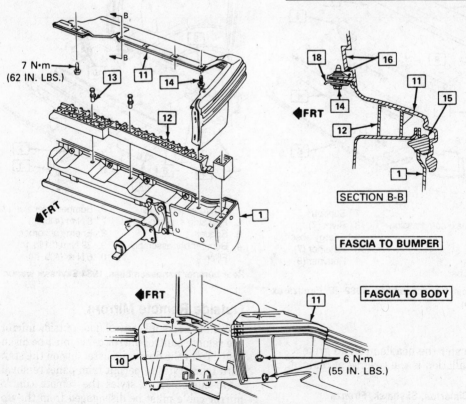

Rear bumper assembly, 1985 Cimarron

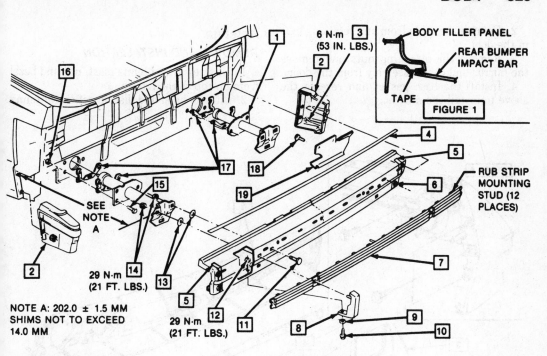

6 N·m (53 IN. LBS.)

BODY FILLER PANEL
REAR BUMPER IMPACT BAR
TAPE
FIGURE 1

RUB STRIP MOUNTING STUD (12 PLACES)

29 N·m (21 FT. LBS.)

SEE NOTE A

NOTE A: 202.0 ± 1.5 MM SHIMS NOT TO EXCEED 14.0 MM

29 N·m (21 FT. LBS.)

1. Energy absorber—rh and lh
2. Extension—rh and lh
3. Nut (4)
4. Protective tape—see figure 1
5. Protective tape—rh and lh
6. Impact bar
7. Impact strip
8. Guard—rh and lh
9. Spacer (2)
10. Screw (2)
11. Bolt (4)
12. Nut (2)
13. Retainer (4)
14. Nut (6)
15. Bolt (6)
16. Nut (6)
17. Shim (3.5 and 1.3 mm—as required)
18. Retainer (4)
19. Shield—rh and lh

Rear bumper assembly, 1987 Cimarron

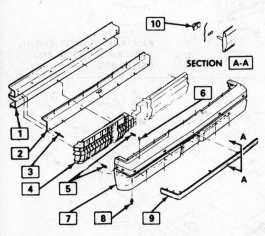

SECTION A-A

1. Bar assembly
2. Support
3. Rivet (7)
4. Energy absorber
5. Retainer (4)
6. Retainer (7)
7. Fascia
8. Retainer (7)
9. Molding assembly
10. Nut (9)

Rear bumper bar assemblies, 1984 Skyhawk except wagon

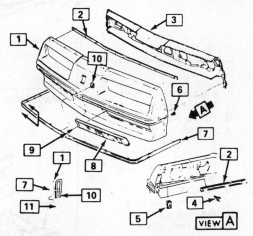

VIEW A

1. Front end panel (fascia)
2. Retainer
3. Reinforcement assembly
4. Screw (9)
5. Nut (16)
6. Screw (6)
7. Moulding
8. Grille (l.h. shown)
9. Screw (16)
10. Nut (15)
11. 3mm max compression

Front end panel and grille assembly, 1982–87 Firenza

2. Detatch the cable from any retaining tabs in the door.

3. Remove the attaching nuts and remove the mirror and cable assembly from the door.

4. Install the base gasket and reverse the above to install the mirror.

Antenna
REMOVAL AND INSTALLATION

1. Unscrew the antenna mast, nut and bezel from on top of the fender.

2. Lift the hood and disconnect the antenna

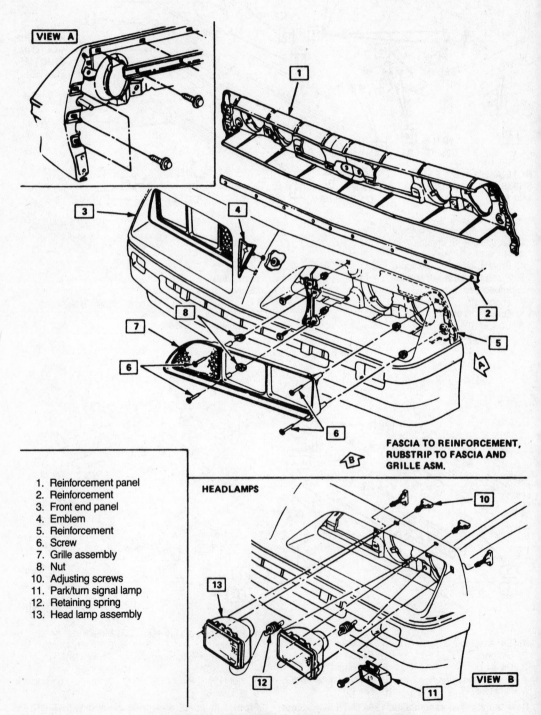

1. Reinforcement panel
2. Reinforcement
3. Front end panel
4. Emblem
5. Reinforcement
6. Screw
7. Grille assembly
8. Nut
10. Adjusting screws
11. Park/turn signal lamp
12. Retaining spring
13. Head lamp assembly

VIEW A

FASCIA TO REINFORCEMENT, RUBSTRIP TO FASCIA AND GRILLE ASM.

HEADLAMPS

VIEW B

Front grille assembly, 1982–87 Sunbird typical non GT

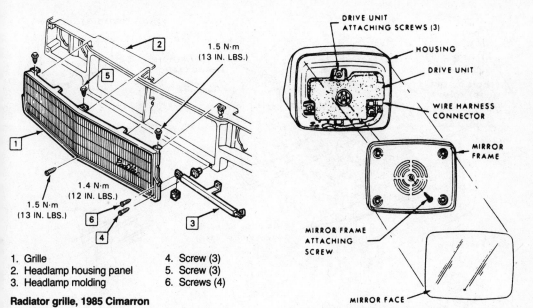

1.5 N·m
(13 IN. LBS.)

1.4 N·m
(12 IN. LBS.)

1.5 N·m
(13 IN. LBS.)

1. Grille
2. Headlamp housing panel
3. Headlamp molding
4. Screw (3)
5. Screw (3)
6. Screws (4)

Radiator grille, 1985 Cimarron

DRIVE UNIT
ATTACHING SCREWS (3)

HOUSING

DRIVE UNIT

WIRE HARNESS
CONNECTOR

MIRROR
FRAME

MIRROR FRAME
ATTACHING
SCREW

MIRROR FACE

Typical power mirror parts

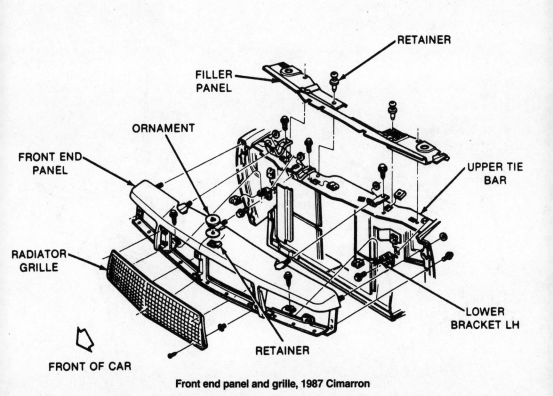

RETAINER

FILLER
PANEL

ORNAMENT

FRONT END
PANEL

UPPER TIE
BAR

RADIATOR
GRILLE

LOWER
BRACKET LH

FRONT OF CAR

RETAINER

Front end panel and grille, 1987 Cimarron

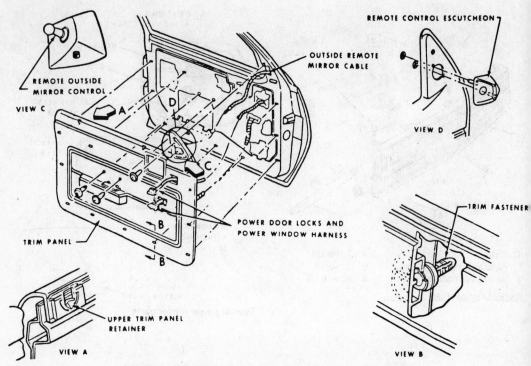

Remote control mirror cable and bezel attachment, standard trim

1. Nut
2. Bezel
3. Cable asm
4. Bolt/screw
5. Front fender asm
6. Stud

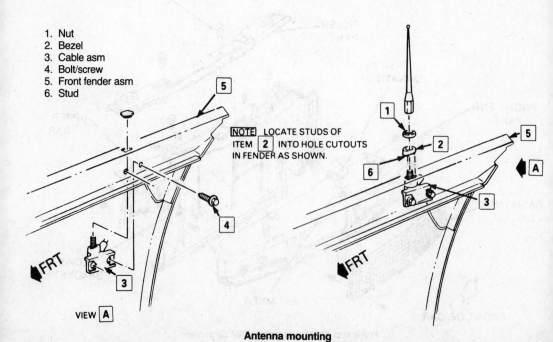

Antenna mounting

cable from the bottom of the antenna base.

3. Remove the two antenna retaining screws from inside the fender.

4. Reverse the above to install. Make sure all connections are tight.

INTERIOR

Door Panel

REMOVAL AND INSTALLATION

1982-87

A one piece trim panel is used on styles with standard trim. The custom trim has an upper metal trim panel. The one piece trim hangs over the door inner panel across the top and is secured by clips down the sides and across the bottom. It is retained by screws located in the areas of the top front of the panel assembly.

1. Remove all door inside handles.

2. Remove the door inside locking rod knob.

3. Remove the screws inserted through the door armrest and pull the handle assembly into the door inner panel or armrest hanger support bracket.

4. On styles with remote control mirrors assemblies, disengage the end of the mirror con-

trol cable from the bezel on the standard trim, or from the upper trim panel on the custom trim. On custom trim, remove the upper trim panel.

5. On styles with power window or door lock controls located in the door trim panel, disconnect the wire harnesses at the switch assemblies. On the four door sedan and the two door hatchback, remove the switch cover by pushing down at the switch area and pulling down at the bottom of the cover. The switch and base may be removed from the trim with the cover removed.

6. Remove the remote control handle bezel screws.

7. Remove the screws used to hold the armrest to the inner panel.

8. Remove the screws and plastic retainers from the perimeter of the door trim using tool BT-7323A or equivalent and a screwdriver. To remove the trim panel, push the trim panel upward and outboard to disengage from the door inner panel at the beltline.

9. On styles with an insulator pad fastened to the door inner panel, use tool J-21104 or equivalent to remove the fasteners and the insulator pad.

10. On styles with the water defector held in place by fasteners, use tool BT-7323A or equiv-

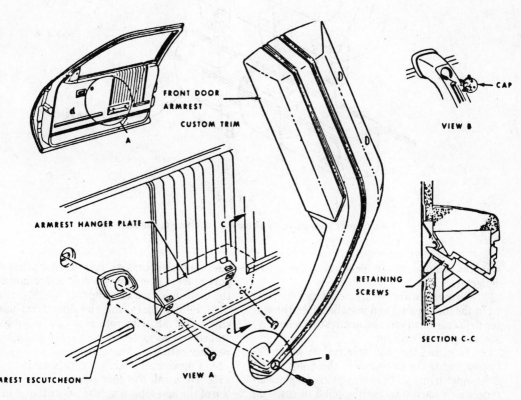

Front door armrest and pull handle attachment, custom trim

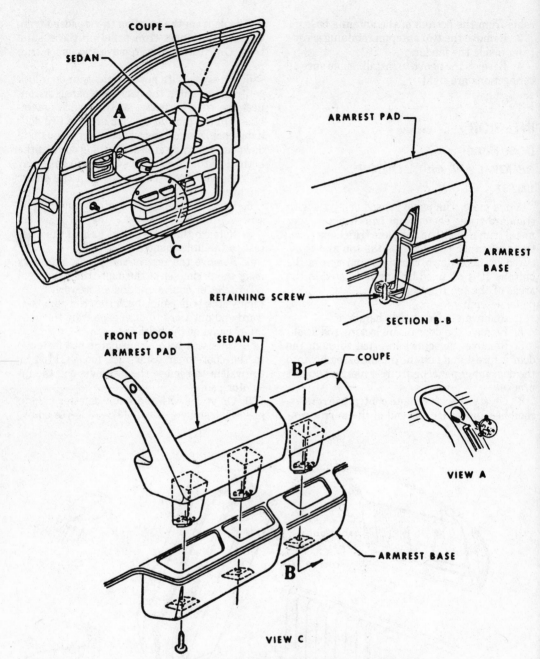

Front door armrest and pull handle attachment, standard trim

alent to remove the fasteners and the water deflector.

11. On styles with the armrest bracket riveted to the inner panel and installed over the water deflector, drill out the armrest bracket rivets using a $\frac{3}{16}$" drill bit.

12. To install the insulator pad or water deflector, locate the fasteners in the holes in the door inner panel and press in place. Replace all tape which may have been applied to assist in holding insulator pad or water deflector in

place. Where necessary, install the armrest support bracket over the water deflector and onto the door inner panel using $\frac{3}{16}$" × $\frac{11}{32}$" rivets.

13. Before installing the door trim panel, check that all trim retainers are securely installed to the assembly and are not damaged. Replace retainers where required.

14. Connect all electrical components.

15. To install the door trim panel, locate the top of the assembly over the upper flange of the door inner panel, inserting the door handle

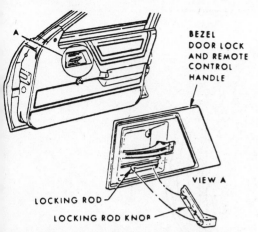

Typical door lock remote control handle and bezel

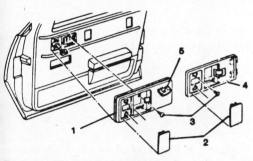

Typical inside door lock handle bezel

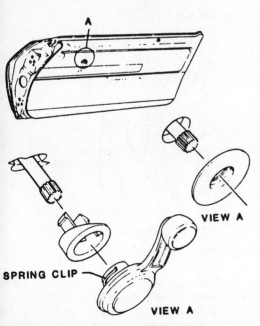

Typical window regulator handle installation

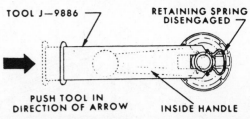

Removing the trim clip retained door inside handle

panel so the trim retainers are align with the attaching holes in the panel and tap the retainers into the holes with the palm of your hand or a clean rubber mallet.

17. Install all previously removed items.

Front Door Lock

REMOVAL AND INSTALLATION

1. Raise the door window and remove the door trim panel and water deflector.

2. Disengage the following rods at the lock assembly:

    a. Inside locking rod.

    b. Inside handle to locking rod.

    c. Lock cylinder to locking rod.

3. Remove the lock screws and lower the lock to disengage the outside handle to the lock rod. Remove the lock from the door.

4. To install, first install the the spring clips to the lock assembly, then reverse the removal procedure. Tighten the lock retaining screws to 80-100 in. lbs.

Rear Door Lock

REMOVAL AND INSTALLATION

1. Remove the door trim and water deflector.

2. Remove the door glass assembly and the stationary vent glass assembly.

3. Disconnect the inside handle to lock rod and inside locking knob to lock rod.

4. Disconnect the outside handle to lock rod.

5. Remove the lock screws and remove the lock through the access hole.

6. To install, reverse the removal procedure and tighten the lock retaining screws to 80-100 in. lbs.

Front Door Glass

REMOVAL AND INSTALLATION

1982-87 Except Cavalier Convertible

1. Raise the door window to the full up position and remove the door trim panel and water deflector.

2. Remove the bolts holding the front glass retainer to the door inner panel and remove the

through the handle slot in the panel and press down on the trim panel to engage the upper retaining clips.

16. Position the trim panel to the door inner

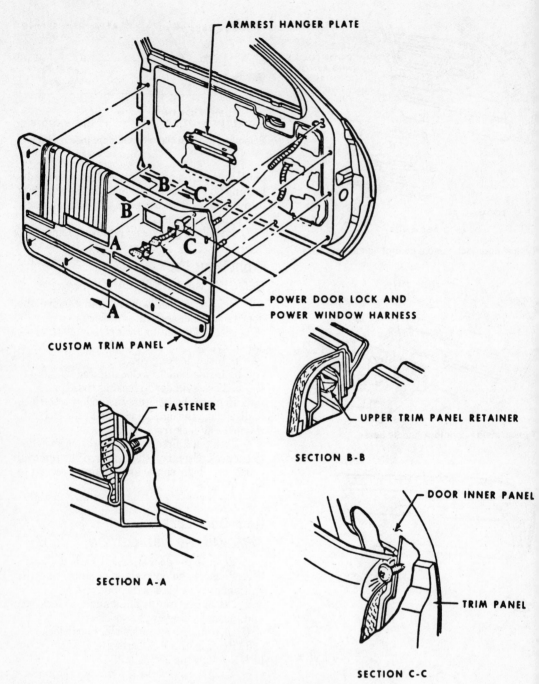

ARMREST HANGER PLATE

POWER DOOR LOCK AND
POWER WINDOW HARNESS

CUSTOM TRIM PANEL

FASTENER

UPPER TRIM PANEL RETAINER

SECTION B-B

DOOR INNER PANEL

SECTION A-A

TRIM PANEL

SECTION C-C

Front door trim panel retention

retainer through the rear access hole. Lower the glass to approximately 3″ above the beltline.

4. Rotate the glass forward to disengage the window regulator roller from the sash channel.

5. Lower the glass into the door to disengage the rear guide (on the glass) from the rear run channel.

6. Using care, raise the glass while tilting forward and remove the glass inboard of the upper frame.

7. To install, tilt the front edge of the glass downward to locate the glass in the door.

8. Apply pressure rearward and snap the glass rear guide into the rear run channel.

9. Lower the glass to about 3″ above the beltline and install the widow regulator roller to sash channel.

10. Run the glass to the full up position.

11. Place the front glass retainer in position and install the bolts.

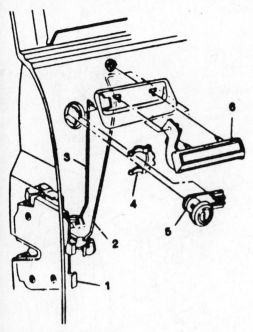

Front door lock system

12. Check the window to make sure it operates correctly, then install the remaining trim parts.

Cavalier Convertible

1. Remove the door trim panel, sound absorber, armrest bracket and water deflector.

2. Position the glass so that the up stop spanner nut on the glass is visible through the access hole.

3. Using tool J-22055 or equivalent, remove the spanner nut, bushing and stop from the glass.

4. Position the glass so the spanner nuts are visible through the access hole.

5. Remove the spanner nuts and bushings.

6. Loosen the upper stabilizers.

7. Disengage the glass from the studs on the sash where the spanner nuts were removed.

8. Lower the regulator to the full-down position.

9. Grasp the glass and pull the glass up, with the front of the glass tilted down and remove the glass.

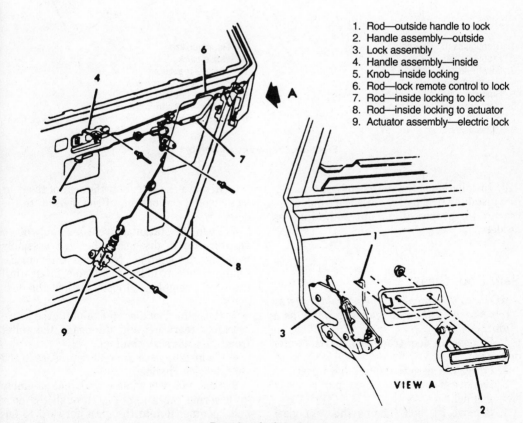

1. Rod—outside handle to lock
2. Handle assembly—outside
3. Lock assembly
4. Handle assembly—inside
5. Knob—inside locking
6. Rod—lock remote control to lock
7. Rod—inside locking to lock
8. Rod—inside locking to actuator
9. Actuator assembly—electric lock

VIEW A

Rear door lock system

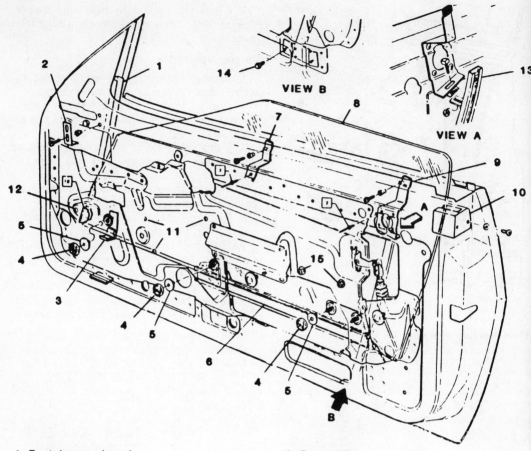

1. Front glass run channel
2. Front up stop
3. Catch—front up stop
4. Glass retainer
5. Bushing
6. Cam assembly door glass
7. Front stabilizer
8. Glass assembly
9. Rear stabilizer
10. Guide block
11. Rivets—regulator
12. Rivets—regulator motor
13. Rear up stop block
14. Rivets—rear cam assembly lower
15. Attaching nuts inner panel cam door reinforcement

Front door hardware, convertible

10. Installation is the reverse of removal. Before installing trim parts, check the window operation for proper alignment and adjust as needed.

Rear Door Glass

NOTE: *The stationary vent assembly must be removed with the rear glass assembly as a unit.*

1. Remove the door trim panel and the water deflector.

2. Lower the glass to the full down position.

3. Remove the screws at the top of the division channel.

4. Remove the bolt holding the vent glass support at the belt.

5. Remove the screws at the rear of the door face holding the bottom of the division to the door.

6. Push the stationary vent assembly down and forward to disengage the vent assembly from the run channel. Now that the vent assembly is inboard of the door frame, lift up until the vent assembly is stopped against the door glass.

7. Raise the door glass 6-8″ and tilt the whole assembly rearward and disengage the roller from the glass sash channel.

8. To install, place the rear door glass in the vent division channel.

9. Load the rear window and vent assembly by lowering the assemblies through the door belt opening. Rotate the glass forward to engage the regulator roller in the glass sash chan-

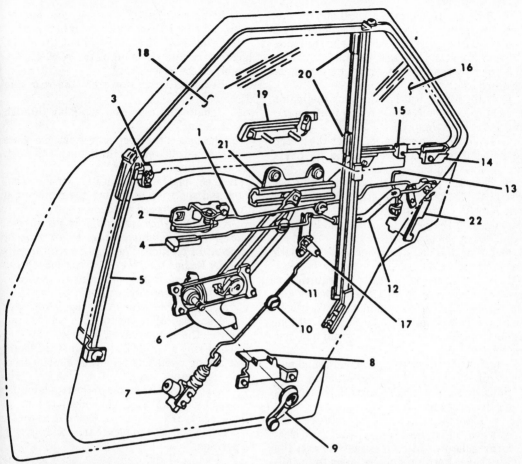

1. Rod—remote control to lock
2. Handle—inside lock remote control
3. Filler—sealing strip—front
4. Knob—inside lock
5. Retainer—glass front run channel
6. Regulator assembly
7. Actuator assembly—door lock
8. Glass down stop
9. Handle—window regulator
10. Shoe—inside locking rods
11. Rod—inside lock to actuator

12. Rod—inside lock knob to lock
13. Rod—outside handle to lock
14. Filler—sealing strip rear
15. Support—vent glass
16. Vent assembly—stationary
17. Bell crank
18. Glass assembly
19. Handle—outside glass
20. Glass guide
21. Glass sash channel
22. Lock assembly

Rear door hardware

nel. Reposition the vent glass into the door frame.

10. Replace the screws at the top of the division channel.

11. Replace the screws at the rear face of the door holding division and lower support in place.

12. Replace the bolt securing the division channel support at the belt.

13. Replace all previously removed trim.

Front Window Regulator And Motor

NOTE: *The following procedure includes both manual and power window regulator re-* *moval and installation. Besides the regulators, window motors and rollers including the washer and pin are serviced separately.*

REMOVAL AND INSTALLATION

1982-87 Except Cavalier Convertible

1. Remove the door trim panel and the water deflector.

2. Raise the glass to the full up position and tape the glass to the door frame using fabric tape.

3. Punch out the center pins of the regulator rivets using a ¼" drill bit. On electric regulators, drill out the rivets supporting the motor to the door inner panel.

4. Move the regulator rearward and disconnect the wiring harness from the motor, if so equipped. Disengage the roller on the regulator lift arm from the glass sash channel.

5. Remove the regulator through the rear access hole.

6. Using a $\frac{3}{16}$″ drill bit, drill out the motor attaching rivets and remove the motor from the regulator, if so equipped.

7. To install, if so equipped, attach the motor to the regulator using a rivet tool and $\frac{3}{16}$″ rivets or $\frac{3}{16}$″ nuts and bolts.

8. Place the regulator through the rear access hole into the door inner panel. If an electric regulator is being installed, connect the wire connector to the motor prior to installing the regulator in the panel.

9. Locate the lift arm roller into the glass sash channel.

10. Using rivet tool J-29022 or equivalent, rivet the regulator to the inner panel of the door using $\frac{1}{4}$″ × $\frac{1}{2}$″ aluminum peel type rivets (part no. 9436175 or equivalent). If a rivet tool is not available, use the following nut and bolt method:

　a. Install U-clips on the regulator and motor (if so equipped), at the attaching locations. Be sure to install clips with clinch nuts on the outboard side of the regulator.

　b. Place the regulator through the rear access hole into the door inner panel. If an electric regulator is being installed, connect the wire connector to the motor prior to installing the regulator in the panel.

　c. Locate the lift arm roller into the glass sash channel.

　d. Align the regulator with the clinch nuts to the holes in the inner panel.

　e. Attach the regulator and motor to the door inner panel with $\frac{1}{4}$″–20 × $\frac{1}{2}$″ screws into $\frac{1}{4}$″ nuts with integral washers. Tighten the screws to 90-125 in lbs.

11. If an electrical window regulator is being installed use a rivet mentioned in step 10 to rivet the regulator motor to the door inner panel.

12. Replace all previously removed parts.

Cavalier Convertible

1. Remove the door trim panel, sound absorber, armrest bracket and water deflector.

2. Using a $\frac{1}{4}$″ drill bit, drill out the rivets supporting the motor to the door inner panel.

3. Disconnect the electrical connector from the regulator motor.

4. Support the door glass in the full-up position, using rubber wedge door stops.

5. Remove the nuts holding the cam assembly door reinforcement to the inner panel and remove the cam assembly.

6. Remove the bolt holding the upper portion of the rear cam assembly to the inner panel.

7. Using a $\frac{3}{16}$″ drill bit, drill out the rivets, holding the lower section of the rear cam assembly to the inner panel.

8. Remove the up stop from the rear cam assembly.

9. Remove the rear cam assembly through the access hole.

10. Disengage the regulator from the glass sash channel and remove the regulator through the access hole.

11. If equipped with an electric window regulator and you wish to remove the motor from the regulator proceed as follows:

CAUTION: *When removing the electric motor from the regulator, the sector gear must be locked in position. The regulator lift arm is under tension from the counterbalance spring and could cause personal injury if the sector gear is not locked in position.*

　a. Drill a hole through the regulator sector gear and backplate and install a bolt and nut to lock the sector gear in position.

　b. Using a $\frac{3}{16}$″ drill bit, drill out the motor attaching rivets and remove the motor from the regulator.

　c. To install the motor to the regulator use a rivet tool J-29022 or equivalent and install $\frac{3}{16}$″ rivets or $\frac{3}{16}$″ nuts and bolts. Remove the bolt and nut used to secure the sector gear in position.

12. To install the regulator, make sure the regulator is in the full up position.

13. Install the regulator arm rollers to the glass sash channel.

14. Install the rear cam assembly using $\frac{3}{16}$″ aluminum peel-type rivets making sure to install the up stop in the cam assembly.

15. Connect the electrical connector to the motor on the regulator.

16. Engage the roller on the regulator lift arm in the cam assembly door reinforcement.

17. Install the cam assembly door reinforcement to the inner panel.

18. Align the attaching holes in the regulator with the holes in the inner panel.

19. Install the regulator to the inner panel, using a rivet gun and $\frac{1}{4}$″ × $\frac{1}{2}$″ aluminum peel type rivets.

Rear Window Regulator

NOTE: *The following procedure includes both manual and power window regulator removal and installation. Besides the regulators, window motors and rollers including the washer and pin are serviced separately.*

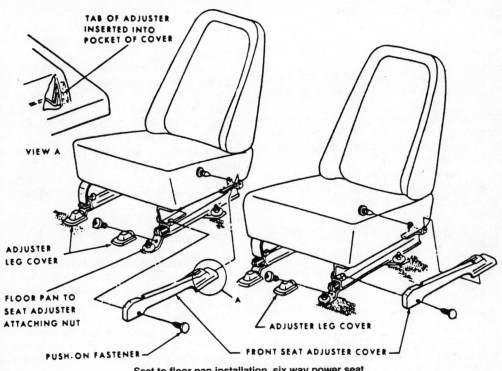

TAB OF ADJUSTER
INSERTED INTO
POCKET OF COVER

VIEW A

ADJUSTER
LEG COVER

FLOOR PAN TO
SEAT ADJUSTER
ATTACHING NUT

A

ADJUSTER LEG COVER

PUSH-ON FASTENER

FRONT SEAT ADJUSTER COVER

Seat to floor pan installation, six way power seat

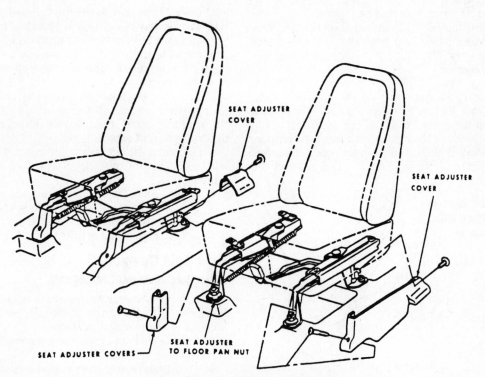

SEAT ADJUSTER
COVER

SEAT ADJUSTER
COVER

SEAT ADJUSTER COVERS

SEAT ADJUSTER
TO FLOOR PAN NUT

Seat to floor pan installation, manual seat

REMOVAL AND INSTALLATION
1982-87

1. Remove the door trim panel and the water deflector.

2. Raise the glass to the full up position and tape the glass to the door frame using fabric tape.

3. Punch out the center pins of the regulator rivets using a ¼" drill bit. On electric regulators, drill out the rivets supporting the motor to the door inner panel.

4. Disconnect the wiring harness from the motor, if so equipped. Disengage the roller on the regulator lift arm from the glass sash channel.

5. Remove the regulator through the rear access hole.

6. Using a ³⁄₁₆" drill bit, drill out the motor attaching rivets and remove the motor from the regulator, if so equipped.

7. To install, if so equipped, attach the motor to the regulator using a rivet tool and ³⁄₁₆" rivets or ³⁄₁₆" nuts and bolts.

8. Place the regulator through the rear access hole into the door inner panel. If an electric regulator is being installed, connect the wire connector to the motor prior to installing the regulator in the panel.

9. Locate the lift arm roller into the glass sash channel.

10. Using rivet tool J-29022 or equivalent, rivet the regulator to the inner panel of the door using ¼" × ½" aluminum peel type rivets (part no. 9436175 or equivalent). If a rivet tool is not available, use the following nut and bolt method:

   a. Install U-clips on the regulator and motor (if so equipped), at the attaching locations. Be sure to install clips with clinch nuts on the outboard side of the regulator.

   b. Place the regulator through the rear access hole into the door inner panel. If an electric regulator is being installed, connect the

wire connector to the motor prior to installing the regulator in the panel.

   c. Locate the lift arm roller into the glass sash channel.

   d. Align the regulator with the clinch nuts to the holes in the inner panel.

   e. Attach the regulator and motor to the door inner panel with ¼"-20 × ½" screws into ¼" nuts with integral washers. Tighten the screws to 90-125 in lbs.

11. If an electrical window regulator is being installed use a rivet mentioned in step 10 to rivet the regulator motor to the door inner panel.

12. Replace all previously removed parts.

Inside Rearview Mirror
REPLACEMENT

The rearview mirror is attached to a support which is secured to the windshield glass. This support is installed by the glass supplier using a plastic-polyvinyl butyl adhesive.

Service replacement windshield glass has the mirror support bonded to the glass assembly.

Service kits are available to replace a detached mirror support or install a new part. Follow the manufacturer's instructions for replacement.

Front Seat
REMOVAL AND INSTALLATION

1. Operate the seat to the full-forward position. If a six way power seat is operable, move the seat to the full-forward and up positions. To gain access to the adjuster to floor pan retaining nuts, remove the adjuster rear foot covers or carpet retainers.

2. Remove the track covers where necessary, then remove the rear attaching nuts. Remove the front foot covers, then remove the adjuster to floor pan front attaching nuts.

3. On seats with power adjusters, tilt the seat rearward and disconnect the feed wire connector.

4. Remove the seat assembly from the car.

5. To install the seat assembly reverse the removal procedure. Tighten the seat adjuster to floor pan attaching bolts or nuts to 15-21 ft. lbs.

Rear Seat Cushion
REMOVAL AND INSTALLATION

1. Remove the rear seat cushion attaching bolts, located at the center of the right and left sections of the rear seat cushion.

2. Lift the cushion upward and remove from the vehicle.

3. To install, reverse the removal procedure. Torque the seat cushion attaching bolts to 14-20 ft. lbs.

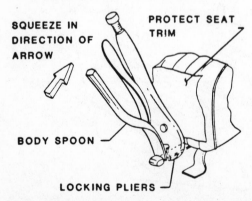

SQUEEZE IN DIRECTION OF ARROW

PROTECT SEAT TRIM

BODY SPOON

LOCKING PLIERS

Removal and installation of the front seat adjuster control arm knob

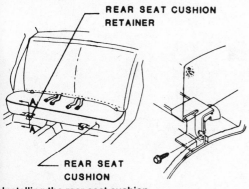

REAR SEAT CUSHION
RETAINER

REAR SEAT
CUSHION

Installing the rear seat cushion

Power Seat Motors

REMOVAL AND INSTALLATION

1. Remove the front seat assembly and place upside down on a clean surface.

2. Disconnect the motor feed wires from the motor.

3. Remove the nut securing the front of the motor support bracket to the inboard adjuster and withdraw the assembly from the adjuster and the gearnut drives.

4. Disconnect the drive cables from the motor and complete the removal of the support bracket with motors attached.

5. Grind off the peened over ends(s) of the grommet assembly securing the motor to the support and separate the motors from the support, as required.

6. To install, reverse the removal procedure except as noted:

   a. Drill out the top end of the grommet assembly using a $\frac{3}{16}''$ drill.

   b. Install the grommet assembly to the motor support bracket and secure the motor to the grommet using a $\frac{3}{16}''$ rivet.

Mechanic's Data

11

General Conversion Table

Multiply By	To Convert	To	
		LENGTH	
2.54	Inches	Centimeters	.3937
25.4	Inches	Millimeters	.03937
30.48	Feet	Centimeters	.0328
.304	Feet	Meters	3.28
.914	Yards	Meters	1.094
1.609	Miles	Kilometers	.621
		VOLUME	
.473	Pints	Liters	2.11
.946	Quarts	Liters	1.06
3.785	Gallons	Liters	.264
.016	Cubic inches	Liters	61.02
16.39	Cubic inches	Cubic cms.	.061
28.3	Cubic feet	Liters	.0353
		MASS (Weight)	
28.35	Ounces	Grams	.035
.4536	Pounds	Kilograms	2.20
—	To obtain	From	Multiply by

Multiply By	To Convert	To	
		AREA	
.645	Square inches	Square cms.	.155
.836	Square yds.	Square meters	1.196
		FORCE	
4.448	Pounds	Newtons	.225
.138	Ft./lbs.	Kilogram/meters	7.23
1.36	Ft./lbs.	Newton-meters	.737
.112	In./lbs.	Newton-meters	8.844
		PRESSURE	
.068	Psi	Atmospheres	14.7
6.89	Psi	Kilopascals	.145
		OTHER	
1.104	Horsepower (DIN)	Horsepower (SAE)	.9861
.746	Horsepower (SAE)	Kilowatts (KW)	1.34
1.60	Mph	Km/h	.625
.425	Mpg	Km/1	2.35
—	To obtain	From	Multiply by

Tap Drill Sizes

National Coarse or U.S.S.

Screw & Tap Size	Threads Per Inch	Use Drill Number
No. 5	40	.39
No. 6	32	.36
No. 8	32	.29
No. 10	24	.25
No. 12	24	.17
1/4	20	8
5/16	18	F
3/8	16	5/16
7/16	14	U
1/2	13	27/64
9/16	12	31/64
5/8	11	17/32
3/4	10	21/32
7/8	9	49/64

National Coarse or U.S.S.

Screw & Tap Size	Threads Per Inch	Use Drill Number
1	8	7/8
1 1/8	7	63/64
1 1/4	7	1 7/64
1 1/2	6	1 11/32

National Fine or S.A.E.

Screw & Tap Size	Threads Per Inch	Use Drill Number
No. 5	44	.37
No. 6	40	.33
No. 8	36	.29
No. 10	32	.21

National Fine or S.A.E.

Screw & Tap Size	Threads Per Inch	Use Drill Number
No. 12	28	.15
1/4	28	3
6/16	24	1
3/8	24	Q
7/16	20	W
1/2	20	29/64
9/16	18	33/64
5/8	18	37/64
3/4	16	11/16
7/8	14	13/16
1 1/8	12	1 3/64
1 1/4	12	1 11/64
1 1/2	12	1 27/64

Drill Sizes In Decimal Equivalents

Inch	Decimal	Wire	mm
1/64	.0156		.39
	.0157		.4
	.0160	78	
	.0165		.42
	.0173		.44
	.0177		.45
	.0180	77	
	.0181		.46
	.0189		.48
	.0197		.5
	.0200	76	
	.0210	75	
	.0217		.55
	.0225	74	
	.0236		.6
	.0240	73	
	.0250	72	
	.0256		.65
	.0260	71	
	.0276		.7
	.0280	70	
	.0292	69	
	.0295		.75
	.0310	68	
1/32	.0312		.79
	.0315		.8
	.0320	67	
	.0330	66	
	.0335		.85
	.0350	65	
	.0354		.9
	.0360	64	
	.0370	63	
	.0374		.95
	.0380	62	
	.0390	61	
	.0394		1.0
	.0400	60	
	.0410	59	
	.0413		1.05
	.0420	58	
	.0430	57	
	.0433		1.1
	.0453		1.15
	.0465	56	
3/64	.0469		1.19
	.0472		1.2
	.0492		1.25
	.0512		1.3
	.0520	55	
	.0531		1.35
	.0550	54	
	.0551		1.4
	.0571		1.45
	.0591		1.5
	.0595	53	
	.0610		1.55
1/16	.0625		1.59
	.0630		1.6
	.0635	52	
	.0650		1.65
	.0669		1.7
	.0670	51	
	.0689		1.75
	.0700	50	
	.0709		1.8
	.0728		1.85

Inch	Decimal	Wire	mm
	.0730	49	
	.0748		1.9
	.0760	48	
	.0768		1.95
5/64	.0781		1.98
	.0785	47	
	.0787		2.0
	.0807		2.05
	.0810	46	
	.0820	45	
	.0827		2.1
	.0846		2.15
	.0860	44	
	.0866		2.2
	.0886		2.25
	.0890	43	
	.0906		2.3
	.0925		2.35
	.0935	42	
3/32	.0938		2.38
	.0945		2.4
	.0960	41	
	.0965		2.45
	.0980	40	
	.0981		2.5
	.0995	39	
	.1015	38	
	.1024		2.6
	.1040	37	
	.1063		2.7
	.1065	36	
	.1083		2.75
7/64	.1094		2.77
	.1100	35	
	.1102		2.8
	.1110	34	
	.1130	33	
	.1142		2.9
	.1160	32	
	.1181		3.0
	.1200	31	
	.1220		3.1
1/8	.1250		3.17
	.1260		3.2
	.1280		3.25
	.1285	30	
	.1299		3.3
	.1339		3.4
	.1360	29	
	.1378		3.5
	.1405	28	
9/64	.1406		3.57
	.1417		3.6
	.1440	27	
	.1457		3.7
	.1470	26	
	.1476		3.75
	.1495	25	
	.1496		3.8
	.1520	24	
	.1535		3.9
	.1540	23	
5/32	.1562		3.96
	.1570	22	
	.1575		4.0
	.1590	21	
	.1610	20	

Inch	Decimal	Wire & Letter	mm
	.1614		4.1
	.1654		4.2
	.1660	19	
	.1673		4.25
	.1693		4.3
	.1695	18	
11/64	.1719		4.36
	.1730	17	
	.1732		4.4
	.1770	16	
	.1772		4.5
	.1800	15	
	.1811		4.6
	.1820	14	
	.1850	13	
	.1850		4.7
	.1870		4.75
3/16	.1875		4.76
	.1890		4.8
	.1890	12	
	.1910	11	
	.1929		4.9
	.1935	10	
	.1960	9	
	.1969		5.0
	.1990	8	
	.2008		5.1
	.2010	7	
13/64	.2031		5.16
	.2040	6	
	.2047		5.2
	.2055	5	
	.2067		5.25
	.2087		5.3
	.2090	4	
	.2126		5.4
	.2130	3	
	.2165		5.5
7/32	.2188		5.55
	.2205		5.6
	.2210	2	
	.2244		5.7
	.2264		5.75
	.2280	1	
	.2283		5.8
	.2323		5.9
	.2340	A	
15/64	.2344		5.95
	.2362		6.0
	.2380	B	
	.2402		6.1
	.2420	C	
	.2441		6.2
	.2460	D	
	.2461		6.25
	.2480		6.3
1/4	.2500	E	6.35
	.2520		6.
	.2559		6.5
	.2570	F	
	.2598		6.6
	.2610	G	
	.2638		6.7
17/64	.2656		6.74
	.2657		6.75
	.2660	H	
	.2677		6.8

Inch	Decimal	Letter	mm
	.2717		6.9
	.2720	I	
	.2756		7.0
	.2770	J	
	.2795		7.1
	.2810	K	
9/32	.2812		7.14
	.2835		7.2
	.2854		7.25
	.2874		7.3
	.2900	L	
	.2913		7.4
	.2950	M	
	.2953		7.5
19/64	.2969		7.54
	.2992		7.6
	.3020	N	
	.3031		7.7
	.3051		7.75
	.3071		7.8
	.3110		7.9
5/16	.3125		7.93
	.3150		8.0
	.3160	O	
	.3189		8.1
	.3228		8.2
	.3230	P	
	.3248		8.25
	.3268		8.3
21/64	.3281		8.33
	.3307		8.4
	.3320	Q	
	.3346		8.5
	.3386		8.6
	.3390	R	
11/32	.3438		8.73
	.3445		8.75
	.3465		8.8
	.3480	S	
	.3504		8.9
	.3543		9.0
	.3580	T	
	.3583		9.1
23/64	.3594		9.12
	.3622		9.2
	.3642		9.25
	.3661		9.3
	.3680	U	
	.3701		9.4
	.3740		9.5
3/8	.3750		9.52
	.3770	V	
	.3780		9.6
	.3819		9.7
	.3839		9.75
	.3858		9.8
	.3860	W	
	.3898		9.9
25/64	.3906		9.92
	.3937		10.0
	.3970	X	
	.4040	Y	
13/32	.4062		10.31
	.4130	Z	
	.4134		10.5
27/64	.4219		10.71

Inch	Decimal	mm
	.4331	11.0
7/16	.4375	11.11
	.4528	11.5
29/64	.4531	11.51
15/32	.4688	11.90
	.4724	12.0
31/64	.4844	12.30
	.4921	12.5
1/2	.5000	12.70
	.5118	13.0
33/64	.5156	13.09
17/32	.5312	13.49
	.5315	13.5
35/64	.5469	13.89
	.5512	14.0
9/16	.5625	14.28
	.5709	14.5
37/64	.5781	14.68
	.5906	15.0
19/32	.5938	15.08
39/64	.6094	15.47
	.6102	15.5
5/8	.6250	15.87
	.6299	16.0
41/64	.6406	16.27
	.6496	16.5
21/32	.6562	16.66
	.6693	17.0
43/64	.6719	17.06
11/16	.6875	17.46
	.6890	17.5
45/64	.7031	17.85
	.7087	18.0
23/32	.7188	18.25
	.7283	18.5
47/64	.7344	18.65
	.7480	19.0
3/4	.7500	19.05
49/64	.7656	19.44
	.7677	19.5
25/32	.7812	19.84
	.7874	20.0
51/64	.7969	20.24
	.8071	20.5
13/16	.8125	20.63
	.8268	21.0
53/64	.8281	21.03
27/32	.8438	21.43
	.8465	21.5
55/64	.8594	21.82
	.8661	22.0
7/8	.8750	22.22
	.8858	22.5
57/64	.8906	22.62
	.9055	23.0
29/32	.9062	23.01
59/64	.9219	23.41
	.9252	23.5
15/16	.9375	23.81
	.9449	24.0
61/64	.9531	24.2
	.9646	24.5
31/32	.9688	24.6
	.9843	25.0
63/64	.9844	25.0
1	1.0000	25.4

AIR/FUEL RATIO: The ratio of air to gasoline by weight in the fuel mixture drawn into the engine.

AIR INJECTION: One method of reducing harmful exhaust emissions by injecting air into each of the exhaust ports of an engine. The fresh air entering the hot exhaust manifold causes any remaining fuel to be burned before it can exit the tailpipe.

ALTERNATOR: A device used for converting mechanical energy into electrical energy.

AMMETER: An instrument, calibrated in amperes, used to measure the flow of an electrical current in a circuit. Ammeters are always connected in series with the circuit being tested.

AMPERE: The rate of flow of electrical current present when one volt of electrical pressure is applied against one ohm of electrical resistance.

ANALOG COMPUTER: Any microprocessor that uses similar (analogous) electrical signals to make its calculations.

ARMATURE: A laminated, soft iron core wrapped by a wire that converts electrical energy to mechanical energy as in a motor or relay. When rotated in a magnetic field, it changes mechanical energy into electrical energy as in a generator.

ATMOSPHERIC PRESSURE: The pressure on the Earth's surface caused by the weight of the air in the atmosphere. At sea level, this pressure is 14.7 psi at 32°F (101 kPa at 0°C).

ATOMIZATION: The breaking down of a liquid into a fine mist that can be suspended in air.

AXIAL PLAY: Movement parallel to a shaft or bearing bore.

BACKFIRE: The sudden combustion of gases in the intake or exhaust system that results in a loud explosion.

BACKLASH: The clearance or play between two parts, such as meshed gears.

BACKPRESSURE: Restrictions in the exhaust system that slow the exit of exhaust gases from the combustion chamber.

BAKELITE: A heat resistant, plastic insulator material commonly used in printed circuit boards and transistorized components.

BALL BEARING: A bearing made up of hardened inner and outer races between which hardened steel ball roll.

BALLAST RESISTOR: A resistor in the primary ignition circuit that lowers voltage after the engine is started to reduce wear on ignition components.

BEARING: A friction reducing, supportive device usually located between a stationary part and a moving part.

BIMETAL TEMPERATURE SENSOR: Any sensor or switch made of two dissimilar types of metal that bend when heated or cooled due to the different expansion rates of the alloys. These types of sensors usually function as an on/off switch.

BLOWBY: Combustion gases, composed of water vapor and unburned fuel, that leak past the piston rings into the crankcase during normal engine operation. These gases are removed by the PCV system to prevent the build-up of harmful acids in the crankcase.

BRAKE PAD: A brake shoe and lining assembly used with disc brakes.

BRAKE SHOE: The backing for the brake lining. The term is, however, usually applied to the assembly of the brake backing and lining.

BUSHING: A liner, usually removable, for a bearing; an anti-friction liner used in place of a bearing.

BYPASS: System used to bypass ballast resistor during engine cranking to increase voltage supplied to the coil.

CALIPER: A hydraulically activated device in a disc brake system, which is mounted straddling the brake rotor (disc). The caliper contains at least one piston and two brake pads. Hydraulic pressure on the piston(s) forces the pads against the rotor.

CAMSHAFT: A shaft in the engine on which are the lobes (cams) which operate the valves. The camshaft is driven by the crankshaft, via a belt, chain or gears, at one half the crankshaft speed.

CAPACITOR: A device which stores an electrical charge.

CARBON MONOXIDE (CO): a colorless, odorless gas given off as a normal byproduct of combustion. It is poisonous and extremely dangerous in confined areas, building up slowly to toxic levels without warning if adequate ventilation is not available.

CARBURETOR: A device, usually mounted on the intake manifold of an engine, which mixes the air and fuel in the proper proportion to allow even combustion.

CATALYTIC CONVERTER: A device installed in the exhaust system, like a muffler, that converts harmful byproducts of combustion into carbon dioxide and water vapor by means of a heat-producing chemical reaction.

CENTRIFUGAL ADVANCE: A mechanical method of advancing the spark timing by using flyweights in the distributor that react to centrifugal force generated by the distributor shaft rotation.

CHECK VALVE: Any one-way valve installed to permit the flow of air, fuel or vacuum in one direction only.

CHOKE: A device, usually a moveable valve, placed in the intake path of a carburetor to restrict the flow of air.

CIRCUIT: Any unbroken path through which an electrical current can flow. Also used to describe fuel flow in some instances.

CIRCUIT BREAKER: A switch which protects an electrical circuit from overload by opening the circuit when the current flow exceeds a predetermined level. Some circuit breakers must be reset manually, while other reset automatically

COIL (IGNITION): A transformer in the ignition circuit which steps of the voltage provided to the spark plugs.

COMBINATION MANIFOLD: An assembly which includes both the intake and exhaust manifolds in one casting.

COMBINATION VALVE: A device used in some fuel systems that routes fuel vapors to a charcoal storage canister instead of venting them into the atmosphere. The valve relieves fuel tank pressure and allows fresh air into the tank as fuel level drops to prevent a vapor lock situation.

COMPRESSION RATIO: The comparison of the total volume of the cylinder and combustion chamber with the piston at BDC and the piston at TDC.

CONDENSER: 1. An electrical device which acts to store an electrical charge, preventing voltage surges.
2. A radiator-like device in the air conditioning system in which refrigerant gas condenses into a liquid, giving off heat.

CONDUCTOR: Any material through which an electrical current can be transmitted easily.

CONTINUITY: Continuous or complete circuit. Can be checked with an ohmmeter.

COUNTERSHAFT: An intermediate shaft which is rotated by a mainshaft and transmits, in turn, that rotation to a working part.

CRANKCASE: The lower part of an engine in which the crankshaft and related parts operate.

CRANKSHAFT: The main driving shaft of an engine which receives reciprocating motion from the pistons and converts it to rotary motion.

CYLINDER: In an engine, the round hole in the engine block in which the piston(s) ride.

CYLINDER BLOCK: The main structural member of an engine in which is found the cylinders, crankshaft and other principal parts.

CYLINDER HEAD: The detachable portion of the engine, fastened, usually, to the top of the cylinder block, containing all or most of the combustion chambers. On overhead valve engines, it contains the valves and their operating parts. On overhead cam engines, it contains the camshaft as well.

DEAD CENTER: The extreme top or bottom of the piston stroke.

DETONATION: An unwanted explosion of the air fuel mixture in the combustion chamber caused by excess heat and compression, advanced timing, or an overly lean mixture. Also referred to as "ping".

DIAPHRAGM: A thin, flexible wall separating two cavities, such as in a vacuum advance unit.

DIESELING: A condition in which hot spots in the combustion chamber cause the engine to run on after the key is turned off.

DIFFERENTIAL: A geared assembly which allows the transmission of motion between drive axles, giving one axle the ability to turn faster than the other.

DIODE: An electrical device that will allow current to flow in one direction only.

DISC BRAKE: A hydraulic braking assembly consisting of a brake disc, or rotor, mounted on an axle, and a caliper assembly containing, usually two brake pads which are activated by hydraulic pressure. The pads are forced against the sides of the disc, creating friction which slows the vehicle.

DISTRIBUTOR: A mechanically driven device on an engine which is responsible for electrically firing the spark plug at a predetermined point of the piston stroke.

DOWEL PIN: A pin, inserted in mating holes in two different parts allowing those parts to maintain a fixed relationship.

DRUM BRAKE: A braking system which consists of two brake shoes and one or two wheel cylinders, mounted on a fixed backing plate, and a brake drum, mounted on an axle, which revolves around the assembly. Hydraulic action applied to the wheel cylinders forces the shoes outward against the drum, creating friction and slowing the vehicle.

DWELL: The rate, measured in degrees of shaft rotation, at which an electrical circuit cycles on and off.

ELECTRONIC CONTROL UNIT (ECU): Ignition module, module, amplifier or igniter. See Module for definition.

ELECTRONIC IGNITION: A system in which the timing and firing of the spark plugs is controlled by an electronic control unit, usually called a module. These systems have not points or condenser.

ENDPLAY: The measured amount of axial movement in a shaft.

ENGINE: A device that converts heat into mechanical energy.

EXHAUST MANIFOLD: A set of cast passages or pipes which conduct exhaust gases from the engine.

FEELER GAUGE: A blade, usually metal, of precisely predetermined thickness, used to measure the clearance between two parts. These blades usually are available in sets of assorted thicknesses.

F-Head: An engine configuration in which the intake valves are in the cylinder head, while the camshaft and exhaust valves are located in the cylinder block. The camshaft operates the intake valves via lifters and pushrods, while it operates the exhaust valves directly.

FIRING ORDER: The order in which combustion occurs in the cylinders of an engine. Also the order in which spark is distributed to the plugs by the distributor.

FLATHEAD: An engine configuration in which the camshaft and all the valves are located in the cylinder block.

FLOODING: The presence of too much fuel in the intake manifold and combustion chamber which prevents the air/fuel mixture from firing, thereby causing a no-start situation.

FLYWHEEL: A disc shaped part bolted to the rear end of the crankshaft. Around the outer perimeter is affixed the ring gear. The starter drive engages the ring gear, turning the flywheel, which rotates the crankshaft, imparting the initial starting motion to the engine.

FOOT POUND (ft.lb. or sometimes, ft. lbs.): The amount of energy or work needed to raise an item weighing one pound, a distance of one foot.

FUSE: A protective device in a circuit which prevents circuit overload by breaking the circuit when a specific amperage is present. The device is constructed around a strip or wire of a lower amperage rating than the circuit it is designed to protect. When an amperage higher than that stamped on the fuse is present in the circuit, the strip or wire melts, opening the circuit.

GEAR RATIO: The ratio between the number of teeth on meshing gears.

GENERATOR: A device which converts mechanical energy into electrical energy.

HEAT RANGE: The measure of a spark plug's ability to dissipate heat from its firing end. The higher the heat range, the hotter the plug fires.

HUB: The center part of a wheel or gear.

HYDROCARBON (HC): Any chemical compound made up of hydrogen and carbon. A major pollutant formed by the engine as a byproduct of combustion.

HYDROMETER: An instrument used to measure the specific gravity of a solution.

INCH POUND (in.lb. or sometimes, in. lbs.): One twelfth of a foot pound.

INDUCTION: A means of transferring electrical energy in the form of a magnetic field. Principle used in the ignition coil to increase voltage.

INJECTION PUMP: A device, usually mechanically operated, which meters and delivers fuel under pressure to the fuel injector.

INJECTOR: A device which receives metered fuel under relatively low pressure and is activated to inject the fuel into the engine under relatively high pressure at a predetermined time.

INPUT SHAFT: The shaft to which torque is applied, usually carrying the driving gear or gears.

INTAKE MANIFOLD: A casting of passages or pipes used to conduct air or a fuel/air mixture to the cylinders.

JOURNAL: The bearing surface within which a shaft operates.

KEY: A small block usually fitted in a notch between a shaft and a hub to prevent slippage of the two parts.

MANIFOLD: A casting of passages or set of pipes which connect the cylinders to an inlet or outlet source.

MANIFOLD VACUUM: Low pressure in an engine intake manifold formed just below the throttle plates. Manifold vacuum is highest at idle and drops under acceleration.

MASTER CYLINDER: The primary fluid pressurizing device in a hydraulic system. In automotive use, it is found in brake and hydraulic clutch systems and is pedal activated, either directly or, in a power brake system, through the power booster.

MODULE: Electronic control unit, amplifier or igniter of solid state or integrated design which controls the current flow in the ignition primary circuit based on input from the pickup coil. When the module opens the primary circuit, the high secondary voltage is induced in the coil.

NEEDLE BEARING: A bearing which consists of a number (usually a large number) of long, thin rollers.

OHM: (Ω) The unit used to measure the resistance of conductor to electrical flow. One ohm is the amount of resistance that limits current flow to one ampere in a circuit with one volt of pressure.

OHMMETER: An instrument used for measuring the resistance, in ohms, in an electrical circuit.

OUTPUT SHAFT: The shaft which transmits torque from a device, such as a transmission.

OVERDRIVE: A gear assembly which produces more shaft revolutions than that transmitted to it.

OVERHEAD CAMSHAFT (OHC): An engine configuration in which the camshaft is mounted on top of the cylinder head and operates the valve either directly or by means of rocker arms.

OVERHEAD VALVE (OHV): An engine configuration in which all of the valves are located in the cylinder head and the camshaft is located in the cylinder block. The camshaft operates the valves via lifters and pushrods.

OXIDES OF NITROGEN (NOx): Chemical compounds of nitrogen produced as a byproduct of combustion. They combine with hydrocarbons to produce smog.

OXYGEN SENSOR: Used with the feedback system to sense the presence of oxygen in the exhaust gas and signal the computer which can reference the voltage signal to an air/fuel ratio.

PINION: The smaller of two meshing gears.

PISTON RING: An open ended ring which fits into a groove on the outer diameter of the piston. Its chief function is to form a seal between the piston and cylinder wall. Most automotive pistons have three rings: two for compression sealing; one for oil sealing.

PRELOAD: A predetermined load placed on a bearing during assembly or by adjustment.

PRIMARY CIRCUIT: Is the low voltage side of the ignition system which consists of the ignition switch, ballast resistor or resistance wire, bypass, coil, electronic control unit and pick-up coil as well as the connecting wires and harnesses.

PRESS FIT: The mating of two parts under pressure, due to the inner diameter of one being smaller than the outer diameter of the other, or vice versa; an interference fit.

RACE: The surface on the inner or outer ring of a bearing on which the balls, needles or rollers move.

REGULATOR: A device which maintains the amperage and/or voltage levels of a circuit at predetermined values.

RELAY: A switch which automatically opens and/or closes a circuit.

RESISTANCE: The opposition to the flow of current through a circuit or electrical device, and is measured in ohms. Resistance is equal to the voltage divided by the amperage.

RESISTOR: A device, usually made of wire, which offers a preset amount of resistance in an electrical circuit.

RING GEAR: The name given to a ring-shaped gear attached to a differential case, or affixed to a flywheel or as part a planetary gear set.

ROLLER BEARING: A bearing made up of hardened inner and outer races between which hardened steel rollers move.

ROTOR: 1. The disc-shaped part of a disc brake assembly, upon which the brake pads bear; also called, brake disc.
2. The device mounted atop the distributor shaft, which passes current to the distributor cap tower contacts.

SECONDARY CIRCUIT: The high voltage side of the ignition system, usually above 20,000 volts. The secondary includes the ignition coil, coil wire, distributor cap and rotor, spark plug wires and spark plugs.

SENDING UNIT: A mechanical, electrical, hydraulic or electromagnetic device which transmits information to a gauge.

SENSOR: Any device designed to measure engine operating conditions or ambient pressures and temperatures. Usually electronic in nature and designed to send a voltage signal to an on-board computer, some sensors may operate as a simple on/off switch or they may provide a variable voltage signal (like a potentiometer) as conditions or measured parameters change.

SHIM: Spacers of precise, predetermined thickness used between parts to establish a proper working relationship.

SLAVE CYLINDER: In automotive use, a device in the hydraulic clutch system which is activated by hydraulic force, disengaging the clutch.

SOLENOID: A coil used to produce a magnetic field, the effect of which is produce work.

SPARK PLUG: A device screwed into the combustion chamber of a spark ignition engine. The basic construction is a conductive core inside of a ceramic insulator, mounted in an outer conductive base. An electrical charge from the spark plug wire travels along the conductive core and jumps a preset air gap to a grounding point or points at the end of the conductive base. The resultant spark ignites the fuel/air mixture in the combustion chamber.

SPLINES: Ridges machined or cast onto the outer diameter of a shaft or inner diameter of a bore to enable parts to mate without rotation.

TACHOMETER: A device used to measure the rotary speed of an engine, shaft, gear, etc., usually in rotations per minute.

THERMOSTAT: A valve, located in the cooling system of an engine, which is closed when cold and opens gradually in response to engine heating, controlling the temperature of the coolant and rate of coolant flow.

TOP DEAD CENTER (TDC): The point at which the piston reaches the top of its travel on the compression stroke.

TORQUE: The twisting force applied to an object.

TORQUE CONVERTER: A turbine used to transmit power from a driving member to a driven member via hydraulic action, providing changes in drive ratio and torque. In automotive use, it links the driveplate at the rear of the engine to the automatic transmission.

TRANSDUCER: A device used to change a force into an electrical signal.

TRANSISTOR: A semi-conductor component which can be actuated by a small voltage to perform an electrical switching function.

TUNE-UP: A regular maintenance function, usually associated with the replacement and adjustment of parts and components in the electrical and fuel systems of a vehicle for the purpose of attaining optimum performance.

TURBOCHARGER: An exhaust driven pump which compresses intake air and forces it into the combustion chambers at higher than atmospheric pressures. The increased air pressure allows more fuel to be burned and results in increased horsepower being produced.

VACUUM ADVANCE: A device which advances the ignition timing in response to increased engine vacuum.

VACUUM GAUGE: An instrument used to measure the presence of vacuum in a chamber.

VALVE: A device which control the pressure, direction of flow or rate of flow of a liquid or gas.

VALVE CLEARANCE: The measured gap between the end of the valve stem and the rocker arm, cam lobe or follower that activates the valve.

VISCOSITY: The rating of a liquid's internal resistance to flow.

VOLTMETER: An instrument used for measuring electrical force in units called volts. Voltmeters are always connected parallel with the circuit being tested.

WHEEL CYLINDER: Found in the automotive drum brake assembly, it is a device, actuated by hydraulic pressure, which, through internal pistons, pushes the brake shoes outward against the drums.

ABBREVIATIONS AND SYMBOLS

A: Ampere

AC: Alternating current

A/C: Air conditioning

A-h: Ampere hour

AT: Automatic transmission

ATDC: After top dead center

μA: Microampere

bbl: Barrel

BDC: Bottom dead center

bhp: Brake horsepower

BTDC: Before top dead center

BTU: British thermal unit

C: Celsius (Centigrade)

CCA: Cold cranking amps

cd: Candela

cm^2: Square centimeter

cm^3, cc: Cubic centimeter

CO: Carbon monoxide

CO_2: Carbon dioxide

cu.in., in^3: Cubic inch

CV: Constant velocity

Cyl.: Cylinder

DC: Direct current

ECM: Electronic control module

EFE: Early fuel evaporation

EFI: Electronic fuel injection

EGR: Exhaust gas recirculation

Exh.: Exhaust

F: Fahrenheit

F: Farad

pF: Picofarad

μF: Microfarad

FI: Fuel injection

ft.lb., ft. lb., ft. lbs.: foot pound(s)

gal: Gallon

g: Gram

HC: Hydrocarbon

HEI: High energy ignition

HO: High output

hp: Horsepower

Hyd.: Hydraulic

Hz: Hertz

ID: Inside diameter

in.lb.; in. lb.; in. lbs: inch pound(s)

Int.: Intake

K: Kelvin

kg: Kilogram

kHz: Kilohertz

km: Kilometer

km/h: Kilometers per hour

$k\Omega$: Kilohm

kPa: Kilopascal

kV: Kilovolt

kW: Kilowatt

l: Liter

l/s: Liters per second

m: Meter

mA: Milliampere

mg: Milligram

mHz: Megahertz

mm: Millimeter

mm^2: Square millimeter

m^3: Cubic meter

$M\Omega$: Megohm

m/s: Meters per second

MT: Manual transmission

mV: Millivolt

μm: Micrometer

N: Newton

N-m: Newton meter

NOx: Nitrous oxide

OD: Outside diameter

OHC: Over head camshaft

OHV: Over head valve

Ω: Ohm

PCV: Positive crankcase ventilation

psi: Pounds per square inch

pts: Pints

qts: Quarts

rpm: Rotations per minute

rps: Rotations per second

R-12: A refrigerant gas (Freon)

SAE: Society of Automotive Engineers

SO_2: Sulfur dioxide

T: Ton

t: Megagram

TBI: Throttle Body Injection

TPS: Throttle Position Sensor

V: 1. Volt; 2. Venturi

μV: Microvolt

W: Watt

∞: Infinity

<: Less than

>: Greater than

Index

Chilton's Repair & Tune-Up Guides

The Complete line covers domestic cars, imports, trucks, vans, RV's and 4-wheel drive vehicles.

RTUG Title	Part No.	RTUG Title	Part No.
AMC 1975-82 Covers all U.S. and Canadian models	7199	**Corvair 1960-69** Covers all U.S. and Canadian models	6691
Aspen/Volare 1976-80 Covers all U.S. and Canadian models	6637	**Corvette 1953-62** Covers all U.S. and Canadian models	6576
Audi 1970-73 Covers all U.S. and Canadian models.	5902	**Corvette 1963-84** Covers all U.S. and Canadian models	6843
Audi 4000/5000 1978-81 Covers all U.S. and Canadian models including turbocharged and diesel engines	7028	**Cutlass 1970-85** Covers all U.S. and Canadian models	6933
Barracuda/Challenger 1965-72 Covers all U.S. and Canadian models	5807	**Dart/Demon 1968-76** Covers all U.S. and Canadian models	6324
Blazer/Jimmy 1969-82 Covers all U.S. and Canadian 2- and 4-wheel drive models, including diesel engines	6931	**Datsun 1961-72** Covers all U.S. and Canadian models of Nissan Patrol; 1500, 1600 and 2000 sports cars; Pick-Ups; 410, 411, 510, 1200 and 240Z	5790
BMW 1970-82 Covers U.S. and Canadian models	6844	**Datsun 1973-80 Spanish**	7083
Buick/Olds/Pontiac 1975-85 Covers all U.S. and Canadian full size rear wheel drive models	7308	**Datsun/Nissan F-10, 310, Stanza, Pulsar 1977-86** Covers all U.S. and Canadian models	7196
Cadillac 1967-84 Covers all U.S. and Canadian rear wheel drive models	7462	**Datsun/Nissan Pick-Ups 1970-84** Covers all U.S and Canadian models	6816
Camaro 1967-81 Covers all U.S. and Canadian models	6735	**Datsun/Nissan Z & ZX 1970-86** Covers all U.S. and Canadian models	6932
Camaro 1982-85 Covers all U.S. and Canadian models	7317	**Datsun/Nissan 1200, 210, Sentra 1973-86** Covers all U.S. and Canadian models	7197
Capri 1970-77 Covers all U.S. and Canadian models	6695	**Datsun/Nissan 200SX, 510, 610, 710, 810, Maxima 1973-84** Covers all U.S. and Canadian models	7170
Caravan/Voyager 1984-85 Covers all U.S. and Canadian models	7482	**Dodge 1968-77** Covers all U.S. and Canadian models	6554
Century/Regal 1975-85 Covers all U.S. and Canadian rear wheel drive models, including turbocharged engines	7307	**Dodge Charger 1967-70** Covers all U.S. and Canadian models	6486
Champ/Arrow/Sapporo 1978-83 Covers all U.S. and Canadian models	7041	**Dodge/Plymouth Trucks 1967-84** Covers all $^1/_2$, $^3/_4$, and 1 ton 2- and 4-wheel drive U.S. and Canadian models, including diesel engines	7459
Chevette/1000 1976-86 Covers all U.S. and Canadian models	6836	**Dodge/Plymouth Vans 1967-84** Covers all $^1/_2$, $^3/_4$, and 1 ton U.S. and Canadian models of vans, cutaways and motor home chassis	6934
Chevrolet 1968-85 Covers all U.S. and Canadian models	7135	**D-50/Arrow Pick-Up 1979-81** Covers all U.S. and Canadian models	7032
Chevrolet 1968-79 Spanish	7082	**Fairlane/Torino 1962-75** Covers all U.S. and Canadian models	6320
Chevrolet/GMC Pick-Ups 1970-82 Spanish	7468	**Fairmont/Zephyr 1978-83** Covers all U.S. and Canadian models	6965
Chevrolet/GMC Pick-Ups and Suburban 1970-86 Covers all U.S. and Canadian $^1/_2$, $^3/_4$ and 1 ton models, including 4-wheel drive and diesel engines	6936	**Fiat 1969-81** Covers all U.S. and Canadian models	7042
Chevrolet LUV 1972-81 Covers all U.S. and Canadian models	6815	**Fiesta 1978-80** Covers all U.S. and Canadian models	6846
Chevrolet Mid-Size 1964-86 Covers all U.S. and Canadian models of 1964-77 Chevelle, Malibu and Malibu SS; 1974-77 Laguna; 1978-85 Malibu; 1970-86 Monte Carlo; 1964-84 El Camino, including diesel engines	6840	**Firebird 1967-81** Covers all U.S. and Canadian models	5996
Chevrolet Nova 1986 Covers all U.S. and Canadian models	7658	**Firebird 1982-85** Covers all U.S. and Canadian models	7345
Chevy/GMC Vans 1967-84 Covers all U.S. and Canadian models of $^1/_2$, $^3/_4$, and 1 ton vans, cutaways, and motor home chassis, including diesel engines	6930	**Ford 1968-79 Spanish** **Ford Bronco 1966-83** Covers all U.S. and Canadian models	7084 7140
Chevy S-10 Blazer/GMC S-15 Jimmy 1982-85 Covers all U.S. and Canadian models	7383	**Ford Bronco II 1984** Covers all U.S. and Canadian models	7408
Chevy S-10/GMC S-15 Pick-Ups 1982-85 Covers all U.S. and Canadian models	7310	**Ford Courier 1972-82** Covers all U.S. and Canadian models	6983
Chevy II/Nova 1962-79 Covers all U.S. and Canadian models	6841	**Ford/Mercury Front Wheel Drive 1981-85** Covers all U.S. and Canadian models Escort, EXP, Tempo, Lynx, LN-7 and Topaz	7055
Chrysler K- and E-Car 1981-85 Covers all U.S. and Canadian front wheel drive models	7163	**Ford/Mercury/Lincoln 1968-85** Covers all U.S. and Canadian models of FORD Country Sedan, Country Squire, Crown Victoria, Custom, Custom 500, Galaxie 500, LTD through 1982, Ranch Wagon, and XL; MERCURY Colony Park, Commuter, Marquis through 1982, Gran Marquis, Monterey and Park Lane; LINCOLN Continental and Towne Car	6842
Colt/Challenger/Vista/Conquest 1971-85 Covers all U.S. and Canadian models	7037	**Ford/Mercury/Lincoln Mid-Size 1971-85** Covers all U.S. and Canadian models of FORD Elite, 1983-85 LTD, 1977-79 LTD II, Ranchero, Torino, Gran Torino, 1977-85 Thunderbird; MERCURY 1972-85 Cougar,	6696
Corolla/Carina/Tercel/Starlet 1970-85 Covers all U.S. and Canadian models	7036		
Corona/Cressida/Crown/Mk.II/Camry/Van 1970-84 Covers all U.S. and Canadian models	7044		

continued on next page

RTUG Title	Part No.	RTUG Title	Part No.
1983-85 Marquis, Montego, 1980-85 XR-7; LINCOLN 1982-85 Continental, 1984-85 Mark VII, 1978-80 Versailles		**Mercedes-Benz 1974-84** Covers all U.S. and Canadian models	6809
Ford Pick-Ups 1965-86 Covers all ¹/₂, ³/₄ and 1 ton, 2- and 4-wheel drive U.S. and Canadian pick-up, chassis cab and camper models, including diesel engines	6913	**Mitsubishi, Cordia, Tredia, Starion, Galant 1983-85** Covers all U.S. and Canadian models	7583
Ford Pick-Ups 1965-82 Spanish	7469	**MG 1961-81** Covers all U.S. and Canadian models	6780
Ford Ranger 1983-84 Covers all U.S. and Canadian models	7338	**Mustang/Capri/Merkur 1979-85** Covers all U.S. and Canadian models	6963
Ford Vans 1961-86 Covers all U.S. and Canadian ¹/₂, ³/₄ and 1 ton van and cutaway chassis models, including diesel engines	6849	**Mustang/Cougar 1965-73** Covers all U.S. and Canadian models	6542
		Mustang II 1974-78 Covers all U.S. and Canadian models	6812
GM A-Body 1982-85 Covers all front wheel drive U.S. and Canadian models of BUICK Century, CHEVROLET Celebrity, OLDSMOBILE Cutlass Ciera and PONTIAC 6000	7309	**Omni/Horizon/Rampage 1978-84** Covers all U.S. and Canadian models of DODGE omni, Miser, 024, Charger 2.2; PLYMOUTH Horizon, Miser, TC3, TC3 Tourismo; Rampage	6845
GM C-Body 1985 Covers all front wheel drive U.S. and Canadian models of BUICK Electra Park Avenue and Electra T-Type, CADILLAC Fleetwood and deVille, OLDSMOBILE 98 Regency and Regency Brougham	7587	**Opel 1971-75** Covers all U.S. and Canadian models	6575
		Peugeot 1970-74 Covers all U.S. and Canadian models	5982
		Pinto/Bobcat 1971-80 Covers all U.S. and Canadian models	7027
GM J-Car 1982-85 Covers all U.S. and Canadian models of BUICK Skyhawk, CHEVROLET Cavalier, CADILLAC Cimarron, OLDSMOBILE Firenza and PONTIAC 2000 and Sunbird	7059	**Plymouth 1968-76** Covers all U.S. and Canadian models	6552
		Pontiac Fiero 1984-85 Covers all U.S. and Canadian models	7571
GM N-Body 1985-86 Covers all U.S. and Canadian models of front wheel drive BUICK Somerset and Skylark, OLDSMOBILE Calais, and PONTIAC Grand Am	7657	**Pontiac Mid-Size 1974-83** Covers all U.S. and Canadian models of Ventura, Grand Am, LeMans, Grand LeMans, GTO, Phoenix, and Grand Prix	7346
		Porsche 924/928 1976-81 Covers all U.S. and Canadian models	7048
GM X-Body 1980-85 Covers all U.S. and Canadian models of BUICK Skylark, CHEVROLET Citation, OLDSMOBILE Omega and PONTIAC Phoenix	7049	**Renault 1975-85** Covers all U.S. and Canadian models	7165
		Roadrunner/Satellite/Belvedere/GTX 1968-73 Covers all U.S. and Canadian models	5821
GM Subcompact 1971-80 Covers all U.S. and Canadian models of BUICK Skyhawk (1975-80), CHEVROLET Vega and Monza, OLDSMOBILE Starfire, and PONTIAC Astre and 1975-80 Sunbird	6935	**RX-7 1979-81** Covers all U.S. and Canadian models	7031
		SAAB 99 1969-75 Covers all U.S. and Canadian models	5988
		SAAB 900 1979-85 Covers all U.S. and Canadian models	7572
Granada/Monarch 1975-82 Covers all U.S. and Canadian models	6937	**Snowmobiles 1976-80** Covers Arctic Cat, John Deere, Kawasaki, Polaris, Ski-Doo and Yamaha	6978
Honda 1973-84 Covers all U.S. and Canadian models	6980	**Subaru 1970-84** Covers all U.S. and Canadian models	6982
International Scout 1967-73 Covers all U.S. and Canadian models	5912	**Tempest/GTO/LeMans 1968-73** Covers all U.S. and Canadian models	5905
Jeep 1945-87 Covers all U.S. and Canadian CJ-2A, CJ-3A, CJ-3B, CJ-5, CJ-6, CJ-7, Scrambler and Wrangler models	6817	**Toyota 1966-70** Covers all U.S. and Canadian models of Corona, MkII, Corolla, Crown, Land Cruiser, Stout and Hi-Lux	5795
Jeep Wagoneer, Commando, Cherokee, Truck 1957-86 Covers all U.S. and Canadian models of Wagoneer, Cherokee, Grand Wagoneer, Jeepster Commando, J-100, J-200, J-300, J-10, J20, FC-150 and FC-170	6739	**Toyota 1970-79 Spanish**	7467
		Toyota Celica/Supra 1971-85 Covers all U.S. and Canadian models	7043
		Toyota Trucks 1970-85 Covers all U.S. and Canadian models of pickups, Land Cruiser and 4Runner	7035
Laser/Daytona 1984-85 Covers all U.S. and Canadian models	7563	**Valiant/Duster 1968-76** Covers all U.S. and Canadian models	6326
Maverick/Comet 1970-77 Covers all U.S. and Canadian models	6634	**Volvo 1956-69** Covers all U.S. and Canadian models	6529
Mazda 1971-84 Covers all U.S. and Canadian models of RX-2, RX-3, RX-4, 808, 1300, 1600, Cosmo, GLC and 626	6981	**Volvo 1970-83** Covers all U.S. and Canadian models	7040
		VW Front Wheel Drive 1974-85 Covers all U.S. and Canadian models	6962
Mazda Pick-Ups 1972-86 Covers all U.S. and Canadian models	7659	**VW 1949-71** Covers all U.S. and Canadian models	5796
Mercedes-Benz 1959-70 Covers all U.S. and Canadian models	6065	**VW 1970-79 Spanish**	7081
Mereceds-Benz 1968-73 Covers all U.S. and Canadian models	5907	**VW 1970-81** Covers all U.S. and Canadian Beetles, Karmann Ghia, Fastback, Squareback, Vans, 411 and 412	6837

Chilton's Repair & Tune-Up Guides are available at your local retailer or by mailing a check or money order for **$13.95** plus **$3.25** to cover postage and handling to:

**Chilton Book Company
Dept. DM
Radnor, PA 19089**

NOTE: When ordering be sure to include your name & address, book part No. & title.